Ghanshyam Sharma, John J. Lowe (Eds.)
Trends in South Asian Linguistics

Trends in Linguistics
Studies and Monographs

Editors
Chiara Gianollo
Daniël Van Olmen

Editorial Board
Walter Bisang
Tine Breban
Volker Gast
Hans Henrich Hock
Karen Lahousse
Natalia Levshina
Caterina Mauri
Heiko Narrog
Salvador Pons
Niina Ning Zhang
Amir Zeldes

Editors responsible for this volume
Chiara Gianollo

Volume 367

Trends in South Asian Linguistics

Edited by
Ghanshyam Sharma and John J. Lowe

DE GRUYTER
MOUTON

ISBN 978-3-11-127733-2
e-ISBN (PDF) 978-3-11-075306-6
e-ISBN (EPUB) 978-3-11-075314-1
ISSN: 1861-4302

Library of Congress Control Number: 2021946766

Bibliographic information published by the Deutsche Nationalbibliothek
The Deutsche Nationalbibliothek lists this publication in the Deutsche Nationalbibliografie;
detailed bibliographic data are available on the Internet at http://dnb.dnb.de.

© 2023 Walter de Gruyter GmbH, Berlin/Boston
This volume is text- and page-identical with the hardback published in 2021.
Printing and binding: CPI books GmbH, Leck

www.degruyter.com

For Peter Edwin Hook

Preface

This volume grows out of the 35th edition of the South Asian Languages Analysis Roundtable (SALA-35) that took place at the National Institute of Oriental Languages and Civilizations (INALCO) in Paris on 29–31 October 2019. Founded at the University of Illinois on the occasion of the 1978 Linguistic Institute of the Linguistic Society of America, SALA has, over many decades, attracted a great number of linguists – both eminent and new – from almost every branch of linguistic inquiry and has been hosted ever since by prestigious academic institutions around the globe. The 35th edition of SALA at INALCO in Paris brought together a large number of linguists (over 130!) with a wide range of interests, backgrounds and methodologies, becoming a major historic event. The present volume, however, does not aim to be the SALA-35 proceedings but contains only a few select papers which broaden our knowledge of many distinctive characteristics found in the languages of South Asia. A major part of the articles present research of substantial empirical breadth while others scrutinize earlier claims paving the way for new fundamental research. Unlike conference minutes, this volume attempts to give a snapshot of some of the structured arguments put forward by the scientific research carried out in the field of South Asian linguistics, mainly in syntax and phonology. We fervently hope that this collection of selected peer-reviewed research papers will give the reader a taste of the depth, diversity, and progress that characterize contemporary work on the South Asian languages. While the bulk of the edited papers in this volume engage mainly with questions of syntax, they do so with quite different research programs as well as different theoretical tools. What is beautiful is that this does not lead to any internal conceptual incoherence; rather, in the best argumentative tradition of the subcontinent, we have research on syntax and phonology that is deepened by its multiplicity of vantage points.

The first three papers in this volume focus on the syntax of embedded clauses. Mark Hale and Madelyn Kissock's paper deals with the syntax of comparative clauses in Vedic Sanskrit, identifying an important new generalization for the interpretation of Vedic comparative clauses, which resolves significant ambiguities in understanding Vedic texts. Likewise, Massimo Vai uncovers a number of subtle features of the Vedic complementizer *yad* and the clauses that it heads, interpreting his observations within a broadly minimalist syntactic perspective. Adriana Molina-Muñoz on the other hand uses sophisticated statistical techniques to uncover the complex interaction of factors affecting the positioning of finite relative clauses in Hindi. Poised to become an important topic of research in syntax, participial agreement in Hindi is the main focus of the following chapter, by Tanmoy Bhattacharya, who considers earlier proposals concerning its optional agreement with the NP – namely agreement in number and gender if the NP is in the direct case (Kachru 2006: 163) – and puts forward a convincing theoretical explanation for participle agreement variation in Hindi at the level of participial object agreement as well. The paper come up with three distinct syntactic operations – valuation, relaying, and copying – which, together with standard Agree applying top-down, derive the full range of the results obtained.

Semantics and syntax of case plays an important and unifying role in putting forward arguments in the following two articles. For instance, through a detailed comparison of cross-linguistic data from both SOV languages, such as Telugu, Tamil, Marathi, Turkish, Japanese, Korean and Persian, and SVO languages, such as Greek and Norwegian, Anuradha Sudharsan's paper develops an analysis of constraints on sentential subjects in Kannada, based on the theory of Case in the minimalist framework. She argues that only nominalized clauses can occupy the canonical subject position whereas non-nominalized clauses can occupy only the object position. According to her, the cross-linguistic facts corroborate this claim and also explain why that-clauses in English tend to extrapose. Similarly, discussing the underlying theme of the semantics of case, Bornini Lahiri's paper investigates the relation between animacy and case-marking in three East Indo-Aryan languages, namely Bangla, Magahi and Bhojpuri. The paper by Dörte Borchers focuses on a paradigmatic gap and its suppletive filler in the participle paradigm in Koints, exploring the relevance of finiteness as a relevant property to explain this suppletion.

In South Asian languages, participles often have a role as main clause predicates, and participles or other non-finite verb forms are often implicated in the formation of 'complex predicates', also known as 'compound verbs'. These are the subject of the papers by Ghanshyam Sharma, Miki Nishioka, and Jean-Luc Chevillard. Sharma investigate the diachronic development of compound verbs in Western Indo-Aryan, providing a finely detailed analysis of the transition between factored verbs and vectored verbs in complex verbal expression. Nishioka focuses on the syntax of the Hindi vector verb *rakhnā* 'put', and compares it with the equivalent Japanese verb, *oku* 'put'. Meanwhile, Chevillard's paper documents what we can learn from one of the earliest accounts of compound verbs in modern Tamil.

Reflexives and reciprocals are the subject of the next two chapters which study two Tibeto-Burman languages, namely Mising and Kokborok. The first paper by Karumuri Subbarao, Tabu Taid and Martin Everaert investigates reflexive and reciprocal strategies in the Tibeto-Burman language Mising, which shows many features typical of the South Asian linguistic area, but also certain unusual or unique features. The second paper by Gargi Roy, Rajesh Kumar and Karumuri Subbarao delves deep into reciprocals in another Tibeto-Burman language, Kokborok, and analyzes the attrition of its inherited reciprocal marking in the face of language contact with Bangla.

The paper by Sajukta Ghosh addresses semantic issues. Ghosh adopts a cognitive linguistic approach to the semantics of locative and spatial construction in Bangla, identifying a number of ways in which languages like Bangla work differently in this respect from more familiar languages like English.

The following chapter by John Lowe provides a bridge between syntax-semantics and phonology and focuses on the Aṣṭādhyāyī. It reviews existing theoretical proposals concerning the Pāṇinian theory of grammar, specifically the question of generative power and rule systems that underlie modern formal linguistic, in particular syntactic and phonological, analysis. Lowe's paper addresses the generative power of the Aṣṭādhyāyī, demonstrating that previous proposals on the topic have misanalysed the facts.

The final two chapters analyze experimental data, report groundbreaking research and share a focus on phonological issues. Paroma Sanyal, Vyom Sharma and Ankita Prasad invoke morphosyntactic and phonological constraints to analyze root allomorphy in Hindi, within the frameworks of Harmonic Grammar and Distributed Morphology. Dinesh Ramoo, Cristina Romani and Andrew Olson, on the other hand, compare resyllabification patterns in English and Hindi; their findings provide support for the existence of syllable structure as a part of the information stored in the mental lexicon.

As the contributions to this volume show, South Asian linguistics is a vibrant and diverse field of research, where work in a variety of linguistic fields on a range of genetically unrelated languages nevertheless displays fundamental interconnectedness and deep unity. Written by leading scholars, all the articles included in the volume establish new lines of research in their respective fields of inquiry and thus undoubtedly open the door to further research in the field of South Asian linguistics. We have no doubt that this volume will be of great help to researchers in South Asian linguistics.

Ghanshyam Sharma, John J. Lowe
Paris & Oxford, September 9, 2021

Contents

Preface —— vii

Acknowledgements —— xiii

Mark Hale, Madelyn Kissock
On the syntax of comparative clauses in Vedic Sanskrit ... *like someone eating the foam off the water* —— 1

Massimo Vai
Some questions about *yád* in Vedic —— 23

Adriana Molina-Muñoz
A statistical model of syntactic and non-syntactic factors affecting relative clause placement in Hindi —— 43

Tanmoy Bhattacharya
Optionality and variation in agreement in some participles in Hindi-Urdu —— 77

Anuradha Sudharsan
A cross-linguistic approach to sentential subjects in Kannada —— 119

Bornini Lahiri
Relation between animacy and case marking in Eastern Indo-Aryan languages —— 173

Dörte Borchers
Participles with a semantic void in Koints —— 191

Ghanshyam Sharma
Competition between vectored verbs and factored verbs in Hindi-Urdu, Marathi and Gujarati —— 207

Miki Nishioka
How similarly do Hindi *rakhnā* and Japanese *oku* PUT behave as a V2? A corpus-based comparative analysis —— 243

Jean-Luc Chevillard
The use of vector verbs in Early Modern Tamil —— 261

Kārumūri V. Subbārāo, Tabu Taid, Martin Everaert
Reflexive and reciprocal marking in Mising —— 291

Gargi Roy, Rajesh Kumar, Kārumūri V. Subbārāo
Reciprocals in Kokborok — A Case of Syntactic Convergence —— 311

Sajukta Ghosh
A cognitive semantic analysis of locative and spatial constructions in Bangla —— 339

John J. Lowe
Revisiting Pāṇini's generative power —— 361

Paroma Sanyal, Vyom Sharma, Ankita Prasad
Hindi root allomorphy: Insights from phonological and morphosyntactic theory —— 381

Dinesh Ramoo, Cristina Romani, Andrew Olson
Lexeme and speech syllables in English and Hindi. A case for syllable structure —— 415

List of contributors —— 463

Index of authors —— 469

Index of languages —— 477

Index of subjects —— 479

Acknowledgements

All the papers included in this volume were double peer-reviewed – a challenging task which necessitated assistance from both internal and external reviewers. Although the internal reviewers performed their services as part of the project, the external reviewers generously provided us with their invaluable services, which were essential for bringing out this volume, gratis. We would like to sincerely thank them all for their support in the accomplishment of the volume: Terje Lohndal (Norwegian University of Science and Technology, Trondheim, Norway), Uma Maheshwar Rao (Hyderabad, India), Jim Benson (Oxford) and Rishi Rajpopat (Cambridge).

We are grateful to Professor Hans Henrich Hock (Illinois), Rajesh Bhatt (Amherst, Massachusetts), Peter Hook (Michigan and Virginia), Anju Saxena (Uppsala), Tanmoy Bhattacharya (Delhi), John Peterson (Kiel, Germany) and Emily Manetta (Vermont) for their valuable support for the organization of the 35th South Asian Languages Analysis at INALCO in October 2019 where most of the papers included in this volume were presented. In addition, we are grateful to the authorities at the following institutions who provided generous financial support to the conference:
- Institut national des langues et civilisations orientales (INALCO), Paris
- Mondes iranien et indien (UMR-7528), Paris
- Laboratoire d'excellence – Empirical Foundation of Linguistics (LABEX-EFL), Paris.

Furthermore, we would like to thank Chiara Gianollo – Mouton's editor for the series *Trends in Linguistics. Studies and Monographs* [TiLSM] – for a favourable review of our proposal and a close reading of the entire manuscript. Without some skilled help from Elisabeth Stanciu of Mouton's production department and valuable assistance from Barbara Karlson of Mouton's editorial department, we would have had to ponder over the CRC of the book for many more months than required: Vielen Dank!

Mark Hale, Madelyn Kissock
On the syntax of comparative clauses in Vedic Sanskrit ... *like someone eating the foam off the water*

Abstract: This paper focusses on the relationship between two aspects of the syntax of a particular type of *iva* comparison clause in mantra Vedic – one with negation in the matrix. Specifically, we examine the relationship between the structural position of the comparison clause relative to the matrix clause and the positive or negative interpretation of the comparison clause itself. We find that when the *iva* clause is syntactically dominated by matrix negation, the *iva* clause is interpreted as "positive", whereas when the *iva* clause is not syntactically dominated by the matrix clause, it is interpreted as "negative". This distribution not only mirrors parallel comparison clauses in living languages but also provides evidence for the prosodic force of both caesura and line boundary.

Keywords: Sanskrit syntax, Comparative clauses, Vedic Sanskrit

1 Preliminaries

Clauses of comparison involving *iva* and *ná* are very, very frequent in mantra Vedic (our focus here), being attested around 2500 times. Various aspects of these clauses have been extensively studied in the previous literature, highlights of which include Bergaigne (1887), Vine (1978), Jamison (1982), and Pinault (1985, 1996, 1997, 2004). As is well-known, *ná* disappears in this function after the mantra period – indeed, there are only a handful of independent (i.e., non-Ṛgvedic) attestations of *ná* in this function in the Atharvaveda and other post-Ṛgvedic mantra texts.

By contrast, *iva* survives into the Vedic prose period, but in the significantly different function of 'as it were' or 'kind of' (for a detailed discussion see Brereton

---

Mark Hale, Concordia University, S-FB 1000-09, Faubourg Building, 1250 Guy, Canada. Email: mark.hale@concordia.ca
Madelyn Kissock, Concordia University, S-FB 1030-11, Faubourg Building, 1250 Guy, Canada. Email: madelyn.kissock@concordia.ca

https://doi.org/10.1515/9783110753066-001

1982) instead of the mantra period function of 'like/as'.[1] Interestingly, it re-emerges quite robustly in the Epics in its original function.

The primary challenge confronting one trying to understand the structure of these clauses is ambiguity of interpretation, which is rampant. Hale (2010), for example, addressed the following passage from the Paippalāda recension of the Atharvaveda:

(1) Atharvaveda Paippalāda recension (henceforth AVP) 6.6.6ab
sindhuprajāno[2]   madhugho | aśva   iva nīyate
Sindhu.born.NOM.SG Madhugha.NOM.SG horse.NOM.SG like is.lead
janām̐   anu ||
men.ACC.PL among
'Madhugha is led like a Sindhu-born horse among men.'
(Griffiths 2009: 84)
'Sindhu-born Madhugha is led like a horse among men.'
(Hale 2010: 3)

In that presentation it was argued that, while syntactic discontinuity of the elements of an *iva*-clause (as envisioned by Griffith's *sindhuprajānaḥ ... aśva iva*) is attested, the particular type of "interrupting" element his translation requires is not, indicating that his interpretation of *sindhuprajānaḥ* as a modifier of *aśvaḥ* (and thus as part of the *iva*-clause) cannot be maintained.

The methodological point of the above exercise was simply to show that, while we must as always interpret the text in some sensible manner, our own prejudices about what a plausible comparison might be, based on semantic considerations, need to be constrained by an understanding of what kinds of structures are permitted (and what kinds are not). We need to make allowances for the fact that the authors of the Vedic text may be saying something that surprises us!

---

1 Pinault (2004) argues that the Brāhmaṇa function is more richly attested in the Ṛgveda than is generally assumed, but even with his rather liberal count of such usages, it is still very much a minority pattern for the Ṛgveda.
2 Just a note on transliteration: for perspicuity, we have undone some vowel contractions which are demanded by the meter. This is indicated with V⌣V. Vowels inserted for scansion are raised; vowels that need to be read as not present are lowered. The ! symbol writes the caesura in trimeter lines. The transcription follows the traditional Indic transcription conventions, not the IPA.

2 A Seemingly General Property of Clauses of Comparison

The structural considerations that are in play in the interpretation of comparison clauses are many and complex, making progress on their untangling slow. We need to think about at least the following issues:

(2a) What is the syntactic structure of the comparison clause? That is, what are the word order possibilities (and their structural correlates) for the elements which make up that clause?
(2b) How is the comparison clause integrated syntactically into the matrix clause? That is, what determines the positioning of the comparison clause relative to the elements of the matrix clause?
(2c) What types of interleaving or interaction between elements from the matrix clause and those from the comparison clause are permitted?

In this paper, we will focus on a relatively small issue, which nevertheless allows us, in our view, to make some progress on both (2b) and (2c). It concerns the relationship between the structural position of the comparison clause relative to its matrix and an interpretational interaction between a negation in the matrix and the (positive or negative) comparison clause itself. It is worthwhile to take a look at some cross-linguistic evidence, which seems fairly robust and interesting. Examine the data below. The commas are intended to represent intonational breaks or resets.[3]

(3a) *Like a decent person, a President does not constantly lie.*
(3b) *A decent person does not constantly lie like Trump.*
(3c) *A President does not constantly lie, like any decent person.*
(4a) *Wie ein anständiger Mensch lügt ein Präsident nicht ständig.*
(4b) *Ein anständiger Mensch lügt nicht ständig wie Donald Trump.*
(4c) *Ein Präsident lügt nicht ständig, wie jeder anständige Mensch.*

The interpretation of these seems to be as follows:

---

[3] German judgements from Sandra Woywod-Pagé, Coordinator, Academic Programs, Concordia University.

(5a) Like a decent person (does not constantly lie), a President does not constantly lie.
(5b) A decent person does not constantly lie like Trump (constantly lies).
(5c) A President does not constantly lie, like a decent person (does not constantly lie).

We will call interpretation of the comparison clause that we find in (5a) and (5c) the "negative" interpretation, and that found in (5b) the "positive" interpretation.

The generalization, which appears at least to some reasonable degree to hold of several other languages as well (see, e.g., Peust 2006 on Old Egyptian), seems to be that if the clause of comparison is outside the scope of the matrix negator, it is interpreted as having a gapped negative, as in (5a) and (5c), whereas if it is not outside the scope of the negator, such as (5b), it is not so interpreted. Anytime we get evidence for an interaction between structure and interpretation, we can, if the generalization in question holds in Vedic as well, use the observation to figure out aspects of the structure of the Vedic clause.

3 Negation and Comparison in Vedic

Such structures are, probably unsurprisingly, somewhat rare in Vedic, but interestingly, they are not absent from the corpus. By our count, there are about forty. In spite of these limited numbers, quite distinct (and illuminating) patterns are revealed by their analysis.

3.1 Preposed Clauses of Comparison

Let us begin with some examples, intended to be parallel to (3a) and (4a), where the comparison clause is initial in the string, prepended to a matrix clause which shows internal negation.

(6)   Ṛgveda 1.124.3cd = 5.80.4cd
        ṛtásya   pánthām ⁝   ánᵘveti   sādhú |
        truth.GEN.SG   path.ACC.SG follow.3SG   straight
        prajānatī͡iva ⁝   ná díśo   mināti ||
        knowing.NOM.SG like   NEG directions.ACC.PL confuse.3SG
        'She follows along the path of truth, straight to the goal.

Like one who knows the way, she does not confound the directions.'
(Jamison and Brereton 2014)

This seems to mean 'just as one who knows the way (does not confound the directions), she does not confound the directions'.

(7) Ṛgveda 10.34.3cd
áśvasya‿iva : járato vásnⁱyasya |
horse.GEN.SG like old.GEN.SG for.sale.GEN.SG
ná‿ahám vindāmi : kitavásya bhógam ||
NEG I.NOM find.1SG gambler.GEN.SG use.ACC.SG
'I find no more use for a gambler than for an old nag up for sale.'
(Jamison and Brereton 2014)

This seems to mean 'just as (I do not find a use) for an old horse up for sale, I do not find a use for a gambler'.

(8) Atharvaveda Śaunaka recension (henceforth AVŚ) 4.20.7cd
vīdhré sū́ryam ịva sárpantaṃ |
clear.sky.LOC.SG sun.ACC.SG like gliding.ACC.SG
mā́ piśācáṃ tirás karaḥ ||
NEG piśāca.ACC.SG conceal.2SG
'Conceal thou not the *piśāca*, like the sun gliding in the clear sky.'
(Whitney 1905)

This would appear to mean something like 'do not conceal the *piśāca*, just as (you do not conceal) the sun gliding in the clear sky'.[4] The voice mismatch is not very adept.

(9) AVŚ 19.50.3cd
gambhīrám áplavā iva | ná tareyur árātayaḥ ||
depths.ACC.SG boatless.NOM.PL like NEG cross.3PL stingy.NOM.PL
'Like those lacking boats the deep, may the stingy ones not cross (it).'

This seems to mean 'like those lacking boats (do not cross) the deep, may the stingy ones not cross (it)'.

---

[4] Whitney (1905) comments: "That is, allow him to be no more concealed than the sun etc.".

(10) AVP 9.18.4d
 tamasi⌢iva ꞉ nihitaṃ na⌢anuvettā ‖
 darkness.LOC.SG like placed.NOM.SG NEG to.be.found
 'Like something placed in a dark place, it is not to be found.'

Parallel to earlier examples, this seems to mean 'like something placed in a dark place (is not to be found), it is not to be found'.

There are, in fact, no "positive" preposed clauses of comparison linked with matrix clauses which contain a negative marker.[5] Additional "negative" examples can be found at Ṛgveda 2.25.3cd, AVŚ 3.39.6ab, and AVŚ 3.39.6cd.

3.2 Postposed Clauses of Comparison

Let us turn now to instances in which the clause of comparison follows the matrix clause. You will recall from our discussion of English and German above that both a negative (as with the preposed cases) and a positive interpretation appears possible, with the negative one generally requiring a major prosodic break between the matrix clause and the clause of comparison. What does the Vedic data look like?

There are three instances in which postposed clauses of comparison have a positive reading, Ṛgveda 3.45.1cd, Ṛgveda 8.1.13ab and Ṛgveda 1.82.1ab, which are cited below.

(11) Ṛgveda 3.45.1c = AVŚ 7.117.1c
 mā́ tvā ké cin ꞉ ní yaman vím ná
 NEG you.ACC.CL anyone.NOM.PL down hold.3PL bird.ACC.SG like
 pāśínaḥ |
 having.a.snare.NOM.PL
 'Let no one hold you down, as men using snares do a bird.'
 (Jamison and Brereton 2014)

This seems to mean 'let someone not hold you down, like men with snares (do hold down) a bird'.

---

[5] The sole difficult, and thus interesting, case, AVŚ 4.36.6cd, will be discussed below.

(12) R̥gveda 8.1.13ab
 má bhūma níṣṭyā iva- |
 NEG be.1PL outsider.NOM.PL like
 -índra   tvád   áraṇā   iva ||
 Indra.VOC.SG you.ABL.SG strangers.NOM.PL like
 'May we not be like outsiders, like foreigners to you, Indra.'
 (Jamison and Brereton 2014)

This seems to mean 'may we not be like outsiders (are), like those estranged from you (are), O Indra'.

(13) R̥gveda 1.82.1ab
 úpo ṣú śr̥ṇuhí gíro |
 PV PTCL listen.IMP hymn.ACC.PL
 mághavan   mā́ átathā   iva ||
 bounteous.VOC.SG NEG nay-sayer.NOM.SG like
 'Listen well to our hymns, bounteous one, not like a nay-sayer.'
 (Jamison and Brereton 2014)

The relevant clause seems to mean 'do not [listen] like one who does not say "*tathā*" ('so be it') [listens]'.

However, a significantly larger number of the postposed clauses of comparison have a negative interpretation. These dozen or so instances fall into two classes. In the first, smaller, subclass, the clause of comparison is prosodically bounded on its left edge by the caesura and on its right by the line-end. We cite three examples below – a fourth likely example (R̥gveda 6.67.9cd) involves philological matters which would take us too far afield in this paper.

(14) R̥gveda 1.143.5a
 ná yó   váraya :   marútām   iva svanáḥ |
 NEG REL.NOM.SG hindering.DAT.SG Marut.GEN.PL like roar.NOM.SG
 'Who is not to be hindered, like the roar of the Maruts.'
 (Jamison and Brereton 2014)

This seems to mean 'who is not to be hindered, like the roar of the Maruts (is not to be hindered)'.

(15) Ṛgveda 10.106.2d
mā́ ‿ ápa sthātam ⫶ mahiṣā́ ‿ iva ‿ avapā́nāt ||
NEG stay.away.IMP buffalo.NOM.SG like waterhole.ABL.SG
'Do not stay away like buffalo from a waterhole.'
(Jamison and Brereton 2014)

This seems to mean 'do not stay away, like a buffalo (does not stay away) from a water-hole'.

(16) Ṛgveda 10.178.3d
ná smā varante | yuvatím ná śáryām ||
NEG PTCL block.3PL youthful.ACC.SG like arrow.ACC.SG
'They do not block him, any more than a youthful arrow.'
(Jamison and Brereton 2014)

Compare Geldner's translation, "wie einen jugendlichen Pfeil hielten sie ihn nicht auf", where the preposing of the comparison indicates that Geldner concurs with Jamison and Brereton (2014) that this means "They do not block him, like [they do not block] a youthful arrow".[6]

In the larger subclass, the clause of comparison is bounded on both sides by the line-boundary.[7]

(17) AVP 13.4.5cd
*na tvām āste 'bhiṣad viṣam | aśmānam
iva sāyakaṃ ||*
NEG you.ACC.SG stay besieger.NOM.SG poison.NOM.SG stone.ACC.SG
like arrow.NOM.SG
'The poison, the besieger, does not stay in you, like an arrow in a stone.'
(after Lopez 2010)

This seems to mean 'the poison ... does not stay in you, like an arrow (does not stay) in a stone'.

---

[6] Not, with Pischel and Geldner (1889: 106), "nicht weist man sie ab, [ebensowenig] wie eine junge Frau den penis" – see Oldenberg (1909: 823) who translates "nicht wehren sie... ab so wenig wie eine jungfräulichen Pfeil", noting "[e]in abgenutzter Pfeil ließe sich eher abwehren".
[7] Additional examples which we do not cite here include AVŚ 5.18.6 and AVP 16.64.2.

(18) AVŚ 3.29.6ab (with a preposed and a postposed comparison)
 írā͡iva   ná͡úpa dasyati |
 drink.NOM.SG like NEG be.exhausted.3SG
 samudrá   iva páyo   mahát ||
 ocean.NOM.SG like drink.NOM.SG great.NOM.SG
 'Like refreshing drink, it is not exhausted, like the ocean, a great draught.'
 (Whitney 1905)

Which seems to mean 'As a refreshing drink (is not exhausted), it is not exhausted, like the ocean, a great draught (is not exhausted)'.

(19) Ṛgveda 8.2.19bc[8]
 mā́ hṛṇīthā   abhⁱy asmā́n ||
 NEG be.angry.IMP at   us.ACC.PL
 mahā́m̐   iva yúvajāniḥ |
 great.NOM.SG like having.young.wife.NOM.SG
 'Stop being angry at us, like a great man with a young wife.'

Which we take to mean 'Do not be angry at us, like a great man with a young wife (is not angry)'.

The contrast between the "positive" and the "negative" clauses of comparison under matrix negation is quite clear in the data we have seen so far. Preposed clauses of comparison are all interpreted as negative clauses. Postposed clauses of comparison show two interpretations, and these two interpretations correlate perfectly with the prosody of the line: if the clause of comparison is "prosodically isolated" (either sitting between the caesura and line end, or between two line-ends) it is interpreted as negative, when it is not prosodically isolated, it is interpreted as positive.

It is worth pointing out how surprising a result like this would be if any of a number of somewhat widely held beliefs were actually true. If the language of the mantra Vedic period was a "free word order" language, for example, we would be in the presence of an astonishing coincidence. Similarly, if the placement of individual words in the string was determined by their metrical properties, i.e., if the word order was largely driven *metri causa*, the observed result could hardly be expected to hold.

---

[8] Other cases of the postposed type will be discussed below because they are of additional interest for one reason or another. These include AVP 6.8.4 and AVP 9.10.1.

The challenges with the interpretation of comparison clauses using only (our) notions of what kinds of things are comparable are well noted by Jamison in her online published commentary on the Jamison and Brereton translation. She writes:

> The context then must determine whether the form is inhibitive or preventive – in particular, the simile 'like a great man with a young wife,' the interpretation of which will be severely affected by interference from our contemporary assumptions about such a situation and by our lack of knowledge about the corresponding assumptions in ancient India. If we assume on the basis of popular Western depictions that young wives have many ways of annoying their old husbands (profligate spending, flirting with younger men, etc.), but also have many wiles to win back their husbands' favor, then an inhibitive would work. [http://rigvedacommentary.alc.ucla.edu/]

The syntax tells us that we are dealing with 'the many wiles', rather than 'the many ways of annoying', in the passage in (19).

Finally, if the caesura were a purely metrical consideration, with no relationship to the actual prosody of speech, it would be just as likely that postposed positive clauses of comparison would span the space between caesura and line-end as it would be that negative clauses of comparison do. But it seems much more likely that the correlation between the prosodic facts initially discussed for English and those found in the Vedas is systematic.

4 Embedded Clauses of Comparison

We have not seen a particularly large number of what we have called "positive" clauses of comparison under matrix negation. This is because the vast majority of these are found in the third possible position of the clause of comparison relative to its negated matrix: embedded. Typical examples include:[9]

(20) Ṛgveda 1.38.5ab
  mā́ vo mr̥gó ná yávase |
  NEG you.DAT.PL wild.animal.NOM.SG like pasture.LOC.SG
  jaritā́ bhūd ájoṣʲyaḥ ||
  singer.NOM.SG be.3SG displeasing.NOM.SG
  'Let your singer not be displeasing to you, like a wild animal in the pasture,'
  (Jamison and Brereton 2014)

---

[9] Not given in full anywhere in this paper are Ṛgveda 2.29.5d and Ṛgveda 8.92.30.

This seems to mean 'let your singer not be displeasing to you, like a wild animal in (one's) pasture (is displeasing)'.

(21) Ṛgveda 1.104.5d
 má no maghâ͡iva: niṣṣapī́ párā dāḥ ||
 NEG us.ACC.PL bounties.ACC.PL like careless.man.NOM.SG hand.over.2SG
 'Don't hand us over, like a careless man his bounties.'
 (Jamison and Brereton 2014)

Which means 'don't hand us over, like a careless man (hands over) his bounties'.

(22) Ṛgveda 8.75.9
 má naḥ samasya dūḍhʲyaḥ |
 NEG us.ACC.PL.CL anyone.GEN.SG bad.intentioned.GEN.SG
 páridveṣaso aṃhatíḥ ||
 hateful.GEN.SG coercion.NOM.SG
 ūrmír ná návam ā́ vadhīt ||
 wave.NOM.SG like boat.ACC.SG beat.down.3SG
 'Let not the coercion of anyone of evil intention and encompassing hatred crash down on us, like a wave on a boat.'
 (Jamison and Brereton 2014)

This means 'Let not the coercion of anyone of evil intention and encompassing hatred crash down on us, like a wave (crashes down) on a boat'.

(23) AVP 7.12.5
 na vai pāṭe pāṭā͡iva͡asi
 NEG PTCL pāṭā.VOC.SG splitter.NOM.SG like be.2SG
 'Not indeed, O Pāṭā, are you like a splitter!'

That is, 'you really are not, O Pāṭā, like a splitter (is)!'

There is, interestingly, a single example of a "negative" embedded clause of comparison – and we think its properties are of use to us in trying to understand with greater precision what is going on with this data. It is found in AVŚ 10.7.43ab:

(24) AVŚ 10.7.43ab
 táyor ahám: parinŕ́tyantyor iva |
 this.GEN.DU I.NOM dancing.about.GEN.DU like

> *ná víjānāmi: yatarā́ parástāt* ||
> NEG distinguish.1SG which.of.two.NOM.SG further.away
> 'Of them, as of two women dancing about,
> I do not distinguish which is further away.'
> (after Whitney 1905)

That is, 'I do not distinguish of the two of them which is the further away, like (I do not distinguish which) of two women dancing about (is further away)'. Notice that in this example, the clause of comparison is once again prosodically isolated – the caesura to its left, the line-end to its right. To help us understand what is going on in this example, we will now turn to some non-Sanskrit data.

When we discussed non-Sanskrit data at the start of this paper, we did not deal with issues surrounding embedded comparisons. Note the English data below:

(25a) *The leaf does not, like a rock, sink in the water.*
(25b) *The leaf, like a rock, does not sink in the water.* (pragmatically odd, since rocks sink)

Embedding alone does not determine whether the comparison clause is interpreted as negative (as in 25b) or positive (as in 25a). It is the position of the embedded clause relative to the negator that appears to be relevant. When the clause of comparison is higher than the negation (25b), it is interpreted negatively, when lower than the negation (25a), positively.

If we assume that the intonational reset (prosodic break), we see in the negatively interpreted postposed examples (14)–(19) above arises due to some kind of rightward dislocation (=attachment high to the right), then the data we have seen will be consistent. In the case of positively interpreted clauses of comparison under negated matrix clauses we find two patterns: embedded under (invariably) clause-initial (and thus "high") negation and clause-final without prosodic isolation. If we take the latter to be simply in situ (that is, not "rightward extraposed"), then these clauses will necessarily be lower than the negation, and the data patterns perfectly.

5 Implications for Less Clear Passages

We have mentioned some structural and prosodic implications of the data we have seen so far, but ultimately these considerations feed into another important mission of the linguistic analysis of Vedic Sanskrit: the interpretation of the texts.[10] In this section we'll discuss some passages where the precise semantics of the clause of comparison was not immediately obvious, at least to us (or, in some cases, to other scholars), with the hopes that our new-found structural understanding will lead us to a particular analysis.

We start with the passage from which the first line of our title is taken, which comes from:

(26) AVP 9.10.1cd (=AVP 2.2.3cd)
rasaṃ   viṣasya   na͡avidam |
essence.ACC.SG poison.GEN.SG NEG find.1SG
udnaḥ   phenam   adann   iva ||
water.GEN.SG foam.ACC.SG eating.NOM.SG like
'Ich habe die Essenz des Giftes nicht gefunden,
wie einer der den Schaum des Wassers isst.'
(Kim 2014)
['I have not found the essence of the poison, like one who eats the foam of the water.']

In this example we have matrix negation, with a postposed clause of comparison. The clause of comparison is bounded on both sides by a prosodic boundary (the line-end), indicating, if our assumptions about prosody in such cases are correct, that this clause is right-dislocated relative to the matrix. Such clauses, as shown above, receive a negative interpretation.

The notion of eating the foam off the water is not entirely clear to us; in particular, it is not clear whether that is supposed to be a poison-ingesting kind of act (since we don't know what kind of 'foam' or what kind of liquid is being referred to), or a completely safe act. Both Kim (2014) on AVP 9.10.1 and Zehnder (1999) on AVP 2.2.3 clearly take it in the latter sense. Kim adds in a comment that

---

10 We will ignore here two passages which are interesting, but not very revealing syntactically as to the interaction with matrix negation. Ṛgveda 10.178.2cd has a *ná* clause that is associated with a *mā́*-negated matrix, but the comparison is inside a vocative phrase, and thus not integrated into the structure of the clause at all. It therefore shows no interaction with the matrix negation, of course. In AVŚ 19.55.1 we find an *iva* comparison with a negated matrix clause, but the comparison is specifically associated with a participial clause: 'night after night bringing to him without mixture, as [=like one bringing–MRH] fodder to a horse that stands, let not us, O Agni, thy neighbors, receive harm, reveling with abundance of wealth, with food (*íṣ*)' [Whitney]. This participial clause, like the vocative, isolates the comparison clause from interaction with the matrix negation.

it should be interpreted as "du bist so wenig vergiftet wie einer, der ... isst" ('you are as little poisoned as someone who eats...'). But knowing what we want the passage to mean is one thing; knowing how it means that, another. Since this clause of comparison must be interpreted negatively, we believe we should take the sentence to mean 'I have not found the effective, i.e. poisoning, part of the poison, like one eating the foam from the water [does not find the effective, e.g., thirst-quenching or whatever, part of the water]'. This has the desired meaning, with an acceptably negative interpretation of the clause of comparison.

The next passage we will consider is Ṛgveda 8.81.3:

(27) Ṛgveda 8.81.3
na-hí   tvā   śūra   devā́ |
NEG-because you.ACC.SG champion.VOC.SG gods.NOM.PL
ná   mártāso   dítsantam ||
NEG mortals.NOM.PL wishing.to.give.ACC.SG
bhīmā́ṃ   ná   gā́ṃ   vāráyante ||
fearsome.ACC.SG like bull.ACC.SG hinder.3PL
'For when you wish to give, o champion, neither gods nor mortals hinder you, any more than they would a fearsome bull.'
(Jamison and Brereton 2014)

This clause involves matrix negation, with an embedded clause of comparison. The embedded clause is manifestly lower than the clause-initial, and thus high, negation. Under our analysis, this means that this clause must be interpreted positively (i.e., like they *do* hinder a fearsome bull). By contrast, Jamison and Brereton (2014) take the comparison in a negative sense (their translation is intended to convey 'like [they *do not* hinder] a fearsome bull'). It's pretty easy to imagine 'gods and men' not being interested in trying to hinder a fearsome bull, but it is also pretty easy to imagine that a fearsome bull is something you probably need to hinder. The syntax indicates that it is the latter, positive notion – that you do need to hinder a fearsome bull – that is being expressed.

In addition, there is some evidence that the need to constrain animals that are *bhīmá-* was something with which the ancient Indians were familiar. Ṛgveda 1.140.6d says *bhīmó ná ... durgŕ̥bhiḥ* 'difficult to grab hold of like a fearsome (bull)' – which seems to indicate that people were familiar with the necessity (and difficulty) of doing that grabbing (similarly *durvártuḥ* 'difficult to obstruct' at Ṛgveda 4.38.8d, Ṛgveda 6.6.5d). That one attempted to constrain such animals in a pen is clearly indicated by Ṛgveda 4.20.6c *ā́ dartā vájraṃ : sthá̄viraṃ ná bhīmā́ḥ* 'he splits open the cowpen as a fearsome (bull) does a sturdy (pen)'. Of course these passages also indicate how hard such constraining is, and thus probably can be equally well cited in support of the Jamison and Brereton (2014) interpretation. Again, in our view, the syntax decides the matter.

The consistency of the patterns we have identified allows us to clarify what for us at least is a fairly unclear comparison at AVŚ 4.36.6cd:[11]

(28) AVŚ 4.36.6cd
śvā́naḥ   siṃhám   iva   dr̥ṣṭvā́ |
dog.NOM.PL   lion.ACC.SG like   having.seen
té   ná   vindante   nyáñcanam ||
they.NOM.PL NEG find.3PL   hiding.place.ACC.SG
'Like dogs on seeing a lion, they do not find a hiding place.'

But do dogs find a hiding place when they see a lion, or some other dangerous predator? In our experience, the unfortunate answer is generally 'no' (e.g., when it comes to the dangers of an interaction with a horse or a skunk). But maybe interaction with lions is different? We can interpret this in one of two ways:

(29a) Like dogs (do not find a hiding place) upon seeing a lion, they do not find a hiding place.
(29b) They do not find a hiding place like dogs (find a hiding place) upon seeing a lion.

The structure – a preposed clause of comparison – is only attested in the presence of 'negative' interpretations, such as that in (29a). It would appear that dogs are just as stupid about lions as they are about skunks.

In R̥gveda 1.53.1cd, Jamison and Brereton (2014) have translated *sasatā́m iva* as 'among those who are, as it were, asleep'. The use of *iva* in the R̥gveda to mean 'as it were' is quite rare (though it is attested), and it seems to us that the alternative, which interprets the *iva*-clause as a positive clause of comparison embedded under the negation within the matrix, is at least as likely.

---

11 Whitney notes that: "[t]he comm[entary] reads *anu* instead of *na* in [pada] d." This would remove the negation from the matrix clause, and thus give the clause of comparison a positive sense – the one in (29b) in the main text below. There is no manuscript support for this modification – it would appear the commentator may have been just as confused about the comparison as we are.

(30) Ṛgveda 1.53.1cd
    nū́ cid dhí   rátnaṃ: sasatā́m   iva⌢ávidan |
    never because treasure.ACC.SG sleeping.GEN.PL like find.3SG
    ná duṣṭutíṛ: draviṇodéṣu   śasyate
    NEG bad.praise.hymn.NOM.SG givers.of.wealth.LOC.PL be.praised.3SG
    'Since it never found a treasure like (it does that) of the sleeping ones, a
    poor praise-hymn among the givers of wealth is not acclaimed.'

The idea, we take it, is that a poor praise hymn only gets rewarded by (i.e., finds the wealth of) patrons who have fallen asleep during the rite (since they won't notice how bad the hymn was), and thus is not worthy of acclaim. But the passage is certainly opaque. The only interpretation that is excluded by our analysis is one in which the *iva*-clause is interpreted negatively. This does not appear to have been suggested by any scholars.

AVP 6.8.4cd offers some interesting philological difficulties. We first give the passage, with the following translations of Lubotsky and Griffiths.[12]

(31) AVP 6.8.4cd
    na tvā́m   *avivyacad   iha- |
    NEG you.ACC.SG make.room.3SG here
    -ukhā⌢iva   śr̥ṅgavac   chiraḥ ||
    pot.NOM.SG like horned.NOM/ACC.SG head.NOM/ACC.SG
    'The horned head here has not given you room like an *ukhā*-pot.'
    (Lubotsky 2002: 40)
    'It (the plant) did not leave space to you here, as a stud bull [reading *ukṣeva*] (does not give space) to a horned head.'
    (Griffiths 2009: 100)

There are several issues here aside from the lexical one (*ukhā́* 'pot' vs. *ukṣā́* 'bull'). Syntactically, there is a question of whether the 'horned head' is the subject of the matrix verb (Lubotsky) or part of the clause of comparison (Griffiths). If it is part of the comparison, it must of course be an accusative direct object (parallel to matrix *tvā́m*), since *ukhā/ukṣā* is nominative.

Both Griffiths and Lubotsky seem to like the idea that bulls, or animals with horned heads in general, don't really like to "make room" for other beings, particularly (as Griffiths emphasizes) if those animals themselves have horned

---

[12] It may be worth noting that an *ukhā*-pot, sometimes translated 'cauldron', appears to be fairly large. It is the pot used in the Ṛgveda for the horse-stew sacrifice.

heads. There is nothing *a priori* objectionable in this, but we can't see what the pot is doing in Lubotsky's version of things (all he says is "[t]he implication seems to be that it is inconvenient here for the Sadānuvās, so that they better leave as soon as possible" – but how is the horned head not giving space 'like a pot'?). The syntax is critical, because if the 'horned head' is part of the matrix, we have an embedded clause of comparison, obviously lower than the (clause-initial) negation, and the comparison should therefore be positive. Griffiths explicitly translates it as negative (but, note, does not consider *śṛṅgavac chiraḥ* to be part of the matrix), and surely whatever exactly Lubotsky has in mind, it can't be 'the horned head here has not given you (Sādanuvās) room like an *ukhā*-pot (gives you room)'. The Sādanuvās are too big for a pot.

Thus, Lubotsky's interpretation is out if our structural analysis of clauses of comparison under matrix negation is correct. If we accept that *śṛṅgavac chiraḥ* is part of the comparison, then we have a postposed, prosodically isolated clause of comparison, which of course indicates that the comparison should be interpreted 'negatively'. Our own sense is that we should read *ukhā* with Lubotsky, and build our analysis around the simple fact that, if you want to put your head into a pot (e.g., to eat grain or water or whatever out of it), and you have horns, you have a problem. Your horns are in the way. So we would interpret this passage as 'it [the plant used in this ritual to ward off the demon] does not accommodate you (the demon) here, like a pot (does not accommodate) a horned head'.

One final passage which superficially shows a comparison clause with a matrix negation is probably corrupt in a way which makes it irrelevant. The passage is AVP 5.27.5.

(32) AVP 5.27.5
 devīm   ahaṃ : nirṛtiṃ   manyamānaḥ |
 goddess.ACC.SG I.NOM Nirṛti.ACC.SG paying.respect.NOM.SG
 pitā͡iva   putram : na sace   vacobhiḥ ||
 father.NOM.SG like son.ACC.SG NEG follow.1SG words.INS.PL
 'Paying respect to the goddess Nirṛti,
 I do not follow [her] with [my] words,
 like a father [does not follow his] son.'
 (Lubotsky 2002)

Note that the clause of comparison is embedded, but above the preverbal negation, so we expect a negative interpretation, just as Lubotsky indicates in his translation. This is satisfying, but would be more so if we could make any sense of what Lubotsky thinks the comparison means. How is a father 'not following' (in genetic succession?) his son like me not following Nirṛti with my words? In general, fathers do accompany their sons.

The passage has parallels in both the Taittirīya saṃhitā and the Kāṭhaka saṃhitā. For our *na sace vacobhiḥ* the Taittirīya saṃhitā passage reads *dasaye vacobhiḥ* 'I exhaust (her) with words', the Kāṭhaka saṃhitā passage *damaye vacobhiḥ* 'I subdue [her] with words'. As Lubotsky notes, the Kāṭhaka saṃhitā reading (and, we would say, the Taittirīya saṃhitā reading as well) give much better sense than that in the AVP. It appears we are dealing with a misreading of *damaye* (or *dasaye*) as *nasace*, not terribly implausible. Under this analysis, the passage would mean 'paying respect to the goddess Nirṛti, I subdue/ exhaust [her] with words, like a father (subdues/ exhausts) his son (with words)'. Both sons and fathers of sons can probably attest to the underlying *realia*. In the end, then, this passage does not actually contain a negation in the matrix clause, and is thus irrelevant to our considerations here.

There remain a number of philologically complex passages which we do not have time to treat in this paper, though none represents, in our view, a challenge to the analysis presented here. We cite them in the interest of completeness: Ṛgveda 6.67.9cd *ná yé devā́ sa óhasā ná mártā | áyajñasāco | ápiyo ná putrā́ḥ* (postposed, prosodically isolated, and expected to be "negative");[13] Ṛgveda 10.62.9ab *ná tám aśnoti káś caná | divá iva sā́nu ārábham* (postposed, prosodically isolated, and expected to be "negative");[14] and Ṛgveda 10.146.1d: *ná tvā bhī́r iva vindatī3m̐*, which Jamison and Brereton (2014) translate as 'Does fear not find you at all?', but which we would take to mean 'Does it not come upon you, like fear (does)?'[15] The clause of comparison would be embedded under the matrix negation in the latter example, and thus be expected to be positive. Finally in Ṛgveda 8.75.8 we have the only instance known to us of a "discontinuous" clause of comparison under matrix negation The discontinuity (interruption by the matrix verb, in our analysis) does not influence the positive interpretation we expect for a clause of comparison embedded under the negation. The interpretation is as in Jamison and Brereton (2014).

---

[13] Unfortunately, the interpretation of the clause of comparison, *ápiyo ná putrā́ḥ*, is not clear.
[14] We would translate 'No one attains him, like (one does not attain) the seizing of the back of heaven'.
[15] There is no clear antecedent for the 'it', we freely admit. The passage is pretty obscure.

6 Conclusions

To conclude, we hope to have shown that when clauses of comparison are within the scope of (i.e., structurally dominated by) a negation in their matrix clause, they are interpreted in a positive manner (i.e., as if the negation in the matrix is not part of the "gapped" material). By contrast, when clauses of comparison are outside the scope of (i.e., not structurally dominated by) a negation in their matrix clause, they are interpreted in a negative manner (i.e., as if the negation in the matrix is part of the "gapped" material).

Given this generalization, clauses of comparison that are to be interpreted positively, in this sense, are generally found embedded, under (usually = to the right of) the negation. This embedding will include both cases in which the clause of comparison is surrounded by material from the matrix clause and cases in which it is (accidentally) *in situ* at the right edge of the matrix clause. In the latter case, it is not generally separated from the matrix clause by a major prosodic boundary.

Clauses of comparison that are to be interpreted negatively, in this sense, are generally found at the left edge of the clause (and thus necessarily linearly before and structurally higher than the matrix negation) or extraposed to the right (and thus outside the scope of the negation). This extraposition is marked by the prosodic isolation of the clause of comparison, which is bounded on its left by a line boundary or caesura, and on its right by a line boundary.

These facts find clear parallels in the structural position and prosodification of clauses of comparison in living languages, and preclude interpretations of the language of the Vedic mantras as displaying "free word order" or a word order determined largely by metrical considerations. They are also consistent with specific interpretations of the prosodic force of the caesura (and line boundary) – in keeping with other well-known observations, e.g., involving clitic distribution relative to these boundaries – and inconsistent with a view which treats such boundaries as a purely metrical phenomenon.

It goes without saying that many issues concerning the internal and external syntax of clauses of comparison remain; we hope to have shown that their investigation can have broad implications for our understanding of these texts.

Abbreviations

1 = first person; 2 = second person; 3 = third person; ABL = ablative; ACC = accusative; CL = clitic; DAT = dative; DU = dual; GEN = genitive; IMP = imperative; INS = instrumental; LOC = locative; NEG = negation marker; NOM = nominative; PTCL = particle; REL = relative; SG = singular

Transliteration

The transliteration of Sanskrit data in this paper follows the standard IAST: https://en.wikipedia.org/wiki/International_Alphabet_of_Sanskrit_Transliteration

References

Bergaigne, Abel. 1887. La syntaxe des comparaisons védiques. *Mélanges Renier*, 75–101. Paris: Vieweg.
Bhattacharya, Dipak. 1997. *The Paippalāda-Saṃhitā of the Atharvaveda*, Volume 1 [Consisting of the First Fifteen Kāṇḍas]. Calcutta: The Asiatic Society.
Bhattacharya, Dipak. 2008. *The Paippalāda-Saṃhitā of the Atharvaveda*, Volume 2 [Consisting of the Sixteenth Kāṇḍa]. Calcutta: The Asiatic Society.
Bhattacharya, Dipak. 2011. *The Paippalāda-Saṃhitā of the Atharvaveda*, Volume 3 [Consisting of the Seventeenth and Eightteenth Kāṇḍas]. Calcutta: The Asiatic Society.
Bhattacharya, Dipak. 2016. *The Paippalāda-Saṃhitā of the Atharvaveda*, Volume 4 [Consisting of the Nineteenth and Twentieth Kāṇḍas]. Calcutta: The Asiatic Society.
Brereton, Joel P. 1982. The particle *iva* in Vedic Prose. *Journal of the American Oriental Society* 102. 443–450.
Griffiths, Arlo. 2009. The Paippalādasaṃhitā of the Atharvaveda, Kāṇḍas 6 and 7: a new edition with translation and commentary [Groningen Oriental Studies XXII]. Groningen: Egbert Forsten.
Hale, Mark. 2010. Some notes on the syntax of *iva*-clauses in Vedic. Paper presented at the 29th East Coast Indo-European Conference, Cornell University, 2010.
Jamison, Stephanie W. 1982. Case disharmony in Ṛgvedic similes. *Indo-Iranian Journal* 24. 251–271.
Jamison, Stephanie W. & Joel P. Brereton. 2014. *The Rigveda: The Earliest Religious Poetry of India*, Volumes 1–3. Oxford: Oxford University Press.
Kim, Jeong-Soo. 2014. Die Paippalādasaṃhitā des Atharvaveda Kāṇḍa 8 und 9: Eine neue Edition mit Übersetzung und Kommentar. Dettelbach a.M.: Verlag J. H. Röll.
Lopez, Carlos A. 2010. Atharvaveda-Paippalāda. Kāṇḍas Thirteen and Fourteen. Text, Translation, Commentary. Cambridge, MA: Harvard University.
Lubotsky, Alexander M. 2002. *Atharvaveda-Paippalāda, Kāṇḍa 5: text, translation, commentary*. Columbia, Missouri: South Asia Books.

Oldenberg, Hermann. 1907. Vedische Untersuchungen 18: Zu den Verbalpräfixen. *Zeitschrift der Deutschen Morgenländischen Gesellschaft* 61. 803–863.
Oldenberg, Hermann. 1909. *Ṛgveda: textkritische und exegetische Noten.* Volume 1. Berlin: Weidmann.
Oldenberg, Hermann. 1912. *Ṛgveda: textkritische und exegetische Noten.* Volume 2. Berlin: Weidmann.
Peust, Carsten. 2006. Die Syntax des Vergleichs mit *mj* 'wie' im Älteren Ägyptisch. In Gerald Moers, Heike Behlmer, Katja Demuß & Kai Widmaier (eds.), *jn.t dr.w: Festschrift für Friedrich Junge,* 485–519. Göttingen: Seminar für Ägyptologie und Koptologie.
Pinault, Georges-Jean. 1985. Négation et comparaison en védique. *Bulletin de la Société de Linguistique de Paris* 80 (1). 103–144.
Pinault, Georges-Jean. 1996. Distribution des particules comparatives dans la Ṛk-Saṁhitā. *Bulletin d'Études Indiennes* 13–14. 307–367.
Pinault, Georges-Jean. 1997. Distribution de la particule négative *ná* dans la Ṛk-Saṁhitā. *Bulletin d'Études Indiennes* 15. 213–246.
Pinault, Georges-Jean. 2004. On the usages of the particle *iva* in the Ṛgvedic hymns. In Arlo Griffiths & Jan Houben (eds.), *The Vedas: texts, language and ritual.* Groningen: Forsten.
Pischel, Richard & Karl F. Geldner. 1889. *Vedische Studien I.* Stuttgart: Kohlhammer.
Schrapel, Dieter. 1970. *Untersuchung der Partikel iva und anderer lexikalisch-syntaktischer Probleme der vedischen Prosa nebst zahlreichen Textemendationen und der kritischen Übersetzung von Jaiminīya-Brāhmaṇa* 2, 371–373. [Gavāmayana I]. Marburg: Marburg University Dissertation.
Vine, Brent. 1978. On the metrics and origin of Rig-Vedic *ná* 'like, as'. *Indo Iranian Journal* 20. 171–193.
Whitney, W. D. 1905. *Atharva-Veda Samhitā* [Translated with a Critical and Exegetical Commentary by William Dwight Whitney. Revised and Brought Nearer to Completion and Edited by Charles Rockwell Lanman]. Cambridge, MA: Harvard University Press.
Zehnder, Thomas. 1999. *Atharvaveda-Paippalāda*, Buch 2: Text, Übersetzung, Kommentar. Idstein: Schulz-Kirchner Verlag.

Massimo Vai
Some questions about *yád* in Vedic

Abstract: This paper considers two problems: the placement of the complementizer *yád* within the sentence and the functional value of *yád* in Vedic. As for the first point, it will be noted that the complementizer *yád*, like other subordinating conjunctions in some ancient and modern Indo-European languages, can be preceded by a topicalized or a focalized phrase in its clause. In particular, in the Ṛgveda there are many cases where *yád* is preceded by an element which seems to have moved from inside the sentence, and also cases where it is preceded by the inflected verb. With regard to the second point, some cases will be discussed showing the use of *yád* to introduce clauses governed by verbs of saying and knowing (not only in the Chāndogya-Upaniṣad and the Kaṭha-Upaniṣad, but also in the Ṛgveda) and a possible syntactic analysis of these structures.

Keywords: Vedic syntax; Indo-European syntax; Vedic clausal Left Periphery; Indo-Aryan complementizers

1 Introduction

A century after Hermann's *Gab es im Indogermanischen Nebensätze?* (Hermann 1985), Kiparsky (1995: 141) claims that:

> On the evidence of Vedic, Greek, and Hittite, the Indo-European proto-language had two left-peripheral operator positions corresponding to those in Hale[1] [...] However, *it lacked the category of complementizer and had no syntactically embedded sentences*. Finite subordinate clauses, including relative clauses and sentential complements, were syntactically adjoined to the main clause, exhibiting "main-clause properties", such as topicalization of constituents to clause-initial position.

The idea that topicalization is only typical of main clauses can be considered superseded by Rizzi's *Left Periphery Theory* (Rizzi 1997), according to which topic

---

[1] According to Hale (1987b: 41): "This "topicalization" process [i.e. fronting a constituent to bring it into special emphasis] can be formally represented as movement into a topicalization slot to the left of the COMP slot: [S2 TOP [S1 COMP [S ...ká...X...]]]".

Massimo Vai, University of Milan, Department of Philosophy, Via Festa del Perdono 7, Milan, Italy. Email: massimo.vai@unimi.it

https://doi.org/10.1515/9783110753066-002

and focus (and related projections) are no longer considered specific to main clauses alone, but also to subordinate clauses. Hale's observations (1987a, 1987b) about the old Indo-European languages can thus be seen as special cases of the articulation of the left periphery of the sentence. Vedic clauses introduced by *yád* (morphologically identical to the neuter singular of the relative pronoun) correspond semantically to propositions of several functions: *yád* seems to behave like an introducer of particular types of sentences which, on the basis of Delbrück (1900: 324), Hettrich (1988: 395) classifies as *Explikativsätze* of temporal, conditional, causal, final, concessive, explanatory value. This paper considers two problems: first, the placement of the complementizer *yád* within the sentence, and second, the functional value of *yád* in Vedic. In order to deal with the first question, let us first make a few remarks about the Left Periphery in the Vedic sentence.

2 The Left Periphery in the Vedic sentence

Hale (1987a, 1987b) considered examples like the following ones:

(1) Ṛgveda 6.27.1b:
  *índraḥ   kím   **asya**   sakhyé   cakāra*
  Indra.NOM what of.it   fellowship.LOC made.PRF.3SG
  'What did Indra create in the fellowship of it?'[2]

(2) Ṛgveda 8.64.9c
  *ukthé   ká   **u**   **svid**   ántamaḥ*
  recitation.LOC who PTCL PTCL closest.NOM
  'Who at the recitation is closest (to you)?'

(3) Ṛgveda 4.12.2a
  *idhmáṃ yás   **te**   jabhárac   chaśramāṇáḥ*
  fuel   REL.NOM to.you bring.PRF.SBJV.3SG laboring.NOM.SG
  'Whoever will labor to bring fuel to you.'

(4) Ṛgveda 2.23.7a
  *utá **vā** yó   **no** marcáyād   ánāgasaḥ*
  also or REL.NOM us harm.SBJV.3SG innocent.ACC.PL
  'Or who is about to injure us who are without offense.'

---

[2] Unless otherwise indicated, the translation of Ṛgvedic passages is from Jamison and Brereton (2014).

In (1)–(4), we see a placement of Wackernagel pronouns or particles that is linearly different from the second position. However, Wackernagel's Law is still regularly applied if we admit that a topicalized initial constituent is "skipped" compared to an actual second position. This is also evident in other languages which use second position clitics; see also Krisch (1990: 71), Adams (1994: 106):

(5) Odyssey 20.47-48
 autàr   egṑ theós eimi   diamperès   hḗ   se
 but   I   god   be.1SG continuously REL.NOM you.ACC
 phulássō
 guard.1SG
 'But I am a god, that guard you to the end in all your toils.'

In (5) we see that the clitic *se* 'you-ACC' is in the second position after the relative *hḗ* (NOM.SG.F.), which is however preceded by the adverb *diamperés* 'continuously', and thus linearly placed in third position.

(6) Cicero, *Epistulae ad Atticum* 7.2.6
 *de   triumpho   autem// nulla **me** cupiditas   umquam tenuit*
 about   triumph.ABL   but   no   me   desire.NOM   ever   held.3SG
 'But as far as the triumph is concerned, no-**me**-desire ever held.'
 (Adams 1994: 106)

Similarly, in (6) *me* is in the second position after *nulla*, which is preceded by the topicalized constituent *de triumpho autem*.

Independently from Hale, Rizzi (1997) proposed an analysis of the initial part of the sentence (*Left Periphery*) in terms of general comparative syntax, and several subsequent studies have confirmed this theory also for genealogically different languages. Rizzi (1997) proposes an articulation of the initial part of the sentence as shown in the following structure:

(7) [ForceP [TopP* [FocP [TopP* [FinP]]]]]

According to Rizzi, the Force of the sentence is encoded in the leftmost projection; as Rizzi suggests, it "looks outside", connecting the sentence with the context or marking it with respect to its clausal type. The rightmost projection looks inside, towards the content of the IP (the choice of the complementizer, for example, has to do with the modality and tense in IP). Thematized and focused phrases are hosted in dedicated functional projections labeled TopP and FocP. Benincà

(2001) proposes a different scheme, claiming that Topics can only be inserted to the left of FocP. She suggests the following structure:

(8) [ForceP [FrameP [TopP [FocP [FinP]]]]]

Hale's observations (1987a, 1987b) can thus be seen as special cases of the articulation of the left periphery of the sentence, see e.g.:

(9) Ṛgveda 6.47.15
 ká   īṃ   stavat   káḥ   pṛṇāt   kó   yajāte
 who   him   praise.SBJV.3SG who fill.SBJV.3SG who   sacrifice.SBJV.3SG
 yád ugrám   ín   maghávā   viśváh_ấvet
 if   strong.ACC PTCL bounteous.NOM   always help.OPT.3SG
 'Who will praise him, who will fill him, who will sacrifice to him, if the bounteous one would always help only the strong?'

(10) Ṛgveda 1.168.8
 áva   smayanta   vidyútaḥ   pṛthivyā́ṃ
 down   smile.INJ.3PL lightning.flashes.NOM   earth.LOC
 yádī ghṛtám   marútaḥ   pruṣṇuvánti
 when ghee.ACC   Marut.NOM.PL   sprinkle.3PL
 'The lightning-flashes smile down on the earth, when the Maruts sprinkle ghee upon her.'

(9) and (10) show that after *yád, yádī*, focused constituents appear in the Left Periphery, in a different order from the expected SOV (*ugrám ín magʰávā, gʰṛtám marútaḥ*), which should imply a syntactic space in which these elements can be placed. Some Indo-European languages also allow the placement of some elements of the sentence on the left of the complementizer (see Fortson 2004: 145):

(11) [XPᵢ [C° [...tᵢ...

Danckaert (2012: 95) called this phenomenon *Left Edge Fronting* (LEF); it is attested in a range of Indo-European languages. For instance, it is quite frequent in Latin, as illustrated in examples (12) and (13):

(12) Cicero, *Epistulae ad Atticum* 9.15.1
 [*Eum*ᵢ[*cum t*ᵢ*uidero*]], *Arpinum pergam*.
 'When I have seen him, I'll proceed to Arpinum.'

(13) Cicero, *Epistulae ad Atticum* 8.15.1
[*Quod*₁ [*cum* t₁ *scies*]], *facies utsciamus*
'When you know this, you will make sure that we know it (as well).'

3 The placement of *yád* in the Vedic sentence

On the basis of Krapova (2010: 1257), Danckaert (2015: 267) analyzes (12)–(13) by hypothesizing that a subordinating conjunction can be merged below ForceP, e.g. in FinP (see also Hsu 2015 for analogous placements of complementizer *je* in Bangla, which can be preceded by a topicalized or focalized phrase in its clause).³ In the R̥gveda there are many cases where *yád* is preceded by an element which seems to have moved from inside the sentence, e.g.:

(14) R̥gveda 3.2.7
ā́ ródasī apr̥ṇad ā́ svàr mahā́j
PTCL two.worlds.ACC fill.IMPRF.3SG PTCL sun.ACC great.ACC
jātáṃ yád enam apáso ádhārayan
born.ACC when him workers.NOM support.IMPRF.3PL
'He filled both world-halves, he filled the great sun, when the (ritual) workers supported him (when he was) just born.'

(15) R̥gveda 4.30.13
utá śúṣṇasya dhr̥ṣṇuyā́ prá mr̥kṣo abhí védanam
and Śuṣṇa.GEN boldly PTCL seize.INJ.2SG PTCL possessions.ACC
púro yád asya sampiṇák
fortresses.ACC when his crush.INJ.2SG
'And you boldly seized the possessions of Śuṣṇa, when you completely crushed his fortresses.'

(16) R̥gveda 1.158.5c
śíro yád asya traitanó vitákṣat
head.ACC when of.him Traitana.NOM cut.off.INJ.3SG
svayáṃ dāsá úro áṃsāv ápi gdha
himself Dāsa.NOM chest shoulders PTCL eat.INJ.MID.3SG
'When Traitana cut off the head, the Dāsa himself ate his own chest and shoulders.'

---

3 Cases of two cooccurring complementizers in the same clause in some Romance varieties also suggest that there can be more than one projection dedicated to the placement of the complementizer (see Paoli 2007).

(17) Ṛgveda 1.164.4
kó   dadarśa   prathamáṃ   jā́yamānam
who see.PRF.3SG   first.ACC   born.PRS.PTCP.ACC
asthanvántaṃ   yád   anasthā́   bíbharti
having.bones.ACC   when   boneless.NOM   carry.3SG
'Who has seen the first one as he is being born, when his boneless (mother) carries the one having bones?'

In (14)–(17), *jātáṃ, púro, śíro,* and *astʰanvántaṃ* are objects placed on the left of *yád* which are governed by verbs introduced by *yád*. If we do not accept the idea of a movement from within CP (extraction), it is difficult to understand which element of the sentence assigns case to the element external to the complementizer. If it had been placed before the subordinate clause then it should have received a default case at the beginning of the derivation of the sentence, see e.g. cases of *nominativus pendens* in Vedic observed by Œrtel (1926):

(18) Āśvalāyana-Śrautasūtra 10.7.1
manur   vaivasvatas   tasya   manuṣyā   viśas
Manu.NOM Vaivasvata.NOM of.him   men.NOM   people.NOM.PL
'Manu Vivasvat's son, his people are men.'

(19) Śatapatha-Brāhmaṇa 4.4.5.1
áth_aitác   chárīram   tásmin   ná   ráso 'sti
now that.NOM   body.NOM   in.it   NEG   sap is
'Now that body, there is no sap in it.'

On the contrary, in the cases present in the Ṛgveda, the element to the left of the complementizer is assigned case by a head which is inside the subordinate clause, e.g.:

(20) Ṛgveda 1.32.14
áher   yātā́ram   kám   apaśya   indra
serpent.GEN   avenger.ACC   who.ACC   see.IMPRF.2SG Indra.VOC
hṛdí   yát   te   jaghnúṣo   bhīr   ágachat
heart.LOC when   of.you   smash.PRF.PTCP.GEN   fear.NOM   come.IMPRF.3SG
'Whom did you see, Indra, as the avenger of the serpent when fear came into your heart after you smashed him?'

(21) Ṛgveda 1.52.10
vṛtrásya   yád   badbadhānásya   rodasī
Vṛtra.GEN   when   press.INT.PTCP.GEN   two.worlds.ACC

máde	sutásyaśávas_ā́bhinac	chírah
exhilaration.LOC	pressed.GEN power.INS split.IMPRF.2SG	head.ACC

'...when, in the exhilaration of the pressed soma, with your vast power you split the head of Vṛtra, who was pressing harder and harder upon the two world-halves.'

(22) Ṛgveda 1.52.6c
vṛtrásya yát pravaṇé durgṛ́bhiśvano
Vṛtra.GEN when torrent.LOC hard.to.grasp.GEN
nijaghántha hánvor indra tanyatúm
struck.PRF.2SG jaws.LOC Indra.VOC thunder.ACC
'When you, Indra, struck your thunder down upon the jaws of Vṛtra, Hard-to-Grasp, in the (waters') torrent.'

In (20)–(22), *hṛdí* "heart" and *vṛtrásya* "of Vṛtra" are governed by heads which are placed to the right of *yád*.[4] There is also another explanation for this particular placement of *yád*. Lowe (2014: 24–26), on the basis of Hettrich (1988: 760–762), assumes that the relative pronoun *yá-* may behave like a syntactic clitic in some contexts. In fact, in Vedic the relative pronoun *yá-* is placed either at the beginning of the relative clause or in a similar position to a Wackernagel clitic, e.g.:

(23) Ṛgveda 3.6.8
uraú **vā yé** antárikṣe mádanti
broad.LOC or REL.NOM.PL midspace.LOC rejoice.3PL
divó **vā yé** rocané sánti devā́ḥ
heaven.GEN or REL.NOM.PL light.LOC be.3PL gods.NOM
'Whether (they be) the gods who rejoice in the broad mid-space or those who are in the luminous realm of heaven, ...'

According to Lowe's hypothesis, the relative pronoun behaves as if it were an element of a clitic cluster *vā yé* which seems to interrupt the phrases [*uraú antárikṣe*] "in the broad midspace" and [*divó rocané*] "in the light of heaven". This behavior, together with the fact that the relative pronoun is frequently preceded by preverbs in tmesis (while this never happens e.g. to the interrogative pronoun

---

4 Interestingly, Viti (2015: 328–329) thinks that the interpretation of a syntactic movement and an extraction from CP for this kind of topicalizations is incorrect, because she considers old subordinating conjunctions as still being frozen forms of relative pronouns: further research should prove useful in this direction.

ká-),[5] leads Lowe to think that Vedic relative pronouns can behave like Wackernagel clitics, even though they are accented. This clearly resembles the same situation found e.g. in Old Irish, as already assumed in Watkins (1963: 29). It seems reasonable to adopt the same explanation in cases where the inflected verb is immediately followed by the complementizer *yád*, which can be analyzed as a syntactically clitic complementizer, e.g.:

(24) Ṛgveda 1.138.2
huvé **yát** tvā mayobhúvaṃ
call.1SG when you.ACC refreshment.being.ACC
devám sakhyā́ya mártyaḥ
god.ACC fellowship.DAT mortal.NOM
'When I, a mortal, call upon you, a god, who are refreshment itself, for fellowship ...'

(25) Ṛgveda 1.153.3
hinóti **yád** vāṃ vidáthe saparyán
spur.3SG when you.two.ACC ceremony.LOC serve.PRS.PTCP.NOM.SG
'When serving you at the ceremony, he spurs you two on.'

(26) Ṛgveda 4.15.7a
bódhad **yán** mā háribhyāṃ kumāráḥ sāhadevyáḥ
awaken.INJ.3SG if me two.bays.INS prince.NOM Sāhadevya.NOM
'If Prince Sāhadevya will awaken me with two fallow bays.'

(27) Ṛgveda 4.44.2
yuvór vápur abhí pṛ́kṣaḥ sacante
you.two.GEN beauty PTCL nourishments.NOM escort.3PL
váhanti **yát** kakuhā́so ráthe vām
convey.3PL when humped.NOM.PL chariot.LOC you.two.ACC
'Nourishments escort your wondrous form when the humped horses [?] convey you on the chariot.'

Perhaps these uses of *yád* are comparable with some relative forms which we find in Celtic, where relative clauses can be realized by means of a relative particle **i̯od* cliticized to the verb:[6] Gaulish *dugiiontiio* < **dugii̯onti-i̯o* and *toncsiiontio* < **tonc-si̯o-nt-i̯o* (see e.g. Thurneysen, Binchy and Bergin 1946: 323; Ziegler 1992:

---

[5] Lowe (2014: 30).
[6] Ziegler (1992: 254): "Es handelt sich um Relativsatzkonstruktionen mit einem unselbständigen Relativaffix, das auf die alte Form des Neutrums **i̯od* mit Abfall des auslautenden *-d* zurückzuführen ist".

254; Holland 1996: 324; Delamarre 2003: 153, 298; *contra* Dunkel 2014, II: 385). Moreover, Old Irish relative verb forms are analyzed in the same way, with a clitic relative particle *e* < PIE *$i̯o$-, e.g.: *bertae* "who bear" <*$beronti$-$i̯o$, 3pl.rel. of *beirid* "bear"; *imm-e-chuirethar* "who carry" 3pl.rel. of *imm-cuirethar* "carry (around)" < PIE *$n̥bhí$-$korH$-$éi̯e$-, where the relative particle is preceded by the preverb in tmesis, like *yád* in Vedic, e.g.:

(28) Ṛgveda 1.39.1
prá yád itth- ā́parāvátaḥ śocír   ná mā́nam   ásyatha
PTCL when so distance.ABL flame.NOM like measure?.ACC cast.2PL
'When from the far distance you cast your measure [/your bellowing], like a flame, just so.'

4 Syntactic category of Vedic *yád*

As we have already seen, according to Kiparsky (1995: 141) "[...] the Indo-European proto-language [...] lacked the category of complementizer and had no syntactically embedded sentences". Krisch disagrees with this conclusion (1998: 359) and claims that, since subordination and subordinating conjunction structures appear everywhere in the Indo-European languages, there is no problem in accepting this structure for the Protolanguage as well: this would also bypass the problem of having to explain why the CP structure came into existence. Lühr (2008: 154–155)[7] suggests that the evolution of the relative pronoun into the conjunction 'that' must be considered part of the Proto-Indo-European language, because of the many explicative clauses documented in older Indo-European languages. In her opinion, however, *that*-clauses in Proto-Indo-European, just like adverbial clauses, were adjoined and not embedded, since they occurred in a subcategorization frame where verbs could subcategorize for nominal/pronominal reference + *that*-clause, that is to say for NPs, but not for CPs.

4.1 Vedic clauses introduced by *yád*

Vedic clauses introduced by *yád* (morphologically identical to relative neuter pronouns) correspond semantically to propositions with several functions. However, unlike the homophonic pronoun *yád*, this kind of *yád* does not take the

---

7 See also Hettrich (1988: 407–408).

place of the argument of the clause in which it occurs, as happens in the following example (see Hettrich 1988: 541; Davison 2009: 227–228):

(29) Ṛgveda 1.179.3
ná mṛ́ṣā śrāntáṃ yád ávanti devā́ḥ
not useless pain REL.ACC help.3PL gods.NOM
'Not in vain is the labor that the gods help.'

In (29) *yád* is co-referent with the subject *śrāntám*, but it functions as the object of *ávanti*. However, in the case of *yád* as the introducer of sentences, *yád* is not an argument of the proposition. This is similar to Italian *(il fatto) che* ('the fact that') which can introduce sentences in which the arguments of the verbs are already completely saturated, e.g.:

(30a) *Il fatto che Gianni ha mangiato la pizza mi rallegra*
Lit.: 'The fact that Gianni ate the pizza makes me happy.'

As opposed to:

(30b) *Il fatto che Gianni mi ha raccontato mi rallegra.*
Lit.: 'The story that Gianni narrated makes me happy.'

We can also find analogous cases in Vedic, where what formally appears as the neuter of the relative *yá-* is not an argument of the verb:

(31) Ṛgveda 1.93.4
ágnīṣomā céti tád vīryàṃvāṃ
Agni.and.Soma.VOC be.conspicuous.AOR.PASS.3SG this deed of.you.two
yád ámuṣṇītam avasáṃ paṇíṃ gā́ḥ
that steal.IMPRF.2DU food niggard/Paṇi.ACC cows.ACC
'Agni and Soma, this heroic deed of you two has become conspicuous, that you two stole the food from the niggard/Paṇi, the cows.'

(32) Ṛgveda 2.13.11
supravācanáṃ táva vīra vīryàṃ
good.to.praise of.you hero.VOC heroism
yád ékena krátunā vindáse vásu
that one.INS power.INS obtain.2SG goods.ACC
'Your heroism, o hero, is good to proclaim: that with your power alone you take possession of goods.'

In (31) and (32), *yád* introduces a proposition of which it is not an argument: *yád* here seems to behave like an introducer of particular types of sentences which Hettrich (1988: 395), following Delbrück (1900: 324), classifies as *Explikativsätze* of a temporal, conditional, causal, final, concessive, explanatory value. As we have already seen in (31) and (32), these sentences may depend on a noun, for which they constitute an explanation;[8] see also e.g.:

(33) Ṛgveda 1.94.14
 tát te bhadráṃ yát sámiddhaḥ své dáme
 this of.you benefit that kindle.PST.PASS.PTCP own.LOC house.LOC
 sómāhuto járase mṛḷayáttamaḥ
 soma.offered.NOM be.awake.PRS.2SG[9] most.merciful.NOM
 'This is your benefit, that, kindled in your own house and be poured with soma, you remain wakeful as the most merciful.'

According to Delbrück (1900: 324), this value of *yád* has developed from temporal sentences, hence: "this is your grace (/ benefit / gift), when ...". Chantraine (1953: 288) instead thinks that "Les propositions déclaratives sont issues de propositions complétives de cause". In any case, they can be introduced by the neuter *hó* < *Hi̯od* also in Greek, *hó* being formally identical to Vedic *yád* (see Delbrück 1900: 319, 326). Delbrück's opinion[10] is that "*yád* erscheint bereits im RV als fertige Conjunction, so dass wir ihre Entwickelung aus dem Neutrum des Relativums in dem überlieferten Sanskrit nicht mehr verfolgen konnen". Lühr (2008: 154) proposes this formal description of the process (which, according to her, must be considered part of the Proto-Indo-European language): the *wh*-phrase originally occupies the specifier position of a CP; following the disappearance of the *wh*-feature, the original relative pronoun would then occupy the previously empty complementizer position and thus become the head of the CP.

In general, *yád*-clauses are propositions that can have different values, for example the value of a subject, as in (34):

(34) = (31) Ṛgveda 1.93.4
 ágniṣomā céti tád vīryàṃ vām
 Agni.and.Soma.VOC be.conspicuous.AOR.PASS.3SG this deed of.you.two

---

8 See Axel-Tober (2017: 41–42) and quoted literature for several proposals of theorical analysis of the explicative clauses.
9 Lubotsky (1997: 492); LIV2 (245–246); Grassmann (1996: 478). √*jar* "rauschen, knistern".
10 Delbrück (1888: 572).

> *yád ámuṣṇītam avasáṃ paṇíṃ gā́ḥ*
> that steal.IMPRF.2DU food niggard/Paṇi.ACC cows.ACC
> 'Agni and Soma, this heroic deed of you two has become conspicuous, that you two stole the food from the niggard/Paṇi, the cows.'

However, they may also have the value of an object, e.g.:

(35) Ṛgveda 1.131.4
vidúṣ ṭe asyá vīryàsya pūrávaḥ
know-PRF.3PL of.you this.GEN deed.GEN Pūru.NOM.PL
púro yád indra śáradīr avā́tiraḥ
stronghold.ACC that Indra.VOC autumnal.ACC bring.down.IMPRF.2SG
sāsahānó avā́tiraḥ
be.victorious.PRF.PTCP.NOM bring.down.IMPRF.2SG
'The Pūrus know of this deed of yours, o Indra, that you brought down the autumnal strongholds, being victorious you brought (them) down.'

In (35) the arguments that saturate the verb *ava-√tṛ-* "bring down" are: the 2SG agent (i.e., *Indra*) and the patient *pur-* "stronghold"; in any case, *yád* is not an argument of the sentence: it has an explanatory value with respect to *vīryàsya* "of the deed".

According to Hettrich (1988), the explanatory proposition can appear without a nominal head in the main clause: in this case, only a demonstrative pronoun can occur in the main clause, which indicates the syntactic function of the explanatory proposition, of a subject or of an object or even of an adverbial function (cf. Hettrich 1988: 398–400):

(36) Ṛgveda 5.31.7
tád ín nú te káraṇaṃ dasma vipra_áhiṃ
this PTCL now of.you deed wondrous.VOC poet.VOC_serpent.ACC
yád ghnánn ójo átr_ámimīthāḥ
yád smash.PRS.PTCP.NOM strength there_measure.IMPRF.2SG
'Just this now is your deed, wondrous poet: that smashing the serpent, you measured your strength there.'

(37) Ṛgveda 1.116.5 (according to Hettrich's analysis)
anārambhaṇé tád avīrayethām anāsthāné agrabhaṇé
unsupporting.LOC this √vīray.IMPRF.2DU unstable.LOC ungraspable.LOC
samudré yád aśvinā ūháthur bhujyúm ástam
sea.LOC that Aśvins.VOC carry.PRF.2DU Bhujyu.ACC home.ACC

'You two have accomplished this as heroic feat, on the unsupporting, unstable and ungraspable sea, that you Aśvins carried Bhujyu home.'

(38) Ṛgveda 1.164.23
yád gāyatré   ádhi   gāyatrám   ā́hitaṃ
that gāyatrī-hymn-LOC PTCL gayatri-line based-PST.PASS.PTCP
traíṣṭubhād   vā   traíṣṭubhaṃ   nirátakṣata
triṣṭubh-hymn-ABL or triṣṭubh-line fashion-IMPRF.MID.3SG
yád vā jágaj jágaty   ā́hitam   padám
that or jagatī jagatī-hymn-LOC based-PST.PASS.PTCP line
yá ít tád vidús   té   amṛtatvám   ānaśúḥ
who PTCL this know-PRF.3PL those-NOM immortality-ACC reach-PRF.3PL
'(The fact) that the *gāyatrī* line is based upon a *gāyatrī* hymn or that a *triṣṭubh* line was fashioned out of a *triṣṭubh* hymn, or that the *jagatī* line is based on the *jagatī* hymn, only those who know this have reached immortality.'

In (38), the arguments of *ā-√dhā-* and *nis-√takṣ-* are the *gayatrī, tristubh, jagatī* lines and the corresponding hymns composed in those meters: in this case *yád* is not an argument of the sentence, but it introduces the propositions whose content is resumed with *tád* in the main clause.[11] We find the same construction also in Homeric Greek (see Chantraine 1953: 289), e.g.:

(39) Iliad.1.120
leússete gàr   tó ge pántes   hó   moi   géras érkhetai állēi
see.2PL in.fact this PTCL all.NOM.PL that to.me prize goes elsewhere
'For you all see this, that my prize goes elsewhere.'

(40) Iliad 9.493
tà   phronéōn hó moi   oúti   theoì   gónon
this.ACC thinking that to.me not.at.all gods.NOM son
exetéleion
accomplish.IMPRF.3PL
'Thinking this, that the gods did not grant me a son.'

---

11 (38) shows that explicative clauses can occur also preposed to the matrix clause, contrary to what Axel-Tober (2017: 56) claims: "... even in Vedic, a language where relative clauses could be pre-, intra-, or postposed, explicative clauses always occurred in postposed position".

4.2 *Yád*-clauses without correlative in the matrix clauses

Interestingly, Speyer (1896: 87) observes that the demonstrative in the main clause is often lacking with verbs of knowing, thinking, believing, etc., where *yád* introduces an object clause, e.g.:

(41) Chāndogya-Upaniṣad 4.10.5
vijānāmy   aham yat prāṇo   brahma
understand.1SG I   that breath.NOM Brahman
kaṃ ca   tu   khaṃ ca   na   vijānāmi   iti
ka   and but kha   and NEG understand.1SG QUOT
'I understand that Brahman is breath. But I do not understand [that Brahman is] *ka* and *kha*.'[12]

(42) Kaṭha-Upaniṣad 1.1.22
devair   atr_āpi   vicikitsitaṃ   kila
gods.INS here_also   doubted.PST.PASS.PTCP   PTCL
tvaṃ ca   mṛtyo   yan na   sujñeyam   āttha
you and death.VOC that NEG well.understandable   say.PRF.2SG
'Even the gods had doubt, indeed, as to this, and you said, O Death, that it is not easy to understand.'[13]

With reference to (39) and (40), Haudry (2012: 22–23) claims that: "La proposition complétive conjonctive régime d'un verbe de ce genre [*scil.* "say" and "know"] est totalement inconnue en védique, y compris dans la prose, et n'apparaît pas avant les *Upaniṣad*... Le védique n'a pas d'équivalent pour les tours *dire que, savoir que*, etc.".[14] Haudry thinks that competition with *iti*-clauses hindered the development from a case like (43): *gṛṇé tád... yád...* to a true completive: **gṛṇé... yád dháṃsi vṛtrám* "je chante que tu frappes à mort Vṛtra" (according to Haudry, Ch. Up. 4.10.5 *vijānāmy ahaṃ yat prāṇo brahma* would be not a good example of completive, because it is a nominal clause).

---

[12] Radhakrishnan (1994: 413): "I understand that life is Brahman. But joy and ether I do not understand".
[13] Radhakrishnan (1994: 604).
[14] See also Viti (2007: 218–219) : "In the Rig-Veda, explicative clauses are adjoined clauses [...] A path of increasing grammaticalization such as lexical antecedent > grammatical antecedent > zero antecedent can be reconstructed, taking into account the frequency of these three types of clause linkage in the Rig-Veda [...] Differently, in Classical Sanskrit, explicative clauses show a higher degree of syntacticization: the antecedent noun is canceled, and the subordinate clause is embedded as the main clause object [...] or as the main clause subject".

(43) R̥gveda 8.62.8
gr̥ṇé   tád indra   te   śáva   upamā́m
sing.MID.1SG this Indra.VOC of.you   strength.ACC highest.ACC
devátātaye   yád dháṃsi   vr̥trám   ójasā
divine.assembly.DAT that smash.2SG Vr̥tra.ACC   might.INS
'I sing that utmost strength of yours, Indra, for the divine assembly, that you smash Vr̥tra with your might, o lord of ability.'

However, Haudry also quotes this example "tout près d'une complétive en dépendance d'un verbe déclaratif":

(44) R̥gveda 1.132.4
nū́   itthā́   te   pūrváthā   ca   pravā́cyam
now especially of.you   previously   and   to.be.proclaimed.NOM.SG.N
yád áṅgirobhyó   'vr̥ṇor   ápa   vrajám
that Aṅgirases.DAT   uncover.IMPRF.2SG   PTCL   enclosure.ACC
'Now as well as it is to be proclaimed of you, that you opened up the enclosure for the Aṅgirases.'

Haudry quotes the following translation by Renou: "maintenant comme autrefois il faut proclamer *cet (acte) de toi*, (à savoir que) pour les Angiras tu as découvert l'enclos", where a noun with the meaning "deed" is understood. On the contrary, according to Lühr (2008: 154) this may be a kind of structure which could be reanalyzed as a "genuine *that*-clause in the function of an object".[15]

According to Lühr (2014: 233), it can be assumed that the clauses introduced by *yád* could occur in a correlative construction associated with a correlative element realized through a dummy NP or a null pronoun.[16] Moreover, Axel-Tober (2017: 54–55) claims that the declarative complement clause developed out of a reanalysis of the correlative construction in the variant with a silent correlative. Interestingly, once the existence of a silent correlative has been posed, Axel-Tober wonders at what stage we can be sure that the structure emerged in which the *that*-clause (in Germanic languages, but we can argue analogously for *yád* clauses in Indo-Aryan) was really a complement of the superordinate verb and not associated with a silent correlative.

---

[15] Lühr (2014: 233), quoting the same example: "Den Wandel zur reinen Konjunktion ‚dass' in Komplementsätzen bezeugen im Altindoiranischen nur wenige Sätze".
[16] See Lühr (2014), quoting Keydana, for the existence of null pronouns in Vedic.

However, we know that some languages allow both structures, i.e. a complementizer with or without a correlative in the matrix clause, e.g. in Italian:
— *dico che...* / *dico questo, che...* (lit. "I say that..." / "I say this, that...").

If we admit the existence of *that*-clauses associated with a silent correlative, then we could argue that not even in Italian we have genuine complement clauses, because we could reanalyze *dico che* "I say that" as "I say Ø, that" with a null pronoun, which seems unnecessary.

Therefore, it is difficult to argue that there must be a null pronoun where there are no independent reasons requiring it: there are no independent reasons to think that (44) – quoted by Haudry and Lühr – must contain a silent correlative and could not be considered a case of "genuine *that*-clause", as stated by Lühr. Thus, there seems to be no reason to think that *yád* in this case is not yet a complementizer in the literal sense of the term. Therefore, we can conclude that Vedic had embedded sentences.

5 Questions about minimality

If we assume that *yád* can behave like a complementizer[17] and occupy the position of a head, we can also resolve a case of apparent violation of minimality, which otherwise would characterize the syntax of Vedic in contrast to modern Indo-Aryan languages.

Davison (2009: 235) quotes a sentence reported by Delbrück (1888: 550) which, according to her, should constitute a case of minimality violation:

(54) Śatapatha-Brāhmaṇa 4.1.5.4
 yát kím ákaraṃ tásmād idám ā́padi[18]
 yád INTER.ACC did.AOR.1SG for.this.reason.ABL this.NOM befall.AOR.3SG
 Eggeling: 'This has come to pass for something or other I have done!'
 (Lit.: 'because I do what?, therefore this happened')

It should be noticed that, according to Speyer (1896: 87): "yad hat ganz die Bedeutung des causalen «weil». Hier ist *tasmād, tena*, in B. auch *etad* correlative", e.g. in the same episode narrated in Śatapatha-Brāhmaṇa:

---

[17] See Lühr (2008: 154).
[18] *ā́padi* in Mādhyandina recension (and Delbrück). In Kāṇva recension 5.1.5.3: *yat kim akaraṃ tata īdṛg āpad iti*.

(55) Śatapatha-Brāhmaṇa 4.1.5.7
 yán n_ā́vediṣaṃ ténā_hiṃsiṣam
 yád NEG_knew.AOR.1SG this.INS injure.AOR.1SG
 Eggeling: 'Because I knew thee not, therefore have I offended thee.'

According to Davison (2009: 233) minimality in Hindi/Urdu (and in other languages like English and Italian), entails that a questioned phrase cannot be extracted from a relative clause, because of minimality violation: $yád_i\ kím_j...t_i\ t_j$. As is known, minimality concerns the good formation of chains between displaced elements and respective traces (or silent copies). Rizzi (1990, 2001) formally defines minimality in these terms:

> Y is in a Minimal Configuration (MC) with X if there is no Z such that:
> (i) Z is of the same structural type as X, and
> (ii) Z intervenes between X and Y

According to Rizzi's *Relativized Minimality*, the intervening element violating minimality should be of the "same structural type": thus, if we admit that *yád* introducing a subordinate clause were a complementizer that is a head, then there should be no minimality violation in case of an intervening phrase (in this case, the interrogative pronoun *kím*).

6 Conclusion

As already claimed by Delbrück (1888: 572), Vedic *yád* already occurs with the value of a subordinating conjunction with the meaning of '(the fact) that', 'when', 'if', and thus its development cannot be followed starting from the neuter of the relative pronoun within the history of Sanskrit.

As regard to the placement in the sentence, the complementizer *yád*, like other subordinating conjunctions in some ancient and modern Indo-European languages, can be preceded by a topicalized or a focalized phrase in its clause; interestingly, Vedic *yád* can sometimes be preceded by the verb of its sentence: this fact could be explained also by the feature of enclisis which seems to characterize also Vedic relative pronouns.

As regards its syntactic category, *yád* can behave as a head: this conclusion is confirmed by the fact that there seems to be no minimality violation in case of extraction of an interrogative phrase.

Vedic finite subordinate clauses introduced by *yád* could be not only adjoined, but also embedded: this is shown by few examples, which however demonstrate that this structure is grammatical in Vedic.

Abbreviations

1 = first person; 2 = second person; 3 = third person; ABL = ablative; ACC = accusative; AOR = aorist; DAT = dative; DU = dual; F = feminine; GEN = genitive; IMPRF = imperfect; INJ = injunctive; INS = instrumental; INT = intensive; INTER = interrogative; LOC = locative; MID = middle; N = neuter; NEG = negation marker; NOM = nominative; OPT = optative; PASS = passive; PL = plural; PRF = perfect; PRS = present; PST = past; PTCL = particle; PTCP = participle; QUOT = quotative; REL = relative; SBJV = subjunctive; SG = singular; VOC = vocative

Transliteration

The transliteration of Sanskrit data in this paper follows the standard IAST. https://en.wikipedia.org/wiki/International_Alphabet_of_Sanskrit_Transliteration

References

Adams, James. 1994. Wackernagel's law and the position of unstressed personal pronouns in classical Latin. *Transactions of the Philological Society* 92 (2). 103–178.
Axel-Tober, Katrin. 2017. The development of the declarative complementizer in German, *Language*, 93 (2). 29–65.
Benincà, Paola. 2001. The position of topic and focus in the left periphery. In Guglielmo Cinque & Giampaolo Salvi (eds.), *Current studies in Italian syntax offered to Lorenzo Renzi*, 39–64. Amsterdam: Elsevier-North Holland Academic Graphics.
Chantraine, Pierre. 1953. *Grammaire Homérique tome II: Syntax*. Paris: Librairie C. Klincksieck.
Danckaert, Lieven. 2012. *Latin Embedded Clauses. The Left Periphery*. Amsterdam & Philadelphia: John Benjamins.
Danckaert, Lieven. 2015. The decline of Latin left-peripheral presentational foci: Causes and Consequences. In Theresa Biberauer & George Walkden (eds.), *Syntax over Time. Lexical, Morphological, and Information-Structural Interactions*, 265–279. Oxford: Oxford University Press.
Davison, Alice. 2009. Adjunction, features and locality in Sanskrit and Hindi/Urdu correlatives. In Aniko Lipták (ed.), *Correlatives Cross-Linguistically*, 223–262. Amsterdam & Philadelphia: John Benjamins Publishing Company.

Delamarre, Xavier. 2003. *Dictionnaire de la langue gauloise*. Paris: Editions Errance.
Delbrück, Berthold. 1888. *Altindische Syntax*. Halle: Verlag der Waisen Hauses.
Delbrück, Berthold. 1900. *Vergleichende Syntax der indogermanischen Sprachen*, III. Strassburg: Karl J. Trübner.
Dunkel, George Eugene. 2014. *Lexikon der indogermanischen Partikeln und Pronominalstämme*, 2vv. Heidelberg: Universitätsverlag Winter.
Fortson IV, Benjamin W. 2004. *Indo-European Language and Culture. An Introduction*. Malden, MA. & Oxford: Blackwell Publishing.
Graßmann, Hermann. 1996. *Wörterbuch zum Rig-Veda. 6.*, [überarbeitete und ergänzte Auflage von Maria Kozianka]. Wiesbaden: Harrassowitz Verlag.
Hale, Mark. 1987a. *Studies in the Comparative Syntax of the Oldest Indo-Iranian Languages*. Cambridge, MA: Harvard University Dissertation.
Hale, Mark. 1987b. Notes on Wackernagel's Law in the language of the Rigveda. In Calvert Watkins (ed.), *Studies in Memory of Warren Cowgill (1929–1985)*, 38–50. Berlin & New York: de Gruyter.
Haudry, Jean. 2012. Genèse de la proposition infinitive. In Alain Christol & Olga Spevak (eds.), *Les évolutions du latin*. Paris: L'Harmattan.
Hermann, Eduard. 1895. Gab es im Indogermanischen Nebensätze? *Zeitschrift für vergleichende Sprachforschung auf dem Gebiete der indogermanischen Sprachen* 33.4, 1895. 481–535.
Hettrich, Heinrich. 1988. *Untersuchungen zur Hypotaxe in Vedischen*. Berlin & New York: Walter de Gruyter.
Hock, Hans Henrich. 1989. Conjoined we stand: theoretical implications of Sanskrit relative structures. *Studies in the Linguistic Sciences* 19.1. 93–126.
Holland, Gary B. 1996. Relativization and Word Order in Old Irish and Vedic Sanskrit. *The Journal of Indo-European Studies* 24, 3 & 4. 323–329.
Hsu, Brian. 2015. Variation in Bangla complementizer order at the syntax-prosody interface. In Thuy Bui & Deniz Özyıldız (eds.), *Proceedings of the 45th Meeting of the North East Linguistic Society*, Massachusetts Institute of Technology. CreateSpace Independent Publishing Platform.
Jamison, Stephanie W. & Joel P. Brereton. 2014. *The Rigveda. The Earliest Religious Poetry of India*. 3 vols. Oxford & New York: Oxford University Press.
Kiparsky, Paul. 1995. Indo-european Origins of Germanic Syntax. In Adrian Battye & Ian Roberts (eds.), *Clause Structure and Language Change*, 140–169. Oxford & New York: Oxford University Press.
Krapova, Iliyana. 2010. Bulgarian relative and factive clauses with an invariant complementizer. *Lingua* 120. 1240–1272.
Krisch, Thomas. 1990. Das Wackernagelsche Gesetz aus heutiger Sicht. In Heiner Eichner & Helmut Rix (eds.), Sprachwissenschaft und Philologie. Jacob Wackernagel und die Indogermanistik heute. Kolloquium der Indogermanischen Gesellschaft vom 13. Bis 15. Oktober in Basel, 64–81. Wiesbaden: Reichert.
Krisch, Thomas. 1998. Zum Hyperbaton in altindogermanischen Sprachen. In Wolfgang Meid (ed.), *Sprache und Kultur der Indogermanen. Akten der X. Fachtagung der Indogermanischen Gesellschaft*, 351–384. Innsbruck: Institut für Sprachwissenschaft der Universität.
LIV2 = Rix, H. 2001. *Lexikon der indogermanischen Verben*, [2nd edn]. Wiesbaden: Dr. Ludwig Reichert Verlag.

Lowe, John J. 2014. Accented clitics in the Ṛgveda. *Transactions of the Philological Society* 112 (1). 5–43.

Lubotsky, Alexander M. 1997. *A Ṛgvedic Word Concordance, 2 Vols.* New Haven, Connecticut: American Oriental Society.

Lühr, Rosemarie. 2008. Competitive Indo-European syntax. In Gisella Ferraresi & Maria Goldbach (eds.), *Principles of Syntactic Reconstruction*, 121–159. Amsterdam & Philadelphia: Benjamins.

Œrtel, Hans. 1926. *The Syntax of Cases in the Narrative and Descriptive Prose of the Brāhmaṇas I. The Disjunct Use of Cases.* Heidelberg: Carl Winter Universitätsbuchhandlung.

Paoli, Sandra. 2007. The fine structure of the left periphery: COMPs and subjects. Evidence from Romance. *Lingua* 117. 1057–1079.

Radhakrishnan, Sarvepalli. 1994. *The Principal Upaniṣads.* New Delhi: Harper Collins.

Rizzi, Luigi. 1990. *Relativized Minimality.* Cambridge, MA: MIT Press.

Rizzi, Luigi. 1997. The fine structure of the left periphery. In Liliane Haegeman (ed.), *Elements of Grammar*, 281–337. Dordrecht: Kluwer.

Rizzi, Luigi. 2001. Relativized Minimality Effects. In Mark Baltin & Chris Collins (eds.), *The Handbook of Contemporary Syntactic Theory*, 89–110. Malden, MA: Blackwell.

Speyer, Jacob Samuel. 1896. *Vedische und Sanskrit Syntax.* Strassburg: Verlag von Karl J. Trübner.

Thurneysen, Rudolf. 1946. *A Grammar of Old Irish.* [Revised and enlarged edition translated from the German by D.A. Binchy & O. Bergin]. Dublin: School of Celtic Studies, Dublin Institute for Advanced Studies.

Viti, Carlotta. 2007. *Strategies of Subordination in Vedic.* Milano: Franco Angeli.

Viti, Carlotta. 2015. *Variation und Wandel in der Syntax der alten indogermanischen Sprachen.* [(Tübinger Beiträge zur Linguistik)]. Tübingen: Narr Farncke Attempto Verlag GmbH.

Wackernagel, Jacob. 1892. Über ein Gesetz der indogermanischen Wortstellung. *Indogermanische Forschungen* 1. 333–436.

Watkins, Calvert. 1963. Preliminaries to a Historical and Comparative Analysis of the Syntax of the Old Irish Verb. *Celtica* 6. 1–49.

Ziegler, Sabine. 1992. Zur Entwicklung der Relativsätze mit dem Relativpronomen*i̯o- in den keltischen Sprachen. *Münchener Studien zur Sprachwissenschaft* 53. 251–270.

Adriana Molina-Muñoz
A statistical model of syntactic and non-syntactic factors affecting relative clause placement in Hindi

Abstract: Hindi is an SOV language that allows scrambling and has null arguments. Finite relative clauses can occupy three different positions: at the left edge of the main clause (left peripheral), at the right edge of the main clause (right peripheral), and immediately after the nominal head they modify (adnominal). The present study applies quantitative methods to a corpus of 2,000 sentences to investigate whether syntactic locality, grammatical weight, linear distance, and information structure affect the position of the relative clause at the left and right peripheries. A Multinomial Logistic Regression was selected as the prediction model. The predictability of the model was tested by means of a Confusion matrix or Error matrix.

Keywords: Grammatical weight, Linear distance, Correlatives, Syntactic locality, Hindi, Information structure

1 Introduction

1.1 Relative clauses in Hindi

Hindi is an SOV language that allows scrambling and has null arguments. Finite relative clauses (RCs) can occupy three different positions: at the left edge of the main clause (MC), (1a); at the right edge of the main clause, (1b); immediately after the nominal head they modify, (1c).[1]

---

[1] Non-finite relative constructions in Hindi are mainly prenominal (i.e. precede the nominal phrase they modify) and do not present a relative pronoun, as shown in (i). They can be based on a participial or adjectival form. Although interesting, this study focuses on finite relative constructions.
(i) [[RC *chaltī*]   gāṛī]   se   mat   utro
    move.PRS.PTCP.SG.F vehicle.SG.F from NEG descend.IMP
    'Do not descend from the moving vehicle.' (Bhatt 2003: 489)

Adriana Molina-Muñoz, Faculty of Linguistics, Philology & Phonetics, Clarendon Institute, Walton Street, Oxford, OX1 2HG, UK. Email: adriana.molina-munoz@ling-phil.ox.ac.uk

https://doi.org/10.1515/9783110753066-003

(1a) Left peripheral relative
[RC *jo kitab sel par hai*] (*vah*) *kitāb acchī hai*
REL book sale on be.PRS DEM book good be.PRS
'Which book is on sale, that book is good.'

(1b) Right-peripheral relative
(*vah*) *kitāb acchī hai* [RC *jo sel par hai*]
DEM book good be.PRS REL sale on be.PRS
'That book is good, which is on sale.'

(1c) Adnominal relative
(*vah*) *kitāb* [RC *jo sel par hai*] *acchī hai*
DEM book REL sale on be.PRS good be.PRS
'That book which is on sale is good.' (Bhatt 2003: 288)

The construction in (1a) is known as *correlative* (Alexiadou et al. 2000; Lipták 2005; Subbarao 2012). In this construction, the relative clause contains a relative pronoun (*jo*) and it is linked to the main clause by an (optional) demonstrative pronoun (*vah*).[2] In languages like Hindi and Sanskrit, correlatives can also occur at the right edge of the main clause, as in (1b). The construction in (1b) is called *extraposed* (Dayal 1996; Srivastav 1991). The one in (1c) is also called *English-type* relative, but as the other two types, it can contain a demonstrative pronoun in the main clause.[3]

The position of the relative clause is fixed with respect to the main clause either at the periphery of the main clause or right-adjacent to the nominal head it modifies.[4] But when a finite complement of a verb (or *ki*-clause) occurs in the

---

[2] All three constructions have roughly the same meaning, which in English is the translation given for (1c). The parentheses are mine in all examples. The optionality of the demonstrative pronoun has been debated in prior work for the construction in (1a) (see Dayal 1996 and Srivastav 1991 for a detailed discussion).

[3] Adnominal relatives are considered an innovation in the language, due to either language contact with Persian or English (Chandola 1963; Puri 2011; Snell 1990) or internal development in Hindi (Marlow 1993). Sanskrit did not have adnominal constructions and apparent embeddings are analyzed as examples of appositives or amplifications (Davison 2009; Hock 1989). Kachru (1978) and McGregor (1972) only refer to left and right-peripheral relatives in their grammars.

[4] For instance, they cannot occur in preverbal position in an intransitive construction, (ii). And a relative clause modifying an indirect object cannot occur between the direct object *kitāb* 'book' and the verb *denā* 'to give' in (iii) (Dayal 1996). Note that the ungrammaticality of (iia) is not due to the repetition of the verb 'to be' (*hai*), as shown in (iib).

(ii) a.*vah laṛkī lambī [RC *jo kharī hai*] *hai*.
DEM girl tall REL standing be.PRS be.PRS

same construction as a right-peripheral relative, the finite complement clause cannot precede the relative clause, as in (2a). The only grammatical order is the one in which the finite complement clause follows the relative clause, as in (2b), which has been explained as a PF linearization restriction on the finite complement clause, not on the relative clause (Manetta 2012).

(2a) *rām-ne us ādmī-ko kahā [$_{CP}$ ki sīta gayī] [$_{RC}$ jo āyā thā]
Ram-ERG DEM man-ACC say.PFV that Sita leave.PFV REL come.PFV be.PST
(2b) rām-ne us ādmī-ko kahā [$_{RC}$ jo āyā thā] [$_{CP}$ ki sīta gayī]
Ram-ERG DEM man-ACC say.PFV REL come.PFV be.PST that Sita leave.PFV
'Ram told that man who had come that Sita had left.'
(from Mahajan 1997; Manetta 2012: 22)

Previous studies have focused on the syntactic relation between the relative clause and the main clause, with a particular interest in left-peripheral relatives (Bhatt 2003; Davison 2009; Dayal 1996; Dwivedi 1994; Mahajan 2000; McCawley 2004; Srivastav 1991). Such syntactic approaches make predictions on well and ill-formed constructions depending on the syntactic structure resulting from movement or adjunction, and not depending on linear order. Regardless of the syntactic analysis assumed for Hindi relative clauses (i.e. movement or base-generated adjunction), speakers have the option of three possible positions to choose from when conveying a message. This selection is not random, but rather motivated.

The different factors that motivate discontinuities have been investigated from both a generative and functionalist perspective, particularly in the case of relative clause extraposition, such as in (3), in English and German (Francis 2010; Francis and Michaelis 2014; Strunk 2014). According to these studies not all factors have an equal effect. For example, it has been reported that length of phrases

---

'The girl who is standing is tall.'
b. *vah laṛkī lambī [$_{RC}$ jo gayī] hai.
DEM girl tall REL go.PFV be.PRS
'The girl who left is tall.' (Dayal 1996)
(iii) a. anu us laṛkī-ko [$_{RC}$ jo vahā̃ kharī hai] kitāb degī
Anu DEM girl-DAT REL there standing be.PRS book give.FUT
b. anu kitāb us laṛkī-ko [$_{RC}$ jo vahā̃ kharī hai] degī
Anu book DEM girl-DAT REL there standing be.PRS give.FUT
c. *anu us laṛkī-ko kitāb [$_{RC}$ jo vahā̃ kharī hai] degī
Anu DEM girl-DAT book REL there standing be.PRS give.FUT
'Anu will give the book to the girl who is standing there.' (Dayal 1996)

(in words) and predicate type are stronger factors than the ones associated with information packaging (i.e. givenness) (Francis and Michaelis 2014; Strunk 2014; Wasow 2002).

(3a) *A letter [$_{RC}$ which was addressed to Mary] arrived yesterday.*
(3b) *A letter arrived yesterday [$_{RC}$ which was addressed to Mary].*
      (Manninen 2002: 4)

Hindi presents an exceptional case given that relative clauses are possible both at the left and right peripheries. The aim of this study is to determine what factor(s) influence the choice of one ordering over the other in Hindi; as well the possibility of a model that will allow us to predict the occurrence of these three relative constructions based on such factors. The remaining part of section 1 discusses the corpus on which this study is based. Section 2 discusses the factors that were investigated, the hypotheses from previous work, and the results of the corpus study. Section 3 presents the statistical model, as well as a discussion on the predictability of the model. Finally, Section 4 presents the conclusions and implications for future research.

1.2 A corpus of Hindi relative clauses

A corpus of Hindi relative clauses was created by extracting all sentences containing a relative clause from a sample of 353 texts of different genres (1,025,411 words total) from the EMILLE/CIIL monolingual written Hindi Corpus, including news websites, educational and fictional literature, administrative and legislation documents, and science and art articles.[5] The extraction was done using Python. The EMILLE/CIIL corpus is not tagged and the annotation was done manually and, then, reviewed by three native speakers. All relevant observations on the annotations are included in the discussion on the examined factors in section 2.

---

[5] The EMILLE/CIIL Corpus is a collaboration between the Enabling Minority Language Engineering (EMILLE) project at Lancaster University, and the Central Institute of Indian Languages (CIIL). This corpus is distributed free of cost for academic endeavors by the European Language Resources Association (ELRA): http://catalog.elra.info/en-us/repository/browse/ELRA-W0037/.

A total of 2,000 sentences with at least one finite relative clause using *jo, jis, jin, jinhoẽ*[6] were annotated. Only 1,704 were examined.[7] Figure 1 provides the overview of the distribution of the different linearization possibilities in the corpus. Only 1,639 were clearly distributed at the left or right peripheries or were clear cases of adnominal constructions.[8] A total of 874 (54%) occurred at the right periphery; 660 (40%) at the left periphery; and 105 (6%) were adnominal.[9]

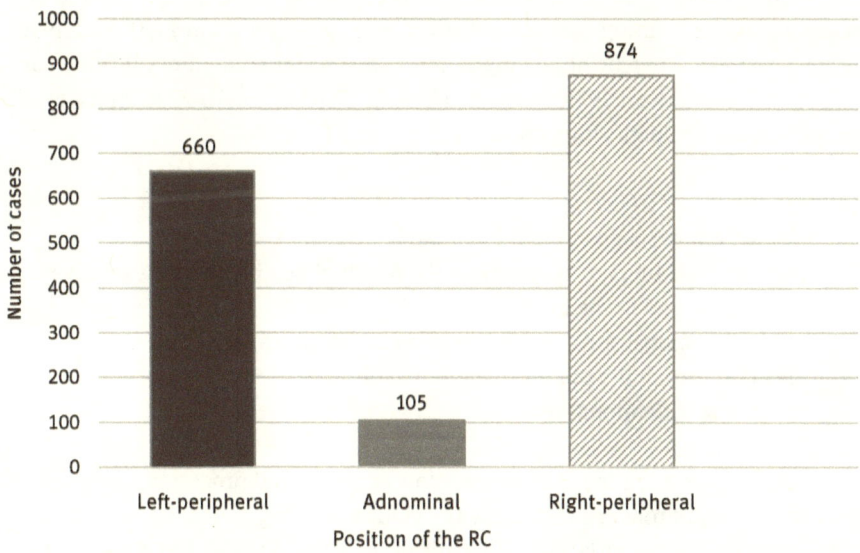

Fig. 1: Linearization patterns of RCs in the corpus

---

6 These forms correspond to the relative pronoun 'who/which' in nominative and oblique singular and plural forms.
7 Constructions where the pronoun *jo* functions as a "reason marker" or a "thematic marker" were excluded (see Gambhir 1981).
8 65 constructions were tagged as *adnominal*, but excluded from Figure 1: 28 were ambiguous between adnominal and right-peripheral (NP RC), 37 were ambiguous between adnominal and left-peripheral (NP RC CC). CC here refers to the main clause with the demonstrative pronoun. The NP seems to have been fronted in both cases.
9 In the corpus, the higher frequency of adnominal (10%) and right-peripheral relatives (62%) are found in news articles.

2 Factors affecting placement of relative clause

Early traditional generative approaches proposed a set of rules to derive relative clauses expanding the NP as in English relative constructions (Kachru 1978; Subbarao 1984; Verma 1966).[10] However, left-peripheral constructions are argued to have the properties in (4), which are argued to differentiate them from the other two constructions. This motivated different analyses. Some group (1b) and (1c) together, while treating (1a) as a distinct relativization strategy (Dayal 1996; Srivastav 1991), whereas others argue for a separate treatment of all three constructions (Donaldson 1971; Dwivedi 1994; McCawley 2004). Note that not all properties are syntactic, they are also semantic.

(4) *Properties of left-peripheral relatives*
   i. a peripheral position of the relative clause,
   ii. the possibility of spelling out the nominal head both in the relative clause and in the main clause,
   iii. the demonstrative requirement on the main clause,
   iv. the availability of multiple relative phrases,
   v. a quantificational reading

Other studies have argued that information structure and processing constraints play an important role in constituent and clause ordering in Hindi (Butt and King 2000; Gambhir 1981; Kidwai 2000; Patil et al. 2008; Prasad and Strube 2000; Verma 1966). A relevant work for the present study is Kothari's (2010). She experimentally investigates the influence of syntactic locality, end-weight and semantic expectations (conditioned by preceding discourse) on online order preferences in Hindi relative constructions. Kothari used a variety of methods, including acceptability judgment tasks, sentence production via fragment-ordering, self-paced reading, and sentence completion.

Nevertheless, Kothari's results were inconclusive, according to the author, due to some methodological limitations. For example, in a production experiment using a fragment ordering task, participants (all native speakers of Hindi) were presented with fragments using PowerPoint. All data were intransitive sentences with subject-modifying non-restrictive relatives, in which the following conditions were controlled: length in number of words of the relative (long/short) and length of the verbal predicate (long/short). The subject was indefinite in all

---

10 A more recent movement approach is found in Bhatt (2003).

items. Participants did not have to write the full sentence, but rather the trial number followed by the sequence of numbers corresponding to their preferred ordering. The results showed a strong bias for the adnominal option (77%) regardless of the condition. Kothari suggests that a possible explanation for this result is that participants selected a single strategy and then consistently applied it. In addition, since all items were non-restrictive, the orders RC-S-VP and RC-VP-S, corresponding to left-peripheral constructions, were excluded as a natural option.

Kothari's study showed that online tasks can be conditioned by the initial decision taken by the speaker and often only one construction was preferred throughout the experiment. Furthermore, more than one processing constraint can apply simultaneously, but not knowing more precisely which factors to control and the extent of their effects made the results not to be conclusive as to what processing patterns can interact with discourse. In the next section, the factors that are argued to influence relative clause extraposition from a generative and a functionalist perspective are discussed in detail, especially in the light of the different properties that have been identified in the analysis of relative clauses in Hindi.

2.1 Syntactic locality

Syntactic locality refers to the fact that closely related elements in a sentence are preferred to be closer to each other. The assumption in generative grammar is that syntactic dependencies are strictly local and apparent long-distance dependencies turn out to be the outcome of a recursive chain of local dependencies. There is conflicting evidence in the literature about locality effects and processing. Some studies argue that the greater the distance between the head and its dependents, the greater the processing difficulty is (Gibson 1998). Other studies argue that with a greater distance processing is facilitated, despite the possibly greater memory requirements, i.e. *anti-locality effects* (Konieczny 2000; Vasishth 2003; Vasishth and Lewis 2006). In the corpus, this notion was examined in terms of *depth of embedding* and *linear distance*.

2.1.1 Depth of embedding of the NP

Chomsky's (1973) *subjacency principle* predicts that a relative clause cannot be extraposed out of a DP that is embedded in another DP. Strunk and Snider (2013) found that the likelihood of extraposition decreases with increasing depth of embedding (in terms of nodes); but according to the authors it should be seen in the context of other factors such as the weight of the extraposed relative clause and the length of the material intervening between the antecedent and extraposed relative clause.

In Hindi, a three-way distinction is made between direct, oblique and vocative case forms (Kachru 2006). The subject has zero marking (direct or nominative case), unless it functions as ergative, in which case it is marked by *ne*. The direct object and indirect object both can be marked by the postposition *ko* 'to'. All other cases are indicated by postpositions. Any position, from subject to oblique, can be relativized using a finite construction in Hindi.

In order to determine whether the grammatical case of the NP determines the position of the relative clause, a Fisher exact test was performed.[11] The results show significant differences in the associations between the position of the RC and grammatical case of the NP ($p < 0.0001$). Figure 2 presents the distribution of the relative clauses according to the grammatical case of the NP.[12]

All three constructions are more frequently used with NPs in subject position (nominative or ergative): 67% of left-peripheral, 74% of adnominal and 42% of right-peripheral. The frequency reduces for left-peripheral in other positions (69% subject > 16% object > 7.5% oblique > 7% genitive > 0.5% predicate). Right-peripheral constructions are more frequent with non-subject NPs (58%): object (16%), oblique (11%) and genitive (14%) and predicate (17%) NPs. Note the use of right-peripheral relatives with NPs in copula constructions (PRED): 17% vs. 0.3% left-peripheral and 0% adnominal. Furthermore, if we split the subject category into nominative and ergative, we observe a difference between adnominal and left-peripheral relatives: 26 ergative NPs (out of 79 subjects) with adnominal relatives vs. 6 (out of 399 subjects) left-peripheral and 4 (out of 356 subjects) right-peripheral.

---

11 Fisher's Exact Test is a statistical significance test used in the analysis of contingency table. It is often employed when sample sizes are small (contrary to the Chi-square test). This is a type of exact test because the significance of the deviation from a null hypothesis (p-value) can be calculated exactly, rather than relying on approximation.
12 Note that only the tokens containing a nominal head were considered: 1,535 instead of 1,639.

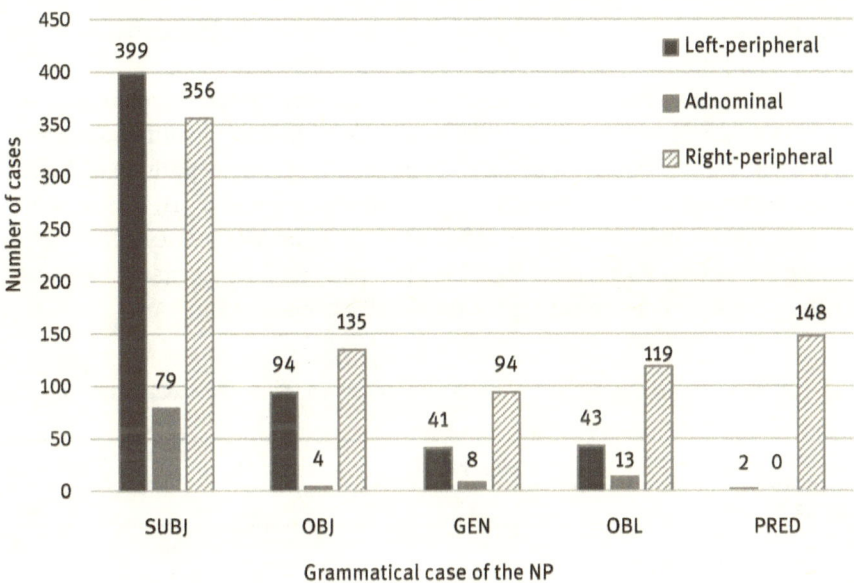

Fig. 2: Grammatical case of the NP according to position of the RC

2.1.2 Linear distance between the NP and the RC

Linear distance between the nominal phrase and the relative clause is another way of measuring syntactic locality. According to Hawkins (2004: 142–146), the likelihood of relative clause extraposition decreases with increasing distance between the nominal head and the extraposed position of the relative clause (i.e. *Minimize Domains*). In other words, the distance between the nominal head and the relative clause should be as small as possible, assuming that a nominal head needs to be retrieved so as to integrate its relative clause with it (Gibson 1998; Hawkins 2004). This hypothesis has been confirmed in corpus studies by Uszkoreit et al. (1998) and Strunk (2014) for German, and by Francis (2010) for English.

In previous studies, linear distance was assumed to be the (hypothetical) extraposition distance in number of words between the nominal head (always subject) and the rightward extraposed relative clause. The material to the left of the nominal head was irrelevant. But given the linearization requirements in Hindi, we need to include this material for the cases in which a left-peripheral construction presents an external nominal head. The measurements (in number of words) considered whether the NP was inside or outside the relative clause, and whether the nominal head was present or not; if absent then the demonstrative pronoun was taken as point of reference. Note that *clause-internal scrambling* is very common, so the position of the nominal phrase is not fixed, nor of the demonstrative.[13]

A One-way Anova test shows that the distance significantly differs according to the type of NP (external, internal or demonstrative) and the position of the relative clause (left-peripheral, adnominal or right-peripheral) [$F (11, 1692) = 36.67$, $p < 0.0001$]. A Bonferroni post hoc test[14] shows interactions between each of the three positions of relative clauses. Table 1 presents the distance means organized by the type of NP and the position of the relative clause.[15]

Tab. 1: Distance means in number of words according to the position of the RC and type of NP

	External NP	Internal NP	DEM only
Left-peripheral	3.7	3.8	5.1
Adnominal	0		0
Right peripheral	2.4		1.6

The results show that the linear distance between the NP and the RC is longer in left-peripheral constructions than in the other two types, and it increases when the nominal phrase is omitted and only the demonstrative pronoun occurs (from

---

13 The relative pronoun usually stands first in its clause, even when it is not the subject. However, sometimes that is not the case, for example, the adverbial phrase "in the exam" occurs at initial position in (iv b). The same is true for a demonstrative phrase in the main clause.

(iv) a. [$_{RC}$ *jo bacca* **parīkshā mẽ** pratham āyā]   vah   lambā hai
       REL child   exam   in   first   come.PFV DEM tall be.PRS

  b. [$_{RC}$ **parīkshā mẽ** *jo bacca* pratham āyā]   vah   lambā hai
       exam   in   REL child   first   come.PFV DEM tall be.PRS

  'The child who came first in the exam is tall.'
  (Kothari 2010: 18)

14 Bonferroni uses t-tests to perform pairwise comparisons between group means. It controls the overall error rate by setting the error rate for each test to the experiment-wise error rate divided by the total number of tests. As a result, the observed significance level is adjusted for the fact that multiple comparisons are being made. Bonferroni is more powerful than Tukey when the number of comparisons is small, like in the case at hand.

15 Note that 35 instances of relative constructions presenting both internal and external heads simultaneously were found: 29 left-peripheral, 4 right-peripheral and 2 adnominal relatives. These were excluded from the counts.

3.7 to 5.1).[16] In right-peripheral constructions, the opposite occurs, the distance is reduced (from 2.4 to 1.6) when the nominal phrase is not overt. Given that clause-scrambling is more frequent in left-peripheral relatives than the other two constructions (Gupta 1986; Kachru 2006), we expect more variation in the position of the relative phrase (*jo* + NP) within the relative clause. Nevertheless, Table 1 shows that the linear distance remains relatively the same whether the NP is inside or outside the relative clause. In other words, we can argue that clause-internal scrambling facilitates the reduction of the syntactic domain.

2.2 Grammatical weight

The *Principle of End Weight* (PEW) states that phrases appear in order of increased weight: "lighter" constituents tend to appear before "heavier" ones. Heavier constituents tend to be longer or structurally more complex than lighter ones.[17] Weight effects on relative clause extraposition have been proven using corpus data in German (Strunk 2010, 2014), English (Francis 2010; Francis and Michaelis 2014), and Persian (Rasekh-Mahand et al. 2016). These studies have measured weight in terms of number of orthographic words, considering the length of the relative clause, the length of the VP (because relative clause extraposition is post-verbal), and the VP-to-RC length ratio (VP length divided by RC length). Hawkins (1994, 2004) claims that grammatical weight is language dependent, and in verb final languages like Japanese a mirror principle applies: *long-before-short* sequences are preferred over *short-before-long* ones (see also Yamashita and Chang

---

16 The reviewer points out that given that relative clauses are most commonly head initial; it is not surprising that left-peripheral relatives have a greater distance. This would be true if distance was taken from the beginning of the relative clause to beginning of the main clause, e.g. (v) below (distance = 5 words). However, distance was taken from the end of the most head-like in the RC to the beginning of most head-like in the MC in the case of left-peripheral constructions, e.g. (vi) (distance = 3 words). This method mitigates against the variable length of the relative clause and tells us more directly about the distance between phrases. The relevant distances are marked in bold:

(v)   [$_{RC}$ **jo kitāb sel par hai**]   [$_{MC}$ (*vah*)   kitāb   acchī   hai]
           REL book sale on be.PRS   DEM   book good be.PRS

(vi)   [$_{RC}$*jo* kitāb **sel par hai**]   [$_{MC}$ (*vah*) kitāb acchī hai]
           REL book sale on be.PRS   DEM   book good be.PRS

17 Wasow (1997) shows that both length and complexity are good indicators of grammatical weight. The assumption is that the longer the sentence, the more likely it contains internal clauses or clause-like constituents.

2001). If Hawkins' prediction is correct, Hindi, being a verb-final language, should behave as Japanese.

2.2.1 Length of the RC and the MC

The length of the 1,639 unambiguous relative clauses was calculated in terms of number of orthographic words. A One-way Anova test shows that the difference between the means of the three types of relatives regarding the length of the relative clause is statistically significant [$F_{(2, 1636)} = 17.53$, $p < 0.0001$]. A Bonferroni post hoc test shows that the adnominal construction differs from the two peripheral ones, and both peripheral constructions differ from each other. Figure 3 displays the mean length of the relative clause according to the three relative constructions. The mean length (in black) of left-peripheral relatives is 9.15; whereas the mean length of right-peripheral is 10.79, and of adnominal is 8.42. In general, right-peripheral relatives are longer than the other two types, especially when considering the outliners.

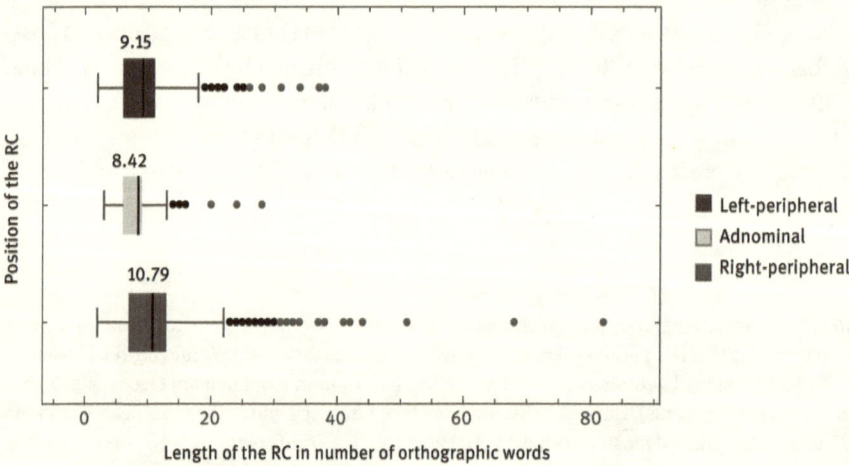

Fig. 3: Mean length of the RC in number of words

A One-way Anova test that the difference between the means of the three types of relatives regarding the length of the main clause is statistically significant [$F_{(2, 1636)} = 13.39$, $p < 0.0001$]. A Bonferroni post hoc test shows significance difference among all three types. Figure 4 displays the length of the main clause according to the three major types of constructions. The mean length (in black) of main clause in left-peripheral constructions is 9.39; whereas the mean length in right-peripheral constructions is 10.58, and in adnominal constructions is 12.25 considering only the material after the relative clause (corresponding to the VP), 17.08 when considering the total main clause length (nominal head + VP). Note the length of the main clause in adnominal constructions is longer even when only the post-relative clause material (VP) is being considered.

Weight effects depend on the relative weights of constituents, not only on the weight of any one (Wasow 2002), hence the MC-to-RC length ratio[18] was also calculated for examining the significance of length of the RC relative to the length of the MC. For the case of adnominal constructions, the mean length of the post-relative materials (VP) was considered instead of the total length of the main clause. A One-way Anova test shows that the interaction between the MC-to-RC length ratio and the position of the relative clause is statistically significant [$F(2, 1636) = 10.34$, $p < 0.0001$]. For the left-peripheral construction the main clause is 1.26:1 compared to the length of the relative clause; for the right-peripheral construction the main clause is 1.28:1 compared to the length of the relative clause; and for the adnominal construction (NP RC VP) the main clause is 2.48:1 compared to the total length (pre- and post-RC material) and 1.72:1 the length of only the post-RC material. In other words, in right-peripheral constructions both the MC and the RC are longer; in left-peripheral constructions both are shorter; and in an adnominal construction the RC is shorter than the MC.

---

18 This ratio consists of the division of the mean length of the main clause by the mean length of the relative clause.

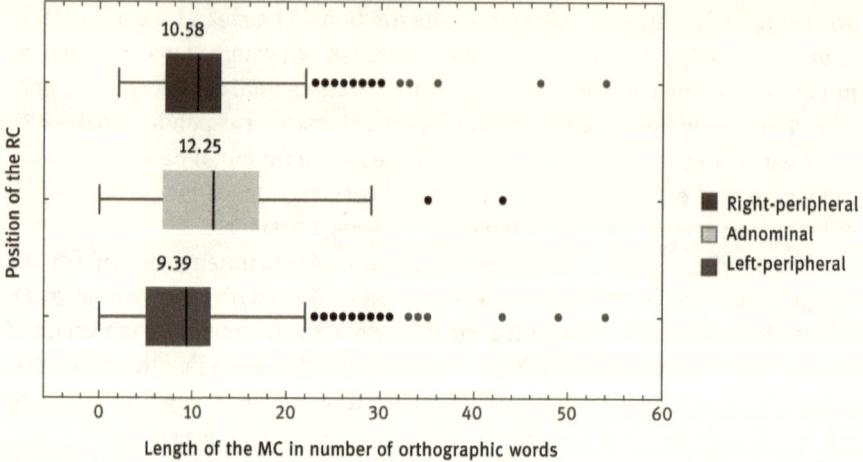

Fig. 4: Mean length of the MC in number of words

Hindi, like English, prefers *short-before-long* for organizing finite relative clauses, and does not pattern with other SOV languages such as Korean or Japanese. The MC-to-RC ratio is not a useful predictor for placement of the relative clause by itself, but in combination with data from RC length and linear distance. Adnominal relatives are preferred when the post-RC material (VP) is longer than the relative clause. Right-peripheral constructions are preferred when the relative clause is longer than the hypothetical extraposition distance. In the case of left-peripheral constructions, both the relative clause and the main clause tend to be shorter.

2.2.2 Complexity of the relative clause and the main clause

The results of two One-way Anova tests, one for complexity of the relative clause [$F(4, 1634) = 152.752$, $p < 0.001$] and one for complexity of the main clause [$F(4, 1633) = 90.62$, $p < 0.001$] show that when a clause is complex (relative or main clause), it is probably long (in number of words), but it does not tell us that if a clause is long (in number of words) it will be complex. The mean lengths are shown in Table 2. As expected, coordinated/stacked and subordinated clauses are longer than clauses containing one finite verb.

Tab. 2: Distance means in number of words according to complexity of MCs and RCs

Complexity[19]	Mean length in number of words in relative clause (RC)	Mean length in number of words in main clause (MC)
Simple	9	9
Postverbal	13	10
Multiple (rel/dem) pronouns	9	12
Coordinated/Stacked	19	19
Subordinated	20	19

Table 3 displays the results of a Fisher exact test of complexity of the relative clause and of the main clause (p = 0.0007). The majority of the constructions in the corpus showed combinations of a simple relative clause with a simple main clause: 1292 (79%). Based on these results, we can now make a distinction between the three different positions in terms of complexity for 79% of the constructions; therefore, length seems to be a better indicator or weight for Hindi relatives.

Tab. 3: Fisher test for MC complexity versus RC complexity

		COORDINATED/ STACKED	MULTI-HEADED	POSTVERVAL	SIMPLE	SUBORDINATED
						RC COMPLEXITY
MC COMPLEXITY	COORDINATED/ STACKED	0	0	0	28	0
	MULTIHEADED	0	1	0	1	0
	POSTVERVAL	1	0	2	21	2
	SIMPLE	103	3	20	1292	52
	SUBORDINATED	5	0	0	102	6

---

19 *Simple*: one finite verb; *coordinated*: coordinated clauses (including omission of the relative pronoun); *stacked*: absence of a conjunction (including omission of the relative pronoun); *subordinated*: containing a *ki*-clause or a relative clause; *multi-headed*: containing more than one relative pronoun; *postverbal*: if either the main or the relative clause presented postverbal elements.

2.3 Givenness of the NP

Givenness, as well as topicality, is related to predictability and the assumption that information that has been mentioned is likely to be mentioned again. The effect of givenness on relative clause extraposition is debatable. Some authors report a large effect, especially in correlation with definiteness (Huck and Na 1990; Rochemont and Culicover 1990); whereas others do not find a strong effect (Francis and Michaelis 2014; Rasekh-Mahand et al. 2016). In the present study givenness of the NP was annotated as: *discourse given* (mentioned earlier), *inferable* (not explicitly mentioned, but inferable), and *discourse new* (truly new) (compare to Francis and Michaelis 2014).

A Fisher exact test shows a significance difference ($p < 0.0001$) between the categories givenness of the NP and the position of the relative clause.[20] Table 4 displays the results of this test. Left-peripheral relatives occur slightly more frequently with discourse given NPs (309 or 53%) than with discourse new ones (200 or 34%); whereas right-peripheral and adnominal relatives occur more frequently with discourse new NPs (544 or 64% and 50 or 48%, respectively).

Tab. 4: Givenness of the NP according to the position of the RC

Position of the RC	Discourse Given	Inferable	Discourse New
Left-peripheral	309	75	200
Adnominal	34	20	50
Right-peripheral	194	109	544
Total	537	204	794

The results in Table 4 also corresponds to the fact that left-peripheral relatives tend to occur more frequently with NPs (internal heads) in subject position (see section 2.1.1). On the other hand, right peripheral relatives also occur frequently with NPs in non-subject position (i.e. predicates), which is usually considered as discourse new. Givenness has also been associated with definiteness. Section 2.4 discusses the relationship between these two factors.

---

[20] For this test, only tokens with nominal phrases were considered: 1,535 instead of 1,639. It also excludes cases of simultaneous internal and external head (35 instances).

2.4 Definiteness of the NP

Previous studies have shown a correlation between definiteness and the probability of relative clause extraposition in English and German (Francis and Michaelis 2014; Strunk 2014). The main claim is that extraposition from definite nominal heads is not possible in English (Guéron and May 1984; Rochemont and Culicover 1990). This restriction was originally formulated for PP extraposition, but later extended to relative clause extraposition. Definiteness has been defined in terms of uniqueness and familiarity of the word (here also understood as givenness), which is argued to be encoded by grammatical markers such as demonstratives, articles, and quantifiers. Nevertheless, this is not an easy task in Hindi, given that it is an article-less language.[21] Srivastav (1991) reports that definiteness of the NP is a main property of left-peripheral relatives, but not of right-peripheral ones (see also Gupta 1986). In the corpus, bare NPs were annotated as definite or indefinite following Singh (1994: 217), whose classification is based on the prototypical thematic roles of NPs, semantics of the verb, and word order information.

Tab. 5: Definiteness of the NP according to the position of the RC

Position of the RC	Definite	Indefinite
Left-peripheral	599	61
Adnominal	98	7
Right-peripheral	614	260
Total	1,311	328

A Fisher exact test of definiteness and position of the relative clause shows significant difference between those categories ($p < 0.0001$). Table 5 displays the results of this test applied to all unambiguous relatives 1,639. All three positions modify more frequently definite NPs (80%); but right-peripherals modify more frequently indefinite heads compared to the other two types: 29%, versus 7%

---

21 Verma (1971), Gambhir (1981) and, more recently, Vasishth (2003), argue that bare NPs can have three possible readings in Hindi: generic, definite, and indefinite. According to Dayal (1999), indefinite readings available to bare singulars can be traced to NP external factors, i.e. not inherent to the bare nominal. The formal semantics of bare NPs is beyond the scope of the present study, but a way to systematically account for the definiteness of a bare NP considering the context is necessary.

(adnominal) 10% (left-peripheral). Overall, definite NPs were more common in the corpus, which also agrees with previous studies (Francis and Michaelis 2014).

The question remains whether there is a direct relationship between givenness and definiteness. A final Fisher exact test was completed to examine the differences between givenness and definiteness of the nominal phrase. The results show a significant difference ($p < 0.001$) between the examined categories. Table 6 displays the results. Observe that definite heads can be given or new (510 and 565, respectively). Indefinite heads, however, are mainly discourse new (230 vs. 25 given).

Tab. 6: Definiteness vs. Givenness of the NP

	Discourse given	Inferable	Discourse New	Total
Definite	510	190	565	1,265
Indefinite	25	15	230	270

2.5 Restrictiveness of the RC

A relative clause is considered *restrictive* if it provides information essential to completing the meaning of the nominal head, as well as restricting its scope. It is *non-restrictive* if it provides additional information, not essential to the meaning of the antecedent.[22] Studies on relative clause extraposition have focused on restrictive relatives, leaving aside non-restrictive constructions. Ziv and Cole (1974) claim that only restrictive sentences can be extraposed, unlike the non-restrictive ones. This claim, however, has been refuted in English and German (Francis and Michaelis 2014; Strunk 2014). In Hindi, the focus has also been on restrictive relatives, and it has been reported that left-peripheral relatives disallow a non-restrictive reading (Dwivedi 1994; Kothari 2010; Srivastav 1991).

A Fisher exact test between the position of relative clause and restrictiveness of the relative clause shows significant differences ($p < 0.0001$). Table 7 displays the results. As reported in previous studies, left-peripheral relatives are primarily restrictive, only two cases of non-restrictive relatives were found in the corpus. Adnominal relatives are primarily non-restrictive; whereas 55% right-peripherals

---

[22] In English, the use of commas and the distinction between *who/which/whom* and *that* help distinguish these two functions, whereas in Hindi these elements are absent.

were non-restrictive and 45% restrictive. The results confirm the tendency of a non-restrictive reading of adnominal and right-peripheral relatives identified in prior work.

Tab. 7: Restrictiveness of the RC according to the position of the RC

Position of the RC	Restrictive	Non-restrictive	Total
Left-peripheral	658	2	660
Adnominal	28	77	105
Right-peripheral	394	480	874

3 A multivariate model of relative clause placement

In the previous sections, I have examined individual factors that are potentially relevant for determining placement of finite relative clauses in Hindi. These and other considered factors are listed in (5). A series of Anova (along with Bonferroni post hoc tests) and Fisher exact tests have shown statistically significant interactions between some of the factors, as well as between the factors and the type of relative clause construction. It remains unclear whether all these factors are required in a model of relative clause placement or whether some of them correlate with each other and are therefore redundant.

(5a) *Nominal head*
Presence or absence, definiteness, givenness, length in number of orthographic words, and complexity, grammatical function, linear distance.

(5b) *Demonstrative*
Presence or absence, definiteness, givenness, grammatical function, linear distance.

(5c) *Relative clause*
Position of the relative clause, length in number of orthographic words and complexity, MC-to-RC length ratio, restrictiveness.

(5d) *Main clause*
Length in number of orthographic words and complexity, direct and cited discourse.

Previous studies on English and German relative clause extraposition used a binary logistic regression for their statistical model (Francis and Michaelis 2016; Strunk 2014). In the present study, a Multinomial Logistic Regression using R was necessary because the dependent variable has more than two categories (left-peripheral, adnominal, right-peripheral). This model helps to predict the probabilities of the different possible outcomes of a categorically distributed dependent variable (position of the relative clause), given the set of independent variables in (5), as well as the risk ratio. This particular model selects a baseline and uses it to compare it with the other two constructions. The baseline was set for adnominal constructions, based on previous studies that propose a derivation of one or both peripheral constructions from the adnominal construction (Bhatt 2003; Srivastav 1991). A total of 36 observations were applied to 1,604 tokens.[23]

3.1 Multinomial logistic regression: Right-peripheral and adnominal relatives

The coefficients of the multinomial logistic regression model that are significantly different from zero (omitting the intercept) and with a significant p-value for the comparison between the right-peripheral construction and the baseline adnominal relative are shown in Table 8. The coefficients are arranged in descending order with respect to their risk ratio.[24] The coefficients with positive values indicate a higher probability of a variable being positively correlated to an outcome; and the coefficients with negative values indicate a higher probability of a variable being negatively correlated to an outcome. Values close to one indicate null association between a variable and an outcome.

According to Table 8, right-peripheral relatives are 1130083.26 times more likely to occur than adnominals when the main clause presents multiple demonstrative pronouns (p = 0.003). In addition, right-peripherals are 1593.9 times more likely to occur than adnominals also when the linear distance between the nominal head and the relative clause increases (p < 0.0001). If the relative clause is restrictive, right-peripheral relatives are 23.86 times more likely to occur than adnominals. On the other hand, right-peripherals are approximately 0.01 times less

---

[23] Once again the 35 constructions presenting simultaneously an internal and external head were left out of the statistical analysis.
[24] Relative risk includes two important features: (i) a comparison of risk between two "exposures" puts risks in context, and (ii) "exposure" is ensured by having proper denominators for each group representing the exposure. The null value is 1.0.

likely to occur than adnominals if the nominal phrase they modify occurs in nominative and accusative (p < 0.04); but only 0.007 and 0.0007 times less likely to occur than adnominals when the nominal phrase was in oblique and genitive case, respectively (p = 0.01 and p = 0.006).

Tab. 8: Coefficients for right-peripheral and adnominal RCs[25]

Factor	Coefficient	Std. Errors	Z stat	P value	Risk ratio
MC complexity (+multi-dem)	11.63	4.02	2.89	0.003	113083.26
Linear distance (head-RC)	7.37	1.26	5.81	6.23×10^{-09}	1593.9
+Restrictive	3.17	1.34	2.36	0.018	23.86
NP in accusative	−4.07	2.06	−1.97	0.04	0.01
NP in nominative	−4.46	1.81	−2.45	0.01	0.01
NP in oblique	−4.90	1.96	−2.49	0.01	0.007
NP in genitive	−7.25	2.13	−3.39	0.0006	0.0007
RC complexity (+multi-headed)	−10.75	2.56	−4.19	2.69×10^{-05}	2.13×10^{-05}

An interesting result comes from complexity of the relative clause, given that right-peripheral relatives are 2.13×10^{-05} times less likely to occur than adnominal relatives when the relative clause is multi-headed. This result is rather problematic given that there were no instances of multi-headed adnominal nor right-peripheral relatives in the analyzed data, only approximately 4 cases, all left-peripheral. The number of tokens available might be affecting the predictability of the model regarding this category. Also, note that in logistic regressions if observations are related to one another, as it seems to be the case according to the previous sections, then the model will tend to overweight the significance of those observations.

---

[25] The coefficients given here are the ones significantly different from zero and p < 0.05.

3.2 Multinomial logistic regression: Left-peripheral and adnominal relatives

The coefficients of the multinomial logistic regression model that are significantly different from zero (omitting the intercept) and with a significant p-value for the comparison between the right-peripheral construction and the baseline adnominal relative are shown in Table 9. The coefficients are arranged in descending order with respect to their risk ratio.

Tab. 9: Coefficients for right-peripheral and adnominal RCs[26]

Factor	Coefficient	Std. Errors	S stat	P value	Risk ratio
NP complexity (+coor/stacked)	11.28	4.15	2.71	0.006	79333.54
Linear distance (head-RC)	7.87	1.27	6.18	6.24×10^{-10}	2631.79
RC complexity (+multi-headed)	6.04	2.56	2.36	0.01	423.8
+Restrictive	4.79	1.91	2.49	0.01	120.53
RC complexity (+simple)	4.53	1.87	2.41	0.01	93.09
NP complexity (+simple)	−18.37	0.03	−462.08	0	1.04
RC length	−0.22	0.09	−2.36	0.01	0.79
+ Quote	−2.84	1.30	−2.17	0.02	0.05
NP complexity (+appositive)	−3.54	0.05	−61.49	0	0.03
NP in ergative	−8.71	0.07	−116.07	0	0.0001

According to Table 9, if the nominal head is coordinated or stacked, left-peripheral relatives are 79,333.54 times more likely to occur than adnominal constructions (p = 0.006). If the nominal head is simple (i.e. no modified just a simple noun) left-peripheral relatives are 1.04 times more likely to occur than adnominal constructions. Similarly, if the nominal head is appositive, left-peripheral relatives are 0.03 times less likely to occur than adnominal constructions (p ≅ 0). If the nominal head is in the ergative case, left-peripheral relatives are 0.0001 less

---

[26] The coefficients given here are the ones significantly different from zero and p < 0.05.

likely to occur than adnominals ($p \cong 0$).[27] As for the complexity of the relative clause, left-peripheral relatives are 423.8 and 93.0941 more likely to occur than adnominal relatives when the relative is multi-headed or simple, respectively (p = 0.01 for both). There is also a significant difference in the length of the relative clause (p = 0.01): left-peripheral relatives are 0.79 times less likely to occur than adnominals if the relative is longer.

Regarding linear distance left-peripheral also differ from adnominals: left-peripheral relatives are 2631.79 times more likely to occur than adnominals if the linear distance increases (p < 0.001). Regarding restrictiveness, left-peripheral relatives are 120.53 times more likely to occur when the relative clause is restrictive (p = 0.01). But if the relative clause occurs in a direct quote, left-peripheral relatives are 0.05 times less likely to occur than adnominal constructions (p = 0.02).

As a summary, there are three factors that are significant for the comparison between adnominal and both the peripheral constructions: linear distance (head-RC), +restrictive, complexity of the RC (+multi-headed). These three factors predict that if the relative clause has multiple relative pronouns (i.e. multi-headed) the relative clause is 2631.79 times more likely to occur at the left periphery than the right periphery (2.13×10^{-05}). The greater the linear distance between the nominal head and the RC, the greater the possibility to occur at the left periphery (2631.79 times) than at the right periphery (1593.9 times). Finally, if the relative clause is restrictive it is more likely to occur at the left periphery (120.53) than the right periphery (23.86). This comparison is presented in Table 10 below.

Tab. 10: Relevant coefficients for comparing adnominal with left-peripheral and right-peripheral RCs

Factor		Linear distance (head-RC)	+ Restrictive	RC complexity (multi headed)
Left-peripheral	Coefficient	7.87	4.79	6.04
	Std error	1.27	1.91	2.56
	z stat	6.18	2.49	2.36
	p value	6.24×10^{-10}	0.01	0.01
	Risk ratio	2631.79	120.53	423.8

---

[27] As the reviewer points out, this probability is rather low given that there were 6 instances of left-peripheral relatives used with NPs marked as ergative, and 26 instances with adnominal relatives. This can also result from overweighting of the model due to the few tokens available.

Factor		Linear distance (head-RC)	+ Restrictive	RC complexity (multi headed)
Right-peripheral	Coefficient	7.37	3.17	−10.75
	Std error	1.26	1.34	2.56
	z stat	5.81	2.36	−4.19
	p value	6.23×10^{-09}	0.018	2.69×10^{-05}
	Risk ratio	1593.9	23.86	2.13×10^{-05}

3.3 Multinomial logistic regression: Left-peripheral and right-peripheral relatives

Given that the baseline of the multinomial logistic regression was set for adnominal relatives, the comparison between both peripheral constructions was not available. This seems to be a shortcoming of the statistical tool for modelling a three-way distinction in which we want to compare all three categories. An additional multinomial logistic regression was done and only the results for the comparison between both peripheral constructions are given in this section. The other results mirror the ones already presented. Table 11 displays the coefficients of the multinomial logistic regression model that are significantly different from zero (omitting the intercept) and with a significant p-value for the comparison between left-peripheral relatives and the baseline right-peripheral relatives. The coefficients are arranged in descending order with respect to their risk ratio.

Tab. 11: Coefficients significantly different from zero and $p < 0.05$ for left-peripheral and right-peripheral RCs

Factor	Coefficient	Std. Error	z value	p value	Risk ratio
Complexity in RC (multi-headed)	13.5	5.8	2.32	0.01	747192.2
Linear distance (head-RC)	0.5	0.11	4.25	2.05^{-05}	1.65
RC Length	−0.25	0.06	−3.72	0.0001	0.77
Quotation	−1.18	0.5	−2.02	0.04	0.3

According to Table 11, linear distance is once again one of the coefficients with the most significant p-value ($p < 0.001$). According to this coefficient, left-peripheral are 1.65 times more likely to occur than right-peripheral constructions when the linear distance is greater. Regarding the length of the relative clause in number of words, left-peripheral relatives are 0.77 less likely to occur than right-peripheral relatives when the relative clause is longer. And in terms of complexity, left-peripheral relatives are 747192.2 times more likely to occur than right-peripheral constructions when the relative clause has multiple relative pronouns. Regarding information structure, one coefficient was marginally significant (p = 0.04) the presence of direct quotation. According to this coefficient, a left-peripheral relative is 0.30 times less likely to occur than a right-peripheral if there is a direct quote.

3.4 Predictability of the model

The predictability of the model was also tested using a method from the field of machine learning called *confusion matrix* or *error matrix*, using R. A confusion matrix is a table that is often used to describe the performance of a classification model or "classifier" on a set of test data for which true values are known. A training data set and a test data set were programmatically selected, each with half of the data of the position of relative constructions from the corpus, to which the following quantitative factors were considered: *linear distance* (nominal head-to-RC), *RC length*, and *MC length*. Note that qualitative factors were not included in this model. The resulting confusion matrix (error rate 0.34) is shown in Table 12.

According to Table 12, the higher success rate was for predicting right-peripheral constructions: 370 constructions were correctly matched with the original, whereas 56 constructions were incorrectly interpreted as a left-peripheral construction, and zero instances were incorrectly interpreted as adnominal. On the other hand, adnominal relatives were incorrectly interpreted as a right-peripheral construction in 51 instances, only one correct match, and zero instances were incorrectly interpreted as left-peripheral. Finally, left-peripheral constructions were correctly matched 154 times, one instance was incorrectly matched with an adnominal construction, and 134 times incorrectly matched with a right-peripheral construction.

Tab. 12: Confusion matrix

		Predicted		
		Right-peripheral	Adnominal	Left-peripheral
Original	Right-peripheral	370	0	56
	Adnominal	51	1	0
	Left-peripheral	154	1	134

There are several reasons why the model was more successful predicting right-peripheral relatives than the other two types. First, the number of tokens is larger for the right peripheral type, hence the model had more input on this construction. Second, right-peripheral relatives present more distinct differences with the other two types in terms of the three considered quantitative factors. Third, it is possible that the distinction between adnominal relatives and left-peripheral constructions depends more heavily on qualitative factors than the considered quantitative ones. Because the former factors were not available, the model was not able to predict correctly.

4 Conclusions

The corpus study confirmed that placement of finite relative clauses in Hindi is motivated by several factors that cannot be reduced to one another, despite the existence of correlations between some of them. Syntactic locality and grammatical weight were stronger predictors than discourse factors in determining the position of the relative clause, which confirms previous claims (Francis and Michaelis 2014, 2016; Rasekh-Mahand et al. 2016; Strunk 2014). The next subsections discuss some of the effects in more detail, as well as methodological considerations, and implications for further research.

4.1 Syntactic locality

The corpus study confirmed locality effects in the placement of relative clauses. Closely related elements in a sentence are preferred to be closer to each other. All relative clauses frequently relativized NPs in subject position (namely nominative). Nevertheless, this was more frequent for left-peripheral relatives than the other two constructions. Right-peripheral relatives also relativized NPs in oblique, genitive and predicate positions. Locality as a factor determining placement of the relative clause is evident when considering that the unmarked word order in Hindi is *Subject–Object–Verb*. Then left-peripheral constructions relativize NPs commonly aligned to the left, whereas right-peripheral constructions relativize NPs commonly aligned to the right (either preverbal or postverbal position). An interesting case is observed with adnominal relatives, since they more frequently relativize NPs as subjects (both nominative and ergative), but no other positions which present oblique case or might be embedded into another NP. Linear distance between the NP and the relative clause further confirms it: 0 words between the NP and the relative clause in adnominal constructions, 2.4 words in the case of right-peripheral ones, and 3.9 in the case of left-peripheral constructions. The results also confirm Kothari's (2010) observation that non-restrictive relatives prefer to be closer to the nominal head they modify.

Linear distance also allows us to observe that despite the fact that clause-internal scrambling is a more frequent phenomenon in left-peripheral constructions, the linear distance remains constant with both internal and external NPs. In other words, one can argue that scrambling preserves locality, i.e. *Minimize Domain*, Hawkins (2004).

Linear distance also accounts for two properties assigned to left-peripheral relatives in prior work: (i) the requirement of a demonstrative pronoun in the main clause and (ii) the possibility of repetition of the nominal head, i.e. simultaneous presence of an internal and external head (Dayal 1996; Srivastav 1991). Linear distance in left-peripheral constructions is greater than the other two constructions: 3.9. The distance increases to 5.1 if the demonstrative occurs alone without a nominal head. I argue that the demonstrative pronoun is required in left-peripheral constructions and not in the other two because of this greater distance. The demonstrative pronoun is then required to pick up the reference of the relative pronoun facilitating processing. Deletion of the demonstrative pronoun is then associated with recoverability and predictability of the reference and the linguistic form. This explains why forms in the nominative (i.e. more recoverable) can be deleted, but not in other cases, especially marked by postpositions (see also Hawkins 2004: 227; Kachru 2006).

On the other hand, the repetition of the nominal head, although marked (only 35 cases in the corpus), it is more frequent in left-peripheral relatives also because of the greater linear distance, confirming Kothari's (2010) hypothesis. In addition, the mean length of the relative clause is longer in those constructions where the nominal head is repeated: 11.11 words versus 9.15 words for the rest of left-peripheral constructions. Hence a need to pick up the reference by repeating the NP.

Finally, linearization requirements such as the ones in (2) can be explained assuming a restriction on locality (minimize domain) on the relative construction and not on the complement clause (*ki-clause*) as it was done previously. Nevertheless, further investigation is required for determining the factors affecting the placement of complement clauses.

4.2 End-weight

Hindi, as English, follows the general principle of end-weight: *short-before-long*, contrary to what is predicted by Hawkins' (2004) mirror principle for verb-final languages. This result can be interpreted as evidence against the claim that directionality of weight effects depends on the language type. Right-peripheral clauses are longer (in number of words) than the other two types, with a mean length of 10.79 words versus 8.42 (adnominal) and 9.15 (left-peripheral) [$F (92, 1636) = 17.53$, $p < 0.0001$]. When considering the length of the main clause, we conclude that the relative clause is shorter when it is adnominal, whereas in left-peripheral constructions both the relative and the main clauses are shorter, and in right-peripheral constructions both the relative and the main clauses are longer. Regarding complexity, the results show that complex clauses are long, which is what we expect. Nevertheless, relative clauses containing multiple relative pronouns are short (9 words), the same length as simple constructions. Also, considering that most combinations involved simple clauses, complexity did not seem to be a good predictor of grammatical weight based on the sampled data.

4.3 The role of information structure

Given and definite entities tend to occur earlier in the utterance than new and indefinite ones. This was partly confirmed by the results, which showed a tendency for relativizing given NPs with left-peripheral constructions, especially as an internal head, whereas new NPs were more frequently relativized by right-peripheral constructions. Overall, 52% of the relativized NPs were annotated as discourse new regardless of the position of the relative clause.

There is not enough evidence in the sample to establish a correlation between discourse givenness and definiteness; nevertheless, most indefinite NPs were also annotated as discourse new (230 or 85%). Overall, 77% of the relativized NPs were definite. This result is similar to the one reported for English (Francis and

Michaelis 2016). This can also be an effect of the pragmatic function of the relative clause itself, as Kuno (1974) claims that restrictive relative clauses assign the discourse role of topic to their heads. Note that in Hindi this seems to be grammaticalized as the "thematic-jo", in which *jo hai* follows a topicalized noun (Gambhir 1981). Furthermore, one can argue that the lack of significance in the results regarding discourse factors can be due to the lack of a systematic framework for definiteness in Hindi, in particular for the analysis of bare NPs.

4.4 The statistical model and its predictability

As mentioned in section 3, previous studies investigating the interaction of competing factors in relative clause extraposition in English and German used a binary regression model. This model was possible because only two conditions were considered: extraposed and integrated. In Hindi, however, there are three categories, namely, left-peripheral, adnominal, and right-peripheral; hence, a multinomial logistic regression was used instead. One shortcoming of this model is that it sets a baseline (either automatically or manually), the baseline establishes only two possible comparisons, i.e. baseline vs. X, and baseline vs. Y, but it does not allow a third comparison, namely X vs. Y. For this study, the model was run twice, changing the baseline in order to compare the peripheral constructions with each other.

One advantage of a multinomial logistic regression is that it considers the totality of the independent variables for calculating the risk ratio, emulating a "real life" situation where the speaker has access to all sort of information (syntactic, semantic, processing, etc.). Nevertheless, if there is interaction between some of the independent variables, the model is claimed to overweight some of the probabilities. We saw this in the case of multi-heading and ergativity, for example. Based on the different Anova and Fisher tests, interactions between some factors were confirmed. The sample size, however, does not allow us to make stronger claims on the overweight effects, if any.

In order to compensate for the limitations of the model, a confusion matrix, a type of classifier, was implemented. This matrix only considered quantitative data (linear distance, RC length, and MC length). The classifier was more successful predicting right-peripheral relatives than the other two types; and as mentioned earlier this could be due to different reasons, such as the number of tokens available for each type and the fact that qualitative factors were excluded (discourse, grammatical case and complexity). For future research, a clustering method using a neural network approach that incorporates quantitative data could be implemented in order to test if the prediction improves for the other two types of constructions. In addition, besides increasing the sample, adding more factors might prove to be fruitful.

Abbreviations

ACC = accusative;   DAT = dative;   DEM = demonstrative;   DEM = demonstrative; ERG = ergative;   F = feminine;   FUT = future;   IMP = imperative;   NEG = negative marker; PFV = perfective; PRS = present; PST = past; PTCP = participle; REL = relative pronoun; SG = singular.

Transliteration

The transliteration of Hindi data in this paper follows the standard ISO-15919. https://en.wikipedia.org/wiki/ISO_15919.

Acknowledgements

I would like to thank the native speakers Mrs. Latika Dhar, Dr. Richa Shrishti and Dr. Tripti Mathur, professors Hans H. Hock and James H. Yoon for their comments on the larger study, and M.A. Oswaldo Navarrete-Carreño and Dr. Rolando Coto-Solano for their advice on the statistical methods; as well as the audience at SALA 35 and the anonymous reviewer for very helpful comments.

References

Adger, David, Cécile de Cat & George Tsoulas. 2004. *Peripheries: Syntactic edges and their effects*. [Studies in Natural Language and Linguistic Theory]. Dordrecht: Springer.

Alexiadou, Artemis, Paul Law, André Meinunger & Chris Wilder. 2000. *The syntax of relative clauses*. Philadelphia, PA: John Benjamins Publishing Company.

Bhatt, Rajesh. 2003. Locality in correlatives. *Natural Language and Linguistic Theory* 21. 485–541.

Butt, Miriam & Tracy Holloway King. 2000. Null elements in discourse structure. *Papers from the NULLS Seminar*. Delhi: Motilal Banarasidass.

Chandola, Anoop Chandra. 1963. Some linguistic influences of English on Hindi. *Anthropological Linguistics* 5 (2). 9–13.

Davison, Alice. 2009. Adjunction, features and locality in Sanskrit and Hindi/Urdu correlatives. In Anikó Lipták (ed.), *Correlatives cross-linguistically*, vi, 223–262. Amsterdam & Philadelphia: John Benjamins Publishing Company.

Dayal, Veneeta. 1996. Locality in wh quantification: Questions and relative clauses in Hindi. Dordrecht & Boston: Springer.

Dayal, Veneeta. 1999. Bare NP's, Reference to Kinds, and Incorporation. *Semantics and Linguistic Theory* 9. 34–51.

Donaldson, Susan. 1971. Movement in restrictive relative clauses. *Studies in the Linguistic Sciences* 1 (2). 1–74.

Dwivedi, Veena Dhar. 1994. *Syntactic dependencies and relative phrases in Hindi*. University of Massachusetts Amherst doctoral dissertation.

Francis, Elaine J. 2010. Grammatical weight and relative clause extraposition in English. *Cognitive Linguistics* 21 (1). 35–74.

Francis, Elaine J. & Laura A. Michaelis. 2014. Why move? How weight and discourse factors combine to predict relative clause extraposition in English. In Edith Moravcsik, Andrej Malchukov & Brian MacWhinney (eds.), *Competing motivations in grammar and usage*, 70–87. Oxford: Oxford University Press.

Francis, Elaine J. & Laura A. Michaelis. 2016. When relative clause extraposition is the right choice, it's easier. *Language and Cognition* 9 (2). 332–370.

Gambhir, Vijay. 1981. Syntactic restrictions and discourse functions of word order in Standard Hindi. University of Pennsylvania.

Gibson, Edward. 1998. Linguistic complexity: Locality of syntactic dependencies. *Cognition* 69 (1). 1–76.

Guéron, Jacqueline & Robert May. 1984. Extraposition and logical form. *Linguistic Inquiry* 15 (1). 1–31.

Gupta, Sagarmal. 1986. *Discourse grammar of Hindi. A study in relative clauses*. New Delhi: Bahri Publications.

Hawkins, John A. 1994. *A performance theory of order and constituency*. Cambridge: Cambridge University Press.

Hawkins, John A. 2004. *Efficiency and complexity in grammars*. Oxford: Oxford University Press.

Hock, Hans Henrich. 1989. Conjoined we stand: Theoretical implications of Sanskrit relative structures. *Studies in the Linguistics Sciences* 19 (1). 93–126.

Huck, Geoffrey J. & Youghee Na. 1990. Extraposition and focus. *Language* 66 (1). 51–77.

Kachru, Yamuna. 1978. On relative clause formation in Hindi-Urdu. *Linguistics* 207. 5–26.

Kachru, Yamuna. 2006. *Hindi*. Amsterdam & Philadelphia: John Benjamins Publishing Company.

Kidwai, Ayesha. 2000. *XP-adjunction in Universal Grammar: Scrambling and binding in Hindi-Urdu*. Oxford & New York: Oxford University Press.

Konieczny, Lars. 2000. Locality and parsing complexity. *Journal of Psycholinguistic Research* 29 (6). 627–645.

Kothari, Anubha. 2010. *Processing constraints and word order variation in Hindi relative clauses*. Stanford University doctoral dissertation.

Kuno, Susumo. 1974. The position of relative clauses and conjunctions. *Linguistic Inquiry* 4. 363–385.

Lipták, Anikó. 2005. Correlative topicalization: The adventures of correlatives in the left periphery. Manuscript, ULCL, Leiden University. https://people.umass.edu/bhatt/752-s05/liptak-hungarian-correlatives.PDF.

Mahajan, Anoop. 2000. Relative asymmetries and Hindi correlatives. In Artemis Alexiadou, Paul Law, André Meinunger & Chris Wilder (eds.), *The syntax of relative clauses*, Linguistik aktuell = Linguistics today, 32, 201–229. Philadelphia, PA: John Benjamins Publishing Company.

Manetta, Emily. 2012. Reconsidering rightward scrambling: Postverbal constituents in Hindi-Urdu. *Linguistics Inquiry* 43 (1). 43–74.

Manninen, Satu. 2002. Extraposition and restrictive relative clauses. *The Department of English in Lund: Working Papers in Linguistics, Volume II*.
https://www.sol.lu.se/fileadmin/media/forskning/workingpapers/engelska/vol02/Satu.pdf

Marlow, Patrick E. (1994). On the origin of embedded relative clauses in Hindi. In Alice Davison & F. M. Smith (eds.), *Papers from the Fifteenth SALA Roundtable Conference* 1993, 167–186. South Asian Studies Program, University of Iowa.

McCawley, James. 2004. Remarks on absentential, adnominal, and extraposed relative clauses in Hindi. In Veneeta Dayal & Anoop Mahajan (eds.), *Clause Structure in South Asian Languages*, 291–311. Dordrecht: Kluwer.

McGregor, Ronald S. 1972. *Outline of Hindi grammar, with exercises*. Oxford,: Clarendon Press.

Patil, Umesh, Gerrit Kentner, Anja Gollrad, Frank Kügler, Caroline Féry & Shravan Vasishth. 2008. Focus, word order and intonation in Hindi. *Journal of South Asian Linguistics* 1 (1). 55–72.

Puri, Vandana. 2011. The influence of English on the history of Hindi relative clauses. *Journal of Language Contact* 4 (2). 250–268.

Rasekh-Mahand, Mohammad, Mojtaba Alizadeh-Sahraie & Raheleh Izadifar. 2016. A corpus-based analysis of relative clause extraposition in Persian. *Ampersand* 3. 21–31.

Prasad, Rashmi & Michael Strube. 2000. Discourse salience and pronoun resolution in Hindi. *Penn Working Papers in Linguistics*, Volume 6.3. 198–208.

Rochemont, Michael & Peter Culicover. 1990. *English focus constructions and the theory of grammar*. Cambridge: Cambridge University Press.

Singh, Mona. 1994. *Perfectivity, definiteness, and specificity: A classification of verbal predicates in Hindi*. Austin, TX: University of Texas doctoral dissertation.

Snell, Rupert. 1990. The hidden hand: English lexis, syntax and idiom as determinants of Modern Hindi usage. *South Asia Research* 10 (53). 53–68.

Srivastav, Veneeta. 1991. The syntax and semantics of correlatives. *Natural Language and Linguistic Theory* 9. 638–686.

Strunk, Jan. 2010. Enriching a treebank to investigate relative clause extraposition in German. In Nicoletta Calzolari, Khalid Choukri, Bente Maegaard, Joseph Mariani, Jan Odijk, Stelios Piperidis, Mike Rosner & Daniel Tapias (eds.), *Proceedings of the Seventh International Conference on Language Resources and Evaluation* (LREC'10), 1911–1917. European Language Resources Association (ELRA): Valetta, Malta.

Strunk, Jan. 2014. A statistitcal model of competing motivations affecting relative clause extraposition in German. In Brian MacWhinney, Andrej Malchukov & Edith Moravcsik (eds.), *Competing Motivations in Grammar and Usage*, 88–106. Oxford: Oxford University Press.

Strunk, Jan & Neal Snider. 2013. Subclausal locality constraints on relative clause extraposition. In Gert Webelhuth, Manfred Sailer & Heike Walker (eds.), *Rightward movement a comparative perspective*, 99–144. Amsterdam: John Benjamins.

Subbarao, Karumuri V. 1984. *Complementation in Hindi syntax*. Delhi: Academic Publications.

Subbarao, Karumuri V. 2012. *South Asian Languages: A syntactic typology*. Cambridge: Cambridge University Press.

Uszkoreit, Hans, Thorsten Brants, Denys Duchier, Brigitte Krenn, Lars Konieczny, Stephan Oepen & Wojciech Skut. 1998. Studien zur performanzorientierten Linguistik. Aspekte der Relativsatzextraposition im Deutschen. *Kognitionswissenschaft* 7. 129–133.

Vasishth, Shravan. 2003. Working memory in sentence comprehension: Processing Hindi center embeddings. Abingdon: Routledge.

Vasishth, Shravan & Richard L. Lewis. 2006. Argument-head distance and processing complexity: Explaining both locality and antilocality effects. *Language* 82 (4). 767–792.

Verma, Manindra. 1966. *The noun phrase in Hindi and English*. Delhi: Motilal Banarsidass Publishers.

Verma, Manindra. 1971. *The structure of the noun phrase in English and Hindi*. Delhi: Motilal Banarsidass.

Wasow, Thomas. 1997. Remarks on grammatical weight. *Language Variation and Change* 9. 81–105.

Wasow, Thomas. 2002. *Postverbal behavior*. Stanford, CA: CSLI Publications.

Yamashita, Hiroko & Franklin Chang. 2001. "Long before short" preference in the production of a head-final language. *Cognition* 81. B45–B55.

Tanmoy Bhattacharya
Optionality and variation in agreement in some participles in Hindi-Urdu

Abstract: Optionality in participial agreement in Hindi was noted in Kachru (2006: 163), where an adverbial participle may optionally agree with the subject NP in number and gender if the NP is in the direct case. For the present paper, I expand this observation further and demonstrate the existence of extensive (syntactic) variation in participial agreement in Hindi with data that has not been reported or analyzed in the literature. In the case of relative participles, where Kachru did not report any variation, the range of judgments indicates a general reluctance of the number feature to be available too low in the structure; this becomes apparent if we use an object relative in these constructions; the optionality in participial subject agreement that Kachru captured seems to take place in the case of participial object agreement as well. For the complex adjectival/ adverbial adjuncts, though Kachru (2006) reported variation by one factor, the extent of variation is found to be much wider. The judgments on these variants indicate that the feature of person seems to be available high up in the clause and gender lower down but it is number that hovers in between. This is in line with the general observation that participle agreement is with number and gender and never with person, unlike subject agreement in general – another reason why this type of agreement should be seen as different from (subject) argument agreement on verbs. Theoretically, the findings indicate that the trigger for the number agreement cannot be lower than at least the main clause aspectual head. The paper proposes three distinct syntactic operations – valuation, relaying, and copying which, together with standard Agree applying top-down, derive the full range of the results obtained.

Keywords: Participles, Agreement, Optionality, Hindi-Urdu

Tanmoy Bhattacharya, Department of Linguistics, University of Delhi, Delhi, 110007, India.
Email: tanmoy1@gmail.com

1 Introduction

This paper is about the role of variation in grammar in general and microvariation in particular (section 3). The discussion in the first three sections broadly problematizes agreement studies in general by pointing out the somewhat skewed development in the area, setting the stage for looking at variation within participles (section 2), and then engaging in specific discussion about variation in the context of Hindi-Urdu participles. Thus, all these three sections work towards contextualizing the problem at hand.[1]

The data on Hindi-Urdu participial agreement is presented in section 4. In section 5, I present the speaker variation in judgments on agreement across the two relevant data-sets – participial relatives and adjectival/ adverbial participial adjuncts; section 6 provides an analysis of the variation data and section 7 concludes.

In the familiar structure of a clause within the generative framework, for various reasons, Agreement was thought to deserve a place, and a new head called AGR found a place in the tree in its own right (see (1) below), which was crucial in obtaining agreement (and case). Soon, however, it was realized that there should be two of them, not one, the latter being a reflection of the research energy being spent mostly studying languages showing the single argument agreement phenomenon, that is, agreement with the subject.

(1)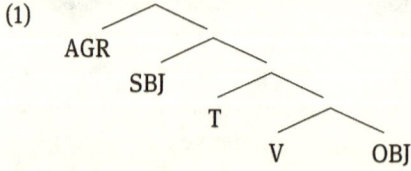

Just to elaborate on this point a little, take a look at the world according to WALS (World Atlas of Language Structures, Siewierska 2013), looking at only 378 languages, where person marking on the verb is depicted (in the legend in the inset) in Figure 1. The color that dominates this map here is black, which stands for languages showing both agent and patient argument agreement, roughly the

---

[1] The discussion in these sections also points to a certain hegemonic approach towards the study of agreement in particular (and maybe syntax in general), which indicates the existence of a much larger problem in the discipline that continues to remain unaddressed.

verb showing both subject and object agreement marking.² Double or multiple agreement therefore seems to be the more common strategy, yet the little history of theoretical linguistics (or more accurately, syntax) that is related to the above through clause structure is dominated by the grey triangles in the map; that is, languages with agreement with only the subject, with the area marked out on the map showing the concentration of Romance and Germanic languages. However, this sample suggests that by far most languages that show agreement also show multiple-argument agreement (>51%).³

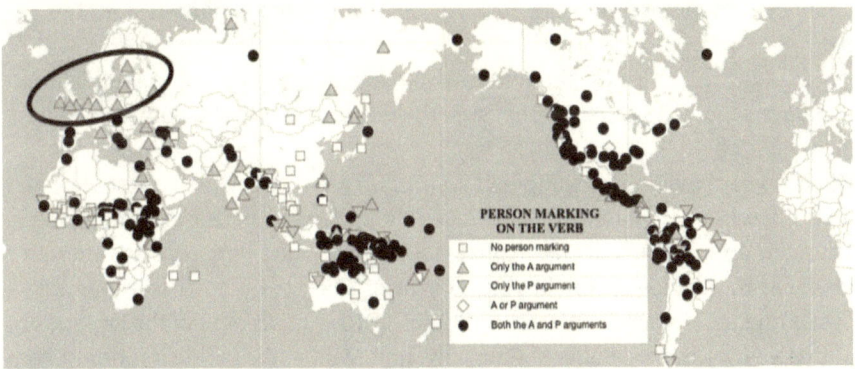

Fig. 1: Map showing person marking on the verb (WALS: Siewierska (2013); http://wals.info)

In Bhattacharya (2016), I tried to show that a group of languages that evolved from Māgadhi Prākrit, namely, languages such as Maithili, Magahi, Angika etc., that are different from languages that evolved from Sauraseni Prākrit, namely, Hindi-Urdu, are multiple-argument agreement languages; making these groups of languages parametrically different from Hindi-Urdu in certainly this aspect of agreement, calling for a different theoretical explanation for the phenomenon. Bhattacharya (2017a,b, 2018b) shows that in the Munda group of languages, at least in the Kherwarian or North Munda languages like Mundari, Santhali and Ho, a different phenomenon of pronominal cliticization obtains where both the subject and the object pronominals cliticize on to the predicate (and/or a pre-

---

2 Equating Agent/ Patient with Subject/ Object is problematic, but this is supposed to be a rough equivalence to make essentially the point that one type of languages is preferred over another.
3 Although counting is not crucial for making a certain syntactic theoretical move (I thank an anonymous reviewer for pointing this out); but the point remains that multiple agreement languages are rarely showcased as typical exemplars of the phenomenon of agreement.

verbal element). This phenomenon, being different technically from agreement, requires a different theoretical treatment. In Bhattacharya (2018a) and Bhattacharya and Sharma (forthcoming), this observation was extended to the agreeing Tibeto-Burman languages across the Himalayan region (including Nepal) and southern Chin languages in Mizoram. Apart from these being microparameters across a contiguous belt extending eastward from the foothills of the Himalayas to Burma, verb-indexation and/or agreement with more than one argument seems not to be that uncommon even within South Asia. Again, syntactic accounts of agreement within the context of at least languages in India have been dominated by studies on Hindi-Urdu, a "sin" I am going to partake in in this paper.

In short, historically, the minority agreement pattern, that is, single-argument agreement, has exerted the most theoretical push in the domain of agreement.

In spite of the limited sample, it is still the case that between the subject and object, subject agreement (19%) is more common than object agreement (6%). Thus, it is no surprise that object agreement in fact makes its entry into generative grammar in the historically important year of 1989, the year of many new proposals and innovations (Bhattacharya 2015–2016 is an account of the importance of that year) – Kayne, Pollock, Chomsky, and Mahajan all made important contributions that year, which could therefore be hailed as the year of agreement since all the four papers make significant contributions to a revision in the clause structure as shown in (1) above in terms of the AGR head(s).

To begin with, there was one AGR node inserted, for the reasons discussed above.[4] Kayne (1989) and Mahajan (1989) are crucially significant in this connection; it can be said that the need for a second AGR projection in the clause was proposed by Kayne and well-supported theoretically (and empirically) by Mahajan. The data for both of these works were based on object agreement of sorts, past participial agreement in French for Kayne, and object agreement in Hindi-Urdu for Mahajan. The proposal for a second AGR position lower in the clause can be termed the Kayne-Mahajan Hypothesis (KMH). In passing, it may also be mentioned that Kayne's (1989) analysis is the basis for the SPEC-HEAD technology that was soon widely adopted.

---

4 In the original proposal by Pollock (1989), the AGR head follows the T head (i.e. T>AGR) but it was soon accepted that the AGR>T order is supported by the Mirror Principle (Baker 1985) and arguments in Belletti (1990). Morpheme order in languages bear this out, for example, *dekh-e-ch-il-am* '(I) had seen' in Bangla, that is, V-ASP-AUX-T-AGR; Chomsky (1995) therefore adopted the AGR>T order.

Participial agreement in Romance is significant in the context of KMH. However, participial agreement in the context of South Asian languages still awaits a complete syntactic treatment. How does participial agreement in these languages line up with the agreement story so far? The current paper is a very initial attempt at finding a theoretical grip on participial agreement in Hindi-Urdu; although participial agreement has been noted in agreement accounts of Hindi-Urdu, most notably in Mahajan (1990) (but also Bhatt 2005, Bhatt and Walkow 2013, and Bhatt and Keine 2017 – the latter discussed further in section 3 in the context of syntactic microvariation), it has been done so far only in passing.

At present, this paper is only a partial account of the participial agreement phenomenon, even while staying within the syntax of participles. However, the paper does not attempt to compare the various characteristics of participial agreement in other languages from other language families within South Asia and outside with the Hindi-Urdu facts, with one exception. This exception highlights the issue of variation that is found in the domain of participial agreement. Is there a theoretical reason for this variation? And how should a formalist look at variation to begin with?

Theoretically, past participle agreement in Romance and other languages was a demonstration of the relation between movement and agreement – it is only the movement of the object that triggers agreement on the verb (see 2 and 3 below). However, as pointed out in Longenbaugh (2018), the dependency between movement and agreement could not be sustained since agreement "at a distance" was shown to operate in many languages. The challenge Longenbaugh (2018) sets up is to account for movement-related agreement and long-distance agreement in general. However, in this paper, I will show that a further challenge is to account for participial agreement itself being "at a distance".

2 Participial agreement in Romance

Kayne (1989) noted that past participles in French optionally agree with an object clitic or a wh-construction instead of the subject. However, he not only noted that this agreement is different from the usual subject agreement but also that this agreement is optional. Thus Kayne's (1989) contribution can be stated as not only proposing a second AGR head in the clausal spine but also showing that it is different from the high AGR head, in addition to a theoretical account of the optionality of participial agreement. The fact that the lower and the upper AGR heads differ can be the basis for marking them differently, as AGR_S and AGR_O, although in Chomsky (1995), these same two heads are considered syntactically identical barring their syntactic position. In Chomsky (1995), these heads are where agreement and case of the subject and object respectively are established via the checking mechanism established through SPEC-HEAD relation, as was the proposal in early Minimalism. This uniformity, which is much celebrated for obvious reasons, is, from this perspective, misplaced. In fact, as was pointed out in Belletti (2001, 2006), past participle agreement in Romance is achieved through a low Agreement position headed by AgrPstPrt, different from the AGR position responsible for case and agreement on the object.

Kayne (1989) presented two basic types of optional object agreement in past participles in French; these are shown in (3) and (4), compared with (2) which shows no agreement:

Object in-situ: no agreement

(2) *Paul a   repeint/*es   les chaises*
     Paul has repainted/*PL the chairs

Object as a clitic: optional agreement

(3) *Paul les   a   repeintes/ repeint*
     Paul them has repainted

Wh-object: optional agreement

(4a) *[les chaises que] Paul a   repeintes/ repeint*
     the chairs   that Paul has repainted
(4b) *[combien de tables] Paul a   repeintes/ repeint*
     how many of tables Paul has repainted

To summarize the data, agreement with the object takes place in French participles only when the object moves from its base position across the participle; however, this agreement is optional. Note that therefore we get a non-canonical order (SOV) in the object agreement configuration. The object movement to the left in these examples can be schematized as in (5).

(5a) Cliticization:
     NP$_{SBJ}$ CL$_i$ AUX   V$_{PTCP}$ [e]$_i$

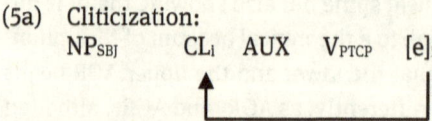

(5b) Wh-movement:
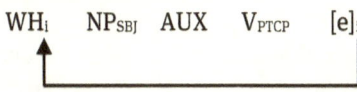
WH$_i$ NP$_{SBJ}$ AUX   V$_{PTCP}$ [e]$_i$

Kayne's suggestion is that the agreement between the moved clitic/ Wh-object is mediated by a lower AGR position in the clause:

(6)   NP$_{SBJ}$ CL$_i$ AUX [e]$_i$ AGR V$_{PTCP}$ [e]$_i$

According to Kayne, the optionality in agreement observed is dependent upon the movement path, which can be shown as follows in terms of (7a) or (7b):

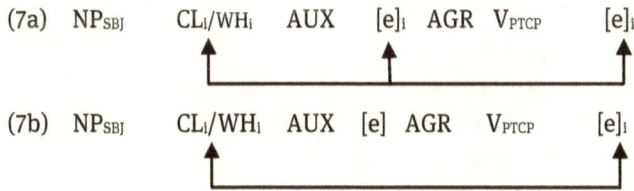
(7a)   NP$_{SBJ}$ CL$_i$/WH$_i$ AUX   [e]$_i$ AGR   V$_{PTCP}$ [e]$_i$

(7b)   NP$_{SBJ}$ CL$_i$/WH$_i$ AUX   [e]   AGR   V$_{PTCP}$ [e]$_i$

In case of the movement path in (7b), no agreement results as the clitic/WH does not stop in the intermediate position nearer the lower AGR. Although the WH and clitic movement are not distinguished in (7a) in the above schema, there is a difference in the movement path of each in Kayne (1989). Specifically, it is proposed that the clitic movement is a substitution to [Spec, AgrP], whereas in the case of the Wh-phrase, it is a case of adjunction. Since this was before the SPEC-HEAD agreement configuration module was crystallized, movement to a "Spec-like" position (that is, the adjoined position) was enough to establish agreement with the head (based on Government). The difference, therefore, is the location of the intermediate *e* position in (7a) for the WH and NP clitic, which can be shown as in (8a) and (8b) respectively:

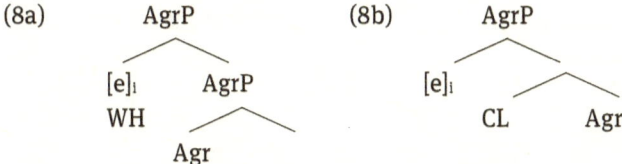

(8a)   AgrP
            [e]$_i$ AgrP
            WH
                        Agr

(8b)   AgrP
            [e]$_i$
                    CL   Agr

Although French does not distinguish empirically the two processes – namely (Wh-)agreement versus cliticization – based on comparative evidence, Kayne claims them to undergo different processes (that is, different movement paths), where the clitic does not adjoin.[5]

Also, it must be the case that for the Wh, there should be another movement to the [Spec, CP] position, whereas for the Clitic movement as schematized in (7), this must be the last phrasal movement before it undergoes head movement. The subcases of Wh past participle and clitic agreement are different; though not visible in French, the difference is clear in Italian (also in Catalan, varieties of Occitan, Beuil dialect, Corsican, Milanese, Cremonese, and Bolognese dialects of Italian), which can be attributed to a difference between adjunction and substitution, respectively:

(9a) *Paolo ha visto le ragazze*
 Paolo has seen.SG the girls
(9b) *Paolo le ha viste/ *visto* CL
 Paolo them has seen.PL/*seen.SG
(9c) *le ragazze che Paolo ha visto/*viste* WH
 the girls that Paolo has seen.SG/*PL
 (Kayne 1989: 33)

Comparing data in (3) and (4) with data in (9) clearly shows variation in participial agreement within Romance. Such variation can be more succinctly captured in the data in contrastive triple in (10), which shows differences across French, Spanish, and Italian:

(10a) *Juan la ha comido/*a* (Spanish: Obligatory non-agreement)
 Juan it.F has eaten.M/*F
 'Juan has eaten it.'
(10b) *Gianni l' ha mangiata/*o* (Italian: Obligatory agreement)
 Gianni it.F has eaten.F/*M
 'Gianni has eaten it.'
(10c) *Jean l' a mangé/ée* (French: Optional agreement)
 Jean it.F has eaten.M/F
 'Jean has eaten it.'
 (Franco 1994: 247)

---

[5] Although Greek clitics have been claimed to be adjoined to TP, where the [Spec,TP] position remains empty, if they are X^0 clitics, they adjoin to the head. Here, too, the movement path of the clitic is supposed to go through a phrasal position (Spec of AgrPstPrtP) and then move into the V head, to highlight the XP/X^0 character of these clitics (Belletti 2006).

Such differences in agreement across languages are not an isolated case, as in French itself many speakers have a Spanish-like obligatory non-agreement in participles. Further, in "substandard" Italian (Parisi 1976: 78), agreement is possible with the in-situ object:

(11) *Paolo ha viste le ragazze*
      Paolo has seen.PL the girls

This version is attested in the Salentino dialect of southern Italy and the Corese dialect as well as in several varieties of Occitan. I address the possibility (and importance) of such cases of dialectal variation, immediately below.

3 Participial agreement as a case of microvariation

Coming back to a point about variation mentioned earlier, any modern agreement account must deal with the reason for such an increased possibility of variation within participles, which perhaps indicates that clausal agreement differs from participial agreement. In Lee (2016), variation was also reported in English in the case of Wh-clefts: *What I really need is/are books*. One can thus claim that the variation in French Wh-object agreement (and no such variation in Italian) is reflected to some extent in English too; the ambiguity, in turn, can be accounted for in terms of movement through [Spec, AgrP] in cases of agreement. Note that specificational copular sentences in Italian show NP2 agreement, contrasting with Wh-objects not agreeing, as reported above in (9c). This again shows that the two types of agreement are different.

Although traditionally variation in judgement has been termed "speaker behavior", it is worth briefly revisiting in the context of the present discussion. It is important to underline that variation in judgment can be accounted for within the paradigm of generative linguistics. The findings will reveal that in each case – that is, for each of the two sets of data described, namely, relative participle and adjectival/ adverbial adjunct – the relevance of what is "clearly disliked" and what is "clearly liked" is pertinent for the analysis; see, for example, the results summarized in Table 6, where the median scores cluster at two ends as '2' (clearly liked) and '5' (clearly disliked). Thus, in spite of the shades of variation, it is broadly true that the set of judgments cluster around what is broadly grammatical and ungrammatical.

It is relevant to consider in this connection the importance of microparametric research in syntax in the last 25 years or so. With the development of Minimalism (Chomsky 1995), a gradual demise of macroparametric research has been noted. However, syntactic studies largely ignore this crucial development and *de facto* practice comparative syntactic research of the type that is more in tune with the 1980s. Take, for example, Bhatt and Keine's (2017: 50) discussion around their observation that in participles (past/passive), among other constructions, number is neutralized in the context of the feminine in Hindi-Urdu; they provide data such as the following for the progressive auxiliary *rahā*:

(12a) *rahā*   *rahe*
      M.SG   M.PL
(12b) *rahī*   *rahī*
      F.SG   F.PL

Note that the two feminine forms in (12b) are identical since the singular-plural distinction is neutralized in the feminine. They also note that in many of the neighboring Indo-Aryan languages – like Punjabi, Sindhi, Kashmiri, and Marathi – this pattern of neutralization does not occur.

This kind of comparative syntactic research is set very much in the mold of parametric research of the early 1980s, when, for example, the null subject parameter (NSP) was considered the most celebrated example of what a parameter is. Note that the NSP was, if not a macro-, certainly a meso- or medio-parameter – Baker (2008) in fact identifies it as such, when comparing the working of this parameter within the Romance group of languages. Looking at one point of difference within broadly northern Indo-Aryan languages like Hindi-Urdu, Punjabi, Kashmiri, etc., is also a case of 1980s-style study of a macro/medio-parameter. If, instead, such studies care to look at dialects of Hindi-Urdu, or dialects of Punjabi, or dialects of Marathi, an entirely different perspective may emerge.

In fact, the dataset that I will be presenting below (see section 4) from Hindi-Urdu participles represents speaker variation in participial agreement in adjuncts. If we take these instances of genuine speaker variation as syntactic variation across languages/ dialects, each of these variants would represent a language/ dialect.[6] That is, the data on speaker variation is really the data on language/ dialect variation. In fact, within the data presented in the next section,

---

6 The variation reported does indicate a trend even if the sample studied for this paper is admittedly small. The fact that, even in such a small sample, wide variations are found only highlights the importance of syntactic variation.

there are various examples containing the passive participle and progressive auxiliary where number neutralization does not take place in the presence of the feminine – see data in (26e), (26g) and (26h). Questions such as where does this data showing feminine plural agreement come from, or how do we account for this data, can no longer be ignored.

Note that this kind of phenomenon is reminiscent of the variation in Romance past participles discussed in section 2. In particular, Kayne (1996) points out in this connection that there are different levels of parameters. For example, one could say that at the surface level the relevant parameter within the domain of past participle agreement in Romance is as noted in section 2; that is, it is optional in French, obligatory in Italian, and absent in Spanish. However, once we go deeper and study the phenomenon in the dialects of these languages, we discover a finer-grained effect of this parameter; for example, some of the dialects (= languages, for Kayne) allow participial agreement in both WH- and clitic constructions, but some only in clitics (Kayne 1989). And once we are prepared to go even further and study the phenomenon in greater detail across the individual dialects, we discover that some of them allow agreement with all object clitics whereas some allow it only with 3rd person objects. Thus, any study looking only at the operation of a parameter among broadly related languages like Hindi-Urdu, Punjabi, Kashmiri, etc., is bound to meet the same fate as NSP, whereby many such macro- or medio-parameters made way for microparameters arrived at by studying closely related dialects instead.

The explosion of microparametric research in the mid-1990s is also in consonance with the theoretical shift that took place with the advent of Minimalism. The place of parameters as such, or more accurately, macro-parameters, became more and more reduced, and as Richards (2008) puts it – UG is maximally emptied of parameters, a change that was heralded with the reaffirmation of the strong minimalist thesis, namely, that the faculty of language is optimally designed for the purpose of its interactions with the semantic and sensorimotor interfaces. The rise of microparametric research in syntax predicted in Kayne (1996), and reaffirmed in Kayne (2005), is the guiding principle for the present work which clearly shows, that for whatever reasons, feminine plural agreement does show up in participles in Hindi-Urdu.[7]

---

[7] Bhatt and Keine (2017: 53 n. 1) note that plural agreement may obtain in the feminine optionally, as shown in data on the internet. The data and arguments in the present paper show that such facts need not reside in footnotes as asides but can be very much a part of the mainstream discussion representing a thriving speech community outside the internet, too, that deserves its due place in scientific research.

4 The participial agreement data in Hindi-Urdu

I begin by looking at reported facts on participial agreement in one of the earliest texts on Hindi-Urdu grammar. Kachru (2006: 163) notes that Hindi has optional participial agreement where the participial adverbial auxiliary may agree with the subject NP in number and gender if the NP is in the direct case (13a); (13b) shows lack of agreement:

(13a) laṛkiyā̃   bhāgtī   huī   āyī̃/   bhāgte   hue   āye
       girl.F.PL   run.IPFV.F   PTCP.F   come.PFV.F.PL   run.IPFV.PL   PTCP.PL   come.PFV.PL
       'The girls came running.'

(13b) laṛkī-ne   [kamre-se   nikalte   hue]
       girl.F-ERG   room.M.SG.OBL-ABL   emerge.IPFV.OBL   PTCP.OBL
       darvāzā   band   kar   diyā
       door.M   shut   do   give.PFV.M.SG
       'The girl closed the door (as she was) leaving the room.'

However, since this is a case of the intransitive predicate, the agreement is with the sole argument, that is, the subject; to create a set that can be compared with the data in Romance easily, let us consider transitives. Let us in fact look at the agreement possibilities in a relative participle clause in Hindi-Urdu which is derived from a transitive base, as in the following:

SET I: (Relative) Participial agreement where the object is relativized:

(14)   ravi-kī   paṛhī   huī   kitābẽ
       Ravi-GEN   read.PFV.F   PTCP.F   book.F.PL
       'Books that have been read by Ravi.'
       (Lit. Ravi's read books.)

Since the subject is case-marked in the case of perfective participles inside a prenominal relative clause, the (past) participial agrees with the object. As in the case of French object agreement in participles, a non-canonical order obtains (SVO), although this is only an NP/DP. The object movement is due to relativization, assuming Bhatt (2002) arguing in favor of a raising analysis of the relative clause. In fact, the agreement facts in the relative participle in Hindi-Urdu can be seen as strong support for the raising analysis of RCs. Apparently, it is not possible to relativize the subject in prenominal relatives, and therefore we do not obtain (15); this has also been pointed out in Mahajan (2018: 93):

(15) *[kitāb paṛhī huī] laṛkiyā̃
     book read.PFV.F PTCP.F girl.F.PL
     *'The book-read girls.' (= The girls who have read the book.)

Thus, we can say that the participle in RCs agrees with the postverbal argument, which can only be the object.

The participles that are adjuncts (and not prenominal RCs), show agreement with the subject, as in the oft-repeated instruction on airplane seats in India:

(16) [bæṭhe hue] kursī ki peṭī bāndhe rakkhē
     sitting.IPFV.OBL PTCP.OBL chair GEN belt tie.OBL keep.2HON
     'Fasten seat belt while seated.'

In such cases, the subject (here 2.HON *pro*) agrees with both the participle in the adjunct[8] (not visible in 16, since the agreement is with an imperative pro-dropped honorific argument, but see footnote 8) as well as the main clause verb. The participial adjunct (both the verb stem as well as the auxiliary) may also show agreement with the object, when the subject is blocked for agreement by case, as in the following, where the subject is case-marked and the object 'birds', may agree in gender with the participial:

---

[8] Although there are no instances, as far as I can see, where the invariant form of the participle (as in 16) is not available, there seems to be both gender and number agreement across different persons. Gender agreement in the singular obtains in 1st and 3rd person for both genders, as well as in the 2nd feminine; for plural, gender agreement only obtains in 2nd and 3rd feminine. For number, again only 2nd and 3rd feminine is marked for some speakers. However, the data collected is not enough to report in the main study. A table such as the following can be drawn in support:

Person	Number	Masculine	Feminine
1	SG	gender/ invariant	gender/ invariant
	PL	invariant	invariant
2	SG	invariant	gender/ invariant
	PL	invariant	invariant/ ?gender-num
3	SG	gender/ invariant	gender/ invariant
	PL	invariant	invariant/?gender-num

(17)   *Ravi-ne   ciṛiyā*   [PRO *uṛte/uṛtī*   *hue/huī*]
       Ravi-ERG bird.F.PL   fly.IPFV.OBL/FLY.IPFV.F   PTCP.OBL/PTCP.F
       dekh-ī/ī̃   *haĩ*
       see-PFV.F./PL   be.3.PL
       'Ravi has witnessed birds flying.'

Note here that although the gender agreement with the object (*ciṛiyā* 'birds') through the object-controlled PRO within the adjunct is optional, the main verb and auxiliary agree with the object,[9] since the subject is case-marked. Similarly, with a dative experiencer subject, agreement in the main clause is with the object but the agreement inside the adjunct is optional:

(18)   *Ravi-ko   ciṛiyā*   [PRO *uṛte/uṛtī*   *hue/huī*]
       Ravi-DAT bird.F.PL   fly.IPFV.OBL/FLY.IPFV.F   PTCP.OBL/PTCP.F
       nazar   āyī̃
       notice   come.3.F.PL
       'Ravi has noticed birds flying.'

Here, the complex predicate (*nazar ānā*) is formed when the noun is denominalized by incorporating it into an empty V which then merges with a light verb head (*v*) *ānā* 'come' (Hale and Keyser 1993, 1998). In both cases (17, 18), the ergative/ dative subject is blocked from agreeing and therefore the object (*ciṛiyā*) agrees with the verb, and in both cases the adjunct can optionally have the invariant form, or it can agree with the gender and number of the object.

SET II: (Complex) Adverbial/Adjectival Participial Agreement[10]

In the present, in their adverbial modifying role, participles in Hindi-Urdu may show agreement with the PRO subject of the participial clause, as in the following (from Kachru 2006):

---

9 Note that the participial agrees with the object-controlled PRO in this example, which is the subject of the adjunct clause as shown in (17) and (18).
10 The clarificatory word "complex" being added to indicate that simple adjectives/ adverbs do not show agreement (p.c. K.V. Subbarao), as in (i):
(i)   *laṛke/ laṛkiyā̃   acchā   gānā   gāte/   gātī(ī̃)   haĩ*
      boys/ girls   good   song   sing.3MPL/ sing.3FPL   be.3PL
In the analysis section, I will comment on them being a case of perhaps concord.

(19) laṛkī [maze mẽ gātī   huī]   jhulā jhul   rahī   hai
    girl.SG fun in sing.IPFV.F PTCP.F.SG swing swing PROG.F.SG be.PRS.3SG
    'The girl is swinging in the swing while singing in gay abandon.'

Note that here in the case of adverbial agreement, we obtain subject agreement. This is so because the subject is not overtly case-marked and the object is incorporated into the verb anyway, and is therefore not available for any possible agreement. For both cases of (14) and (19), what is of interest is that we find agreement inside the adjunct.

With regards to the example in (19), Kachru (2006: 228) notes that the participle agreement (of the adjunct) is optional:

(20) laṛkī [maze mẽ gāte   hue]   jhulā jhul   rahī   hai
    girl.SG fun in sing.IPFV.OBL PTCP.OBL swing swing PROG.F be.PRS.3S
    'The girl is swinging in the swing while singing in gay abandon.'

Here, the adjunct shows the invariant form [V-*te hue*] and therefore does not agree with the main clause subject. However, as I will immediately show, the extent of variation in the data is much more than what is reported in Kachru (2006).

5 Variation in Hindi-Urdu participial agreement

For the current paper, I have tested sentences of the pattern in (14) and (19)/(20), that is relative participle and complex adverbial participles respectively, for variation. I will present here two sets of judgments from 5 and 6 native speakers, respectively.[11]

---

[11] The speakers for the two sets are different but they do overlap; in total there were 8 speakers, all of them have lived and studied/worked in Delhi or nearby regions. If I am pushed to assign a variety to them, then I would say 4 of them are perhaps "Delhi Hindi" speakers and the rest speak some version of "Uttar Pradesh Hindi". With an average age of about 45 years, there were 6 females and 2 males. The data was collected in 2015.

5.1 Variation in relative participles

Let us first look at the judgement for the relative participle case. Note that Kachru did not report any variation in this case. The following are the 4 variants obtained – in (21) – over which the total judgments are reported as in Table 2:

(21a) *paṛhī huī kitābē*   (GND in both V and PTCP)
      read.F PTCP.F book.F.PL
      'Read books' (= Books that have been read.)
(21b) *paṛhĩ huī kitābē*   (NUM + GND in V, GND in PTCP)
      read.F.PL PTCP.F book.F.PL
(21c) *paṛhī huĩ kitābē*   (GND in V, NUM + GND in PTCP)
      read.F PTCP.F.PL book.F.PL
(21d) *paṛhĩ huĩ kitābē*   (NUM + GND in both V and PTCP)
      read.F.PL PTCP.F.PL book.F.PL

In reporting the results of the two sets of data – relative participles (Set I) and adjectival/ adverbial adjuncts (Set II) – a Likert scale of 4 values (for Set I) and 5 values (Set II) are used in order to obtain ordinal data in terms of numbers. As is well known, Likert scales are one of the most effective ways of measuring attitudes; for example, shades of grammatical judgments on a construction, in our case. Since the distances between the various responses in such cases are not measurable, ranking is often the most effective way of measuring attitudes, even as uncommonly as measuring attitude towards a sentence. The underlying variable that is being tested in each case through the various items, that is, the example sentences together with their associated responses, is the nature of the agreement with its head noun of a prenominal relative participle (Set I) and with the subject for a participle inside an adjectival/ adverbial adjunct (Set II).

In the case of Set I, the following four values are used (see Table 1); note that although the scale is bivalent (ranging from 'acceptable' to 'unacceptable'), it is not symmetrical since there is no obvious neutral choice measuring central tendencies among four given choices, although [2] is clearly a neutral choice:

Tab. 1: Likert scale values of grammatical judgements for Set I

Standard diacritic	L-scale value	L-scale rank
✓	'acceptable'	[1]
?	'neither fully grammatical nor fully unacceptable'	[2]
??	'almost unacceptable'	[3]
*	'unacceptable'	[4]

Speaker judgments on the 4 variants in (21a)–(21d) above are shown in Table 2, values for 5 speakers arrived at using the Likert scale established above:

Tab. 2: Speaker judgments on the 4 variants in relative participle agreement

Sentence type	[1]	[2]	[3]	[4]
a.	2	1	2	–
b.	–	–	3	2
c.	4	–	–	1
d.	–	2	1	2

In terms of speaker behavior, although not revealed in the Likert values, we may note that except for one speaker, who is very strict in their judgment, all the rest show a great range of variation. Among the variants, it is first of all surprising that there is little agreement on the so-called standard form in (21a) in terms of speakers' judgments. Secondly, the variant (21c) is most preferable, more than the standard form that is (21a).

In the following (see Table 3) is provided the summary of the distribution of ϕ-features along with a somewhat controversial concept of an "average" judgment in the last column based on speaker behavior and regional information. Note first that one of the advantages of a 4-value scale is that it avoids the disadvantages of a central tendency observed in a symmetrical 5-value scale; 4 value scales are also effective with small samples like the present one, although Set II employs a standard 5-value scale. Secondly, note that calculating the average of a Likert scale is generally not a good idea, since sometimes it is meaningless to assign a value to something like 'almost unacceptable', for example. Instead, it is considered better to calculate the Median score or/ and the Inter-Quartile Range; however, since the sample size here is very small, quartile values are not feasible. Therefore, whenever "average" judgment is mentioned, what is implied is the associated median score (calculated as the average of two numbers lying exactly in the middle), as shown in the last column of Table 3.[12]

Tab. 3: Distribution of φ-features and Median score ('average' judgment)

VARIANT	RELATIVE CL.		RELATIVIZED NP	Median Score ('average' judgment)
	V	PTCP		
a.	Gender	Gender	Gender + Number	2
b.	Gender Number	Gender	Gender + Number	3
c.	Gender	Gender Number	Gender + Number	1
d.	Gender Number	Gender Number	Gender + Number	3

One thing that using a Likert scale (along with the median scores) in this case reveals, which simple speaker-based grammaticality judgments do not, is that nothing is completely unacceptable (since a Median score of 4 does not obtain). The results can be summarized as follows:

(22)　Results for relative participle agreement:
　　　i. agreement in gender on both the verb and participle preferred (21a)
　　　ii. number agreement on V is not acceptable (21b)
　　　iii. number agreement on the participle is preferable (21c)
　　　iv. number agreement on both V and participle is not acceptable (21d)

The table in general is very instructive and we can take the following to be the main syntactic finding of the exercise:

(23)　Given the judgments for the variants (21b) and (21d), there is a general reluctance of the number feature to be available too low in the structure.

This can be schematically shown as follows:

---

[12] Note that a blank in the tables (shown by an en-dash) indicates absence of any response for a given judgment.

(24) [RC V   AUX] NP   (Set I, Phrase)
         GND   GND   GND
         *NUM   (NUM) NUM

5.2 Variation in participial adverbials

Let us now move on to the next construction tested for this study, that is, the complex adjectival/ adverbial adjunct. As we saw in (19) and (20), repeated here as (25), Kachru (2006) already observed variation (by one factor) in these examples:

(25) laṛkī ⎡ (i) maze mẽ gātī   huī ⎤ jhulā jhul rahī hai
             ⎣ (ii) maze mẽ gāte   hue ⎦
         ⎡ (i) fun in sing. IPFV.F   be.F.SG ⎤
         ⎣ (ii) fun in sing. IPFV.OBL   be.OBL ⎦

However, as noted earlier, the extent of variation is much broader than only one factor, as shown by the observations in the current study. As before, the following is a list of the 8 variants tested in the study:

(26a) laṛkī   [maze mẽ gāte   hue] jhulā jhul   rahī   hai
      girl.SG fun in sing.IPFV.OBL be.OBL swing swing PROG.F.SG be.PRS.3SG
      'The girl is swinging in the swing while singing in gay abandon.'
(26b) laṛkī   [maze mẽ gātī   huī] jhulā jhul   rahī   hai
      girl.SG fun in sing.IPFV.F   be.F.SG swing swing PROG.F.SG be.PRS.3SG
(26c) laṛkīyã̄ [maze mẽ gāte   hue] jhulā jhul   rahī   hai
      girl.PL fun in sing.IPFV.OBL be.OBL swing swing PROG.F.SG be.PRS.3SG
(26d) laṛkīyã̄ [maze mẽ gātī   huī̃] jhulā jhul   rahī   hai
      girl.PL fun in sing.IPFV.F   be.F.PL swing swing PROG.F.SG be.PRS.3SG
(26e) laṛkīyã̄ [maze mẽ gātī   huī̃] jhulā jhul   rahī̃   hai
      girl.PL fun in sing.IPFV.F   be.F.PL swing swing PROG.F.PL be.PRS.3SG
(26f) laṛkīyã̄ [maze mẽ gātī   huī] jhulā jhul   rahī   hai
      girl.PL fun in sing.IPFV.F   be.F.SG swing swing PROG.F.SG be.PRS.3SG
(26g) laṛkīyã̄ [maze mẽ gātī   huī] jhulā jhul   rahī̃   hai
      girl.PL fun in sing.IPFV.F   be.F.SG swing swing PROG.F.PL be.PRS.3SG
(26h) laṛkīyã̄ [maze mẽ gātī   huī(ī̃)] jhulā jhul rahī(ī̃) haĩ
      girl.PL fun in sing.IPFV.F   be.F.(PL) swing swing PROG.F.SG(PL) be.PRS.3PL

Note that this is not an exhaustive list of combinations of a sprinkling of the φ-features; there are other possible combinations, especially the ones with the number marking on finiteness carrying auxiliary of the main clause, as is the case with variant (26h). However, in spite of the non-exhaustiveness of the set, the judgments on these eight variants already tell us something which is of interest.

The Likert scale values and attributes used for this set of data are shown in Table 4:

Tab. 4: Likert scale values of grammatical judgments for Set II

Standard diacritic	L-scale value	L-scale rank
✓✓	'strongly acceptable'	[1]
✓	'acceptable'	[2]
?	'neither fully grammatical nor fully unacceptable'	[3]
??	'almost unacceptable'	[4]
*	'unacceptable'	[5]

Note that the scale in Set II is both bivalent and symmetrical; however, since this is too small a sample, hopefully, the usual pitfalls of a central tendency are avoided.

The judgments on these variants for 6 speakers are captured in Table 5:

Tab. 5: Speakers' judgments on the 8 variants in adjectival/ adverbial adjunct agreement

Variant	[1]	[2]	[3]	[4]	[5]
a.	1	4	1	–	–
b.	–	4	2	–	–
c.	–	–	–	–	6
d.	–	–	–	–	6
e.	–	1	2	2	1
f.	–	–	–	–	6
g.	–	1	2	1	2
h.	–	5	1	–	–

The table represents the judgments of 6 speakers on a 5-point scale (from [1] to [5]) for the variants (26a) to (26h). As can be clearly seen, none of the 6 speakers liked the variants (26c), (26d), and (26f) as all 6 speakers marked them [5] or 'unacceptable' (see Table 4).

Given the first look at the variation noticed above in the relative participle and the adverbial participle in Hindi-Urdu, one thing that becomes more or less clear with regards to agreement in this language is shown schematically in (27). This observation that person lies in the outermost periphery, gender in the innermost, and number in between, seems to be one conclusion that has been pointed out in several studies by different authors, working on or commenting on the agreement phenomenon in this language:

(27)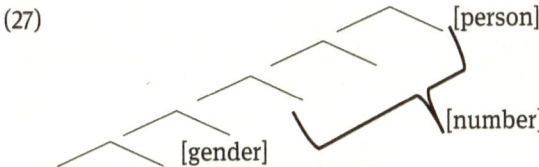

This has also been the general consensus regarding the positioning of these features. That is, person seems to be available high up in the clause and gender lower down but it is number that hovers in between, except that the results in this paper show that number cannot be too low in the structure (see 23). This is also in line with the general observation that participle agreement is with number and gender and never with person, unlike subject agreement in general, another reason this type of participle agreement should be seen as different from (subject) argument agreement on verbs.[13] Note that the distribution of features as above also implies that participial agreement has to be lower in the clausal spine if participial agreement is restricted to only gender and number.

In the following is provided the summary of the distribution of ϕ-features along with the concept of an "average" judgment based on Median score, in the last column, arrived at by looking at the distribution of the responses:

---

[13] As noted by Mahajan (2017), person does not show up in object agreement cases in Hindi-Urdu either (Mahajan 2017: 9, n. 10).

Tab. 6: Summary of distribution of ϕ-features and Median score ('average' judgment)

VARI-ANT	SUBJ_MAIN NUMBER	ADJUNCT		MATRIX CL.		Median Score ('average' judgment)
		V	PTCP	ASP	AUX	
a.	Singular	Oblique invariant		Gender	Person	2
b.	Singular	Gender	Gender	Gender	Person	2
c.	Plural	Oblique invariant		Gender	Person	5
d.	Plural	Gender	Gender Number	Gender	Person	5
e.	Plural	Gender	Gender Number	Gender Number	Person	3.5
f.	Plural	Gender	Gender	Gender	Person	5
g.	Plural	Gender	Gender	Gender Number	Person	2
h.	Plural	Gender	Gender (Number)	Gender (Number)	Person Number	2

First, note that the results here demonstrate exactly the point raised and discussed in section 3, that the strength of studies on syntactic variation lies in the conviction that existing theoretical proposals are adequate to provide an account of variation as well since, in spite of the gradation noticed in speakers' judgments, it is still the case that results seem to verge on clearly acceptable and clearly unacceptable. We see the same pattern here in Table 6, where a., b., g., and h. are obviously acceptable, whereas c., d., and f. are clearly unacceptable.

A couple of results stand out in this dataset; again, it has to do with where and how deep the number feature is visible/accessible. First, looking at the judgments for the variants (26a) and (26b), it is clear that whether there is agreement inside the adjunct or not, does not really matter. Note here that the main clause subject is in the singular and the default value for singular being null, the result here can also be interpreted as saying there is number agreement in the main clause. However, the theoretically interesting question, how does one account for the optionality in agreement inside the adverbial adjunct in these examples, will be taken up in the next section. For now, we can note that the following is the first result in the case of adverbial adjuncts:

(28) Result 1: Within the Adverbial participle, presence or absence of number agreement with the sentential subject does not matter in the case of singular subjects.

With a plural matrix clause subject, the story is more complicated (and as mentioned above with relation to judgment 26h, not complete), but one result that can be considered a finding is the average judgment for variant (26e) and (26g); the former seems to be marginally acceptable whereas the latter is plain acceptable. In light of the fact that for plural subject number, agreement on the main clause finiteness carrying element (Aux here) is the only way to get full grammaticality (the variant 26h here), these results for (26e) and (26g) are interesting. The shading in the table above indicates that somewhere in the matrix clause the number feature needs to be visible – this can be seen in the Median score of 5 ('unacceptable') for examples in (26c), (26d), and (26f) which fail to meet this requirement; its availability only in the adjunct does not fulfill the requirement (variant 26d). Note also that (26e) and the acceptable (26h) are in conflict with what Bhatt and Walkow (2013: 954), and as pointed out earlier, Bhatt and Keine (2017: 50) observe:

(29) Agreement markers on participles (habitual, perfective/passive, progressive) and infinitives distinguish singular and plural forms for masculine, but not feminine.

Comparing the results in (26e), (26g), and (26h), we infer that having [NUM] in the matrix clause is better (26g, 26h) than having it in the matrix and the participial adjunct (26e). We can summarize the observation with regards to Table 6 as the following:

(30) Result 2: Number agreement either just on the main clause ASP (26g) or on the participle and the main clause aspect (26e), is (marginally) acceptable.

Note in this connection the judgment (26d), where number agreement is available only on the participle in the adjunct. Therefore, Result 2 cannot be interpreted as indicating that the visibility of the number agreement *anywhere* is still more acceptable to some extent than its complete invisibility, otherwise (26d) would have been acceptable. We can thus refine Result 2 as follows:

(31) Result 3: Number agreement either with the participle and the main clause aspect, as in (26e), or just on the main clause ASP, as in (26g), is preferable to number agreement just on the participle, as in (26d).

Note that this result is very similar to what we noted with respect to the Relative Participle example, as noted in result (23) (that number cannot be too low). This is a desirable unifying finding about a general character of the number agreement in the language. Both (23) and Result 2/3 above, point in the same direction.

Theoretically, this refined result indicates that the trigger for the number agreement cannot be lower than *at least* the main clause aspectual head. This can be schematized as follows:

(32a) [$_{PtcPP}$ V-*tā/ī* PTCP-NUM] ASP^0-NUM ↑ AUX^0
(32b) [$_{PtcPP}$ V-*tā/ī* PTCP] ASP^0-NUM ↑ AUX^0

If the trigger for number agreement is below ASP^0, then we cannot account for either (32a) or (32b) (since the Aspect must get it too); therefore, the trigger has to be above ASP^0, which would imply that it could be the T^0 itself, as is standard. However, placing the trigger in T^0 would make it difficult to account for the surprising variants (26e) and (26g) (though not 26h), since for both of these, the number features are *not* available in the matrix Aux. The empirical facts thus tell us that there must be a trigger for number agreement *also* between ASP^0 and AUX^0, in addition to T^0 (for 26h); this is indicated in (32) by a vertical arrow.

Finding the trigger for number agreement above ASP^0 argues against what is stated in Bhatt (2005: 764), since it is claimed that case-licensing of objects in Hindi-Urdu is independent of what appears above the *v*P; Butt (1995) is also cited there as supporting the same claim. Note that Bhatt (2005) states this in the context of case-licensing rather than agreement; as far as I can see, there is no empirical evidence in Bhatt (2005) that argues against higher positioning of the trigger. My suggestion (to be elaborated in the next section) of placing the trigger for agreement higher than ASP^0, as indicated in (32), therefore implies that aspectuality of the clause does have something to do with the agreement inside *v*P – the insight in Mahajan (1989) with regards to Case that Bhatt was arguing against. I will take this up in the next section.

6 Analysis

By consolidating the results in Table 3 and Table 6, we obtain the following generalized pattern:

(33a) [$_{RC}$ V   AUX] N   (Set I, Phrase)
           GND   GND   GND
           *NUM (NUM) NUM

(33b) [$_{ADJ/ADV\ PTCP}$ V   AUX] ASP   AUX   (Set II, Clause)
                        GND   GND   GND   PER
                        *NUM (NUM) (NUM) (NUM)

Combing these two, we derive the following findings:

(34a) The feature [PER] is at the outermost periphery, while [GND] is the innermost one, and [NUM] is something that is in between the two.
(34b) It is only the [NUM] feature that shows optionality – it being optional on AUX (Set I), AUX$_{EMBEDDED}$, or AUX$_{MAIN}$, and ASP (Set II).
(34c) [NUM] clearly cannot sit on V (Set I & II), but it can sit on AUX$_{EMB/MAIN}$ and ASP (Set II).

Given the above findings, the analysis presented here reaffirms the operation of the standard Agree model (Chomsky 2000, 2001), rather than its various later versions like Multiple Agree (Nevins 2007, 2011), Cyclic Agree (Béjar and Řezáč 2009), reverse Agree (Adger 2003; Bošković 2007; Zeijlstra 2008, 2012), and indeed, agreement as feature-sharing as in Pesetsky and Torrego (2007), and its various extensions.[14]

A lack of agreement in raising constructions (in English) seems to be the reason for Pesetsky and Torrego (2017: 280 n. 9) to critique Chomsky-Agree, where [uϕ] on probes is the source for case on goal NPs. However, the languages we deal with show agreement in such cases as well as in participles (the topic of the present paper) and at long-distance; there is no strong reason therefore to reject Chomsky-Agree. Additionally, the summaries of the findings in (33) and (34) suggest that to apply a feature-sharing model, all values of α will be shared with β

---

[14] For example, Agree as feature-sharing as applied to different domains, such as for negative concord as in Haegeman and Lohndal (2010).

and ɣ, and all values of β will be shared with ɣ if the probes are at α and β, respectively, as shown in (35):

(35a)

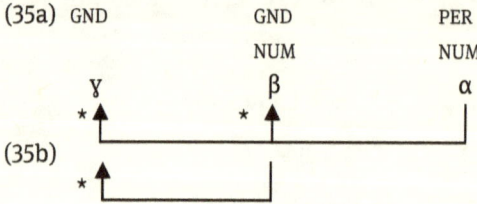

(35b)

As shown in (35a), the system will wrongly copy [PER] value on AUX and ASP, and both [PER] and [NUM] value on V; (35b) shows that the system will wrongly copy [NUM] value on V. Thus, since in the Pesetsky and Torrego system all instances of a particular uninterpretable feature must share the same value, there is no scope of differential or partial φ-feature access in this system. For example, in their demonstration of the case of raising infinitivals, Pesetsky and Torrego show that finally when valuation does take place in the domain of the finite v, all three instances of [uT], namely, on the subject DP (moved to the [Spec,vP$_{matrix}$]), on the non-finite embedded T, and on embedded v, get the [uT:val] of the matrix v.

Following standard Agree assumes using the definition of Agree as in Chomsky (2000, 2001), as follows:[15]

(36) Agree:
(i) An uninterpretable (and unvalued) feature F on a Probe (a head) seeks for another (valued) instance of F on a Goal with which to Agree in its c-command domain.
(ii) The value of the Goal is assigned as the value of the Probe and all instances of uninterpretable features deleted.

For the purpose of this paper, staying with standard Agree, I will assume that Agree takes place in a top-down fashion, that is, v-Agree follows T-Agree (T-Agree > v-Agree). Furthermore, based on (27), I will assume that a strict structural φ-feature hierarchy such as the following exists:

(37)   PER > NUM > GND

---

[15] This definition combining the two works of Chomsky is summarized somewhat differently in Pesetsky and Torrego (2007: 265).

That is, the ϕ-features are accessed strictly in the order specified. Note that this is different from prominence hierarchies and is specific to syntactic mechanisms involving differential ϕ-feature access.[16] With this, we are ready to tackle the cases of syntactic variation reported here.

As we saw in Result 1, the presence or absence of agreement inside the adjunct does not matter when the subject of the main clause is in the singular. With regards to the placement of the adjunct, I will assume that it is adjoined at the VP level since these adverbial or adjectival adjuncts modify the VP in terms of manner. Syntactically, the finding of Result 1 indicates that the adjunct can be somewhat independent, or more technically, there can be a trigger of agreement inside the adjunct as well. The fact that there is no visible number agreement on the matrix finiteness carrying verb, namely, the AUX in instances where the matrix subject is in the singular, tells us that we cannot really decide about the agreement process inside the adjunct. In particular, we cannot decide – as shown by a '?' mark on the last copying stage in (38) – whether or not the agreement process – which now I shall identify as Agree – inside the adjunct is *dependent* on the trigger for agreement in the main clause.

Result 1 is therefore obtained by establishing a simple Agree relation from the matrix T. Note that, in this example, no Agree relation can be established within the VP-shell – with the little *v* – as the object is noun-incorporated into the main V. At the most, we can say that there is a split in the ϕ-features whereby person and gender are copied and/or relayed on to the appropriate heads differentially. This is roughly shown below in (38) for (26a) and (26b) (details to be worked out as we proceed).[17]

In the case of the result for the variant in (26b), where there is gender agreement inside the adjunct, it is possible to say that the T inside the adjunct can probe the gender feature of the PRO at the subject position of the adjunct TP. However, one has to be careful in designing the mechanism in such a manner that only a reduced set of the subject's features are available as a PRO (that is, the full set of ϕ-features is not available in the base-generated PRO position, being controlled by the matrix subject). Note also that given the discussion in footnote 19, these adjuncts are not really fully-fledged TPs, since T seems to be defective.

---

[16] See relevant references on differential ϕ-feature access theories in Bhattacharya (2016) and Bhattacharya and Sharma (forthcoming).

[17] Note especially with regard to relaying of the [GND] feature on to the lower AUX head from T, that a default [GND] feature is assumed to be passed on, which is later copied on the ASP head in step 2; however, the AUX never shows up the [GND] feature in the singular, making this move non-sustainable. I will resolve this issue in the revised structure presented further below. I will also clarify the process of "relay" and how it is different from "copy".

Thus, if there is independent probing inside the adjunct, it has to be the *v* and not the T, making the accessibility of the PRO inside the adjunct questionable. I will come back to this aspect of Agree inside the adjunct right at the end of this section.

(38)

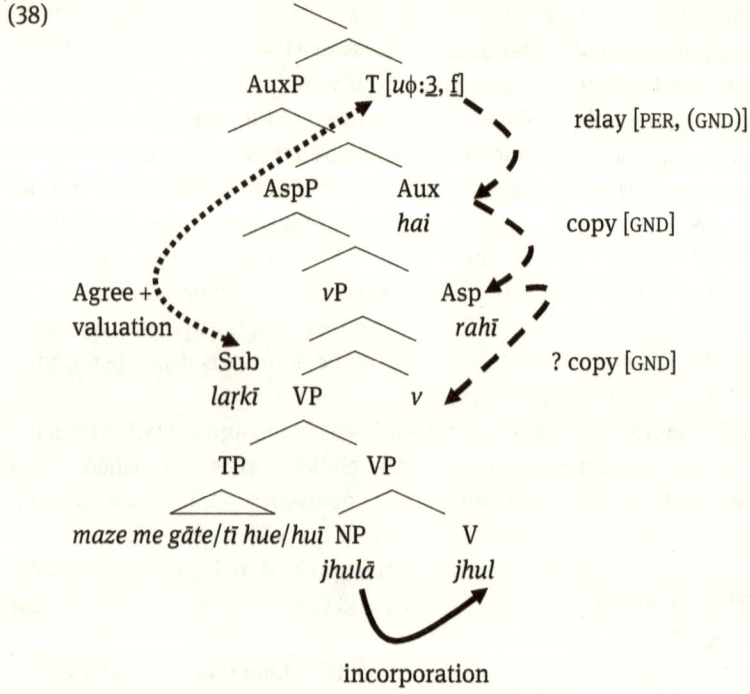

The split between the φ-features is going to become important as we proceed to analyze the rest of the data in this paradigm. Let us now switch attention to the cases when the matrix subject is plural (i.e. (26c)–(26h) and Table 6). As we reported through the findings in Results 2 and 3, the trigger for the number feature cannot be too high or too low, given the results for variants (26e) and (26g). For various reasons, this will become impossible to implement (as I will show), unless we allow the possibility of probing into the adjunct from the matrix *v*, (rather than a reduced Agree inside the adjunct as conjectured in the previous paragraph with regards to 26b), *if and only if* the matrix *v* is higher in the structure.

That is, we need to revise the structure in (38) by placing the matrix *v* in between the Aux and Asp head. Although there is no substantial morphological evidence in favor of such a structure, given the results for the variants in (26e) and (26g), we are pushed towards this conclusion. Furthermore, MacDonald (2006:

65) also settles for a structure of the vP where the order of the heads are V-ASP-v-AUX-T; this is especially justified to account for aspectual distributions of bare plurals and mass nouns. In addition, with this, we have now found a Probe position as suggested through the arrowheads in (32). (39) represents the data set in (26):

(39)

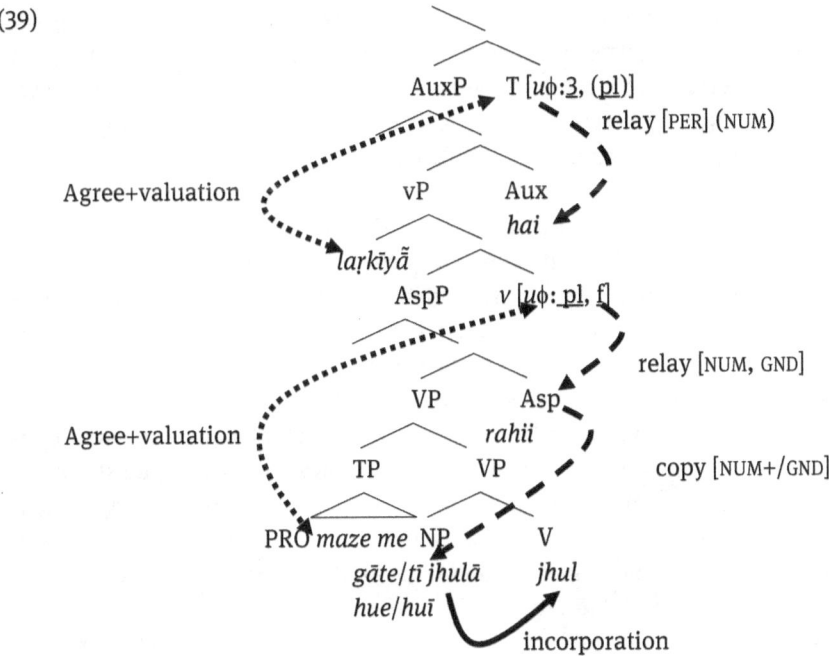

Note that we are making a distinction between three Agree-based operations: valuation, relaying and copying – this will become apparent immediately below in (42). The different aspects of these three operations are noted below:

(40) 3 Agree-based operations:
VALUATION: This is familiar from standard Agree models whereby the uninterpretable features of a Probe get valued by the interpretable features of the Goal, as seen in the definition of Agree in (36).
RELAY: This mechanism is assumed by everyone but never formalized; for example, English subject-verb agreement is obtained in classic textbook fashion by relaying the valued features from the T head onto the v (see for example Adger 2003: 221). I will call this relay and not Agree as otherwise,

a reverse Agree will result. Thus, copying of features from a just valued head is relay in this proposal.[18] I will also restrict relaying to a one-step-only process. We will see that *under-relaying*, that is, copying a partial set of values, is a violation.

COPYING: Copying of a feature is like relay but it is a "lower-level" process since it cannot copy more than one feature at a time; however, it is not restricted to a one-step-only process. It is suggested here that the copying process is restricted between contiguous non-probing heads. Note that copying is copying of an already relayed feature from a higher head – a kind of valuation through relay. We will see that *over-copying*, that is, copying more than one value at a time, is a violation.

The copying process is familiar from Norris (2014), Åfarli (2016), Velle (2016) and others, where at least in the domain of adjectival agreement (both attributive and predicative agreement), it has been realized that *both* Agree and copy are required. The copying process is also reminiscent of Bhatt's (2005) attempt to capture the dependency between the finite head and the participle in terms of agreement in Hindi-Urdu – Bhatt calls it "covaluation" (Bhatt 2005: 769).

Note that dispersal of the [NUM] feature in both sets of data is indicative of the operation of either relay or copy as a one-step process since the data shows that there is no instance of the feature being copied/ relayed more than once, that is, there is no instance of its occurrence more than 2 times in consecutive heads. Consider, for example, data (21c) and (21d) for Set I, and (26e) and various versions of (26h). I will therefore restrain relay to a one-step only operation – and copy too when it comes to the feature [NUM] – whereas copying can be done more than once. Furthermore, I distinguish copying as a low-level operation and therefore restrict it to copying only one feature per copy operation; or else, it ends up *over-copying*, as is the case with (43e).

Furthermore, for Bhatt (2005), covaluation is proposed as a(n) (desirable) alternative to probing from two heads (T and Asp, in Bhatt's case); for the data-results being presented here, I will show that both copying and probing by different heads is required. One way of restraining copying, I will assume, can be achieved if dominance plays a role (Norris 2014) – the syntactic account provided

---

18 Although, the Chomsky definition of Agree assumes that once Agree takes place, no history of the operation is remembered for the purpose of the derivation (Pesetsky and Torrego's 2007 feature-valuation proposal crucially differs in this respect), and therefore a just-valued feature can participate in Agree again. I will, however, invoke relay rather than another Agree in such cases.

for both the paradigm cases this paper deals with incorporate this restriction on copying. By assuming a second probing from the matrix *v*, the result obtained with regards to the variant d. easily falls out – if there is no "valued-[number] copy" in the head immediately dominating the adjunct (namely, ASP), then there cannot be a "valued-[number] copy" inside the adjunct either. Thus, the contiguity or adjacency effect of copying is scanned from a "bottom-up" direction as follows:

(41) If a head has a feature, it must be the case that the immediately dominating head too has the same feature but not the other way round.

With regards to the results obtained for the standard (26h), and the surprising results (26e) and (26g) (which forced us to position the matrix *v* higher in the structure, now being able to probe into the adjunct), the following rough schema is suggested to be elaborated for each case immediately further:

(42a) Matrix T probes matrix subject in [spec,*v*P] and gets part of φ-set valued, namely [PER] (and [NUM] for (26h);
(42b) The features are relayed on to the immediately dominated head, namely, AUX (as in 26h);
(42c) Matrix-*v* then probes (as copying is only between contiguous non-probing heads, and Probe *v* intervenes copying features from AUX to ASP) the PRO into the adjunct and gets valued for [NUM] and [GND], as a *v* can never probe a [PER] feature;
(42d) The features are relayed onto the immediately dominated head, ASP, as in (26e), (26g) and (26h);
(42e) These valued features from ASP can be copied into the adjunct in one step, as in (26e) and (26h);
(42f) No valued features can be copied into the adjunct if that feature is not available in the immediately dominating head, as in (26d).

Note that by doing this, we are now creating a conflict with what we conjectured with regards to the optional agreement of [GND] inside the adjunct in the case of a singular subject, namely the result for variant b. This conflict can be resolved if we uniformly adopt the second probing possibility from matrix *v* for singular subject cases also; since the [NUM] feature does not matter for singular anyway, only the [GND] features will be copied into the adjunct. Giving up Agree inside the adjunct is a good thing anyway; unless we are willing to adopt a Bidirectional/ reverse Agree (Preminger and Polinsky 2015; Wurmbrand 2012; Zeijlstra 2012, among others), there is no way to access the PRO (in [Spec, *v*P]) from *v* inside the adjunct; Bidirectional Agree can probe upward from PRO and value the ϕ-features of *v*.

I will now elaborate each derivation of Set II schematically. Note that the feature access hierarchy noted in (37) and the T-Agree > *v*-Agree work hand-in-hand along with the stated restrictions on relay and copy to produce the results; the letter-number indicates the sentence type as in (26), strikethrough indicates valuation, shaded indicates valued already, light font indicates not relevant, double asterisks indicate violation of feature access hierarchy:

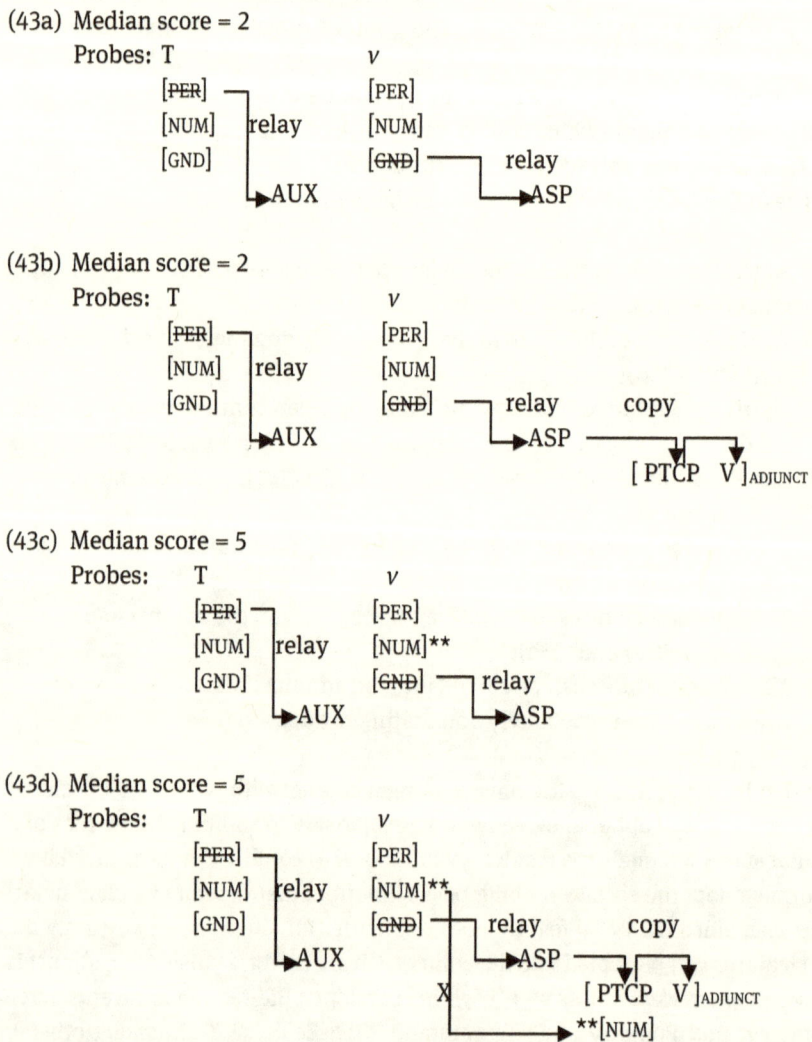

Optionality and variation in agreement in some participles in Hindi-Urdu — 109

(43e) Median score = 3.5

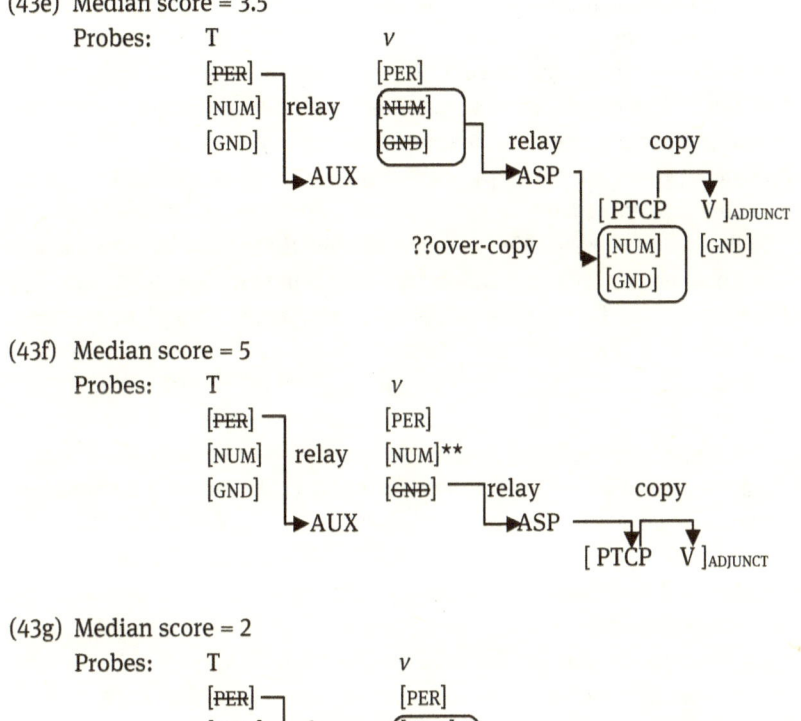

(43f) Median score = 5

(43g) Median score = 2

(43h) Median score = 2

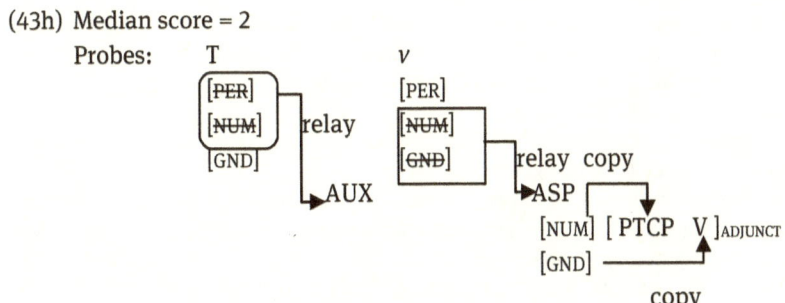

From the above schema, we can now easily match the Median score with the derivation to figure out that those with the score of 5 (c., d. and f. in Table 6) have skipped a step in the feature-access hierarchy in the *v*-Agree cycle and instead valued the lowest feature, namely, [GND]. Similarly, the 3.5 Median score for e. is accounted for by *over-copying*, copying two features at a time from ASP to PTCP into the adjunct. Note that for the derivation in (26h), although there is no violation of hierarchy or copy, the [NUM] feature is accessed by both the Probe heads, and furthermore, there are two copy operations from the same head ASP. However, since (26h) is a condensed version of at least 4 different examples and since data for all the various possibilities are not available, these extra steps in the derivation may be seen as a reflex of collapsing 4 different variations together.

With regards to the first paradigm (Set I), that is, the relative participle case, the general picture of the derivation remains the same as in the adverbial participle case, and is given in (46), for the so-called standard result, namely (21a), where the copying of the [NUM] feature does not take place. However, we saw that the (21c) variety, where the [NUM] feature is copied onto the participle, is in fact better than the standard. However, the result in (21d) cannot be explained through the above derivation, because if the [NUM] feature is available at the PTCP (as a result of copying it from *v*), then it should be able to copy into the V as well (or the V will pick it up by head movement), yet the result is not acceptable. Here, then, we have to reconsider the standard T-Probe story. Recall that unlike in the adverbial adjunct participle case, here we are dealing with Agree within the relative participle itself, and given the nature of participles, T cannot act as a legal Probe as it is not clear if a full TP is available in such structures. Given that negation within the RC is not admissible, as in (44), it is highly likely that even if there is a T, it is highly defective:[19]

---

[19] I thank Ayesha Kidwai for pointing this out to me. Although, note that as pointed out in Mahajan (2017: 86), the lack of Tense (as well as relative pronouns and a subject) seems to be a feature of the prenominal relative clauses (and not the postnominal ones); interestingly, the example Mahajan uses for the point does contain a time adverb, as in the following:
(i) [tumhāre kal kharīde hue] vo phūl bahut acche haĩ
    your yesterday buy.PFV.M.PL be.PFV.M.PL those flower.M.PL very nice.M.PL be.PRS.PL
    'The flowers that you bought yesterday are very nice.'
It is also fine to include a temporal adverb inside an adverbial adjunct (*kal gānā gāte hue* 'yesterday while singing songs'). However, temporal adverbs are event modifying ones and therefore are taken to attach at the *v*P/ VP level (Ernst 2002, Haider 2000). Note though that if a sentence adverbial like *sac mẽ* 'in truth' "truly" is stuck at the initial position of the RC, it is odd if it is interpreted inside the RC in (i), or indeed inside an adverbial adjunct. I take this to mean that even if T is available in the RC, it is of a reduced nature, perhaps φ-incomplete, not being able to either participate in case marking (of a possible subject) or carrying finiteness. Note here that Mahajan identifies the so-called invariant participle form identified by Kachru (2006), V-*te hue*, as plural.

(44) *Ravi-kī nahī̃ paṛhī   huī   kitabẽ
     Ravi-GEN not   read-F PTCP.F books.F.PL
     'The books not read by Ravi.'

In this derivation, therefore, given the discussion in footnote 19, I will assume that the relative participle clause is perhaps not a full TP with a ɸ-complete T,[20] and therefore probing for ɸ-features is initiated from *v* instead. A point that needs to be stated here is that Mahajan (2018: 93) makes a claim that even the *v* head is not available in these highly reduced prenominal relative clauses. This claim is based on the empirical fact that direct objects cannot remain in-situ in prenominal relatives with perfect participles, showing in turn that there is no case assigning head inside the relative clause. I will not adopt this stance here since the agreement facts clearly indicate that there is some Agree relation taking place inside the relative clause. In fact, I will take the stance more as in Mahajan (2017) which considers these clauses to have a *v* that is unable to assign case.[21] On the other hand, with regards to imperfective prenominal relative clauses, since the DO is allowed to remain inside such a clause, they ought to have an active *v*:

(45) kitāb paṛh-tī   (huī)   laṛkī
     book   read-IPFV.F (be.PFV.F.SG) girl
     'The book-read girl.'

As before, relaying of features is a one-step process each, and copying here too is by default a one-step process since there is one Agree cycle only; additionally, I will consider that the last copying step cannot be copying [NUM], which also ensures that the [NUM] feature does not get copied "too deep", in consonance with findings in (23) and Result 2/3. The derivation sketched below in (46) represents the derivation for (21c) which has a Median score of 1, being judged more acceptable than the standard in (21a).

---

20 Apart from the reasons given in the text, this is also because the verb in prenominal participial relative clauses is always non-finite, as also noted in Mahajan (2017).
21 Note that one reason for this *v* being different could be because it is ɸ-incomplete due to lack of [person] feature, but I will not pursue it further here, noting that for our purposes, this incomplete *v* can still act as a Probe.

(46)

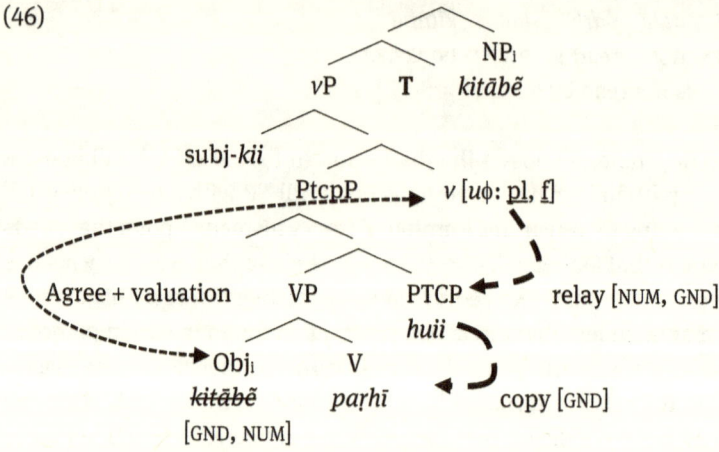

The standard in (21a) scoring less than the above is explained by looking at the schematic derivation in (47), which shows the phenomenon of *under-relaying*; that is, although both the [NUM] and [GEN] features are accessed (and valued) in the v-Agree cycle, only the latter is relayed on to the PTCP head in the adjunct:

(47) Median score = 2

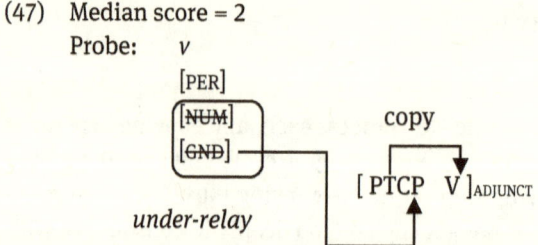

The result in (21b) is ruled out in the above derivation by prohibiting the copying of a feature that is not available on the immediately dominating head (see 41); since the PTCP head does not have the [NUM] in that variant, it is not possible to copy it onto the lower head V. Copying by default here is only a one-step operation that refers to the immediately dominating head. Derivation of the result in (21d) – where both the V and PTCP carry both [GND] and [NUM] – can be ensured by invoking the requirement that copying is always a lesser operation than relaying; that is, it deals with a smaller set of features. Thus, if two features are relayed, then one feature is copied.²² In any case, the result in Set I being consistent with the result in Set II in not allowing the [NUM] feature to be copied too deep, any constraining principle should satisfy this requirement.

As noted, no further indep0endent Probe is available inside the adjunct; we considered this possibility with respect to the adverbial participles too (in 38). As mentioned previously, the adjunct T is highly deficient; for one, the verb form inside these adjuncts is always non-finite, making the adjunct T, if present, ineligible to act as a Probe by itself. It is also mentioned that the *v* too in these adjuncts is weak; however, even if *v* were to act as a Probe inside the adverbial adjunct, it would not be able to find the PRO as a Goal (assuming standard Agree), since due to a weak T, the PRO remains at [Spec, *v*P] position. In this paper, therefore, a system of probing from the main clause into the adjunct is established for Set II data, in particular through the matrix *v*, which finds the PRO inside the adjunct as the nearest Goal to Agree with, as is the case with derivation (39). Keeping to a phase-based derivation, I assume with Fischer and Høyem (2017) that PRO can be displaced at the edge of the adjunct for it to be licensed or accessed for Agree. Since the adverbial participles are all attached under the domain of T, an Agree relation between the matrix *v* and the PRO in the adjunct can be considered as establishing (obligatory) control.

7 Conclusions

This paper has laid out first the data and then the analysis of that data in support of the theory that microvariation ought to be studied more syntactically. The paper shows that the understanding of the agreement phenomenon in Hindi-Urdu obtained through broad comparative studies paints a picture perhaps more simplistic than it really is – a microparametric comparison, on the other hand, reveals minute details of agreement that are otherwise easily missed in the broad strokes.

The extent of variation reported in the domain of participial agreement in the two sets of data studied in this paper is given a syntactic analysis using the existing standard Agree model, which is shown to be capable of dealing with the

---

22 Note that since gender can be low in these cases of agreement, the [GND] feature does not have this restriction; this is confirmed by data such as the following where all are ungrammatical, showing that the [GND] features are copied all the way to V.
(i) *[paṛhā   huī]   kitāb/kitābe/kitābẽ
    read-PFV.M be.PFV.F book/ book.OBL/ book.F.PL

extent of variation observed. One common observation that emerged from the data is that although the availability of the number feature should be lower than the person feature, it cannot be too low in the structure; this observation was captured in an analysis that proposed a system of locality by using the notion of relay – which is restricted to a one-step mechanism – and copying that has the restriction of copying one feature at a time.

The alignment of ϕ-features also implicates their accessibility in terms of T- and then v-Agree in consecutive cycles. The differential ϕ-feature access also indicates that participial agreement has to be lower in the clausal spine if participial agreement is restricted to only number and gender. As far as the alignment of different heads is concerned, this paper's findings suggest that they should be aligned as V-ASP-v-AUX-T – this is obtained through the variation data that shows that the [NUM] feature valuation can be a result of two different probes, either T or v. The similarities between the two sets of data also prompted an analysis that employed similar syntactic processes to account for the extent of variation.

Abbreviations

1 = first person; 2 = second person; 3 = third person; ABL = ablative; ADJ = adjective; ADV = adverb; AGR = agreement; ASP = aspect; AUX = auxliary; CL = clitic; DAT = dative; ERG = ergative; F = feminine; GEN = genitive; GND = gender; HON = honorific; IPFV = imperfective; M = masculine; NUM = number; OBJ = object; OBL = oblique; PER = person; PFV = perfective; PL = plural; PROG = progressive; PRS = present; PTCP = participle; RC = relative clause; SBJ = subject; SG = singular

Transcription

The transliteration of Hindi data in this paper follows the standard ISO-15919. https://en.wikipedia.org/wiki/ISO_15919

Acknowledgements

Versions of this paper were presented at the 34th SALA conference in Konstanz, the AcqVA workshop in Trondheim, and at the 12th Asian GLOW in Seoul; I am grateful to audiences at these three conferences for commenting and asking questions that improved the paper substantially. I am especially indebted to Rajesh

Bhatt, Anoop Mahajan, K.V. Subbarao, Ayesha Kidwai, Žjelko Bošković, Tor Åfarli, Terje Lohndahl, and Inghild Høyem. I thank Terje Lohndahl for reading through a draft of the paper and making valuable comments on it, all of which have been useful in improving the present version. Finally, I thank the following for providing data judgements (and sticking to them!) over a period of time on the Hindi-Urdu data sets used in the paper: Anoop Mahajan, Ayesha Kidwai, Dipti Misra Sharma, K.V. Subbarao, Mahima Gulati, Mukul Priyadarshini, Sakshi Bhatia and Shiti Malhotra.

References

Adger, David. 2003. *Core Syntax: A Minimalist Approach*. Oxford: Oxford University Press.
Åfarli, Tor A. 2016. Agreement is not an essential ingredient of finiteness: Evidence from impersonal sentences in Norwegian dialects and in English. In Kristin M. Eide (ed.), *Finiteness Matters*, 171–188. Amsterdam: John Benjamins Publishing Company.
Baker, Mark. 1985. The mirror principle and morphosyntactic explanation, *Linguistic Inquiry* 16. 373–415.
Baker, Mark. 2008. The Macroparameter in a Microparametric World. In Theresa Biberauer (ed.), *The Limits of Syntactic Variation*, 351–373. Amsterdam: John Benjamins Publishing Company.
Béjar, Susana & Milan Řezáč. 2009. Cyclic Agree. *Linguistic Inquiry* 40. 35–73.
Belletti, Adriana. 1990. *Generalized Verb Movement: Aspects of Verb Syntax*. Turin: Rosenberg and Sellier.
Belletti, Adriana. 2001. Agreement Projections. In Mark Baltin & Chris Collins (eds.), *The Handbook of Contemporary Syntactic Theory*, 453–510. Oxford: Blackwell Publishing Ltd.
Belletti, Adriana. 2006. (Past) Participle Agreement. In Martin Everaert & Hen van Riemsdijk (eds.), *The Blackwell Companion to Syntax*, Vol III, 493–521. Oxford: Blackwell Publishers.
Bhatt, Rajesh. 2002. The raising analysis of relative clauses: Evidence from adjectival modification. *Natural Language Semantics* 10. 43–90.
Bhatt, Rajesh. 2005. Long distance agreement in Hindi-Urdu. *Natural Language and Linguistic Theory* 23. 757–807.
Bhatt, Rajesh & Martin Walkow. 2013. Locating agreement in grammar: an argument from agreement in conjunctions. *Natural Language and Linguistic Theory* 31. 951–1013.
Bhatt, Rajesh & Stefan Keine. 2017. Tense and the realization of feminine plural in Hindi-Urdu. In Gautam Sengupta, Shruti Sircar, Madhavi G. Raman & Rahul Balusu (eds.), *Perspective on the Architecture and Acquisition of Syntax*, 49–76. Singapore: Springer Nature.
Bhattacharya, Tanmoy. 2015–2016. পোলকের বাক্য-ভঙ্গ অথবা বাটারফ্লাই এফেক্ট [in Bangla: Pollock's Sentence-breaking or the Butterfly Effect]. *Ebong Mushaira*, Vol 22 (3–4). 21–32.
Bhattacharya, Tanmoy. 2016. Inner/Outer Politeness in Central Māgadhan Prākrit Languages: Agree as Labeling. *Linguistic Analysis*, vol. 40 (3–4). 297–336.
Bhattacharya, Tanmoy. 2017a. Agreement and Pronominalisation: Two different ways to Agree. Plenary address at 33rd SALA, Adam Mickiewicz University, Poznań.

Bhattacharya, Tanmoy. 2017b. Pronominalisation in South Asian Languages: Of People and their Actions. Keynote address at 38th Nepal Linguistic Society conference, Tribhuvan University, Kathmandu.
Bhattacharya, Tanmoy. 2018a. The syntax of argument indexation in the languages of India: A case of Macro- or Micro-variation? Talk at Sikkim University.
Bhattacharya, Tanmoy. 2018b. Pronominalisation in south Asian languages: of people and their actions. *Nepalese Linguistics* vol. 33 (1). 60–68.
Bhattacharya, Tanmoy & Jyoti Sharma. (forthcoming). 'Indexation switch' and multiple agreement in two Tibeto-Burman languages. In Andrew Nevins, Anita Peti-Stantić, Mark de Vos & Jana Willer Gold (eds.), *Angles of Object Agreement*. Oxford: Oxford University press.
Bošković, Željko. 2007. On the locality and motivation of Move and Agree: An even more minimal theory. *Linguistic Inquiry* 38. 589–644.
Butt, Miriam. 1995. *The Structure of Complex Predicates in Urdu*. [Dissertations in Linguistics]. Stanford, CA: CSLI Publications.
Chomsky, Noam. 1986. *Barriers*. Cambridge, MA: MIT Press.
Chomsky, Noam. 1995. *The Minimalist Program*. Cambridge, MA: MIT Press.
Chomsky, Noam. 2000. Minimalist inquiries. In Roger Martin, David Michaels & Juan Uriagereka (eds.), *Step by step: Essays on minimalist syntax in honor of Howard Lasnik*, 89–155. Cambridge, MA: MIT Press.
Chomsky, Noam. 2001. Derivation by phase. In Michael Kenstowicz (ed.), *Ken Hale: A life in language*, 1–52. Cambridge, MA: MIT Press.
Ernst, Thomas. 2002. *The Syntax of Adjunct*. Cambridge: Cambridge University Press.
Fischer, Silke & Inghild Flaate Høyem. 2017. Adjunct Control. Paper presented at 32nd Comparative Germanic Syntax Workshop, NTNU, Trondheim [Sept.].
Franco, Jon. 1994. On the absence of Spanish past participial object clitic agreement: The AGRo parameter in Romance. *Anuario del Seminario de Filología Vasca*, XXVIII (1). 247–262.
Haegeman, Liliane & Terje Lohndal. 2010. Negative Concord and (Multiple) Agree: A Case Study of West Flemish. *Linguistic Inquiry* 41 (2). 181–211.
Haider, Hubert. 2000. Adverb placement – convergence of structure and licensing. *Theoretical Linguistics* 26. 95–134.
Hale, Kenneth & Samuel J. Keyser. 1993. On Argument Structure and the Lexical Expression of Syntactic Relations. In Kenneth Hale & Samuel Jay Keyser (eds.), *The View from Building 20*, 53–110. Cambridge, MA: MIT Press.
Hale, Kenneth & Samuel J. Keyser. 1998. *Bound Features, Merge and transitivity Alterations*. Cambridge, MA: MIT Press.
Kachru, Yamuna. 2006. *Hindi*. Amsterdam: John Benjamins.
Kayne, Richard. 1989. Facets of Romance past participial agreement. In Paola Benincà (ed.), *Dialect variation and the theory of grammar*, 85–103. Dordrecht: Foris Publications.
Kayne, Richard. 1996. Microparametric Syntax: Some Introductory Remarks. In James R. Black & Virginia Motapanyane (eds.), *Microparametric Syntax and Dialect Variation*, ix-xviii. Amsterdam: John Benjamins.
Kayne, Richard. 2005. Some notes on comparative syntax, with special reference to English and French. In Guglielmo Cinque & Richard Kayne (eds.), *The Oxford Handbook of Comparative Syntax*, 3–69. New York: Oxford University Press.
Lee, Seung-Ah. 2016. Verb agreement in English Wh-Cleft: A corpus-based study. *English Studies*. DOI: 10.1080/0013838X.2016.1198141

Longenbaugh, Nicholas. 2018. *Past participle agreement revisited*. Cambridge, MA: Massachusetts Institute of Technology doctoral dissertation.

MacDonald, Jonathan Eric. 2006. *The Syntax of Inner Aspect*. New York: Stony Brook University doctoral dissertation.

Mahajan, Anoop K. 1989. Agreement and Agreement Phrases. In Itziar Laka & Anoop K. Mahajan (eds.), *Functional Heads and Clause Structure, No. 10* [MIT Working Papers in Linguistics, MITWPL], 217–252. Cambridge, MA: MIT.

Mahajan, Anoop K. 1990a. *The A/A-bar distinction and Movement Theory*. Cambridge, MA: Massachusetts Institute of Technology doctoral dissertation.

Mahajan, Anoop K. 2017. Accusative and Ergative in Hindi. In Jessica Coon, Diane Massam & Lisa Travis (eds.), *The Oxford Handbook of Ergativity*, 86–108. Oxford: Oxford University Press.

Mahajan, Anoop K. 2018. Case licensing in Hindi prenominal relative clauses. In Ghanshyam Sharma & Rajesh Bhatt (eds.), *Trends in Hindi Linguistics*, 85–106. Berlin: De Gruyter Mouton.

Nevins, Andrew. 2007. The representation of third person and its consequences for person-case effects. *Natural Language and Linguistic Theory* 25 (2). 273–313.

Nevins, Andrew. 2011. Multiple agree with clitics: Person complementarity vs. omnivorous number. *Natural Language and Linguistic Theory* 29 (4). 939–971.

Norris, Mark. 2014. *A Theory of Nominal Concord*. Santa Cruz: University of California, Santa Cruz doctoral dissertation.

Parisi, Domenico. 1976. The Past Participle. *Italian Linguistics* 1. 77–106.

Pesetsky, David & Esther Torrego. 2007. The syntax of valuation and the interpretability of features. In Simin Karimi, Vida Samiian & Wendy K. Wilkins (eds.), *Phrasal and clausal architecture: Syntactic derivation and interpretation*, 262–294. Amsterdam: John Benjamins Publishing.

Pollock, Jean-Yves. 1989. Verb movement, Universal Grammar and the structure of IP. *Linguistic Inquiry* 20. 365–424.

Preminger, Omer & Maria Polinsky. 2015. Agreement and semantic concord: a spurious unification. Ms.

Richards, Mark. 2008. Varieties of Competition. In Fabian Heck, Gereon Müller & Jochen Trommer (eds.), *Linguistische Arbeits Berichte 87*, 133–162. Leipzig: Universität Leipzig.

Siewierska, Anna. 2013. Verbal Person Marking. In Matthew S. Dryer & Martin Haspelmath (eds.) *The World Atlas of Language Structures Online*. Leipzig: Max Planck Institute for Evolutionary Anthropology. (Available online at http://wals.info/chapter/102, Accessed on 2021-01-31.)

Velle, Ingvil Håberg. 2016. *Partisippkongruens og formelle subjekt i herøydialekta: ein dialektsyntaktisk studie*. Trondheim: Norwegian University of Science and Technology MA thesis.

Wurmbrand, Susi. 2012. The syntax of valuation in auxiliary-participle constructions. In Jaehoon Choi, E. Alan Hogue, Jeffrey Punske, Deniz Tat, Jessamyn Schertz & Alex Trueman (eds.), *Coyote Working Papers: Proceedings of the 29th West Coast Conference on Formal Linguistics* (WCCFL 29), 154–162. Tucson: University of Arizona.

Zeijlstra, Hedde. 2008. Negative Concord is syntactic agreement. Ms. University of Amsterdam. Lingbuzz/000645.

Zeijlstra, Hedde. 2012. There is only one way to Agree. *The Linguistic Review* 29. 491–539.

Anuradha Sudharsan
A cross-linguistic approach to sentential subjects in Kannada

Abstract: In Kannada, only nominalized clauses can occupy the canonical subject position whereas non-nominalized clauses can occupy only the object position. Nominalized clauses have an overt D head, whereas non-nominalized clauses lack it. Two factors explain this subject/object asymmetry. Firstly, finite T is always +Case, whereas only transitive *v* has Case. Secondly, the fact that only nominalized clauses can occupy Case positions shows that only an overt nominal head can receive Case. A (Non-)Overt Head Constraint is proposed to exclude non-nominalized clauses from Case positions. Cross-linguistic facts corroborate this claim and also explain why that-clauses in English tend to extrapose.

Keywords: Nominalized clauses, overt head, case positions, non-nominalized clauses, Caseless positions, (non-)overt head parameter

1 Introduction

This paper examines asymmetries in the behavior of sentential subjects (hereafter SSs) and sentential objects (hereafter SOs) in Kannada and in other languages, in the light of controversies regarding the subjecthood of the initial *that*-clause in English, and attempts to resolve these controversies by offering an alternative account of *that*-clauses. In languages like Kannada, nominalization of CP (and IP) clauses are available while in languages like English nominalization of CP clauses is not available. It is this distinction that determines the distribution of SSs and SOs across languages.

An analysis of Kannada data shows that only nominalized clauses can occupy the Case-marked canonical subject position whereas non-nominalized clauses are not allowed in this position, but are allowed in the object position. Nominalization converts a CP clause (or an IP clause) into a DP clause with an overt D head. Non-nominalized clauses, on the other hand, are bare CP clauses without a D head, overt or non-overt, and hence they are not eligible for Case. This asymmetry in the behavior of the subject and object clauses comes from two

Anuradha Sudharsan, EFLU, Hyderabad, India. Email: asudharsan@yahoo.com

https://doi.org/10.1515/9783110753066-005

factors. Firstly, it is due to the distinct Case-licensing properties of the functional heads T and *v*. Case/D feature is always available on finite T/I. Therefore, SpecIP position is always Case-marked. As for *v*, it determines the argument structure of a clause and assigns theta-roles to its arguments, but does not always assign Case. Only transitive verbs assign Case, especially when they subcategorize for a DP argument. So *v* is +Case when it subcategorizes for a DP argument and it is -Case when it subcategorizes for a CP argument. This way, Spec*v*P is not always Case-marked unlike SpecIP. Secondly, the fact that only DP clauses can occupy a Case position shows that only an overt nominal head is eligible for Case. An Overt Head Constraint (hereafter OHC) is proposed to exclude non-nominalized clauses from Case positions.

Requirement of an overt nominal head for Case-marking is not specific to Kannada. Data from several genetically and typologically unrelated languages in which clausal nominalization is available also show that they obey this constraint. Availability of clausal nominalization distinguishes languages like Kannada from languages like English in which nominalization of CP clauses is not available. This goes to show that there is an Overt Head Parameter which determines the distribution of SSs and SOs across languages. I use the term "parameter" in the sense of "typological difference" to describe the difference between Kannada-type languages and English-type languages. Finally, on the basis of cross-linguistic facts, I try to resolve the controversies regarding *that*-clauses in English.

1.1 Are subjects nominal?

In this section, we will consider why subjects are generally considered nominal categories and why NP-hood is a criterion for subjects to be able to occupy the canonical subject position.

The notion of "subject" features prominently in traditional grammars and in the generative framework as well. In the traditional approach, every sentence has a subject. In the generative framework, this requirement is expressed by the Extended Projection Principle (hereafter EPP). "Subjecthood" stands for a cluster of properties. In other words, subjects can be defined along several parameters. Firstly, they can be defined in terms of the position they occupy in a clause, secondly, in terms of their semantic properties or the thematic roles they bear, and, thirdly, in terms of their morphosyntactic properties. In the generative framework, these properties are specified at two levels, namely, the lexical level, or what is called *v*P projection, where semantic/thematic roles are assigned to the arguments of a verb, and at the Inflectional phrase level, or IP projection, where morphosyntactic features of subjects are manifested. These characteristics are cross-linguistically attested to be general properties of subjects. Let's take a closer look at each of these characteristics.

A subject generally occupies the initial position of a clause in languages like Kannada and in many other languages as well. Within the generative framework, the clause initial position is referred to as specifier position of the Inflectional Phrase. This position is higher than any other argument position in the structural hierarchy of a clause and it is generally referred to as the canonical subject position (McCloskey 1997).

Secondly, subjects, in general, are bearers of semantic/thematic roles like Agent, Experiencer, and also CAUSE, as mentioned in McCloskey (1997: 197). In these cases, subjects are NPs or pronouns because NPs alone can be Agents or Experiencers. As noted earlier, theta-roles of the external and internal arguments of a verb are specified within vP projection. This means that the subject also originates within vP, but eventually moves to the specifier of IP position. So, as McCloskey (1997: 216) observes, the surface position of a subject NP is a derived position and there is no single subject position where all the properties of a subject are realized and licensed. "Rather", he observes further, "subject properties are distributed over a sequence of derivationally linked positions".

Besides, these nominal subjects inflect for number and Case – and for person and gender also in the case of pronouns. These morphosyntactic features trigger verb-agreement generally in finite clauses and it is at the inflectional phrase level that these morphosyntactic properties of subjects are licensed. The functional head T(ense) is a Case assigner and the SpecIP/TP position is a Case-marked position where subjects finally land. Only nominal categories can occupy this position as they alone can receive Case. Chomsky (1981) and Lasnik (1999) also argue that only nominal phrases can satisfy the subject requirement in English and this is true of Kannada and several other languages.

Davies and Dubinsky (2009) claim that even PP and APs can occupy the canonical subject position as they are said to be contained within a DP projection when they occupy the subject position. The occurrence of PPs in the subject position is known as the phenomenon of locative inversion. Safir (1998３: 731) observes that PPs and APs in the subject position, which he calls "honorary NPs", are allowed only in copular constructions, though they do not act like NPs in any other context. I will not go into the details of the claim about the NP-hood of PPs and APs, since it demands a detailed analysis which is beyond the scope of this paper. My main objective is to show that nominalized clauses are clearly nominal whereas bare CP clauses are not.

In the following sections, I will demonstrate that in Kannada only nominalized clauses can occupy the canonical subject position since they meet the above-mentioned criteria for subjecthood, while non-nominalized CP clauses fail to meet these requirements. Earlier, I stated that nominalized clauses have an overt nominal head, i.e., D, that possesses Case feature, which means it can occupy the specifier position of IP/TP which is a Case position. Another important property of a nominalized clause is that it can be an external argument of psych verbs such as *worry* or *disappoint*. In contrast to agentive verbs like *kill* or *hit*, psych verbs do not generally assign the thematic role Agent to their subject; these verbs express a psychological state and hence take an Experiencer or a Patient as their internal argument. For instance, in Kannada, a transitive psych verb like *kāḍu*, 'worry/bother' assigns a subject theta-role to its clausal subject and an Experiencer or Patient theta-role to its internal NP/DP argument, which is invariably human. The clausal argument represents a state of affairs and so, it is assigned, let's say, a Cause theta-role, to use McCloskey's (1997: 197) term. So the clausal subject originates at SpecvP. Consequently, the D feature on the clausal head D matches with the D/Case feature on T, forcing the DP clause to raise to SpecIP position where these features are checked. This way DP clauses are eligible to occupy the canonical subject position, that is the SpecIP position, since they meet the minimum requirements to occupy that position. In addition, a DP clause can be the object of a Case-assigning transitive verb. Besides, nominalized clauses can be topicalized just like simple non-clausal NPs/DPs. They are also easily available in the subject position of embedded clauses and of NP-NP clauses. This way, nominalized clauses act just like simple (non-clausal) NPs/DPs.

The non-nominalized CP clause, on the other hand, lacks an overt nominal head and hence it is totally excluded from all Case positions. It is not allowed in any of the positions that a nominalized clause can occupy. It can, however, be an internal argument of verbs of *speaking* and *thinking* which do not always assign Case to their arguments. In the subsequent sections we will consider in detail several Case-marked and non-Case-marked positions where the nominalized and non-nominalized clauses, respectively, are licit.

My main claim in this paper is that only an overt nominal head is eligible for Case and since nominalized clauses have an overt nominal head, they alone can occupy a Case position. Secondly, my main objective is to show that the nominative-marked subject position contrasts in important ways with the object position which is not always Case-marked.

1.2 The controversial *that*-clauses in English

The question regarding the distribution of SSs and SOs across languages has provoked a hot debate among scholars for several years. And this debate has raised several interesting questions regarding the syntax of SSs in different languages. By way of setting the stage for our discussion, I will address, in this section, an important line of enquiry which is concerned with the controversies regarding the structural position of *that*-clauses in English. An overview of these accounts will introduce concepts central to the notion of subjecthood, particularly of SSs in the light of these controversies.

Central to this line of enquiry is the question whether the initial *that*-clause in English occupies the canonical subject position or topic position in the left periphery of the main clause. Some scholars argue against the subjecthood of initial *that*-clause since it doesn't have an NP status, and a few others argue in support of its subjecthood as it exhibits certain characteristics associated with real subjects. The debate remains unresolved. This debate is mainly concerned with the relation between the following sentences.

(1)   [That he passed the exam] surprised us all.
(2)   It surprised us [that he passed the exam].

Scholars are divided in their opinion regarding the structural position of the bracketed clause in (1). Studies such as Rosenbaum (1967), Delahunty (1983) and more recently Davies and Dubinsky (2009) and Han (2005) argue that the initial clause in (1) occupies the canonical subject position as it exhibits NP characteristics.

Rosenbaum (1967) presented one of the earliest accounts of (1) and (2) within the transformational framework. In his analysis, all sentential subjects are generated as complements to a subject pronoun *it* so that (1) and (2) have the same underlying structure, as shown in (3).

(3)   [$_{NP}$ it [$_S$ that he passed the exam]] surprised us all.

In (1), the pronoun deletes, leaving the S in subject position, dominated by a headless NP projection. In (2), when the S extraposes to the end of the clause, the pronoun *it* is left behind in subject position. Delahunty (1983) also proposes a similar analysis. Besides, he analyzes sentential subjects as NPs and sentential complements as S-bars, because the latter does not exhibit certain NP characteristics such as clefting (Delahunty 1983: 389). Davies and Dubinsky (2009) analyze

SSs as DPs with a null D head which gets Case-marked, and analyze SOs as CP clauses devoid of nominal characteristics.

On the other side, Koster (1978), Stowell (1981), Adger (2003), and Alrenga (2005) take a different stand and argue that the clause in (1) is in topic position and that something else occupies the SpecIP position. These two opposite views have led to a very interesting debate about the distribution of SSs and SOs across languages in general. We will now take a closer look at these opposite views.

According to Koster (1978), the initial *that*-clause in (1) is not in the canonical subject position, but is in a "satellite" position outside the main clause and gets extraposed to the final position in normal situations, as in (2). He argues, in terms of Case-theoretical constraints on the distribution of arguments, that only nominal phrases can occupy the canonical subject position, since the subject position is a Case position and that only NPs can bear Case. This predicts that SSs like *that*-clauses lack a head and exocentric PS rules such as:

(4)   NP → S

are ruled out by the principles of X-bar system. Hence, *that*-clauses cannot sit in the subject position.

Subsequently, Stowell (1981) proposed the Case Resistance Principle (hereafter CRP) in order to explain why the *that*-clause moves to the postverbal position, as in (2). CRP states that Case may not be assigned to a category like S or S-bar which bears a Case-assigning feature. Several accounts of SSs and SOs - including the present one - have presented overwhelming evidence against CRP. Although Koster (1978) and Stowell (1981) take a different approach, both argue in terms of Case factors that initial *that*-clauses are not real subjects.

Dryer (1980), who offers a detailed account of the distribution of simple (non-clausal) NPs and sentential NPs across languages, observes that there is a significant difference between sentential NPs and simple non-clausal NPs. Sentential NPs exhibit a strong tendency to occur in the clause-final position whereas the normal position for simple non-clausal NPs is clause-initial position. Extraposition of a simple NP will only result in ungrammaticality, as shown in the following sentences, cited in Dryer (1980: 124).

(5a)   That John is tall is obvious.
(5b)   It is obvious that John is tall.
(6a)   The conclusion is obvious.
(6b)   *It is obvious the conclusion.

The above sentences demonstrate an important asymmetry between simple (non-clausal) NPs/DPs and sentential NPs. Both Grosu and Thompson (1977) and Dryer (1980) offer a non-syntactic explanation for the strong tendency of *that*-clauses to occur in clause-final position. They argue that this tendency is rooted in psycholinguistic factors.[1] I will not go into the details of these issues; the reader can refer to the original articles for a detailed discussion.

More recent studies such as Davies and Dubinsky (2009) argue that initial *that*-clauses are real subjects as they exhibit characteristics associated with subjects such as:
— They raise to canonical subject position obligatorily;
— They trigger subject-verb agreement;
— They license quantificational adverb which occur with NPs;
— They host emphatic reflexive *itself* just like NPs.

Davies and Dubinsky further argue that initial *that*-clauses are DPs with a null D head and the null D is Case-marked whereas *that*-clauses in the object position are CPs since they lack these NP characteristics. They suggest that the DP analysis of subject CPs in English can be extended to other languages in which SSs exhibit NP-like characteristics. Cross-linguistic studies have also shown that SSs and SOs exhibit an asymmetry in that the former behave like DPs/NPs whereas the latter do not.

There are problems in these accounts. Firstly, as for the obligatory raising of the *that*-clause to SpecIP, as shown in (1), we cannot say for sure whether it is in

---

[1] Grosu and Thompson (1977) and Dryer (1980) are among the earliest studies that tried to account for the distributional differences of SSs across languages in terms of psycholinguistic factors. Grosu and Thompson's account is based on the psycholinguistic evidence that a basic task in processing a clause lies in identifying the matrix predicate and its arguments, which is done early in sentence processing. This process becomes easier if the arguments are endocentric than if they are exocentric. So, in order to facilitate clause processing, languages use the strategy of postposing SSs that are exocentric. This is why *that*-clauses get extraposed, since according to them they are "headless" exocentric clauses. They observe that only SSs with an initial complementizer show a tendency to occur clause-finally. Dryer (1980), on the other hand, cites a number of languages in which SSs without initial complementizers also occur clause-finally. Dryer offers an alternative explanation according to which a language in which SOs and relative clauses are right-branching would present problems in processing clause-initial SSs which are left-branching. So SSs tend to occur in the final position so that clauses will uniformly be right-branching. However, in languages like Greek, Persian, and Norwegian, relative clauses are right-branching, but nonetheless, SSs occur in the initial subject position. Going by the data that they cite in their works, Grosu and Thompson and Dryer's generalization that SSs exhibit a strong tendency to occur clause-finally is true only of non-nominalized clauses.

SpecIP or SpecCP. That's what the controversy is all about. Secondly, verb-agreement does not guarantee that the subject sits in the SpecIP position from where it can check agreement on I, given that there are cases of long-distance agreement in several languages of the world, such as in Hindi ergative constructions wherein the ergative subject occupies the canonical subject position and the verb shows agreement with a constituent inside its clausal argument, as shown in Bhatt (2005). Lohndal (2014) also argues that subject-verb agreement is no guarantee for the subjecthood of SSs.

Another diagnostic used for the subjecthood of sentential SSs is the subject-auxiliary inversion. Koster (1978: 53) shows that CP subjects in English fail to undergo subject inversion in questions, such as the following.

(7) *Did [that John showed up] please you?
(8) *What does [that he will come] prove?

Delahunty (1983) gives counter examples to Koster's to show that sentential subjects do invert in questions. Here is an example from Delahunty (1983: 387)

(9) Does [that the world is round] bother as many people as it did 500 years ago?

My informants feel that sentence (9) would become more acceptable if it is rephrased as *Does (the fact that the world is round) bother as many people as it did 500 years ago?* Davies and Dubinsky (2009) also provide some examples to show that SS Invert in wh-questions.[2]

(10) To whom is [that pigs can fly] most surprising?
(11) Is [that I am done with this homework] really amazing?

They argue that parsing considerations such as phrasal weight and prosody play an important role in determining the acceptability of SSs in questions. Lohndal (2014: 9) remarks that this line of argumentation has problems in that native speakers "notoriously disagree" on the above judgments. Some speakers agree with Delahunty's data, others disagree.

As we see, there are as many arguments for the subjecthood of the *that*-clause as against it. The debate remains unresolved. Lohndal (2014: 8) attempts to

---

[2] Some of my informants who are teachers of English feel that there is "something wrong with sentences (10) and (11)".

reconcile these two positions by arguing that there are speaker variations regarding the acceptability of initial *that*-clauses. He remarks that the CP subjects in English are either ambivalent or there are "two grammars among the speakers of English: one that allows sentential subjects in SpecIP, and one that treats them as topics". It looks like that there is no consensus among speakers about the structural position of the initial *that*-clause.

Further, Koster (1978) points out that sentential subjects are less acceptable in the subject position of embedded clauses than in main clauses. Alrenga (2005: 195) is also of the view that sentential subjects are not acceptable in embedded clauses even for speakers who find them acceptable in main clauses. Similarly, Lohndal (2014: 20) observes that there is definitely inter-speaker variation regarding whether the SS is in the canonical subject position or in a topic position and "this variation is especially pronounced when it comes to subject-auxiliary inversion and embedded environments".[3]

In the following sections, I will examine the subject/object asymmetry exhibited by complement clauses in Kannada and in other languages in the light of these controversies and will offer an explanation for this asymmetry in terms of an OHC according to which only an overtly headed clause can occupy a Case position. I will also try to resolve the issues related to the structural position of initial *that*-clauses by making a distinction between Kannada-type languages and English-type languages in terms of the availability of nominalization of clausal arguments, particularly of CP clauses. In languages like Kannada, CP (and IP) clauses can be nominalized and in languages like English, CP clauses cannot be nominalized. It is this distinction which is responsible for the differences in the distribution of sentential complements in these two types of language.

The present account differs from the earlier accounts we have just considered in important ways. Firstly, in Davies and Dubinsky's (2009) and Delahunty's (1983) accounts, the initial *that*-clause is a DP/NP and has a null D head which gets Case-marked. Secondly, neither of them consider nominalized clauses. Following Davies and Dubinsky (1998), Han (2005) also assumes a null D for the *that*-clause and treats it on a par with an overt nominal head in Korean SS. The present study makes a clear distinction between an overt nominal head and a null/zero head for purposes of Case and argues that only an overt nominal head is eligible for Case. I provide further supporting evidence from several other languages to show that these languages also obey the OHC. The OHC which is based on cross-linguistic facts can be used to explain why *that*-clauses exhibit a strong tendency to get extraposed to the clause-final position. One of the defining characteristics

---

3 See Lohndal (2014: 16–19), for a detailed discussion.

of nouns is to be Case-marked. But I argue that the complementizer *that*, although derived historically from a nominal base, is not "nominal enough" to receive Case directly on its own. This is because *that* has lost much of its original nominal character due to grammaticalization - and this is true of complementizers in several languages. Therefore, it has to be "nominalized" in order for it to receive Case. In English, as we know, nominalization of CP clauses is not possible.

We will now turn our attention to SSs in Kannada.

2 Sentential subjects in Kannada

In Kannada,[4] nominalized clauses behave just like simple (non-clausal) NPs/DPs. Some of the defining characteristics of simple NPs/DPs are as follows: they can bear Case, they can be topicalized, and they are available in the subject position of embedded clauses. Bare CP clauses lack these NP characteristics.

In Kannada, both finite and non-finite clauses can be nominalized. This paper focuses on finite clauses which are of two types; CP and IP clauses. CP clauses are fully finite in the sense that they possess all the properties of root clauses except that they are dependent clauses and are signaled by the presence of a complementizer. The embedded verb inflects for tense and aspect and licenses a nominative subject. It inflects for agreement only if the clause is non-negative and non-modal (indicative). So the function of agreement is to complete the statement of a positive indicative clause. Negative and modal verbs in general are invariant and so do not inflect for agreement. In other words, the presence of agreement is contingent upon the presence of tense which means it can occur only in tensed clauses. But tense is independent of agreement since gerunds, adverbial and relative clauses inflect for tense/aspect and license a nominative subject, but lack agreement. Therefore, it is tense which renders a clause finite. Kannada is a nominative-accusative language and it is the nominative subject/NP that triggers agreement on the verb.

There are, mainly, three types of CP clauses in Kannada: the *embudu*-clause, which is a nominalized CP clause, the *emba*+DP clause, which is a Complex DP clause i.e. a CP clause with a lexical head, and the *endu*-clause which is a bare CP

---

4 Although I am a native speaker of Kannada, I preferred to double-check the Kannada data with other native speakers and Kannada scholars. My special thanks are due to Dr. Tarakeshwar, Department of Translation Studies, The English & Foreign Languages University, and Prof. Padikkal, Centre for Applied Linguistics and Translation Studies, Hyderabad Central University, Hyderabad, for their valuable feedback.

clause. There are two kinds of complementizers in Kannada: *emba* and *endu*, both of which are derived from the verb *en*, 'say'. *Emba* is a relative or adjectival participial form of *en*, and *endu* is an adverbial participial form of the same verb. These complementizers can be analyzed as follows:

(12a) en+-a
       verb+REL.PTCPL→emba
(12b) en+-u
       verb+ADV. PTCPL→ endu

It is an important characteristic of Kannada phonology that in some cases whenever Sandhi takes place, there is an increment of a new sound to the base form. In the above examples, a bilabial plosive /b/ comes as an increment in (12a) as a result of which the alveolar /n/ assimilates to the following /b/, and in (12b), a dental /d/ comes as an increment. The suffix -*a* has several uses in Kannada. It is used as a relativizer in the formation of relative clauses. It is also used in forming adjectives, as in *gājina gombe*, 'glass doll', *maṇṇina mane*, 'mud house', etc. *Emba* is a deverbal adjective and being an adjective, either it has to be used before a noun or it has to be nominalized. Complementizers with an N (nominal) feature alone can be nominalized in Kannada. Since *emba* is an adjective, it has an N (nominal) feature and hence it can be nominalized by the pronominal or nominalizing suffix -*udu*.[5] This results in a nominalized *embudu*-clause. Alternatively, *emba* can have a lexical head like *samācāra* 'news' or *viṣaya* 'subject' to form a Complex DP construction (hereafter CDPC), that is, the *emba*+DP clause. The *embudu*-clause and the *emba*+DP clause are contained within a DP projection, with a functional and a lexical head, respectively. As stated earlier, these clauses are indicative and are fully finite.

---

5 Nadkarni (1977: 15–17) analyzes *embudu* as *emba+adu*, consisting of the complementizer *emba* and the independent pronoun *adu* 'that' as its head. If this was so, then *embudu* should be pronounced as *embadu* with a medial vowel -*a*-, in conformity with Kannada phonological rules. But the fact is that the nominalized Comp is always pronounced as *embudu*, with a medial vowel -*u*-. Nadkarni is of the view that *udu* is a variant of *adu*. On the contrary, -*udu* is a nominalizing suffix and it is derived historically from an independent pronoun *udu*. Ramachandrarao (2005: 169) observes that there were three demonstrative pronouns in Old Kannada: the distal *udu* 'that', the proximal *idu* 'this', and *udu*, which he categorizes as an intermediate demonstrative pronoun which, we can say, corresponds to the English pronoun *it*. I assume that over time the demonstrative *udu* got grammaticalized and reanalyzed into a nominalizing suffix. Until recently -*udu* was also used as a 3rd person, singular, neuter agreement inflection. In contemporary Kannada, it functions only as a nominalizing suffix.

In addition to these two clause types, Kannada has a gerund clause; the nominalizing suffix *-udu* is attached to the tensed verb of an IP clause to form a gerund clause. The gerund clause lacks agreement but can have a nominative subject. This clause is a (nominalized) non-indicative finite clause, while the *embudu-*clause is a (nominalized) indicative clause.

In contemporary Kannada, the suffix *-udu* functions basically as a nominalizing suffix and it is used to derive verbal nouns, such as *ījuvudu* 'swimming', *kuḍiyuvudu* 'drinking', *ōduvudu* 'reading', *naḍeyuvudu* 'walking', and so on. It is also used to nominalize finite clauses. It is not used to nominalize non-finite clauses. Until recently *-udu* was used as an agreement inflection also and it stood for 3rd person, singular number, neuter features. The suffix is, therefore, a determiner since it has pronominal features. The functional head *-udu* and its CP clause complement together form a Case Phrase (hereafter KP) which is licensed in a Case position. It is the head D which gets Case-marked and consequently its complement CP (or IP) clause is also licensed in a Case position.

As for the complementizer *endu*, it is an adverbial form of the verb *en*, 'say' It lacks N(nominal) feature and therefore it cannot be nominalized. Hence, the *endu*-clause is barred from a Case position.

In the classical minimalist framework, specifier-head-complement is assumed to be the universal underlying word order from which surface word orders of different languages are derived. Kannada is a verb-final language and deriving SOV from the underlying SVO order would involve several unmotivated movements in order to arrive at the surface SOV order. So I assume specifier-complement-head as the underlying order for Kannada from which the surface SOV is derived. For my analysis, I have used the formal/written variety of Kannada as it is more transparent morphologically. I have, however, provided examples of the colloquial/spoken variety wherever required. Below is an example of a transitive sentence in Kannada (e.g. 13) and its diagrammatic representation is given in (14).

(13) *rāmanu   nāyiyannu   hoḍedanu*
     Rama.NOM   dog.ACC   beat.PST.3M.SG
     'Rama beat/hit the dog.'

The tree in (14) gives a very sketchy view of the structure of a transitive clause in Kannada. As shown in the tree, I have assumed Kannada to be underlyingly SOV, wherein all functional and lexical heads follow their complements. The external argument of a transitive verb, i.e., the subject, originates at SpecvP and subsequently raises to its surface SpecIP position, where its D feature gets realized. In sentence (13), the NP *rāmanu* is the subject which originates at SpecvP, as shown in (14), and then finally moves to SpecIP, as shown in the diagram. I will not go into further details at this point. In section 2.2, I will discuss both subject- and object-raising in greater detail.

(14) Tree diagram

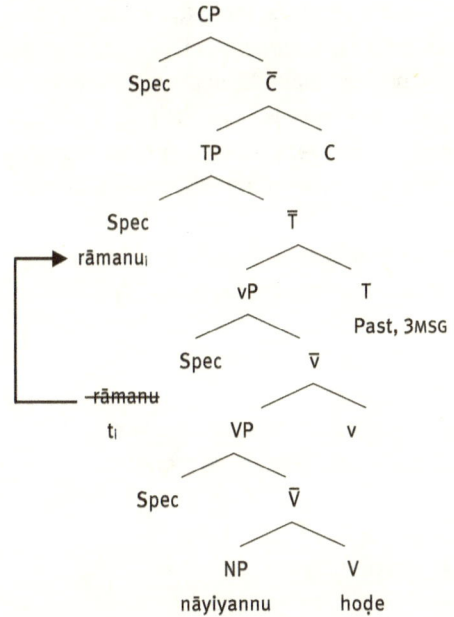

We will now turn our attention to nominalized clauses. Take a look at these sentences:

(15) [DP[CP[IP *nanna magan-ige innū kelasa sikk-illa-v-*] *emba*] *-udu*]
      my   son-DAT yet   job   got-NEG-∅- COMP -NMLZ
    nannannu   kāḍ-utt-ade.
    I.ACC   worry-PST-3N.SG
    'That my son hasn't got a job yet worries me.'

(16) *nān-u* [DP[CP[IP *śānti-yu   endigū avana kaibiḍu-vudu-illa*]
    I-NOM   Shanti-NOM never   his   hand.let.go-FUT-NEG
    emba]*-udu*]*-annu*   *nambuttīni.*
    COMP-**NMLZ**-ACC   believe.1SG
    'I believe that Shanti will never let him down.'

The *embudu*-clause in (15) is in the subject position and is non-overtly marked nominative. As stated earlier, in Kannada, nominative Case is invariably marked non-overtly, and occasionally in written/formal Kannada it gets realized as *-u*. The matrix verb with a 3rd person, singular, neuter inflection shows agreement with its clausal subject. The transitive (psych) verb *kāḍu* 'worry/bother' assigns a subject theta-role to the *embudu*-clause, its external argument. The clause refers to a state of affairs, and we can assume that it receives, let's say, a Cause theta-role. The object noun *nannannu* 'me', an internal argument of the verb, receives an Experiencer/Patient theta-role. This way, the nominalized clause meets these important criteria for subjecthood. In (16), the clause is in the object position; it receives Theme theta-role and is marked accusative, while the subject pronoun *nānu* 'I' is the experiencer. *Embudu* translates as 'the thing', 'the news', 'the saying', etc.

Now take a look at the (nominalized) gerund clause which also has the nominalizing suffix *-udu* attached directly to its tensed verb; once the nominalizing suffix is attached, the verb cannot take agreement inflection. This clause is also contained within a DP, headed by the functional *-udu*, as shown in (17).

(17) [DP[IP *kālēj   huḍugaru   sigareṭ   sēdu-]vudu]-annu   namma*
          [college   boys(NOM)   cigarette smoke-NMLZ]-ACC   my/our
      tande   khaṇḍisu-utt-āre.
      father   criticize-PRS-3PL(HON)
      'My father criticizes college boys' smoking cigarettes.'
      (My Father is critical of college boys smoking cigarettes.)

Now consider the CDPC, that is the *emba*+DP clause, given in (18). The *emba*-clause in CDPC takes a lexical head such as *samācāra, suddi* 'news', *viṣaya* 'subject'.

(18) [DP [CP [IP *narēśa(nu)   prītiyannu   guṭṭāgi   maduve   māḍikoṇḍanu]*
              Naresh.NOM   Priti.ACC   secretly   marriage   do.REFL.PST.3M.SG
      emba]   viṣaya]-(vu)   ūri-ge-ella   haraḍu-ide.
      COMP   news-NOM   town-DAT-all   spread-be.3N.SG
      'The news that Naresh married Priti secretly has spread all over the town.'

In the example (18), the *emba*-clause is in the subject position and is headed by the noun, *viṣayavu*, 'the news'. Here, *viṣaya (vu)* gets nominative Case and so the entire CDPC is in the nominative-marked subject position. Invariably, the nominative Case is not realized overtly on the nominal head as indicated by the bracketed Case inflection in (18).

In sum, the nominalized *embudu-clause*, the gerund clause, and the *emba*+DP clause, are all DP projections, with an overt nominal head that requires Case. An important point to be noted here is that these nominalized clauses and the *emba*+DP clause are used widely in formal/ written Kannada whereas their informal/colloquial counterparts *annuvudu*-clause and *annuva*-clause, respectively, are widely used in colloquial Kannada. The complementizers in the formal and the spoken varieties are derived from the roots *en* and *an* respectively, both of which mean 'say'.

Kannada being a verb-final language, the main verb generally sticks to the sentence-final position in the written variety and therefore, the formal variety *embudu*-clause, the gerund clause (and also the *emba*+DP clause) do not generally occur in the clause-final position. However, their colloquial counterparts, the *annodu*-clauses, do occur in the postverbal position, as shown in (19).

(19) *nannan tumba kāḍtā-ide* [DP[CP[IP *jan kaṣṭapaṭṭu*
I.ACC very.much worry.PRS.PROG-be.3N.SG [John hard
*kelasa māḍ-ōd-illa] anno]-udu].
work do-PRS-NEG COMP]-NMLZ.(NOM)
'It worries me very much that John does not work hard.'
(That John does not work hard worries me very much.)

An important point worth taking note is that the occurrence of the nominalized clause in the non-Case-marked clause-final position as in (19) does not in any way discredit my claim that nominalized clauses occur in the Case-marked subject position. Once the DP clause is checked for Case in the SpecIP position, it can be "scrambled" to the postverbal position, in which case it carries its Case with it. This happens especially in spoken/colloquial Kannada. What is crucial to my claim is the fact that the bare (non-nominalized) CP clause is totally excluded from the Case-marked subject position or from any Case position (see examples (25) and (26) below in section 2.1).

Like simple (non-clausal) DPs, nominalized clauses can also occur in dative, locative, instrumental Cases, etc. Here is an example of the *embudu*-clause in the instrumental Case.

(20) [DP[CP *avanu bahumandi hengasar-ige mōsa-māḍid-anu*]
he.NOM many women-DAT cheating-done-PST.3M.SG

> *emba-udu]-rinda-lē   ellarū   avanannu   dwēṣisu-utt-āre.*
> COMP-**NMLZ**-INST-EMPH all.NOM   he.ACC   hate-PRS-3PL
> "Everybody hates him for (the reason that) he cheated many women"

Since my main focus is on nominalized clauses in the nominative-marked subject position, I will not consider non-nominative positions. I will, however, consider the object position only in so far as it enables me to demonstrate that the subject position is obligatorily Case-marked while the object position is not obligatorily Case-marked. Nominalized clauses can also be topicalized like non-clausal DPs. The topicalized SSs can be easily distinguished from SSs in the subject position as they carry topic markers, as shown in (21) and (22).

(21) [DP[IP *bengaḷūrin-alli   mane   māḍu]-vudu]* -**andare**, (*adu*)
          Bangalore-LOC house make.PRS-**NMLZ**]   TOP   (that)
      aṣṭu   sulabhave?
      that.much   easy.Q
      'As for making a home in Bangalore, is (it) that easy?'

(22) [DP [CP [IP *avanu   bengaḷūrin-alli   doḍḍa mane   māḍ-idd-āne*]
              he.NOM Bangalore-LOC   big   house   made-iru-3M.SG
      emba]-udu] **ideyallā,** *adu barī   suḷḷu.*
      COMP-**NMLZ** TOP   that plain lie
      '(The news) that he has made a big house in Bangalore, it is a plain lie.'

Notice, the demonstrative pronoun *adu* 'that' inserted in the subject position in (21) shows that the subject clause has moved to the topic position. There are several topic markers in Kannada and there are constraints on which topic marker can be attached to which clause. For instance, the *embudu*-clause cannot take the topic marker *endare/andare*, since *endare* is also based on the verb *en/an* 'say'. The non-nominalized *endu*-clause, on the contrary, cannot be topicalized, as shown in the ungrammatical (23).

(23) *[CP[IP *avanu   bengaḷūrin-alli   doḍḍa mane   māḍ-idd-āne*]
            he.NOM Bangalore-LOC   big   house   made-iru-3M.SG
      -*endu*] **ideyalla** *adu   barī   suḷḷu.*
       COMP   TOP   that plain lie
      'That he has made a big house in Bangalore, it is a plain lie.'

It is generally observed that only a simple (non-clausal) DP can be the subject of an embedded clause and that sentential arguments cannot appear in this position. In Kannada, however, nominalized clauses are easily available in embedded clauses also. Here is an example.

(24) [DP[CP[IP śāntiyu   dinēśanannu guṭṭāgi maduve   māḍikoṇḍaḷu]
         Shanti.NOM Dinesh.ACC secretly   marriage do.PST.3F.SG
  emba]-udu] [CP[IP avaḷa tande   tāyiyarige gottu]   endu]]]
  COMP-NMLZ   her   father mother.DAT (is).known COMP
  rājanu   tanna hendạtige hēḷid-anu.
  Raja.NOM self wife.DAT tell.PST-3M.SG
  'Raja told his wife that (the fact that) Shanti married Dinesh secretly is known to her parents.'

In this sentence the nominalized *embudu*-clause is in the subject position of the embedded *endu*-clause.

2.1 The non-nominalized *endu*-clause

We will now turn our attention to the non-nominalized *endu*-clause. The *endu*-clause is contained within a CP projection. We noted earlier that the comp *endu*, being adverbial, lacks a N(ominal) feature and so it cannot be nominalized. Therefore, the *endu*-clause is not allowed in a Case position, as shown in (25) and (26).

(25) *[CP [IP ṇanna magan-ige innū kelasa sikk-illa] **endu-udu**]
         [my   son-DAT   yet   job   got-NEG COMP-NMLZ]
  ṇann-annu kāḍ-utt-ade.
  I-ACC   worry-PRS-3N.SG
  'That my son hasn't got a job yet worries me.'
(26) *[CP [IP nanna magaḷu   kaṣṭapaṭṭu ōdu-vudu-illa] endu]
         my   daughter.NOM hard   study-PRS-NEG COMP]
  nann-annu kāḍ-utt-ade.
  I-ACC   bother-PRS-3N.SG
  'That my daughter does not study hard bothers me.'

The ungrammatical (25) shows that nominalization of *endu* is not allowed, and the ungrammatical (26) shows that even the bare CP clause is not licit as the subject of a transitive verb like *kāḍuttade* 'bothers'. Only the *embudu*-clause can be the subject of *kāḍuttade* (e.g. 15). However, the CP clause can be an internal argument/complement of verbs of *saying* and *thinking* such as *hēḷu* 'say' or *yōcisu* 'think', which do not necessarily assign accusative Case to their internal arguments, as shown in (27) and (28).

(27) cp [ip *jān kaṣṭapaṭṭu kelasa māḍu-vudu-illa*] endu] *nānu andu-kon-ḍe*
John hard work do-PRS-NEG COMP] I.NOM feel-koḷ-1SG
'I feel that John does not work hard.'

(28) [cp [ip *śāmanu ōdalu amērikā-ge hōg-utt-āne*] endu]
Shama.NOM study.INF America-DAT go-PRS-3M.SG COMP]
nanna tangi nanage hēḷid-aḷu.
my younger.sister.NOM I.DAT inform.PST-3SG
'My younger sister told me that Shama will go to America to study.'

A point we need to note here is that in Kannada, the internal clausal arguments of verbs generally occur either in the preverbal object position or they are pushed further back to the left of the matrix clause. The longer the clause, the greater its tendency to move to the left of the matrix clause.

Just like the *embudu*-clause, the *endu*-clause is used generally in formal and written Kannada and it is invariably placed in the preverbal position. Its colloquial counterpart, the *anta*-clause, does occur postverbally very often, as shown in sentence (29).

(29) *nanna tangi nanage hēḷidlu* [cp [ip *śāmanu*
my younger.sister.NOM I.DAT tell.PST.F.SG Shama.NOM
ōdalu amērikā-ge hōg-utt-āne] anta].
study.INF America-DAT go-PRS-3M.SG COMP
'My younger sister told me that Shama will go to America to study.'

We noted in section 2, that the postposition of the (nominalized) DP clause does not counter my claim that DP clauses occur in the case-marked subject position. The DP clause gets postposed only after it has checked its Case at SpecIP. What provides crucial evidence for my claim is the total exclusion of the non-nominalized CP clauses from the canonical subject position as demonstrated by the ungrammatical examples (25) and (26). In the following sections, I will provide more evidence in support of my claim.

Although the *endu*-clause is not allowed in the canonical subject position, it can be treated as the understood subject of certain empty expletive constructions. The subject position in these sentences is empty. The verb in these constructions, particularly in non-negatives and non-modals, has the default 3rd person, singular, neuter inflection in fulfilment of the finiteness requirement of the clause. Consider these expletive constructions:

(30) Pro_EXPL [CP [IP *mundina śukravāra śālege   raja]   endu]*
              next   Friday   college.DAT holiday COMP]
tōr-utta-ade.
seem-PRS-3N.SG
'It seems/appears that next Friday is a holiday for the college.'

(31) Pro_EXPL [CP[IP *kṛṣṇanu   paramātmana swarūpa]   vendu]*
              Krishna-NOM God's   incarnation COMP
bhāgavatad-alli   hēḷalāgide.
Bhagavata-LOC   say.al.āgu.be.PRS.PRF.3N.SG
'It has been said in the Bhagavata that Krishna is an incarnation of God.'

Consider the raising verb *tōru* 'to seem', and the composite verb *hēḷal+āgu+iru*, roughly meaning 'has been able to say', in the examples (30) and (31), respectively. Sentence (31) has a passive meaning; both of these verbs have an empty expletive subject. As we know, these verbs do not θ-mark their subject position, nor do they have the ability to assign Case to their internal arguments. The Caseless *endu*-clause is an internal argument of these verbs. Although the subject position is non-thematic and Case-marked, the CP clause cannot move to this position to check Case on T either, because it lacks a D/Case feature. So, it stays back in the verb's complement position. Besides, there is no movement of the embedded subject to the non-thematic subject position of the main clause, either. This is because raising verbs in Kannada subcategorize for a bare CP clause, i.e., the *endu*-clause which is a finite clause. Hence the subject of the *endu*-clause does not have to move to the non-thematic matrix subject position for Case, unlike in English in which the subject of a non-finite embedded clause moves to the matrix subject position. Thirdly, Kannada lacks an (overt) expletive that can be inserted in the matrix subject position. So, an empty expletive corresponding to the English *it* is postulated for the subject position. This means that the subject position in these constructions is totally empty. However, one can argue that the CP clause in (30) and (31) can be looked upon as the "logical" or "understood" subject of these constructions for the following reasons. The clause serves as an answer to a question like "what seems or appears (to me)... or what is said in the *Bhāgavata?*" Accordingly, the clause can be interpreted as the "logical" subject because it is perceived as the "understood" subject of the main verb. So, the CP clause can be analyzed as the "understood" subject of the constructions, and accordingly it can be coindexed with the empty subject position. Since the subject position does not get realized overtly in these constructions, and since we get to hear only the *v*P part of the sentence, these can be treated as bare *v*P structures. Following these observations, I propose that the canonical subject position, i.e., the SpecIP position, gets realized only at LF when the CP clause raises covertly to SpecIP, not for Case-checking, but to meet FI and also to satisfy EPP. This suggests that in Kannada, the EPP requirement may be met at LF also. All this demonstrates that although the *endu*-clause is perceived as the "understood/underlying" subject of raising or passive verbs, it cannot occur in the Case-marked subject position, because it is Caseless. This further corroborates Chomsky's (1981) view that only nominal phrases can meet the subject requirement.

Before I examine *endu*-clauses in greater detail, I will digress here a bit to give an account of how the nominalized clause, originating at Spec*v*P, finally ends up at SpecTP/IP. For this purpose, I will adopt Pesetsky and Torrego's (2004) approach to Case checking.

2.2 Deriving DP and CP clauses

In Pesetsky and Torrego's (2004) approach, nominative Case is uninterpretable T(uT) on D. In other words, nominative Case is the realization of D-feature, that is EPP, on T and this feature is always present there which means that SpecIP position is obligatorily Case-marked. In Kannada also, it is T that licenses a nominative subject. According to Chomsky (1995), the EPP requires that all sentences must have a subject by a strong D-feature on the functional head T(ense). So subjects raise to SpecIP not only to check Case but also to meet the EPP requirement. We noted that the overt D head of a DP clause has a D feature, just like T. As Chomsky (1995) observes, a categorial D-feature is intrinsic to DP. It is the matching features on the *Probe* T and the *goal*, i.e. the subject DP, that enter into the Agree relation, which force the subject to raise to SpecIP. The bare CP clause which lacks an overt head lacks a D feature and hence does not raise to SpecIP.

As for the Case feature on the functional head *v*, it depends upon the internal arguments that it takes. Only transitive verbs take an object which needs Case. So, the head *v* is +Case only if the verb is transitive. Unaccusatives, passive verbs and intransitive ergatives lack the ability to assign Case and hence their internal (nominal) arguments have to move to SpecIP where Case is assured. So Case may not always be present on *v*; but *v* does determine the argument structure of a clause, unlike T which is merely a Case licensor. This is an important difference between the functional heads T and *v*. We know that DP clauses have a D-feature; and following Chomsky (1995) we said that D-feature on T is EPP. Adopting the notion of Generalized EPP (Chomsky 1998), we can assume that the functional head *v* also has a D-feature only when the verb is transitive, especially when it takes a DP object. Consequently, the D-feature on DP and on *v* translates into accusative Case which is also a structural Case. Therefore, we assume that D feature in general gets realized as structural Case. However, there is a difference between T and *v* in this respect. Since Case is always present on T, it triggers obligatory raising of the DP clause to SpecIP. The functional head *v*, on the other hand, has a D-feature only when the transitive verb has a DP object. We will see in section 2.3 that certain verbs take only DP clause argument and certain other verbs take a DP clause and a CP clause as well as their argument, in which case the verb will be +Case or -Case. Accordingly, when the verb has a DP object, the D/Case feature on *v* attracts the DP clause to Spec*v*P, and when the verb takes a CP complement, the CP clause does not raise to Spec*v*P.

2.3 CP and DP clauses as complements of nouns and verbs

I will now demonstrate that the bare CP *endu*-clause occurs in several Case-less environments where the nominalized DP clause and the CDPC clause are not allowed and vice versa. Earlier we noted that since nominal heads require Case, the *endu*-clause cannot be the complement of a nominal head. Only the *emba*-clause can be the complement of nominals like *samācāra/ suddi/ vārte* 'news' as in (32) below. The ungrammatical (33) below demonstrates that the *endu*-clause is not allowed as the complement of these nouns.

(32) [DP[CP[IP *mānya   pradhānamantri narēndra mōdiyavaru   īdina*
             honorable Prime.Minister Narendra Modi.HON.NOM today
     haiderabād-ge bar-utt-āre]   emba] samācāravu]
     Hyderabad-DAT come-PRS-3M.SG COMP]   news.NOM
     ellarigū   tiḷidide.
     all.DAT   known-is
     'The news that the Honorable Prime Minister Narendra Modi will come to Hyderabad is known to all.'

(33) *[CP[IP *mānya   pradhānamantri narēndra mōdiyavaru   īdina*
            honourable Prime.Minister Narendra Modi.HON.NOM today
     haiderabād-ge bar-utt-āre]   endu] samācāravu ellarigū tiḷidide.
     Hyderabad-DAT come-PRS-3M.SG COMP]] news.NOM   all.DAT known-is
     'The news that the Honourable Prime Minister Narendra Modi will come to Hyderabad is known to all (everybody).'

However, certain abstract nouns such as *bhāṣe/mātu* 'promise', *pratigñe* 'vow' can take either the *endu*-clause or the *emba*-clause as their complement. Another property of these nouns is that they can also afford to do without Case. As the object of a transitive verb, when an abstract noun such as *bhāṣe/mātu* takes the *endu*-clause as its complement, it cannot raise to the SpecvP position for Case, since its complement, *endu*-clause, cannot occupy a Case position along with it. So the noun moves away from the clause and combines with the verb to form a N+V composite predicate. When the noun combines with the verb, it does not need Case, as in the case of incorporated nouns (Baker 1988). However, I would not call this a case of noun incorporation.[6] Following Miner (1982, 1983), I would rather call this a case of noun stripping or a case of "loose noun incorporation" whereby a noun is stripped of its Case inflections. However, both of these phenomena are similar in several respects. In noun incorporation, the noun and the verb become a single word and they undergo certain morphophonemic and semantic changes. In the case of noun stripping, there are no morphophonemic or semantic changes and the noun retains its independent status. Nonetheless, as Miner observes, adjacency is mandatory between the stripped noun and the verb and nothing can intervene between them. In the Kannada case, the noun retains its independent status although nothing can intervene between the stripped noun and the verb, so that it meets the adjacency criterion. This way, the *endu*-clause is in fact the underlying complement of the Case-stripped noun.

But when the abstract noun takes the *emba*-clause complement, as in the case of CDP constructions, it has to stay in-situ with its clausal complement and raise to SpecvP and gets Case-marked. This is because *emba* which is a (deverbal) adjective requires a nominal support so that it can stand as a clause along with its head. Consider the examples below:

(34a) *bhīṣmanu   satyavati-ge   [CP[IP tānu   endigū*
    Bhishma.(NOM)   Satyavati-DAT   self   always
    *bramhacāriyāgi-yē   iru-utt-ēne] endu]   bhāṣe/*bhāṣeyannu*
    unmarried-EMPH   remain-PRS-1SG COMP]   promise/promise.ACC
    koṭṭanu.
    gave.3M.SG
    'Bhishma gave a promise to Satyavati that he will always remain a bachelor.'

---

6 In Sudharsan (1998, 2002), I analyzed these structures as noun-incorporated structures. Subsequently, in Sudharsan (2019), I revised my views and analyzed them as cases of noun stripping or loose incorporation since they did not exhibit all the characteristics associated with noun incorporation per se.

(34b) *bhīṣmanu*   *satyavati-ge* [$_{DP}$[$_{CP}$ [$_{IP}$ *tānu endigū bramhacāriyāgi-yē*
Bhishma.NOM   Satyavati-DAT   self   always   unmarried-EMPH
iru-utt-ēne]   **emba**]   *bhāṣe*]-*(annu) koṭṭanu.*
remain-PRS-1SG] COMP   promise-ACC   gave.3M.SG
'Bhishma gave a promise to Satyavati that he will always remain a bachelor.'

In the perfectly grammatical sentences (34a) and (34b), the *endu*-clause and the *emba*-clause occur as the complement of the predicate, *bhāṣe* 'promise'. Generally, in Kannada, abstract nouns such as *bhāṣe, pratigñe, mātu,* are overtly marked for Case only in formal Kannada, as shown in (34b). We observe that in examples (34a) and (34b), the noun *bhāṣe* immediately follows its clausal complement. How do we know that the noun *bhāṣe* in (34a) is separated from the *endu*-clause and has combined with the verb and that in (34b) it is in the Case-marked object position along with its complement, the *emba*-clause? By using the adjacency test, I will show that in (34a) *bhāṣe* has combined with the verb whereas in (34b) it has stayed in-situ with its complement the *emba*-clause. In (34a) and (34b), the indirect object *satyavatige* can be moved around within the clause although there are some restrictions on its movement. Consider these sentences.

(35a) *bhīṣmanu* [$_{CP}$ [$_{IP}$ *tānu endigū bramhacāriyāgi-yē iru-utt-ēne*]**endu**]
Bhishma.(NOM)   self   always   unmarried-EMPH   remain-PRS-1SG]COMP]
satyavati-ge   **bhāṣeyannu/**bhāṣe***   *koṭṭanu.*
Satyavati-DAT   promise.ACC/ promise   gave.3M.SG
'Bhishma gave a promise to Satyavati that he will always remain a bachelor.'

(35b)*bhīṣmanu [$_{CP}$ [$_{IP}$ *tānu endigū bramhacāriyāgi-yē iru-utt-ēne*]**endu**]
Bhishma.(NOM)   self   always   unmarried-EMPH   remain-PRS-1SG]COMP]
bhāṣe   ***satyavati-ge***   *koṭṭanu.*
promise   Satyavati-DAT   gave.3M.SG
'Bhishma gave a promise to Satyavati that he will always remain a bachelor.'

In the grammatical sentence in (35a), the occurrence of the dative NP *satyavatige* immediately after the *endu*-clause demonstrates that the noun *bhāṣe* is separated from the *endu*-clause and that it has combined with the verb.[7] This is further confirmed by the ungrammatical instance of the accusative marked *bhāṣe* in (34a) and (35a); when the noun combines with the verb it becomes a part of the verbal predicate and so it does not need Case. Again, in the ungrammatical (35b), the occurrence of *satyavatige* between *bhāṣe* and the verb *koḍu* shows that the noun has not combined with the verb and that it is in a Caseless position. Now look at (36).

(36) **bhīṣmanu* [DP[CP[IP *tānu endigū bramhacāriyāgi-yē*
Bhishma.(NOM)　self　always　unmarried-EMPH
iru-utt-ēne]**emba**]]　　**satyavati-ge bhāṣe**　*koṭṭanu*.
remain-PRS-1SG] COMP]]　Satyavati-DAT　promise　gave.3M.SG
'Bhishma gave a promise to Satyavati that he will always remain a bachelor.'

The *emba*-clause, on the contrary, cannot be separated from its nominal head. But in (36), the dative NP *satyavatige* intervenes between the *emba*-clause and its head *bhāṣe* which renders the sentence ungrammatical. It works the same way in Telugu and Tamil also. See Telugu examples (4) and (5) and Tamil examples (8) and (9) in the Appendix.[8]

The *endu*-clause can also function as the complement of abstract nouns such as *santōṣa* 'happy', *hemme* 'proud', *matsara* 'jealousy', *ātaṅka* 'anxiety', etc., since these nouns are not Case-assigning predicates. These nouns select a human (Experiencer) subject which is marked dative. They can also be used with the light verb *paḍu* 'to suffer, experience', to form N+V complex predicates such as *hemmepaḍu* 'feel proud', *santōṣapaḍu* 'feel happiness' and so on. These complex predicates are intransitive and they also select a human subject; but their subjects are marked nominative as *paḍu* is marked for tense and agreement. This way, these predicates select not only their subject but decide their Case feature also, as shown in the following examples:

---

[7] Bhatt (p.c.) makes an important observation about (35a). He says that when the noun *bhāṣe* combines with the verb, the *endu*-clause functions as an adjunct. This is probably because the complementizer *endu* is basically an adverbial. This clause does often function as an adjunct.
[8] All the Telugu and Tamil examples cited in the Appendix have been checked with native speakers of Telugu and Tamil. I thank them all for providing me with detailed data.

(37) [CP [IP *nanna magaḷu   bahaḷa cennāgi hāḍ-utt-āḷe]   endu] nanage
           my   daughter very   well   sing-PRS-3F.SG COMP] I.DAT
    hemme/ santōṣa.
    pride/ happiness
    'I am proud that my daughter sings very well.'

(38) [CP [IP *nanna magaḷu   bahaḷa cennāgi hāḍ-utt-āḷe]   endu] nānu
           my   daughter very   well   sing-PRS-3F.SG COMP] I.NOM
    santōṣa-paḍuttīni.
    happiness-feel.1SG
    'I feel happy that my daughter sings very well.'

In (37), the matrix predicate is a nominal, that is *hemme* or *santōṣa*, and hence the subject is in dative Case, whereas in (38), the matrix clause has an (intransitive) N+V complex predicate and so the subject is in nominative Case.

The nominalized *embudu*-clause, on the other hand, cannot be the complement either of these nouns or even of the complex predicates, as the ungrammatical (39) shows. Because neither can these predicates assign Case to their internal clausal argument, nor can the nominalized clause move to the subject position since the subject position is theta-marked, as shown in (39).

(39) *[DP[CP [IP *nanna magaḷu   bahaḷa cennāgi hāḍ-utt-āḷe]   **emba**] **-udu**]
             my   daughter very   well   sing-PRS-3F.SG COMP] NMLZ
    nanage   hemme/santōṣa.
    I.DAT   pride/happiness
    'I am proud that my daughter sings very well.'

Kannada has NP- NP (or DP- NP) clauses wherein only a DP or an NP can occupy the subject position and so only the nominalized clauses or the complex DP construction can occur in the subject positions of these clauses. But the non-nominalized CP clause is excluded from this position. The NP-NP clauses can have abstract nouns, such as *satya* 'truth', *suḷḷu* 'falsehood', as their predicates; these abstract nouns are quite different from the abstract nouns *hemme* 'pride', *santōṣa* 'happiness' which we have just looked at. Firstly, they do not select a human Experiencer subject like the nouns *hemme* 'pride' etc. Secondly, they can have only nominative subjects, unlike the other nouns which take a dative subject. I analyze the DP clause in these constructions as a complement of these nouns; and since these nouns do not assign Case, it moves to the subject position for Case. Although the NP-NP clauses have non-verbal predicates, they are potentially tensed because in the past tense, these nouns occur with the linking verb *āgu* 'become' and the auxiliary *iru* 'be', which is marked for tense and agreement. So we can posit an abstract tense feature for these clauses even when there is no linking verb. This way the subject receives nominative Case. Consider these examples:

(40) [DP [CP [IP *avanu guṭṭāgi sigareṭ sēd-utt-āne*]
    he.NOM secretly cigarette smoke-PRS-3M.SG]
  emba]-*udu*] *nija*.
  COMP]-NMLZ] truth
  'That he smokes cigarette secretly is true.'

(41) [DP[IP *avanu guṭṭāgi sigareṭ sēdu*] -*vudu*] *nija*.
    he.NOM secretly cigarette smoke.PRS] NMLZ] truth
  'His smoking cigarette secretly is true.'

(42) *[CP[IP *avanu guṭṭāgi sigareṭ sēd-utt-āne*] *endu*] *nija*.
    he.NOM secretly cigarette smoke-PRS-3M.SG] COMP] truth
  'That he smokes cigarette secretly is true.'

In (40) and (41), the nominalized *embudu*- and the gerund -*udu* clauses, respectively, occupy the canonical subject position and are (non-overtly) marked nominative. The ungrammatical (42) demonstrates that the *endu*-clause is not allowed in this position. Examples of Telugu and Tamil DP-NP clauses in the Appendix provide further supporting evidence for my claim regarding DP-NP clauses in Dravidian languages in general. See Telugu examples (11)–(14) and Tamil examples (15)–(18) in the Appendix.

So far we have looked at several non-Case-marked positions where only the *endu*-clause can occur and several Case-marked positions where only DP clauses can occur. We will now consider verbs which subcategorize for a CP clause and a DP clause as well. For instance, verbs like *hēḷu* 'say', or *ghōśisu/ prakaṭisi* 'announce', subcategorize for a CP (*endu*-) clause and a DP (*embudu*-) clause as well. So, these verbs have a dual status and accordingly they are marked +Case or -Case in the lexicon. In other words, when a verb such as *prakaṭisu* 'announce' takes a nominalized clause as its internal argument, it will be +Case and when it takes a CP complement, it will be marked -Case. Here are some examples.

(43) Pro$_{ARB}$[CP[IP *jūn ippattonadaneya tārīku antarrāṣṭrīya yōgada*
    June twenty.first   date international yoga
  divasa] *endu*] *ella samācāra patrikegaḷalli prakaṭisiddāre*.
  day   COMP all news   papers.LOC announce.PRF.3PL
  '(They) have announced in all newspapers the 21st of June as Yoga Day.'

(44) Pro$_{ARB}$[$_{DP}$[$_{CP}$[$_{IP}$ *jūn   ippattonadaneya tārīku antarrāṣṭrīya yōgada*
June   twenty.first   date   international yoga
divasa] **emba-udu**]*-annu ella samācāra patrikegaḷalli*
day   COMP]-**NMLZ**]-ACC all news   papers.LOC
prakaṭisiddāre.
announce.PRF.3PL
'In all newspapers, (they) have announced that 21st of June will be (observed as) Yoga Day.'

The null subject in these sentences has an arbitrary reference. The *endu*-clause in (43) and the nominalized *embudu*-clause in (44) originate in the preverbal complement position, since Kannada is a Verb-final language. I argue that although these clauses occur preverbally, they do not occupy exactly the same position. When the verb has a DP object the functional head *v* has a D feature. The DP clause then raises to Spec*v*P in obedience to the (Generalized) EPP (Chomsky 1998), and its Case is checked. Since the bare (non-nominalized) CP clause lacks D/Case feature, it does not raise to Spec*v*P, but rather stays in-situ in its original complement position within VP. However, in Kannada, word order is quite flexible. Besides, there is no adjacency requirement for accusative Case assignment. Adverbs can be freely scrambled around and placed between the verb and its DP or CP complement. So it is difficult to show in terms of surface word order that the DP complement and the CP complement occupy different positions preverbally. But the fact that the DP clause is overtly marked for Case, as seen in the example (44), shows that it has moved to Spec*v*P where its Case is licensed.

In sum, the subject/object asymmetry in Kannada arises from an interaction between the distinct Case-licensing properties of the functional heads T and *v* and the OHC according to which only an overt nominal head – that is, a morphologically realized head – is eligible for Case.[9] The OHC can be stated as follows:

(45) In Kannada, only an overt nominal head is eligible for Case, morphological or abstract.[10]

---

[9] It would be worthwhile to investigate further this Case-related constraint to find out what implications it has for a theory of Case in general.

[10] One of the anonymous reviewers remarks that: "The claim made in (45) really looks like a version of the Visibility Condition on case assignment (which was intended to replace the Case Filter) - proposed in Chomsky's 1986 and related to theta-marking". The Visibility Condition proposed in Chomsky (1986) was a condition on theta-role assignment and it was in a way condition on argumenthood. In order to circumvent the problem posed by the Caseless argument PRO, Chomsky proposed that PRO gets null Case. The OHC is not related to the Visibility Condition in

The nominalizer, as we have seen, is the head of CP and IP clauses and it is this head which receives Case and enables its CP and IP complements to sit in a Case position. This constraint rules out non-nominalized (CP) clauses from Case positions, since they lack an overt nominal head. It also states that Case need not be realized morphologically on the nominal head. The presence of an overt head is itself a realization of Case. This takes care of the fact that nominative Case in Kannada is invariably abstract; and in several other languages which we will consider in section 3, it is marked non-overtly.

3 Sentential subjects cross-linguistically

The OHC is not unique to Kannada. Cross-linguistic data show that several genetically and typologically unrelated languages in which clausal nominalization is available also obey this constraint. I have looked at seven such languages, namely, Marathi, Japanese, Turkish, Korean, Persian, Greek, and Norwegian. Data for these languages come from papers published in journals, from books, and from personal communication with the authors of these papers.[11] Clausal nominalization is available in all of these languages, and in none of them is a non-nominalized (CP/IP) clause allowed in the subject position, which lends further support to my claim about nominalized clauses. As for the object position, these languages exhibit differences which we will consider shortly.

---

any way, as far as I can see at this point. It states that overtness of the nominal head is a requirement for Case-marking. I have proposed this constraint solely on the basis of observed cross-linguistic facts. In fact, in Sudharsan (1998: 129–131, 2005), I have argued against the Visibility Condition by pointing out that expletives which are non-arguments get Case-marked in English. Besides, in Sudharsan (1998), I have developed a Case theory in which I have done away with the Visibility Condition and also the Null Case hypothesis. The present study provides further support for my stand against Visibility Condition. We have seen that non-nominalized CP clauses in Kannada, and in other languages - which we will consider in sections 3 - are all arguments, but are not Case-marked.

11 While working on these languages, I contacted several scholars in the field who helped me with the data crucial to my claims. I am deeply indebted to Jaklin Kornfilt (Syracuse University), Shoichi Iwasaki (University of Hawaii), Kuzuha Watanabe (California State University), and Terje Lohndal (NTNU, Trondheim) who patiently answered all my questions regarding Turkish, Japanese, and Norwegian, respectively. I would also like to thank Ms. Yukino Amemiya, Mr. Pankaj Narke and Mr. Ashyrberdi Rejetov, research scholars at the English & Foreign Languages University, Hyderabad, for discussing Japanese, Marathi, and Turkish data, respectively, with me.

3.1 Sentential subjects in SOV languages

Sections 3.1.1–3.1.5 will consider five SOV languages, namely, Marathi, Turkish, Korean, Japanese, and Persian in which nominalization of CP/IP clauses is available. All these SOV languages strictly obey the OHC and confirm my claims about the distribution of DP and CP clauses. The discussion will focus on those aspects which are relevant to my claims. For a more detailed discussion of complement clauses in these languages, the reader is referred to the original works cited in the paper.

3.1.1 Marathi

Marathi, an SOV language belonging to the Indo-Aryan family, has two types of complement clause: the Indo-European type *ki*-clause which is head-initial; and the head-final *he*-clause, which is similar to the (nominalized) gerund clause found in the Dravidian languages, namely, Kannada, Telugu and Tamil. The complementizer *ki* in *ki*-clause cannot be nominalized and so the clause can be analyzed as contained within a CP projection. It occurs exclusively in the postverbal object position, as in (46), and is excluded from the Case-marked subject position, as shown in the ungrammatical (47).

(46) he satya āhe [cp ki [ip jān   vivāhit āhe]].
      it true is [COMP   John married is]
      'It is true that John is married.'
(47) *[cp ki   [ip jān vivāhit āhe]] satya āhe.
           COMP   [John married   is]   true is
      'That John is married is true.'

In (46), the expletive pronoun *he* 'it' is in the nominative subject position and the *ki*-clause follows the linking verb *āhe* 'is' and the postverbal position is not a Case position.

The head-final *he*-clause, on the other hand, is formed by inserting the pronominal *he* in the final positional of an IP clause. The pronominal *he* corresponds to *it* in English and it is the head of the IP clause and this clause can occupy the canonical subject position, as shown in (48).

(48) [DP [IP jān   vivāhit āhe] he] satya āhe.
          [John(NOM)   married is] it] true   is
      'That John is married is true.'

The 3ʳᵈ person, singular, neuter pronoun *he* is also used as an independent lexical pronoun like the English *it* and it occurs in thematic positions also. Notice that *he* is in a non-thematic subject position in (46) and is in a thematic object position in (49) below.

(49) *mala* **he** *āvaḍte.*
     I.dat it like
     'I like it.'

Here is another example of *he* occurring in the non-thematic subject position of a raising predicate.

(50) **he** *śakya   āhe* [cp *ki*   [ip *jān   pudhcya varṣi USA   la jaēl*]].
     it possible/likely is   COMP John next   year   USA   to go.FUT
     'It is possible/likely that John will go to the USA next year.'

The *ki*-clause in (50) is in the postverbal position. As the object of a transitive verb, the *he*-clause occurs in the pre-matrix position as in (51). If we replace the *he*-clause by a *ki*-clause in (51), the *ki*-clause has to occur postverbally, as in (52):

(51) [DP [IP *rāhulne   kutryāla mārle*] *he*] *sarvajan   mʰantāt.*
         Rahul.ERG dog.DAT hit   it   everybody says
     'Everybody says that Rahul hit the dog'
(52) *sarvajan mʰantāt* [cp *ki* [ip *rāhulnekutryāla mārle*]].

Examples (51) and (52) show that the nominalized *he*-clause and the non-nominalized *ki*-clause can be the object of verbs of *saying*, although the former occurs preverbally and the latter occurs only postverbally. The *ki*-clause being head initial follows the verb whereas the head-final *he*-clause can occur in preverbal or in postverbal positions.

3.1.2 Turkish

Turkish, another SOV language, exhibits similar constraints on the distribution of clausal arguments. Kornfilt (2007) discusses two types of nominalized clauses in Turkish: one which has the suffix -*DIK* in place of tense, aspect and mood morphemes of a fully finite verb, and the other type with the nominal suffix -*mA*. She characterizes -*Dik* as a factive nominal and -*mA* as a non-factive nominal. Kornfilt

(2007) characterizes nominalized clauses as finite, irrespective of whether they are factive or non-factive and says that agreement on the nominalized verb licenses a genitive subject. And in the non-nominalized clauses, the tensed verb licenses a nominative subject. Göksel and Kerslake (2005) discuss nominalized clauses which are formed by attaching the nominalizing suffix *yacağ*. Example (53) is from Göksel and Kerslake (2005: 367) and examples (54) and (55) are from Kornfilt (2007: 316)

(53) [Orhan-ın birşey yap-ma-dığ-ı] belliydi.
[Orhan-GEN anything do-NEG-VN-3SG.POSS] obvious
'It was obvious [that Orhan *wasn't doing/hadn't done* anything].'

(54) [sen-in sınav-ı geç-tig-in]-i san-ıyor-um.
you-GEN test-ACC pass-FN-2SG-ACC believe-PRSPR-1SG
'I believe (that) you passed the test.'

(55) [sen-in sınav-ı geç-me-n]-i isti-yor-um.
[you-GEN test-ACC pass-NFN-2SG]-ACC believe-PRSPR 1SG
'I believe (that) you should pass the test.'

As we notice, in (53), the nominalized SS occurs preverbally unlike *that*-clause in the English translation in which it occurs clause-finally; and in (54)–(55) again, the SOs occur preverbally. As shown in (56) which is taken from Göksel and Kerslake (2005: 368), the sentential object occurs clause-internally.

(56) O gün Suzan bana [artık dayan-a-ma-**yacağ-ın**]-ı
that day Suzan to.me [any.longer bear-PSB-NEG-VN-3sg.POSS-ACC
söylemişti.
told
'That day Suzan told me [that she couldn't bear (it) any longer].'

As for the postverbal occurrence of nominalized clauses, some of my Turkish scholars ruled out examples (57) and (58) as unacceptable.

(57) ?belliydi [Orhan-**ın** birşey yap-ma-**dığ**-ı].
Obvious Orhan-GEN anything do-NEG-VN-3SG.POSS
'It was obvious [that Orhan *wasn't doing/hadn't done* anything].'

(58) ?isti-yor-um [sen-in sınav-ı geç-me-n]-i.
believe-PRSPR-1SG [you-GEN test-ACC pass-NFN-2SG]-ACC
'I believe (that) you should pass the test.'

However, another Turkish scholar[12] observed that both simple DPs and clausal DPs (nominalized clauses) could be freely postposed to clause final position in Turkish and gave the following examples in support of her statement – which seems to go against the judgement about (57)–(58).[13]

(59a) **Ali   kofte-yi   ye-di.**
        Ali   meatball-ACC eat-PST
        'Ali ate the meatball.'
(59b) *köfte-yi ye-di Ali.*
(60a) [**Ali-nin   kofte-yi   ye-me si**]   Oya-yı   kız-dır-dı.
        Ali-GEN   meatball-ACC eat-NOM-3SG Oya-ACC angry-CAUS-PST
        'Ali's eating the meatball made Oya angry.'
(60b) *Oya-yı kız-dır-dı* [**Ali-nin kofte-yi ye-me-si**].

What was crucial to my study was to find out if Turkish allowed non-nominalized clauses in the canonical subject position. So, with the help of the available data, I constructed a sentence with a CP clause inserted in the subject position, as shown in the example (61), and checked it with the Turkish speakers. As expected, the Turkish (student) informants[14] ruled out the sentence as unacceptable.[15] They, in fact, came up with "better" versions of (61) which are cited below as (62a)–(62d).

(61) *[*Ali sınav-ı   geçecek] beni mutlu   edecek.*
      [Ali exam-ACC   will.pass] me   happy   will.make
      'That Ali will pass the test will make me happy.'

---

12 I thank the scholar for the examples (59a), (59b), (60a) and (60b). Unfortunately, I am unable to recollect her name. My sincere apologies to her.
13 Kornfilt (p.c.) agrees with the Turkish scholar who says that both simple DPs and clausal DPs can be extraposed to the clause-final position in Turkish and cites examples (59a–b) and (60a–b) in support of her observation. She observes that a nominalized clause can have a postverbal position and that sentences like (57), (58) and (60b) do occur frequently in colloquial Turkish. As for the Turkish students' view of sentences (57) and (58) as unacceptable, Kornfilt says that "there might an issue of phonological imbalance" in these sentences, as "the main verb is the only constituent in the main clause while the embedded clause is quite a bit longer".
14 I thank the Turkish speakers who are students at the English and Foreign Languages University, Hyderabad, for their feedback on Turkish data.
15 Kornfilt (p.c.) further confirms that non-nominalized clauses cannot occur in the canonical subject position, "They *can* occur as objects with certain matrix verbs, however". So, she rules out sentence (61) as "ill-formed". She also considers the examples (62a)–(62d) given by the Turkish students as perfectly acceptable as none of them contain a non-nominalized clause in the subject position.

(62a) [*Ali-nin sınav-ı geçme-si*] *beni mutlu edecek.*
Ali-GEN exam-ACC will.pass-NOM me happy will.make
'That Ali will pass the test will make me happy.'
(62b) [*Ali sınavı geçip*] *beni mutlu edecek.*
(62c) [*Ali sınavı geçerek*] *beni mutlu edecek.*
(62d) [*Ali sınavı geçerek*] *ve* [*benomutlu edecek*].

As in Kannada, in Turkish also, non-nominalized clauses are excluded from the canonical subject position, as demonstrated in (61). Another trait that Turkish shares with Kannada is that it allows postposition of nominalized clauses, as shown in (60b).

3.1.3 Japanese

In Japanese, complement clauses are nominalized by the nominalizers *koto* and *no*, both of which are pronominals, which indicates that the nominalized clauses are DPs (Simpson 2003); topic markers or Case-markers are attached to these nominalizers. Nominalized clauses occur as topics, or as subjects or as objects. According to Iwasaki (p.c.) and Watanabe (p.c.), since Case markers have to be attached to an overt nominal head, the occurrence of non-nominalized clauses in the subject position results in ungrammaticality. However, in most of the languages considered in this paper, nominative Case is marked non-overtly, which shows that it is the overtness of the nominal head that is crucial to Case assignment. In Japanese, the subject occurs clause-initially with the subject marker *ga*.

(63) [*kinoo itta koto*]-*ga bareta.*
yesterday went NMLZ SUBJ revealed
'The fact that I went yesterday was found out.'

Here is an example in which a SO occurs preverbally as the object with the object marker -*o*.

(64) [[*john ga hon yonda to*] *bill ga itta koto*]-*o*
John SUBJ book read COMP Bill SUBJ said COMP-OBJ
Mary wa sitte-imasu.
Mary SUBJ knows
'Mary knows that Bill said that John read the book.' (Dryer 1980: 163)

As for the object position, Iwasaki (2013: 224) observes that "a subset of verbs of *speech* and *thought*" take either a quotative *to*-clause or a complement clause as their object, as demonstrated in (65a) and (65b).

(65a) *hannin wa [jibun   gayatta] to   jihaku-shita.*
      culprit TOP self.NOM do.PST   QT   confession-do.PST
      'The culprit confessed that he did (it).'

(65b) *hannin wa [jibun   gayatta] koto-o   jihaku-shita.*
      culprit TOP self.NOM do.PST   NMLZ-ACC confession-do.PST
      'The culprit confessed to the fact that he did (it).'

In (65a), the verb has a non-nominalized (quotative-*to*) clause as its object, and in (65b), the same verb has a nominalized clause as its object. Iwasaki observes that although (a) and (b) are similar in meaning, there is a clear "factivity" difference between them. Complement clauses are factive while the quotative *to*-clauses are non-factive. What is relevant to our discussion is that both nominalized and non-nominalized (CP) clauses can occur in the preverbal object position, as in Kannada. In Kannada also, verbs of *saying* and *thinking* do subcategorize for a DP clause and a CP clause as well.

The sentence in (66) is a crucial piece of evidence to show that in Japanese non-nominalized clauses are barred from the Case-marked subject position (Iwasaki, p.c.).

(66) **[kinoo   itta]-ga   bareta.*[16]
     yesterday went SUBJ revealed
     'The fact that I went yesterday was found out.'

3.1.4 Korean

Korean further corroborates my claim regarding the non-occurrence of non-nominalized clauses in the subject position. Han (2005) shows that declarative subject CP clauses have to be nominalized by the nominalizer *kes*, which is morphologically a dependent noun (e.g. 67). The ungrammatical (68) demonstrates that nominalization of the subject CP clause is mandatory.

---

[16] I thank Prof. Iwasaki for the examples (63) and (66).

(67) [NP [CP ku-ka   apu-ta   nun kes]-i   sasil-i-ani-ta.
         he-NOM sick-COMP MOD NMLZ-NOM true-be-not-COMP
     'That he is sick is not true.'
(68) *[NP [CP ku-ka   apu-ta]-(ka)   sasil-i-ani-ta.
          he-NOM sick-COMP-NOM true-be-not-COMP
     'That he is sick is not true.'

As in SOV languages like Kannada and Japanese, nominalized SOs in Korean generally occur preverbally. Here is an example from Simpson (2003: 13)

(69) na-nun [ku-ka   oasstanun]-kes-ul   mollaessta.
     I-TOP   he-NOM   came   NMLZ-ACC did.not.know
     'I didn't know that he came.'

Han argues that the overtly Case-marked declarative subject CP clause in Korean cannot be accounted for if one assumes Adger's (2003) analysis of the *that*-clause in English. In Adger's account, the subject CP is base-generated in the SpecCP (topic) position and is associated with a null DP in the SpecIP position where the null D checks Case on T. Han goes on to argue that the overt Case marker on the CP subject in Korean cannot appear on a null host, that is, a null DP. Besides, there are problems in associating a CP in the topic position with a null DP in the subject position.

Adopting Davies and Dubinsky's (1998) approach to SSs in English, Han (2005) analyzes SSs in Korean and several other languages within a DP/NP shell. Han observes that there are parallels between SSs in English and the overtly Case-marked SSs in Korean. He further argues that the null D in English corresponds to the sentence nominalizing suffix *-kes* in Korean and so posits an NP-shell for the Korean nominalized subject CPs.

There are problems with Han's analysis. Firstly, Han does not take into account the difference in the distribution of *that*-clauses in English and those in languages like Korean, Greek, Spanish, etc. in which only nominalized clauses can occupy a Case position. We have noted that the structural position of the clause-initial *that*-clause is a highly controversial matter; but the most natural position for nominalized clauses in Korean, and in several other languages we have looked at is the Case-marked canonical subject position. Secondly, he treats the so-called null D in the *that*-clause and the overt D/N in nominalized SSs alike. Thirdly, Han does not explain why non-nominalized clauses are barred from the subject position in Korean and in other languages. In sum, Han's account fails not only to explain why *that*-clauses generally occur in the postverbal position but also why non-nominalized clauses are excluded from the subject position in Korean.

3.1.5 Persian

Persian is not a consistent SOV language as it possesses some SVO traits such as prepositions, head-initial complement clauses, etc. Farudi (2007) demonstrates that in Persian, nominalization of a *ke*-clause is mandatory when it occurs in the canonical subject position or the preverbal object position, both of which are Case-marked in Persian. But the bare non-nominalized *ke*-clause must occupy only the postverbal position, as demonstrated in the following examples (70a), (70b), and (70c).

(70a) *man   mi-du-am*   [cp *ke* [IP *Giti mi-ā-d*]].
     I   DUR-know-1SG   COMP   Giti DUR-come-3SG
     'I know that Giti is coming.'
     [Farudi, 2007: 5]
(70b) **man* [cp *ke   giti khub-e*]   *mi-dunest-am*.
     I   that Giti good-be.3SG   DUR-know-1SG
     'I know that Giti is good.'
     [Farudi, 2007: 39]
(70c) ***[cp*ke   giti khub-e*]   *man mi-dunest-am*.
          that Giti good-be.3SG I   DUR-know-1SG
     'I know that Giti is good.'
     [Farudi, 2007: 39]

Farudi says that the *ke*-clause can occur as a "subconstituent" of a DP – to use Farudi's term – consisting of *in*, a demonstrative, and a dummy NP. The dummy NP is selected from a closed set of expressions such as *vaqiat* 'fact', *eded'ā* 'claim', *dāstan* 'story', *xabar* 'news', and other nouns which stand for a proposition. The presence of the demonstrative *in* is obligatory, while that of the dummy nominal is optional. Farudi describes this clause as a CDPC, but I would rather call this clause a "nominalized" clause, as the presence of the demonstrative *in* alone is mandatory. Having said this, we can assume that the *ke*-clause turns into a "nominalized" construction when it has an overt nominal head, that is, the Case-bearing demonstrative *in*, whose presence is mandatory, as demonstrated in (71), taken from Farudi (2007: 10)

(71) [DP *in* [CP *ke to u-rā da'vat na-kard-i*]] *mādar-at-ro*
     this COMP you he-OBJ invitation NEG-did-2SG mother-2SG-OBJ
     nārāhat kard.
     upset did.2SG
     'That you did not invite him made your mother upset.'

Here is another example from Farudi (2007: 9) in which CDPC occurs in the topic position as well.

(72) [DP ***in*** [CP *ke to u-ro bāyāt da'vat bo-kon-i*]]
     this COMP you he-OBJ should invitation SUBJ-do-2SG
     mādar-at-ro behet t₁ goft.
     mother-2SG-OBJ to.2SG said.3SG.
     'That you should invite him, your mother told you.'

The nominalized *ke*-clause can also occur in the preverbal object position or as the object of prepositions, as shown in examples (73) and (74), taken from Farudi (2007: 10, 9, respectively).

(73) *hamme* [DP *in-ro* [CP *ke Ramin bigonah-e*]] *mi-pazir-an.*
     all this-OBJ COMP Ramin innocent-be.3SG DUR-accept-3PL
     'Everyone accepts this that Ramin is innocent.'
(74) *Sārā* [PP ***az*** [DP *in* [CP *ke darin mosābeqe barande*
     Sara from this COMP in.this competition winner
     na-shode xeli sharmande ast.
     NEG-become.PRT.3SG very ashamed be.3SG
     'Sara is very embarrassed at this that she didn't win the competition.'

Farudi observes that there are three possible ways of Case-marking the CDPC. Firstly, the dummy nominal head can be marked for Case, as in (75a). Alternately, the entire DP can be marked for Case, as in (75b). When the dummy nominal head is not present, the demonstrative *in* itself is marked for Case as in (75c). Consider the following from Farudi (2007: 8):

(75a) *Hamme* [DP *in edde'a-ro* [CP *ke Ramin bigonah-e*]]
      all DEM claim-RA that Ramin innocent-be.3SG
      mi-pazir-an.
      DUR-accept-3PL
      'Everyone accepts the claim that Ramin is innocent.'

(75b) [DP in   dāstān [CP ke   davoud varshekaste shode]-**ro**
         this story   that Davoud bankrupt   become.PART]-OBJ
      bavar na-dār-am.
      belief NEG-have-1SG
      'I do not believe this story that Davoud has become bankrupt.'
(75c) *man be u*   [DP *in-**ro*** [CP *ke   to   ketāb-ro be ali dād-i*]]
       I   to him   this-OBJ   that you book-OBJ to Ali gave-2SG
      na-goft-am.
      NEG-said-1SG
      'I did not tell him you gave the book to Ali.'

We notice that only accusative (objective) Case gets realized overtly, as in (73) and (75a)–(75c).

We noted earlier that bare CP complements cannot occur preverbally. As for DPs, there are two possibilities. They can occur only preverbally, either as the subject or as the preverbal object of a verb because the preverbal subject and object positions are Case-marked, while the postverbal position is not Case-marked. An interesting feature about the CDPC, particularly in the object position, is that it can be discontinuous. In other words, its associate CP can be separated from its DP head and moved to the postverbal Caseless position. Consider (76a) and (76b) which Farudi (2007: 36, 38) cites as examples.

(76a) *sara* [DP *in-o*   [CP *ke   man giti-ro   da'vat   kard-am*]] *mi-dun-e.*
       Sarah   this-OBJ   that I   Giti-OBJ invitation did-1SG]] DUR-know-3SG
      Sarah knows (this) that I invited Giti.'
(76b) *sara* [DP *in-o*]   *mi-dun-e*   [CP *ke   man giti-ro   da'vat*
       Sarah   this-OBJ   DUR-know-3SG   that I   Giti-OBJ invitation
      kard-am].
      did-1SG
      'Sarah knows (this) that I invited Giti.'

In (76a), the CDPC is in the preverbal object position. In (76b), the CP associate of CDPC is separated from its DP constituent and has been moved to the postverbal position while the demonstrative *in* 'this' stays in-situ. This is an interesting phenomenon. We noted above that in Persian, there are three options available to Case-mark DP clauses (cf. examples (75a)–(75c)). I think it is these Case-marking options that enable the bare CP complement to be disassociated from the DP clause.

Farudi accounts for the positional difference between CDPCs and bare CPs within the Antisymmetric framework in which all movement (including scrambling) is leftward. Hence the underlying order for Persian would be SVO from which the surface SOV is derived. So accordingly, the subject complex DP construction originates to the left of the finite verb at SpecvP, and moves to the SpecIP for checking. In this case, the embedded DP (*in* NP) alone cannot move out of the CDPC leaving the associate CP behind at SpecvP, because CP clauses cannot stay in Case positions, as shown in the ungrammatical (77) where the adverb *hatman* 'certainly' adjoined to *v*P intervenes between the subject DP and its associate CP and shows that CP hasn't moved along with its DP associate (Farudi 2007: 48).

(77) *[DP *in*   *mozu'e*]   *hatman* [CP *ke*   *reza*   *tabra'e*   *shod*]]
        this   matter   certainly   that   Reza   innocent   became.3SG
        sābet   *mi-kon-e*   [CP *ke*   *qāzi*   *monsef-e*].
        prove   DUR-do-3SG   that   judge   fair-be.3SG
        'This matter that Reza was found not guilty certainly proves that the judge is fair.'

As for the object DP and CP clauses, both are generated in the postverbal complement position. In the case of the complex DP clause, either the entire DP moves to the preverbal Case-marked object position or only the embedded DP (*in* or *in* NP), moves to the preverbal position leaving the bare CP clause behind in the postverbal Caseless position. Farudi refers to this as the STRANDING analysis. As for the bare CP complement of the verb, there is no leftward movement since it lacks Case feature.

Farudi observes further that in most cases the CP associate of the subject DP cannot extrapose. However, she cites an example from Aghaei (2006: 152) of an extraposed CP associate of the subject DP in the postverbal position which according to Aghaei is possible only in contexts wherein the object DP is scrambled over the subject DP and the finite verb occurs to the left of the subject CP, as demonstrated in (78).

(78) [DP *bigonah-i*   *ali*]-*ro* [DP *in*   *haqiqat*]   *sābet*   *mi-kon-e*
        innocence-EZ Ali-OBJ   this   fact   prove   DUR-do-3SG
        [CP *ke*   *dishab*   *dar manzel-e maqtul na-bud-e*]].
        that   last.night   in   house-EZ victim NEG-was-PART
        'His innocence, this fact that he was not in the victim's house last night, proves.'

The reader is referred to Farudi (2007) for details about the various approaches she discusses. Persian, as we noted above, differs from other SOV languages such as Kannada, Japanese, and Turkish, in that it does not allow a nominalized clause in the Caseless postverbal position which is reserved exclusively for CP clauses. A possible reason for this could be that the *ke*-clause being head-initial follows the verb, as it happens in most cases of head-initial complement clauses.

3.2 Sentential subjects in non-SOV languages

We will now consider two non-SOV languages which provide further supporting evidence for OHC.

3.2.1 Greek

An account of complement clauses in Greek by Roussou (1991) further supports my claim about the occurrence of nominalized and non-nominalized clauses in mutually exclusive environments.

The *oti*-clause in Greek is a CP clause with a clause-initial complementizer *oti* 'that'. *Oti* clause can be nominalized by inserting the definite article *to* in front of the clause so that nothing can intervene between the determiner and the CP. Nominalization of *oti*-clause is mandatory in the subject position as in example (79). The ungrammatical (80) shows that a non-nominalized clause is not licit in the subject position.

(79) [DP *to* [CP *oti ehis filus*]] *simeni pola.*
 the.NOM that have.2SG friends.ACC means much
 'That you have friends means a lot.'

(80) *[CP *oti lei psemata*] *apodhikni tin enohi tis.*
 that tell.3SG lies.ACC prove.3SG the-ACC guilt her.GEN
 'That she tells lies proves her guilt.'

Here are examples of the *to*-clause as the object of a verb (81) and complement of a preposition (82), respectively.

(81) [*to oti perase*] *to ksero.*
 the.ACC that passed.3SG it.ACC know.1SG
 'That he passed I know.'

(82) apo   to   oti   etreme
     from the.ACC   that was.shaking.3SG
     'From the fact that he was shaking'

The case of SO of a verb is somewhat less straightforward than that of SS. Roussou accounts for this in the following way. Usually object NPs follow the verb in Greek. But sometimes they occur preverbally, and are associated with a clitic in the main clause. Tsimpli (1990) analyzes these preverbal objects associated with a clitic as base-generated topics. Following Tsimpli (1990), Roussou analyzes preverbal object *oti* clauses associated with a clitic as base-generated topics. Consider sentence (83).

(83) (to)   oti   perase   to   ksero.
     the.ACC that passed.2SG it.ACC know.1SG
     'That he passed I know.'

As the example (83) shows, the optionality of the determiner *to* does not result in ungrammaticality for the following reasons. Verbs like *ksero* 'know' and *protimo* 'prefer' subcategorize for a DP and a CP as well. Whenever there is a clitic, the preverbal CP (without the determiner *to*) can be interpreted as a base-generated topic. Then the clitic *to* is assigned accusative Case and therefore the CP does not need Case. If, on the other hand, the determiner *to* is also present, then Case is realized on the determiner. Roussou explains this by assuming a Case-sharing relation between the determiner and the clitic. If the *oti*-clause occurs postverbally with the verb *ksero* or *protimo*, then *to*-insertion leads to ungrammaticality, as shown in (84) and (85).

(84) *ksero   to   oti   efighe.
     know.1SG   the.ACC that   left.3SG
     'I know that he left.'
(85) *protimo   to   na   **fevgho**.
     prefer.1SG the.ACC PRT leave.1SG
     'I prefer to leave.'

Examples (84) and (85) show that the postverbal position in Greek is not Case-marked, hence only a CP clause can occupy this position. Greek patterns more or less like Persian in this respect. Non-nominalized SOs occur postverbally in both languages although their word order is different. Another property they share is that their CP clauses are head-initial and head-initial CP clauses generally follow the verb.

3.2.2 The Norwegian case

Lohndal (2014) examines the distribution of SS in English and Norwegian. In section 1.2, we considered several accounts of the controversial *that*-clauses including Lohndal's. Lohndal examines in detail earlier analyzes of the initial *that*-clause both as a subject and as a topic. Since we already considered Lohndal's account of English in section 1.2, I will only summarize his main observations about *that*-clauses. Lohndal observes that there are more arguments in favor of the clause as a subject than as a topic. However, he goes on to say, the topic analysis of SS seems to account better for the lack of SS in embedded clauses. In conclusion, he remarks that there is variation among speakers' judgments about the structural position of SS and this variation is most pronounced regarding subject-auxiliary inversion and the availability of SS in embedded environments. Either way, there is indeterminacy about the structural position of SS in English. The reader is referred to Lohndal (2014) for more details.

In this section we will consider Lohndal's analysis of SS in Norwegian. Using the V2 property as a test for deciding the structural status of SSs, Lohndal (2014) argues that SSs in Norwegian are not allowed in the SpecIP position and, following Koster (1978) and Alrenga (2005), he analyzes sentential subjects in the initial position as a topic, as shown in this example from Lohndal (2014: 20):

(86) At   han kom så sent, ødela   festen.
     that he   came so late ruined the.party
     'That he arrived so late ruined the party.'

The topic analysis of the sentential subject is further confirmed by the fact that an expletive can be inserted in the subject position, as is done in Dutch. Lohndal (2014:20) cites the following examples from Norwegian (87) and from Dutch (88):

(87) At   han vil   komme, (det)   er klart.
     that he   will   come, (that) is clear
     'That he will come is clear.'
(88) Dat   hij komt   (dat) is duidelijk.
     that he   comes (that) is clear
     'That he will come is clear.' (Koster 1978)

Again, Lohndal uses the V2 property to test whether sentential subjects can occur in SpecIP in Norwegian. If a non-subject occurs in SpecCP, the sentential subject should follow the verb and thereby occupy the SpecIP position. He uses a nominal subject as a baseline as shown in (89a). If the object is fronted, then the subject sits in SpecIP, as in (89b). When the PP is fronted also, the subject John sits in SpecIP. Lohndal says all these sentences are grammatical (Lohndal 2014: 21):

(89a) *John overrasket alle deltakerne i fjor.*
 John surprised all the.participants in last.year
 'John surprised all the participants last year.'
(89b) *Alle deltakerne, overrasket John i fjor.* [fronted object]
 all the.participants surprised John in last.year
 'All the participants, John surprised last year.'
(89c) *I fjor overrasket John alle deltakerne.* [fronted PP]
 in last.year surprised John all the.participants
 'Last year, John surprised all the participants.'

Lohndal says that in (89b), *alle deltakerne* 'all the participants' is focused so that it will not have the interpretation that it was the participants who surprised John last year. The above examples demonstrate that a simple NP or a non-sentential subject can occupy the SpecIP position in Norwegian. Lohndal (2014: 22) goes on to show that if a sentential subject is inserted in the same position as *John* in the above examples, only the first one (i.e. 90a) turns out to be grammatical, as demonstrated in the following:

(90a) *At John vant prisen, overrasket alle deltakerne i fjor.*
 that John won the.prize surprised all the.participants in last.year
 'That John won the prize surprised all the participants last year.'
(90b) **Alle deltakerne overrasket at John vant prisen, i fjor.*
 all the.participants surprised that John won the.prize in last.year
 Intended meaning: 'It surprised all the participants that John won the prize last year.'
(90c) **I fjor overrasket at John vant prisen, alle deltakerne.*
 in last.year surprised that John won the.prize all the.participants
 Intended meaning: 'Last year, it surprised all the participants that John won the prize.'

Sentence (90a) is grammatical because the sentential subject is in the topic position. The ungrammatical (90b) and (90c) demonstrate that a SS cannot occupy the SpecIP position. This further demonstrates further that Norwegian distinguishes between a simple (non-clausal) NP subject and a sentential subject.

Lohndal further observes that the above unacceptable examples can be "rescued" if a nominal determiner *det* 'it' is inserted so that the *that*-clause modifies this determiner. Consider these examples from Lohndal(2014:22)

(91) Alle deltakerne   overrasket **det** at   John vant prisen,   i fjor.
      all   the.participants surprised it that John won the.prize in last.year
      'The fact that John won the prize last year surprised all the participants.'
(92) I fjor   overrasket **det** at   John vant prisen,   alle
      in last.year surprised   it that John won   the.prize all
      deltakerne.
      the.participants
      'Last year, the fact that John won the prize surprised all the participants.'

The determiner *det* functions as a nominal head in (91) and (92) and receives Case and consequently the CP clause is also licensed in a Case position. In the above examples, the CP clause with a *det* inserted just before the complementizer *at* patterns like the *to*-clause in Greek and the CDPC in Persian and hence it can be treated as a nominalized clause. These examples demonstrate that in Norwegian also only a nominalized CP clause has an NP/DP status which enables it to sit in the Case-marked subject position.

Another piece of evidence to show that there are distributional differences between a sentential subject and sentential subject embedded within a nominal phrase in Norwegian is that the latter is easily available in the subject position of an embedded clause whereas the former is not, as shown in the following examples from Lohndal (2014: 23)

(93) ??*Peter forteller* [CP [*at*   John kom forsent] vil *irritere mange*].
      Peter says   that John came too.late will annoy   many
      'Peter says that the fact that John came too late will annoy many.'
(94) *Peter forteller* [CP at [**det** [*at* John kom forsent*]] vil *irritere mange*].
      Peter says   that it   that John came too.late will annoy   many
      'Peter says that the fact that John came too late will annoy many.'

Lohndal (2014: 23) demonstrates that this difference between a CP subject and a SS embedded within a nominal phrase in Norwegian is found between *that*-clause and the *fact*-clause in English also, as shown in the following examples:

(95a) *Did [that John showed up] please you?
(95b) Did [the fact [that John showed up]] please you?

As for the object complements in Norwegian, consider the sentences given in (96) and (97)[17] which are not discussed in Lohndal (2014). Lohndal (p.c.) observes that there is no need to insert *det* in the object position and that Norwegian allows complements much like English. However, this is possible only with some verbs such as the one used in the following sentences.

(96) *Jeg hørte* [CP *at Paul kom hjem*].
　　 I　 heard　　that Paul came home
　　 'I heard that Paul came home.'

(97) *Jeg hørte* [DP ***det***[CP *at Paul kom hjem*]].
　　 I　 heard　 it　 that Paul came home
　　 'I heard that Paul came home.'

So verbs like *hørte* 'heard' subcategorize for a CP clause and a DP clause as well. In sum, Lohndal demonstrates that complement clauses in Norwegian can occur in the canonical subject position when they are "embedded" within a DP phrase.

In the foregoing sections, we looked at data from eight different languages which clearly distinguish between a nominalized DP clause and a bare CP clause. The cross-linguistic data demonstrate that subjects that are clearly nominal alone can occupy the canonical subject position and that only nominalized clauses meet this criterion of being clearly nominal. The presence of an overt nominal head makes them perfect endocentric nominal phrases. Cross-linguistic data further demonstrate that complementizers cannot function as nominal heads that can bear Case.

4 Concluding remarks

This paper offers an explanation for the non-occurrence of a bare CP clause in the canonical subject position in terms of an OHC according to which only an overt nominal head can occupy a Case position. The canonical subject position is a Case position and the CP clause cannot sit in this position because the functional head C cannot bear Case on its own, as we have seen in the foregoing discussion.

---

[17] I thank Prof. Terje Lohndal for the examples (96) and (97).

Roussou (1991: 85), following Kayne (1982), observes that a complementizer in clauses functions as a nominalizer and thereby gives the clause the status of a nominal category so that it can function as an argument. True, CP does function as an argument even in Kannada and in several other languages which we have considered. We are aware that complementizers in many languages of the world are derived historically from nominal categories such as demonstrative pronouns, or interrogative pronouns or determiners. This is the case of Norwegian *det*, Greek *to*, English *that*, and of complementizers in several other languages. This way, complementizers in many Indo-European languages originate from a nominal base. In Kannada, on the other hand, the complementizers *emba* and *endu* are derived from a verbal base, that is, from the verb *en* 'say'. But only the deverbal adjective *emba* can be nominalized since it has the N feature. The adverbial *endu* cannot be nominalized as it lacks the N feature. One of the defining characteristics of nouns is the ability to bear Case. However, if C is a nominalizer and CP has a nominal status why can't C receive Case on its own? Why should it be nominalized at all? A plausible answer lies in the history of the complementizers. Nominal categories such as interrogative pronouns, demonstratives, and determiners, etc., from which complementizers in many languages are derived historically, underwent grammaticalization and were reanalyzed into functional categories as a result of which the reanalyzed forms lost much of their nominal characteristics. They became abstract functional elements devoid of any semantic and nominal content. Of course, the original nouns also continued to be used alongside the grammaticalized forms. This is the reason why these complementizers cannot receive Case on their own. They have to be "nominalized" in order to receive Case.

We have noted that the clause-initial position is where subjects occur frequently. However, in English *that*-clauses exhibit a strong tendency to get extraposed and the initial occurrence of *that*-clauses is considered "marked" or to be more precise "rare" or not so "frequent" (see Haspelmath 2006).

The present study suggests that a possible explanation for the tendency of the *that*-clause to occur postverbally lies in two factors: Firstly, it is a head-initial CP clause. We noted earlier that head-initial complement clauses generally follow the verb, unless they are nominalized in which case they occur in the preverbal position as in the cases of Greek and Persian. Secondly, it lacks an overt nominal (Case-bearing) head because it cannot be nominalized. These two factors push the clause to the far end of the clause. In fact, the foregoing cross-linguistic observations lend support not only to Koster's (1978) view that the initial *that*-clause is not in the subject position, but is in the Topic position, but also to Safir's (1982) hypothesis that S-bars (or CPs) are not Case-marked. Interestingly,

Dryer (1980: 143) observes that "in Old English sentential subjects always occur in clause-final position, while other subjects most commonly occur in clause-initial position". Traugott (1972: 103) also observes that initial *that*-clauses are a recent innovation. What this suggests is that a historical study of how and in what contexts *that*-clauses came to be used in the initial position will probably lead to a better understanding of these clauses.

Appendix

CP clause as a complement of Case-stripped nouns: More evidence from Telugu and Tamil

Telugu

In Telugu and Tamil also, only nominalized clauses and the CDPC can occupy a Case position while the CP clauses are excluded from all Case positions.

The *ani*-clause in Telugu cannot occur in a Case position because it cannot be nominalized. The *anna*+DP clause, the nominalized *annadi*-clause, and the gerund -*adi*-clause can all occupy a Case position.

Consider sentences (1)–(5). When the object noun *māṭa* 'promise' takes the Caseless *ani*-clause as its complement, as in (1), it moves away from its complement and combines with the transitive verb *ivvu* 'give', since it cannot raise to Spec*v*P along with its clausal complement to check its Case. When the noun has *anna*-clause complement, as in (2), the noun has to stay in-situ with its complement, and raise to Spec*v*P along with its complement for Case, as shown by the accusative-marked *māṭani*, because *anna* being an adjectival category needs the support of a noun. As for the grammatical sentence (3), the indirect object *vaḷḷa talliki* is placed between the *ani*-clause and the object noun *māṭa* which shows that the noun has moved away from its complement clause. But sentence (4) in which the indirect object intervenes between the noun *māṭa* and the verb *ivvu* 'give' indicates that the noun *māṭa* has not combined with the verb which results in ungrammaticality. Notice again, in example (5), the indirect object *vaḷḷa talliki* is placed between the *anna*-clause and its nominal head *māṭa* which leads to ungrammaticality, because the *anna*-clause is left dangling without the support of its nominal head *māṭa*.

Telugu data

(1) *rāju vaḷḷa talliki* [DP[CP[IP *pro śāntinē pelḷicēsukuṇṭānu*]
    Raju his mother.DAT pro Shanti.EMPH marry.FUT.1SG
    ani] *māṭa*]] *iccāḍu*.
    COMP word give.PRF.3SG
    'Raju has given a word to his mother that he will marry Shanti alone.'

(2) *rāju vaḷḷa talliki* [DP [CP[IP *pro śāntinē pelḷicēsukuṇṭānu*] **anna**]
    Raju his mother.DAT pro Shanti.EMPH marry.FUT.1SG COMP
    māṭa(-ni) *iccāḍu*.
    word-ACC give.PRF.3SG
    'Raju has given a word to his mother that he will marry Shanti alone.'

(3) *rāju* [CP [IP *pro śāntinē pelḷicēsukuṇṭānu*] *ani*]
    Raju pro Shanti.EMPH marry.FUT.1SG COMP
    vaḷḷa talliki māṭa/*māṭani iccāḍu.
    his mother.DAT word word.ACC give.PRF.3SG
    'Raju has given a word to his mother that he will marry Shanti alone.'

(4) **rāju*₁ [CP [IP*pro*₁ *śāntinē pelḷicēsukuṇṭānu*] *ani*] **māṭa**
    Raju pro Shanti.EMPH marry.FUT.1SG COMP word
    vaḷḷa talliki iccāḍu.
    his mother.DAT give.PRF.3SG
    'Raju has given a word to his mother that he will marry Shanti alone.'

(5) **rāju*₁ [DP [CP [IP*pro*₁ *śāntinē pelḷicēsukuṇṭānu*] **anna**]
    Raju pro Shanti.EMPH marry.FUT.1SG COMP
    *vaḷḷa talliki **māṭa** iccāḍu*.
    his mother.DAT word give.PRF.3SG
    'Raju has given a word to his mother that he will marry Shanti alone.'

Tamil data

In Tamil, the *enrə*-clause is a Caseless CP clause. The *enrə*+DP clause and the nominalized *enbadu*-clause are Case-marked clauses. The complementizers *enrə* and *enra* end with vowels /ə/ and /a/, respectively; both are derived from the same verb root *en* 'say'. The *adu*-clause is a gerund clause.

In (6), since the abstract noun *vākku* 'promise' has the non-nominalized *enrə*-clause as its complement, it moves away from its complement and combines with the verb where it does not have to have Case. Hence the ungrammaticality of the Case-marked instance of *vākkai* in (6). When *vākku* has the *enrə*-clause as its complement, as in (7), it has to stay with it, because *enra* being an adjectival complementizer needs a nominal support. This way, the object noun and its complement together raise to Spec*v*P for Case, as shown by the Case-marked *vākkai*. Again, in the ungrammatical (8), in which the *enrə*-clause is the complement of the object noun, the indirect object *tannoḍeya ammāvukku* 'his/self's mother' is inserted between *vākku* and the verb *kuḍu* 'give' which shows that the noun has not combined with the verb. In sentence (9), the indirect object is placed between the adjectival complementizer *enra* and its nominal head *vākkai* which renders the sentence ungrammatical. By contrast, in (10), the complement *enra*-clause is not separated from its nominal head *vākku*, since the indirect object is placed after the object noun *vākkai*. So, both the noun and its complement raise to Spec*v*P to check Case.

(6) *rāju tannoḍeya ammāvukku* [cp [ip *nān śāntiyei kalyāṇam*
 Raju his mother.DAT I.NOM Shanti.ACC marriage
 seidikoḷḷugirēn] ***enrə***] *vākku/*vākkai kuḍuttirikkirān.*
 make.REFL.1SG COMP word/word.ACC give.PRF.3M.SG
 'Raju has given a promise to his mother that he will marry Shanti.'

(7) *rāju tannoḍeya ammāvukku* [DP[CP *nān śāntiyei kalyāṇam*
 Raju his mother.DAT I.NOM Shanti.ACC marriage
 seidikoḷḷugirēn] ***enra***] ***vākk(-ai)***)] *kuḍuttirikkirān.*
 do.REFL.1SG] COMP word-ACC give.PRF.3M.SG
 'Raju has given a promise to his mother that he will marry Shanti.'

(8) **rāju* [*nān śāntiyei kalayāṇam seidikoḷḷugirēn*] ***enrə***
 Raju I.NOM Shanti.ACC marriage do.REFL.1SG COMP
 vākku *tannoḍeya ammāvukku kuḍuttirikkirān.*
 word his mother.DAT give.PRF.3M.SG
 'Raju has given a promise to his mother that he will marry Shanti.'

(9) **rāju* [*nān śāntiyei kalyāṇam seidikoḷḷugirēn*] ***enra***
 Raju I.NOM Shanti.ACC marriage make.REFL.1SG COMP
 tannoḍeya ammāvukku vākku *kuḍuttirikkirān.*
 his mother.DAT word give.PRF.3M.SG
 'Raju has given a promise to his mother that he will marry Shanti.'

(10) *rāju* [*nān śāntiyēi kalyāṇam seidikoḷḷugirēn*] ***enra***
 Raju I.NOM Shanti.ACC marriage make.REFL.1SG] COMP
 vākkai *tannoḍeya ammāvukku kuḍuttirikkirān.*
 word.ACC his mother.DAT give.PRF.3M.SG
 'Raju has given a promise to his mother that he will marry Shanti.'

DP clauses as the subject of NP/DP- NP clauses in Telugu and Tamil

In Telugu also, only nominalized clauses are allowed in the canonical subject position of NP–NP clauses. The ungrammatical sentence in (14) shows that the non-nominalized CP clause cannot occupy the subject position whereas the nominalized clauses and CDPC are allowed in the subject position, as in (11), (12), and (13).

(11) [DP[IP *ataḍu   guṭṭuga/rahasyanga poga   trāga]-a-**di**]   nijam.*
      he.NOM   secretly/secretly   cigarette smoke-PRS-NMLZ   true
      'That he smokes cigarette secretly is true.'

(12) [DP[CP[IP *ataḍu   guṭṭuga/rahasyanga poga   trāgatāḍu]*
      he.NOM   secretly/secretly   cigarette smoke.PRS.3M.SG]
anna-adi]] *nijam.*
COMP-NMLZ true
'That he smokes cigarette secretly is true.'

(13) [DP[CP[IP *ataḍu guṭṭuga poga   trāgatāḍu]   **anna viśayam**]] nijam.*
      he.NOM secretly cigarette smoke.PRS.3M.SG COMP the.subject true
'The fact that he smokes cigarette secretly is true.'

(14) *[CP [IP*ataḍu   guṭṭuga poga   trāgatāḍu]   **ani**] nijam.*
      he.NOM   secretly cigarette smoke.PRS.3M.SG COMP true
'That he smokes cigarette secretly is true.'

Example (18) below shows that in Tamil also a non-nominalized CP clause, i.e. the *enrə*-clause, cannot occupy the subject position of an NP-NP clause. Only DP clauses are licit in this position, as demonstrated in sentences (15), (16) and (17).

(15) [DP [IP*avan   ragasyamāga sigarēṭ   piḍikkira]-(**a)du**]   unmai.*
      he.NOM   secretly   cigarette hold.PRS.3M.SG-NMLZ   true
'That he smokes cigarette secretly is true.'

(16) [DP [CP [IP*avan   ragasyamāga sigarēṭ piḍikkirān]   **enba**]-(**a)du**] unmai.*
      he.NOM secretly   cigarette hold.PRS.3M.SG COMP-NMLZ   true
'That he smokes cigarette secretly is true.'

(17) [DP [CP [IP*avan   ragasyamāga   sigarēṭ   piḍikkirān]*
      he.NOM   secretly   cigarette hold.PRS.3M.SG
enra] **seidi** *unmai.*
COMP   news   true
'The news that he smokes cigarette secretly is true.'

(18) *[_CP_[_IP_ *avan   ragasyamāga sigarēṭ   piḍikkirān]   **enrə**] *unmai.*
           he.NOM   secretly   cigarette   hold.PRS.3M.SG COMP   true
    'That he smokes cigarette secretly is true.'

Abbreviations

ACC = accusative; ADV = adverbial; AP = adjective phrase; ARB = arbitrary (*pro*); CDPC = complex DP construction; COMP = complementizer; CP = complex predicate; CRP = case resistance principle; DAT = dative case; DP = determiner phrase; EMPH = emphasis; EPP = extended projection principle; EXPL = expletive; F = feminine gender; FUT = future; GEN = genitive case; GER = gerund; HON = honorific; INF = infinitive; INST = instrumental case; IP = inflectional phrase; KP = case phrase; LOC = locative case; M = masculine gender; N = neuter gender; NEG = negative (verb); NMLZ = nominalizer; NOM = nominative case; NP = noun phrase; OHC = overt head constraint; PL = plural number; PP = preposition phrase; PRF = perfect tense; PROG = progressive aspect; PRS = present tense; PST = past tense; PTCPL = participle; Q = question marker; REFL = reflexive verb; REL = relativizer; SG = singular number; SO = sentential object; SPEC = specifier; SS = sentential subject; TOP = topicalizer (topic marker); TP = tense phrase; VP = verb phrase.

Transliteration

The transliteration of South Asian languages in this paper follows the standard ISO-15919. https://en.wikipedia.org/wiki/ISO_15919

Acknowledgements

This is an expanded and improved version of an earlier version of the paper. A summary of the earlier version was presented at SALA-35, hosted by INALCO, Paris, France, on Oct 29–31, 2019. I thank the audience in general, and Professor Rajesh Bhatt in particular, for their comments, etc., which helped me put some points in clearer perspective and improve the paper on the whole. I would also like to express my gratitude to the anonymous reviewers for raising some important questions which I had overlooked and which helped me to incorporate important points into my paper and to organize the discussions more coherently.

References

Adger, David. 2003. *Core Syntax: A Minimalist Approach*. Oxford: Oxford University Press.

Aghaei, Behrad. 2006. *Clausal complementation in modern Persian*. Austin, TX: University of Texas at Austin doctoral dissertation.

Alrenga, Peter. 2005. A sentential subject asymmetry in English and its implications for complement selection. *Syntax* 8. 175–207.

Baker, Mark. 1988. *Incorporation: a theory of Grammatical Function Changing*. Chicago: University of Chicago Press

Bhatt, Rajesh. 2005. Long distance agreement in Hindi-Urdu. *Natural Language & Linguistic Theory* 23. 757–807.

Chomsky, Noam. 1981. *Lectures on Government and Binding*. Dordrecht: Foris Publications.

Chomsky, Noam. 1995. *The minimalist Program*. Cambridge, MA: The MIT Press.

Chomsky, Noam. 1998. Minimalist Inquiries: The Framework. *MIT Occasional Working Papers in Linguistics* 15.

Davies, William D. & Stanley Dubinsky. 1998. Sentential Subjects as Complex NPs: New Reasons for an Old Account of Subjacency. In M. Catherine Gruber, Derrick Higgins, Kenneth S. Olson & Tamra Wysocki (eds.), *Proceedings of the Chicago Linguistic Society 34, Part 1: Papers from the Main Session*, 83–94. Chicago: Chicago Linguistic Society, University of Chicago.

Davies, William. D. & Stanley Dubinsky. 2009. *On the Existence (and Distribution) of Sentential Subjects*. Scholar Commons, University of California.

Delahunty, Gerald P. 1983. But Sentential Subjects Do Exist. *Linguistic Analysis* 12 (4). 379–397.

Dryer, Mathew S. 1980. The positional tendencies of sentential noun phrases in universal grammar. *The Canadian Journal of Linguistics* 25/2. 123–195.

Farudi, Annahita. 2007. An antisymmetric approach to Persian clausal complements. Ms, University of Massachusetts, Amherst.

Göksel, Asli & Celia Kerslake. 2005. *Turkish: A Comprehensive Grammar*. London & New York: Routledge.

Grosu, Asli & Sandra A. Thompson. 1977. Constraints on the distribution of NP clauses. *Language* 53 (1). 104–151

Han, Hye Jin. 2005. A DP/NP-shell for subject CPs. In Rebecca T. Cover & Yuni Kim (eds.), *Proceedings of the 31st annual meeting of the Berkeley Linguistics Society: General session and parasession on prosodic variation and change*, 133–143. Berkeley: Berkeley Linguistics Society.

Haspelmath, Martin. 2006. Against markedness (and what to replace it with). *Journal of Linguistics* Vol. 42, No. 1. 25–70.

Iwasaki, Shoichi. 2013. *Japanese*. [London Oriental and African Language Library 17]. Amsterdam: John Benjamins.

Kayne, Richard. S. 1982. Predicates and arguments: verbs and nouns. *Glow Newsletter*. 8. 24.

Kornfilt, Jaklin. 2007. Verbal and nominalized finite clauses in Turkish. In Irina Nikolaeva (ed.), *Finiteness: Theoretical and Empirical Foundations*, 305–332. Oxford: Oxford University Press.

Koster, Jan. 1978. Why subject sentences don't exist. In Samuel Jay Keyser (ed.), *Recent transformational studies in European languages*, 53–64. Cambridge MA: The MIT Press.

Lasnik, Howard. 1999. *Minimalist analysis*. Malden, MA: Blackwell.
Lohndal, Terje. 2014. Sentential subjects in English and Norwegian. *Syntaxe et Sémantique* (15). 81–113.
McCloskey, James. 1997. Subjecthood and Subject Positions. In Liliaene Haegeman (ed.), *Elements of Grammar*, 197–235. Dordrecht: Kluwer Publications.
Miner, Kenneth. L. 1982. Object Stripping in Some Oceanic Languages. *Mid-American Linguistics Conference papers*. Lawrence, KS: University of Kansas Department of Linguistics, 129–140.
Miner, Kenneth L. 1983. Noun Stripping and loose incorporation in Zuni. *Kansas Working Papers in Linguistics* Vol. 8, No 2. 242–254.
Nadkarni, M. V. 1972. Sentential Complements on Nouns in Kannada. *Indian Linguistics* 3. 1–23.
Pesetsky, David & Esther Torrego. 2004.Tense, Case, and the nature of syntactic categories. In Jacqueline Guéron & Alexander Lecarme (eds.), *The Syntax of Time*, 495–537. Cambridge, MA: The MIT Press.
Ramachandrarao, B. 2007. *Kannaḍa Bhāṣeya Itihāsa* (Evolution and Modernization of Kannada). Mysore: D. V. K. Murthy Publications.
Rosenbaum, Peter S. 1967. *The grammar of English predicate complement constructions*. Cambridge, MA: The MIT Press.
Roussou, Anna. 1991. Nominalized clauses in the syntax of Modern Greek. *UCL Working papers in Linguistics* 3. 77–100.
Safir, Kenneth. 1982. *Syntactic chains and the definiteness effect*. Cambridge, MA: MIT doctoral dissertation.
Safir, Kenneth. 1983. On Small Clauses as Constituents. *Linguistic Inquiry* 14. 730–735
Simpson, Andrew. 2003. On the Reanalysis of Nominalizers in Chinese, Japanese and Korean. In Audrey Yen-hui Li & Andrew Simpson (eds.), *Functional Structure(s), Form and Interpretation: Perspectives from East Asian Languages*, 131–160. London: Curzon Routledge.
Stowell, Tim. 1981. *The Origins of Phrase Structure*. MIT doctoral dissertation. Cambridge, MA: The MIT Press.
Sudharsan, Anuradha. 1998. *A minimalist account of null subjects in Kannada*. Hyderabad, India: Hyderabad University doctoral dissertation.
Sudharsan, Anuradha. 2002. Noun-incorporation in Kannada. International conference on the Architecture of Grammar, CIEFL (EFLU), January 15–17, 2002.
Sudharsan, Anuradha. 2005. PRO and Syntactic Theory. *CIEFL Special Bulletin*, Vol 15, #1.
Sudharsan, Anuradha. 2019. Noun stripping or loose noun incorporation in Telugu and Kannada. Telugu Linguistics Forum, Osmania University, Organizers: Centre for Advanced Study of Linguistics, Osmania University, and The Central Institute of Indian Languages, Mysore.
Traugott, Elizabeth C. 1972. *A History of English Language*. New York: Holt, Rineheart & Winston.
Tsimpli, Ianthi-Maria. 1990. The Clause Structure and Word Order in Modern Greek. *UCL Working Papers in Linguistics*: Vol.2. 226–255.

Bornini Lahiri
Relation between animacy and case marking in Eastern Indo-Aryan languages

Abstract: Case markers in eastern Indo-Aryan languages mark the animate and inanimate objects differently. Most of the case markers of eastern Indo-Aryan languages are sensitive to animacy features of nouns and pronouns and this is reflected in the morphology. It is seen that the linguistic manifestation of animacy does not follow the biological dimension of animacy in case marking. It is perceived that despite strong preferences for a specific animacy value of nouns, speakers may conceptualize nouns differently from this preferred value in different contexts. In these contexts, an inanimate object can get case marked as an animate object. But in these cases, there are certain restrictions which need to be followed. For example, the verb plays an important role. The present paper explores the relationship between animacy and case marking in eastern Indo-Aryan languages. It also lists the various conditions in which inanimate objects are marked as animate objects, while maintaining the difference between animate and inanimate objects.

Keywords: Animacy, Eastern Indo-Aryan, Case markers, Locative case, Objective case, Bangla, Magahi, Bhojpuri

1 Introduction

Animacy plays an essential role in case selection and marking in languages across the world. Studies have shown that the relation between cases and the animacy feature is diverse (Aristar 1997; Malchukov 2008). Diversity also lies in the encoding of this relationship. In some languages, the case markers for marking the same case vary depending on the animacy feature of the host. Such is the case in Nepali, where ergative case /le/ can be used on both animate and inanimate transitive subjects. However, its use on animate transitive subjects is sensitive to tense and aspect, while its use on inanimate transitive subjects is not sensitive to tense and aspect (Li 2007). Whereas in some languages, the difference

---

Bornini Lahiri, Humanities and Social Sciences, Indian Institute of Technology Kharagpur, B265, 721302, Kharagpur, West Bangal, 721302, India.
Email: borninilahiri.ra@jadavpuruniversity.in

between animate and inanimate objects is reflected through marking one and not marking the other. For example, in Hindi, the accusative/dative case is mostly unmarked on inanimate objects but it is mandatory to mark it on animate objects (see Mohanan 1990).

It may be argued that the differences in case marking, which are due to differences in the animacy feature, can be explained in terms of semantic roles. Many semantic roles inherently involve animate participants like Agent and Comitative, whereas other semantic roles are taken to be inherently inanimate like Instrumental and Goal. It could be argued that, rather than the animacy features, the semantic roles decide the different case markers. However, in certain case relations, the semantic role fails to explain the difference in case marking. For example, in Bangla, an animate patient is case marked overtly for the objective case while the inanimate patient is not overtly marked (however, in certain instances, the inanimate object also can be marked overtly, explained in the following sections). In the following Bangla examples, it can be seen that there is an Experiencer and a Source of experience. In the following example (1a) *amar* 'I' is the Experiencer and $c^h ele$ 'boy' is the Source of anger. In (1b) *bari* 'house' is the Source of the experience. In the same position the object is overtly case marked with the animate object (1a) and not overtly case marked with the inanimate object (1b).

(1a)　am-ar c^hele-ta ke dek^{h}e rag　holo. (Bangla)
　　　I-GEN　boy-CLF OBJ see　　anger happen
　　　'I was angry to see the boy.'

(1b)　am-ar bari-ta　　dek^{h}e rag　holo. (Bangla)
　　　I-GEN　house-CLF see　　anger happen
　　　'I was angry to see the house.'

Semantic roles cannot always explain the use of different markers, as also shown in the following examples. In the following Bangla examples, it can be seen that the semantic role Goal takes two different case markers depending on the animacy feature of the Goal. The difference between the two sentences is that the Goal in one sentence (1c) is animate whereas it is inanimate in the other sentence (1d). In the following sentences, it is the animacy feature that determines the case markers (Bhattacharya & Simpson 2007).

(1c)　ami bari-ṭe　　ek-ta　citt^{h}i　pat^{h}alam. (Bangla)
　　　I　 house-LOC　one-CLF letter　sent
　　　'I sent a letter to (my) house.'

(1d) *ami raɟu-ke ek-ta citt*ʰ*i paṭ*ʰ*alam.* (Bangla)
I Raju-OBJ one-CLF letter sent
'I sent a letter to Raju.'

The present paper discusses the relationship between animacy and case in the eastern Indo-Aryan (EIA) languages. The topic has not been much explored. One of the reasons for this is that "animacy, or the distinction between animate and inanimate entities, is so pervasive in the grammars of human languages that it tends to be taken for granted and become invisible" (Dahl and Fraurud 1996: 47). Moreover, what should be marked as animate and what should be marked as inanimate often becomes a debatable issue as it does not relate to biological criteria.

There are some studies on animacy and asymmetries of case marking (Malchukov 2008; Aissen 2003; Corbett 2000; Malchukov 1984; Silverstein 1981). However, it is hard to find any such study on the EIA languages. The EIA languages are the languages which lie on the eastern belt of the Indo-Aryan languages (Grierson 1931; Chatterji 1926, Katre 1968). Among other languages, Asamiya, Bangla, Bhojpuri, Maithili, Magahi and Odia are part of this group. The present paper explores these languages to identify the relationship between case marking and animacy.

2 Case marking in EIA Languages

Cases are morphologically marked in EIA languages. The case markers in EIA languages distinguish between inherent characteristics and contingent features. Cases are marked in EIA languages by inflectional marking or by postpositions (Blake 2001; Masica 1991). Some cases need both an affix and a postposition to be realized. Such postpositions have been termed as secondary postpositions by Blake (2001). Blake (2001) remarks that most of the postpositions, generally in the Indo-Aryan languages, need the "oblique" marker to precede them. However, EIA languages are an exception to this phenomenon.

In the following example, a sentence in Hindi, the oblique form of the noun is used before the postposition, whereas in Bangla the root form of the noun is used, which is followed by the postposition because in Bangla the postpositions do not always need an oblique marker to precede them.

(2a) lərke   ko   bulao. (Hindi)
     boy.OBL ACC/DAT   call
     'Call the boy.'
(2b) cʰele ke   dako. (Bangla)
     boy   ACC/DAT   call
     'Call the boy/son.'

The above examples show that in Bangla, like many other EIA languages, oblique marking is not always needed for the postposition to occur. However, at times the genitive marker or the objective marker in EIA languages behave as the oblique marker, which is followed by the postpositions. The genitive marker mostly occurs when the object is animate in Bangla and Asamiya. However, the objective marker also behaves as an oblique marker and precedes the postpositions in many other EIA languages, as in (3b).

(3a) raja bʰãɾ-er   tʰeke taka   nilo. (Bangla)
     king clown-GEN   ABL   money   took
     'The king took money from the clown.'
(3b) hɔm to-ɾa   se   mitʰai ləiləi he. (Magahi)
     I   you-OBL ABL   sweet   took   AUX
     'I took sweets from you.'

The use of the oblique marker is affected by the animacy feature in EIA languages. Example (3a) can be contrasted with (3c) where the oblique marker is dropped as the object is inanimate (a detailed description follows in the next section). Both the sentences have the homophonous word /bʰãɾ/ as their object, but in example (3a) it means 'clown' (animate) and in the following example (3c) it means 'pot for collecting money' (inanimate), so in example (3a) the genitive marker precedes the ablative postposition. In example (3c) the genitive marker is not used as the object is inanimate.

(3c) raja bʰãɾ   tʰeke taka   nilo. (Bangla)
     king pot (money chest)   ABL   money   took
     'The king took money from the money chest.'

The case markers of EIA languages are multifunctional in nature. One case marker often goes beyond the function of marking a case relation. One of the examples of such usage is the genitive case marker in Bangla and Asamiya, which is used with the experiencer subject. The difference between the experiencer and the agent is marked by the use of different case markers (cf. Verma and Mohanan, 1990; Bossong, 1998; Aikhenvald et al., 2003; Bickel et al., 2015, Verbeke et al. 2015). In some of the EIA languages like Asamiya, the experiencer is marked by the genitive and the agent is marked by the agentive case marker, while in other EIA languages the agentive is mostly unmarked and the experiencer is marked with the objective or genitive case markers. Both the experiencer and the agent are always animate.

3 Case marking and animacy in EIA languages

In most of the EIA languages, case markers differentiate between animate and inanimate hosts. The most common hierarchy of animacy (Swart, Lamers and Lestrade 2008), which is characterized as a three-step scale – human > animals (animate) > inanimate – is maintained in these languages. In the following sections, I describe the different cases and their relations with the feature of animacy.

3.1 Local case

Local cases are used to mark the position or location of an object, which is always stated in reference to another salient object. As noted by Miller and Johnson-Laird (1976) and Talmy (1983), if the objects are unequal in size or mobility, the larger and more stable object is invariably encoded as the reference object.

Locative as a thematic role is taken as the place where the action or event denoted by the predicate is situated, and is inherently treated as inanimate. Thus, in many languages, when the location is animate, the case marker is different from that of the inanimate locative case marker.

In Maithili, two locative markers are used to mark the static position of an object: /me/ or /mẽ/, and /pər/.

(4a) jʰora me   ṭərkari   əic.   (Maithili)
     bag   in/LOC   vegetable AUX
     'There is a vegetable in the bag.'
(4b) lərka oi per   bəisəlje. (Maithili)
     child it on/LOC sat
     'The child sat on it.'

When the host noun/pronoun (location) is animate, then /me/ follows the affix /-ra/ or /ka/. The affix does not precede the marker /me/ if the object hosting the case marker is inanimate (4a–b). The marker /-ra/ or /ka/ is preceded by the locative marker (5a–b) when the object is animate. The pattern is followed in many EIA languages like Magahi, Angika and Bhojpuri.

(5a) həm-ra   me   himmət   əic. (Maithili)
      I-OBL   in/LOC   valour   AUX
      'I have valour in me.'

(5b) bəcca   hun   ka   upər   bəis gele. (Maithili)
      child   (s)he   GEN   on/LOC sat gone
      'The child sat on him/her.'

Creissels (2009) notes that in many languages there is a general tendency to express spatial relations with "human beings as the reference point in an indirect way, through a Genitival construction ('at N's place')" (Creissels 2009: 612). It can also be argued that when the location point is an animate body, then the whole construction is perceived as a genitive construction rather than a locative construction (e.g. (5b)).

In some other EIA languages like Bangla, Asamiya, and Odia, the locative marker cannot be used with an animate host (Lahiri 2013). The locative marker with an animate host is replaced with a genitive marker. Asamiya, Bangla, and Odia have only one locative marker each: /ɔt̪/, /t̪e/ and /re/ respectively. These are used to mark the inanimate location, but the animate location is marked by the genitive case markers which are /ɔr/, /er/ and /ra/ in Asamiya, Bangla, and Odia respectively. There is no vowel in these suffixes if the host noun/pronoun ends with a vowel sound. In the following examples, the contrasts between the animate and the inanimate hosts are shown.

(6a) tʰoli-t̪e   sobji   acʰe. (Bangla)
      bag-LOC   vegetable   AUX
      'There is a vegetable in the bag.'

(6b) ram-er   kʰɔmot̪a   acʰe. (Bangla)
      Ram-GEN   capacity   AUX
      'Ram has the capacity.'

(6c) *ram-e   kʰɔmot̪a   acʰe. (Bangla)
      Ram-LOC   capacity   AUX

(7a) pua-t̪i   jʰiɔ-t̪i-ku   paṇi-re   ḍʰɔkka   marila. (Odia)
      boy-CLF   girl-CLF-OBJ   water-LOC   push   hit
      'The boy pushed the girl in the water.'

(7b) se-manɔŋkə-ra bahut̪ sahɔs. (Odia)
 (s)he-PL-GEN very valor
 'They have valor.'

Ablative case is often taken as the marker of dynamic location. It shows the movement of an object. The relation which marks the separation of an object from a source is marked by the ablative case. In Bangla, when the source is animate, the ablative marker follows the genitive marking. Here the genitive marking works like an oblique case marker. In Bangla, when an object is separated from an animate source, then it is marked with ablative marker /t̪ʰeke/ which follows the genitive marker /-er/ or /-r/.

(8a) cʰele-ta skul t̪ʰeke palie gæ lo. (Bangla)
 boy-CLF school ABL escape went
 'The boy escaped from the school.'
(8b) cʰatro ʃikəkʰɔk-er t̪ʰeke boi nilo. (Bangla)
 student teacher-GEN ABL book took
 'Student took book from the teacher.'

3.2 Instrumental

Palancar (2002) defines an instrument as an object, which is manipulated by the agent to bring some change in the patient. Although the instrumental marker serves as agentive and comitative in many languages, it has been identified as a typical case for inanimate objects (Narrog 2009). This feature of being unpopular with animates makes the instrumental stand differently from comitative and agentive (Nilsen 1973). All the EIA languages overtly mark the instrumental case with the inanimate instruments.

(9a) xikʰok-ɟon-e chalk-dal-ere likʰise. (Asamiya)
 teacher-CLF-AGT chalk-CLF-INST writing
 'The teacher is writing with the chalk.'
(9b) lukɔ-ti kat̪ʰi-re gʰɔrə t̪iari kɔlə. (Odia)
 man-CLF wood-INST house make did
 'Man built the house with the wood.'
(10c) cʰele-ta pat̪ʰor d̪ie ɟanlata bʰeŋe d̪ilo. (Bangla)
 boy-CLF stone INST window break gave
 'Boy broke the window with the stone.'

(10d) ləika sãpə ke laṭʰi se mərələk. (Bhojpuri)
     boy snake OBJ stick INST killed
     'Boy killed the snake with the stick.'

Mahapatra (2007) while discussing the case syncretism of Odia, points out that instrumental /-re/ of Odia can always be replaced by /ḍwara/. However, the Odia locative marker /-re/ cannot be replaced by any other marker. But it is interesting to note that the /-re/ marker for both the instrument and location is used to mark only inanimate objects. For both animate locations and animate instruments, the language has different markers.

The instrumental case marker is widely used with the agent of passive sentences. According to Bhatta (1989), Pāṇini states that non-agentive cases such as 'instrument' can mark the agents of different actions. In the following examples, we can see, that the agents of the sentences are marked by the instrumental markers. But in these sentences, the agent does not have control over the situation.

(11)   mu ḍwara ṭelɔ sisi bʰɔŋgi gɔla. (Odia)
       I INST oil bottle broke went
       'The bottle of oil got broken by me.'
(12)   telo-r botol-tu mo-r ḍara bʰagil. (Asamiya)
       oil-GEN bottle-CLF I-GEN INST broke
       'The bottle of oil got broken by me.'
(13)   am-ar ḍara ʃiʃi-ti baŋia gælo. (Bangla)
       oil-GEN INST bottle-CLF broke went
       'The bottle got broken by me.'

These were called *oblique constructions* (cf. Hook 1990; Verbeke et al. 2015). Abbi (1994) suggests calling them "non-agentive constructions" as there is only an affected nominal without the power of an agent in such constructions which also justifies the use of the instrumental marker with the agent. The use of the instrumental marker shows the loss of control of the agent over the action.

In many Indo-Aryan languages, the adjunct agent-causee of a causative construction is marked by an instrumental marker (Masica 1991; Saksena 1982; Kachru 1980; Hook 1979). In similar constructions, Asamiya uses the genitive marker /-r/ followed by the postposition /ḍara/ to mark the agent-causee. In such constructions there is a main agent followed by an agent-causee. The action is done by the agent-causee. The agent-causee performs the action but does not control the action. The action is controlled by the main agent through the agent-causee.

(14a) rɔza-i   mo-r   ɖara zuɖɖʰɔ kɔrowale. (Asamiya)
      king-AGT I-GEN   INST war   did.CAUS
      'The king made me fight in the war.'
(14b) loɽa-tu-e   kukur-tu-r   ɖara mo-k kamurale. (Asamiya)
      boy-CLF-AGT   dog-CLF-GEN   INST I-OBJ bite.CAUS
      'The boy made the dog bite me.'

Odia uses /-re/ to mark the inanimate instrument. The postposition /ɖwara/ is used in Odia to mark the agent-causee. But unlike Asamiya, /ɖwara/ does not precede the genitive marker. But when the marker /ɖwara/ is used the verb is then in the causative or passive form in both Asamiya and Odia. Below are some examples showing the use of /ɖwara/ in Odia. In these examples, it can also be seen that the agent-causee has no control over the action. The use of an instrumental marker with animate bodies, in these languages always shows the loss of control of the agent (passive agent and agent-causee) over the action.

(15a) cʰua-ti   kukur ɖwara moṯe   kamoraila. (Odia)
      boy-CLF   dog   INST   I-OBJ bite.CAUS
      'The boy made the dog bite me.'
(15b) maḻi   ɖwara bɔgica sapʰa kɔrau. (Odia)
      gardener   INST   garden clean do.CAUS
      'Get the garden cleaned by the gardener.'

3.3 Objective

The objects of the transitive sentences and the indirect objects of the ditransitive sentences are case marked in the EIA languages by what is referred to here as the objective case. In this group of languages, the objective case is marked mostly when the object is animate and dropped when the object is inanimate, as can be seen in the following examples.

(16a) lərka: lərki: kə   ɖekʰalkai. (Angika)
      boy   girl   OBJ saw
      'The boy saw the girl.'
(16b) lərka: gʰər   ɖekʰalkai. (Angika)
      boy   house   saw
      'The boy saw a house.'

(17a) *ami raja ke ḍekʰlam.* (Bangla)
　　　I　　king OBJ　saw
　　　'I saw the king.'
(17b) *ami bari ḍekʰlam.* (Bangla)
　　　I　　house　saw
　　　'I saw a house.'

It is interesting to note that unlike Hindi (Mohanan, 1990), in Bangla and Asamiya the objective marker is not used to mark specificity or definiteness. This is so because Bangla and Asamiya have classifiers, which are used to mark the object as definite. The classifiers have other uses also in these languages. If the noun of a sentence is definite, then the presence of the classifier is obligatory, as the classifiers give the definite reading of the object, as is the case with (17c).

(17c) *ami bari-ta ḍekʰlam.* (Bangla)
　　　I　　house-CLF　saw
　　　'I saw the house.'

The objective case marker is mainly the case marker of animate objects in EIA languages, which can also be proven by the fact that when the object in these languages behaves like an inanimate Goal argument, i.e., like an inanimate location, then it is marked with the locative marker. But when the Goal argument is an animate object, then the locative marker is not used and the objective marker is used in Bangla (Bhattacharya & Simpson 2007). I here repeat the examples which I used in section 1, to show the contrast between Asamiya and Bangla. In Asamiya, both the animate and the inanimate goal use the same marker, unlike Bangla.

(18a) *ami bari-ṭe　　ek-ta　　cittʰi paṭʰalam.* (Bangla)
　　　I　　house-LOC　one-CLF　letter　sent
　　　'I sent a letter to (my) house.'
(18b) *ami raju-ke　　ek-ta　　cittʰi paṭʰalam.* (Bangla)
　　　I　　Raju-OBJ　one-CLF　letter　sent
　　　'I sent a letter to Raju.'
(19a) *mu raju-ku　gote　ciṭʰi　lekʰili.* (Asamiya)
　　　I　　Raju-OBJ　one　letter　wrote
　　　'I wrote a letter to Raju.'
(19b) *mu mo gʰara-ku gote ciṭʰi lekhili.* (Asamiya)
　　　I　　my　home-OBJ　one　letter　wrote
　　　'I wrote a letter to my home.'

Under certain conditions the objective case is used with the inanimate objects in the EIA languages. In the following cases, the inanimate object is obligatorily marked by the objective case marker.
— Inanimate object (lexical meaning) carrying animate reading
— Depending on the semantics of the verb
  i. Animate Verb
  ii. Impingement Verb

At times, an inanimate object can be perceived as an animate object and in that context the inanimate object carries animate reading. In EIA languages, if an inanimate noun/pronoun in the object position shifts from its lexical meaning (-animacy) to convey a meaning of an animate object, then the objective marker is used with it. If we insert the objective marker with an inanimate pronoun, then it gives an animate reading. This can be seen in the following Bangla example (21b).

(20a) *ami   o-ta   ḍekʰlam.*
      I   it-CLF   saw
      'I saw it(-animate).'
(20b) *ami   o-ta   ke   ḍekʰlam.*
      I   it-CLF   OBJ   saw
      'I saw it(+animate : him/her).'

Here, the lexical meaning of /o/ is inanimate (so it is marked with the classifier denoting an inanimate definite object, /ta/) but the use of /ke/ in the sentence (20b) has made it animate. Here, the inanimate pronoun /o/ is being used to refer to a person. The use of an inanimate pronoun with the inanimate marking classifier for a human is used to show disrespect to the human. The human is referred to as an object in a derogatory manner. But since the real-life referent is animate the obligatory object marking has been used.

The objective marker is also obligatory with two types of verb. One is verbs which can be used only with animate objects, like causatives of *eat, feed, see, hear* (as these actions cannot be done by the inanimate objects). I call these verbs *Animate Verbs* (AV). These are the verbs, which mainly take animate objects as their arguments. These verbs impose animacy on their objects which makes the use of the objective case marker obligatory. In the following examples, the verb used in the sentences obligatorily takes the animate object as its argument, so the objective marker is used.

(21) ləiki-ja əpən guṛij-a ke kʰana kʰiləlakəi:. (Magahi)
    Girl-CLF self doll-CLF OBJ food feed
    'The girl fed food to her doll.'
(22) *ləiki-ja əpən gurij-a kʰana kʰiləlakəi:. (Magahi)
    Girl-CLF self doll-CLF food feed
(23a) ami puṭul-ta ke jama pɔralam. (Bangla)
    I doll-CLF OBJ dress wear
    'I made the doll wear the dress.'
(23b) ami puṭul-ta (ke) baŋlam. (Bangla)
    I doll-CLF (OBJ) broke
    'I broke the doll.'

The above example (23a) stands in contrast with (23b). In (23a) the verb is AV, so the objective marker is obligatory. However in example (23b.) the verb 'break' is not AV as it can be used with inanimate objects (e.g. *ami kɔela baŋlam* 'I broke coal'), so the use of an objective marker is optional. If one wants the 'doll' to be perceived as an animate object, then the objective marker has to be used, otherwise, it may be dropped.

The second type of verb with which the objective marker is used are the *Impingement Verbs* like *hit, kick, punch*. Impingement Verbs (IV) (Longacre 1976) are those verbs that involve *power, force*, and *contact* by the agent to the object and leave the object physically affected.

(24) lərka gĕṇḍkə laṭʰ marəlke. (Angika)
    boy ball OBJ kick hit
    'The boy kicked the ball.'
(25) *lərka gĕṇḍ laṭʰ marəlai. (Angika)
    boy ball kick hit
(26) lərka səb ḍiwalke gʰusa marlək. (Bhojpuri)
    boy all wall OBJ punch hit
    'Boys punched the wall.'
(27) *lərka səb ḍiwal gʰusa marlək. (Bhojpuri)
    boy all wall punch hit

Except for the above-stated conditions, in certain instances the objective marker can be used with inanimate objects in some EIA languages. In the above-stated conditions, it is obligatory to use the objective marker, the absence of which makes the sentence ungrammatical. However, when the object is definite then the objective case marker can also be used with an inanimate object, in some EIA languages. However, the absence of the marker does not make the sentence ungrammatical as shown in the following examples.

(28a) *fʰiɔ-ti   dabba-guɽi-ku   bɔfarɔ   patʰaila.* (Odia)
       girl-CLF box-PL-OBJ   market   sent
       'The girl sent the boxes to the market.'
(28b) *fʰiɔ-ti   dabba-guɽi   bɔfarɔ   patʰaila.* (Odia)
       girl-CLF box-PL   market   sent
       'The girl sent the boxes to the market.'
(29a) *aḍmi   ḍibba   sab   ke   bəjar   pəhũcelək.* (Maithili)
       man   box   all   OBJ   market   sent
       'The man sent the boxes to the market.'
(29b) *aḍmi   ḍibba   sab   bəjar   pəhũcelək.* (Maithili)
       man   box   all   market   sent
       'The man sent the boxes to the market.'

4 Discussion

It is assumed that cases, besides marking the relationship between two nouns or a noun and a verb, also help in discriminating between the different arguments of a verb and work as the reflector or the index marker of certain semantic properties like animacy, humanness or definiteness. Discriminating the arguments of the verbs based on case marking is often referred to as a discriminatory approach (cf. Comrie 1989). The index marking and the discriminating function often go together. The index marking encodes specific semantic/pragmatic information about the nominal arguments of the sentence. Cases identify some semantic or thematic properties as well. For example, in Asamiya, the agentive case marks high agentivity (i.e. the agent is in control of the event). So the agentive case marker can only be used with animate subjects. It should be noted, that the agent in this language should be the real doer of the action. It means it should have the capacity to perform the action; hence it should be volitional and have control over the action ([+Control]). The inanimate objects are supposed to lack this control, so the agentive case cannot be used with them, as can be seen in the following Asamiya examples.

(30a) *kukur-tu-e   bʰuki   uṯʰil.* (Asamiya)
       dog-CLF-AGT   bark   rose
       'The dog barked.'

(30b) *bol-tu   ghurile.* (Asamiya)
     ball-CLF rolled
     'The ball rolled.'

The loss of control in animate subjects is marked by the genitive marking. The difference is shown in the following examples. In the following sentence (31a), the subject has control over the feeling of shame whereas in (31b) the subject has no control over the feeling of shame. The subject with control is marked by the agentive marker whereas the subject which does not have control over the situation is marked by the genitive marker.

(31a) *mo-i   laȷ   palu.* (Asamiya)
     I-AGT   shame   felt
     'I felt ashamed.' (+control)
(31b) *mo-r   laȷ   lagilə.* (Asamiya)
     I-GEN   shame   do
     'I was ashamed.' (−control)

Kakati (1941) also focuses on the fact that the agentive marker in Asamiya helps to differentiate between the subject and the object, which he elaborates with the following examples (Kakati 1941: 285). The examples show that the use of the agentive marker makes the subject an agent with control over the situation.

(32a) *manuh   mare.* (Asamiya)
     man   dies
     'Man dies.'
(32b) *manuh-e   mare.* (Asamiya)
     man-AGT beats
     'Man beats.'

Like the objective case marker, the agentive case marker of Asamiya too can be used with the Animate Verbs and Impingement Verbs described in the previous section. These verbs are perceived as the verbs of animates and their arguments are treated as animate objects. So the agentive case can be used with the arguments of such verbs in Asamiya.

(33a) *bɔl-tu-e   mu-k   kʰundiele.* (Asamiya)
     ball-CLF-AGT I-OBJ   hit
     'The ball hit me.'

(33b) bɛt-e   bɔl-tu   marile. (Asamiya)
       bat-AGT ball-CLF hit
       'The bat hit the ball.'

The literature on Differential Object Marking (Comrie 1986, 1989; Croft 1988; Lazard 1982, 1984; Bossong 1983, 1984; Silverstein 1976, 1981) focuses on the idea that when an object is higher in prominence, it is more likely to be overtly case-marked. Prominence includes the features of animacy and definiteness (Aissen 2003). The usual explanation for DOM relies on the concept of markedness. The unmarked animate object is more prominent than the unmarked inanimate object. Moreover, in a canonical transitive construction, the object is lower than the subject on the animacy/definiteness scale. If the object is inanimate, then it is unmarked, so when the object is animate in a transitive construction, then it is marked, which means it should be case marked as well.

Aissen (2003) discusses a ranking, according to which if there are two unmarked objects, one animate and the other inanimate, then the inanimate one is the unmarked one. So in the examples that we saw in the earlier sections, the objects are marked either because they are animate or they are marked due to the presence of certain types of verbs (Animate Verb and Impingement Verb). The presence of an Animate Verb and Impingement Verb raises the object's category from an unmarked object to a marked object; from an inanimate to an animate object.

Tab. 1: Distribution of Case Markers based on Animacy

Languages			Angika Bhojpuri Magahi Maithili	Asamiya	Bangla	Odia
Case Markers	Locative	+A	mə, pər	-ɔr	-r	-r
		-A	mə, pər	-ɔt̪	-te	-re
	Ablative	+A	sə, se, sə̃	Gen + pora	Gen + tʰeke	tʰaru
		-A	sə, se, sə̃	pora	tʰeke	tʰaru
	Instrumental	+A	sə, se, sə̃	dara	dara/ke die	dwara
		-A	sə, se, sə̃	-re/ -di	die	-re
	Objective	+A	-ra/ ke	-ək	ke	ku
		-A	N	N	N	N

Legend: +A = Animate object; –A = Inanimate object; N = Not marked

The above table shows that all the languages discussed here differentiate between animate and inanimate objects through different case marking. The difference is maintained in at least one case in some languages (e.g. Magahi, Maithili, Angika, and Bhojpuri). In a language like Bangla, the difference is maintained in all the four cases mentioned in the table above. This shows that animacy plays an essential role in choosing the case markers in EIA languages. In some languages, for almost all case relations, the feature of animacy plays a significant role in choosing the case markers. In the other languages, the role of animacy is limited to one or two case relations. It is difficult to find any EIA language where animacy has no role to play in the distribution of case markers.

5 Conclusion

It was seen in the previous sections that animacy plays a vital role in choosing the cases and their markers in EIA languages. The notion of animacy is not clear-cut as the linguistic manifestation of animacy does not follow the biological dimension (Swart, Lamers and Lestrade 2008). It is perceived that despite strong preferences for a specific animacy value of nouns, speakers may conceptualize nouns differently from this preferred value in different contexts. So it can be seen that an object which is inanimate is perceived as animate, as in (20a) and (20b). Both the examples are context-bound hence the meaning is beyond the lexical value. As has been mentioned in the literature, "despite strong preferences for a certain animacy value of nouns, speakers may conceptualize nouns differently from this (the) preferred value in different contexts" (Swart, Lamers and Lestrade 2008: 135).

In EIA languages, it can be seen that only animate objects get marked for the objective case, although there are some exceptions with some verbs (Animate Verbs & Impingement Verbs, discussed in 3.3). This is so because these verbs subcategorize mainly for animate objects and so when an inanimate object is the argument, then it is treated as an animate object. In a specific context, namely, when the inanimate object needs an animate reading, then the presence of the object marking is obligatory.

The locative case markers also differentiate objects based on their animacy features. Instead of a locative marker, the genitive case marker is used with animate objects, to mark the location (see 2.2.2). It is a common phenomenon among languages to use different markers for animate and inanimate objects to mark a location (Malchukov 2008; Swart, Lamers and Lestrade 2008; Aristar 1997; Dixon 1994). "Cross-linguistically locative case marking is most often used with NPs expressing locations, which tend to be inanimate" (Swart, Lamers & Lestrade 2008: 134). A pattern can be observed in the relations between animacy and case marking, which has a universal character, and needs to be explored further.

All the EIA languages distinguish between animate and inanimate objects for at least one of the cases. All the languages discussed here mark the objective case differently based on the animacy feature of the object. It was shown that in the maximum number of languages discussed here, the difference in case marking for the objective case is maintained. The objective case is overtly marked for the animate objects while it remains unmarked when the object is inanimate. The locative and the instrumental cases in Asamiya, Bangla and Odia use different markers for animate and inanimate objects. It is evident that the difference in animacy is also marked in the ablative case in Asamiya and Bangla. Bangla and Asamiya cases are therefore most sensitive to animacy among the EIA languages.

References

Aissen, Judith. 2003. Differential Object Marking: Iconicity vs. Economy. *Natural Language and Linguistic Theory* 21. 435–483.
Aristar, Anthony R. 1997. Marking and hierarchy types and the grammaticalization of case markers. *Studies in Language* 21. 313–368.
Bhatta. V. P. 1988. Theory of Karaka. Bulletin of the Deccan College Post-Graduate and Research Institute, Vol. 47/48. 15–22.
Bhattacharya, Tanmoy & Andrew Simpson. 2007. Argument prominence and the nature of superiority violations. In Eric J. Reuland, Tanmoy Bhattacharya & Giorgos Spathas (eds.), *Argument Structure*, 175–211. Amsterdam: John Benjamins Publishing Company.
Bickel, Balthasar. 2015. Distributional typology: statistical inquiries into the dynamics of linguistic diversity. In Bernd Heine & Helko Narrog (eds.), *The Oxford handbook of linguistic analysis*, 901–923. Oxford: Oxford University Press.
Blake, Barry. 2001. *Case*. Cambridge: Cambridge University Press.
Bossong, Georg. 1983–1984. Animacy and Markedness in Universal Grammar. 39 *Glossologia* 2-3: 7–20. Retrieved from http://www.rose.uzh.ch/seminar/personen/bossong/Bossong_39.pdf
Chatterji, Suniti K. 2002 [1926]. *The Origin and Development of the Bengali Language*. Reprint. New Delhi: Rupa & Company.
Creissels, Denis. 2009. Spatial cases. In Andrej Malchukov & Andrew Spencer (eds.), *The Oxford handbook of case*, 609–625. Oxford: Oxford University Press.
Dahl, Östen. 2008. Animacy and egophoricity: Grammar, ontology and phylogeny. *Lingua* 118 (2). 141–150.
Dahl, Östen & Kari Fraurud. 1996. Animacy in grammar and discourse. In Thorstein Fretheim & Jeanette K. Gundel (eds.), *Reference and Referent Accessibility*, 47–64. Amsterdam & Philadelphia: John Benjamins Publishing Company.
Dixon, Robert M. W. 1994. *Ergativity*. Cambridge: Cambridge University Press.

Grierson, George A. 1968 [1903]. *Linguistic Survey of India*. Vol. V. Reprint. Delhi: Motilal Banarsidass.
Hook, Peter E. 1979. Hindi Structures: Intermediate Level. *Michigan Papers on South and South East Asia* 16. Ann Arbor, MI: University of Michigan.
Kachru, Yamuna. 1976. On the semantics of the causative construction in Hindi/Urdu. In Masayoshi Shibatani (ed.), *The Grammar of Causative Constructions*, Vol 6 [Syntax and Semantics], 353–370. New York: Academic Press.
Kakati, Banikanta. 1941. *Assamese, Its formation and development*. Assam: Government of Assam in the department of Historical and Antiquarian studies. Retrieved from http://ena-jori.com/wp-content/uploads/2012/11/Assamese-Its-Formation-and-Development.pdf
Katre, Sumitra M. 1968. *Problems of reconstruction in Indo-Aryan*. Shimla: Indian Institute of Advanced Study.
Lahiri, Bornini. 2013. A typological study of Local cases of EIA languages. *Journal of Universal Language* 14 (1). 85–115.
Lazard, Gilbert. 1998. *Animacy*. Berlin & New York: Mouton de Gruyter.
Li, Chao. 2007. Split ergativity in Nepali and its typological significance. In *Proceedings of the 30th Annual Penn Linguistics Colloquium*. Vol 13. 169–182.
Longacre, Robert E. 1976. *An Anatomy of Speech Notions*. Michigan: Peter de Ridder Press.
Mahapatra, Bijay. P. 2007. *A Synchronic Grammar of Oriya* (Standard spoken and written). Mysore: Central Institute of Indian Languages.
Malchukov, Andrej L. 2008. Animacy and asymmetries in differential case marking. *Lingua* 118. 203–221.
Masica, Colin P. 1991.*The Indo-Aryan Languages*. Cambridge: Cambridge University Press.
Miller, George A. & Philip Johnson-Laird. 1976. *Language and Perception*. Cambridge, MA: Harvard University Press.
Mohanan, Tara. 1990. *Arguments in Hindi*. Stanford, CA: Stanford University doctoral dissertation.
Narrog, Heiko. 2009. A Diachronic Dimension in Maps of Case Functions. *Linguistic Discovery* 8 (1). 233–25.
Nilsen, Don L. F. 1973. *The instrumental case in English*. The Hague: Mouton.
Palancer, Enrique L. 2002. *The origin of agent markers. Studia typologica*, Vol 5. Berlin: Akademie Verlag.
Saksena, Anuradha. 1982. *Topics in the Analysis of Causatives: With an Account of Hindi Paradigms*. [University of California publications in linguistics]. Berkeley, CA: University of California Press.
Silverstein, Michael. 1976. Hierarchy of features and ergativity. In Robert M.W. Dixon (ed.), *Grammatical categories in Australian languages* II, 2–171. Canberra: Australian Institute of Aboriginal Studies, Linguistic Series 22.
Silverstein, Michael. 1981. Case marking and the nature of language. *Australian Journal of Linguistics* 1. 227–244.
Swart, Peter de, Monique Lamers & Sander Lestrade 2008. Animacy, argument structure, and argument encoding. *Lingua* 118. 131–140. Retrieved from http://www.sciencedirect.com/science/article/pii/S0024384107000307
Talmy, Leonard. 1983. How language structures space. In Herbet L. Pick & Linda P. Acredolo (eds.), *Spatial orientation: theory research and application*. 225–282 New York: Plenum Press.
Verbeke, Saartje, Leonid Kulikov & Klaas Willems. 2015. Oblique case-marking in Indo-Aryan experiencer constructions: Historical roots and synchronic variation. *Lingua* 163. 23–39.

Dörte Borchers
Participles with a semantic void in Koints

Abstract: Koints ([kɔĩts]; English: Sunwar, Sunuwar; Nepali: सुनुवार Sunuvār) is a Kiranti language spoken in eastern Nepal. With about 38,000 speakers, Koints is one the larger languages of the 123 languages of Nepal (Central Bureau of Statistics 2012: 164). The past tense participle paradigm of transitive verbs of Koints has a semantic void for a first person singular when the participle functions as main verb. Speakers of Koints fill this void spontaneously with the first person singular past tense form of the same lexeme. Koints finite past tense forms, which have person and number indexes of the subject, and forms from the past tense participle, which is not indexed for participants, are in general used interchangeably. It is hypothesized that the void and its filler might be a gap or a case of suppletion. The reason for the occurrence of the void, which always has the same filler, might be a language-internal rule of Koints. According to that rule, forms referring to first person subjects of transitive verbs are at least as finite or even more finite than those referring to other subjects. Finiteness refers in this context only to the morphological marking of participants. This qualitative study is based on data from Koints texts that different persons collected at different times in different locations in Nepal and on data from elicitations undertaken with three speakers of Koints during the past five years. It will be shown that the semantic void in the past tense participle's paradigm is a semantic gap rather than a case of suppletion, even though it has a regular filler. The gap is odd because it occurs with a large number of verbs, and is limited to only one function of a form that has several functions.

Keywords: Koints participle, Semantic void, Tibeto-Burman

1 Introduction

Koints is spoken in villages along the river *Likhu Khola*, about a hundred kilometres east of Nepal's capital Kathmandu (see Figure 1). The speakers of Koints and their children refer to themselves as *Koints* or *Kointsmur*, 'Koints' or 'Koints people'. There is some regional variation within the Koints language which does not

---

Dörte Borchers, University of Graz, Institute of Linguistics, 70 Merangasse, 8010 Graz, Austria.
Email: dborchers9@web.de

https://doi.org/10.1515/9783110753066-007

hinder communication (Rapacha 2009: 120). Rather, speakers of Koints are able to identify each other's place of origin based on their pronunciation.

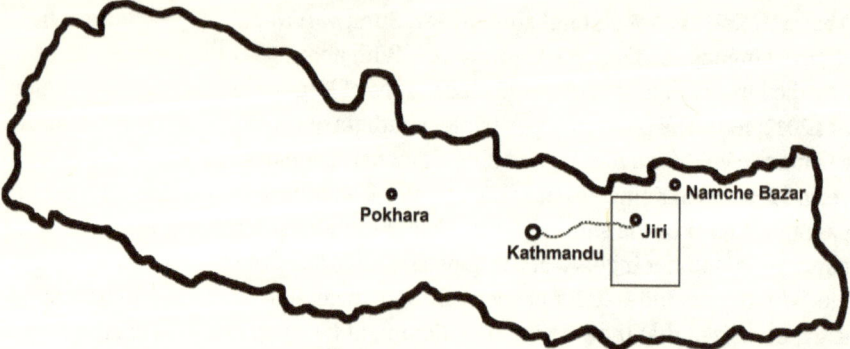

Fig. 1: Nepal, with the square indicating the area traditionally inhabited by Koints speakers

Koints verbs can be finite for tense and agreement. Traditionally, Koints indexed the subject and the object on the verb (Genetti 1988) but except for a few single occurrences in texts from the 1970s (Bieri, Schulze and Hale 1973) there is no evidence of that system in the few text collections.

Forms occurring abundantly in reports about past events belong to the finite past tense paradigm, in which the subject but not the object is indexed, or to the paradigm of the past tense participle.

Past tense participles show no person or number morphology. They can be main verbs and are then used interchangeably with finite past tense forms. A peculiarity of past tense participles is that such participles of transitive verbs have a semantic void for a first person singular (see for example 1a).[1] Koints speakers readily and uniformly fill the semantic void in the past participle's paradigm with a finite past tense verb form indexed for a first-person singular subject (see 1b). Past tense participles of intransitive verbs don't have this void – they can refer to a first person singular subject (see 1c). Morphologically, there is no difference between transitive and intransitive past tense participles.

---

[1] A Koints pronoun unmarked for plurality is unmarked for number and may refer to a singular, dual, or plural entity.

(1a) go   sil   pa -ʃo
     1   dance   do -PST.PTCP
     'We (DU/PL) danced.'
     (Borchers 2020; elicitation with speaker from Bhuji, Ramechap district)

(1b) go   sil   pa -taŋ
     1   dance   do -PST.1SG
     'I danced.' (not: 'We (PL) danced', or 'We (DU) danced')
     (Borchers 2020; elicitation with speaker from Bhuji, Ramechap district)

(1c) go   ip   -ʃo
     1   sleep -PST.PTCP
     'I slept.' or 'We (DU/PL) slept.'
     (Borchers 2020; elicitation with speaker from Bhuji, Ramechap district)

The past tense participle also functions as an adnominal modifier (see 2a) and as a noun (2b; cf. Borchers 2008: 192), and it may be followed by one of three copulas to express different evidential categories (DeLancey 1997; DeLancey 1997: 33–35, 43; see 2c).

The function of the past tense participle in a specific context is indicated by the syntax. Nominal modifiers precede a noun. A past tense participle employed as a noun may be preceded by a modifier and can have nominal affixes.

(2a) dom -ʃo   waiʃal -kali caklet
     be.fat -PST.PTCP   boy   -OBJ   chocolate
     blo   -ʃo   dum   -t
     taste.good -PST.PTCP   become -PST.3SG
     'The fat boy likes to eat chocolate [likes the taste of chocolate].'
     (Borchers 2018; elicitation with speaker from Saipu (Ramechap district))

(2b) dom -ʃo   -kal   caklet
     be.fat -PST.PTCP -OBJ   chocolate
     blo   -ʃo   dum   -t
     taste.good -PST.PTCP   become -PST.3SG
     'The fat one likes to eat chocolate [likes the taste of chocolate].'
     (Borchers 2018; elicitation with speaker from Saipu (Ramechap district))

(2c) go   sil   pa -ʃo   ba -ti
     1   dance   do -PST.PTCP   be -1SG.PST
     'I was dancing.' (speaker sees herself on TV or in a dream and is surprised)
     (Borchers 2020; elicitation with speaker from Bhuji (Ramechap district))

The void that occurs when the participle is used as main verb raises the questions of why there is a void at all, and why it is in the slot where it is.

One hypothesis is that the void and its filler are a case of a gap or of suppletion and might therefore be explained by causes for these phenomena. Another hypothesis is that there is a language-internal tendency in Koints to refer to first person singular subjects of transitive verbs by forms that are more finite than the forms referring to other participants.

This second hypothesis is based on the observation that in Genetti's (1988) data the first person singular form in the subject-indexing past tense paradigm takes the same subject and object indexes as the corresponding person in the biactantial paradigm (see Table 1 in section 2.1).

The term finite is used here to refer exclusively to morphologically expressed agreement, and not to other categories of finiteness such as tense for which the verb may be morphologically marked. The category of agreement is the one that is relevant for the second hypothesis. The term "degrees of morphological finiteness" refers here to the relative number of participants indexed on the verb. The term is used here in the same sense as used by Utz Maas (2004: 368), who speaks of degrees of morphological finiteness and thereby refers to valency that differs for different nominal and verbal lexemes. Koints verbs may agree with the subject and object, or with only the subject, or with no participant. Cross-linguistically, verbs of independent clauses are expected to be finite (Nikolaeva 2007a: 3, 169; Evans 2007: 366). The Koints past tense participle can be the main verb of a declarative clause despite being morphologically non-finite. Some might assume the presence of a silent copula following past tense participles, as suggested by a reviewer. Here, the presence of a silent copula is not assumed because the past tense participle, when used as main verb, may be substituted by a finite past tense form, and not by a participle with a finite copula. Non-finite main verbs of declarative clauses are cross-linguistically rare but they do occur in other languages too (Nikolaeva 2007b: 169–174).

In the following section, the literature about Koints past tense participles and about the Koints finite past tense paradigm will be reviewed, followed by a look at the literature about gaps and suppletion in paradigms. Section 3 informs about the data basis of the analysis. The analysis follows in section 4. A conclusion and a summary are presented in sections 5 and 6 respectively.

2 Literature review

Data on Koints have been collected at different times and different locations since the end of the 19th century. These data contain various verbal forms, among them finite past tense forms and non-finite past tense participles, which are used interchangeably to refer to past events.

In this section, the literature about past tense participles and about the finite past tense paradigm in Koints is reviewed first, followed by a look at literature about gaps and suppletion in verbal paradigms.

2.1 Koints past tense participles and finite past tense forms

Stan Konow (1909) was the first to identify and label the Koints finite past tense forms and past tense participle. Finite past tense forms have morphological tense and agreement markers. Past tense participles have no tense or agreement morphology; they are formed by suffixing the morpheme '-ʃo' to a verb stem (Konow 1909; Borchers 2008: 192–194). Konow also published Koints language data. He collected the data in the 19th century in Kathmandu (Nepal) and Sikkim (India), and pointed out that his sample text, a translation of a Bible text from English into Koints, shows features more typical of English than of a Kiranti language, for example with regard to word order. The text sample contains a few finite past tense forms but not enough to fill a complete paradigm. There are past tense participles of two verbs in Konow's text. Each of the participles is followed by a copula and none has a first person singular subject. The text thus shows that finite past tense verbal forms and past tense participles were already part of the language more than a hundred years ago, but there is no information about a possible semantic void in the past participle's paradigm.

Carol Genetti (1988) analysed Koints verbal paradigms with complex past tense forms, which are morphologically marked for person and number of both subject and object, as well as past tense forms with only subject indexes. Participles were not part of her study. Genetti's subject-indexing finite past tense paradigm has only one form for each person and number, except for a first person singular, for which there are several forms, and these are the same as those found in the complex paradigm in the corresponding first person singular subject slots (see Table 1). For indexing a first person singular subject therefore a choice had to be made according to the person and number of the object. This peculiarity is relevant for the following analysis.

Both existent descriptive grammars of Koints by Lal Rapacha (2005) and by Dörte Borchers (2008) discuss form and function of the Koints past tense participle and of the finite past tense and provide similar descriptions. The finite past tense paradigm has only subject and no object indexes. The participle functions as a nominal modifier (Rapacha 2005: 160, 202; Borchers 2008: 192–194). Borchers mentions explicitly that the past participle functions as a noun too, and that the past tense participle is used interchangeably with finite past tense forms (2008: 192–193). She mentions in a footnote that during elicitations of finite past tense forms speakers would offer past tense participles too. Borchers (2008: 193) also points out that past tense participles, when employed as main verb, never refer to a first person singular subject, but she does not say here that this is limited to participles of transitive verbs.

Table 1: The past tense participle and the finite past tense paradigm

Subject (person & number)	Finite transitive past tense person and number indexes (subject and object indexes) (Genetti 1988)[2]	Finite transitive past tense person and number indexes (subject indexes) (Genetti 1988)	Finite transitive past tense person and number indexes (subject indexes) (Borchers 2008)	Past tense participle (Borchers 2008)
1sg	-tān, -tānsi, -tānni (Object 1, 2, 3 dual) -tāŋ, -tāŋsi, -tāŋmi (Object 1, 2, 3 plural)		-ŋ	
2sg	(various)	-yi	-ī	-ʃo
3sg	(various)	-u	-u	-ʃo
1du	(various)	-sku	-sku	-ʃo
2du	(various)	-si	-si	-ʃo
3du	(various)	-s(e)	-s(e)	-ʃo
1pl	(various)	-k(a)	-k(a)	-ʃo
2pl	(various)	-ni	-ni	-ʃo
3pl	(various)	-m(e)	-m(e)	-ʃo

---

[2] The various non-first person singular indexes are not specified here because they would enlarge the table and are of no relevance in this context.

2.2 Paradigm gaps, and suppletion

A paradigmatic gap, or paradigmatic defectivity, is defined as the absence of morphological forms of lexemes of a specific class. The absent morphemes do not exist even though they could exist and would be expected to exist based on what is known about the morphology of the majority of lexemes belonging to the same category (Halle 1973: 5–6; Baronian and Kulinich 2012: 1; Daland, Sims and Pierrehumbert 2007: 943; Sims 2006: 7, 18; Sims 2015: 26). Gaps are often defined as a morphological phenomenon, but semantic gaps (Stump 2010: 207; Baerman and Corbett 2010: 2, 9) and syntactic gaps (Reis 2016: 261; Strobel and Weiß 2019: 112) are studied too.

Baerman and Corbett (2010: 2) point out that the detection of a gap depends on the limits of the lexical subset that is probed. In the case of Koints, a look exclusively at transitive verbs will not reveal a gap or a suppleted form but looking at all verbs shows that there is a large group of verbs, namely the transitive ones, with a void.

The occurrence of gaps may be semantically, pragmatically, morphologically, or phonologically motivated. Semantic defectiveness concerns verbs that due to their lexical meaning have no morphological form referring, for example, to a first person singular subject, like the Russian verb *šelestet* 'to rustle (of leaves)' (Sims 2006: 284–285). Instances of gaps due to semantic constraints can be found in many languages, and Sims (2006: 284–285) as well as Baerman and Corbett (2010: 2) ask whether such transparent cases can even count as cases of defectiveness. Other gaps can only be explained by language-specific morphological rules (Stump 2010: 192). Stump illustrates such rules with an example from Sanskrit. Several Sanskrit neuter nouns of the *an*-stem declension have no singular, dual or plural Nominative/Vocative/Accusative forms. This gap is filled with the corresponding forms of a synonymous noun, a process Stump (2010: 192) labels as borrowing. The domain of the gap, namely the singular, dual and plural Nominative/Vocative/Accusative forms, is determined by the syncretism of these forms in most neuter declensions in Sanskrit (Stump 2010: 192).

A frequent explanation for the persistence of gaps is that the gaps persist not for morphological reasons but because the forms that could fill the gaps occur rarely, and speakers are used to avoiding the gaps by using alternative forms (Daland, Sims and Pierrehumbert 2007: 936, 937, 943; Reis 2016: 258; Sims 2006: 18).

Suppletion, the occurrence of an unexpected and morphologically odd item in a paradigm, looks like a proper counterpart to a gap. One should, however, keep in mind that suppletion may also occur without the prior presence of a gap (Corbett 2007: 13–14).

Suppletion refers to cases in which the paradigm of a lexeme contains forms that are unexpected and unpredictable on the basis of the form inventory of other lexemes of the same category (Mel'čuk 2000: 510; Veselinova 2006: xv, 9). Like gaps or defectivity, cases of suppletion occur only with a limited number of lexemes of one lexical category.

Some linguists speak of suppletion only when a lexeme's stem is affected (Hippisley et al. 2004: 387), while others also speak of suppletion when inflectional affixes are concerned (Juge 1999: 183, 194; Veselinova 2006: xv; Mel'čuk 2000: 514), as in Koints.

Suppletion may be the result of sound change, analogy, or incursion (Juge 1999: 184; Pomino and Remberger 2019: 472, 474, 476). Suppletion is considered to be strong when the suppleted element shares no phonological features with regular elements in a paradigm, and weak when some phonological elements are shared (Mel'čuk 2000: 518; Veselinova 2006: 152; Veselinova 2015: 47; Juge 1999). Whether irregular forms are cases of suppletion or not is a matter of perspective. Unlike Veselinova (2006: 152–153), Juge (1999: 184) accepts irregular forms as cases of suppletion. He describes suppletion as a continuum from weak cases, including irregular forms, to strong cases.

Juge (1999) explores the concept of overlapping suppletion, in which forms of one lexeme occur in the paradigm of another lexeme, resulting in a syncretism of forms across lexemes. According to Juge (1999: 186), overlapping suppletion may happen to any paradigm, whether defective, suppletive or regular. What Juge (1999: 186) describes as overlapping suppletion in the case of a defective paradigm would be analysed by Stump (2010: 192) as a gap in a paradigm of one lexeme, which is filled with an item borrowed from a paradigm of another lexeme.

Corbett (2007) developed Juge's notion of overlapping suppletion further by differentiating instances in which the direction of suppletion is synchronically transparent from those in which it is not. Corbett labels instances in which the direction of suppletion is synchronically transparent "directional overlapping" and the opaque instances "nondirectional overlapping" (Corbett 2007: 26).

3 Data basis

This qualitative study is based on data from elicitations undertaken predominantly with three speakers of Koints from villages in the districts of Ramechap and Okhaldhunga during the past five years. These data are supplemented by data from three Koints text collections that were compiled at different times in different locations in Nepal.

The first text collection of 12 texts was compiled by Dora Bieri and Marlene Schulze (Bieri, Schulze and Hale 1973) in the 1960s and 1970s in the village of Sabra (Ramechap), another collection of four texts was compiled by Lal Rapacha (2005) between 1995 and 2001 with speakers from the villages Khiji, Ragani and Gorumare Bhanjyang (Okhaldhunga), and from Sikkim (India), and the third collection of 18 texts was compiled by Borchers (2008) with speakers from the villages of Saipu (Ramechap), Bhuji (Ramechap) and Khiji (Okhaldhunga).

The text collections contain material on a variety of themes, such as culture, recent events, mythology, recipes and so on. For this study, texts referring to past events were used because these predominantly contain past tense participles and finite past tense forms. Texts about general procedures, about mythology or about the future contain none or almost none of these forms and were therefore excluded. From the collection of Bieri and Schulze four texts (1, 1A, 2, 3) were included, none from the collection by Rapacha and three (15, 16, 18) from the collection by Borchers.

In the texts, finite past tense forms and past tense participles used as main verbs were counted with the aim to find out whether texts with first person narrators have, as expected, a different proportion of finite past tense forms and past tense participles used as main verbs than non-first person narrations.

Elicitation sessions took place in the house of two speakers in Kathmandu, and with the third speaker in her house in Kathmandu and recently in spring 2020 via Skype. During elicitation sessions, the acceptability and the meaning of different constructions with past tense participles and finite past tense forms with varying subjects and verbs was tested.

(3a) go   umtsili tʰiẽ   bara   bars- -ṅā
     I   small   be.PST.1SG   twelve year   -GEN
     'I was small, only twelve years old.'

(3b) ã̄   bara   bars -ma mina āma   be   -ʃo
     1POSS   twelve year -LOC and   mother   die -PST.PTCP
     'I was twelve years old and then my mother died.'

(3c) āma   be -m   patshʰi boge   -m   tʰul -ʃo
     mother   die -NMLZ after   grandmother -ERG feed -PST.PTCP
     'My grandmother raised me after mother's death.'

(3d) māma   maigyu -mī   tʰul -ʃo   meke -le
     uncle aunt   -ERG   feed -PST.PTCP   there -from
     'Since then, I was raised by my uncle and aunt.'

(3e) min go māma hoṅkoṅ   -mī tʰiyo
     and I   uncle Hongkong -LOC be.PST.3SG
     'Later my uncle was in Hong Kong.'

(3f) māma hoṅkoṅ   -mī tʰiyo   minu pʰeri ã̄   -kal
     uncle Hongkong -LOC be.PST.3SG and again 1POSS -OBJ
     māma -mī māma ā-   kāka   kʰĩ   -mī hoi -tu
     uncle -ERG uncle his- paternal.uncle house -LOC keep -PST.3SG
     'My uncle later went to Hong Kong. He (took) me in and my uncle kept (me) at his uncle's house.'
     (Borchers 2008: 253-255; text 16: Uttar Kumar Sunuvar's live)

(4a) go -puki ake -le   la -ʃa ṅa mina, saber
     I -PL   here -from go -PF and then a.few.days.ago
     'mar 'pa -ʃo   dēn -ʃa hana, erikʰa monikʰa
     what do -PST.PTCP say -PF if   Erika Monika
     go -puki sān   ake -le   hawaydzãdz -m dziri dzam la -ʃo
     I -PL   three here -from plane   -LOC Jiri to   go -PST.PTCP
     'Now let's see what we did when we left from here a few days ago. The three of us, Erika, Monika, and I, went by plan from here to Jiri.'

(4b) mekele meko nãʔdo 'ip   -ʃo
     there that night sleep -PST.PTCP.
     'There we slept that night.'

(4c) minu asuni   bōʔ   -ʃa ṅa mina,
     and next.morning get.up -PF and then
     kur -b   mur mal -ʃa, sabra gãʔ -tsa tʰale   -ʃo
     carry -NPST.PTCP man search -PF Sabra walk -INF begin -PST.PTCP
     'And having gotten up the next morning, and having searched for porters, we started to walk towards Sabra.'
     (Bieri, Schulze and Hale 1973: 435-440; text 1a: The language helper reports on a survey trip in the Sabra area)[3]

Examples (3) and (4) present the first phrases of two texts that illustrate in context the use of past tense participles used as main verbs. These participles are not preceded by a finite copula, the scope of which might apply to them. The text samples show that both texts have first person singular narrators talking about their own activities.

---

[3] The transcription and the glosses of this text have been slightly adapted to the transcription and glosses in Borchers (2008) in order to avoid confusion.

The study of Koints texts showed that, contrary to expectation, Koints texts (Bieri, Schulze and Hale 1973; Borchers 2008) about past events with first person narrators talking about their own activities do not in general contain relatively more finite past tense forms than past tense participles.

4 Analysis

Before this study, it was known that past tense participle and finite past tense forms can be used interchangeably. Past tense participles of transitive Koints verbs have a semantic void for the first person singular subject, when the participle is used as a main verb. The only filler of this void is the first person singular of the finite past tense paradigm.

It was hypothesized that the void in Koints might be a gap or its filler might be a suppleted form. Compared with paradigmatic gaps and suppletion discussed in the literature, the first person singular void in the past tense participle's paradigm is odd. The void occurs regularly with a large number of verbs and has only one filler. The paradigmatic gaps mentioned, for example, in Sims' study (2006: 18), tend to have two or more possible fillers, which are avoided by speakers. The filler of the void in the Koints participle's paradigm shares the lexical stem and thereby phonological and morphological material with other items in the paradigm, and the form of the filler is easily analysable. This is different from regular cases of suppletion (Veselinova 2006: 14). Even though the same form occurs in Koints in two verbal paradigms, this is different from overlapping suppletion (Juge 1999) because the paradigms that share a form in Koints belong to the same lexeme.

The interpretation of the void's filler as a suppleted form becomes less convincing when we consider the fact that transitive verbs do have a morphological form of a past tense participle that refers to a first person singular. This form occurs with a following copula (see example (2c)). When the participle is followed by a copula, the participle cannot be replaced by a finite past tense form (see example (5)). Additionally, when the participle is used with its adnominal or nominal function, it cannot be replaced by a finite past tense form. This shows that the finite past tense form is not generally an alternative to the participle referring to a first person singular, but replaces the participle only in one of its functions. The existence of the morphological form of a past tense participle that, when followed by a copula, may refer to a first person singular also shows that the void is not a phonological or morphological one but a semantic one.

(5) *go sil pa -taŋ   ba -ti
    1   dance do -PST.1SG be -1SG.PST
(Borchers 2020 elicitation with speaker from Bhuji, Ramechap district)

The second hypothesis formulated earlier concerns the motivation for the void. It was mentioned that the void in Koints is motivated by a language-internal rule. Such a language-internal motivation is a criterion for a regular gap according to Baerman and Corbett (2010: 2) and Sims (2006: 284–285). According to the language-internal rule, past tense main verbs have first person singular forms that are at least as or more finite than corresponding forms referring to other participants.

The basis for formulating this rule is data collected by Genetti (1988). Genetti (1988) presents two transitive verbal paradigms that share the forms for a first person singular subject. In one of the paradigms, the verb is marked morphologically for subject and object, while in the other the verb is marked only for subject. In the latter paradigm, the first person singular slot has six fillers, which also index the object (see Table 1). In other words, the complex past tense paradigm and the subject-only indexing paradigm share the forms for first person singular subjects, just like the transitive past tense participle (when used as a main verb) and the finite past tense paradigm share the form for a first person singular subject. Different degrees of finiteness within the same paradigm seem not to have been reported from other languages. This phenomenon clearly occurs in Koints and has been documented for two different paradigms at different locations and two different points in time.

The analysis of the void in Koints shows that it is an odd gap and that its filler is not a good example of a suppleted form. The oddity of the void leads to questions about its historical emergence and about similar odd voids in other languages. Was the void always there? Do other languages have voids that on the one hand occur with a large number of lexemes, and on the other hand are so limited that they concern only one of several functions of a form? And do other languages have verbal paradigms showing different degrees of morphologically marked finiteness with regard to person and number agreement?

For Koints there are no historical data to document the emergence of the past tense participle. Nothing can be said about the development or about the persistence of the void in Koints. Should it have existed for a long time, then the reason would probably not be an avoidance strategy as observed in other languages (Daland, Sims and Pierrehumbert 2007: 936, 937, 943; Sims 2006: 18), since the void is regularly filled with the same morphological form.

5 Conclusion

It seems unlikely that Koints is the only language with an odd void. For a better understanding of the typological status of such a void as in Koints, a cross-linguistic study of similar voids might be helpful. The Surrey Typological Database on Defectiveness (Baerman, Brown and Corbett 2009) is a very useful tool for such a language comparison, and the database does contain one example of a gap that resembles the void in Koints on the surface. The example comes from Tamashek (Afro-Asiatic, Berber), and the source of the information in the database is Heath (2005). In Tamashek, stative or adjectival verbs are expected to have a first person plural form that is homophonous with the form for the third person singular from the same paradigm. However, that form refers exclusively to a third person singular, and cannot refer to a first person plural. Reference to a first person plural is expressed by one of two alternative forms. The gap in Talashek is clearly not morphologically or phonologically motivated but seems to be the result of homophony avoidance (Heath 2005 cited according to Baerman, Brown and Corbett 2009). This example from Tamashek shows that other languages have gaps that resemble the one in Koints but the differences are obvious too.

The gap in Tamashek does not have a single filler, it has nothing to do with finiteness, and its language-internal motivation differs from the one in Koints.

A comparative study with data from more languages is desirable, and such a typological study of similarly odd voids could also contribute to exploring and redefining the edges of the concepts of gaps and suppletion.

6 Summary

The Koints past tense participle is employed as the main verb of clauses and is in this function used interchangeably with finite past tense forms (see Table 1), with one exception. The past tense participle of a transitive verb cannot refer to a first person singular subject. The past tense participle has in this case a void that is regularly filled with a finite first person singular form. This void is an odd gap because it occurs with all transitive verbs, and its filler is a form from a different paradigm of the same verb.

In Koints, there are more examples of verbal paradigms, in which first person singular subject forms of transitive verbs are more finite than forms indexed for other participants (see section 2.1). There is no phonological or syntactic reason for the odd gap but there seems to be a language-internal rule of Koints that forms referring to first person subjects of transitive verbs are at least as finite or even more finite than those referring to other subjects.

Abbreviations

DU=dual; ERG=ergative; GEN=genitive; LOC=locative; NMLZ=nominalizer; NPST=nonpast; OBJ=object; PL=plural; POSS= possessive; PST=past; PTCP=participle; SG=singular; 1=first person; 3=third person

Transliteration

The Koints data are presented by a broad transcription using symbols of the international phonetic alphabet with two exceptions. Vowel length is represented here by a line above the vowel sign, for example /ā/, and the velar nasal is represented by the sign for a dental nasal with a dot above /ṅ/.

Acknowledgements

I thank an anonymous reviewer for critical comments on an earlier version of this paper.

References

Baerman, Matthew, Dunstan Brown & Greville G. Corbett. 2009. *Surrey Typological Database on Defectiveness*. University of Surrey. http://dx.doi.org/10.15126/SMG.21/1; http://www.smg.surrey.ac.uk/defectiveness/typological (10 Septemebr 2020)

Baerman, Matthew & Greville Corbett. 2010. Introduction: Defectiveness: Typology and Diachrony. Defective paradigms: Missing forms and what they tell us. In Matthew Baerman, Greville G. Corbett & Dunstan P. Brown (eds.), *Defective Paradigms: missing forms and what they tell us*, 1–18. Oxford: Oxford University Press.

Baronian, Luc & Elena Kulinich. 2012. Paradigm gaps in Whole Word Morphology. In Thomas Stolz, Hitomi Otsuka, Aina Urdze & Johan van der Auwera, (eds.), *Irregularity in Morphology (and beyond)*, Studia Typologica 11, 81–100. Berlin: Akademie Verlag.

Bieri, Dora, Marlene Schulze & Austin Hale. 1973. An Approach to Sunwar Discourse. In Austin Hale (ed.), *Clause, Sentence, and Discourse Patterns in selected languages of Nepal*, 433–462. Norman: Summer Institute of the University of Oklahoma.

Borchers, Dörte. 2008. *A Grammar of Sunwar. Descriptive grammar, paradigms, texts and glossary* [Languages of the Greater Himalayan Region 7]. Leiden: Brill Publications.

Central Bureau of Statistics. 2012. *National Population and Housing Census 2011* (National Report). Kathmandu: Government of Nepal, National Planning Commission Secretariat. https://unstats.un.org/unsd/demographic/sources/census/wphc/Nepal/Nepal-Census-2011-Vol1.pdf (accessed 21 March 2017).

Corbett, Greville G. 2007. Canonical Typology, Suppletion, and Possible Words. *Language* 83(1). 8–42.

Daland, Robert, Andrea D. Sims & Janet Pierrehumbert. 2007. Much ado about nothing. A social network model of Russian paradigmatic gaps. In Annie Zaenen & Antal van den Bosch (eds.), *Proceedings of the 45th Annual Meeting of the Association of Computational Linguistics*, 936–943. Prague: Association for Computational Linguistics. https://www.aclweb.org/anthology/P07-1.pdf (2020-07_15).

DeLancey, Scott. 1992. Sunwar copulas. *Linguistics of the Tibeto-Burman Area* 15(1). 31–38.

DeLancey, Scott. 1997. Mirativity: The grammatical marking of unexpected information. *Linguistic Typology* 1(1). 33–52. DOI: https://doi.org/10.1515/lity.1997.1.1.33 (accessed 30 June 2020).

Evans, Nicholas. 2007. Insubordination and its uses. In Irina Nikolaeva (ed.), *Finiteness: Theoretical and Empirical Foundations*, 366–431. New York: Oxford University Press.

Genetti, Carol. 1988. Notes on the structure of the Sunwari transitive verb. *Linguistics of the Tibeto-Burman Area*. 11(2). 62–92.

Halle, Morris. 1973. Prolegomena to a theory of word formation. *Linguistic Inquiry* 4(1). 3–16. https://pdfs.sematicscholar.org/2054/4d69621d6846d369e62458b2495618e7d7b8.pdf (accessed 19 June, 2020).

Hippisley, Andrew, Marina Chumakina, Greville G. Corbett & Dunstan Brown. 2004. Suppletion: frequency, categories and distribution of stems. *Studies in Language* 28. 387–418.

Juge, Matthew L. 1999. On the rise of suppletion in verbal paradigms. *Berkeley Linguistics Society* 25. 183–194.

Konow, Stan. 1909. Sunwār or Sunuwār. In George Abraham Grierson (ed.), *Linguistic survey of India III: Tibeto-Burman family, Part I: General introduction, specimens of the Tibetan dialects, the Himalayan dialects, and the North Assam group*, 198–205. Calcutta (Kolkata): Superintendent of Government Printing, India, http://dsal.uchicago.edu/books/lsi/lsi.php?volume=3-1&pages=670#page/29/mode/1up (accessed 18 March 2019).

Maas, Utz. 2004. "Finite" and "nonfinite" from a typological perspective. *Linguistics* 42(2). 359–385.

Mel'čuk, Igor. 2000. Suppletion. In Geert Booji, Christian Lehmann & Joachim Mugdan (eds.), *Morphologie. Ein internationales Handbuch zur Flexion und Wortbildung* 1, 510–522. Berlin & New York: de Gruyter.

Nikolaeva, Irina. 2007a. Introduction. In Irina Nikolaeva (ed.), *Finiteness: Theoretical and Empirical Foundations*, 1–19. New York: Oxford University Press.

Nikolaeva, Irina. 2007b. Constructional economy and nonfinite independant clauses. In Irina Nikolaeva (ed.), *Finiteness: Theoretical and Empirical Foundations*, 138–180. New York: Oxford University Press.

Pomino, Natascha & Eva-Maria Remberger. 2019. Verbal suppletion in romance synchrony and diachrony: the perspective of distributed morphology, *Transactions of the Philological Society* 117(3). 471–497; doi: 10.1111/1467-96X.121 https://onlinelibrary.wiley.com/doi/full/10.1111/1467-968X.12170 (accessed 18 August 2020).

Rapacha, Lal Shankyarelu. 2005. *A descriptive grammar of Kirānti-Kōits*. New Delhi, India: Jawaharlal Nehru University doctoral dissertation.
Rapacha, Lal. 2009. *Vanishing Ethnicity, Cultures and Languages of Nepal*. Kathmandu: Institute of Kirantology.
Reis, Marga. 2017. Grammatische Variation und realistische Grammatik. In Marek Konopka & Angelika Wöllstein (eds.), *Grammatische Variation. Empirische Zugänge und theoretische Modellierung*, 255–282. Berlin & Boston: de Gruyter.
Sims, Andrea. 2006. *Minding the gaps: Inflectional defectivity in a paradigmatic theory*. Graduate School of The Ohio State University dissertation https://linguistics.osu.edu/sites/linguistics.osu.edu/files/Sims_dissertation_2006.pdf. (accessed 20 June 2020).
Sims, Andrea. 2015. *Inflectional Defectivity* [Cambridge Studies in Linguistics]. Cambridge: Cambridge University Press.
Strobel, Thomas & Helmut Weiß. 2019. Von sprachlichen und nicht-sprachlichen Lücken. In Gerrit Kentner, Frank Kügler, Beata Moskal & Stavros Skopeteas (eds.), *Tweets 'n greets for Caroline Féry on the occasion of her farewell from Goethe-University Frankfurt*, 111–117. https://www.linguistik-in-frankfurt.de/blog/wp-content/uploads/2019/09/Tweet-n-greets_CarolineFery.pdf (accessed 4 September 2020).
Stump, Gregory. 2010. Interactions between defectiveness and syncretism. In Matthew Baerman, Greville G. Corbett & Dunstan P. Brown (eds.), *Defective Paradigms: Missing forms and what they tell us*, 181–210. Oxford: Oxford University Press.
Veselinova, Ljuba N. 2006. Suppletion in verb paradigms: Bits and pieces of a puzzle. Amsterdam: John Benjamins.
Veselinova, Ljuba N. 2013. Suppletion According to Tense and Aspect. In Matthew S. Dryer & Martin Haspelmath (eds.), *The World Atlas of Language Structures Online*. Leipzig: Max Planck Institute for Evolutionary Anthropology. http://wals.info/chapter/79 (accessed 29 June 2020).

Ghanshyam Sharma
Competition between vectored verbs and factored verbs in Hindi-Urdu, Marathi and Gujarati

Abstract: In this paper, we present a comparison of Hindi-Urdu verb-verb sequences with those of Marathi and Gujarati. Although such sequences in Marathi and Gujarati are less frequent than they are in Hindi-Urdu, there are good evidence for their proliferation – at least in Marathi – over the past six or seven centuries (Hook 1991; Pardeshi 2021). Assuming that the expansion in their use and scope continues along a path similar to the paths taken by Hindi-Urdu and Panjabi (Marathi and Gujarati's more compound-verb-rich peers), the paper makes use of the differences between verb-verb sequences in the three languages as a way to sketch a scenario for the replacement of factored verbs by vectored verbs over time and put forward an explanation for that gradual replacement as being the consequence of the progressive assumption of more abstract semantic and grammatical functions by unmarked vector verbs like *de-* GIVE and *le- / ghe-* TAKE. As shown in many studies such gradual replacements are a typical feature of grammaticalization: more specific lexical phenomena yield over time to encroachment by more general – hence more abstract – grammatical ones (Andersen 2003; Harris and Campbell 1995; Hopper and Traugott 1993).

Keywords: Vectored verbs, Factored verbs, Hindi-Urdu, Marathi, Gujarati

1 Introduction

Before we embark on the main topic of this paper – i.e. a comparison of Hindi-Urdu verb-verb complexes with those of Marathi and Gujarati – it would be worthwhile looking at the complex yet widespread phenomenon of verb-verb sequences in New Indo-Aryan languages. The verb-verb sequences in these languages – variously called "compound verbs" or "explicator compound verbs" by South Asian linguists – come in at least three flavors: vectored compound verbs, factored compound verbs and serialized compound verbs.

Ghanshyam Sharma, INALCO, 65 rue de Grands Moulins, Paris 13, France.
Email : hindi.paris@gmail.com

1.1 Three types of V1-V2 complexes

1.1.1 Vectored verb complexes

A vectored compound verb is one in which the main verb – also known as the "polar verb"[1] – is followed by one of the semantically bleached vectors[2] (or vector verbs). Published lists of such vector verbs attested in New Indo-Aryan languages vary somewhat from language to language, but typically include a number of items etymologically and phonologically corresponding to basic main verbs.[3] When employed as vectors, these items assign to V-V complexes, among others, meanings such as GO, COME, GIVE, TAKE, POUR, PUT or THROW, FALL, GET UP, SIT DOWN, MOVE, DIE, KILL, KEEP, RELEASE or LET GO.[4] These items are homophonous with lexical main verbs in that they both convey their primary meaning as main verbs and as vectors function like semantically bleached light verbs. Compare the examples (1a) and (1b) from Hindi-Urdu:

(1a) Simple verb: *jā-* 'go'
 bāhar   jāo.
 outside go-2IMP
 'Go outside!'

(1b) Vectored compound verb: *ā-* 'come' + *jā-* 'GO'
 andar   ā   jāo.
 inside come GO-2IMP
 'Come inside!'

The Hindi-Urdu verb *jā-* 'go' conveys its primary lexical meaning as a main verb in (1a), whereas its homophonous form is employed as a bleached vector in (1b), not contributing any lexical element to the overall verbal construction. These vector verbs may superficially be called "auxiliaries" because, instead of typically adding their primary lexical meaning to the compound constructions, they enrich them with some semantic or pragmatic ingredients which have to do with

---

1 The term "polar verb" was introduced by Dasgupta (1977).
2 The term "vector" was first introduced in Pray (1970) and then adopted by Hook (1974).
3 According to Slade (2021: 271), Hindi has 12 vectors: *de* 'GIVE', *jā* 'GO', *ā* 'COME', *paṛ* 'FALL', *baiṭh* 'SIT', *ḍāl* 'PUT', 'THROW', *le* 'TAKE', *rakh* 'KEEP', *uṭh* 'RISE', *cal* 'MOVE', *mar* 'DIE', *mār* 'KILL'.
4 In this paper we use capitals to represent semantically bleached vector verbs and normal case to represent factor verbs. However, unlike different letter shapes, differences between factor and vector are not always clear-cut.

Aktionsart and argument structure etc., even though they do not behave in the same manner as auxiliaries in many European languages, especially English. Let us consider some more examples from Hindi-Urdu:

(2a) Simple verb: *ā-* 'come'
 are suno, dūdhwālā āyā hai.
 hey listen-IMP.2PL milkman come-PFV.M.SG be.PRS.SG
 'Hey listen, the milkman has come (i.e. is here).'
(2b) Vectored verb complex: *ā-* 'come' + *jā-* 'GO'
 are suno, dūdhwālā ā gayā hai.
 hey listen-IMP.2PL milkman come GO.PFV.M.SG be.PRS.SG
 'Hey listen, the milkman has come (i.e. finally or unexpectedly).'

The Hindi-Urdu example in (2a) shows a simple verb, namely *ā-* 'come', whereas the example (2b) exhibits the polar verb *ā-* 'come' followed by the vector verb *jā-* 'GO'. Needless to say that the vector *jā-* 'GO' in (2b), quite the opposite of *ā-* 'come', does not add any lexical element to the overall structure of the compound verb except determining an aspectual profile of the compound construction in question. As mentioned above, the exact number of the vector verbs varies from language to language in the group of New Indo-Aryan languages. In general, most of the V2s in a vectored compound construction exhibit a consonant transitivity matching characteristic – i.e. transitive vectors come with transitive main verbs and intransitive vectors come with intransitive main verbs – although exceptions to this generalization can also be found. For example, some intransitive Hindi vectors such as *jā-* 'GO' or *baiṭh-* 'SIT' can show up with the transitive main verbs such as *khā-* 'eat' or *pī-* 'drink' as in (3a) and (3b) respectively. Similarly, some transitive vectors such as *le* 'TAKE' and *de* 'GIVE' can be seen in concert with a handful of intransitive main verbs such as *baiṭh-* 'sit', *so-* 'sleep' and *muskurā-* 'smile', as in (3c), (3d) and (3e) respectively:

(3a) Vectored verb complex: V1 transitive + V2 intransitive
 *śer use mārkar **khā gayā**.*
 lion him kill.ABS eat GO.PFV.M.SG
 'The lion killed and ate him up.'
 http://ayodhyap.blogspot.com/2013/05/blog-post_3465.html
(3b) Vectored verb complex: V1 transitive + V2 intransitive
 śāndār jīt se utsāhit ṭīm kahī̃ holī khelne me magn
 beautiful victory for excited team may be Holi play.OBL in engrossed

        *hote   bhāg   na **pī**   baiṭhe.*
        be.PRT cannabis not drink SIT.SUBJ.SG
        'Excited by the spectacular victory, lest the team drink cannabis while engrossed in playing Holi.'
        https://www.jagran.com/blogs/sadguruji/भारतीय-टीम-शानदार-जीत-के-स/

(3c) Vectored verb complex: V1 intransitive + V2 transitive
        ittī   dūr   āe   ho,   to
        that much distant come.PFV be.2PL then
        *pal-bhar   mere ghar   bhī **baiṭh lo**.*
        moment-just my house also sit TAKE.2.IMP
        'If you have come this far, then sit at my house for a moment.'
        http://www.hindisamay.com/premchand%20samagra/karm-bhoomi/karmbhoomi.htm

(3d) Vectored verb complex: V1 intransitive + V2 transitive
        *ṭhanḍ lage to   oṛh-ke   **so**   **lo**.*
        cold have then cover with-ABS sleep TAKE.2.IMP
        'If it is cold, then cover yourself up (with it) and sleep.'
        http://www.hindisamay.com/upanyas/dukkham-sukkham-mamta-kaliya/dukkham-sukkham-2.htm

(3e) Vectored verb complex: V1 intransitive + V2 transitive
        *Saṅgītā **muskurā dī**.*
        Saṅgītā smile GIVE.PFV.F.SG
        'Sangeeta smiled.'
        http://atmkatha3.blogspot.com/2014/12/blog-post_19.html

While discussing a vectored complex, we need to bear in mind a few more considerations. First, regardless of the type of V2 – i.e. whether it is a transitive or an intransitive verb – the vectored compound as a whole remains a monoeventive construct as we have seen in (1b), (2b) and (3a)–(3e) above. As it can be seen, *jā-* 'GO' in (1b), (2b) and (3a), *baiṭh-* 'SIT' in (3b), *le-* 'TAKE' in (3c) and (3d), and *de-* 'GIVE' in (3e) do not supply any new event or state of affair to the vectored compound. Second, vectors do not normally appear before the main verb, i.e. in a reversed order, as is the case with several factored verb complexes, which we will discover later. However, some rare exceptions to this generalization can be found in sentence examples such as the following one where a vectored verb complex *mār de-* 'hit + give' is materialized in a reversed order, i.e. *de mār-* 'give + hit':

(4)   *... mā   kā mobāil uṭhāyā   aur   jor   se*
     ...mother of mobile pick up.PFV.M.SG and force with

dīvār par **de**   **mārā**.
wall on GIVE hit.PFV.M.SG
'(He) picked up mother's mobile and hit it hard on the wall.'
http://kuchehsaas.blogspot.com/2008_04_01_archive.html

1.1.2 Factored verb complexes

A factored verb-verb complex, on the other hand, is one in which the second component – the factor verb – has retained to a greater degree its primary lexical sense, which contributes to the overall meaning of the verb-verb complex. To figure out the identifying characteristics of factored compounds, let us examine the following sentence examples from Hindi-Urdu:

(5a) Simple verb: *bhāg* 'run'
    qaidī   qaid se   bhāgā.
    prisoner prison from run.PFV.M.SG
    'The prisoner fled/ran away from the prison.'
(5b) Simple verb: *nikal* 'go/come out' or 'exit'
    qaidī   qaid se   niklā.
    prisoner prison from come out.PFV.M.SG
    'The prisoner came out of the prison.'
(5c) Factored verb complex: *bhāg* 'run' + *nikal* 'come/go out' or 'exit'
    qaidī   qaid se   **bhāg** **niklā**.
    prisoner prison from run   come out.PFV.M.SG
    'The prisoner escaped (running) from the prison.'

While *bhāg-* 'run' and *nikal-* 'come out, go out, exit' are used as simple verbs in (5a) and (5b) respectively, in (5c) the main verb *bhāg-* 'run' picks *nikal-* 'go out, exit' as a factor verb which retains its primary meaning. Remarkably, V2 in this example adds a semantic component which makes it as if it were the main verb, rather than a factor verb. In actual fact, the verb "exit" is the principle component rather than "run". In view of this, it can be argued that a factored compound verb is significantly different from a vectored compound verb as, unlike the latter, an overall meaning of the former is typically composed of elements supplied by both V1 and V2, as can be seen in the case of *bhāg-* 'run' and *nikal-* 'come out, go out, exit' in (5c). Hence, the blended meaning of this verb complex is "escaped".

Furthermore, although both the vectored and factored verbs are monoclausal and monoeventive, their internal structures are notably different from one another. For example, at times the meaning of V1 in a factored complex is similar to the meaning of a manner adverbial attested in expressions such as *bhāgte hue niklā* 'went out running' or an absolutive participial construction such as *bhāgkar niklā* 'went out having run' as in (5c). Notice that this is never the case with a vectored compound verb construction.

This being said, the meaning of V1 in examples such as (5c) cannot be deemed to be completely identical with a manner adverbial such as *bhāgte hue niklā* 'went out running'. In truth, actions of "running" and "coming out" are blended into one. This blended semantic construct necessarily contains some degree of idiomaticity which gives rise to a new concept meaning, namely "escape". It does not necessarily mean that the prisoner left the prison "running", for he might have escaped it stealthily! Similarly, he might have left the prison on a motorbike or a helicopter provided to him by a conspirator. Hence, such constructions should be called factored compound verbs and differentiated from other types of V1-V2 complexes.

Notice also that the simple verbs *bhāg-* 'run' and *nikal-* 'go out, come out', in (5a) and (5b) respectively, can both be employed as V1, and have a vector V2 as well, thereby producing vectored compound verbs as in (6a) and (6b). In such circumstances, while V1 retains its lexical meaning, the contribution of V2 as a vector to the verbal construction as a whole can be understood in terms of Aktionsart or argument structure only as it does not add any lexical ingredient to the verb complex:

(6a) Vectored verb complex: *bhāg* 'run' + *paṛ* 'FALL'
 ham ḍar gae aur haṛbaṛāhat mẽ **bhāg paṛe**.
 we fear GO.PFV.M.PL and panic in run FALL.PFV.M.PL
 'We got scared and fled in panic.'
 http://www.abhivyakti-hindi.org/kahaniyan/2014/chor.htm

(6b) Vectored verb complex: *nikal* 'go/come out' + *paṛ* 'FALL'
 sab sāmān lekar Bīrbal agle din nagar se **nikal**
 all goods take-ABS Birbal next day city from come out
 paṛe.
 FALL.PFV.M.PL
 'Taking all the goods, Birbal left the city the next day.'
 http://gaunkichaupal.blogspot.com/2010_09_01_archive.html

Another distinguishing characteristic of a factored verb complex is that, as mentioned above, sometimes we can find the V1-V2 sequences in a reversed order whereas in the case of a vectored verb complex this is extremely rare, as we have seen above in (4). Thus, we can find a standard factored V1 and V2 sequence *bhāg nikal*, 'run + exit', in (7a) in a reversed sequence *nikal bhāg*, 'exit + run' in (7b):

(7a) Factored verb complex: *bhāg-* 'run' + *nikal-* 'come/go out, exit'
 vah bhī tīnõ   bhāiyõ ke sāth **bhāg niklā**.⁵
 he   also the.three brothers together run   exit.PFV.M.SG
 'He too, together with the three bothers ran away.'

(7b) Factored verb complex with reversed order: *nikal* 'come out' + *bhāg* 'run'
 vah maukā dekh beṭe ke sāth asptāl se **nikal bhāgā**.
 he occasion see son with   hospital from exit run.PFV.M.SG
 'Seeing the opportunity, he ran away from the hospital with his son.'
 http://anvarat.blogspot.com/2011_07_01_archive.html

Therefore, the reversibility of V1 and V2 sequence can be considered to be one of the not quite widespread yet hugely important characteristics of a factored verb complex. This phenomenon of reversed verb sequence in factored verb complex requires a detailed survey of the data. Nevertheless, it can be affirmed that, for the most part, the reversed order is the result of emphasis laid by the speaker or writer. A close scrutiny of the following two data sets reveals that the examples (8b) and (9b) in fact carry some kind of emphasis (i.e. speaker or writer's astonishment, etc.) which is absent in (8a) and (9a):

(8a) ek din dhobī   ke ghar mẽ koī cor **ghus āyā**.
 one day washerman of house in one thief enter come.PFV.M.SG
 'One day a thief broke into the washerman's house.'
 http://dadimaakikahaniyan.blogspot.com/2011_01_01_archive.html

(8b) nadī se   nikalkar   rihāyasī ilāke mẽ ā   **ghusā**
 river from come out.ABS residential area in come enter.PFV.M.SG
 magarmacch.
 crocodile.M.SG
 'Out of the river, a crocodile broke in the residential area.'
 https://hindi.news18.com/news/bihar/west-champaran-crocodile-entered-in-residential-area-of-bagha-in-bihar-bramk-3175674.html

(9a) (vo) miṭṭī se bhare jūte   andar hī **ghusā**   **lāyā**.   Oh!
 (he) dirt of filled shoes inside emp cause.to.enter bring.PFV.M.SG Oh!
 '(He) has brought shoes filled with dirt inside. Oh!'
 APC Pushpak (Hindi Textbook) - Class 2, P. 67

(9b) jā̃c ke bīc cunāv kahā̃ se **lā** **ghusāyā**.
 probe of middle election where from bring cause.to.enter.PFV.M.SG

---

5 *Čičo* in *čā̃dnī rātē – sahāyak pustak mālā*. New Delhi: Hemkunt Press, p. 18.

'From where have you brought the (question of) election amid the investigation?'
https://twitter.com/dharambandpuri/status/1296011282726793216

At any rate, further work is required to discover some systematicity in the semantics of factored verbs, which will include a detailed survey of the data as well as an in-depth investigation into the interaction of the polysemy networks of both constituents of factored complexes, too ambitious an aim to pursue in this paper. Nevertheless, it can be argued that two elements of a factored verb complex equally participate in the framing of a new semantic concept through idiomaticity. As a matter of fact, two verb constructs, namely "gather + come", "think + extract" and "drag + bring" in (10), (11) and (12) respectively, give birth to new concepts which are obtained through idiomaticity:

(10) *jab   tak   ham   nīce   pahŭce   andherā   pūrī tarah*
     when until we   down.below arrive.PFV.M.PL darkness completely
     ghir   *āyā*   *thā.*
     gather.to.besiege come.PFV.M.SG be.PST
     'By the time we reached the bottom, it was completely dark.' (Lit. 'the darkness had gathered to besiege.')
     http://www.hindisamay.com/mohan-rakesh-sanchayan/mohan-rakesh-travelogue-4.htm

(11) *islie maĩne tīsrā bahānā* **soc**   *nikālā.*
     thus   I.ERG third excuse   think   extract.PFV.M.SG
     'So, I figured out a third excuse.' (Lit. 'I distilled the third excuse through thinking.' or 'I extracted the third excuse through digging deep into mind = thinking.')
     http://www.hindisamay.com/premchand%20samagra/Mansarovar1/Akhiri-Heela.htm

(12) *abkī   maĩ   inhẽ   **ghasīṭ   lāyā.***
     this time I   he/she.ACC.PL drag   bring.PFV.M.SG
     'This time, I have dragged him/her along.'
     http://www.hindisamay.com/contentDetail.aspx?id=193&pageno=7

As can be seen in the aforementioned examples, unlike a vectored verb complex, the factored verb complexes in (10), (11) and (12), namely *āyā* 'come', *nikāl-* 'extract' and *lā-* 'bring' all contribute, albeit in different manners, to the unified lexical meaning of overall constructions. In view of this and for the sake of clarity, it is important to draw a distinction between vectored compound verbs and factored compound verbs.

It must be noted, however, that not all factored verbs belong to a single group or class of verbs. There are different types of factored verbs which necessitate an in-depth research into the topic, preferably comparing data from different languages. At any rate, it would be inappropriate if we continue to disregard the well-established distinction between vectored and factored classes of verbs.

1.1.3 Serialized verb complexes

Akin to a factored verb, a serialized verb complex is that V1-V2 sequence in which both components contribute towards the formation of a new compound unit. Analogous to a vectored verb and a factored verb, a serialized verb complex is monoclausal. Dissimilar to a factored verb, though, a serialized verb is multieventive – rather than monoeventive – and therefore the two events that constitute it are clearly discernible. For example, (13) reports two interrelated yet independent actions which may have a time interval as well. For example, the author of the letter in (13) may have written it on a particular day and sent it the next day.

(13) *us.ne*   **likh   bhejā**   *hai*:
      he.ERG   write   send.PFV.M.SG   be.PRS.SG
      acchā   ab   māf   bhī   kar do   nā.
      alright now   pardoned   also   do give please
      'He has written: 'Okay, now you will forgive me, won't you?'
      http://meraapnajahaan.blogspot.com/2009/07/blog-post.html

To better understand the independence of two events reported by the serialized complex *likh- bhej-* 'write + send' in (13), let us compare its two versions in causative constructions (14a) and (14b) where this verb construct can have two different agents:

(14a) *maĩ.ne xat*   **likh   bhijvāyā**.
      I.ERG   letter   write   send.CAUS.PST
      'I wrote the letter and have it delivered (by a third party).'
      https://www.ekpehalbymadhubhutra.com/pahli-mohabbat-pahla-khat/
(14b) *nābālig-ne   sahelī-se   patr* **likhvā**
      minor.girl-ERG female.friend-by   letter write.CAUS

pulis-ko **bhejā.**
police-DAT **send**.PFV.M.SG
'The minor sent a letter to the police having got it written by a friend.'
https://www.bhaskar.com/harayana/rewari/news/latest-rewari-news-042003-2255806.html

This clearly demonstrates that the two events reported in (13) are indeed independent even though they are joined together to form a macroevent. Hence, the meaning of *likh bhejā* in (13) is not similar to the meaning obtained by a manner adverbial construction (*likhte hue bhejā*), as was the case with a factored verb construct, but rather as *likhkar bhejā* ('sent having written') or *likhne ke bād bhejā* ('sent after having written').

There are other cases, slightly different from the one above, which can also be classified as examples of serialized verb complex, although the two actions reported in these examples do not involve any time interval as is the case with the verb construct in (13). For instance, *ho ā-* 'be + come' and *jā ā-* 'go + come' both meaning 'has been to' are composed of two verbs representing to events, even though the two events in question conceptualize a new verb construct which is rendered in English by "has been to":

(15a) *beṭā* **ho āyā** *thā.*
son be come.PFV.M.SG be.PST.M.SG
'The son had been (there).'
http://apnailakaa.blogspot.in/

(15b) *vah Mīnū se milne mahīne mẽ ekādh bār*
she Meenu with meet.OBL month in a few times
jā āyā *kartī hai.*
go come.PFV.M.SG do.IPFV.F.SG be.PRS.SG
'She used to go to see Meenu a few times in a month.'

Notice that there are three actions indicated by the serialized verbal complexes *ho ā* 'be + come' and *jā ā* 'go + come' in (15a) and (15b), namely:
— going to a place,
— being at the place, and
— coming back from the place.

The serialized verb complexes, as exemplified in (15a) and (15b), are elliptical since (15a) omits "going to a place" whereas (15b) omits "being at a place". Interestingly, the corresponding English construct "has been to" omits two events (for example, *He has been to Paris recently*), namely "going to a place" and "coming back from the place".

A serialized verb complex may be made of more than two verb sequences. For instance, in (16) there are three verbs which mark three independent actions or events (i.e. *khī̃c* 'pull', *le* 'take' and *jā* 'go') and jointly form a new verbal construct:

(16) use pichvāṛe kī taraf   paṛne vālī   pahāṛī par
     him backyard of towards   fall the one that hill   on
     khī̃c le   gayā   thā.
     drag take   go.PVF.M.SG   be.PST.M.SG
     'He was dragged to the hill facing the backyard.'
     http://www.hindisamay.com/contentDetail.aspx?id=2835&pageno=1

The meaning of three verbal elements in (16) are not blended as is the case with the category of factored verbs discussed in 1.1.2.

1.2 Cases of a blurred divide

In spite of the fact that the aforesaid three distinct complex verb categories have their own identifying characteristics, the V1-V2 phenomenon in New Indo-Aryan languages is much more complex due to the often polysemous nature of the two verbs that constitute a verbal complex. For instance, if we keep to the defining characteristics of the aforementioned three verb complexes, in (17a) V2 *paṛ-* 'lie' adds a meaning which makes it a factored verb through idiomaticity whereas in (17b) the same verb seems to add a meaning which makes it more a serialized verb complex rather than a factored verb complex:

(17a) ye   Raṅgrājan kahā̃ se   **ṭapak paṛā**.
      this Raṅgrājan where from   drip   lie-PFV.M.SG
      'Where has this Rangarajan (out of the blue) come from?'
      https://blogs.navbharattimes.indiatimes.com/dineshraidwivedi/satire-on-indian-politics-and-news-of-high-gas-prices/

(17b) bāhar kūdte hī   baccā zamīn par **gir paṛā**
      outside jump EMPH   child ground on fall lie.PFV.M.SG
      aur so   gayā.
      and sleep GO.PFV.M.SG
      'As soon as he jumped out, the child fell on the ground and fell asleep.'
      http://balsansar.blogspot.com/

1.3 More on the vectored and factored divide

The term and concept "factor" was first introduced for Hindi-Urdu in Hook (1974: 76–83). To distinguish the two categories in question, an array of syntactic tests (e.g. 'object agreement', 'control', 'anaphora') have been proposed by some scholars.[6] It is argued in the literature that one of these tests – namely, 'argument structure' – successfully demonstrates that both parts of a factored compound verb must have the same predicate argument structure: "transitives" go with "transitives" (e.g. *khoj nikāl-*, 'find out, discover, unearth, uncover', etc.) and "intransitives" go with "intransitives" (e.g. *ā pahũc-* 'arrive, reach', etc.). As has been seen above, this is not always the case for vectored compound verbs like *khā jā-* [eat + GO] 'gobble up'.

It is also argued that in vectored verbs it is the V1 that carries the causative morphology whereas in factored verbs it is the V2 that exhibits it. At a first glance this generalization seems to hold, but a closer look reveals a more complex picture of the situation. For example, in conformity with the said generalization, in (18a) it is the V1 – namely, *marvā-* 'get/have killed by someone' – that exhibits the causative morphology. However, in (18b) and (18c) it is the other way around. In fact, it is the V2 which displays the causative morphology in the following examples:

(18a) *iske āge   mujhe nahī̃ mālūm ki   usne   use*
      this further to I.DAT not   known that he.ERG he.ACC
      marvā   ḍālā   *yā kuch aur   kiyā.*
      kill.cause THROW.PFV.M.SG or something else do.PFV.M.SG
      'Beyond this I do not know whether he/she got him/her killed or did anything else.'
      http://www.hindisamay.com/contentDetail.aspx?id=2348&pageno=15

(18b) *us-ne ṭhekedār   ravīndr sinh-ko   jīem ophis-ke-andar hī*
      he-ERG contractor Ravindra Singh-ACC G.M. office-of-inside EMPH
      *apne ādmiyõ-se **mār ḍal-vā-yā**   thā.*
      self's men-INS   kill THROW.CAUS.PST be.PST.M.SG
      'He had the contractor killed by his own men right in the GM's office.'
      [prabhatkha-bar.com/state/]

---

6 Under a different term – namely, 'co-eventual verb' – Raina (2011) discusses the syntax and semantics of factored verbs. Applying an array of syntactic tests – viz. 'object agreement', 'control' and 'anaphora' – to vectored CVs and factored CVs ("compound verbs" and "co-eventual verbs" respectively in Raina's terminology), she shows that both of them are monoclausal.

(18c) *buddhimān ānyang-ne ... tīn bahādur logõ-ko*
intelligent Anyang-ERG three brave people-ACC
jān se **mār** *ḍal-vā-yā* ...
life from kill THROW-CAUS.PFV.M.SG
'The wise Anyang had three brave people killed ...'
http://hindi.cri.cn/baike/mjcs/fjgs/902/20170815/17261.html

In light of examples (18b) and (18c), we believe that the test named "causal modification" requires further investigation. As has been noted above, in a factored compound verb, the V2 may be a transitive verb or an intransitive verb. If the factored compound has a transitive verb as V2, then the test named "causal modification" becomes quite tricky in that there may be two different agents for V1 and V2. For instance, in (18a) above, it is the same agent of two actions, whereas in (18b) and (18c) there may be two different agents of *mār-* 'kill' and *ḍāl-* 'throw', even though in default of further information, it is thought to be the same agent. Thus, taking into account the fact that unlike a vectored compound verb, a factored compound verb is the composite of two lexical units, either one of the composing units can exhibit causative morphology. The same could be said about the examples (19a) and (19b) which were discussed above in (14a) and (14b). In (19a) the agent writes the letter himself and gets it delivered by a third party, whereas in (19b) the agent gets the letter written by a third party and delivers the letter herself.

(19a) *maĩne xat* **likh** *bhijvāyā.*
I.ERG letter.M write send.CAUS.PFV.M.SG
'I wrote the letter and have it delivered (by a third party).'
https://www.ekpehalbymadhubhutra.com/pahli-mohabbat-pahla-khat/

(19b) *nābālig-ne sahelī-se patr* **likhvā** *pulis-ko*
little.girl-ERG female.friend-by letter.M.SG write.CAUS police-DAT
bhejā.
send.PFV.M.SG
'The minor sent a letter to the police having got it written by a friend.'
https://www.bhaskar.com/harayana/rewari/news/latest-rewari-news-042003-2255806.html

The pattern of causation of vectored compound verbs – widely seen in Hindi-Urdu and quite common in Kashmiri (Kaul 2006: 71) – is encountered in Marathi and Gujarati, too, as exemplified in (20) and (21):

(20) Marathi
rāṇi-tsā tevhā.ts parābhav kar-un ṭāk-avi-lā hi goṣṭ
queen-GEN then defeat do-GER THROW-CAUS-PST this thing
kharo.khar cira-smaraṇiy ase koṇ mhaṇ-el?
really long-memorable such who say-FUT
'Who would contend that (X) had the queen (Lakshmibai) defeated is really such an unforgettable thing?'
[Parasnis 2016: 148]

(21) Gujarati
makāno-ni marāmat kar-āv-vā tathā tem-ne
houses-GEN repair make-CAUS-INF and them-ACC
pāḍ-i naṅkh-āv-vā sārū.
demolish-GER THROW-CAUS.INF good
'(X is) good for having houses repaired as well as for having them knocked down.'
[Bhanderi 1993: 103]

The next test – namely, "distribution of negation" – does not seem to distinguish FC verbs from VC verbs as both types exhibit the same constraints on negative polarity items. In fact, as is evident, both (22b) and (23b) are ill-formed Hindi-Urdu sentences, whereas the negation in hypothetical constructions is acceptable in both FC verb constructions and VC verb constructions, as can be seen in (22c) and (23c).

(22a) Hindi-Urdu
andar ā jāo
inside come GO.2IMP
'Come inside!'

(22b) Hindi-Urdu
*andar na ā jāo
inside not come GO.2IMP
'Don't come inside!'

(22c) Hindi-Urdu
jab tak vo andar na ā jātā, vo uskā
until he inside not come GO.IPFV.M.SG she he.GEN
intzār kartī rahtī
wait do.IPFV.F.SG remain.IPFV.F.SG
'She used to continue waiting for him until he would come in!'

(23a) Hindi-Urdu
   usne   ciṭṭhī   likh   bhejī.
   he.ERG letter.F write send.PFV.F.SG
   'He sent a letter (having written).'

(23b) Hindi-Urdu
   *usne   ciṭṭhī   nahī̃ likh   bhejī.
   he.ERG letter   not   write send.PFV.F.SG
   'He didn't send a letter (having written).'

(23c) Hindi-Urdu
   jab tak   vo use   ciṭṭhī nahī̃ likh   bhejtā tab tak
   until when he she.DAT letter not   write send   until then
   vo   nahī̃ āegī
   she not   come.FUT.F.SG
   'Until/unless he writes and sends a letter to her, she will not come.'

Against this background, we must rely on differences in argument structure as syntactic properties to distinguish them, although, the components of factored compound verbs may show differences in argument structure, too:

(24) Hindi-Urdu
   cār   mustaṇḍe unhẽ   gāliyā̃   de-de-kar   gā̃v-se
   four toughs   them.ACC curses   give-give-ABS village-from
   bāhar bhagā āe.
   out   drive   come.PFV.M.PL
   'Several village toughs uttering curses and imprecations drove them out of town.'
   [http://sarokarnama.blogspot.com/2012/02/blog-post_5029.html]

This leaves us with little more than our intuitions as guide in the discussion of various types of verb complexes.[7] As far as the exact number of Hindi vectors and factors is concerned, there are roughly two dozen Hindi verbs – both transitive and intransitive – which can appear as V2 in V1-V2 complexes.[8] Their detailed

---

[7] For a detailed discussion of factor verbs in Marathi see Ozarkar (2014).
[8] For example, according to the inventory of 1,319 basic Hindi verbs in Sharma (2004), there are about eighteen verbs – "transitive" in their primary meaning – which can appear as V2 – either as a vector or a factor– namely, le 'take' (901); de 'give' (748); dāl 'put in' or 'throw' or 'pour' (583); mār 'kill' (119); rakh 'put' (65); phẽk 'throw' (27); paṭak 'dash down' or 'throw down' (26); dikhā 'show' or 'display' (11); čhoṛ 'leave' (8); dhar 'place' or 'put' (7); baiṭhā 'seat' or 'cause to be seated' (2); dekh 'see' or 'look' (2); lā 'bring' (2); nikāl 'take out' (1); bhej 'send away' (1); khā

classification into vectors and factors requires an in-depth study. However, following the aforementioned discussion of various types of ā verb complexes in Hindi, we can safely determine at least three basic categories of different verb complexes, namely:
1. Vectored V-V complexes
   - V1-**V2** [a vector verb]
   - **V1** [a vector verb]-V2 (i.e., a reversed vectored verb sequence)
2. Factored V-V complexes
   - V1-**V2** [a factor verb]
   - **V1** [a factor verb]-V2 (i.e., a reversed factored verb sequence)
3. Serialized V1-V2 verb complexes

1.4 Zooming in on the vectored and factored divide in Hindi-Urdu

In addition to the aforementioned tests, it would be worth trying out some other criteria to establish a fuzzy – yet helpful – line of demarcation between a vectored CV and a factored CV. To begin with, considering examples from Table 1, it can be affirmed that the composite meaning of V1 and V2 in a VC verb does not correspond to the meaning derived from a conjunctive participle of V1, nor does it contain any element akin to an adverbial (i.e. *te-hue* construction). An FC verb, on the other hand, is semantically very much similar to a V1-kar+V2 construction. This is so because while in a VC verb, V1 is a polar verb and V2 a bleached verb; in an FC verb, both V1 and V2 contribute to the overall meaning, although V2 is the main verb. We can therefore draw a striking parallel between an FC verb and a V1-kar+V2 construction, since an FC verb contains either a reduced absolutive of V1 or an adverbial. That said, the FC verbs are not synonymous with V1-kar+V2 constructions, as we will see later.

'eat' (1); *girā* 'cause to fall' or 'throw' (1); *bāhar kar* 'drive off' or 'remove' or 'move away' (1). Besides, Hindi has about sixteen verbs – "intransitive" in their primary meaning – to appear as V2, namely, *jā* 'go' (568); *paṛ* 'fall' (211); *uṭh* 'get up' or '*rise up*' (182); *ā* 'come' (124); *baiṭh* 'sit' (113); *čal* 'walk' (15); *mar* 'die' (15); *nikal* 'come out', 'go out' or 'exit' (7); *bhāg* 'run away' or 'flee' (3); *pahūč* 'arrive' (2); *ban* 'be made' (1); *dhamak* 'fall with a thud' (1); *gir* 'fall' (1); *bas* 'settle down' (1); *rah* 'live' or 'stay' (1); *khaṛā ho* 'stand up' (1). The aforementioned transitive and intransitive vectors may change their gender in use. The number in brackets after the verb indicates its frequency in the Hindi verb inventory of 1,319 verbs. Notice, however, that some of the aforementioned vector verbs act both as a vector and factor verbs.

Tab. 1: Semantics of Vectored verbs (legends: = means equal to; ≠ means "not equal to"; ≈ **means** "almost equal to"; * means "ill-formed"; ? means "anomalous"

Vectored verb	V1-kar + V2	V1 as an adverbial
(a) ā $_{Intr}$ + jā $_{Intr}$ come + GO = 'come'	≠ ākar jānā 'to leave having come'	? āte hue jānā 'to leave while coming'
(b) paṛh $_{tr}$ + ḍāl $_{tr}$ read + THROW = 'read'	? paṛhkar ḍālnā 'to throw having read'	? paṛhte hue ḍālnā 'to throw while reading'
(c) uṭh $_{Intr}$ + jā $_{Intr}$ get up + GO = 'wake up', 'get up'	≠ uṭhkar jānā 'to leave having got up'	? uṭhte hue jānā 'to leave while getting up'
(d) likh $_{tr}$ + ḍāl $_{tr}$, write THROW = 'write', 'draft'	≠ likhkar ḍālnā 'to throw having written'	≠ likhte hue ḍālnā 'to throw while writing'
(e) juṭ $_{Intr}$ + jā $_{Intr}$ be involved + GO = 'become involved'	≠ juṭkar jānā 'to leave having been involved'	? juṭṭe hue jānā 'to leave while being involved'
(f) dekh $_{tr}$ + le $_{tr}$ see + TAKE = 'see'	≠ dekhkar lenā 'to take having seen'	≠ dekhte hue lenā 'to take while seeing'
(g) uchal $_{Intr}$ + paṛ $_{Intr}$ jump + FALL = 'jump'	≠ uchalkar paṛnā 'to fall having jumped'	≠ uchalte hue paṛnā 'to fall while jumping'
(h) baiṭh $_{Intr}$ + jā $_{Intr}$, sit + GO = 'sit down'	≠ baiṭhkar jānā 'to leave having sat'	? baiṭhte hue jānā 'to go while sitting'
(i) so $_{Intr}$ + jā $_{Intr}$, sleep + GO = 'fall asleep'	≠ sokar jānā 'to leave having slept'	≠ sote hue jānā 'to go while sleeping'
(j) hās $_{Intr}$ + paṛ $_{Intr}$, laugh + FALL = 'burst out laughing'	* hāskar paṛnā 'to fall having laughed'	* hāste hue paṛnā 'to fall while laughing'
(k) pī $_{Intr}$ + ḍāl $_{Intr}$ drink + THROW = 'drink', guzzle'	* pīkar ḍālnā 'to throw having drunk'	≠ pīte hue ḍālnā 'to throw while drinking'

Tab. 2: Semantics of factored verbs (legends: = means equal to; ≠ means "not equal to"; ≈ means "almost equal to"; * means "ill-formed"; ? means "anomalous"

Factored verb	V1-kar + V2	V1 as an adverbial
(a) soc $_{tr}$ + nikāl $_{tr}$ think + extract = 'find out'	≈ sockar nikālnā 'to extract having thought'	≠ socte hue nikālnā 'to go out while thinking'
(b) mār $_{tr}$ + girā $_{tr}$ hit + cause to fall = 'hunt down, kill'	≈ mārkar girānā to cause to fall having hit	≈ mārte hue girānā 'to cause to fall while hitting'
(c) mār $_{tr}$ + bhagā $_{tr}$ beat + casue to flee = 'chase'	≈ mārkar bhagānā 'to cause to flee having beaten'	≈ mārte hue bhagānā 'to cause to flee while beating'
(d) bhāg $_{Intr}$ + nikal $_{Intr}$ run + go out = 'escape'	≈ bhāgkar nikalnā 'to escape having run'	≈ bhāgte hue nikalnā 'to escape while running'
(e) nikal $_{Intr}$ + bhāg $_{Intr}$ go out + run = 'escape'	≈ nikalkar bhāgnā 'to run having escaped'	≠ nikalte hue bhāgnā 'to run while escaping'
(f) bah $_{Intr}$ + nikal $_{Intr}$ flow + go out = 'flow'	≈ bahkar nikalnā 'to flow out'	≈ bahte hue nikalnā 'to go out flowing'
(g) uṭh $_{Intr}$ + baiṭh $_{Intr}$ get up + sit down = 'get up'	≈ uṭhkar baiṭhnā 'to sit down having got up'	? uṭhte hue baiṭhnā 'to sit down while getting up'
(h) dekh $_{tr}$ + rakh $_{tr}$ see + keep = 'choose', 'select'	≈ dekhkar rakhnā 'to choose having seen'	? dekhte hue rakhnā 'to choose while looking at'
(i) uchāl $_{tr}$ + phēk $_{tr}$ toss up + throw = 'throw down'	≈ uchālkar phēknā 'to throw down having tossed up'	≈ uchālte hue phēknā 'to throw down while tossing up'
(j) bac $_{Intr}$ + nikal $_{Intr}$ escape + go out = 'escape (from)'	≈ backar nikalnā 'to go out having escaped'	≠ bacte hue nikalnā 'to go out escaping'
(k) daboc $_{tr}$ + dhar $_{tr}$ pounce on + hold = 'pounce on', 'swoop on', 'spring out at someone'	≈ dabockar dharnā 'to hold having pounced on'	≠ dabocte hue dharnā 'to hold while pouncing on someone'

Tab. 3: Semantics of serial verbs (legends: = means equal to; ≠ means "not equal to"; ≈ means "almost equal to"; * means "ill-formed"; ? means "anomalous"

Serialized verbs	V1-kar + V2	V1 as an adverbial
(a) ho _Intr_ + ā _Intr_ be + come back = 'be to and come back'	≈ hokar ānā 'to come back having been to'	≠ hote hue ānā 'to come back passing by'
(a) jā _Intr_ + ā _Intr_ go + come back = 'go and come back'	≈ jākar ānā 'to come back having gone to'	? jāte hue ānā 'to come back while going'
(c) dekh _tr_ + ānā _Intr_ see + come back = 'see and come back'	≈ dekhkar ānā 'to come back having look at'	≈ dekhte hue ānā 'to come back while looking at'
(d) likh _tr_ + bhej _tr_ write + send = 'write and send'	≈ likhkar bhejnā 'to send having written'	≠ likhkte hue bhejnā 'to send while writing'
(f) uṭh _Intr_ + baiṭh _Intr_ get up + sit down = 'wake up and sit down'	≈ uṭhkar baiṭhnā 'to sit down having got up'	? uṭhte hue baiṭhnā 'to sit down while rising up'
(g) dekh _tr_ + rakh _tr_ see + keep = 'check and keep aside'	≈ dekhkar rakhnā 'to keep aside having seen'	≠ dekhte hue rakhnā 'to keep aside while looking at'

If we consider the grammatical role played by each type, both display similarities. For example, both types behave in the same manner as far as passivization and nominalization are concerned. Despite all that, there is clear evidence for maintaining the divide between a vectored CV and a factored CV, although more research is needed to give a full picture of the phenomenon.

In spite of the fact that a factored verb seems semantically similar to a V1-kar-V2 construction in Hindi, these two types do not behave similarly in the language. This is so because the two lexical elements in a factored verb are merged to make a single verb, whereas in a V1-kar+V2 construction both the elements have their own grammatical function. For instance, unlike a factored compound verb in (25a), a V2 in a V1-kar+V2 construction can take a vector as in (25b):

(25a) *us.ne ciṭṭhī likh bhejī.*
      he.ERG letter write send.PFV.F.SG
      'He sent a letter (having written it).'

(25b) *us.ne ciṭṭhī likh-kar bhej dī.*
      he.ERG letter write-kar send GIVE.PFV.F.SG
      'He sent away a letter having written it.'

To conclude this line of reasoning, we consider the aforementioned divide between VC verbs and FC verbs a very important tool to understand the phenomenon of complex predicate in New Indo-Aryan languages, although only a detailed study of complete verb inventories in these languages can provide us with further proofs to arrive at a unified theory of this aspect. Similarly, we believe that it is difficult to compile comprehensive lists of vector verbs and factor verbs as a single verb can play a dual role: at times functioning as a vectored compound verb, as in (26a) where V2 functions as a vector, and at times as a factored verb as in (26b) where the V2, namely *baiṭh-* 'sit up', contributes its lexical element to the whole factored verb:

(26a) *hamārā baccā āj chah baje hī* **uṭh baiṭhā**.
our child today six o'clock EMPH get up **SIT UP**.PFV.M.SG
'Our child **woke up** at six o'clock today.'

(26b) *dabā khāte hī rogī bistar mẽ* **uṭh baiṭhā**.
medicine eat EMPH patient bed in get up sit up.PFV.M.SG
'The patient **sat up** in bed as soon as he ate the medicine.'

2 Vectored and factored verbs in Hindi-Urdu, Marathi and Gujarati

As illustrated above, vectored verbs may alternate with simple verb counterparts as in (27b) with little or no change of meaning easily rendered in English or Sanskrit or other languages lacking them:

(27a) Hindi-Urdu: Vectored verb
bhāg-o, bhāgo, pulis ā **gaī** *hai.*
run.away-IMP run.away-IMP police come WENT[9] be.PRS.SG
'Run! Run! The cops have come!' [*www.panjabkesari.in*]

(27b) Hindi-Urdu
pulis **āī** *tab bhāge sab, andhere mẽ hāth*
police came then ran.away all darkness in hand
nahī̃ āyā koī.
NEG came anyone

---

[9] In order to facilitate the counting of verb frequencies in Hindi-Urdu, Marathi and Gujarati, from now on, only an English translation of verb form (for example "WENT") – rather than a full gloss (e.g. GO.PFV.F.SG) – will be provided.

'[When] the police came everybody ran; in the dark nobody was caught.'
[*srijangatha.com*]

It is possible to discuss the differences in meaning that distinguish (27a) from (27b). For instance, the coming of the cops in (27a) is a salient or feared event expressed in a main clause while their arrival in (27b) is (sardonically?) expressed as a routine event, maybe an ineffective one, and set in a backgrounded clause (the relative adverb *jab* 'when' is understood). Such conjectured distinctions, however, have only begun to be put to a statistical test and are probably not valid for all of Indo-Aryan.[10] For instance, speakers of Marathi, like those of nearly all Indo-Aryan languages, frequently use compound verbs.[11] However, the Marathi homolog of Hindi-Urdu (27a) has a very different sense and in fact cannot be considered to harbor a vectored or even a factored compound verb as in (28). In Marathi the sequence *ye-un ǰā-* {come-GER go-} is the serialized conjunction of two independent actions:

(28) Marathi
*ekā-pāṭh-o-pāṭh   ek ase sagḷe sainik   **ye-un   gele**.*
one-back-and-back one so all   soldiers come-GER WENT
'... one by one all the soldiers came and [then] went [away].'
[*www.myvishwa.com*]

Nor is every vector so clearly bleached as vector GO in (27a) [where the literal meaning of *gayā* (< *jā-* 'go') is a foursquare contradiction to the meaning of the main verb *ā-* 'come']. To some degree vectors may seem to retain a trace of the senses of their counterparts among basic lexemes. Compare (29a) with (29b):

(29a) Marathi
*je   saŋg-āy-tsa-y te   **sāŋg-un ṭāk!**   goṭh-le-lyā*
what say-INF-GEN-is that say-GER   TOSS   freeze-PST-PRT
manā-lā   vitaḷ-un   ṭāk.
mind-ACC thaw-GER   TOSS
'Say what you want to say! Unfreeze your frozen heart!'
[*nagvekarkomal.blogspot.com*]

---

10 Burton-Page (1957), Hacker (1958), Hacker (1961), and Hook (1993a) are early attempts at approaching an analysis of the semantic and pragmatic conditions on the alternation of compound verbs with their non-compound counterparts.
11 Among the few Indo-Aryan languages that lack vectored compound verbs are most varieties of Shina.

(29b) Marathi
> hi   phula   kaśi ban.av-l.i-s   te   **sāŋg** nā.
> these flowers how make-PST-2SG that say no
> 'Tell me how you made these flowers, will you?'
> [www.rainbow-arts.in]

In (29a) there is a peremptory demand for final and decisive action. The addressee is told to spit out whatever it is that he or she has been keeping pent up inside. The imperative *sāŋg-un ṭāk* 'speak up' or 'blurt out' can be thought of as expressing a throwing off or tossing away of a burden, one with which the basic lexical sense of *ṭāk-* 'toss' converges. By contrast the unvectored imperative *sāŋg* in (29b) – followed by the appeasing particle *nā* to express supplication – is milder. However, since many occurrences of *ṭāk-* with polar verbs [see (30)] cannot be seen as involving an actual or metaphorical throwing away, we must count *ṭāk-* as a vector but one that compared to *jā-* GO in Hindi-Urdu (27a) is less completely grammaticalized:

(30) Marathi
> āt   dzā āṇi   dzhop...   **dzhop-un** ṭāk!   sakāḷi   uṭh-lā.s
> inside go and sleep sleep-GER TOSS morning get.up-PST.2SG
> ki   dzhā.lā.s   tu   māṇus.
> that became you man
> 'Go inside and sleep. Go sleep! You'll wake in the morning a human again.'
> [www.haaram.com]

Analysis of V1s (the main or "polar" verbs) and the contexts in which the second elements in verb-verb sequences occur leads to the conclusion that there is a range of degrees of bleaching,[12] a spectrum of "vectorality" if you will, that informs the phenomenon of compound verbs in Indo-Aryan. Not every vector is as fully grammaticalized as every other. Some candidates for the designation "vector" are in fact

---

12 Moreover, there are a few vectors whose meanings cannot plausibly be considered to be semantically "bleached". They have simply and sharply shifted from the meanings of their basic lexical counterparts:
(a) *he   mi   kāy   kar-un bas-lo!*   [Marathi]
   this I.NOM what do-GER SIT-PST.1SG
   'What have I done!!'
   [www.maayboli.com/node/63872]
The use of vector {SIT} to express regretted or misguided action is common to many New Indo-Aryan languages (see Table 20 in Masica 1976: 146). Is sitting a semantic component of regret?

better regarded as being themselves main verbs that are linked to other main verbs in conventional sequences. It is these that we term "factor verbs" [or just "factors"] and it is to them that we will turn our attention now.

A "factored compound verb" is a verb-verb sequence in which each lexeme refers to a [notionally] discriminable element in the action expressed by the entire verb-verb sequence. In examples (31a), (31b) and (31c) from Hindi-Urdu, Gujarati and Marathi respectively, the first verb indicates the orientation of motion toward a reference point; the second verb, the achievement of arrival:

(31a) Hindi-Urdu: factored compound verb
haŋgāme-kī xabar sun-kar pulis bhī yahā̃ ā **pahŭc.ī.**
riot-GEN news hear-GER police also here come arrived
'Hearing word of the riot the police also showed up here.'
[khabar.ibnlive.in.com/news]

(31b) Gujarati: factored compound verb
karm.cārio ane vāyar.men-no kāfilo ghaṭnā-sthaḷ-e
officers and wiremen-GEN convoy accident-scene-LOC
ā-vi pohŏc.yo.
come-GER arrived
'A convoy of officers and linemen arrived at the scene of the accident.'
[www.sandesh.com]

(31c) Marathi: factored compound verb
15 minṭ-āt tsunami-ci rākṣasi lahar phukuśimā
15 minute-in tsunami-GEN monstrous wave Fukushima
yethe **ye-un pohots.li.**
here come-GER arrived
'In 15 minutes a tsunami's monstrous wave arrived in Fukushima.'
[envis.maharashtra]

In contrast to (31a), (31b) and (31c) the two lexemes {arrive + GO} in the V-V sequences *pahŭc gaī* in (32a), *pohŏci gai* in (32b) and *pohotsun geli* in (32c) are not equipollent. The V-V sequences in (32a), (32b) and (32c) may refer to the same situation of arrival and be taken as nearly synonymous to those in (31a), (31b) and (31c). But the second element [vector GO] lacks the deictic sense of motion away from a reference point that is proper to its basic lexical counterpart:

(32a) Hindi-Urdu: vectored compound verb
xabar mil-ne-par pulis bhī yahā̃ **pahŭc gaī**.
news get-INF-on police also here arrive WENT

'On getting the news the police showed up here, too.'
[*www.amarujala.com*]

(32b) Gujarati: vectored compound verb
samj-ā-y.che   ke   ā   (kāyā) to
understand-PASS-3SG.PRS that this (body) TOP
kāṭh-e   pōc-i   gaib.
edge-LOC arrive-GER WENT
'You realize that this body has reached the end of the line.'
[*www.readgujarati.com*]

(32c) Marathi: vectored compound verb
*gharā-paryant āg **pohots-un** geli   hoti.*
house-up.to fire arrive-GER   GONE had
'The fire had gotten as far as the house.'
[tarunbharat.net/ftp/e-paper]

As with many analytic categories posited by linguists, the distinction between factor verbs and vector verbs is not clear-cut. There is a fuzzy boundary between the two in which it is difficult to decide how to characterize some V2s. Nevertheless there are some V2s such as *nikāl-* in Hindi-Urdu and *kāḍh-* in Marathi and Gujarati meaning 'take out' or 'bring out' that all clearly fall on the factorial side of the factor ⇔ vector continuum, the side that is opposite to Hindi-Urdu's vector *jā-* GO.[13] Thus, in (33a) *nikāl-* expresses the successful bringing to light or bringing about as result of the action denoted by *khoj-* 'search for' as does *kāḍh-* in both Gujarati (33b) and in Marathi (33c) with respect to the action of searching denoted by *śodh-*:

(33a) Hindi-Urdu: factored compound verb
*us-ne vo kitāb **khoj   nikālī** hai jo rāj ṭhākre-ke*
he-ERG that book search taken.out has that Raj Thackeray-GEN
dādā-ne   likhī.thī.
grandfather-ERG wrote
'He has found the book which RT's grandfather had written ...'
[uttaranchal.yuku.com]

---

[13] It should be kept in mind that just as not every vector verb is as bleached as every other, similarly not every factor verb is as "factoral" as every other. If it occurs at all, the evolution from factor verb to vector verb may proceed at different rates for different verbs in different languages, even in those that are as closely related to each other as are these three.

(33b) Gujarati: factored compound verb
*e-ṇe   bepāri-ni   dukān **śodh-i   kāḍhi.***
he-ERG merchant-GEN shop   search   took.out
'He found the merchant's shop.'
[www.gujaratsamachar.com]

(33c) Marathi: factored compound verb
*kolambasā-na amerikā **śodh-un   kāḍhli.***
Columbus-ERG America search-GER took.out
'Columbus discovered America.'
[saneguruji.net]

In this paper we use the verb "profile" to indicate that the lexemes in a factored compound verb express some elements of a composite action that may be thought of as having notionally discriminable although tightly integrated constituent parts. In profiling the components of complex actions, the second element in sequences like *khoj nikāl-* is similar to the second element in verb-verb constructions found in many languages spoken in Asia and elsewhere:

(34a) Japanese: factored compound verb
*haha.no-hi-no   purezento-o yatto   **sagaši-dašita!***
Mother's-Day-GEN present-ACC finally search-took.out
'I finally found a gift for Mother's Day!'
[twitter.com/makirom]

(34b) Korean: factored compound verb
*yongtol-i   tu.ti.eo   "alphi" chaek-ul **chac-a   naessta.***
Yong Dol-NOM finally Alfie   book-ACC search-GER took.out
'Yong Dol finally found the book [named] "Alfie".'
[windlov2.tistory.com]

(34c) Chinese-Mandarin: factored compound verb[14]
*zuì.zhōng wǒ **zhǎo   chū**-le   dá.àn !*
finally   I   search come.out-PFV answer
'I finally found the answer!'
[yuqing.people.com.cn/n1/2016/...]

---

14 In Chinese, profiles of actions or events that in other languages are expressed as transitive factored verbs (or transitive vectored verbs) feature reactive intransitives as second element. See Liang and Hook (2021).

However, compared to what we observe in languages like Japanese, Korean, and Chinese (as well as in Gujarati and Marathi), **factor** verb sequences like *khoj nikāl-* are relatively less common in Hindi-Urdu. To a greater or lesser degree they have been eclipsed by **vector** verb sequences like *khoj lī* {search TOOK} in (35):

(35) Hindi-Urdu: vectored compound verb
apne thīsas-ke.liye us-ne bād-mẽ koī aur kitab khoj lī.
self's thesis-for he-ERG later some other book search TOOK
'Later on for his thesis he found some other book …' [*pratilipi.in*]

Evidence for this assertion of "eclipse" can be seen in the more frequent use and wider scope of the factor verb *kāḍh-* in Marathi and Gujarati versus the less important role played by the corresponding factor verb *nikāl-* in Hindi-Urdu. The direction of this difference runs counter to the difference between the three languages in the frequency of use and the breadth of scope of vector verbs. To better illustrate these two opposed differences, we first measure the frequency of vector verb compounding in the three languages. For reasons of feasibility this general measure must be carried out by summing a number of individual counts:[15]

Tab. 4: Frequency of Hindi-Urdu, Gujarati and Marathi vector verbs meaning 'drown' or 'sink'

	Hindi-Urdu	Gujarati	Marathi	H-U	G	M
Simple	*ḍūbī hogī* drowned 'X must have drowned (sunk).'	*ḍubi hati* drowned 'X must have drowned (sunk).'	*buḍ(ā)li āhe* drowned 'X must have drowned (sunk).'	21	40	96
Vectored	*ḍūb ga(y)ī hogī* drowned GONE 'X must have drowned (sunk).'	*ḍubi gai hati* drown GONE 'X must have drowned (sunk).'	*buḍūn geli āhe* drown GONE 'X must have drowned (sunk).'	17	42	19

---

15 The numbers given here come from Google searches carried out in early October of 2012 and subsequent searches made in May 2020. To reduce the difficulty encountered in culling *n*-tuplicates the minimal or near-minimal pairs searched include some additional words to bring down the total number of hits to manageable levels (fewer than 100). Since Hindi-Urdu's online presence vastly exceeds Marathi's and Gujarati's, strings have to be longer in Hindi-Urdu searches than they do in Marathi and Gujarati ones. Care was taken to include alternate spellings and to exclude robo-translations in Hindi-Urdu, Marathi and Gujarati (marked in on-line addresses with "ru." or "it.")

Tab. 5: Frequency of Hindi-Urdu, Gujarati and Marathi vector verbs meaning 'reach'

	Hindi-Urdu	Gujarati	Marathi	H-U	G	M
Simple	dīlī pahūcā Delhi arrive 'X reached Delhi.'	dilhī pahōcyo Delhi arrive 'X reached Delhi.'	dilli-paryant pohotslā Delhi-up.to arrive 'X reached up to Delhi.'	85	65	30
Vectored	dīlī pahūc gayā Delhi arrive WENT 'X reached Delhi.'	dilhī pahōcī gayo Delhi arrive WENT 'X reached Delhi.'	dilli-paryant pohotsun gelā Delhi-up.to arrive WENT 'X reached up to Delhi.'	90	35	1

Tab. 6: Frequency of Hindi-Urdu, Gujarati and Marathi vector verbs meaning 'send' a note, etc.

	Hindi-Urdu	Gujarati	Marathi	H-U	G	M
Simple	ciṭṭhī bhejī note sent 'X sent a note.'	ciṭṭhi mokali note sent 'X sent a note.'	ciṭṭhi pāṭha/vali/vili note sent 'X sent a note.'	72	71	35
Vectored	ciṭṭhī bhej dī note send GAVE 'X sent a note.'	ciṭṭhi mokali didhi/āpi note send GAVE 'X sent a note.'	ciṭṭhi pāṭhvun dili note send GAVE 'X sent a note.'	79	5	0

Tab. 7: Frequency of Hindi-Urdu, Gujarati and Marathi vector verbs meaning 'leave' a job, etc.

	Hindi-Urdu	Gujarati	Marathi	H-U	G	M
Simple	yah naukarī choṛī this job left 'X left this job.'	sarkāri nokari choḍi govt. job left 'X left this job.'	hi nokari soḍli this job left 'X left this job.'	1	9	27
Vectored	yah naukarī choṛ dī this job leave GAVE 'X left this job.'	sarkāri nokari choḍi didhi/āpi govt. job leave GAVE 'X left a government job.'	hi nokari soḍun dili this job leave GAVE 'X left this job.'	32	8	11

Summing these four datasets (representing the two least marked vectors GO and GIVE), we find that vector compounds are over four times more frequent in Hindi-Urdu than they are in Marathi with CV flux in Gujarati coming somewhere between that found in the other two:

Tab. 8: Summary of Hindi-Urdu, Gujarati and Marathi vectored verb frequency and their percentage

	Hindi-Urdu	Gujarati	Marathi
Simple verb	179	185	188
Vectored verb	218	90	31
Total	397	275	219
Percent vectored	55%	33%	14%

This degree of difference in CV flux among these three languages is in good agreement with that found in other independent studies.[16]

Even when vectored forms of a verb are in the minority in all three languages, the degree to which they are preferred is greater in Hindi-Urdu than it is in Gujarati or Marathi as can be noted in table 9:

Tab. 9: Vectored verb preferences in Hindi-Urdu, Gujarati and Marathi

	Hindi-Urdu	Gujarati	Marathi	H-U	G	M
Simple	*dīllī pahūcā* Delhi arrived 'X reached Delhi.'	*dilhī pahōcyo* Delhi arrived 'X reached Delhi.'	*dilli-paryant pohotslā* Delhi-up.to arrived 'X reached up to Delhi.'	85	65	30
Vectored	*dīllī pahūc gayā* Delhi arrive WENT 'X reached Delhi.'	*dilhī pahōcī gayo* Delhi arrive WENT 'X reached Delhi.'	*dilli-paryant pohotsun gelā* Delhi-up.to arrive WENT 'X reached up to Delhi.'	90	35	1
			Total	175	100	31
			Percentage	56%	35%	3%

---

16 In other counts the CV flux in Hindi-Urdu is approximately four to five times greater than that found in modern Marathi. That in turn is three times greater than in Old Marathi. See Hook (1991), Hook (1993b), and Hook and Pardeshi, MS.

Tab. 10: Frequency of simple and vectored verbs in Hindi-Urdu, Gujarati and Marathi meaning "to learn"[17]

	Hindi-Urdu	Gujarati	Marathi	H-U	G	M
Simple	...*hindī sīkhī thī* ... Hindi learned was. '(X) had learned Hindi.'	*ghaṇū šikhy@ che* a lot learned was '(X) had learned a lot.'	*marāṭhī šikhl@* Marathi learned '(X) learned Marathi.'	20	52	158
Vectored	...*hindī sīkh lī thī* ... Hindi learn TAKEN was '(X) had learned Hindi.'	*ghaṇū šikhi lidhū/gay@ che* a lot learn taken/WENT was '(X) had learned a lot.'	*marāṭhī šikhun ghetl@* Marathi learn TOOK '(X) learned Marathi.'	4	6	16
			Total	24	58	174
			Percentage	16%	10%	11%

Against the great abundance of vectored verbs in Hindi-Urdu there is a relative poverty of factored verbs. For instance, the factored verb {search + take.out} in Hindi-Urdu is about as frequently encountered as {search + TAKE} whereas in Marathi {search + take.out} is practically the only choice speakers have. In the meaning of 'find a way / path' we found one single instance in Marathi of the vector sequence {search + TAKE} against dozens and dozens of the factored sequence {search + take.out}:

(36) Marathi
tyā-ne āplā mārg ātā **śodh-un ghet-lā** *āhe.*
he-ERG self's path now search-GER take-PFV is
'Now he has found his path ...'
[sureshdwadashiwar.blogspot.com]

Trilingual numbers (garnered through Google searches made in October 2012) follow suit:

---

[17] The symbol "@" covers the concord endings of adjectives, verbs, and participles. They show agreement with nouns or pronouns.

Tab. 11: Vectored versus factored verbs in three languages (35)

	Hindi-Urdu	Gujarati	Marathi	H-U	G	M
Vectored	*mārg khoj liyā* path search TOOK '... found a path.'	*mārg šodh.i lidho* path search TOOK '... found a path.'	*mārg šodh-un ghetlā* path search TOOK '... found a path.'	22	4	1
Factored	*mārg khoj nikālā* path search TOOK OUT '... found a path.'	*mārg šodh.i kāḍh.yo* path search TOOK OUT '... found a path.'	*mārg šodh-un kāḍhlā* path search TOOK OUT '... found a path.'	19	9	69
			Total	41	13	70
			Percentage	46%	70%	98%

Thus, in Hindi-Urdu the factor verb {take.out} has a less prominent role than it does in Gujarati, and in Gujarati, {take.out} has a less prominent role than in Marathi. In combination with {search for} the vector verb TAKE has begun to compete with the factor verb {take.out} in Gujarati and has drawn even with it in Hindi-Urdu.[18]

Incorporating the data in (31) and (35), Figure 1 shows representative trend lines for the relative importance of factored {search + take.out} versus vectored {search + TAKE} V-V compounds in Marathi, Gujarati and Hindi-Urdu. Geographically these three languages lie on a line running from south to north with Marathi to the south, Hindi-Urdu to the north and Gujarati in between. Since the flux of vectored verbs is increasing in all three of them, we may use the spatially oriented differences between them as substitute for unavailable chronology (also known as "apparent time"):

---

18 It is hard to find comparable datasets across all three languages. In a reduced set, counting just Marathi and Hindi-Urdu, in which *phĕk de-, phekun de-* are compound verbs, and *phĕk mār-, phekun mār-* are factor verb sequences, we may observe a tendency parallel to those seen in Table 11 and Table 12 for Hindi-Urdu to prefer the CVC over the FCV and for Marathi to favor the FCV over the CVC:

(a) Hindi-Urdu   Marathi   H-U   Marathi
     Y par čappal phĕk dī   *čappal phek-un dilā*   15   0
     Y par čappal phĕk mārī   *čappal phek-un mārlā˜*   6   25
     Y-on chappal throw /GAVE//hit/   chappal throw /GAVE//hit/   21   25
     'X threw a chappal at Y.'   'X threw a chappal (at Y).'   29%   100%

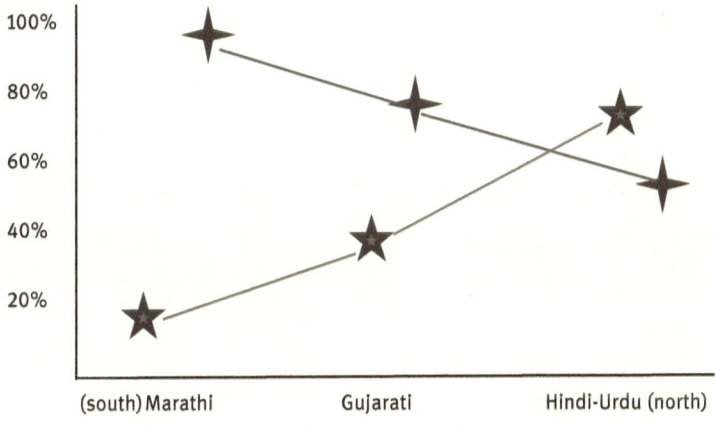

Fig. 1: Vector ★ verb frequency versus ✛ factor verb frequency

Searching another contrastive pair (VCV 'home arrive WENT' versus FCV 'home come arrive') an identical geotypological skew can be observed for the same triplet of languages:

Tab. 12: Frequencies of vectored and factored verbs in Hindi-Urdu, Gujarati and Marathi (36)

	Hindi-Urdu	Gujarati	Marathi	H-U	G	M
Vectored	*mere ghar pahūc gayā* my home arrive WENT '... reached my home.'	*ghare pohōci gayo* home arrive WENT '... reached home.'	*ghari pohots-un gelā* my home arrive WENT '... reached my home.'	25	55	0
Factored	*mere ghar ā pahūcā* my home come arrived '... reached my home.'	*ghare ā-vi pohōc.yo* home arrive come arrived '... reached home.'	*ghari ye-un pohots.lā* home come arrived '... reached home.'	9	55	25
			Total	175	100	31
			Percentage	33%	50%	100%

However, subsequent searches revealed an ostensible counter-example. Preterence for a particular factored V-V, namely {exit + flee} 'run away (from X), escape (X)' (37) or {flee + exit} 'ditto' (38) over the corresponding vectored (or factored) V-V {flee + go} (39), is much greater in Hindi-Urdu than it is in Marathi (40, 41):

(37) Hindi-Urdu
pita-kī   ḍā̃ṭ-se   kṣubdh ho.kar
father-GEN scolding-from angry   becoming
ghar-se   nikal bhāgī.
home-from exit   ran
'Enraged by her father's scolding (she) ran away from home.'
[amarujala.com]

(38) Hindi-Urdu
pati-ke   zulm-se   pareśān ho.kar   vo
husband-GEN cruelty-INS tormented becoming she
ghar-se   bhāg nikalī.
house-from run exited
'Tormented by her husband's cruelty she ran away from home.'
[bbc.com/hindi/]

(39) Hindi-Urdu
ek laṛkī apne   boy-phreṇḍ-se śādī.kar-ne ke.lie
one girl self's boy-friend-with marry-INF   for
ghar-se   bhāg gaī.
house-from run WENT
'A girl ran away from home in order to marry her boyfriend.'
[m.patrika.com/]

(40) Marathi
ti ek sāmāny āyuṣy jag-ṇyā-sāṭhī ḍubai-tun   paḷ-un   nighā.li.
she one normal life live-INF-for Dubai-from flee-GER exited
'She ran away from Dubai in order to live a normal life.'
[divyamarathi]

(41) Marathi
tyā-nantar mulgi ti.cyā priyakarā-sobat gharā-tun paḷ-una geli.
that-after girl her   lover-with   home-from run-GER
?went/WENT
'Subsequently the girl ran away from home with her lover.'
[mahanayakonline.com]

Table 13 shows a clear preference in Marathi for *dẓā* 'go' over factor *nigh* 'escape, depart':

Tab. 13: Frequency of vectored, factored and inverted factored verbs in Hindi-Urdu, Gujarati and Marathi

Hindi-Urdu	Gujarati	Marathi	H-U	G	M
ghar se bhāg gaī	bhāg-i gai	paḷ-un geli	90	>80	50
ghar se bhāg nikalī	bhāg-i nikaḷi	paḷ-un nighāli	45	65	6
ghar se nikal bhāgī	nikaḷ-i bhāgi	nigh-un paḷāli	60	20	0
'ran away from home.'	'ran away…'	'… ran away.'			
		Percentage	46%	49%	87%

One possible explanation for this discrepancy is that {go} when occurring as V2 with V1's expressing unbounded motion retains its nature as a factor verb in Marathi, Gujarati and Hindi-Urdu. The progressions seen in Table 11 and Table 12 illustrate the competition and replacement of a factor verb by a vector. The dataset in Table 13 illustrates competition among three factor verbs: {flee}, {exit}, and {go}. As such the tendency posited by Anderson (2003) has simply failed to occur.[19]

---

19 We may posit a specific possible explanation for the discrepancy seen in Table 13 that ʤā- 'go' in Marathi is felt to be more of a factor than a vector. Prima facie evidence for this is the inability for ʤā- 'go' in Marathi to serve as a vector to V1s that contradict the literal sense of ʤā- 'go'. As shown in the discussion above of (27a) versus (28), unlike Hindi-Urdu's ā- 'come', V1s such as ye 'come' do not allow ʤā- 'go' to serve as vector in Marathi. This aversion extends to non-displacement change-of-state verbs like ho 'be, become' in which use of ʤā- 'go' connotes disappearance or departure from life:
(b) čhatrapati śivāji mahārāʤ ase ek-ats mahān vyaktimatv ho-un gele
    Emperor Shivaji Maharaj such one-only great figure become-GER went
    'Emperor Shivaji, this one towering figure came (and went)…' [mywordshindi.com]
Contrast this connotation of departure with the departure-free becoming of ho gayā in Hindi-Urdu:
(c) ek-bār jo netā ho gayā yah hameśā ke-lie netā ho gayā.
    once who leader become WENT this always for leader become WENT
    'Once somebody became a leader they became a leader forever.' [Shree 2007]
It is not that vectorial use of ʤā 'go' does not exist in Marathi. It is found with verbs of emotion:
(d) tyā (kalpanā) aik-un sāti mohar-un gelā.
    those (ideas) hear-GER Satie be.enthralled-GER WENT
    'Hearing those (ideas) Satie was enthralled.' [Purandare n.d., p. 115]
But the common change-of-state use observed in Hindi-Urdu's completive badal gayā 'change WENT; changed' is of negligible frequency in Marathi. With ʤā 'go' continuing with verbs of unbounded motion as a factor rather than as a vector its resistance to replacement by a different factor such as nigh- / nikaḷ- / nikal- 'exit' does not materially affect the adherence of Marathi,

3 Concluding remarks

In the spirit of Andersen's (2003) conception of innovating "I-variants" moving in on older "O-variants", this paper argues for positing a competition between more than one possible way of looking at certain events or situations as seen for instance in Table 11 and Table 12: 1. Profiling of physical result or direction: An entity is sought out or located in space or time (*khoj nikāl-* {search + take out} and *ā pahũc-* {come arrive}). 2. Profiling of interest: The speaker is aware that the searcher wants to be sure that his/her own position is maintained or that he/she is benefitted as a result of the action (*khoj le-* {search + TAKE}) or that from his/her point of view the action is complete prior to some other action (*pahũc jā-* {arrive GO}). As orientation of action with respect to an actor's interests is of more general concern [and less predictable] than orientation of result or onset in space or time, we may speculate that this drift in usage toward profiling the former is not unexpected, especially given common assumptions about human motivations. However, all three of these languages are commonly believed to derive from a single source: OIA Sanskrit. Why might Gujarati speakers lag behind Hindi-Urdu speakers over the centuries? And why might Marathi speakers lag behind Gujarati speakers? These are questions for historians and areal linguists.

Abbreviations

ABS = absolutive; ACC = accusative; CAUS = causative; DAT = dative; EMPH = emphatic; ERG = ergative; F = feminine; FUT = future; GEN = genitive; GER = gerund; IMP = imperative; INF = infinitive; INS = instrumental; IPFV = imperfective; LOC = locative; M = masculine; NEG = negative; NOM = nominative; OBL = oblique; PASS = passive; PFV = perfective; PL = plural; PRS = present; PRT = participle; PST = past; SG = singular; SUBJ= subjunctive; TOP = topic marker

Transliteration

The transcription of language data in the paper is largely based on the ISO-15919 system: https://en.wikipedia.org/wiki/ISO_15919.

Gujarati and Hindi-Urdu to the diachronic generalization proposed by Andersen (2003), Harris and Campbell (1995), and Hopper and Traugott (1993).

Acknowledgement

This is an expanded and updated version of a draft which was archived as a "project report" by Peter Edwin Hook when he was a Visiting Professor at NINJAL [The National Institute of Japanese Languages and Linguistics] in 2012. I am grateful to Peter Hook for assigning the task of redoing the paper. Peter Hook is grateful for the generous support that he received (both financially and intellectually) during his stay in Tokyo from NINJAL's Director, Taro Kageyama, and his host there, Prashant Pardeshi. Needless to say, all errors in this revised version are my own.

References

Akiyama, Ken & Shinsuke Murofushi (eds.). 2011. *genji monogatari daijiten* [a comprehensive dictionary of the genji monogatari]. Tokyo: Kadokawa Gakugei Shuppan.

Andersen, Henning. 2003. Actualization and the (Uni)directionality of change. In Henning Andersen (ed.), *Actualization: Linguistic Change in Progress*, 227–248. Amsterdam: John Benjamins.

Bhanderi, Kalpesh. 1993. *pañcāyat rāj.nīti* [Panchayat policy]. Gujarat Panchayat Authority.

Burton-Page, John. 1957. Compound and Conjunct Verbs in Hindi. *Bulletin of the School of Oriental and African Studies* 19. 469–78.

Butt, Miriam. 2010. The light verb Jungle: Still hacking away. In Mengistu Amberber, Brett Baker & Mark Harvey (eds.) *Complex Predicates: Cross-Linguistic Perspectives on Event Structure*, 48–78. Cambridge: Cambridge University Press..

Chhabra, Usha. nd. *Pushpak* (Hindi Textbook) - Class 2. New Delhi: Arya Publishing Company.

Dasgupta, Probal. 1977. The internal grammar of Bangla compound verbs. *Indian Linguistics* 38 (2). 68–85.

Hacker, Paul. 1958. *Zur Funktion einiger Hilfsverben im Modernen Hindi.* Mainz: Akad Wissen. und Literatur.

Hacker, Paul. 1961. On the Problem of Treating the Compound & Conjunct Verbs in Hindi. *Bulletin of the School of Oriental and African Studies* 24. 484–516.

Harris, Alice & Lyle Campbell. 1995. *Historical syntax in cross-linguistic perspective.* Cambridge: Cambridge University Press.

Hook, Peter E. 1974. *The Compound Verb in Hindi*. Ann Arbor: Center for South and Southeast Asian Studies, The University of Michigan.

Hook, Peter E. 1978. The Hindi Compound Verb: What it is and What it Does. In Kripa Shankar Singh (ed.), *Readings in Hindi-Urdu Linguistics*, 129–154. Delhi: National Publishing House.

Hook, Peter E. 1991. The Emergence of Perfective Aspect in Indo-Aryan. In Elizabeth C. Traugott & Bernd Heine (eds.), *Approaches to Grammaticalization*, 59–89. Amsterdam & Philadelphia: John Benjamins Publishing Company.

Hook, Peter E. 1993a. Seven Variables Controlling the Use of the Compound Verb in Hindi-Urdu Texts. *South Asian Language Review* 3. 59–70. New Delhi: Creative Publishers.

Hook, Peter E. 1993b. Aspectogenesis and the Compound Verb in Indo-Aryan. In Manindra K. Verma (ed.), *Complex Predicates in South Asian Languages*, 97–113. New Delhi: Manohar Books.

Hook, Peter E. 1996. The Compound Verb in Gujarati and its Use in Connected Text. In R.T. Vyas (ed.), *Consciousness Manifest: Studies in Jaina Art and Iconography and Allied Subjects in Honour of Dr. U.P. Shah*, 339–356. Vadodara & New Delhi: Oriental Institute & Abhinav Publication.

Hook, Peter E. 2021. The Hindi-Urdu compound verb and its covert semantics. Births, earthquakes, meteors, and other autogenous expressions. In Taro Kageyama, Peter E. Hook & Prashant Pardeshi (eds.) *Verb-Verb complexes in Asian Languages*, 274–299. Oxford: Oxford University Press.

Hook, Peter E. & Prashant Pardeshi. MS. Inflation in the Marathi Compound Verb: 1300–2000.

Hopper, Paul J. & Elizabeth C. Traugott (eds.). 1993. *Grammaticalization*. Cambridge: Cambridge University Press.

Koul, Vijay K. 2006. *Compound verbs in Kashmiri*. Delhi: Indian Institute of Language Studies.

Kulkarni, Aaditya. 2019. *Synchrony and diachrony of compound verbs in Marathi*. Pune: Deccan College, University of Poona M.A. thesis.

Liang, Hsin-hsin & Peter E. Hook. 2021. Verb-verb sequences in Mandarin and Hindi-Urdu: a comparison. In Taro Kageyama, Peter E. Hook & Prashant Pardeshi (eds.), *Verb-Verb Complexes in Asian Languages*, 521–544. Oxford: Oxford University Press.

Ozarkar, Renuka & Gillian Ramchand. 2018. Structure Matching and Structure Building in Marathi Complex Predicates. *Journal of South Asian Linguistics*, Volume 8/1. 3–28.

Ozarkar, Renuka. 2014. *Structures of Marathi verbs*. Mumbai: Mumbai University doctoral dissertation.

Parasnis, Raobahadur Dattatray Balvant. 2016. *Jhānśi-ci rāni Lakṣmibāi*. Nachiket E-books.

Pardeshi, Prashant. 2003. The Explicator Compound Verb in Marathi: Definitional Issues and Criteria for Identification, *Indian Linguistics*. Vol. 64. 19–36.

Pardeshi, Prashant. 2021. Classification of complex verbs and the evolution of the compound verb in Marathi. In Taro Kageyama, Peter E. Hook & Prashant Pardeshi (eds.) *Verb-Verb Complexes in Asian Languages*, 223–248. Oxford: Oxford University Press.

Pray, Bruce R. 1970. *Topics in Hindi-Urdu Grammar*. [Research Monograph number 1.]. Berkeley: South and South-East Asia Studies, University of California at Berkeley.

Premchand. 1988 [1936]. *Godan*. [Rajkamal Paperbacks]. New Delhi: Rajkamal Prakashan.

Purandare, Madhuri. (undated). *Pikaso (Picasso)*. Pune: Purandare Prakashan.

Raina, Achla. 2011. The co-eventual verb in Hindi. In Omkar N. Koul (ed.), *Indo-Aryan Linguistics*, 135–152. Mysore: Central Institute of Indian Languages.

Sharma, Ghanshyam. 2004. *Dizionario hindi-italiano e italiano-hindi*. Bologna: Zanichelli Editore.

Shree, Geetanjali. 2007. *Hamārā śahar us baras (Our town that year)*. Delhi: Rajkamal Prakashan.

Slade, Benjamin. 2021. Development of verb-verb complexes in Indo-Aryan. In Taro Kageyama, Peter E. Hook & Prashant Pardeshi (eds.) *Verb-Verb Complexes in Asian Languages*, 249–274. Oxford: Oxford University Press.

Miki Nishioka
How similarly do Hindi *rakhnā* and Japanese *oku* PUT behave as a V2? A corpus-based comparative analysis

Abstract: This paper aims to use an online Hindi corpus in order to investigate the restrictions in Hindi on the co-occurrence of the stem form of the main verb (V1) plus the vector *rakhnā* PUT or KEEP together with negative particles (*nahī̃, na,* and *mat* for imperative forms); and, using Japanese translations of Hindi short stories and a novel, to examine how similarly or differently this Hindi construction works compared with *oku*, the Japanese equivalent verb as V2.

Keywords: compound verbs, Hindi, Japanese, comparative analysis, corpus, *oku, rakhnā*

1 Introduction

The topic of compound verbs or complex predicates, that is, V1 + V2 concatenations, has been popular in South Asian linguistics. Regarding Hindi V2s, there is an endless list of studies on special V2s in V1 + V2 concatenations, i.e., the supposed *compound verbs* defined by Kellogg (1876: 187–191). Masica (1991: 326–330), Hook (1974), and other noteworthy 20th century scholars have termed such V2s *intensifiers, operators, explicators,* or *vectors*. Snell (2010: 188–190; 277–279) and Jagannathan (1981: 264–273) give a list of main Hindi V2s such as *jānā* GO, *denā* GIVE, *lenā* TAKE, *ḍālnā* POUR or PUT, *baiṭhnā* SIT, *paṛnā* FALL, *uṭhnā* RISE, and *rakhnā* PUT or KEEP. According to Masica (1991: 326), all of these V2s express "manner specification".

Japanese, though of a different language family from Indic languages, has similar devices to the V2s in Hindi. These are generally treated as auxiliary verbs in Japanese language and education, and are given as *shimau* PUT AWAY, *ageru* GIVE, *morau* TAKE or GET, *oku* PUT, *miru* SEE, etc. These V2s are usually connected to the *te* form, a non-finite past form equivalent to past/perfect participles in Indo-European languages.

Miki Nishioka, University of Osaka, Japan. Email: miki.nishioka@gmail.com

https://doi.org/10.1515/9783110753066-009

As for restrictions on the co-occurrence of the STEM form of the main verb (V1) plus vectors in Hindi, Jagannathan (1981: 272) points out that *jānā*, *lenā*, or *denā* rarely co-occur with negative particles like *nahī̃*, *na* or *mat* (used for the imperative) in Hindi. Snell (2014), apparently in support of this claim, explains that "compound verbs give a specific sense of the way in which a particular action is done. It therefore follows that a sentence that's negative or general won't use them; ..." [Snell 2014: 210]. He provides an illustrative dialogue as follows.

Rājū: *maĩ ne   khānā   khā   liyā   hai.*
      I   ERG   food   eat.STEM   TAKE.PFV   COP.PRS
      'I have had my meal.'
Gītā: *acchā? maĩ ne to nahī̃   khāyā   hai.*
      really I   ERG TOP NEG   eat.PFV   eat.PRS
      'Really? I haven't.'

As we see in Gita's reply, she drops TAKE in order to form a negative answer. This example indicates that speakers do not use TAKE when giving a negative answer, even though the question contains TAKE as V2. This is one of the pragmatic issues that native speakers are only vaguely aware of, and thus they find the usage of difficult to explain to non-native speakers – as the native speakers have already acquired competence in the target language and command it unconsciously.

Of the V2s for compound verbs, we will turn to PUT, that is, *rakhnā* and *oku* in Hindi and Japanese respectively, and examine how similarly or differently the Hindi *rakhnā* works compared to *oku* as V2, especially when used with negative particles.

2 PUT: Serial verbs vs. Compound verbs

There are various types of V1 + V2 concatenations, and the difference between so-called serial verbs and compound verbs often becomes controversial.

(1a) *maĩ ne   us   kārḍ ko   apnā   samajh-kar   rakh   liyā.*
     I   ERG that   card ACC   one's   understand.STEM.CONJ   put.STEM   TAKE.PST
     'I took the card as my own and kept it.'   [By courtesy of Peter Hook]
(1b) *ise   baṛe bhāī   kā   pyār   samajh-kar*
     this.ACC big   brother   GEN   love   understand.STEM-CONJ
     rakh   lo.
     put.STEM TAKE.IMP

'Take this as a token of brother's love.'
https://navbharattimes.indiatimes.com/navbharatgold/we-the-people/employment-crisis-due-to-lockdown/story/75776993.cms

Semantically speaking, (1a) is a serial verb sequence or construction and it involves two actions. One is to understand and the other is to keep. On the contrary, (1b) is a pseudo-serial verb sequence, since it does not contain two separate actions.[1] In other words, the V2 does not provide the original meaning, PUT. That means the V2 in this sentence functions as a vector verb. The concatenation V1 + V2 does not consist of STEM + V2 but STEM-*kar* + V2, which is basically added as a conjunctive marker. The following are ambiguous examples.

(2a) *mehandū jī ke pās savāī bhoj ne us kā ādhā*
Mehandu sir GEN near Savai Bhoj ERG she.OBL GEN half
zevar choṛ-kar rakhā hai.
ornament leave.STEM-CONJ PUT.PFV COP.PST
'Savai Bhoj has left half of her ornaments with Mehandu.'
http://ignca.gov.in/coilnet/devn038.htm

(2b) *mehandū jī ke pās savāī bhoj ne us kā ādhā*
Mehandu sir GEN near Savai Bhoj ERG she.OBL GEN half
zevar choṛ rakhā hai.
ornament leave.STEM PUT.PFV COP.PST
'Savai Bhoj has left half of her ornaments with Mehandu.'

Examples (2a) and (2b) have almost the same meaning with PUT as V2. This kind of pair can also be found in Japanese V1 + V2.

(3a) *watashi wa musukoni sono okane wo nokoshi-te oita.*
I TOP son-DAT that money ACC leave-*te*-form PUT.PST
'I left that money with (my) son.'

(3b) *nokoshi oku koto no ha-gusa*
leave.*renyoukei* (STEM) PUT.NONPST.ATTR saying GEN leaf-grass
'(lit.) Leaf-grass of sayings which (someone) leaves'
Itoh Kashitaro Takeaki[2]

---

[1] This idea is suggested by Peter Hook. I am immensely grateful to him.
[2] Shimozawa Kan (1929) *Shinsengumi ibun*, revised in 1997, Tokyo: Chuuoukouron shinsha. He was a member of Shinsengumi at the end of the Edo period.

The predicate of (3a) consists of a verbal *te*-form + PUT. (3b) is a noun phrase with an attributive form of the verb, that is, a kind of participial modifier. In the example, *renyoukei* + PUT is used for the complex predicate or the verb concatenation. When we compare the Japanese pair to the Hindi one, the former is equivalent to STEM-*kar* and the latter is a non-finite conjunctive form which carries imperfective aspect. The *te*-form in Japanese is said to be derived from *-ta*, the suffix for the definite past form, and is used as a conjunctive, comparable with STEM-*kar* in Hindi. Thus, the pair is parallel to *dekh-kar* vs. *dekh* or *choṟ-kar* vs. *choṟ* in non-finite conjunctive forms with aspect of perfective vs. imperfective. As in (2), there is no difference in meaning between *nokoshi-te* vs *nokoshi*. However, the former contains the meaning 'done' due to the suffixation of *-ta*, i.e., the finite past morpheme, and the latter form is not used commonly in modern Japanese. Therefore, the structure in (3b) sounds archaic to native speakers of modern Japanese. Regarding Hindi PUT, we, as non-native speakers of Hindi, cannot say anything definite about the subtle difference between *choṟ-kar* and *choṟ*. However, it is inferred that the difference between them can be analogous to the difference between the pair *nokoshi-te* and *nokoshi*.

At any rate, though we are not able to specify the semantic or pragmatic difference between STEM + V2 and STEM-*kar* + V2 in Hindi precisely, still as far as we have seen, we can tell that the latter is substituted for serial verb sequences as well as compound verbs, while the former is not. The latter is usually used as a serial verb sequence rather than a compound verb. Therefore we will focus only on STEM + PUT here.

3 Compound verbs and PUT

Regarding *rakhnā* in Hindi, Snell (2010: 279) points out that the basic sense of 'to keep, maintain' can imply a firmness of action, or one whose results or implications might last over time. The following are illustrative examples of Hindi *rakhnā* (4a) and its Japanese translated equivalent verb *oku* (4b).

(4a) *māsṭar, samjhe?   yah   bāt   bhalī bhā̃ti   soc   rakho.*[3]
       master understand.PST this speech good kind   think.STEM   PUT.IMP
       'Master, do you understand? Think it out properly!'

---

[3] Ramakrishna Math (2018) *Anandadham ki Or*.
https://books.google.co.jp/books?id h9ddDwAAQBAJ&printsec frontcover&hlja#v onepage&q&f false, accessed 3 Feb, 2020.

(4b) wakari   mashita   ka? konokoto wo yoku kiite
      understand.STEM AUX.POL.PST Q   this word ACC well listen.*te*[4]
      oite   kudasai.
      PUT.*te* GIVE.POL.IMP
      'Master, please listen to this (word) carefully.'
      [my own translation]

Snell (2014) does not clearly specify how *rakhnā* co-occurs with a negative particle, although he does do so regarding the often-used *jānā* GO, *denā* GIVE, and *lenā* TAKE. Jagannathan (1981: 268–269) explains that *rakhnā* as a V2 denotes a "stative" mood and is used in a resultative construction instead of a perfective form + (perfective copula) + copula; yet he does not mention the co-occurrence of the V2 with a negative particle. It seems that only Liperovskiĭ (1984: 182–183) points out a certain limitation in V1 + V2 with negative particles. He also provides an illustrative example with *rakhnā* and a negative particle, as follows:

(5) maĩ ne koī ānāthālay nahī̃ khol   rakhā   hai!
     I   ERG any orphanage NEG open.STEM PUT.PFV COP.PRS
     'I am not running an orphanage!'

Example (5) is an exclamatory sentence, not a declarative sentence. Liperovskiĭ himself has claimed that this kind of limitation occurs in utterances expressing apprehension, surprise, denial of a supposed possibility, rhetorical questions, etc. As he explains regarding the example, it renders "complete denial which is in the nature of assurance". This is because the sentence is an exclamatory one. The studies I have performed on *jānā*, *denā*, and *lenā* and even on the Japanese *shimau* PUT AWAY, which functions similarly to the Hindi verbs as the V2,[5] essentially prove Liperovskiĭ's (and even Jagannathan's) claims, especially on the following points: negative particles can co-occur with the V2s in exclamatory, interrogative, or some specific imperative sentences; there seem to be no restrictions on using the V2s with a negative particle in adverbial clauses such as conditional, subjunctive, or adjectival clauses or noun clauses; a negative particle does not negate an affirmative proposition, which would be sentential negation, but rather negates a part of the proposition, which is a partial or constituent negation. Therefore, it can be said that example (5) is possible, since the sentence is not

---

[4] Hereafter, I will abbreviate *te*-form (the allomorph *de* included) as *te*.
[5] These papers have been presented at SALA-31, 32, 33, and 34 in 2015–2018.

only exclamatory but also includes a constituent negation triggered by the word *koī*.

With all of this in mind, I examined the circumstances under which V1 + PUT with a negative particle *nahī̃, na, mat* in Hindi and *-nai* (its allomorphs included) in Japanese actually occurs in Web corpora. In particular, I checked for the same situation with two patterns, namely P1: NEG + V1 + PUT [*rakhnā*] and P2: V1 + NEG + PUT [*rakhnā*].

4 What do the corpora tell us?

We investigated P1 and P2 in COSH, a large web corpus of Hindi language, using a specific formula[6] to retrieve the results. The total number of V1 + *rakhnā* PUT instances in COSH is 6,769. Regarding V1 + *rakhnā* with a negative particle, I investigated two patterns, P1 and P2 as described above. The number of results for P1 is 131 and the number for P2 is 69.[7] Tables 1, 2, and 3 below indicate the breakdown for each type of sentence, mood, and declarative sentence.

Tab. 1: Types of sentence

	P1	P2
Exclamatory	0	4
Interrogative	9	9
Declarative	121	54
Imperative	1	2
Total	131	69

Table 1 represents types of sentences with NEG + *rakhnā* as a V2. Declarative sentences occupy more than 90% in P1 and almost 80% in P2 as well. Table 2, below, shows the moods of sentences. About 86% is occupied by the indicative mood in P1 and 65% in P2. When looking into the declarative sentences, Table 3, below,

---

6 The formula for affirmative sentences is [pos! "VM;0;.*"] [pos "VM;0;.*"] [lemma "रख"] [lemma! "दे" &lemma! "ले"]

7 The formulas for each pattern are [pos "NEG.*" & word! "मना"] [pos "VM;0;.*"] [lemma "रख"] and [pos "VM;0;.*"] [pos "NEG.*" & word! "मना"] [lemma "रख"]

tells us declarative sentences' share of indicatives. For P1, declaratives occupy 85% and for P2, 61%.

Tab. 2: Sentential moods

Moods	P1	P2
Indicative	113	45
Subjunctive	17	22
Imperative (infinitive usage included)	1	2
Total	131	69

Tab. 3: Declarative and subjunctive sentences

Moods	P1	P2
Indicative	104	33
Subjunctive	17	21
Total	121	54

Source: Data compiled from the Corpus of Spoken Hindi

In regard to the frequency of V1 with PUT, i.e., *rakhnā* in Hindi, the results are as below:

Tab. 4: Frequency of V1 with *rakhnā*: P1

	V1	meaning	Frequency
1	pahan	wear	27
2	uṭhā	raise	19
3	choṛ	release	14
4	lagā	attach	13
5	kar	do	9
6	pī	drink	8
7	le	take	7
8	de	give	5

	V1	meaning	Frequency
9	chipā	hide	5
10	banā	make	4
11	pāl	protect	4
12	bā̃dh	bind	3
13	sun	hear	2
14	bacā	save	2
15	nikāl	take out	2
16	lagvā	cause to be attached	1
17	paṛh	read	1
18	ḍāl	throw down	1
19	jamā	cause to be fixed	1
20	caṛhā	cause to rise up	1
21	khol	open	1
22	khā	eat	1
		Total	131

Tab. 5: Frequency of V1 with *rakhnā*: P2

	V1		Frequency
1	uṭhā	raise	30
2	kar	do	26
3	chipā	hide	2
4	dabā	press	2
5	pakaṛ	catch	2
6	soc	think	2
7	cuk	be finished	1
8	choṛ	release	1
9	pahan	wear	1
10	pī	drink	1
11	rok	stop (vt)	1
		Total	69

Additionally, we searched the "Balanced Corpus of Contemporary Written Japanese" (hereafter BCCWJ) for V1 + *oku* in Japanese, and retrieved 31,943 results. Since these are too many, here we present only the top 20 V1s with PUT and their frequency. As we can see, *shite oku*, that is, 'do' + PUT is by far the most frequent result in this pattern.

Tab. 6: Top 20 V1s with *oku*

	V1 {OKU}	Meaning	Frequency
1	して[shite]{おく}	do	3658
2	放って[houtte]{おく}	leave	839
3	入れて[irete]{おく}	put ... in	829
4	言って[itte]{おく}	say	781
5	せて[sete]{おく}	let ... V1	669
6	知って[shitte]{おく}	know	647
7	置いて[oite]{おく}	put	590
8	覚えて[oboete]{おく}	remember	530
9	つけて[tsukete]{おく}	put ... on	448
10	残して[nokoshite]{おく}	save/leave	420
11	見て[mite]{おく}	look/see/watch	420
12	書いて[kaite]{おく}	write	383
13	確認して[kakunin shite]{おく}	confirm	381
14	作って[tsukutte]{おく}	make	369
15	用意して[youi shite] {おく}	prepare	328
16	申し上げて[moushiagete]{おく}	say (a humble form)	318
17	とって[totte]{おく}	get/pick	315
18	考えて[kangaete]{おく}	think	290
19	紹介して[shoukai shite]{おく}	introduce	282
20	止めて[tomete]{おく}	stop (vt)	280

Compared to total the number of V1 + *rakhnā* instances, the number of results for V1 + *oku* is much larger.[8] As an example for checking co-occurrence with a negative particle, we took *shite* 'do' + *oku* and selected a random sample of 500 out of 3,658 results. We found out that *shite* 'do' + *oku* with NEG has only 14

---

[8] It is worth mentioning that the BCCWJ website claims to contain 109,102,192 words, whereas COSH contains 179,979,464 words (Nishioka and Akasegawa 2016).

results.[9] 13 results out of these are used in embedded clauses, and only one result is imperative. These results provide clear evidence to support the results we obtained when we examined the tendency of the other vectors: *shimau* in Japanese[10] and *jānā, denā,* and *lenā* as often used in Hindi.

5 Comparison with Japanese *OKU* as a V2

In this section, we observe how similarly or differently both vectors behave in Hindi and Japanese. As we have mentioned, there are many examples of V1 + *rakhnā* or V1 + *oku* found in the corpora or other reading materials and explaining them all would be a Sisyphean problem. Therefore we will demonstrate some salient examples here. To begin, the following are examples from short stories by Premchand, *Īdgāh* and *Do bailõ kī kathā*. Example (6a) below is from *Īdgāh*.

(6a) isīlie badmāś ne apne paise bacā rakhe the.
so villain ERG own money save.STEM PUT.PFV COP.PST
'For this the villain/ naughty boy saved up his own money.'
[Singh (n.d.)]

(6b) dakara aitsu wa jibun no okane wo nokoshi-t(e[11])
so he TOP self GEN money ACC save-te
oita n(o) da.
PUT.PFV.ATTR GEN COP.PRS
'So he (Hamid) saved up his money (for the tongs).'

(6b) is a Japanese translation by Matsuoka (1990: 101) for (6a). Adding PUT to V1 generally means 'to do something in advance', 'to leave something in a certain state' or 'to keep something in a certain state'.[12] The Japanese translation with *oku* expresses 'save his money just in case' for buying the tongs.

Examples (7a) below is from *Do bailõ kī kathā*. (7b) is a translation by Sakata (1990: 64).

---

9 The default formula is *shite* [te.form] + *oka-nai* [put-NEG]. The negative particle *-nai* is conjugated to express past vs. non-past in Japanese.
10 See Nishioka (2013) for details.
11 Elision often happens in colloquial Japanese, e.g., *-t(e)* + *oku* --> *-toku*.
12 'Shimau' in *Imiwa?* [Application: A free multilingual Japanese dictionary for iOS] <http://www.imiwaapp.com/>, accessed 3 Feb, 2020.

(7a) *jise   unhonne apnā ghar samajh   rakhā   thā,*
     REL.ACC they ERG own house understand.STEM PUT.PFV COP.PST
     vah āj   un   se   chūṭ   gayā   thā.
     that.COR today they.OBL ABL be.released.STEM GO.PFV COP.PST
     'What they thought was their home had been left behind.'
     [Unknown translator (2014)]

(7b) *jibun no ie   da   to omotte   ita   tokoro kara*
     own   GEN house COP.PRS AP think.te COP.PFV.ATTR   place ABL
     dasa-rete, ...
     put.out-PASS.*te*
     '(They had been displaced from the home) which they had considered as their own.'

This example is not translated word for word, and *samajh rakhā* is translated into *omotte ita*, which is syntactically or morphologically equivalent to *samjhā thā* in Hindi, and which is used to express a typical resultative meaning in Japanese. We have found an example with *rakhnā* as well as a negative particle:

(8a) *ham ne to tumhārī sevā   karne   mẽ koī kasar*
     we ERG TOP you.GEN service do.INF.OBL LOC any loss
     nahĩ uṭhā   rakhī.
     NEG   raise.STEM PUT.PST
     'We have served you with all our devotion.'
     [Unknown translator (2014)]

(8b) *hone-oshimi   shi-nai-de   shikkari hataraite*
     bone-sparing do.STEM-NEG-*te* hard   work.*te*
     kita   de   wa   nai desu   ka.
     COME.PFV.ATTR   COP.*te* TOP NEG AUX.POL.PRS Q
     '(We) have worked hard without sparing ourselves, haven't we?'
     [Sakata: 63]

We can also observe that (8a) is the same as (5), that is, an exclamatory or emphatic sentence. In addition, it contains the word *koī* as a trigger that co-occurs with the negative particle *nahĩ*. The sentence is assumed to be of a constituent *kasar* 'loss' negation, as we have seen in (5). Looking back at the Japanese, (8b) is again translated freely by the same translator. NEG+ *uṭhā rakhī* is not equivalent to *hataraite kita*, literally, 'working came'. Incidentally, the Japanese COME as a V2 expresses the same certain resultative meaning as *āj tak karte āe haĩ* in Hindi. In Japanese, COME adds a time vector from past to present when the utterance occurs. As we have seen in examples (6), (7) and (8), PUT in Hindi denotes a resultative meaning slightly different from the normal resultative that consists of PFV + COP.

Now we shall observe rare and peculiar examples that we have found in the corpora. Example (9) below is a Japanese example from BCCWJ. The part of the compound verbs consists of *die* + PUT. Table 4 and 5 show that almost all V1s with PUT are transitive verbs. Thus it is clearly not possible to translate them into Hindi word for word. *Oku* as a V2 expresses here 'leave someone dead for the time being'. This is possible since it is a blog about a video game. The use of the combination of *die* + PUT is limited to a specific context.

(9)   a   *chinamini*   *akirakani*   *bag ppoi*   *node*   *shinde oki*
       oh incidentally   clearly   bug like   because.of   die.*te*   PUT.STEM
       mashita.
       AUX.POL.PST
       '(lit.) Since this game clearly has some bugs, I left (him – the main character in the game) dead (for the time being, not forever).'

BCCWJ shows another example in which *die* + PUT is used in an embedded clause. We found only two results of this collocation in the corpus. *Die* + PUT behaves as resultative expression in (10). This example is from a blog about a freelance journalist who returned from a hostage crisis in Syria. The sentence cannot be translated into Hindi word for word either.

(10)   *koitsu*   *wa*   *shinde oita*   *hou*   *ga*   *yokatta*   *n-ja-ne?*[13]
       this guy   TOP   die.*te*   PUT.PFV.ATTR   way   NOM   good.PST   TAG
       'Would it have been better if we left this guy for dead?'

On the other hand, COSH provides other two notable examples in the results of P1 and P2. Example (11) is *take* + PUT with a negative particle. It is supposedly a declarative sentence. However, the sentence that contains the compound verbs is followed by a contrastive conjunction *lekin*, and the negative particle *nahī̃* negates *yah sevā*, not the compound verbs themselves/verb itself.

(11)   *maleśiyan*   *eyarlāins ne*   *yah sevā*   *nahī̃*   *le*
       Malaysian   Airlines   ERG   this   service   NEG   take.STEM

---

13 This is a short form of *no dewa nai* [GEN COP.ATTR TOP NEG] which is literally equivalent to 'It is not that ...'. Here the phrase works as a tag question (TAG).

```
rakhī        hai          lekin...
PUT.PFV      COP.PRS      but
```
'Malaysian Airlines has not installed this service but...'

Example (12) below is an example of (8a) *raise* + PUT in P2. As we have seen in the previous section, the number of P2 is generally far less than the number of P1. (12) is also a declarative sentence as (11) above. Seemingly there is a slight difference in the negation between (8a) and (12), which is difficult to render into English.[14]

```
(12)  modī   aur   amit śāh   kī    jorī   ne    koī    kasar   uṭhā
      Modi   and   Amit Shah  GEN   pair   ERG   any    loss    lift.STEM
      nahī̃   rakhī.
      NEG    PUT.PST
```
'The pair of Modi and Amit Shah spared no efforts.'

In addition, we have observed a few rare examples on the internet as in (13) and (14) below. We see *be* + PUT, i.e., *ho* + *rakhnā* used here. Few grammarians have introduced such a combination in their Hindi grammar books. The part of *be* + PUT in Hindi is presumed to express a resultative meaning. This supports what Jagannathan has pointed out. Incidentally, Japanese *be* + PUT (for example, *naru* + *oku*) is a possible combination, yet it will render a nuance of 'for the time being' as in (9) and (10). If we translate the part of the verb predicates, we will have to use a resultative construction.[15]

Example (13) is an affirmative sentence with *ho* + *rakhnā* and (14) is an interrogative sentence with the same V1 + V2.

```
(13)  ājkal       ek    tārīkh      ko    le-kar            bolīvuḍ     mẽ
      recently    one   date        ACC   take.STEM-CONJ    Bollywood   LOC
      filhāl        billī-bā̃ṭ         ho          rakhā       hai.[16]
      at present   cat-dividing      be.STEM     PUT.PFV     COP.PRS
```
'There is an argument going on in Bollywood over a date these days.'

---

14 It is inferred that P1 is an unmarked negative and P2 is a marked one which expresses a kind of emphatic meaning. (Narsimhan, p.c.). I will not go deeply into this matter in this paper.
15 See (15) below.
16 'Īd 2020 kī rilīz par akṣay-salmān mẽ jo lafṛā ho rakhā thā, usmẽ ek aur ṭvisṭ ā gayā', <https://www.thelallantop.com/news/salman-khans-movie-dabang3-or-kick2-clashes-with-akshay-kumars-film-laxmi-bomb/>, 15 Feb, 2020.

(14) āp   kā   plug kahā̃   connect ho   rakhā   hai?[17]
      you GEN plug where connect be.STEM PUT.PFV COP.PRS
      'Where has your plug been connected?'

Both (13) and (14) are again presumed to be resultative expressions. As is the case with (12), Japanese does not allow us to translate the compound verbs into the *be* + PUT. If the author were allowed to translate (14) into Japanese, it would be:

(15a) anata no   puragu wa   doko   ni   setsuzoku
      you   GEN   plug   TOP where LOC connect
      sa-rete   iru?
      do.STEM-PASS.*te*   COP.PRS
      'Where has your plug been connected?'

(15b) anata no   puragu wa   doko   ni   setsuzoku
      you   GEN   plug   TOP where LOC connect
      shite   aru?
      do.*te*   COP.PRS
      'Where have (you) connected your plug?'

Example (15a) and (15b) are typical Japanese resultative constructions that consist of -*te* + *iru* /*aru*. *Iru* and *aru* are existence verbs equivalent to a copula or auxiliary in Hindi. The former is used for animate and the latter for inanimate nouns. If we replace *iru* or *aru* with *oku*, (15a) will not make sense and (15b) will be rendered as a resultative meaning with 'in advance'.[18]

6 Conclusion

Regarding V1+PUT in combination with the negative marker, we have found a tendency towards the co-occurrence of *rakhnā* with a negative particle, and found this combination's behavior in the context of pragmatics to be quite similar to that of *jānā* GO, *denā* GIVE, and *lenā* TAKE. As shown for declarative sentences in the indicative mood in tables 1, 2 and 3, the numbers of P1 and P2 with a negative

---

[17] '*āp kā plug kahā̃* connect *ho rakhā hai*? Paul Hindi Bible – Gospel' https://www.youtube.com/watch?v S-_QXEqAsoI, 14 Feb, 2020.
[18] Incidentally, although Japanese and Hindi do not belong to the same langue family, the construction of the Japanese example in (15b) is similar to the ergative construction found in Hindi.

particle are quite small: P1 constitutes one fiftieth of the total, and P2 only one hundredth. Regarding Japanese V1 + PUT in BCCWJ, the same tendency was observed as for the Hindi V1 + PUT. The actual number of Japanese V1 + PUT instances is 4 times as in Hindi. We extracted 500 results of *shite oku* 'do PUT' randomly, and examined how frequently V1 + PUT occurred with a negative particle. The results showed only 15 combinations with a negative suffix, none of them declarative sentences in the indicative mood. This tendency is also quite similar to Hindi.

Another point we have found is that in most of the indicative sentences in Hindi, *koī* (or *kisī*) has shown up along with a negative particle, rather than particles such as *to*, *hī*, *bhī* with a negative particle. The particles *to*, *hī*, and *bhī* tend to occur with GO, GIVE and TAKE rather than with PUT. Although *koī* tends to appear with PUT as a V2, it still means that the negative particle does not negate an affirmative proposition or verbal predicate, but rather negates part of the proposition (i.e., a constituent negation), as for example 'orphanage' in (5). We have found some exceptions, such as (11). However, these seem to express, e.g., a 'stative' or a kind of resultative mood or meaning, instead of a simple perfective form such as, e.g., *lī hai*. Incidentally, the Japanese *-te aru*, which renders a resultative, can be used in this case. In addition, there is also a possibility that the negative particle negates only the part of 'this service' in (11).

Most of the V1s frequently used in the Hindi corpus are similar to those found in the Japanese corpus – such as 'do', 'leave', 'say/tell', 'save', 'see/look', 'think', 'stop', 'hear/listen', etc. However, *die* as the V1 in Japanese never happens as the V1 in Hindi with PUT, and *be* in Hindi never occurs as the V1 in Japanese. It is worth noting that both verbs are so-called intransitive verbs, and constitute rare cases. In regard to meaning and pragmatic function, the Hindi *rakhnā* expresses a resultative meaning, while the Japanese *oku* adds a kind of modal meaning such as 'in advance' or 'for the time being', as well as a resultative meaning.

Abbreviations

ABL = ablative; ACC = accusative; AP = appositive; ATTR = attributive; AUX = auxiliary; CONJ = conjunctive; COP = copula; COR = correlative; DAT = dative; ERG = ergative; GEN = genitive; IMP = imperative; INF = infinitive; INST = instrumental; IPFV = imperfective; LOC = locative; NEG = negative; NOM = nominative; OBL = oblique form; PASS = passive; PFV = perfective; POL = polite form; PRS = present; PST = past; Q = question marker; REL = relative; TOP = topic marker

Transliteration

Hindi Devanagari letters have been Romanized following the ISO system of transliteration (https://en.wikipedia.org/wiki/ISO_15919). Japanese examples are transliterated following Kunrei-shiki Romanization system: https://www.bunka.go.jp/kokugo_nihongo/sisaku/joho/joho/kijun/naikaku/roma/honbun.html

Acknowledgements

This research was supported by Grant-in-Aid for Scientific Research No. JP15K02517 from the Ministry of Education, Culture, Sports, Science and Technology (MONKASHŌ), Government of Japan. I thank my Indian colleague and friend Dr. Ranjana Narsimhan (Department of East Asian Studies, University of Delhi) for being a delightful consultant on Hindi and Japanese.

References

Balanced Corpus of Contemporary Written Japanese (BCCWJ), National Institute for Japanese Language and Linguistics, Lago Institute of Language. (2012–2018) NINJAL-LWP for BCCWJ. Available at http://nlb.ninjal.ac.jp/.
Bhatia, Tej K. 1995. *Negation in South Asian Languages*. Patiala: Indian Institute of Language Studies.
Hook, Peter E. 1974. *The Compound Verb in Hindi*. Michigan: University of Michigan, Center for South and Southeast Asian Studies.
Jagannathan, V. R. 1981. *Prayog aur prayog*. Delhi: Oxford University Press.
Kellogg, Samuel Henry. 2011 [1938]. *A Grammar of the Hindi Language: in which are treated the High Hindī, Braj, and the Eastern Hindī of the Rāmāyan of Tulsī Dās, also the colloquial dialects of Rājputānā, Kumāon, Avadh, Rīwā, Bhojpūr, Magadha, Maithila, etc., with copious philological notes* (2nd edition). London: Kegan Paul, Trench, Trubner and Co.
Liperovskiĭ, Vladimir Petrovich. 1984. *Hindi language - Verb*. Moscow: Institut vostokovedeniia (Akademiia nauk SSSR).
Masica, Colin. P. 1976. *Defining a Linguistic Area: South Asia*. Chicago: University of Chicago Press.
Masica, Colin. P. 1991. *The Indo-Aryan Languages*. Cambridge: Cambridge University Press.
Matsuoka, Tamaki. 1990. Īdogāha. In Teiji Sakata (ed.), *Genkan no yoru: Premchand tampen shū*, 83–108. Tokyo: Nihon Asia Bungaku kyōkai.
Nishioka, Miki. 2013. Te-kei + Shimau to Hiteiji to no Kyōki Seigen to Sono Kankyō ni tsuite: Hindīgo to no Taishōgengogakuteki Shiten kara (Co-occurrence Restrictions on the '-te Form + shimau' and Negation in Japanese: A Contrastive Analysis with Hindi). *Matani ronshū*, vol. 7, 47–73. Osaka: Nihongo Nihon Bunka Kyōiku Kenkyūkai.

Nishioka, Miki & Shiro Akasegawa. 2016. The Development of a Web Corpus of Hindi Language and Corpus-based Comparative Studies to Japanese. In *Proceedings of the 6th Workshop on South and Southeast Asian Natural Language Processing (WSSANLP2016)*, 114–123. <https://www.aclweb.org/anthology/W16-3712/>

Nishioka, Miki, Lago Language Institute. 2016–2018) Corpus of Spoken Hindi (COSH) and COSH Conc [Software]. Available at <http://www.cosh.site>.

Premchand, Munshi. 1956. "Īdgāh (Idgah)". In *Premcaṃd kī sarvaśreṣṭh kahāniyāṁ*, 11–26. Banāras: Sarasvatī press.

Premchand, Munshi. n.d. *Idgah*, translated by Kushwant Singh, available from https://archive.org/stream/Idgah-English-Premchand/idgah_djvu.txt, Accessed: 25 Dec 2018.

Premchand, Munshi. 2014 [1931]. Do bailõ kī kathā. In *Mansarovar 1* (Hindi Edition). General Press: Kindle version.

Premchand, Munshi. 2014. Premchand's Short Story Do Baillon Ki Katha: A Tale of Two Oxen. Translated by unknown translator, available from <http://ghai-tc.blogspot.com/2014/09/prem-chands-short-story-do-baillon-ki.html>, accessed 3 Feb, 2020.

Sakata, Teiji (ed.). 1990. Nitō no Ushi. In *Genkan no yoru: Premchand tampen shū*, 59–82. Tokyo: Nihon Asia Bungaku kyōkai.

Snell, Rupert & Simon Weightman. 2010. *Complete Hindi: A Teach Yourself Guide*. London: McGraw-Hill.

Snell, Rupert. 2014. *Get Started in Hindi*. London: Hodder & Stoughton.

Jean-Luc Chevillard
The use of vector verbs in early modern Tamil

Abstract: The posthumous *Vocabulario Tamulico com a Significaçam Portugueza* (VTCSP) compiled by Antam de Proença (1625–1666) was printed in 1679 in Ambalacatta (now in Kerala). Although the VTCSP contains 16,217 entries printed on 508 pages, it does not deal with 16,217 distinct lexemes because it is non-lemmatized and stands in fact between a grammar and a dictionary. A number of entries have to be grouped into families, scattered over several pages. Limiting ourselves to the verbal morphology, which takes up 39% of the total count, we can say that (almost) all families of entries contain a citation form (ending in -*kkiṟatu*, -*kiṟatu*, or -*ṟatu*) but that many families also contain a separate entry for the relative participle or for a verbal noun ending in -*kai*. The central focus of this paper is an in-depth analysis of a group of 298 entries, in which we see the earliest clear attestation of the use of vector verbs in compound verbal expressions in Tamil. Fifteen distinct vector verbs are represented in the VTCSP, of which the most frequently attested are the following four: *pōṟatu* 'to go' (42%), *koḷḷukiṟatu* 'to take' (20%), *irukkiṟatu* 'to sit' or 'to be' (17%), and *pōṭukiṟatu* 'to put' (10%). An additional important element of information provided by the VTCSP is the collection of Portuguese glosses that are provided with each of these entries, which are in some cases accompanied by concrete examples of use. These glosses and examples allow us to see how these compound forms were perceived to differ, or not to differ, from the corresponding simple forms.

Keywords: Early modern Tamil, vector verbs, Tamil grammar

1 Introduction

In the present contribution, my focus will be on the examination of one specific feature in a "work-in-progress-1", which is itself part of a larger "work-in-progress-2". Both of these subparts belong to the larger domain called "History of Descriptive Linguistics". More specifically, the first work-in-progress – which

---

Jean-Luc Chevillard, CNRS, Laboratoire d'Histoire des Théories Linguistiques, Case postale 7034, 5 rue Thomas Mann, 75205 Paris cedex 13, France. Email: jean-luc.chevillard@univ-paris-diderot.fr

https://doi.org/10.1515/9783110753066-010

started in 2013 and is nearing completion – consists in preparing an electronic edition of the 17th century *Tamil-Portuguese Vocabulario Tamulico Com a Significaçam Portugueza* (henceforth VTCSP),[1] printed in 1679. Although the second work-in-progress started a long time ago, it is still at an earlier stage because of its larger scope,[2] and consists in preparing an electronic Corpus (henceforth CETGD) of (potentially) all the Early Tamil Grammars & Dictionaries, some of them written in Portuguese and some in Latin. These grammars and dictionaries were written in the 16th, 17th and 18th centuries by Europeans[3] (see section 5), the first among them being Henrique Henriques (1520–1600). These Westerners were trying to learn, use, and teach several varieties of Tamil. As for the specific feature of the VTCSP – the topic of present research – it can be defined concisely as being what is common to the members of a subset (see section 6) of 298 entries (out of a total of 16,217 entries for the whole VTCSP), seen as early linguistic observations of the presence of "compound verbs" in which we see the frequently repeated use, as the second component, of what several 20th-century linguists have called "vector verbs".[4] This subset is quantitatively described in section 9 and some of the relevant pre-modern technical explanations, which belong to the same long period as the VTCSP and precede the appearance and the rise of English in India, are evoked in section 10. The reason for choosing this particular feature as the central object of this study is the fact that the observations made by those Westerners constitute the earliest substantial evidence for the presence of vector verbs in complex or compound verbal expressions in (Modern) Tamil. Being outsiders, these Westerners had not yet become accustomed to the diglossic attitude of native speakers. This attitude is the reason why many of the specific features of spontaneously spoken Tamil are masked in all the early native descriptions, where the sole focus is on the poetical language variety.

---

1 The primary preliminary data entry for that work-in-progress was recently completed.
2 I have presented this larger project in Chevillard (2015) and Chevillard (2017).
3 Although they did not all write in Latin, I have (Chevillard 2017) referred to those early Western descriptors of Tamil as the *Grammatici Tamulici*, because even those who wrote in Portuguese were following the Latin model. See also Muru (2018) for more information on the *Grammatici Tamulici* and Aussant & Chevillard (2020) for a discussion of "Extended Latin Grammar".
4 Liang & Hook (2007: 109–110) note that: "Compound verb is not a given or self-evident category. On the basis of its shared properties in the languages of South Asia and Central Asia the compound verb may be defined as a sequence of two verbs AB (main verb A plus auxiliary or "vector" verb B) that alternates with main verb A with very little difference in meaning translatable into languages which do not have compound verbs (such as Sanskrit or English)". It must be mentioned however that the three linguists mentioned in Table 6 do not use the term "vector verb".

This being a work in progress, I shall try to avoid drawing premature conclusions and shall try to focus on making elements of information available to other researchers that are usually inaccessible because of the difficulty in reading the original sources. These sources are vast and necessitate a simultaneous mastery of several languages, which is rarely found nowadays. In the concluding section, I shall try to bring together several of the recurrent threads and make suggestions for a possible future collective work, entitled "Multi-Lingual Dictionary of Early Linguistic Terminology" (MLDELT).

2 Preliminary exploration of a non-lemmatized vocabulary which makes use of a pre-modern spelling system

The VTCSP, which is our main source of linguistic observations in this article, was compiled by Antam de Proença (1625–1666) and printed posthumously in 1679 in Ambalacatta (= Ambazhakad in present day Kerala, India). As per my count, on the basis of my preliminary entering of the text into XML format,[5] which has recently reached completion, the VTCSP contains 16,217 entries. However, this does not mean that it deals with 16,217 lexemes, as will be made clear later. The reason for this is that the VTCSP is not lemmatized, and stands in fact between a dictionary and a grammar. This is the reason why its entries received a number of grammatical category labels, such as "V", "PE", "INF1", etc. in the process of my XML encoding, as we shall see in the following examples where some of the labels will be discussed.

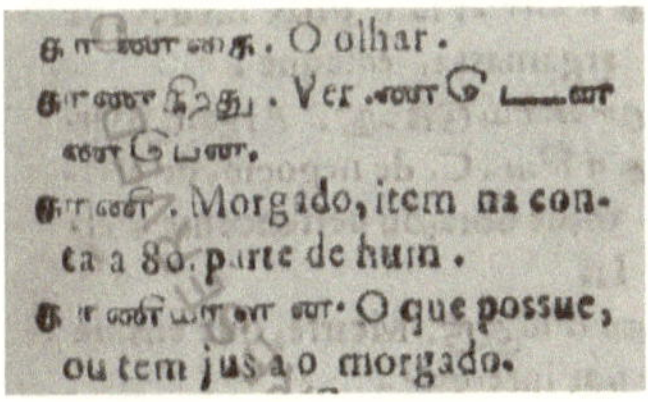

Fig. 1: Entries 281_L_n to 281_L_q in VTCSP_1679

---

5 See a sample in (1), below.

As the processing of the XML text is not yet completed, it is not possible to state precisely how many lexemes the VTCSP deals with. However, on the basis of the available data, I shall later on provide an estimate of the number of "verbs" which the VTCSP contains (see section 4, Table 3). It will become clear, however, as we progress in the description, that a simple answer is not possible. One of the reasons for this is the pervasiveness of verbal compounding, which on the one hand, is used for extending the lexicon, and on the other hand, can have grammatical functions, being used for the creation of periphrastic paradigms (see section 6).

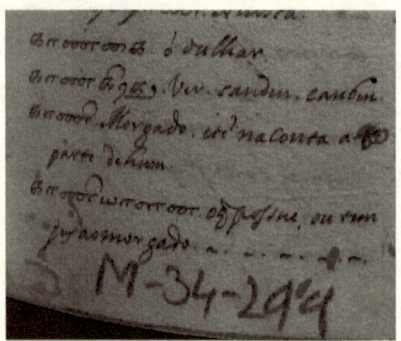

Fig. 2: Same entries in a Goa MS predating VTCSP_1679

As a first illustration, I provide a fragment from the left column of page 281 in the VTCSP (Figure 1) which contains four entries to which I have ascribed the coordinates 281_L_n to 281_L_q.[6] As can be seen, each entry consists of a head, in Tamil script, followed by a body, containing explanations in Portuguese and, at times, additional segments in Tamil script. This is the case in entry 281_L_o, although an earlier MS of the VTCSP preserved in Goa – which predates the printed book[7] – sometimes makes use of a form of Roman script transliteration for the Tamil words contained in the body of the entries. An example of this can be seen in Figure 2 which contains the passage from the GOA manuscript which

---

6 My coordinate system is explained in Chevillard (2017): the first component is the (notional) page number, the second component is the column (L or R) and the third component is a lower case letter indicating the rank of the entry inside the column. For instance, item 281_L_o is the 15th item on the left side of page 281. There are no visible page numbers in the VTCSP_1679, but the folio numbers printed on many of them are unfortunately unusable, because they are inconsistent.

7 See Gregory James (2007).

corresponds to the content of Figure 1. However, it seems that in the case of entry 281_L_o, some teachers or users decided that the information provided was not clear enough. Both the truncated sequence in Tamil script (in the 1679 VTCSP) and the Roman script transliteration (in the Goa MS) must have seemed ambiguous. Our conviction is based on the fact that a later copy of the same *Vocabulario* – preserved in the Bibliothèque Nationale de France (henceforth BnF) in Paris under shelfmark "Indien 221" and reproduced here in Figure 3 – contains an improved rendering of the elements of information which are given in the entry body. This can be seen in Table 1, which compares image fragments from the three sources and explains possible transcription strategies.

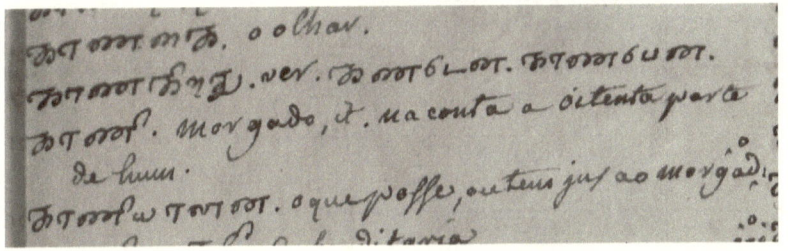

Fig. 3: Same entries in a Paris MS which is later than VTCSP_1679

It is important to note here the ambiguity of the early Tamil writing system and that transcribing the content of an ancient Tamil book or manuscript is very frequently an act of interpretation. One must for instance decide whether a long "ē" or a short "e" was intended, whether a consonant stands alone or possesses an inherent "a", whether a particular symbol, conventionally represented here in Table 1 by "#", stands for "ra" (Modern "ர"), or for "r" (Modern "ர்"), or for a "long ā" vowel modifier (Modern "ா") etc.

However, it is not always desirable or possible to perform that interpretive step. For that reason, I also use a VERBATIM "Raw transcription" system in parallel with the "standard" transcription in my electronic edition of the VTCSP_1679, as illustrated in Table 1. For the purposes of this article, and for readers unfamiliar with the Tamil script, I provide references here using the standard transliteration scheme for modern Tamil. The reader should, however, keep in mind that this is only *my* interpretation.

Tab. 1: Comparing the treatment of entry 281_L_o in the VTCS_1679 and in a Goa and Paris MS

	Entry Head	Past	Habitual - future
Goa MS	*[handwritten Tamil]*	canden.	canben.
VTCSP_1679	*[handwritten Tamil]*	*[handwritten Tamil]*	*[handwritten Tamil]*
BnF (Indien 221)	*[handwritten Tamil]*	*[handwritten Tamil]*	*[handwritten Tamil]*
RAW Verbatim representation of Tamil words	க#ணகிறது	கண@டன	க#ண@பன
Standardized Tamil spelling	காண்கிறது	கண்டேன்	காண்பேன்
Transliterated version of the standardized spelling	kāṇkiṟatu	kaṇṭēṉ	kāṇpēṉ

A sample XML encoding for the entry 281_L_o could be as follows:[8]

(1)   <entry coordinates="281_L_o">
      <entry_head> க#ணகிறது </entry_head>
      <Intended_Modern_Spelling> காண்கிறது
      [kāṇkiṟatu]</Intended_Modern_Spelling>
      <CATEGORY>V</CATEGORY>
      <entry_body>Ver <p>ண@டன</p> // <p>ண @ பன</p>
      </entry_body>
      <Variation>
      <Variant_Goa>Ver . canden. canben</Variant_Goa>
      <Variant_VTCSP>Ver. ண@டன // ண @ ப ன.</Variant_VTCSP>
      <Variant_Indien_221>ver. கண@டன. க # ண @ பன
      </Variant_Indien_221>
      </Variation>
      </entry>

---

8 This is a simplified encoding for the purposes of illustration.

3 How to encode a non-lemmatized vocabulary

The content of the two XML elements named "entry_head" and "entry_body" in the fragment of XML encoding presented in (1) corresponds to what is really present in the VTCSP, if we overlook the added layer of explicit information tagged for verbal conjugation using the "p" element (for "paradigm") in the "entry_body". Other elements such as "Intended_Modern_Spelling", "CATEGORY" and "Variation" are part of the added interpretive layer. This is also true of the attribute "coordinates" which appears in the opening tag of the "entry" element. We shall now move from page 281 of the VTCSP to page 264, where we find in the left column an entry whose content is provided here both in image form (see Figure 4) and in text form (see 2a and 2b, below).

Fig. 4: VTCSP entry 264_L_a

Compared with (1), the structure in (2a) is a simplified one, where the "Variation" element is not visible, in order not to burden the reader. The simplified XML version is followed in (2b) by a non-XML compact version, in which the conventions implicitly followed can be deduced by comparison with (2a). This simplified version is the model which I shall use for the remainder of this article. Where possible, an English translation will also be provided between double brackets for the compact version.

(2a)   <entry coordinates="264_L_a">
<entry_head>கண்ட</entry_head>
<Intended_Modern_Spelling>கண்ட
[kaṇṭa]</Intended_Modern_Spelling>
<Under>281_L_o</Under>
<CATEGORY>PE</CATEGORY>
<entry_body>C. que ulo, ou foi // uifta </entry_body>
</entry>

In this type of VTCSP entry, the head would be called a *"peyar eccam"* (henceforth PE),[9] by traditional Tamil grammars, and is nowadays referred to in English as a "past relative participle".[10] From the point of view of my XML encoding scheme, this type of entry is a "secondary entry", which is categorized as "PE" by means of the "CATEGORY" element. The fact that the entry *kaṇṭa* [264_L_a] is a secondary entry is indicated within the XML structure that I use by the presence of the XML element "Under" (see 2a, above). This element contains a pointer towards the primary entry *kāṇkiṟatu*, in the form of a string, making its coordinates "281_L_o". I now repeat the same information in a more compact manner in (2b), a human-reader-friendly model.

(2b) *kaṇṭa* [264_L_a] "C. que uio, ou foi uifta". (PE) (Under 281_L_o) ((([entity][11] which saw or which was seen))

It is to be noted that modern Tamil dictionaries, such as the Madras Tamil Lexicon (henceforth MTL) or the Cre-A dictionary, do not reserve a separate entry for an item such as *kaṇṭa*, as it is considered the task of a grammar, and not the task of a dictionary, to deal with morphology. In the case of the MTL, the user would have found the relevant lexeme on p. 857, where a 31-line entry starts with:

(3) காண் (ணு)-தல்[12] kāṇ- , 13 v. [T. kānu, K. M. kāṇ.] tr. 1. To see, perceive, view, descry; [...] (MTL, p. 857)

Users of the MTL would then have to be told, or would have to discover, that the indication "13 v." indicates that this verb belongs to the 13th class. They could

---

9 More precisely, this type of *peyar-eccam* is called a "*ceyta v-eṉṉum vāyppāṭṭu-p peyar-eccam*". Because this is statistically the most frequent type, I have chosen the "PE" abbreviation for noting it. Other types are tagged using longer strings such as "PE_pr", "PE_neg", etc.

10 Many other designations have been used in the course of history. It will be the role of the MLDELT, mentioned in the introduction and conclusion of this article, to list them all.

11 Here, there is a translation dilemma. Literally, *kaṇṭa* translates nowadays as "which saw OR who saw OR which was seen OR who was seen OR ...". In order to explain the Portuguese gloss, I can say that *C.* stands for *cousa*, and is a kind of place-holder for the head-noun which will follow the relative participle *kaṇṭa* in actual use. Therefore, 'thing' would not be a good translation for *cousa* here in English, in case the "entity" referred to by the head-noun is a human being.

12 The citation form chosen by the MTL for the entry head, which in direct transliteration would be *kāṇ(ṇu)-tal* and is in fact realized as *kāṇtal* in actual use, illustrates a type of verbal noun (ending in *-tal*) that is frequently attested in the VTCSP, in which I have so far tagged 151 such forms (identified as category "INF2"). This is the citation form for verbs in all the traditional Tamil grammars and thesauri.

consult p. lxvii in the MTL, where they would discover that the 13th class groups together irregular verbs, but they would not be told that there is a change of vowel length for this particular verb when going from the present stem to the past stem. This particular example is of course especially unsuitable for beginners because the other 12 classes do have a predictable morphology. The VTCSP is, in a sense, more user-friendly in this instance, although it must not have been easy for a beginner to guess that the primary entry *kāṇkiṟatu* [281_L_o] associated with the secondary entry *kaṇṭa* [264_L_a] will be found 17 pages later due to the difference in vowel length.

In the first non-autochthonous grammar of Tamil, composed in Portuguese in the 16th century by Henrique Henriques (henceforth HH, see section 5), a different classificatory scheme for the verbal morphology was adopted (see Table 2, below). The primary citation form used by HH was the first person form of the present. As can be seen on p. 96 in the critical edition by H.J. Vermeer, the whole paradigm of the verb which I have chosen as a first example, and which turns out to be the model chosen by HH for the "nona conjugaçaõ" (ninth conjugation), starts with the present form *canguiren* "veio" (Vermeer, 1982, p. 96) where no vowel lengths (for what is now transliterated as *kāṇkiṟēṉ*) are indicated in HH's MS. This head of enumeration is followed by all the forms derived from the present stem. This is then followed by a second group of forms belonging to the past stem, in which the initial item is *candhen* "eu olhei" (now transliterated *kaṇṭēṉ*). Then comes a third group of forms belonging to the future stem, in which the initial item is *canpen* "olharei" (now *kāṇpēṉ*). This is followed still by other groups, with almost one hundred forms mentioned in total.

Tab. 2: Morphology of 9th conjugation in HH's 16th-century grammar

canguiren "veio" [I see]	*candhen* "eu olhei" [I saw]	*canpen* "olharei" [I shall see]	47 other forms belonging to imperative, negative and infinitive groups
(along with 19 other forms, such as *canguiRadu*)	(along with 12 other forms, such as *candha*)	(along with 15 other forms)	

It must be noted at this stage that the forms *candhen* and *canpen*, that I have just mentioned in this brief account of HH's grammar, also appear in a slightly different notation, namely *canden* and *canben*, in the Goa MS partly reproduced in the second column of Table 1. This is a trace of the reorganization which was going on, but should of course be examined in parallel with the grammars which were current at the time of the VTCSP.¹³ On the other hand, the main citation form for verbs in the VTCSP, which has been so far represented by the entry *kāṇkiṟatu* [281_L_o], appears for that same lexeme as *canguiRadu*, (see Vermeer (1982: 96)).¹⁴ We can conveniently refer this to as "Present tense, subtense J" if we adopt the scheme proposed by Jeanne Hein and V.S. Rajam on page 195 in their 2013 English translation of HH's grammar (HOS-76).

In a parallel manner, the VTCSP entry *kaṇṭa* [264_L_a] is locatable in HH's grammar as item "*candha*", which is one of the items making up the "past stem group", starting with *candhen* (see Vermeer (1982: 97)). We can refer to it conveniently as "Past tense, subtense J" following Hein & Rajam (2013: 196), although of course such a designation is less palatable than the native PE (*peyar eccam*).¹⁵

Compared with HH's grammar, the treatment of the Tamil verbal morphology in the 1679 VTCSP contains a number of innovations. For example, a constituent of the Tamil verbal paradigm which is prominent in the VTCSP but silently omitted by HH's *Arte*¹⁶ is a type of verbal noun ending in -*kai*. This type of verbal noun has in fact already been seen by the readers of this article because it appears in Figure 1, Figure 2 and Figure 3, just above entry *kāṇkiṟatu* [281_L_o], that is, entry [281_L_n] (produced as (4a) and (4b) below).

(4a)   <entry coordinates="281_L_n">
       <entry_head>க # ணா @@ க</entry_head>
       <Intended_Modern_Spelling> காண்கை [kāṇkai]</Intended_Modern_Spelling>
       <Under>281_L_o</Under>
       <CATEGORY>INF1</CATEGORY>
       <entry_body>O olhar.</entry_body>
       </entry>
(4b)   kāṇkai [281_L_n] "O olhar". (INF1) (Under 281_L_o)((the seeing))

---

13 My colleague Cristina Muru has been preparing the edition of such an unpublished grammar, the ARTE TAMULICA by Balthasar da Costa SJ (c. 1610–1673), for several years. See Muru (2020).
14 Note that there is a second *canguiRadu* on the page, which should have been *canguiRaducu*, but a syllable was left out by mistake. See Hein & Rajam (2013: 195 fn. 351).
15 Native designations, such as *peyar eccam*, did eventually become familiar to Western scholars. For example, although Ziegenbalg (1716) does not mention such indigenous terms, Beschi (1738: 65) writes: *Participium autem vocant* பெயரெச்சம், *defectus nominis* [...].
16 Interestingly, however, even though the INF1 type of verbal noun is not described in HH's grammar, HH has made use of it in a book which he composed, *Flos Sanctorum* என்ற அடியார் வரலாறு, a collection of the lives of Saints.

As indicated by the content of the "Under" XML element, this is a secondary entry, which is part of the "family" of forms in which *kāṇkiṟatu* [281_L_o] is the primary entry. The apparent discrepancy between the Portuguese translations "O olhar" for 281_L_n, "Ver" for 281_L_o and "C. que uio, ou foi // uiſta" for 264_L_a, however, could lead one to suspect that this is not the same lexeme. HH's grammar, though, also contains an alternating translation, with suppletion between "ver" and "olhar", in *canguiren* "veio" ('I see'), *candhen* "eu olhei" ('I saw') and *canpen* "olharei" ('I shall see'), already presented in Table 2. I must add that the CATEGORY label INF1 was chosen for the simple reason that, inside the VTCSP, this type of verbal noun, having the ending *-kai*, is the most frequent (see section 4) and is always translated by a Portuguese infinitive preceded by an article.

4 How many "verb families" does the VTCSP contain?

In order to conclude the exposition started in the previous section, in this section I will provide figures concerning the frequency of the V, INF1 and PE types of secondary element in the work-in-progress-1, namely my entry of the VTCSP into XML format. In this section, I also provide some information on chronology, before moving into the core topic in section 5.

Out of a total of 16,217 entries, which are printed in 1,016 columns, limiting ourselves to the CATEGORY labels with which we are familiar, we can say that:
— The value "V"[17] is found inside the "CATEGORY" element of 3,156 items
— "INF1" occurs 1,121 times
— "PE" occurs 719 times

Regarding the distribution of primary and secondary entries, the basic facts are that:
— There are 3,471 occurrences of the "Under" element in the 16,217 completed "entry" elements and these 3,471 occurrences are pointers towards 1,413 primary target entries. This means that an average targeted primary entry is associated with an average of 2.46 Secondary entries.

---

17 I must at this stage specify that I give the label V to verbal forms ending in *-kkiṟatu*, or *-kiṟatu*. Some of these occasionally appear in a variant form ending in *-ṟatu*. Examples are *keṭukkiṟatu* [289_R_l], *kāṇkiṟatu* [281_L_o] and *pōṟatu* [242_L_h], which is a variant of *pōkiṟatu* [238_R_f].

— In addition, there are also 1,475 entries which are categorized as V, but which are neither primary entries with respect to other entries, nor secondary entries with respect to a primary entry. I shall refer to those entries as singleton entries.

When we include both groups in global statistics about families, we obtain the distribution of verbal forms described in the following table.

Tab. 3: Distribution of 6,359 entries belonging to the verbal paradigm in the VTCSP

Singleton entries	Entries which are primary with respect to one or several other entries	Secondary entries	Total
1,475	1,413	3,471	
	2,888 heads of families (including singleton families)		6,359
An average family of verbal forms contains 1 primary entry and 1.2 secondary entries			

However, due to a number of factors – some of which will be discussed in what follows, while others will remain undiscussed – such a figure is only very roughly indicative.[18] The hard fact nevertheless is that out of a total of 16,217 entries found in the VTCSP, ca. 6,359 are devoted to verbal morphology (and semantics), which represents 39% of the VTCSP.

5 Elements concerning chronology

In this section, I shall provide chronological information concerning the early Western descriptors of Tamil.[19] These early descriptors, who wrote in Portuguese and in Latin, are followed in the timeline (Table 4) by later descriptors who wrote in English.

---

18 For instance, if the 548 CAUSATIVE verbs which are currently identified were to be declared as "Secondary" to their base, and not as standalone singleton items, the global proportions would be different.
19 Their works will hopefully someday be part of the CETGD (Corpus of Early Tamil Grammars and Dictionaries) mentioned in the introduction and conclusion.

Tab. 4: Timeline for five early missionary descriptions of Tamil and a broad chronology

Abbreviation & title	Early Authors' name, dates of Birth and Death (and stay in India)	Work Date, type & Meta-language used	English translations (and critical editions)
HH Arte em Malauar	Henrique Henriques 1520–1600 (1546–1600)	16th c. MS grammar (in Portuguese)	Hans J. Vermeer (1982) [critical edition] // J. Hein & V.S. Rajam (HOS 76, 2013) [translation]
AP Vocabulario Tamulico	Antaõ de Proença[20] 1625–1666 (1647–1666)	1679 Printed vocabulary (in Portuguese)	No
BZ Grammatica Damulica	Bartholomæus Ziegenbalg 1682–1719 (1706–1714 & 1716–1719)[21]	1716 Printed grammar (in Latin)	Daniel Jeyaraj (English transl. 2010)
CJB Grammatica Latino-Tamulica	Constantius Joseph Beschi 1680–c.1746 (1710–1746)	1738 Printed grammar (in Latin)	Horst (1806[1], 1813[2]) Mahon (1848)
CTW Observationes Grammaticæ	Christoph Theodosius Walther 1699–1741 (1724–1740)	1739 Printed grammar (in Latin)	No

Later Names	Period
Horst Mahon	Translators of Beschi from Latin into English (early 19th cent.)
G.U. Pope, Arden	Grammarians (late 19th century)
Harold Schiffman, E. Annamalai, Sanford B. Steever	Linguists (late 20th century)

6 A first encounter with verbal composition and with VE1 forms

Building on the framework given in section 4, we can now turn our attention to the subset of 298 elements that illustrate "grammatical compounding" (see

---

[20] Proença's dictionary has been extensively studied by G. James in several publications. See bibliography.
[21] BZ made a two-year journey (1714–1716) to Europe. See Jeyaraj (2010).

section 8), in which we see the presence of what have been called "vector verbs" by some authors (see footnote 5). This subset represents 8.6% of the 3,471 secondary verbal entries which have been mentioned in the third column of Table 3.[22] The manner in which those 298 entries can be categorized as secondary entries, with respect to other entries, is probably more difficult to justify, as was the case for the "relative participles" (label PE) discussed previously.

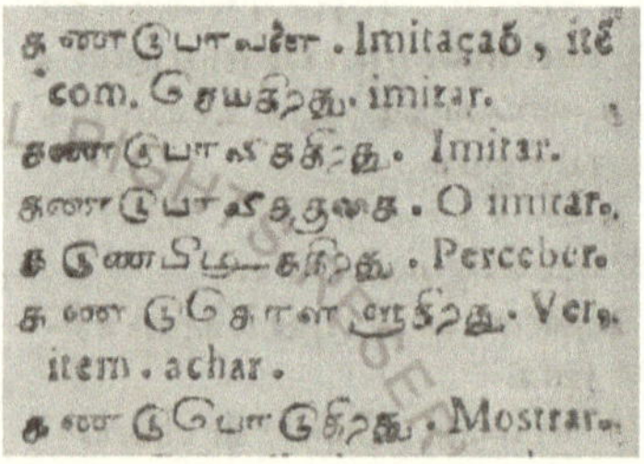
. Imitaçaõ, itẽ
com. செய்கிறது. imitar.
. Imitar.
. O imitar.
. Perceber.
. Ver.
item. achar.
. Mostrar.

Fig. 5: items 264_R_c to 264_R_i in the VTCSP (1679)

The morphology of the elements of our subset is more complex than the morphology of the secondary items which we have examined in (2) and in (4) in the previous sections. All of the 298 elements are "compound verbs", which occur as a result of the combination of two verbs; one of them being the verb which is their primary entry, accessible via an "Under link" as we have seen previously, and the other one being what has been called a "vector verb" by some and an "auxiliary verb" by others. Another point to be noted is that I use more than one category tag in order to characterize those items with enough precision. A final general remark is that verbal composition is a much larger domain, the study of which will not be exhausted by dealing with the phenomenon at hand. This is to say that our set of 298 elements is a subset of a larger set, the CVS (for "Compound Verb Set"), of all the verbs found in the VTCSP which are obtained by combining two verbs. I will be using the following abbreviations in the examples moving forward:

- The 298 items shall be said to belong to the G-CVS (Grammatical Compound Verbs Subset)

22 By extrapolation, the corresponding subset in the whole of the VTCSP probably contains 298 elements.

- The other items shall be said to belong to L-CVS (Lexical Compound Verbs Subset)

At this stage, it is not possible to precisely determine the size of the L-CVS, but I have provided representatives of both subsets, G-CVS and L-CVS, below. We will begin with six entries related to the verb *kāṇkiṟatu* [281_L_o], discussed above. These six entries appear in Figure 5, where they are followed by a seventh. All seven entries appear in the R(ight) column on p. 264 of the 1679 printed version of the VTCSP. Using the aforementioned designation of "families", we can say that the six entries represent four verbal families:

- The first three items (264_R_c to 264_R_e) are three components of a family:

(5a) *kaṇṭupāvaṉai* [264_R_c] "imitaçaõ [...]" (VN_aṉai) ((imitation)), a secondary entry which is a verbal noun with the suffix -*aṉai*;[23]
(5b) *kaṇṭupāvikkiṟatu* [264_R_d] "Imitar" (V)[24](VE1-V) ((to imitate)), which is the family head, alias Primary entry in the family, to which I have also given a second categorization for reasons which have to do with its belonging to L-CVS;
(5c) *kaṇṭupāvikkukai* [264_R_c] "O imitar" (INF1) ((imitating)), a secondary entry which is a verbal noun with the suffix -*kai*.[25]

- The fourth item, which contains a typographical mistake,[26] can be transcribed after correction as:

(6) *kaṇṭupiṭikkiṟatu* [264_R_f] "Perceber" (V)(VE1-V) ((to understand, to comprehend)), a "singleton" (as per the conventions presented in Table 3); I have also given it a second categorization, "VE1-V", as I had done for 264_R_d.

- The fifth item, which can be transcribed as:

---

23 This is in fact a Sanskrit suffix because *pāvaṉai* is the Tamilized version of Sanskrit *bhāvanā* 'imagination'.
24 As already explained, I use the V category label for items ending in -*kkiṟatu*, -*kiṟatu* or -*ṟatu*.
25 This verbal noun belongs to the same morphological category (INF1) as the item *kāṇkai* [264_L_a] discussed in (2) in section 3.
26 In the RAW transcription, கடுணபிடிககிறது, the second and third symbol should be inverted. A normalized modern rendering is "கண்டுபிடிக்கிறது" [kaṇṭupiṭikkiṟatu].

(7) *kaṇṭukoḷḷukiṟatu* [264_R_g] "Ver, item. achar" (V)(VECTOR_CONSTRUCTION) (Under 281_L_o) ((to see, or to think/ to guess)), is a secondary entry falling under primary entry *kāṇkiṟatu* [281_L_o].

— The sixth item, which can be transcribed as:

(8) *kaṇṭupōṭukiṟatu* [264_R_h] "Mostrar." (V)(VECTOR_CONSTRUCTION) (Under 281_L_o) ((to display, to exhibit)) , I have tentatively labelled this a secondary entry falling under the same primary entry *kāṇkiṟatu* [281_L_o], although the Portuguese meaning provided might be a reason for recategorizing this entry as a member of L-CVS.

Leaving aside the two secondary items belonging to the *kaṇṭupāvikkiṟatu* family (items 5a and 5c, above), labeled respectively as VN_aṉai and as INF1, we will here examine in more detail those items labelled V (5b, 6, 7, and 8). The first point to be noted is that all four of these items share a common feature: the presence of the same first morphological component *kaṇṭu*, a form which belongs to the paradigm of the verb *kāṇkiṟatu* [281_L_o] and has received a number of designations in the course of history. Among these designations, we must first of all mention the standard designation given by the Tamil grammarians, which is either concisely (but ambiguously) *viṉai-y-eccam* (henceforth VE), or verbosely (and unambiguously) "*ceyt-eṉṉum vāypāṭṭu viṉai-y-eccam*", i.e. "VE of the *ceytu* type". I abbreviate this type as VE1 as it is the first to be mentioned in traditional enumerations. From the point of view of the *Grammatici Tamulici* (enumerated in Table 4), on the other hand, we see the following:

(A1) In HH's grammar, while describing the "Nona comjugaçaõ" (Vermeer 1982: 97), i.e. 'ninth conjugation', there is a gap in the enumeration of the forms derived from the preterite *candhen*. We might have expected to find *candhu* here in a position which, in the terminology adopted by Hein & Rajam (2013), should be referred to as preterite tense, Subtense G.[27] Nevertheless, when discussing the equivalent form, *vichuuaditu*, which belongs to the paradigm of the "primeira cõjugaçaõ" ('first conjugation'), HH refers to it as a "tẽpo que parece quasi gerũdio" (Vermeer 1982: 40)[28] and says that it is frequently used. Elsewhere, he gives additional pieces of information to which we will return in (B1) in section 10.

---

27 See Hein and Rajam (2013: 196).
28 Hein and Rajam (2013: 91) translate: "it seems almost like a gerund".

(A2) Proença, while explaining the uses of *koḷḷukiṟatu* (entry 299_L_o), says that it can be combined "com o gerundio de qualquer uerbo" [with the gerund of any verb], a statement to which we shall return in (12) in section 7. However, unlike his treatment of the "relative participle" (alias PE),[29] he reserves almost no entries for the VE1 type items. Many of VE1 forms, however, are present as the first component of a compound form included in other entries.

(A3) Ziegenbalg, in his 1716 grammar (BIB), composed in Latin, refers to it as the "*gerundium*" (Ziegenbalg 1716: 72).

(A4) Beschi, in his grammar printed in 1738, also refers to it as the *gerundium* (see Caput III, § VI. pp. 63–65) but adds that the VE1 corresponds only to the "*gerundium in do*", and that other solutions are required for rendering the other types of Latin gerund (in *di* and in *dum*).

(A5) Walther, in his book printed in 1739, also refers to it as the *gerundium* (see Caput III, § III. pp. 24–26)

(A6) In the modern period, forms of the VE1 type have also been called a "Verbal Participle", "Converb", or "Ad-verbal Participle". If not using the label "VE1", I shall myself use "converb".

7 Two examples of lexical compounding

In this section and in the following, we will turn our attention to the second component of the four entries, first introduced in (5b), (6), (7) and (8), namely *kaṇṭu-pāvikkiṟatu* [264_R_d], *kaṇṭu-piṭikkiṟatu* [264_R_f], *kaṇṭu-koḷḷukiṟatu* [264_R_g] and *kaṇṭu-pōṭukiṟatu* [264_R_h]. Each of these four second components can be located as an independent entry inside the VTCSP. Transcriptions of the first two are as follows:

(9) *pāvikkiṟatu* [215_L_d] "Representar, imaginar". (V) ((to have a mental representation of, to imagine))

(10) *piṭikkiṟatu* [234_R_d] "Pegar, item prēder [...]" (V) ((to catch, OR[30] to take))

These two elements offer us an opportunity to illustrate lexical compounding. For clarity, I remind the reader that here we have the original meaning of two items

---

[29] See my statement in section 4: "PE" occurs 656 times in CC".
[30] The word "item" is used in the VTCSP for itemizing, i.e. for separating the successive meanings enumerated in the body of an entry.

which, after combining with *kaṇṭu*, VE1 (alias 'Gerund/.../Converb') of *kāṇkiṟatu* [281_L_o] 'to see', become the lexical entries earlier presented in (5b) and in (6), in section 6. We could paraphrase the process with a minimal symbolic notation, using exponentiation for representing the converbs as left-specifiers of main verbs in equations of the form $^{\text{CONVERB1}}$-VERB2 = VERB3. Describing the process thusly:

(11a) ^{Seeing}-Catch = Understand ('to_see_AND_THEN to_catch' = 'to_understand') (When Left-specified by the converb of 'to see', 'to catch' becomes 'to understand' [i.e. 'to grasp'])

(11b) ^{Seeing}-Imagine = Imitate ('to_see_AND_THEN to_imagine' = 'to_imitate') (When Left-specified by the converb of 'to see', 'to imagine' becomes 'to imitate')

These two examples are comments on the relationship between the two entries *kaṇṭu-pāvikkiṟatu* [264_R_d] and *kaṇṭu-piṭikkiṟatu* [264_R_f], on the one hand, and the two entries *pāvikkiṟatu* [215_L_d] and *piṭikkiṟatu* [234_R_d], on the other. They illustrate what I refer to as lexical compounding, and therefore items 264_R_d and 264_R_f are, in this scheme, members of the L-CVS set evoked in section 6.

8 The VTCSP explanations concerning grammatical compounding

We now come to the second set, namely G-CVS, which contains the elements found in the VTCSP which are the result of grammatical compounding.

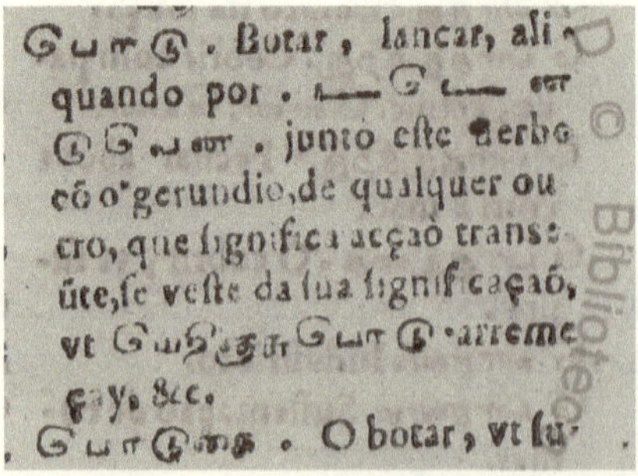
. Botar, lancar, ali-
quando por .
. junto este verbo
cõ o gerundio, de qualquer ou
tro, que significa acçaõ trans-
ite, se veste da sua significaçaõ,
vt arreme-
çay, &c.
. O botar, vt su-

Fig. 6: VTCSP entries 243_E_e & 243_R_f

The logic underlying the formation of grammatical compounds is explicitly presented inside the VTCSP in the following two entries, (12) and (13) (see also the images of these entries from the VTCSP in Figure 6, Figure 7 and Figure 8). A complete translation of these two entries can only be provided step-by-step. This is due to the density of information they contain and the great number of intertextual links that must be established with other parts of the VTCSP, where we find many illustrations, and with other components of the CETGD.

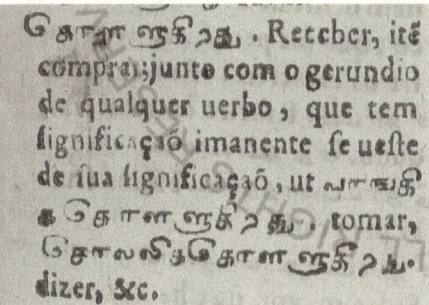

Fig. 7: VTCSP entry 299_L_o

(12) *koḷḷukiṟatu* [299_L_o]. "Receber, itẽ comprar; junto com o gerundio de qualquer uerbo, que tem fignificaçaõ imanente fe uefte de fua fignificaçaõ, ut வ # ங கி க @ க # ள ரு கி ற து. tomar, @ ச # ல லி க @ க # ள ரு கி ற து. dizer, &c.". (V)

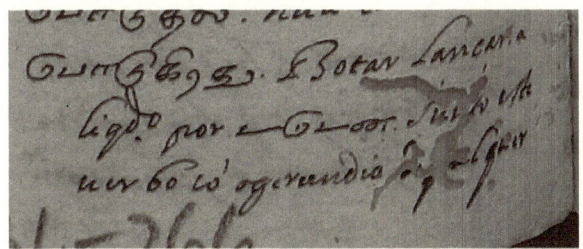

Fig. 8: Initial part of entry 243_R_e in Goa MS

(13) *pōṭu[kiṟatu]*[31] [243_R_e] "Botar, lançar, aliquando por. [...]. junto efte uerbo cõ o gerundio de qualquer outro, que fignifica acçaõ transeũte, fe vefte da fua fignificaçaõ, vt @ யறிஞ்ச @ ப # டு, arremeçay, &c." (V)

The step-by-step approach I have adopted for the translation of (12) is as follows:
— we started in (7) with the entry *kaṇṭu-koḷḷukiṟatu* [264_R_g], in section 6
— we discussed its first component, *kaṇṭu*, labelled as VE1, in section 6
— we located its second component, *koḷḷukiṟatu* [299_L_o], in (12)
— we are now told in (12) that
    — WHEN *koḷḷukiṟatu* is a standalone verb, it means "Receber, itē comprar" ('to receive', OR 'to buy')
    — WHEN *koḷḷukiṟatu* is combined with the gerund of any verb which has an immanent signification (*junto com o gerundio de qualquer uerbo, que tem fignificaçaõ imanente*), THEN it becomes vested with its signification (*fe uefte de fua fignificaçaõ*)
    — This second possibility is then illustrated by two examples
        — *vāṅkik koḷḷukiṟatu* "tomar" (see 14a and 14b, below)
        — *collik koḷḷukiṟatu* "dizer" (see 15a and 15b, below)
— we started in (8) with the entry *kaṇṭu-pōṭukiṟatu* [264_R_h], in section 6
— we discussed its first component, *kaṇṭu*
— we located its second component, *pōṭukiṟatu* [243_R_e], in (13)
— we are now told in (13) that
    — WHEN *pōṭukiṟatu* is a standalone verb, it means "Botar, lançar, aliquando por" ('to throw, to toss', sometimes 'to put')
    — WHEN pōṭukiṟatu is combined with the gerund of any transitive verb (*junto efte uerbo cõ o gerundio de qualquer outro, que fignifica acçaõ transeũte*), THEN it becomes vested with its signification (*fe vefte da fua fignificaçaõ*)
    — This second possibility is then illustrated by one example:
        — *yeṟiñcu-pōṭu* "arremeçay. &c." (see 16a and 16b, below)

The next task is to locate the three examples provided in the VTCSP for our grammatical compound examples, or less anachronistically (more precisely), for those examples where "a verb has been vested with the signification of another verb combined with it as a 'gerund'". We started with two pairs of verbs and we now

---

[31] As can be seen by comparing Figure 6 and Figure 8, the entry head of 243_R_e is mistakenly truncated in the printed book where we see "@ப# டு" where we should see "@ ப#டுகிறது", as in the earlier Goa MS.

have five pairs. The new items will be presented in the same order, with the simple verb coming first and the compound verb following it.

(14a) *vāṅkiṟatu* [421_R_a2] "Tomar, receber da maõ doutrem" ((to take, to receive from the hand of someone else))
(14b) *vāṅkik koḷḷukiṟatu* "idem mais uzado" [421_R_b] ((same [as preceding entry, i.e. 421_R_a2], [but] more frequent in usage))
(15a) *collukiṟatu* "Falar, dizer" [494_L_o] ((to speak, to say))
(15b) *collik koḷḷukiṟatu* [494_L_q] "Fazer que se fala delle, ou ſer // falado. [...]³² item absolute dizer" ((to cause others to talk about oneself, OR to be talked about, ALTERNATELY, [when used] absolutely to say))
(16a) *eṟikiṟatu* [74_R_b] [[Atirar com pedra, aremeçar, item dar couzes. ((to throw stones [at somebody], to hurl [a weapon at somebody], OR to give kicks))
(16b) *eṟiñcu-pōṭukiṟatu* [74_R_h] "Aremeçar" ((to hurl [a weapon at somebody]))

These three pairs of examples confirm what we have already seen in (12) and (13), but there is more to be said about them. When we compare (15a) and (15b), we see that it is (partly) true that *collik koḷḷukiṟatu* and *collukiṟatu* can have the same meaning, namely "dizer" ('to say'), as was announced in (12). We also see, however, that other meanings are possible and that the overlap is therefore limited. We observe the same situation in the comparison between (16a) and (16b): they have been designated with the common Portuguese gloss "aremeçar" 'to hurl', but they are certainly not globally identical. In the case of (14a) and (14b), the VTCSP tells us that they mean the same thing, but that the compound form is found more frequently. Another example of partial overlap appears in a pair belonging to our original set of examples: the compound form *kaṇṭukoḷḷukiṟatu* [264_R_g] first examined in (7), contrasted with *kāṇkiṟatu* [281_L_o], first examined in (1). The common stated meaning is "ver" ('to see'), whereas another meaning is proposed for the compound form, namely "achar" ('to think, to suppose, to guess'). The most difficult pair seems to be the one consisting of *kaṇṭupōṭukiṟatu* [264_R_h] "mostrar" ('to display, to exhibit'), first presented in (8) for which the meaning given differs from the meaning "ver" of the same *kāṇkiṟatu* [281_L_o].

---

32 The passage set aside is an example: "நலலவ@னனறு@ச #லலிக@க#ணட #ன. ſes q~ o tiueſẽ por bom, ou q~ foſſe chamado bom".

9 A global view of grammatical compounding, as seen in the VTCSP

I have so far acted, for "self-pedagogical reasons", as if I were making an original discovery of my own while exploring the VTCSP in the early 21st century. The truth is, however, that I had a preconceived notion of what I hoped to find in the VTCSP because of my familiarity with articles and books written about Tamil by authors such as H. Schiffman, E. Annamalai and S. B. Steever (see the lower part of Table 4 and see Bibliography), who have written at length on items such as *koḷḷukiṟatu*, *pōṭukiṟatu*, and other such items. On the other hand, I also know, because of long practice, that the ancient native Tamil tradition totally ignores those phenomena, although they must certainly have existed at least since the medieval period.[33]

The three modern linguists (whom I first mentioned in Table 4) refer to the items under consideration either as "aspect markers" (Schiffman), "Auxiliary Verbs [AV]" (E. Annamalai) or "Auxiliary verbs in an AVC"[34] (Steever). Following them, I have used the label AUX in Table 5 (see below) for referring to the second component in the items which have been labelled as VECTOR_CONSTRUCTION in the CATEGORY element of my XML encoding of the VTCSP. When placing their own work in a historical context, these authors refer to earlier descriptions written in English in the 19th century, for instance, works by authors such as G.U. Pope, Arden, and others. Those 19th century authors themselves had been partly relying on a particularly important translation from Latin into English, made in the early 19th century by Horst and by Mahon. This Latin book translated into English by Horst and Mahon was the 18th c. *Grammatical Latino-Tamulica* of C. J. Beschi, printed in 1738 in Tranquebar. Of course, Beschi himself, as is clear when reading his grammar, also had predecessors. Although he used Latin as a meta-language, he both depended upon and continued the work of earlier descriptions (grammars and dictionaries) written in Portuguese. However, a significant part of the information contained in those early descriptions ceased at some point of time to be transmitted. It is with the intention of restoring a kind of longer memory in the history of the description of Tamil that I have started the task on

---

33 There are traces of the use of grammatical compounding in the *Tēvāram*, a collection of hymns to Shiva which may have been composed in the 7th and the 8th centuries. However, space and time prevent me from doing more here than mentioning as an example the use of forms like *uyttiṭṭu, ceytiṭṭu, niṟuviṭṭu, oṉṟiṭṭu, aṭṭiṭṭu* and *uṇṭiṭṭē* in the *Tēvāram* hymn 1_126. The *Tēvāram* contains many such forms, as can be seen when exploring the concordance provided in the Digital Tevaram CD (see bibliography).
34 AVC = Auxiliary verb construction.

which I am currently reporting. I was initially surprised to see the presence inside the VTCSP of so many items resulting from grammatical compounding. Such items, which modern lexicographers entrust to the care of their grammarian colleagues, had obviously been considered important by Proença. This is why he included ca. 298 of them as standalone entries in his VTCSP. The following chart provides a basic set of elements in six columns, concerning each of the groups of items in which the same AUX is found. The groups are ordered by decreasing frequency, the most frequent AUX, "*pōṟatu*", being at the top, found in 118 items in the current stage of the "work-in-progress". It is followed by "*koḷḷukiṟatu*" (57 items), "*irukkiṟatu*" (48 items), "*pōṭukiṟatu*" (27 items), "*viṭukiṟatu*" (8 items), "*vaikkiṟatu*" (5 items) and 9 more items having even lower frequencies. For each group, I give the reference to the page numbers in the book or, in the case of Schiffman, in the journal issues, where the specific auxiliary has been discussed.

Tab. 5: Auxiliaries in the VTCSP (by descending frequencies)

Group Rank	Group Count	AUX Value for the group[35]	H. Schiffman (in *JTS*[36])	E. Annamalai (1985)	S.B. Steever (2005)
1	126 items	pōṟatu @ ப #றது	*JTS* 04 (p. 49–50)	pp. 104–108	pp. 281–285
2	60 items	koḷḷukiṟatu @ க# ளுகிறது	*JTS* 04 (pp. 51–54)	pp. 113–123	pp. 195–208
3	52	irukkiṟatu இ ருக்கிறது	*JTS* 06 (pp. 31–43)	pp. 124–136	pp. 168–185
4	30	pōṭukiṟatu @ ப #டுகிறது	*JTS* 04 (pp. 33–39)	pp. 45–47	pp. 274–277
5	8	viṭukiṟatu வி டு கிறது	*JTS* 04 (pp. 39–41)	pp. 69–103	pp. 185–195
6	6	vaikkiṟatu @@ வக்கிறது	*JTS* 09 (pp. 98–103)	pp. 39–44	pp. 225–225
9 to 15	16	9 low-frequency items			
	298	TOTAL			

---

[35] Technically, in the XML file, each "entry" element containing a "CATEGORY" element which has "VECTOR_CONSTRUCTION" as a value, also contains two other elements called "CONSTITUENT_VE" and "CONSTITUENT_AUX".
[36] *The Journal of Tamil Studies*.

10 What other "Grammatici Tamulici" tell us about grammatical compounding

To conclude, it would be worthwhile here to briefly revisit the remarks of other grammarians on the phenomena that have been the focus of our attention in order to place them in the context of our discussions so far. The first among them is HH (16th century). He briefly commented on the use of *Porhuren*, which is his citation form for our *pōṭukiṛatu*,[37] as part of his report on the "Septima cõjugaçaõ" (seventh conjugation). Page 92 in the 1982 critical edition by Vermeer contains his statement on *Porhuren* (17a), the original of which appears in Figure 9. The 2013 translation by Hein & Rajam is provided in (17b).

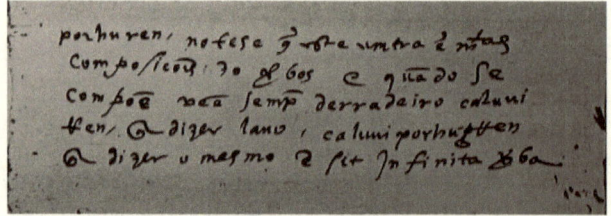

Fig. 9: folio 110v (Lisboa MS of HH's grammar)

(17a) Porhuren. Notese que este emtra ẽ muitas composiçoĩs do[s] verbos ; e quãdo se compoẽ, veẽ sempre derradeiro : caluuiRen quer dizer lauo, caluuiporhuRen quer dizer o mesmo, et sic jnfinita verba. (Vermeer, 1982, p. 92)

(17b) Porhuren.[38] Note that this [verb] enters into many compound verbs and when the parts are put together, porhuren always comes after [the verb with which it is combined]. caLuviRRen means 'I wash', caLulvi porhuRRen means the same. It is so with countless verbs. (Hein & Rajam, 2013, p. 185)[39]

---

37 As exemplified in Table 2, HH uses the 1st person singular form of the present tense as the main citation form.
38 A reader surprised by the discrepancy between (7a) and (17b) can examine the MS fragment in Figure 9. I have discussed the difference between the transcription systems of Vermeer (1982) and Hein & Rajam (2013) in Chevillard (2017).
39 As noted by Hein & Rajam, in a footnote on the same page, we find illustrations of that phenomenon in *Flos Sanctorum,* already mentioned in footnote 16. To which we can add that the

The most striking fact in (17a) and (17b) is the assertion that the items *caluuiRen* and *caluuiporhuRen* have the same meaning and can both be translated by lauo "I wash". The corresponding item, 259_R_b *kaḻuvukiṟatu* "Lauar" ('to wash'), can be identified in the VTCSP, but the equivalent of the compound form, which should be *kaḻuvippōṭukiṟatu*, cannot. However, if we examine the collection of 30 forms which are referred to in row 4 of Table 5, we find that in almost all cases the same meaning has been given in Portuguese for both the simple and the compound form. To mention just a few, in order of occurrence:
- both *arikiṟatu* [28_R_f] and *ariñcupōṭukiṟatu* [28_R_p] are said to mean "cortar" ('to cut')
- both *avikkiṟatu* [41_L_f] and *aviccuppōṭukiṟatu* [41_R_g] are said to mean "apagar" ('to extinguish')
- both *māṟukiṟatu* [127_L_b] and *māṟippōṭukiṟatu* [126_R_a] are said to mean "trocar" ('to exchange [money]') etc.

Anyone who has read H. Schiffman's article in *JTS* 04 (Schiffman 1973), where he describes "The Aspect Marker /pōṭu/, 'Malevolent'", or pp. 45–47 in E. Annamalai's (1985) monograph, where he describes "pooṭu: the verb of casualness", would expect to see a difference of meaning between the two items. Although S.B. Steever (2005) also has a similar title, namely "Auxiliary of abruptness: pōṭa", for the section on pages 274–277 of his book, the solution to our problem with the interpretation of the Portuguese glosses might be found in a comment he makes at the beginning of the section (p. 274). He remarks here that there are Tamil dialects which do not differentiate between *pōṭa* and *viṭa*, instead merging them into a single item, *piṭa*. That remark of course raises a difficult question: which variety of Tamil is described by the VTCSP? This topic, however, has been dealt with elsewhere.[40]

Bringing this section to a close, I simply want to point to a few locations in the CETGD corpus which are possible entry points for continuing this exploration of early Western descriptions of Tamil:

(B1) A group of two examples, *vamduuirhugiren* and *poivirhugiren*, given by HH in the lower part of fol. 48r,[41] in which we see the combination of the VE1 *vamdu* (resp. *poi*) with the verb which he writes *uirhugiren* (resp.

---

preface to the VTCSP tells us that HH has used the *Flos Sanctorum* as one of the sources of his compilation.
40 See Chevillard (2017), section 10 "Which language to describe?".
41 See Vermeer (1982: 41) and Hein and Rajam (2013: 91–92).

virhugiren), his citation form for the *viṭukiṟatu* auxiliary (5th item in Table 5 of this work). These two examples, with *vamdu* and *poi*, are provided by HH as a context for understanding one of the roles of the VE1 forms. His main model for this is *vichuuaditu*, introduced at the bottom of fol. 47v and continued at the top of fol. 48r. I have already mentioned this in (A1), in section 6.

(B2) Turning now to BZ, the grammarian following HH and AP chronologically in Table 4, it may be useful to examine the short section titled *De Verborum Compofitione*, pp. 83–84 in Chapter VI (*De Verbo*), in his 1716 *Grammatica Damulica*.

(B3) The logical continuation would then be to read the longer presentation made by Beschi in his 1738 *Grammatica Latino-Tamulica*. In *Caput IV* (*De Syntaxi*) there is a §. IV titled *De Compositione Verborum*, spanning pp. 109 to 116, that provides specific paragraphs for specific auxiliaries.

(B4) After that, it would also be necessary to read Walther's 1739 *Observationes*, where we find in the first paragraph of the section *De Verbis Auxiliaribus* (Caput IV, § XV, pp. 53–55) the statement: « *Ut linguæ vernaculæ duo verba componunt et adunant, quorum alterum vocatur auxiliare; ita et fit in tamulica;* e.g.
   — நான்போயிருக்கிறேன்
   — *eo profectus fum quondam,*
   — *german. ich bin gegangen,*
   — *lufit. eu foi ido &c.* »

(B5) Finally, it would also be important to compare those Latin texts with their English translations.

11 Not a conclusion: Toward an MLDELT

As stated in the introduction, the elements contained in this short article are fragments extracted from a work in progress. Explaining why it might nevertheless be useful to circulate those elements will be the goal of this final paragraph, organized as a collection of brief statements:
— because of the domination of English as a scientific lingua franca, any source which is redacted in another language is in danger of being ignored.
— a number of pioneers have made efforts to render some of the primary sources accessible to the general community of descriptive linguists, redacted in Portuguese, Dutch and Latin. Apart from them, one could cite Désoulières (1982), Bhatia and Machida (2008), Pytlowany (2018) for

Hindustānī; Rocher (1977), Van Hal and Vielle (2013) for Sanskrit and Vermeer (1982), Jeyaraj (2010), Hein and Rajam (2013) for Tamil.
— Much, however, remains to be done, at least as far as Tamil is concerned.

Finally, I wish here to express my interest, on the basis of my experience in preparing the VTCSP, and as I meditate on the ideal format for the CETGD, in a future collective undertaking which would consist in working towards a "Multi-Lingual Dictionary of Early Linguistic Terminology" (MLDELT), centered on the Latin Linguistic Terminology but also incorporating Portuguese terminology, as seen in the VTCSP and in the treatise studied by Désoulières (1982), Dutch terminology, as seen in Bhatia & Kazuhiko (2008), etc. I am aware, of course, of the fact that there is a long way from the cup to the lips, but Tamil studies should not live in a ghetto.

Acknowledgements

This is the final written version of a presentation which was given at SALA 35 (INALCO, Paris, 29–31 October 2019). The original title was: "On 17th century strategies for explaining by means of Portuguese glosses the use of vector verbs in Early Modern Tamil, as seen in Antam de Proença's posthumous *Vocabulario Tamulico com a Significaçam Portugueza (1679)*". I am grateful to the anonymous reviewers and to my colleagues Erin McCann and Ghanshyam Sharma who made several important suggestions for improving my article after reading an earlier version.

References

Annamalai, E. 1985. *Dynamics of verbal extension in Tamil*. Trivandrum: Dravidian Linguistics Association of India.

Aussant, Émilie & Chevillard, Jean-Luc. 2020. Foreword. In Émilie Aussant & Jean-Luc Chevillard (eds.), *Extended Grammars*, Topical issue of *Beiträge zur Geschichte der Sprachwissenschaft 30.1*, 3–8. Münster: Nodus Publikationen.

Bhatia, Tej K. & Kazuhiko Machida. 2008. *The Oldest Grammar of Hindustānī. Contact, Communication and Colonial Legacy* (3 vol.). Tokyo: Research Institute for Languages and Cultures of Asia and Africa, Tokyo University of Foreign Studies.

Beschi, Constantius Joseph. 1738 [1728]. *Grammatica Latino-Tamulica, ubi de Vulgari Tamulicæ Linguæ Idiomate* கொடுந்தமிழ *[KOṬUNTAMIḺ] dicto*. Tranquebar: Typis Miffionis Danicæ [Danish mission press].

Beschi, Constantius Joseph. 1831 [1806]. *A Grammar of the Common Dialect of the Tamulian Language, Called Koṭuntamiḻ.* [Translated by Christopher Henry Horst]. Madras: Vepery Mission Press.

Beschi, Constantius Joseph. 1848. A Grammar of the common dialect of the Tamul Language, called கொடுந்தமிழ் [KOṬUNTAMIḺ], composed for the use of the Missionaries of the Society of Jesus by Missionary of the said Society in the district of Madurai [Translated from the original Latin by Mahon, George Wiliam]. Madras, Vepery: Christian Knowledge Society's Press.

Chevillard, Jean-Luc. 2015. The challenge of bi-directional translation as experienced by the first European missionary grammarians and lexicographers of Tamil. In Émilie Aussant (ed.), *La Traduction dans l'Histoire des Idées Linguistiques*, 107–126. Paris: Librairie Orientaliste Paul Geuthner.

Chevillard, Jean-Luc. 2017. How Tamil was described once again: towards an XML-encoding of the Grammatici Tamulici. *Histoire Epistémologie Langage* 39 (2). 103–127. Paris: SHESL/EDP Sciences.

Cre-A Dictionary of Contemporary Tamil / kriyāviṉ taṟkālat tamiḻ akarāti (Tamil-Tamil-English). Chennai: Cre-A Publishers.

Désoulières, Alain. 1982. *Gramatica Indostana 1778, Étude critique et traduction d'un manuel d'hindoustani.* Mémoire pour un diplôme de Doctorat de troisième cycle en Études Indiennes. Paris : Université of Paris (Sorbonne Nouvelle Paris III) doctoral dissertation.

Hein, Jeanne & V. S. Rajam. 2013. *The Earliest Missionary Grammar of Tamil. Fr. Henriques' Arte da Lingua Malabar: Translation, History and Analysis.* Harvard Oriental Series (v. 76). Cambridge, MA: Harvard University Press.

Henrique Henriques. 1967 [1586]. *Aṉṯirīkku aṭikaḷār iyaṟṟiya Flos Sanctorum eṉṟa aṭiyār varalāṟu.* [Edited by Ca. Irācamāṇikkam]. Tūttukkuṭi, India: Tamiḻ Ilakkiyak Kaḻakam.

James, Gregory. 2000. Colporuḷ, A History of Tamil Dictionaries. Chennai: Cre-A.

James, Gregory. 2007. The manuscript and printed versions of Antão de Proença's Vocabulario tamulico (1679), no:kku, 1. (article accessed on the Academia page of the author)

James, Gregory. 2009. Aspects of the structure of entries in the earliest missionary dictionary of Tamil. In O. Zwartjes, R. Arzápalo & T. Smith-Stark (eds.), *Missionary Linguistics IV / Lingüística misionera* IV, 273–301. Amsterdam: John Benjamins Publishing Company.

Jeyaraj, Daniel. 2010. *Tamil Language for Europeans: Ziegenbalg's Grammatica Damulica (1716).* [Translated from Latin and Tamil. Annotated and commented by Daniel Jeyaraj]. Wiesbaden: Harrassowitz Verlag.

Liang, Hsin-hsin & Peter E. Hook. 2007. The Compound Verb in Chinese and Hindi-Urdu and the Plausibility of the Indo-Turanian Linguistic Area. In Colin P. Masica (ed.) *Old and New Perspectives on South Asian Languages. Grammar and Semantics*, 109-143. [MLBD Series in Linguistics, volume XVI]. Delhi: Motilal Banarsidass.

Muru, Cristina. 2018. Early Descriptors and Descriptions of South Asian Languages from the 16th Century Onwards. *Journal of Portuguese Linguistics* 17 (1). 8. [Online publication https://jpl.letras.ulisboa.pt/articles/10.5334/jpl.202]

Muru, Cristina. 2020. Grammaire Latine Étendue. Two Portuguese missionary Tamil Arte (17th century). In Émilie Aussant & Jean-Luc Chevillard (eds.), *Extended Grammars*, Topical issue of *Beiträge zur Geschichte der Sprachwissenschaft 30.1*, 59–73. Münster: Nodus Publikationen.

MTL : Madras Tamil Lexicon. 1982 [1924–1939]. *Tamil Lexicon*. [Six volumes and one supplement published under the authority of the University of Madras]. Madras: University of Madras.

Pytlowany, Anna K. 2018. *Ketelaar rediscovered. The first Dutch grammar of Persian and Hindustani (1698)*. Amsterdam: Amsterdam Center for Language and Communication doctoral dissertation.

Rocher, Ludo. 1977. *Dissertation on the Sanskrit language by Paulinus a S. Bartholomaeo: with an introductory article, a complete English translation, and an index of sources.* Amsterdam: John Benjamins.

Schiffman, Harold. 1973. The Tamil aspectual system: A transformational grammar. Chapter III, Aspectual markers and their derivation. *Journal of Tamil Studies* 4. 33–54.

Schiffman, Harold. 1974. The Tamil aspectual system: A transformational grammar. The aspect marker /IRU/. *Journal of Tamil Studies* 6. 31–43.

Schiffman, Harold. 1976. The Tamil aspectual system: A transformational grammar. The aspect marker /vay/, "future utility". *Journal of Tamil Studies* 9. 98–112.

Steever, Sanford B. 2005. *The Tamil Auxiliary Verb System*. [Routledge Asian Linguistics Series]. London & New York: Routledge.

Subramanya Ayyar, V. M., Jean-Luc Chevillard & S.A.S. Sarma (eds.). 2007. *Digital Tēvāram* (kaṇiṉit tēvāram). [with complete English gloss of the late V.M. Subramanya Ayyar]. Collection Indologie no. 103 [CD-ROM]. Pondichéry: Institut Français de Pondichéry / École française d'Extrême-Orient.

Thani Nayagam, Xavier S. 1966. *Antaõ de Proença's Tamil-Portuguese Dictionary A.D. 1679*, [University of Malaya, Kuala Lumpur]. Leiden, The Netherlands: E.J. Brill.

Vermeer, Hans J. 1982. *The first European Tamil grammar. A critical edition*. [English version by Angelika Morath]. Heidelberg: Julius Groos Verlag.

Van Hal, Toon & Christophe Vielle (eds.). 2013. *Grammatica Grandonica. The Sanskrit Grammar of Johann Ernst Hanxleden S.J. (1681–1732)*. [With a photographical reproduction of the original manuscript by Jean-Claude Muller]. Potsdam: Universitätsverlag.

Walther, Christoph Theodosius. 1739. *Observationes Grammaticae, quibus Linguae Tamulicae idioma Vulgare in usum operariorum in messe Domini inter gentes vulgo malabares dictas, illustratur a Christophoro Theodosio Walthero*. Trangabariae: Typis Missionis Regiæ [Royal mission press].

Ziegenbalg, Bartholomaeus. 1716. *Grammatical Damulica,* Halae Saxonum (Halle): Orphanotrophei [Orphanage]

Kārumūri V. Subbārāo, Tabu Taid, Martin Everaert
Reflexive and reciprocal marking in Mising

Abstract: The study of anaphora has been the focus of attention for the last three to four decades. Studying this phenomenon in different languages brings new facts, challenges existing theories, and helps us to uncover the nature of language. This paper shows that there are certain specific aspects of the behavior of anaphors and pronouns in Mising, a Tibeto-Burman language spoken in Assam, which are fascinating from a cross-linguistic point of view (cf. König and Gast 2008; Lust et al. 2000). We show that Mising exhibits an intricate combination of anaphoric (reflexive and reciprocal) strategies. Like other languages it exhibits the strategy of reflexivizing the predicate by reduplication of an anaphoric element, but it simultaneously marks the predicate with a 'self' element (cf. Subbārāo 2012). The same elements play a role in the reciprocity strategies in Mising.

Keywords: Reflexive and reciprocal marking, Mising

1 Overview of the reflexive strategies in Mising

Mising[1] has nominal and verbal reflexives markers. Mising exhibits a strategy of reflexivizing the predicate by having an anaphoric element in an argument position (nominal reflexive), but simultaneously marking the predicate with a 'self' element, a verbal reflexive, glossed VR (cf. Subbārāo 2012). This is illustrated in (1). Note that the nominal reflexive as a subcategorized argument is not obligatory (cf. (1)–(2)). If the verbal reflexive is dropped, the nominal reflexive is obligatory (cf. (3)–(4)):

---

[1] Glottolog: Sino-Tibetan, Macro-Tani, Tani, Eastern Tani, Mising.

K.V. Subbārāo, Formerly Professor of Linguistics, Department of Linguistics, University of Delhi, India. Email: kvs2811@gmail.com
† Tabu Taid, Formerly professor of English, Cotton College, Guwahati University, Assam, India
Martin Everaert, University of Utrecht, Department of Linguistics, 10 Trans, 3512KJ, The Netherlands. Email: m.b.h.everaert@uu.nl

https://doi.org/10.1515/9783110753066-011

(1) kɔ.kidɨ   də   aɨə-aɨə-m   luyit-su-to.
    children DEF self.NOM-self-ACC   praise-VR-PST
    'The children praised themselves.'
(2) kɔ.kidɨ   də   luyit-su-to.
    children DEF praise-VR-PST
    'The children praised themselves.'
(3) *kɔ.kidɨ də   luyit-to.
    children DEF praise-PST
    'The children praised themselves.'
(4) kɔ.kidɨ   DEF aɨə-aɨə-m   luyit-to.
    children def self.NOM-self-ACC praise-PST
    'The children praised themselves.'

1.1 The nominal/argumental reflexive

We begin by questioning what the basic nominal reflexive element *aɨə* is. Tabu Taid observes "*-ə* is the nominative suffix for common nouns with generic reference", and he speaks of the nominal anaphor containing a nominative case marker: *aɨ.ə*. We have interpreted this as follows: the nominative marker *-ə* in *aɨ.ə* is grammaticalized, meaning that *aɨə* is the root to which the accusative marker *-m* is attached.[2]

As you see in (1) and (4) the nominal reflexive marker appears as a reduplicated/doubled element *aɨə-aɨə-m*, and the structural case-marking of the position is suffixed to the second element. However, note that reduplication is not necessary. Take as an example (5). It is an example of an Exceptional Case-Marking (ECM) construction. The reflexive *aɨə* 'self' is case-marked accusative by the matrix verb in spite of the fact that there occurs a final complementizer *əm.na*, the quotative form of the verb *say* (Emeneau 1956; Masica 1976).

(5) *Shikha-bɨ   aɨə-m   kangkandag əm.na   lu.su-dag.*
    Shikha-PM[3] self.NOM-ACC   beautiful   COMP(QUOT)   say.VR-PRS
    'Shikha considers herself beautiful.'
    Literally: 'Shikha says to herself that (is) beautiful.'

---

2 One could say that given the forms *aɨ-də-m* and *aɨə-m* (cf. (5)–(6)) that *aɨ* and *aɨ.ə* are, in fact, two allomorphs.
3 In Mising proper nouns take a pronominal copy, which we glossed as "person marker" (PM).

The example in (6) shows that 'When two persons are involved in the context, the specifying or the definite suffix -də is used' (Taid 2016: 126). That is, -də functions as a specificity marker.

(6) Sika-bɨ   ai-də-m   lu-po-su-dung.
    Shika-PM   self-DEF-ACC   talk-PLM-VR-PRS
    'Shika talks to herself.'

It is important to observe that aiə, the nominal anaphor and -su- also function as emphatic markers. The nominal emphatic marker aiə is optional when -su-, the verbal emphatic, occurs. In the following we indicate the optional occurrence of aiə in parentheses:

(7) sə   ager-səm ngongo (aiə)   ger-su-yə.
    this   work-PM I   (myself)   do-VR-FUT
    'I'll do this work myself.'

If aiə is left out, the sentence will convey the same meaning, but its use adds the element of emphasis – 'I myself', (not anybody else)'.

Thus, to sum up, the nominal reflexive is "inherently" nominative case-marked, and will carry the case marking of the position the anaphor occupies, the structural accusative marker [-m] in (1), (4) and (5) above. Mising has a simplex (cf. (5)–(6)) and a complex (cf. (1) and (4)) form. The phonological form of the complex form suggests a form of reduplication. We will come back to this issue in section 3.1, although it cannot be fully dealt with in this article.

1.2 The verbal reflexive

The verbal reflexive -su- occurs to the right of the verb stem, and to the left of the tense marker. Thus, it is a suffix just as the verbal reflexive in all the Dravidian and in the Kuki-Chin languages of the Tibeto-Burman language family.

(8) Sika-bɨ   ai-di-m   lupo-**su**-dung.
    Shika-PM   self-DEF-ACC   talk-VR-PRS
    'Shika talks to herself.'

The VR marks the relation between two semantic arguments, not necessarily expressed as syntactic arguments, as the example in (2), here repeated as (9), illustrates:

(9) kɔ.kidɨ də   luyit-su-to.
    children DEF praise-VR-PST
    'The children praised themselves.'

In some cases, the VR conveys the interpretation of 'inadvertently' (cf. (10)). In Telugu (Dravidian) (cf. (11)) we find a similar sentence with a VR and it carries the same interpretation of 'inadvertently':

(10) Talom-bɨ   ayo-əm   rək-su-to.
     Talom-PM   tongue-ACC bite-VR-PST
     'Talom bit his tongue [inadvertently].'
(11) Talom   nālika   karucu-konn-ā.du.
     Talom   tongue   bite-VR-PST.3SG.M
     'Talom bit (his) tongue [inadvertently].'

Finally, the VR in Mising can also function as an inchoative marker.

(12) okum-də   dār-su-kang.
     house-DEF collapse-VR-PST
     'The house collapsed on its own.'
     (Taid 2016: 128)

2 Overview of the reciprocal strategies in Mising

Mising has a reduplicated form (*akon-ə akon*) and the verbal reciprocal marker *-su* and *-min.su* to express reciprocal meaning.

(13) Sika lang Dorika bɨnyɨ akon.də akon.də-m   lu-po-su-dag.
     Shika and Darika PM   one.DEF one.DEF-ACC talk-PLM-VREC-PRS
     'Shika and Darika talk to each other.'

The example in (14) suggests that in Mising the occurrence of the verbal reciprocal is *optional*, while the occurrence of the nominal reciprocal is obligatory.[4]

---

4 "When the reciprocal pronouns are used, the marking of the verb for reciprocal action is optional." (Taid 2010: 57).

(14) bi.nyi   akon-ə/akon-də   akon-də.m   ai.ma:pɨə   mə:-dag.
    he/she.two one-NOM/one-DEF one-DEF.ACC good.NEG.ADV feel/think-PRS
    'The two of them do not like each other.'
    (Taid 2010: 57; Taid 2016: 126)

Taid comments that *ai.ma:pɨ* 'good.NEG.ADV' may be considered as an example of part of a *group verb ai.ma:pɨə mə:-dag*, as the intended meaning is conveyed by the two together, perhaps allowing the VREC not necessarily to be there. Taid (2016: 127) makes two significant observations: 'When the reciprocal pronouns are not used in a sentence, reciprocal action is marked obligatorily by adding the suffix *mɨn.su* or *kā.mɨn.su*[5] to the verb root, e.g. *gē.mɨnsu-* (<*ge* 'scold' - *mɨnsu* [suffix, marking a reciprocal action]) 'to quarrel', *ding.kā. mɨnsu* (*dī-* 'to beat' -*kā* 'to see' *mɨnsu* [suffix, marking a reciprocal action] 'to beat up each other', etc.[6] (Cf. section 2.2). Taid (2016) further observes: "When the reciprocal pronouns are used, the marking of the verb for reciprocal action is optional".[7] The example in (17) without the VREC is illustrative:[8]

(15) bulu akon-də   akon-də-m   luyum-dug.
    they one-DEF   one-DEF-ACC praise-PRS
    'They admired each other.'

Based on these observations and the data presented above, we can say that Mising exercises the following three options.
— the nominal reciprocal alone,
— the verbal reciprocal alone, and
— the nominal reciprocal as well as the verbal reciprocal.

---

5 The occurrence of *kā* to the left of the verbal reciprocal deserves mention. *kā ~ka* means 'to see, to look at', "[...] *-mɨn.su-* can replace *-kā-mɨn.su-* in most cases, especially when it suggests a confrontation, a clash, etc., e.g. *lu-kā-mɨn.su > lu-kā-mɨn.su* 'to quarrel', *tup-kā-mɨn.su > tub-mɨn.su-*, etc. However, in the case of an action, suggestive of competition, a consensual reciprocal action, etc., the use of *-kā-mɨn.su-*appears to be obligatory, *duk.kā.mɨn.su-* 'to run a race in some competition'." (Taid 2016: 197).
6 Also, according to Dipak Kr Doley, the VREC is always obligatory in these cases.
7 This would be in sharp contrast to Mizo and the other Kuki-Chin languages and all Dravidian languages, where the occurrence of the verbal reciprocal is obligatory, while the occurrence of the nominal reciprocal is optional.
8 Note that in Meithei (Tibeto-Burman), the verbal reflexive is optional while the occurrence of the verbal reciprocal is obligatory.

2.1 The nominal reciprocal

The first component of the reciprocal *akon* 'one' carries a case copy of the subject, the nominative case marker *-ə*. The second part of the reciprocal *akon* 'one' carries the structural case marker of the direct object, the accusative case marker *-m*.

Here too the question arises whether we should analyse the nominative marker as grammaticalized, incorporated in the root: "*-ə* is the nominative suffix for common nouns with generic reference in *akon.ə* and in *akon.ə-m*, *-m* is the accusative suffix. Therefore, literally, the reciprocal *akon.ə-akon.ə-m* means 'another (subject case marker)-another (object case marker)'." (Taid 2016: 126). Again, it is not clear whether we have to take *akonə* as an uninflected morpheme. Summarizing, Taid (2016) says:

— The word *akon* (derived from *ako* 'one') means 'another'. *-ə* is the nominative suffix for common nouns with generic reference in *akonə* and in *akonəm -m* is the accusative suffix: literally, therefore, *akonə akonəm* means 'another (subject) another (object)'.
— When two persons are involved in the context, the specifying or the defining suffix-*də* is used: *akonə akonəm* or *akondə akondəm*.

What we see here could be a case of "case copying" (Subbārāo 2012): the first part of the reciprocal takes the case of the antecedent (nominative), while the second part takes the case of the position. If we could analyse these instances as case copying, the phenomenon is the opposite of the one found in Dravidian: first the reciprocal is marked with the case of the position, then the reciprocal with the case copied from the subject. (See 3.1).

In the case of reciprocals too, definite markers occur. There are two instances:

(i) The definite marker occurs only on the second constituent of the anaphor:[9]

(16) *bɨ.nyi   akon-ə   akon-də-m   aimāpə   mə:dang.*
 he.two other-NOM other-DEF-ACC well.not feel
 'The two of them do not like each other.'
 (Taid 2016: 126)

---

[9] Taid (2016) notes: "*bɨnyi* (*bɨ* 'he/she' *-nyi* clipped from *annyi* 'two'), used as a marker of the dual number".

(ii) The definite marker may occur on the first as well as the second constituent of the anaphor. When the definite marker occurs, the nominative marker cannot occur. In other words, they are in complementary distribution (cf. footnote 4).

(17) bɨ.nyi   akon-də-akon-də-m   aimāpə mə:dang.
      two.of.them   other-DEF-other-DEF-ACC   well.not feel
      'The two of them do not like each other.'
      (Taid 2016: 126–127)

Why the definite marker is used on each component of the reciprocal is a puzzle to us: We hypothesize that it is used simply to emphasize the definiteness.
    Thus, to summarize, these are the options:
— akon-ə-akon-ə-m
— akon-ə-akon-də-m
— akon-də-akon-də-m

Moreover, note that there is more than one way to express reciprocity with a nominal reciprocal:[10]

(18) bulu akon-asak lədu-pə gi-minsu-ka.
      they each-other back-to go-VREC-PST
      'They followed each other in a line.'
(19) Bill-bɨ   la(ŋ) Jane bulu kekon kesak-pə
      Bill-PM   CONJ   Jane PM   each other-to
      tet-la-dung / *tet-mɨn-la-dung.
      sit-PROG-exist sit-VREC-PROG-exist
      'Bill and Jane are sitting next to each other.' (lit. side by side)

2.2 The verbal reciprocal marker

The reflexive marker -su- is also used as the verbal reciprocal in Mising. The verbal reciprocal may carry the group or participation marker mɨn to its left thus

---

[10] Observe that the verbal reciprocal marker in (19) is not allowed, perhaps like in Dravidian languages where it occurs only when the lexical anaphor occurs in a subcategorized position. In the Mising example in (19) 'next to each other' is not a subcategorized argument of the predicate 'sit' (see also section 3.5).

yielding the form *mɨn.su*. Following the suggestion of Tabu Taid, we gloss *mɨn* as a "participation marker", indicating that there are at least two persons participating in the event.[11]

(20) *Punyam-bɨ   Migom-bɨ   akonə   akon-əm   luyit-su-mɨnsu-to.*
     Punyam-PM   Migom-PM   one.NOM   one-ACC   praise-VREC-PCM-PST
     'Punyam and Mignom praised each other.'
     (Prativa Payeng, Dipika Pegu, p.c.)

Considering the occurrence of such particles in some other Tibeto-Burman languages such as Liangmai (Naga)[12] and Meithei (Subbārāo 2012: 303) and Khasi (Austro-Asiatic) (Subbārāo 2012: 302), we analyze *mɨn* 'together' as an adverb. Interestingly, in all the afore-mentioned languages, this adverb is incorporated in the predicate and it does not occur as a free morpheme.

Note that other languages have been analyzed as having a participation marker in the domain of reciprocity (Wolof; Creissels and Nouguier-Voisin 2008): they call it a 'reciprocal co-participation' marker. And there is a striking similar case described by Geniušiene (1987) for Lithuanian [our underlining]:

> The reflexive morpheme *-si-/-s* is traditionally called a particle in Baltic linguistics and here it is termed a reflexive-middle marker due to its origin and range of functions [...] <u>Reciprocity is also encoded by the complex *su-si-* comprised of a prefix with the meaning 'together (with)' and obligatory reflexive-middle marker</u>, on a limited number of derived verbs, cf.: (4) *žvelgti* 'to glance' → *su-si -žvelgti* 'to exchange glances/glance at each other' *švilpti* 'to whistle' → su-si -švilpti 'to exchange whistles/whistle to each other' *šnek˙eti* 'to talk' → *su-si -šnek˙eti* 'to (begin to) understand each other.'

The VREC is also used in the case of a reciprocal possessor reading:

(21a) *bulu   dumit   səp-mɨnsu-ka/   səp-ka-mɨnsu-ka.*
      they   hair   cut-VREC-PST / cut-see[13]-VREC-PST
      'They cut each other's hair.'
(21b) *bulu   akon asak-kə   doyiŋ-əm   kɨ-mɨnsu-ka.*
      they   each other-GEN   story-ACC   talk-VREC-PST
      'They talked about each other's story.'

---

11 The form *su-mɨnsu* will be discussed in section 3.4.
12 In Liangmai (Naga) the participation maker is *ŋisəm* 'together' and in Meithei it is *-min-* 'together'. Thanks to Wicham Mataina for providing data on Liangmai (Naga).
13 With some predicates such as *səp* 'cut', the verb *ka* 'see' occurs to the right, optionally.

Though the interpretation holds of a relation between an argument (the antecedent) and the (implicit) reciprocal possessor object the verbal reciprocal marker *minsu* occurs. In Telugu (Dravidian) the verbal reciprocal cannot occur in such cases.

Another interesting example in this respect is (22):

(22) Bill-bɨ   guest-kɨdɨ-də-m   kaŋkin-minsu-mo-ka.
     Bill-PM   guest-PL-DEF-ACC   introduce-VREC-make-PST
     'Bill introduced the guests to each other.'
     'Bill made the guests introduce each other.' (literal translation)

The verbal reciprocal marks a reciprocal relation in which the 'antecedent' *guest-kɨdɨ* 'guests', is the direct object. In Telugu (Dravidian) the verbal reciprocal cannot occur if the antecedent is a non-subject, so an example such as (22) would be ungrammatical. A plausible explanation is given in (23):

(23) Bill [s the guests know each other] CAUS

In the embedded S the verbal reciprocal takes the embedded subject as 'the antecedent'. A similar situation obtains in other languages of the Kuki-Chin subfamily such as Thadou, Hmar, Mizo, etc.

The examples in (21)–(22), and the contrast with Telugu, need some further research.

3 Diverse aspects of the anaphoric strategies in Mising

3.1 Swapping

The nominal reflexive and reciprocal in most of the South Asian languages is polymorphemic and it exhibits a bipartite structure (cf. Lust et al. 2000). Both the parts of the reciprocal are case-marked. While one of the parts may carry a case copy of the antecedent, the other may carry the structural case marker of the position in which it occurs. Such case marking in the first place is not found uniformly and the part on which such case marking takes place is parametric.

In some languages the first part of the bipartite structure may be structurally case-marked with an overt lexical case marker and the second part may carry a case copy of the antecedent which is normally the subject of the specific clause. Interestingly, in Dravidian languages, except in some cases, Malayalam (Subbārāo and Everaert 2011), and in some Tibeto-Burman languages the first and second parts can be swapped (Sarju Devi and Subbārāo 2002). The first part which we label as X can be swapped with the second part which we label as Y, for convenience: XY → YX.

If swapping is allowed, it is an indication that what we see is not a case of standard reduplication (44a), a morphological process, but a case of syntactic reduplication (Stolz 2009) – also called repetition, doubling. And Mising is one of the Tibeto-Burman languages that does exhibit swapping. In (23) after swapping the parts of the nominal anaphor, the first part of the reciprocal contains the *accusative case marker* and the second the *nominative case marker*. To quote Taid (2010: 57): "[...] the reciprocal pronoun used in Mising is *akonə akonəm* or *akonəm akonə* [...] The order of the two words can be reversed without any change in meaning".

(24a) *Punyam-bɨ   Migom-bɨ   akon-əm   akon-ə   luyit-su-mɨn.su-to.*
Punyam-PM Migom-PM one-ACC one-NOM praise-VR-VREC-PST
'Punyam and Migom praised each other.'

(24b) *bɨ.nyi   akon-ɨ /   akon-dɨ akon-dɨ.m   ai.ma:pɨ   me-dang.*
he/she.two one-NOM one-DEF one-DEF.ACC good.NEG.ADV feel/think-PRS
'The two of them do not like each other.'
(Taid 2010: 57)

Based on Taid's observation, confirmed by native speakers' intuitions, (25)–(27) shows Mising reflexives might also allow swapping:

(25) *kɔ.kɨdɨ   də   aiə-aiə-m   luyit-su-to.*
children DEF self.NOM-self-ACC praise-VR-PST
'The children praised themselves.'

(26) *kɔ.kɨdɨ   də   aiə-m-aiə   luyit-su-to.*
children DEF self-ACC-self.NOM praise-VR-PST
'The children praised themselves.'

If (25) and (26) are correct, we would have additional evidence that *aiə* is really nominative marked, given the fact that reversal/swapping is generally permitted if and only if the two components reciprocal carry overt case markers. We have evidence from all the Dravidian languages (except Malayalam), Meithei

(Manipuri), Adi (Padam) and Adi (Minyong) in support of our claim. This supports the claim that *aiə* is nominative marked.

3.2 Special features of the verbal reciprocal marker

As we noted above, according to Tabu Taid (2010: 565) *mɨn* is a "suffix added to an appropriate verb root to denote participating in some action or following someone in some action".[14]

(27) {*gɨ*" to go/come' + *mɨn* > gɨ. *mɨn* 'to go somewhere with someone'
jē' 'to shout' + *mɨn* > *jē* . *mɨn* 'to join someone in shouting', etc.}

The suffix *mɨn* is also used: "to denote two or more persons engaged in a reciprocative [reciprocal] or mutual action (e.g., a combat, a competition, a collision, etc. etc.): *ge:-* 'to abuse or scold' + *mɨn.su* → *ge:* + *mɨn.su* 'to quarrel with each other', *tub-* 'to knock with the head' + *mɨnsu* → *tub. mɨn.su* (of animals) to knock against each other's head', etc.". (Taid 2010: 565).

We analyze *mɨn* 'together' as an adverb, considering the occurrence of such particles in some other Tibeto-Burman languages such as Liangmai (Naga) and Meithei (Subbārāo 2012: 333). Interestingly, in all the above-mentioned languages, this adverb *mɨn* is incorporated in the predicate and it does not occur as a free morpheme. The position of the participation marker is parametric.

There are some verbs in Mising that carry the verbal reflexive/ reciprocal *-su-* inherently, and they may occur even when there is no reflexive/reciprocal nominal: it occurs with some verbs such as: *lupo.su* 'talk', *rik.su* 'meet', *rupo.su* 'quarrel'. When the verbal reciprocal is grammaticalized, it (often) presupposes the participation of two participants, though there is no plural subject (antecedent) with which it can be coindexed as in (29)–(31):

(28) ŋo bɨ-m   lambə-do   rik.su-to.
     I PM-ACC road-on.the meet-PST
     'I met him/her on the road.'

(29) Sika-bɨ   Dorika-mɨ   lupo-su-ka.
     Shika-PM   Darika-ACC talk-VREC-PST
     'Shika talked to Darika.'

---

14 The discussion is based on preliminary observations, but explains what the wider implications might be if further corroborated.

(30) *Shikha-bɨ   Darika-mə   sɨ:lu:-do   rik.su-to.*
Shikha-PM Darika-with(?) forest-in meet.VREC-PST
'Shikha met Darika in the forest.'

Such grammaticalization also takes place in Telugu (Dravidian) with verbs such as *peḷḷi ceesu konu* 'marriage do VREC', that is, 'marry', *kalusu konu* 'meet VREC', *talacu konu* 'remember VREC', *muddu peṭṭu konu* 'kiss keep-VREC', that is 'to kiss', etc.

In the case of symmetric predicates there are several options:

(i) The VREC does *not* occur. The adjective *lək* 'together' functions like a verb in (31) and the numeral *ako* 'one' is incorporated in the verb. It is a phenomenon that is quite robust in Tibeto-Burman languages. In this case *ko-* is derived from *ako* 'one'. The initial vowel gets deleted when preceded by an adjective like *lək* 'together' (as shown in (32)).

(31) *bulu lək-ko-dak.*
they together-one-PRS
'They are similar.'
(32) *lək + ako   → lək + ko*
together + one   'similar'

(ii) The VREC does occur:

(33) *bulu lək-ko-mɨn.su-dak.*
they together-one-VREC-PRS
'They are similar.'

When *lək* 'together' is used a free adverb, the adverbial suffix *pə* occurs:[15]

(34) *bulu lə.ko-pə   gi-dak.*
they together.one-ADV go-PRS
'They are going together.'/ 'They go together.'

In Dravidian languages too this holds. For example, the verb *kalus* 'meet' in Telugu requires the verbal reciprocal, when X meets Y, as in (35).

---

[15] The adverbial suffix *pə* also occurs in expressions such as: *akon-akon pə* 'one by one'.

(35) mādhavi tana bharta ni kalusu-kon-i santōṣinca lēdu.
     Madhavi self's husband ACC meet-VREC-CPM feel.happy not
     'Madhavi did not feel happy meeting her husband.'
     (Subbārāo 2012, web materials)

In Mising a similar phenomenon obtains with a difference. With a specific set of predicates in Mising, the marker -po- occurs, which according to Taid (2010), is a happiness or pleasure marker (PLM).

(36) Sika-bɨ   aɨ-də-m   lu-po-su-dung.
     Shika-PM self-DEF-ACC talk-PLM-VR-PRS
     'Shika talks to herself.'

3.3 Verbal reflexive as an emphatic/benefactive marker

As far as we know, it is cross-linguistically not often the case that verbal markers are used as an emphasis marker. In Tibeto-Burman languages such as Hmar, Thadou, Vaiphei (of the Kuki-Chin subgroup) and Khasi[16] (Mon-Khmer) and Kharia (Munda) the verbal reflexive functions as a verbal emphatic marker (Subbārāo 2012). In Mising too, the verbal marker -su- functions as an emphatic marker. The following examples from Mising are illustrative: i-su- 'to go somewhere (by) oneself', ger-su- 'to do something myself'.

(37) sə   ager-səm ŋo ger-su-yə.
     This work-PM   I   do-VR-FUT
     'I'll do this work myself.'

If aɨə is left out, the sentence will convey the same meaning, but its use adds the element of emphasis – 'I myself, (not anybody else)'. Another example:

(38) koaɨ   də   aɨda   yup-su-kāng.
     child   DEF by himself sleep-VR-PST
     'The child slept by himself.'

To account for the 'on/of its own accord' interpretation of the verbal reflexive -su- in Mising and the other South Asian languages we propose that the verbal

---

[16] Cf. Subbārāo (2012: 64) for a Khasi verbal reflexive functioning as an emphatic marker.

emphatic keeps the external theta role "syntactically visible", visible enough to license an adjunct interpretation like 'on its own' (that needs an agent/external theta role). A similar analysis may be extended to account for the function of the verbal emphatic -*la*- in Dimasa, -*in*- in Hmar, -*ki*- in Thadou and Vaiphei, -*hi*- in Khasi and, *jom* in Kharia. Interestingly, the nominal reflexive and the nominal emphatic may optionally be dropped when the verbal reflexive or the verbal emphatic is present in the verb in the Tibeto-Burman languages mentioned above. Thus, not only is there *symmetry* in the position of occurrence of the verbal anaphor and the verbal emphatic, there is a correspondence in the optional deletion of the nominal anaphor and the nominal emphatic and the obligatory occurrence of the verbal anaphor and emphatic, respectively.

The verbal reflexive also performs the function of a self-benefactive.

(39) *Anam-bɨ   nammɨr-əm   git-su-tɔ.*
 Anam-PM   beard-ACC   shave-VR.BEN-PST
 'Anam shaved himself.'
 Literally: 'Anam shaved his beard (for his own benefit).'

(40) *ŋolu ŋolu.k   alag-əm   sābun-kokki   mɔ-su-dɔ.*
 we   we.GEN   hands.ACC   soap-with   wash-VR.BEN-PST
 'We washed our hands with soap.'

The occurrence of the marker -*su*- with a verb such as *tig* 'to cut with a large knife' may have two interpretations:
(i) to cut somewhere in one's body oneself, and
(ii) to cut (a bamboo etc. with a large knife) oneself. etc.
 (Taid 2010: 254)

While in interpretation (i) it is the verbal reflexive, in interpretation (ii) it is a self-affective or self-benefactive.

3.4 Grammaticalization and the triple occurrences of the anaphor in Mising

In (41) below the nominal reciprocal and the verbal reciprocal co-occur:

(41) *Sika   lang Dorika bɨnyɨ   akon.də akon.də.m   lupo-su-dag.*
 Shika and   Darika they(PM)   one.DEF one.DEF.ACC   talk-VREC-PRS
 'Shika and Darika talk to each other.'

The examples (42) and (43) below carry:
— the nominal reciprocal *akon.də akon.dəm* 'one.DEF one.ACC',

- the grammaticalized verbal reciprocal in the verb *rik.su* 'meet.VREC', and
- the participation marker (PCM) *min* 'together' and the verbal reciprocal *-su-*.

(42) ŋo.nyi lambə-do   akon.də akon.də.m   rik.su-min-su-ka.
     we.two road-on-the one.DEF one.DEF.ACC meet.VREC-PCM-VREC-PST
     'We two met each other on the road.'

(43) ko-kidi-də   (akon.də akon.də.m)   (ka)-rik.su-min-su-ka.
     boy-Pl-DEF   one.DEF one.DEF.ACC   (see)-meet.VREC-PCM-VREC-PST
     'The boys met each other.'

Thus, we find that co-occurrence is manifested not only by the nominal reciprocal alone, but also, by the occurrence of the verbal reciprocal twice and the verbal participation marker *min* 'together'. That is reciprocity is expressed by four elements which leads to triple redundancy in Mising. This, we think, is a very unique feature not observed in any language to the best of our knowledge.

3.5 Blocking the verbal marker when the nominal anaphor occurs in a non-subcategorized position

When the nominal reciprocal occurs in a non-subcategorized position, the occurrence of the verbal reciprocal is prohibited. Such non-occurrence is observed across languages. Subbārāo (2012: 83) points out: "a polymorphemic anaphor and the VR are permitted only if the locative PP is a *subcategorized argument*. If it is not, neither of them is permitted". In (44) below, *bulu kekon kesak-pə* 'side by side-to' is a non-subcategorized argument. Hence, the verbal reciprocal is not permitted.

(44) Bill-bi la(ŋ)   Jane bulu kekon kesak-pə   tet-la-duŋ/* tet-min-la-dung.
     Bill-he CONJ   Jane they each other-to   sit-PROG-exist/ sit-PCM-PROG-exist
     'Bill and Jane are sitting next to each other (side by side, literally).'

Here *bi* 'he' and *bulu* 'they' occur as copy pronoun ("person marker") for Bill, and Bill and Jane respectively. The first and second person pronouns respectively are: *ŋ-lu* 'we', *no-lu* 'you'. These too may occur as copy pronouns.

3.6 The occurrence of a verbal suffix as a 'happiness or pleasure marker'

The occurrence of the suffix -*po*- with certain predicates and its non-occurrence with some other predicates is still under investigation.

According to Taid (2010) *lu.po* means: "to speak before somebody else (in a meeting, or discussion". The precise meaning of the morpheme -*po*-, according to (Taid 2010: 351), is "a suffix, added to denote something being pleasurable/ nice/ easy, etc. to do", e.g.:

(45) *do*- 'to eat'+ -*po*-   →   *do.po*- 'to be tasty to eat'
  yub- 'to sleep + -*po*- →   *yup.po*[17] 'to be nice to sleep', etc.
  dosug- 'kiss' + -*po*-   →   *dosuk.po lu-po-su* 'converse'
  gonggab 'hug'+ -*po*-   →   *gonggap.po*

In (46), the marker -*po*- functions as a happiness or pleasure marker (PLM).

(46) Sika   lang   Dorika bɨnyɨ   akon.də akon.dəm   lu-**po**-**su**-dung.
  Shika   and   Darika PM   one.DEF one.DEF.ACC talk-PLM-VREC-PRS
  'Shika and Darika talk to each other.'

To verbs such as *dosug* 'kiss' and *gonggab* 'hug', -*po*- can also be added.

The case of the predicate *rik.su-mɨn.su* 'meet.VREC-PCM.VREC' deserves mention. With this predicate the pleasure marker -*po*- cannot occur as (48) shows. Such non-occurrence needs further investigation.

(47) *ko-kɨdar*[18] (*akon.də akon.dəm*)   (*ka*)-*rik.su-mɨn-su-ka*.
   boy-PL   one.DEF one.DEF.ACC   (see)-meet.VREC-PLM-VREC-PST
   'The boys met each other.'
(48) *ko-kɨdar* (*akon.də akon.dəm*)   (*ka*)-**rɨk-po-su-mɨn-su-ka*.
   boy- PL   one.DEF one.DEF.ACC   (see)-meet-PLM-VREC-PCM-VREC-PST
   'The boys met each other.'

---

[17] The final consonant /-b/ changes to /-p/ due to regressive assimilation, a phenomenon that is more predominant in South Asian languages than progressive assimilation.
[18] Note that the plural marker -*kɨda* in Mising has alternate forms: -*kɨdar*, -*kɨdɨng*, -*kɨrɨng*, -*kɨlɨng*. In case of pronouns, it is -*lu*, (for instance) (40), and in case of proper names (personal), the marker -*bulu* (for instance) (44)), is used.

The pleasure marker -po- also does not occur with the adjective aipə mə:. Thus, *aipə mə:.po and is not permitted.[19]

4 Conclusion

Mising shows reflexivity/reciprocity strategies that are not crucially different from other South Asian languages. However, there are certain features that need further scrutiny because they seem to be atypical/unique. To encode reciprocity, multiple affixes are employed. Such multiplicity in the occurrence of affixes leads to "redundant" marking of reciprocity through verbal affixes. The occurrence of the verbal reflexive is crucially dependent on occurrence of nominal reflexive/reciprocal appearing in argument (subcategorized) position. Just as in some other South Asian languages, the nominal anaphor is complex and has a bipartite structure. The first part of the anaphor carries a case copy of the subject while the second part is structurally case-marked by the predicate. The two parts of the complex anaphor may be swapped as in Dravidian languages, and Meithei, Liangmai and Adi (Paadam). Further, the definite marker is used on each component of the reciprocal and we hypothesize that it is used simply to emphasize the definiteness. The occurrence of the pleasure marker -po- with a set of predicates and wits non-occurrence with a specific set of some other predicates deserves further investigation.

Abbreviations

ACC = accusative; ADV = adverb; BEN = benefactive; CAUS= causative; COMP(QUOT) = complementizer (quotative); CONJ = conjunction; CPM = conjunctive participial marker; DEF = definite; FUT = future; GEN = genitive; M = masculine; NEG = negation; NOM = nominative; PCM = participation marker; PL = plural; PLM = pleasure marker; PM = person marker; PROG = progressive; PRS = present; PST = past; SG = singular; VR =verbal reflexive; VREC = verbal reciprocal.

---

[19] We need more data to be able to reach at any specific conclusion regarding the nature of the pleasure marker -po-.

Transliteration

The Mising data are transcribed using a broad IPA phonemic transcription. The long vowels are marked by a macron over the vowel.

Acknowledgements

The authors based their analysis on the field work done in Tezpur with several language consultants, among which Tabu Taid, Dipika Pegu and Dipak Kr Doley, all native speakers of Mising. Our co-author Tabu Taid died on August 17, 2019 while working on this paper. The late Tabu Taid was the editor of *A Dictionary of the Mising Language* (Mising to Mising, Assamese, English) and the author of *An Introduction to Mising Phonology and Grammar*, a contribution that is full of deep insights into the Mising language. We dedicate this paper to him. The data were collected in 2011, and then in 2014 and 2015 from language consultants, who spoke Mising as their first language. Some of our informants are speakers of the Moing and Pagro dialects of Mising. We are thankful to Dr. Dipok Doley, Dipika Pegu, Prativa Payeng, Ratneswar Mili, Jugen Pegu, Shikha Dole, and Darika Pegu. The article is based on a paper presented at South Asian Languages Analysis Roundtable 35 at INALCO, Paris in 2019. We are thankful to Professor Ghanshyam Sharma for his help in several ways. We want to thank the reviewer of this article for thoughtful comments.

References

Creissels, Denis & Sylvie Nouguier-Voisin. 2008. Valency-changing operations in Wolof and the notion of co-participation. In Ekkehard König & Volker Gast (eds.), *Reciprocal and Reflexives, Theoretical and typological explanations*, 289–305. Berlin & New York: Mouton de Gruyter.
Emeneau, Murray B. 1956. India as a linguistic area. *Language* 32 (3). 3–16.
Everaert, Martin, Kārumūri V. Subbārāo & Mataina Wichamdinbo. 2014. Lexical Anaphors and Pronouns in Liangmai. *Lingua Posnaniensis* 55 (2). 41–47.
Geniušiene, Emma. 1987. *The Typology of Reflexives*. Berlin: Mouton de Gruyter.
König, Ekkehard & Volker Gast (eds.). 2008. *Reciprocals and Reflexives. Theoretical and Typological Explorations*. Berlin & New York: Mouton de Gruyter.
Lust, Barbara, Kashi Wali, James. W. Gair & Kārumūri V. Subbārāo (eds.). 2000. *Lexical reflexives and pronouns. Selected South Asian Languages: A Principled Typology*. Berlin: Mouton de Gruyter.
Masica, Colin P. 1976. *Defining a Linguistic Area: South Asia*. Chicago: The University of Chicago Press.

Sarju Devi, T. & Kārumūri V. Subbārāo. 2002. Reduplication and case copying: The case of lexical anaphors in Manipuri and Telugu. *Linguistics of the Tibeto-Burman Area* 25 (2). 47–72.

Subbārāo, Kārumūri V. 2012. *South Asian languages: A Syntactic Typology*. New York: Cambridge University Press.

Subbārāo, Kārumūri V. & Martin B. Everaert. 2011. Verbal and Nominal Reciprocals in South Asian Languages (SALs) and Obligatory Order Reversal in the Nominal Anaphor in Dravidian. Paper presented at South Asian Languages Analysis (SALA-29) and also at *Formal Approach to South Asian Languages* (FASAL). Boston, MA: Massachusetts Institute of Technology, 2012.

Stolz, Thomas. 2009. Total Reduplication: Syndetic vs Asyndetic Patterns in Europe. *Grazer Linguistische Studien* 71. 99–113.

Taid, Tabu R. (ed.). 2010. *Mising Gomipir Kumsung. A Dictionary of the Mising Language*. Guwahati, Assam: Anundoram Borooah Institute of Language, Art & Culture.

Taid, Tabu R. 2016. *An Introduction to Mising Phonology and Grammar*. Guwahati, Assam: Anundoram Borooah Institute of Language, Art & Culture.

Gargi Roy, Rajesh Kumar, Kārumūri V. Subbārāo
Reciprocals in Kokborok — A Case of Syntactic Convergence

Abstract: This paper presents a detailed description of the reciprocals in Kokborok (Tibeto-Burman) and provides evidence to suggest that the syntactic convergence in Kokborok reciprocals resulted from language contact. The paper focuses on the reduplicated form of the verbal reciprocal *-lai lai-*, a rare indigenous feature across South Asian languages that performs the specific function of reciprocity. This feature has receded over a few decades due to the influence of the dominant language Bangla, an Indo-Aryan language that has been spoken in the proximity of Kokborok for a prolonged time.

Keywords: reciprocal, verbal reciprocal, nominal reciprocal, reduplication, Binding Theory

1 Introduction

Studies of language contact on the South Asian subcontinent have demonstrated a number of contact-induced changes. Evidence of language contact can be observed in various syntactic features and is commonly found in clausal subordination, for example in relative clauses, complementizer clauses, and control constructions. This section presents a brief introduction to contact-based changes in the clausal constructions of some South Asian languages (henceforth SALs).

The correlative strategy in relative clause constructions is predominantly found in SOV languages and more specifically in Indo-Aryan and Dravidian languages (Downing 1978; Keenan 1985; Cardona and Jain 2003; Bhatt 2003; Subbārāo 2012a). Relative-correlative clauses are constructions in which the relativized noun phrase in the embedded clause is coindexed with a correlate (either

---

Gargi Roy, IIT-Madras, Humanities and Social sciences, 600036, Chennai, India. Email: findgargiroy@gmail.com
Rajesh Kumar, IIT-Madras, Humanities and Social sciences, 600036, Chennai, India. Email: thisisrajkumar@gmail.com
K.V. Subbārāo, 13/704, Formerly Professor of Linguistics, University of Delhi, India. Email: kvs2811@gmail.com

https://doi.org/10.1515/9783110753066-012

a pronoun or an NP) in the matrix clause. In this type of construction, both the matrix and the embedded clauses are [+finite].[1]

Sentences (1) and (2) are examples of relative-correlative clauses in Hindi-Urdu (Indo-Aryan) and Telugu (Dravidian), respectively. The relative pronouns *jis* 'which' in Hindi-Urdu and *ē* 'which' in Telugu function as the relative determiners and *vō/ā ammāyi*, which function as the correlate, occur in the matrix clause.

(1) Hindi-Urdu (Indo-Aryan)
[*jis   laṛkī$_i$-ko mãĩ-ne ek kitab   dī*]   *vō$_i$*
which girl-DAT I-ERG one book.3SG.F give.PST.3SG.F she
merī dōst   hai.
my   friend be.PRS
'The girl who(m) I gave the book to is my friend.'

(2) Telugu (Dravidian)
[[[*ē   ammāyi-(aitē)$_i$ mā   inṭi-ki   vaccind(i)]-ō*]
  which girl-become.COND our home-to came-DUB.MKR
ā$_i$ ammāyi meḍisin   caduv kondi].
that girl medicine studied
'The girl who came to my house studied medicine.'

The correlative strategy is also found in the Tibeto-Burman language family, as well as some Munda languages, due to intense contact with surrounding Indo-Aryan languages. For example, the correlative strategy in Rabha, Bodo, Kokborok (Tibeto-Burman) Santali, and Kharia (Munda) (see Subbārāo 2012b, Roy, Kumar and Subbārāo 2020) is a result of language contact with Indo-Aryan. Rabha and Bodo have been in contact with Assamese (Indo-Aryan), Kokborok and Santali with Bangla (Indo-Aryan), and Kharia[2] with Sadani (Indo-Aryan). The indigenous relativization pattern of the Munda and the Tibeto-Burman languages, as discussed in Subbārāo (2012a), is a gap strategy[3] in which the overt relativized Head

---

1 Whether relative-correlative clauses are indigenous to the Dravidian language family is controversial. Lakshmi Bai (1985) argues that relative-correlative clauses are indigenous to Dravidian, whereas Nadkarni (1970), Krishnamurti and Gwynn (1985), Sridhar (1990), and Asher and Kumari (1997) maintain that this is a borrowed construction from Sanskrit.
2 Kharia takes either the relative pronoun *je* (due to Indo-Aryan influence) or the interrogative pronoun *ata* (due to Dravidian influence; see Peterson 2011).
3 In this strategy, the overt head is expressed either in the matrix or the embedded clause and is coindexed with a null operator. The Kokborok examples are illustrative. In IHRCs (typical of Tibeto-Burman languages), the overt Head occurs in the embedded clause, while in EHRCs it

is expressed either in the matrix or the embedded clause and the embedded verb usually appears in the [-finite] form. This strategy is manifested in two forms: Internally Headed Relative Clauses (IHRCs), in which the relativized Head is expressed overtly inside the embedded clause, and Externally Headed Relative Clauses (EHRCs), in which the relativized Head is expressed overtly in the matrix clause. Thus, the appearance of the correlative strategy in the Tibeto-Burman and Munda languages is a clear contact phenomenon. The Rabha (Tibeto-Burman) example in (3) illustrates a relative correlative clause. The relative pronoun *ja*, which functions as the relative determiner, is followed by the correlate *o* in the matrix clause.

(3) Rabha (Tibeto-Burman)
 [*ja-kay   cusar   ini-para   mica-be   cika*
  which-CL   well   of-from   lady-NOM   water
  rai-nata]   o-kay-be   thu-a.
  bring-PFV.PFV CORR-CL-NOM   deep-PRS
 'The well from which the lady has just brought water is deep.'
 (Subbārāo 2012b: 113)

Another instance of contact-centric change occurs in the relativization pattern of some Indo-Aryan languages such as Konkani and Dakkhini, which are spoken in the larger Dravidian region. This pattern is typically attributed to Dravidian influence, as suggested by Nadkarni (1975) and Hock and Bashir (2016). Nadkarni (1975) shows a gradual change in the correlative clause of Kannada-type Konkani (Indo-Aryan) in which the relative pronoun was replaced by an interrogative pronoun followed by a post-sentential question particle. This is due to the influence of Kannada (Dravidian), which is spoken in the proximity of Konkani.

---

occurs in the matrix clause. The embedded verb is usually in the form of [-finite] (participial form in Indo-Aryan, Dravidian, and Munda families and infinitival (nominalized) in the Tibeto-Burman family).
– Internally Headed Relative Clause (IHRC) in Kokborok:
(i) [tini   bɔrɔkᵢ   ani nɔg-ɔ   phai-mani] Øᵢ   ani kicɪŋ.
   today   person   my house-in come-NMLZ   my friend
   'The person who came to my house today is my friend.'
– Externally Headed Relative Clause (EHRC) in Kokborok:
(ii) [tini   Øᵢ ani nɔg-ɔ   phai-mani] bɔrɔkᵢ   ani kicɪŋ.
    today   my house-in come-NMLZ person   my friend
    'The person who came to my house today is my friend.'

The existence of Backward Control in Dakkhini, a transplanted Hindi-Urdu variety spoken in Telangana – a state in southern India in which the majority of the population speaks Telugu (Dravidian) – is a consequence of Telugu influence. Telugu exhibits both Forward and Backward Control,[4] whereas Hindi-Urdu allows only Forward Control.[5] Thus, the alternative strategy of Backward Control in Dakkhini is due to contact with Telugu (refer to Subbārāo 2012b for details of the consequences of contact in control constructions). Example (4) represents a Backward Control structure in Dakkhini. As the ungrammaticality of (5) suggests, the same structure is not feasible in Hindi-Urdu.

(4) Dakkhini (Indo-Aryan)
[ham loga$_i$ ya-ku ā-ke] Ø$_i$ das sāl ho gaye.
we here-to come-CPM ten years.3P.M happened.3P.M
'It is ten years since we came here.'
(Subbārāo 2012b: 306)

(5) Hindi-Urdu (Indo-Aryan)
[*ham$_i$ yahã ā-kar] Ø$_i$ das sāl hue.
we here-to come-CPM ten years.3P.M happened.3P.M
'It is ten years since we came here.'
(Subbārāo 2012b: 305)

---

4 Control here refers to a type of syntactic subordination in which the overt subject/object in one clause c-commands the coindexed null subject of the other clause in a sentence. The null subject in the literature is labelled as PRO, which represents a null pronominal in the subject position. In Forward Control, the overt subject/object occurs in the matrix clause and is coindexed with PRO in the embedded clause, whereas in Backward Control, it is the null subject that occurs in the matrix subject position and is coindexed with the overt NP in the matrix clause.

5 Hindi-Urdu exhibits no Backward Control except for the instance of case alternations between instrumental and accusative case markers in infinitival clauses when the verb occurs as *kahnā* 'to say' in the matrix clause (Subbārāo 2012b). The examples below illustrate the context of Backward Control in Hindi-Urdu. Ø stands for an obligatorily null element.

Hindi-Urdu (Indo-Aryan)
– Forward Control
(iii) rādhā-ne mujh$_i$-se [PRO$_i$ dillī jā-ne ke liye] kahā.
Radha-ERG I-with Delhi go-to in order asked
'Radha asked me to go to Delhi.'
(Subbārāo 2012b: 61)

– Backward Control
(iv) rādhā-ne [mujh$_i$-ko dillī jā-ne ke liye] Ø$_i$ kahā.
Radha-ERG I-ACC Delhi go-to in order asked
'Radha asked me to go to Delhi.'
(Subbārāo 2012b: 61)

In addition to the borrowed constructions, there are cases in which the borrowed categories get nativized in the language and thus often undergo syntactic reanalysis. Arora and Subbārāo (1989) demonstrate that the correlate *so* and the Initial Complementizer (IC) *ki* in Hindi-Urdu undergo syntactic reanalysis when they occur in Dakkhini. Here, we present an example of the correlate *so* and show how its function has changed upon borrowing into Dakkhini. The correlate *so* in Hindi-Urdu occurs as the Final Complementizer (FC) in Dakkhini which is different from its function in the source language, Hindi-Urdu. As most of the Dravidian languages exhibit only FC structures, Telugu (Dravidian) also manifests this type. As a result, Dakkhini (Indo-Aryan), adopts the Telugu configuration and uses *so* as a final complementizer (see Arora and Subbārāo 1989, Subbārāo 2012b for the details of FC *so*, and see Arora and Subbārāo 2004 for a discussion of other aspects of contact-induced changes in Dakkhini). Examples (6) and (7) are illustrative of the use of *so* in Hindi-Urdu and Dakkhini respectively.

(6) Hindi-Urdu (Indo-Aryan)
 jo sotā hai so khotā hai.
 who sleep PRS he lose PRS
 'Whoever sleeps, loses.'
 (Subbārāo 2012a: 196)

(7) Dakkhini (Indo-Aryan)
 bālammā gayē so mere-ku naĩ mālum.
 Balamma went FC(COMP) I-DAT neg knowledge
 'I do not know that Balamma has gone.'
 (Arora and Subbārāo 1989: 10)

2 Kokborok and the language contact situation

The phenomenon of language contact between Kokborok and Bangla is several centuries old. It was during the reign of Ratna Manikya (1464–1468) that several Bengali professionals from neighboring Bangladesh were provided with patronage to help the state run its administrative and economic affairs smoothly. The common people in the Kokborok community depended on their traditional cultivation for their livelihood which did not yield any surplus production. This led the kings to initiate revenue collection through the expansion of wet rice cultivation, which eventually led to the growth of agricultural production (Ghoshal 2012). Jacquesson (2008) suggests that ever since the 16th century, the Kings of Tripura had promoted Bangla in the higher social circle of the royal court, which continued even during the lifetime of Rabindranath Tagore, who was one of the King of Tripura's favorite royal guests. The contact became more intense when there was a large influx of Bengalis from Bangladesh, who settled mostly in north-eastern regions of India such as Tripura, Assam, and some parts of West Bengal.

This longstanding contact with Bangla has led to changes in the indigenous syntactic features of Kokborok. As already mentioned, the widespread correlative strategy in Kokborok – resulting in the relative-correlative clause, the multi-head correlative clause, the free relative clause, and some oblique PP relativization (ablative and comitative) – is worth-noting (see Roy, Kumar, and Subbārāo 2020 for details). Here, we present an instance of a multi-head correlative clause in Kokborok (8) to show how the non-indigenous correlative strategy borrowed from Bangla has been nativized in Kokborok to produce a different type of correlative structure. Example (9) shows a multi-head correlative structure in Bangla.

(8) Kokborok (Tibeto-Burman)
 je   ja   pai-kha abɔ   bebak-nɔ   pɔri-kha.
 who what buy-PST he/she all-EMPH   read-PST
 Literally: 'Who bought what, he/she read all of that.'

(9) Bangla (Indo-Aryan)
 je   ja   kin-e-chi-l-o   še
 who what buy-CPM-PFV-PST-3   he/she
 ta   šɔb   pɔṛ-e-chi-l-o.
 that all   read-CPM-PFV-PST-3
 Literally: 'Who bought what, he/she read all of that.'

Another instance of contact-induced change in Kokborok is exhibited in control structures. For example, predicates expressing physical ailments take both nominative and genitive subjects. The case of genitive subjects in Kokborok, as in (10), is borrowed from Bangla, as shown in (11).

(10) Kokborok (Tibeto-Burman)
 khumti-(ni)   kulum iŋ-kha.
 Khumti-GEN   heat   be-PST
 'Khumti had a fever.'

(11) Bangla (Indo-Aryan)
 kɔmola-r   jɔr   ho-ye-ch-e.
 Kamala-GEN   fever be-CPM-PFV.PRS-3
 'Kamala had a fever.'

Subbārāo, Hakacham, and Sarju Devi (2007) suggest that most of the Tibeto-Burman languages take only nominative subjects. The Angami data in (12) is illustrative.

(12) Angami (Tibeto-Burman)
   a-e   a-tsɨ   chɨ   ba.
   I-NOM   1.SG-head pain   is
   'I have a headache.'
   (Mimi Kevichusa, p.c.)

The genitive subject in Kokborok has implications for the Copy Control[6] structure, especially in the presence of the physical ailment predicates, as shown in (13). In the absence of the genitive subject in the embedded clause, the Copy Control structure is not achieved. Example (14) illustrates its ungrammaticality.

(13) Kokborok (Tibeto-Burman)
   [khumti₁-ni   kulum   iŋ-ii]   khumti₁   thui-kha.
   Khumti-GEN   heat   be-CPM   Khumti.NOM   die-PST
   'Having had fever, Khumti died.'

(14) Kokborok (Tibeto-Burman)
   *[khumti₁   kulum   iŋ-ii]   khumti₁   thui-kha.
   Khumti   heat   be-CPM   Khumti.NOM   die-PST
   'Having had fever, Khumti died.'

The cases discussed above suggest that there has been a gradual drift in the syntax of Kokborok due to long-term contact with Bangla (Indo-Aryan), the dominant[7] language spoken in Tripura. The remainder of this paper is divided into

---

6 Copy Control is the phenomenon of control in which the controller NP and the controllee NP occur overtly in both the matrix and embedded clauses, and thus occur in apparent violation of Linear Axiom Correspondence (Kayne 1994). There is no PRO as found in forward and backward control. In (v), both the controller and the controllee are overtly expressed (see Haddad 2007, 2011, for details of Copy Control). The example below is illustrative of a Copy Control structure.
(v) Assamese (Indo-Aryan)
   [ram₁-ɔr   bhok   lag-i]   ram₁-e   bhat   khal-e.
   Ram-GEN   hunger   feel-CPM Ram-NOM   rice   ate-3
   'Having felt hungry, Ram ate rice.'
   (Haddad 2007: 157)
7 Although both Kokborok and Bangla are the official languages of Tripura, Bangla is the dominant one, as Kokborok is not much used in official domains. Therefore, most of Kokborok

three sections. Section 2 presents a typology of reciprocals across SALs. Section 3 describes reciprocals in Kokborok, focusing on the rare instance of the reduplicated form of the verbal reciprocal *lai lai*. Section 4 discusses the effects on Kokborok reciprocals of language contact, which has led to the phenomenon of syntactic convergence.

3 An account of the typology of reciprocals

Cross-linguistically, the typology of reciprocals is essentially diverse. The work of König and Kokutani (2006), which is considered the "first step towards systematizing our knowledge on the encoding of reciprocity" by König and Gast (2008), divides reciprocals into two basic categories: nominal and verbal. Various languages allow both nominal and verbal reciprocals. However, several others allow only either a nominal or a verbal reciprocal. Lust, Wali, Gair, and Subbārāo (2000) and Subbārāo (2012a), discussing reflexives and other critical syntactic features, present a panorama of reciprocals across SALs.

We present some instances of reciprocals from SALs and later show a few from other language groups. Most Indo-Aryan languages have nominal anaphors. Therefore, in the Indo-Aryan group, the nominal device is the only strategy for expressing reciprocity in action. Sinhala exhibits both nominal and verbal reciprocals (Gair and Karunatillake 2000: 726). On the other hand, Dravidian languages[8] and most of the Tibeto-Burman languages exhibit both nominal and verbal reciprocals. Amongst SALs, it is the Munda group of languages in which the verbal device alone is the only indigenous anaphoric device[9] available in these languages (Subbārāo 2012a: 57).

---

speakers are bilingual (speaking both Kokborok and Bangla fluently), whereas Bangla speakers are not.

8 There are differing views on the subject of occurrence of verbal anaphoric devices in Malayalam and Toda (Dravidian). For example, Subbārāo (2012a: 45) considers Malayalam and Toda exceptions to the Dravidian group, as these two languages exhibit only nominal anaphors whereas other studies such as Emeneau (1984: 174), Asher and Kumari (1997: 165), and Steever (2013: 4), do record instances of verbal reflexives in Malayalam and Toda. Thus, the question requires further investigation.

9 There are some Munda languages that exhibit nominal reflexives owing to intense contact with neighboring Indo-Aryan languages. For example, Kharia has both nominal and verbal reflexives. The nominal device is borrowed from neighboring Indo-Aryan language Sadani, as Peterson (2011) observes.

– Verbal reflexive in Kharia (Munda)

In Sinhala (15), the verb *gatta* 'take' functions as the verbal reciprocal and *ekekkənāTə* 'one-one' functions as the nominal reciprocal. The verbal reciprocal *gatta* is obligatory, as in its absence the reading of reciprocity is not achieved.

(15) Sinhala (Indo-Aryan)
 edā ēgollə ekekkənāTə tǣgi dī-gatta.[10]
 that.day those.people one.one.ANIM.DAT gifts give-VRECP.PST
 'That day those people gave gifts to each other (i.e. to one another).'
 (Gair and Karunatillake 2000: 726)

The Telugu (Dravidian) verbal reciprocal *konn*, as in (16), is obligatory, except in the dative subject construction. The nominal reciprocal *okari-ki okaru* 'one-DAT one.NOM' in Telugu is a reduplicated form. The first component of the bipartite structure of the reciprocal is dative case-marked by the verb and the second component carries the case copy of the subject.

(16) Telugu (Dravidian)
 muttaiduvalu okari-ki okaru vāyinālu iccu-konn-ā-ru.
 married.women one-DAT each.NOM gifts give-VRECP-PST-AGR
 'The married women each gave gifts to each other.'
 (Subbārāo and Lalitha Murthy 2000: 262)

In Mizo too, as in (17), the nominal reciprocal occurs in a bipartite form. Each component is composed of a personal possessive pronoun plus *māh* 'self'. The

---

(vi) pro₍ᵢ₎ yo-ḍom₍ᵢ₎-ki-kiyar₍ᵢ₎.
 they see-vrefl-middle.pst-dual
 'They saw themselves (e.g. in the mirror).'
 Peterson (2011: 294)
– Nominal reflexive in Kharia (Munda)
(vii) pro₍ᵢ₎ aina-te apan₍ᵢ₎-te yo-yo?-j₍ᵢ₎.
 I mirror-in self-ACC see-ACTIVE.PST-1SG
 'I saw myself in the mirror.'
 Peterson (2011: 295)
10 In the absence of the verb *gatta*, the action of reciprocity is not conveyed as (viii) shows.
– Sinhala (Indo-Aryan)
(viii) *edā ēgollə ekekkənāTə tǣgi dunna.*
 that.day those.people one.one.ANIM.DAT gifts give.PST
 'That day those people gave gifts one by one.'
 Gair and Karunatillake (2000: 726)

first element is conjoined with the second by the conjunction *leh* 'and'. The reciprocal exhibits no case inflection. The verbal reciprocal *in* is obligatory.

(17) Mizo (Tibeto-Burman)
zova leh zovi an-māh-ni leh an-māh-ni an-in-fop.
Zova and Zovi they-self-PL and they-self-PL 3PL-VRECP-kiss
'Zova and Zovi kissed each other.'
(Lalitha Murthy and Subbārāo 2000: 783)

Sentence (18) illustrates nominal and verbal reciprocals in Juang (Munda). Although the verbal device is indigenous to the Munda languages, it is optional in Juang in the presence of the nominal reciprocal. The nominal reciprocal is reduplicated in structure, whereas the verbal reciprocal is monomorphemic as in other SALs, and has the form *ku*. Subbārāo (2012a: 45) suggests that the nominal device in Juang has been borrowed from Oriya due to intense contact with Oriya for several centuries. Other Munda languages, such as Kharia, Ho, and Santali, exhibit nominal anaphoric devices due to contact with neighboring Indo-Aryan languages such as Sadani, Hindi-Urdu, and Bangla.

(18) Juang (Austro-Asiatic)
rāma-ba sāma-ba āpein āpein-te sugāi ḍia(ku)bujiki.
Ram-CONJ Shyam-CONJ self self-ACC very love(VRECP)PL
'Ram and Shyam love each other.'
(Patnaik and Subbārāo 2000: 844)

Nominal reciprocals are further divided into pronominal and quantificational strategies, and verbal reciprocals into synthetic and compound strategies. The following examples, drawn from König and Kokutani (2006: 276) and König and Gast (2008: 11–12), represent different strategies involving nominal and verbal reciprocals in various languages. Examples (19) and (20) illustrate nominal reciprocals. German (19) exhibits the pronominal strategy, with a reflexive pronoun expressing 'reflexivity/reciprocity', while English (20) exhibits the quantificational strategy with the nominal reciprocal *each other*. Examples (21) and (22) present verbal reciprocals. In Swahili (21), the reciprocal *-an-* is incorporated within the predicate, whereas Mandarin adopts a compound strategy, as in (22) where the predicate *dǎ* 'beat' reduplicates to express reciprocity in the action of 'beating'.

3.1 Nominal reciprocal

Nominal reciprocals are of two types: pronominal and quantificational.

3.1.1 Pronominal strategy

In the pronominal strategy, the reciprocal occurs as an NP and functions as a reflexive pronoun exhibiting the role of reflexivity and reciprocity. For example, the form *sich* in German, as in (19), occurs either as a reflexive or a reciprocal.

(19) German
  seidem   meiden   sich   die beiden Professoren.
  since.then avoid   REFL/RECP   the both   professors
  'The two professors have avoided each other ever since.'

3.1.2 Quantificational strategy

Quantification is a different nominal strategy for expressing reciprocity. Here, the reciprocal generally takes a bipartite structure, contrasting two or more participants involved in the action and highlighting the relationship between the participants rather than the participants themselves. The English example in (20) is illustrative. The reciprocal *each other* is a bipartite structure that represents the relationship shared between two participants, John and Pete.

(20) English
  John and Pete hate each other.

3.2 Verbal Reciprocal

In contrast to nominal reciprocals, verbal reciprocals are categories that occur inside the verbal complex. They are manifested in two strategies: synthetic and compound. The following examples are illustrative.

3.2.1 Synthetic strategy

The synthetic strategy represents one of the two verbal devices that can express reciprocity in action. In this strategy, a morpheme indicating reciprocation is inserted into the verbal stem. Subbārāo (2012a: 44) labels this verbal category as "verbal clitic". In the Swahili example (21), the form *-an-* is the verbal reciprocal.

(21) Swahili
 ali na fatuma wa-na-pend-an-a.
 Ali and Fatuma 3PL-PRS-love-RECP-FV
 'Ali and Fatuma love each other.'

3.2.2 Compound strategy

Compound strategy is another verbal device for expressing reciprocity. The verbal root undergoes reduplication. For example, in the Mandarin example (22), the verb 'beat' reduplicates to indicate reciprocation in the action of beating.

(22) Mandarin
 tamen da-lai-da-qu.
 3.PL beat-come-beat-go
 'They beat each other.'

As developed in Nedjalkov (2007) and further classified in Haspelmath (2007), the cross-linguistic study of reciprocals identifies more structural types. We do not reiterate these structural types here. Rather, we directly move to the next section to explore reciprocals in Kokborok.

4 Kokborok Reciprocals

Kokborok has two types of reciprocals: nominal and verbal. Both occur either in a reduplicated or a polymorphemic form. Nominal reciprocals are generally polymorphemic/complex in form, as a result of which reciprocals do not participate in non-local/long-distance binding. The nominal reciprocal in Kokborok is a reduplication of the word *khɔrɔk* meaning 'person'. The reciprocal is *khɔrɔk-sa tai khɔrɔk-sa* 'person-CL and person-CL' where the components are joined by the conjunction *tai*. Case inflection is exhibited on the second component of the reciprocal. The verbal reciprocal *lai lai* in Kokborok also shows reduplication, a rare phenomenon in SALs. As far as we know, among SALs, only Kokborok and Bodo (two Tibeto-Burman languages belonging to the Bodo-Garo sub-branch) exhibit a reduplicated form of the verbal reciprocal with two identical components. Here, it should be mentioned that Roy, Subbārāo, Kumar, and Everaert (2020) demonstrate a unique binding phenomenon of Kokborok where the complex reflexive *sak baithaŋ* exhibits an apparent violation of Principle A of Binding Theory (Chomsky 1981). Similarly, reciprocals in Kokborok also exhibit a unique phenomenon of binding. Although the form of the verbal reciprocal *lai lai* is identical to the form in Bodo, the function of the Kokborok form is significantly different. We discuss the phenomenon in detail below.

4.1 The nominal reciprocal: *khɔrɔk-sa tai khɔrɔk-sa*

Binding of the nominal reciprocal in Kokborok is strictly local and thus obeys Principle A of binding theory. Examples (23) and (24) illustrate local binding. Example (23) is a simple sentence in which the nominal reciprocal *khɔrɔk-sa tai khɔrɔk-sa-nɔ*, in the object position, is coindexed with the subject antecedent of the same clause. Example (24) shows a bi-clausal structure in which the reciprocal occurs in the object position of the embedded clause. The reciprocal *khɔrɔk-sa tai khɔrɔk-sa-nɔ* is coindexed with PRO (subject of the embedded clause), which in turn is co-indexed with the object of the matrix clause *cirai-rɔk* 'child-PL'. Coindexation with the long-distance antecedent (subject of the matrix clause) is not permitted and thus conforms with Principle A. The group marker *-lai-*, expressing collaborative effort, is optional in the presence of the nominal reciprocal. However, the group marker[11] is obligatory when there is no reciprocity of action but only a group activity, as in (25). Note that the group marker in (25) does not function as a verbal reciprocal. We discuss the verbal reciprocal in the next section.

(23) Kokborok (Tibeto-Burman)
 bɔrɔk$_i$ khɔrɔk-sa tai khɔrɔk-sa$_i$-nɔ sɔkat ri-kha.
 they person-CL and person-CL-ACC prize give-PST
 'They gave the prize to each other.'

---

[11] The use of the group marker is not frequently found amongst the younger generation of speakers. This could plausibly be the result of prolonged contact with Bangla.

(24) Kokborok (Tibeto-Burman)
*phiyɔgnai-rɔk*₁ *cirai-rɔk*ₖ-*nɔ* [PRO·₁/ₖ *khɔrɔk-sa tai*
teacher-PL child-PL-ACC person-CL with
*khɔrɔk-sa*ₖ/·₁-*nɔ mɔtɔm su-(lai)-nani] sa-kha*.
person-CL-ACC whiff take-GR.MKR-INF tell-PST
'The teachers asked the children to kiss each other.'

(25) Kokborok (Tibeto-Burman)
bɔrɔk thancakhe him-(lai)-kha*.
they together walk-GR.MKR-PST
'They walked together.'

4.2 The verbal reciprocal *-lai lai-*

Kazenin (2001: 918) and Subbārāo (2012a: 59) suggest that verbal anaphors are morphologically simplex. Kokborok and Bodo are the two SALs to exhibit polymorphemic/complex verbal reciprocals. In Bodo, the verbal reciprocal occurs with any action of reciprocity, whereas in Kokborok it is highly restrictive and has special functions. The verbal reciprocal in Kokborok is used only with special predicates that exhibit inherent reciprocity or when the predicate exhibits intimate reciprocity of action. We illustrate with examples. In (26) and (28), the predicates *kiss* and *kick* entail inherent reciprocity, and therefore the verbal reciprocal is preferred (although not obligatory), even in the presence of the nominal reciprocal. The informants we consulted say that *-lai lai-* appropriately reflects the inherent reciprocity implied in the action. The same applies to other similar predicates like *love* and *hug*, which express inherent reciprocity. Note that in the case of the predicate *see*, *-lai lai-* is not permitted because the verb does not inherently convey any action of reciprocity, as in (30). The simple form *-lai-* in (30) is only a group marker and not a reciprocal. Contrary to (30), the verbal reciprocal *-lai lai-* in (31) is obligatory, as the action implies intimacy in the relationship between the participants. It happens only when there is mutual cooperation in the form of eye contact. Although there is no close physical contact, eye contact is an intimate act in which both participants are intensely involved in the action, satisfying the condition of intimacy. Examples (26) to (32) show that the verbal reciprocal takes over the function of reciprocity in the absence of the nominal reciprocal.

(26) Kokborok (Tibeto-Burman)
jæk bai jil khɔrɔk-sa tai
Jack and Jill person-CL and

khɔrɔk-sa-nɔ   mɔtɔm   su-(lai-lai)-kha.
person-CL-ACC   whiff   take-VRECP-PST
'Jack and Jill kissed each other.'

(27) Kokborok (Tibeto-Burman)
jæk   bai   jil   mɔtɔm   su-lai-lai-kha.
Jack and   Jill whiff   take-VRECP-PST
'Jack and Jill kissed each other.'

(28) Kokborok (Tibeto-Burman)
jæk   bai   bil   khɔrɔk-sa   tai   khɔrɔk-sa-nɔ   lathi-ri-(lai-lai)-kha.
Jack and   Bill person-CL   and   person-CL-ACC kick-give-VRECP-PST
'Jack and Bill kicked each other.'

(29) Kokborok (Tibeto-Burman)
jæk   bai   bil   lathi-ri-lai-lai-kha.
Jack and   Bill kick-give-VRECP-PST
'Jack and Bill kicked each other.'

(30) Kokborok (Tibeto-Burman)
jæk   bai   jil   khɔrɔk-sa tai   khɔrɔk-sa-nɔ   nai-(lai)-kha.
Jack and   Jill person-CL and person-CL-ACC see-GR.MKR-PST
'Jack and Jill saw each other.'

(31) Kokborok (Tibeto-Burman)
jæk   bai   jil   khɔrɔk-sa tai   khɔrɔk-sa-nɔ   nai-*(lailai)-kha.
Jack and   Jill person-CL and person-CL-ACC see-VRECP-PST
'Jack and Jill looked at each other with affection/love.'

(32) Kokborok (Tibeto-Burman)
jæk   bai   jil   nai-lai-lai-kha.
Jack and   Jill see-VRECP-PST
'Jack and Jill looked at each other with affection/love.'

It should be mentioned here that such an instance of mutuality and simultaneity is also found in Kannada (Dravidian), as Amritavalli (2000: 54) suggests. The examples in (33) and (34) are illustrative. The non-occurrence of the verbal reciprocal *koḷ* in (33) results in a slight change in meaning, as the sense of mutuality and simultaneity seems to be missing in the action of reciprocity. In (34), the use of *koṇ* (boldfaced) (*koḷ* changes to *koṇ* due to phonological conditioning) is meant to express a kind of desire to reciprocate the action. However, in (33), the desire to become involved in the act of 'seeing each other' is missing. It could be a matter of chance, or perhaps an effortful activity in the act of 'seeing' characterized by a lack of warmth in the action.

(33) Kannada (Dravidian)
    vara-vadhu   obbaranna   obbaru   nōḍidaru.
    bridegroom-bride   one.ACC   one.NOM   saw
    'The bride and bridegroom saw each other.'
    (Amritavalli 2000: 54)
(34) Kannada (Dravidian)
    vara-vadhu   obbaranna   obbaru   nōḍi**konḍ**aru.
    bridegroom-bride   one.ACC   one.NOM   saw
    'The bride and bridegroom looked at each other.'
    (Amritavalli 2000: 54)

Note that the Kokborok simplex form -*lai*- does not imply reciprocity as it only imparts the meaning of group activity. Here, the group marker -*lai*- is not to be mistaken for the verbal reciprocal. In sentences (35), (36), and (37), the group marker in the absence of the nominal reciprocal conveys only the reading of group activity and not reciprocity. In (37), Jack and Jill's act of kissing their daughter is a collaborative effort, and therefore the reduplicated form of -*lai lai*- is strictly barred in this context. The sentence in (38) is illustrative. In (35) and (36), the use of the simplex form -*lai*- conveys only the group activity of kicking somebody and looking at somebody together respectively. Thus, it can be concluded that the reduplicated form -*lai lai*- in Kokborok is the verbal reciprocal, while the simplex form -*lai*- is the group marker.

(35) Kokborok (Tibeto-Burman)
    jæk   bai   bil   lathi-rɨ-lai-kha.
    Jack and   Bill   kick-give-GR.MKR-PST
    'Jack and Bill kicked something together.'
(36) Kokborok (Tibeto-Burman)
    jæk   bai   jil   nai-lai-kha.
    Jack and   Jill   see-GR.MKR-PST
    'Jack and Jill saw something together.'
(37) Kokborok (Tibeto-Burman)
    jæk   bai   jil   bɔrɔg-ni   sajug-nɔ   mɔtɔm   su-lai-kha.
    Jack and   Jill   they-GEN   daughter-ACC   whiff   take-GR.MKR.PST
    'Jack and Jill kissed their daughter together.'
(38) Kokborok (Tibeto-Burman)
    *jæk bai   jil   bɔrɔg-ni   sajug-nɔ   mɔtɔm   su-*lai-lai-kha.
    Jack and   Jill   they-GEN   daughter-ACC   whiff   take-VRECP-PST
    'Jack and Jill kissed their daughter.'

In Bodo, however, this is not the case. The verbal reciprocal in Bodo is obligatory and occurs in the presence of all predicates. However, the reduplicated form of the verbal reciprocal is not obligatory. Examples (39) to (41) are illustrative.

(39) Bodo (Tibeto-Burman)
meri arə bil-ya naŋ-lai-(lai)-dəŋ-mən.
Mary and Bill-NOM argue-VRECP-PFV-PST
'Mary and Bill argued with each other.'

(40) Bodo (Tibeto-Burman)
bisərə gau-zen-gau səu-lai-(lai)-dəŋ-mən.
they.NOM self-with-self punch-VRECP-PFV-PST
'They punched each other.'

(41) Bodo (Tibeto-Burman)
jɔn arə meri-ya gau-zəŋ-gau nu-lai-(lai)-dəŋ-mən.
John and Mary-NOM self-with-self see-VRECP-PFV-PST
'John and Mary saw each other.'

In Bodo, the reduplicated form is not permitted when the nominal reciprocal occurs in a non-subcategorized position. This is permissible in Kokborok, as it encodes a kind of reciprocity in which the participants involved exhibit internal symmetry in the action of reciprocity. This is why -lai lai- in Kokborok is not dependent on the subcategorized position of the nominal reciprocal. Thus, the reduplicated form of the verbal reciprocal in Kokborok is unique to SALs. The Bodo example (42) shows that reduplication leads to ungrammaticality when the reciprocal *gau-zen-gau* occurs in the adjunct position (a non-subcategorized position). However, in Kokborok, it is permissible as (43) and (44) suggest. The reduplicated form is obligatory, as the context of sitting together exhibits intimacy in the relationship between Bill and Mary. This suggests that both participants are equally involved in the action and may be in close physical contact with each other, imparting the reading of intimacy. Without the reduplication, there is no clear sense of intense reciprocation, as this implies that the two people sitting together may not be familiar with each other. It could also be a case of mere chance that two persons named Bill and Mary are sitting together. In that case, the group marker -lai- in the predicate does not communicate the desired meaning of reciprocation. Only the verbal reciprocal -lai lai- is appropriate to the context, and therefore it is obligatory. In the absence of the nominal reciprocal, it is the verbal reciprocal -lai lai- which conveys the interpretation of reciprocity coupled with a deep sense of mutuality and intimacy.

(42) Bodo (Tibeto-Burman)
jɔn arə meri-ya gau-zen-gau khathi-yao
John and Mary-NOM self-with-self near-LOC
zirai-lai-*lai-dəŋ.
sit-VRECP-IPFV
'John and Mary are sitting next to each other.'

(43) Kokborok (Tibeto-Burman)
bil bai meri khɔrɔk-sa tai khɔrɔk-sa-ni
Bill and Mary person-CL with person-CL-GEN
ganaɔ acuk-ii-tɔŋ-lai-lai-ɔ.
near sit-CPM-PROG-VRECP-PRS
'Bill and Mary are sitting next to each other.'

(44) Kokborok (Tibeto-Burman)
bil bai meri ganaɔ acuk-ii-tɔŋ-lai-lai-ɔ.
Bill and Mary near sit-CPM-PROG-VRECP-PRS
'Bill and Mary are sitting next to each other.'

Let us take another example in which the reciprocal occurs as the modifier of the object (a non-subcategorized position). In this case, the verbal reciprocal -lai lai- is strictly barred in Kokborok. Note sentence (45). The incorporation of -lai lai- is incompatible with the predicate cut, as the verb does not entail any intimacy in the action of cutting each other's hair. The sentence is grammatical only in the absence of the verbal reciprocal (46). However, in Bodo it is only the simplex form that occurs in the predicate. In Bodo, the simplex form -lai- is also a verbal reciprocal, and it manifests only in the non-subcategorized position (47). Reduplication leads to ungrammaticality, as shown in (48).

(45) Kokborok (Tibeto-Burman)
bɔrɔk khɔrɔk-sa bai khɔrɔk-sa-ni khinai ra-*lai-lai-kha.
they person-CL with person-CL-GEN hair cut-VRECP-PST
'They cut each other's hair.'

(46) Kokborok (Tibeto-Burman)
bɔrɔk khɔrɔk-sa bai khɔrɔk-sa-ni khinai ra-kha.
they person-CL with person-CL-GEN hair cut-PST
'They cut each other's hair.'

(47) Bodo (Tibeto-Burman)
bisərə-ə gau-zen-gau khanai ha-sɔ-lai-dəŋ-mən.
they-NOM self-with-self hair cut-down-VRECP-PFV-PST
'They cut each other's hair.'

(48) Bodo (Tibeto-Burman)
    bisərə-ə   gau-zen-gau   khanai   ha-sɔ-lai-*lai-dəŋ-mən.
    they-NOM self-with-self   hair   cut-down-VRECP-PFV-PST
    'They cut each other's hair.'

Unlike in Bodo, the verbal reciprocal in Kokborok conveys the traditional concept of reciprocity, coupled with a sense of deep mutual cooperation and an implied sense of close contact between the participants. Therefore, -lai lai- in Kokborok is restricted to certain contexts, while the equivalent construction in Bodo is diverse in function, as it is used in various events of reciprocity. In the case of the verbs like *kick* and *kiss*, the action already involves close physical contact, which is why -lai lai- in Kokborok is optional, although it is preferred (speakers say that its use in the case of *kick* and *kiss* is apt for the inherent meaning, or deepens the intensity of the reciprocal component). In the case of verbs like *sit* or *see*, in which the existence of close contact is unclear, the reduplicated verbal reciprocal plays a crucial role in imparting the meaning of deep involvement in the action of reciprocity, and hence it is obligatory in such contexts in Kokborok. A similar instance is found in Kuuk Thaayore, a non-South Asian language spoken on the Cape York Peninsula in Australia (Gaby 2008). In Kokborok, the verbal reciprocal -lai lai- is restricted to certain kinds of predicates, *sit* and *see* which do not exhibit inherent reciprocity. The Kokborok reciprocal is employed to characterize a deep sense of reciprocation arising out of intimacy, whereas in Kuuk Thaayore, reciprocity is expressed in two forms: either the traditional sense of reciprocity or a type of reciprocation coupled with symmetric events. The verbal device of reciprocity in Kuuk Thaayore therefore expresses various kinds of symmetry in the event of reciprocity. We present several representative examples of this in the following section.

4.2.1 Verbal reciprocity in Kuuk Thaayore

Gaby (2008: 284) elaborates on the implications of verbal reciprocity in Kuuk Thaayore (a Paman language) and distinguishes between two forms of verbal anaphor: -e- (reflexive) and -rr- (reciprocal). The reciprocal marker -rr- is employed to express the traditional concept of reciprocity, while the reflexive marker -e- expresses symmetric events in the action. Gaby shows that the -e- marker appears only when the following three conditions are met:

— The occurrence of the event depends on each of the participants playing a particular role;

- There is a blurring of the individual roles played by participants; and
- There is close contact between the participants.

Consider the Kuuk Thaayore example in sentence (49). The marker -*e*- occurs only because all of the three aforementioned conditions are fulfilled in the action. Unless the participants lean in the appropriate direction, they would not support each other and thereby satisfy the first condition. The individual roles in the act of leaning are blurred, as the participants are involved in the action together. This meets the second condition. There is definitely close physical contact amongst the participants, as their backs are touching each other, thereby satisfying the third condition.

(49) Kuuk Thaayore (Paman)
*pul   mut-u   thā.yōyoŋk-**e**-ø.*
3DU.NOM/ERG   back-DAT   lean.RDP-REFL-NONPST
'They are leaning (on each other) back to back.'
(Gaby 2008: 283)

We provide another example from Gaby (2008) in which a distinction is drawn between the two reciprocity markers. The crucial difference between (50) and (51) is that in (50) the participants look into each other's eyes at the right time, which is an intimate act of reciprocity because making eye contact implies close (though not necessarily physical) contact between the participants, thereby satisfying all three of the above conditions. However, in (51), the reciprocal -*rr*- expresses only the action of looking, which is devoid of the subtleties of intimacy or close contact.

(50) Kuuk Thaayore (Paman)
*pul   nhānhath-**e**-ø.*
3DU.NOM   look.RDP-REFL-NONPST
'They are looking (into) each other('s eyes).'
(Gaby 2008: 284)

(51) Kuuk Thaayore (Paman)
*pul   mēr-e   nhāth-**rr**-r.*
3DU.NOM/ERG   eye-ERG   look-RECP-PST.PFV
'They looked at each other (one after the other).'
(Gaby 2008: 284)

Quite like Kuuk Thaayorre, the reduplicated form of the verbal reciprocal -*lai lai*- in Kokborok, a rare indigenous phenomenon unique to SALs, is a special technique employed to express a deep sense of intimacy, close contact, and mutual involvement in the reciprocal action.

5 Reciprocals and syntactic convergence in Kokborok

As discussed in the earlier sections, verbal anaphors are found in the Munda, Dravidian, and Tibeto-Burman families, as well as in a few Indo-Aryan languages such as Marathi, Gujarati, and Sinhala. In the Munda family, the verbal device is the only indigenous anaphoric device, although some Munda languages, such as Santali, Kharia, Ho, and Juang, exhibit the nominal anaphoric device, a strategy borrowed from neighboring Indo-Aryan languages. The polymorphemic form of verbal reciprocal -*lai lai*- in Kokborok and Bodo (two sister languages in the Bodo-Garo sub-branch of the Tibeto-Burman family) is a rare phenomenon. As discussed in section 3.2, the verbal reciprocal in Bodo is diverse as it is used in various reciprocal events, whereas in Kokborok it is restricted to specific contexts. One plausible reason could be the long-term contact with Bangla (Indo-Aryan spoken in proximity), as Bangla does not exhibit any verbal anaphoric devices. This explanation is supported by the precedence of the nominal reciprocal over the verbal device in Kokborok, and also by the gradual disappearance of the indigenous verbal device in the younger generation speech.

During our field work, we noticed that the speakers aged between 16 and 30 (n = 15) did not prefer the adverbial incorporation in the verb stem which is typical of the Tibeto-Burman family[12]. For example, the reduplicated form of -*lai lai*- was used less by these speakers and in their speech the essence of reciprocity was reduced to collaborative/group activity. The reduplicated form functioned only as a group marker in their speech, and therefore they frequently dropped one of the components due to redundancy, as the group marker -*lai*- already exists in Kokborok. In some cases, these speakers did not use group marker incorporation in the predicate, as they preferred to use a separate adverb indicating 'togetherness'.

---

[12] The Kokborok speakers we consulted with, in our field work, were born and brought up in Tripura and aged between 16 to 75.

The impending loss of the function of *-lai lai-* as a reciprocal is possibly due to contact with Bangla, as Bangla does not exhibit any verbal incorporation phenomena. The speech of some ten speakers in the older group (aged 50 to 75) exhibits the use of *-lai lai-* (as a verbal reciprocal) only in specific contexts. However, there were still a few who considered its use to be redundant in the presence of the nominal reciprocal. The remainder of speakers, who were aged between 30 and 50, used *-lai lai-* sporadically. A thorough investigation with a larger sample size is necessary to capture the impact of contact on the grammar of reciprocity in the Kokborok community. However, the results discussed in this paper suggest that the indigenous device of reciprocity in Kokborok has undergone change, as have other structures such as control and relative clause constructions (mentioned in the previous sections) due to long-standing contact with Bangla. As far as this fieldwork is concerned, this structural change in reciprocals was observed mostly amongst the younger speakers. These speakers, in comparison to the older group, are more exposed to multilingual diversity due to education, and experience more intense language contact in their day-to-day work patterns.

Several examples show the differences in the use of *-lai lai-* between speakers. Let us take the example of the verb *kiss*. In (53), the act of 'kissing their daughter' is a collaborative effort, and therefore the group marker *-lai lai-* (as the reduplicated form is reduced to a group marker) can be optionally used. However, as illustrated in (38) above – repeated here as (52) – the reduplicated form is strictly barred when there is no reciprocity of action. However, this is acceptable for the younger speakers, as shown in (53). Moreover, when it comes to the reciprocal action as in (54), the group marker *-lai-* can be optional (the younger generation does not prefer its use), as the nominal reciprocal already imparts the reading of reciprocation.

(52) Kokborok (Tibeto-Burman)
 *jæk bai jil bɔrɔg-ni sajug-nɔ mɔtɔm su-*lai-lai-kha.
 Jack and Jill they-GEN daughter-ACC whiff take-VRECP-PST
 'Jack and Jill kissed their daughter.'

(53) Kokborok (Tibeto-Burman)
 jæk bai jil bɔrɔg-ni sajug-nɔ mɔtɔm su-lai(lai)-kha.
 Jack and Jill they-GEN daughter-ACC whiff take-GR.MKR-PST
 'Jack and Jill kissed their daughter together.'

(54) Kokborok (Tibeto-Burman)
 jæk bai jil khɔrɔk-sa tai khɔrɔk-sa-nɔ mɔtɔm su-(lai(lai))-kha.
 Jack and Jill person-CL and person-CL-ACC whiff take-GR MKR-PST
 'Jack and Jill kissed each other.'

We provide another example with the verb *sit*. Unlike example (43) in section 3.2, in which the reduplication of *-lai lai-* is obligatory, the younger generation in this case prefers the reduplicated form only as the group marker, as in (55). The form *-lai lai-* is optional, as it only describes group activity (the group marker itself is largely optional for this generation of speakers). Therefore, the sense of reciprocity in the action of 'sitting' is missing here, as there is barely any sense of close contact between the participants coupled with the impression of intimacy in the action. Thus, it is not clear if the two persons are familiar with each other, or if it is a matter of chance that they are sitting together. However, in (56), a clear-cut meaning of reciprocity is expressed in the use of the nominal reciprocal. At this point, it is quite plausible to argue that the essence of the verbal reciprocal *-lai lai-* is gradually fading away probably due to the contact influence of the dominant language Bangla. Verbal reciprocal is not indigenously available in Bangla, and therefore gradual fading of this device in Kokborok could perhaps be the result of language contact with Bangla.

(55) Kokborok (Tibeto-Burman)
bil bai meri ganaɔ acuk-ïi-tɔŋ-(lai-lai)-ɔ.
Bill and Mary near sit-CPM-PROG-GR.MKR-PRS
'Bill and Mary are sitting together.'

(56) Kokborok (Tibeto-Burman)
bil bai meri khɔrɔk-sa tai khɔrɔk-sa-ni
Bill and Mary person-CL with person-CL-GEN
ganaɔ acuk-ïi-tɔŋ-(lai-lai)-ɔ.
near sit-CPM-PROG-GR.MKR-PRS
'Bill and Mary are sitting next to each other.'

The meaning of reciprocity in *-lai lai-* is lost in the speech of the younger generation, as it has transformed into a group marker. In fact, the reduplicated form as the group marker has become quite redundant, as it no longer performs any syntactic function. For the older generation of speakers, the indigenous verbal reciprocal *-lai lai-* exhibits specific functions of reciprocity and this is distinctly conveyed in their speech. This variation in Kokborok, as far as our fieldwork is concerned, is plausibly due to prolonged contact with Bangla, which is widely spoken in Tripura.

6 Conclusion

This paper has attempted to capture the phenomenon of the gradual loss of the reduplicated form of the indigenous verbal reciprocal -*lai lai*- and its special syntactic functions in Kokborok. It appears that this loss is the result of intense contact with the genetically different language Bangla (Indo-Aryan), the dominant language spoken in Kokborok's proximity for centuries. The reduplicated form of the verbal anaphor in Bodo and Kokborok is a rare phenomenon, as it is not found in any other SALs so far studied. In Bodo, the verbal reciprocal -*lai lai*- is meant for various reciprocal actions, whereas in Kokborok it is restricted only to specific contexts of reciprocity. The reduplicated form in Kokborok classically invokes mutuality and a deep sense of intimacy and contact in the reciprocal action. However, the influence of Bangla appears to have resulted in the precedence of the nominal reciprocal over the verbal device in Kokborok, which is reflected mostly in the younger generation of speakers. This could be due to the fact that these speakers are more exposed to the contact with Bangla due to education, business and workspace.

Abbreviations

1=first person; 3=third person; ACC=accusative case; AGR=agreement; ANIM=animate; CL=classifier; CONJ=conjunction; CPM=conjunctive participle marker; DAT=dative case; ERG=ergative case; FV=finite verb; GEN=genitive case; GR.MKR=group marker; IPFV=imperfective aspect; INF=infinitive; LOC=locative; NMLZ=nominalizer; NOM=nominative case; PFV=perfective aspect; PL=plural; PRS=present tense; PROG=progressive aspect; PST=past tense; RECP=reciprocal; REFL=reflexive; SG=singular; VREFL=verbal reflexive; VRECP=verbal reciprocal

Transliteration

The transcription of language data in the paper is largely based on the ISO-15919 system. (https://en.wikipedia.org/wiki/ISO_15919). However, as there is no special symbol available in ISO-15919 to transcribe a centralized /i/ found in Kokborok (as well as in other Tibeto-Burman languages), a special symbol, namely /ɨ/, has been borrowed from the IPA inventory of symbols.

Acknowledgements

We are immensely grateful to our language consultants, Mr. Manik Debbarma, Mr. Mukthang Koloi, Mr. Bosong Jamatia, and Mr. Yakchu Debbarma for the Kokborok data and their comments on variations in the data. We express our heartfelt thanks to Mr. Sansuma Brahma and Ms. Ganga Brahma for the Bodo data.

References

Amritavalli, Raghavachari. 2000. Lexical Anaphors and Pronouns in Kannada. In Barbara Lust, Kashi Wali, James W. Gair & Karumuri V. Subbarao (eds.), *Lexical Anaphors and Pronouns in Selected South Asian Languages: A Principled Typology*, 49–112. Berlin & New York: Mouton de Gruyter.

Arora, Harbir & Karumuri V. Subbarao. 1989. Convergence and Syntactic Reanalysis: The Case of *so* in Dakkhini. *Studies in the Linguistic Sciences* 19. Urbana, IL: University of Illinois.

Arora, Harbir & Karumuri V. Subbarao. 2004. Syntactic Change and Convergence. In Peri Bhaskararao & Karumuri V. Subbarao (eds.), *Non-Nominative Subjects*, vol I, 25–48. Amsterdam & Philadelphia: John Benjamins.

Asher, Ronald E. & T. C. Kumari. 1997. *Malayalam*. London & New York: Routledge.

Bhatt, Rajesh. 2003. Locality in Correlatives. *Natural Language and Linguistic Theory* 21. 485–541.

Cardona, George & Dhanesh Jain (eds.). 2003. *Indo-Aryan Languages*. London & New York: Routledge.

Chomsky, Noam. 1981. *Lectures on Government & Binding*. Dordrecht: Foris Publication.

Downing, B. T. 1978. Some Universals of Relative Clause Structure. In Joseph H. Greenberg, Charles A. Ferguson & Edith A. Moravcsik (eds.), *Universals of Human Language*, vol. IV, 375–418. Stanford, CA: Stanford University Press.

Emeneau, Murray B. 1984. *Toda Grammar and Texts*. Philadelphia: American Philosophical Society.

Gaby, Alice. 2008. Distinguishing Reciprocals from Reflexives in Kuuk Thaayorre. In Ekkehard König & Volker Gast (eds.), *Reciprocals and Reflexives: Theoretical and Typological Explorations*, 259–288. Berlin: Mouton de Gruyter.

Gair, James W. & W. S. Karunatillake. 2000. Lexical Anaphors and Pronouns in Sinhala. In Barbara Lust, Kashi Wali, James W. Gair & Karumuri V. Subbarao (eds.), *Lexical Anaphors and Pronouns in Selected South Asian Languages: A Principled Typology*, 715–776. Berlin & New York: Mouton de Gruyter.

Ghoshal, Anindita. 2012. Changing Mentality of the Bengalee Refugees: The Story of Tripura (1946–1971). *Refugee Watch*. 18–34.

Haddad, Youssef A. 2007. *Adjunct Control in Telugu and Assamese*. Gainesville, FL: University of Florida doctoral dissertation.

Haddad, Youssef A. 2011. *Control into Conjunctive Participle Clauses: The Case of Assamese*. Berlin: De Gruyter Mouton.

Haspelmath, Martin. 2007. Further Remarks on Reciprocal Constructions. In Vladimir P. Nedjalkov (ed.), *Reciprocal constructions*, 2087–2115. Amsterdam: Benjamins.
Hock, Hans Henrich & Elena Bashir (eds.). 2016. *The Languages and Linguistics of South Asia*. Berlin: De Gruyter Mouton.
Jacquesson, François. 2008. *A Kokborok Grammar: Agartala Dialect*. Agartala: Kokborok Tei Hukumu Mission.
Kayne, Richard. 1994. *The Anti-Symmetry of Syntax*. Cambridge, MA: MIT Press.
Kazenin, Konstantin I. 2001. Verbal Reflexives and the Middle Voice. In Martin Haspelmath, Ekkehard König, Wulf Oesterreicher & Wolfgang Raible (eds.), *Language Typology and Language Universals*, 916–927. Berlin: Mouton de Gruyter.
Keenan, Edward L. 1985. Relative Clauses. In Timothy Shopen (ed.), *Language Typology and Syntactic Description*, vol. II, 141–170. Cambridge: Cambridge University Press.
König, Ekkehard & Volker Gast. 2008. Reciprocity and Reflexivity – Description, Typology and Theory. In Ekkehard König & Volker Gast (eds.), *Reciprocals and Reflexives: Theoretical and Typological Explorations*, 1-31. Berlin: Mouton de Gruyter.
König, Ekkehard & Shigehiro Kokutani. 2006. Toward a Typology of Reciprocal Constructions: Focus on German and Japanese. *Linguistics* 44 (2). 271–302.
Krishnamurti, Bhadriraju. & John P. L. Gwynn. 1985. *A Grammar of Modern Telugu*. Delhi: Oxford University Press.
Lakshmi Bai, Balachandran. 1985. Some Notes on Correlative Constructions in Dravidian. In Veneeta Z. Acson & Richard L. Leed (eds.), *For Gordon H. Fairbanks*, 181–190. Honolulu: University of Hawaii Press.
Lalitha Murthy, Balemarthy & Karumuri V. Subbarao. 2000. Lexical Anaphors and Pronouns in Mizo. In Barbara Lust, Kashi Wali, James W. Gair & Karumuri V. Subbarao (eds.), *Lexical Anaphors and Pronouns in Selected South Asian Languages: A principled typology*, 777–840. Berlin & New York: Mouton de Gruyter.
Lust, Barbara, Kashi Wali, James W. Gair & Karumuri V. Subbarao (eds.). 2000. *Lexical Anaphors and Pronouns in Selected South Asian Languages: A Principled Typology*. Berlin: Mouton de Gruyter.
Nadkarni, Mangesh V. 1970. *Noun Phrase Embedded Structures in Kannada and Konkani*. Los Angles: University of California (UCLA) doctoral dissertation.
Nadkarni, Mangesh V. 1975. Bilingualism and Syntactic Change in Konkani. *Language* 51. 672–683.
Nedjalkov, Vladimir P. (ed.). 2007. *Reciprocal Constructions*. Amsterdam: John Benjamins.
Patnaik, Manideepa & Karumuri V. Subbarao. 2000. An Initial Note on Lexical Anaphors and Pronouns in Juang. In Barbara Lust, Kashi Wali, James W. Gair & Karumuri V. Subbarao (eds.), *Lexical Anaphors and Pronouns in Selected South Asian Languages: A Principled Typology*, 841–860. Berlin & New York: Mouton de Gruyter.
Peterson, John. 2011. *Kharia: A South Munda Language*. Leiden & Boston: Brill Publications.
Roy, Gargi, Rajesh Kumar & Karumuri V. Subbarao. 2020. Relative Clauses in Kokborok — A Case of Syntactic Convergence. *International Journal of Dravidian Linguistics* XLIX (2). 116–145.
Roy, Gargi, Karumuri V. Subbarao, Rajesh Kumar & Martin Everaert. 2020. Kokborok and the Simple-Complex Reflexive Distinction. *Studies in Language*. Amsterdam: John Benjamins Publishing Company. http://doi.org/10.1075/sl.19091.roy
Sridhar, Shikaripur N. 1990. *Kannada*. London: Routledge.

Steever, Sanford. 2013. *Review: South Asian Languages: A Syntactic Typology*. Cambridge: Cambridge University Press.

Subbarao, Karumuri V. 2012a. *South Asian Languages: A Syntactic Typology*. New York: Cambridge University Press.

Subbarao, Karumuri V. 2012b. *South Asian languages: A Syntactic Typology*. Retrieved from https://www.academia.edu/6666513/South Asian_Languages_A_Syntactic_Typology

Subbarao, Karumuri V. & Harbir Arora. 1989. Extreme convergence: The case of Dakkhini Hindi-Urdu. In Aditi Mukherjee (ed.), *Language change and language variation*, 359–386. Hyderabad: Centre of Advanced Study, Osmania University.

Subbarao, Karumuri V. & Balemarthy, Lalitha Murthy. 2000. Lexical Anaphors and Pronouns in Telugu. In Barbara Lust, Kashi Wali, James W. Gair & Karumuri V. Subbarao (eds.), *Lexical Anaphors and Pronouns in Selected South Asian Languages: A Principled Typology*, 217–276. Berlin & New York: Mouton de Gruyter.

Subbarao, Karumuri V., Upen R. Hakacham & Thokchom Sarju Devi. 2007. Case-marked PRO: Evidence from Rabha, Manipuri, Hindi-Urdu and Telugu. In Roland Bielmeier & Felix Haller (eds.), *Linguistics of the Himalayas and Beyond*, 291–322. Berlin: Mouton de Gruyter.

Sajukta Ghosh
A cognitive semantic analysis of locative and spatial constructions in Bangla

Abstract: This paper examines certain spatial constructions in Bangla by identifying and describing locative and spatial postpositions used in different spatial constructions. The initial data are based on the Topological Relation Picture Series (TRPS) description. This is an exploratory study for Bangla locative and spatial postpositions in a cognitive semantics framework. For describing location, Bangla uses two main types of construction: first, Trajector-Landmark + Locative marker-copula and, second, Trajector-Landmark + GEN-Postposition-Verb-Copula. Bangla is observed to have 14 spatial postpositions for the TRPS picture description. These are derived from spatial nouns and are marked with locative case. The paper shows that apart from postpositions and locative markers, the copula verb also plays an important role in the cognition of space in Bangla.

Keywords: Spatial constructions, spatial postpositions, locative, copula, Bangla, TRPS, cognitive semantics

1 Introduction

Languages differ in the way they express the concept of space and this difference is crucial in understanding the relation between language and thought. This issue is explored in cognitive semantics as the relation between the conceptual category of space and linguistic categories like case markers, pre/postpositions, certain verbs, nouns, etc. The relation of language and space has been one of the major research areas within cognitive semantics, cognitive psychology and cognitive science in general.

This paper is an attempt to describe the locative and spatial postpositions of Bangla using the Topological Relation Picture Series (TRPS) description. In doing so, the TRPS (Bowerman and Pederson 1992) pictures are described in Bangla using a "where" question in relation to the position of Trajector and Landmark. These pictures describe a situation where one object is located in a particular

---

Sanjukta Ghosh, Department of Humanistic Studies, IIT (BHU), Varanasi, India 221005. Email: sanjukta.hss@iitbhu.ac.in

place (the Figure or the Trajector) in relation to some other object (the Ground or the Landmark). This picture series is one of the most widely used picture series for exploring the spatial semantic constructions of a language. It was first developed by Melissa Bowerman and has been subsequently extended in collaboration with Eric Pederson and Penelope Brown on the basis of their experiences of a number of non-Indo-European languages; it comprises 71 pictures (as given in the appendix). The Bangla sentences were generated by the author (myself) as a result of the description of the pictures. The sentences were generated based on the question "Where is X?", where X is the object pointed out in the picture. The data was later cross-checked with another native speaker. The results of the description were then categorized and analyzed to understand the semantics of spatial constructions in the language.

The paper aims to find and point out the linguistic tools that Bangla uses for describing Basic Locative Constructions (BLC). Bangla is historically derived from Sanskrit, a highly inflectional Indo-Aryan language which primarily uses case markers (*vibhakti* in Sanskrit) to express all types of case relations. The postpositions found in Bangla are mainly derived from different nouns and verbs, and are later developments in the history of Bangla. This paper addresses the following questions.
— To what extent do the spatial constructions of Bangla use locative case markers?
— Where are the spatial postpositions used?
— Is one of these constructions unmarked or default compared to the other?
— How is Bangla different from or similar to English?

The paper has five sections. The second section provides the background of the study by discussing some of the major works in spatial semantics in the last couple of decades, especially within cognitive linguistics and cognitive psychology. It also introduces the major terms used in literature on spatial semantics. The third section discusses the sentences generated from the TRPS and presents a brief analysis of those sentences. The fourth section summarizes the observations and the findings. The fifth section presents the concluding remarks.

2 Spatial semantics research: A brief review

2.1 Spatial semantics in cognitive linguistics

Spatial semantics has been a topic of discussion in cognitive linguistics over a long period of time (Talmy 2000; Levinson 2004; Hickman and Robert 2006, Zlatev 2007; Levinson and Maira 2003; Majid et al. 2004; Bloom et al. 1996; Pütz and Dirven 1996). Universality is one of its core characteristics as spatial experience is a universal human experience across languages and it therefore constitutes a good source to look for language universals. Space is often considered to be a basic concrete experience and other abstract experiences like time, social and psychological distance etc. are expressed through spatial expressions across languages. Putz and Dirven rightly point out "Space is at the heart of all conceptualization" (Putz and Dirven 1996: xi). Therefore, the importance of the study of spatial relations in cognitive linguistics and cognitive science is easily understood.

The long tradition of research in spatial cognition has generated academic debate. On the one side, there are universalists like Pinker (1996), Landau and Jackendoff (1993), and Li and Gleitmann (2002), who take the position that languages merely reflect the universal conceptual categories. For them, there are certain conceptual spatial primitives like containment, contiguity, proximity etc. These conceptual primitives are directly coded in the languages mostly as adpositions (pre- or post- positions). These are universal in nature as they are grounded in our neuro-cognition. The alternative viewpoint assumes that language plays a role in the cognitive understanding of space. However, there are two different views about this role of language. Majid et al. (2004) argue that language structures spatial cognition but Levinson and his colleagues hold the view that there is a universal understanding of space and different languages partition that differently (Levinson and Maira 2003). Levinson and his colleagues, in a different work (Levinson et al. 2002) based on different languages, suggested that egocentric languages (like English) which use terms like "left" and "right" also identify an object with respect to the speaker's position. But languages which use absolute spatial terms like "north" and "south" (e.g. Tzeltai) encode the position of an object in more global absolute terms. Therefore, they conclude that our spatial language repertoire influences and restructures the understanding of the concept of space. Feist and Gentner (2007) also show, through a series of experiments, that spatial language influences memory for spatial scenes. Gentner et al. (2013) showed that deaf children who do not have a conventional sign language and use "homesigns" to communicate, cannot express spatial relations. Their study confirms that spatial language facilitates spatial cognition.

2.2 Different spatial terms

There is debate even on what should be considered a spatial term in language. The most common way of defining spatial semantics is in terms of a class of expressions like "spatial prepositions" (Cuyckens 1991; Landau and Jackendoff 1993), "closed class forms" (Talmy 1983) or "spatial grams" (Svorou 1994). However, these classifications are problematic, as pointed out in Zlatev (2007), because they do not distinguish between spatial and non-spatial senses of the prepositions and do not include verbs, nouns and adverbs that provide spatial senses. Alternatively, spatial expressions are defined as those that express some spatial relations (Langacker 1987; Sinha and Thorsheng 1995) in terms of the Trajector and Landmark or Figure and Ground. An entity whose location or translocation is relevant is called a Trajector (Langacker 1987). The Trajector can be static or dynamic. The Landmark is the reference entity in relation to which the Trajector is located or the Trajectory of the motion of the Trajector is specified.

The examples in (1) and (2) illustrate the relation between a Trajector and a Landmark.

(1) The *apple* is in the bowl. (*Apple* is the static Trajector, *bowl* is a Landmark)
(2) The *boat* is in the river. (*Boat* is a dynamic Trajector, *river* is a Landmark)

The Trajector is referred to as "Figure" and Landmark as "Ground" by Talmy (1983).

There may not be an explicit Landmark in a construction. For instance, in the sentence, *the balloon went up*, the balloon is the Trajector but there is no specific Landmark. There is no need of an explicit Landmark to understand the construction.

Alternatively, Zlatev (2007) pointed out that the objects of the study of Spatial Semantics are the "spatial expressions, that is, conventional specifications of the location or change of location (translocation) of a given entity in space" (Zlatev 2007). To locate an object in a space in relation to other objects, languages use Frames of Reference (hereafter FoR). FoR refers to one or more reference points and a coordinate system of axes and angles (Zlatev 2007). Levinson describes three FoRs, grammaticalized or lexicalized, in a language, as given below.

a. Intrinsic FoR: the main reference point coincides with the landmark, and axes and angles are projected on the basis of its geometry, as in (3).

(3)   *The girl was sitting* in front of the car.

The car has an intrinsic front and the reference is made on this basis.

b. Relative FoR: a real or imaginary viewpoint serves as a reference point and co-ordinates are projected on the basis of this viewpoint, as in (4).

(4)   *The girl is in front of the bush.*

The bush does not have an intrinsic front or back, so the front is in relation to the speaker's viewpoint.

c. Absolute FoR: the system is anchored in fixed geo-cardinal positions, as in (5).

(5)   *Delhi is to the west of Varanasi.*

The location is stated with reference to geographical position.

3 Spatial constructions of Bangla

Bangla uses two main types of Basic Locative Constructions. The frame for the first type is Trajector-Landmark+Locative marker-copula. The locative marker of Bangla is *-te* or *-e* and the copula verbs that are used in the "where" constructions are *aṭʰ* 'to be, exist, have' and *rɔa* 'to stay', often preceded by the verb *rakʰa* 'to keep'. The spatial knowledge comes from both the locative marker and the copula. Out of the 71 pictures of TRPS, the Locative marker is used for 32 cases in my translations of the pictures. These are picture numbers 1, 2, 5, 7, 9, 10, 11, 12, 18, 21, 22, 26, 27, 28, 32, 33, 35, 37, 39, 41, 42, 44, 45, 46, 48, 50, 51, 54, 57, 61, 62 and 69. In some of these cases, alternatively a postposition may also be used for some specification of the location. These are picture numbers 1, 12 and 68 in my translations of the picture. For instance, in the first picture of the TRPS data, *a cup is on the table* may be represented by the following sentences.

(6) *kapṭa ṭebile aṭʰe.* [generic]
    cup.CLF table.LOC be.PRS.3
    'The cup is on the table.'

(7) *kapṭa ṭebiler opor rakʰa aṭʰe.* [specific]
    cup.CLF table.GEN on put.PASS be.PRS.3
    'The cup is (kept) on the table.'

Though the two examples given above have similar English translations, a careful investigation shows that the use of these constructions depends on the contexts. The second construction with the postposition is more specific about the location of the Trajector. The second sentence may be used in contrast to *ṭebiler dʰare* 'at the edge of the table' or *ṭebiler niṭe* 'under the table' etc. The physical three-dimensional shape of the table can also be highlighted by using the second type of construction with a spatial postposition. If the speaker simply asks, "where is the cup?", the first response will be sentence (5). But suppose the addressee checks the table and could not find it, or the speaker presupposes that the addressee may have difficulty in finding it; the speaker may then be more specific in answering the question about the location, often using a focus marker *-i* with the postposition. This observation has been confirmed by some other native speakers of the language.

The second type of construction is Trajector-Landmark+GEN-Locative Postposition- Verb+Copula. These postpositions are derived from different spatial nouns and are marked with locative marker *-e*. The copula used in this construction is always *aṭʰ* and it is used as an auxiliary after a content verb. Often, the Trajector and Landmark have no direct contact, as in (8) and (9).

(8) *ṭʰeleṭa aguner paſe boſe aṭʰe.* [TRPS 38]
    boy.CLF fire.GEN side.LOC sit.PFV be.PRS.3
    'The boy is sitting beside the fire.'

(9) *baṛir tʃari dike bɛṛa dea aṭʰe.* [TRPS 15]
    house.GEN four side.LOC fence put.PASS be.PRS.3
    'There is a fence around the house.'

3.1 Postpositions derived from body parts

When a postposition is derived from a body part, the distance between the Trajector and the Landmark disappears. The postpositions *gae* and *matʰae* are derived from words meaning *body* and *head* and they directly refer to the body or top of the Landmark. A total of nine occurrences of the postposition *gae* are found in my data. For example, pictures 3, 4, 54, 58, 66 and 68 may be described using the postposition *gae* (literally body-LOC).

(10) stɛmpta kʰamer gae ʃãta atʃʰe. [TRPS 3]
 stamp.CLF envelop.GEN body.LOC paste.PASS be.PRS.3
 'The stamp is pasted on the envelope.'

The sentence in (10) is my translation of picture 3. The other speaker with whom I cross-checked the data translated the picture with *opore* 'on'. She offered an interesting opinion regarding the use of the postposition *gae*. She uses it only when a vertical or a three-dimensional shape is associated with the Landmark. In the last example, the envelope lacks vertical dimension. Therefore, it is not preferable to use *gae* with it. The examples (11)–(13) have a vertical dimension and are appropriate for using *gae*. In picture 68 (example 14), the T-shirt is worn by a man and that provides a perception of the T-shirt in three dimensions with a vertical height.

(11) mombatir gae pʰiteta dʒɔɾano atʃʰe. [TRPS 4]
 candle.GEN body.LOC ribbon.CLF fasten.PASS be.PRS.3
 'The ribbon is fastened around the candle.'
(12) dealer gae pokagulo lege atʃʰe. [TRPS 54]
 wall.GEN body.LOC insects attached be.PRS.3
 'The insects are on the wall.'
(13) moita dealer gae rakʰa atʃʰe. [TRPS 58]
 ladder.CLF wall.GEN body.LOC kept be.PRS.3
 'The ladder is kept against the wall.'
(14) tiʃarter gae iusiele lekʰa atʃʰe. [TRPS 68]
 T-shirt.GEN body.LOC UCLA written be.PRS.3
 'UCLA is written on the T-shirt.'

The data discussed above reveal that the postposition *gae* can be used for a situation where the Trajector and the Landmark have direct contact: either encirclement (pic. 4) or sticking on a vertical surface (pic. 54, 68) or support against a vertical surface (pic. 58). The data also support the notion that the geometric shape of an object plays a crucial role in the use of a postposition. Levinson (1994) also observes that "quite precise and complex axial geometry seems to be involved in so-called topological concepts".

Matʰae 'at the top', which I use in the context of three pictures (34), (56) and (65), is the other postposition derived from a body-part. This is metaphorically used for the topmost part of anything. In example (16), we may alternatively use *dɔgae* (literally, locative of 'top of a plant') 'at the top' in a similar sense. This postposition *dɔgae* may be used in two examples of TRPS of my data. This, however, does not occur at all in the other speaker's data. In all these examples, the other speaker uses *opore* 'on'. I cannot use *opore* 'on' because it is ambiguous with two readings of *on* and *above* when the Trajector and the Landmark may or may not have contact. But *matʰae* ensures contact between the Trajector and the Landmark.

(15) *lokʈa baɽir   matʰae   roetʃʰe.* [TRPS 34]
     man.CLF house.GEN head.LOC stay.PRS.PRF.3
     'The man is on the top of the house.'

(16) *pɔtakaʈa bãʃer   matʰae / dɔgae   uɽtʃʰe.* [TRPS 56]
     flag.CLF bamboo pole.GEN head.LOC/top.LOC fly.PRS.PROG.3
     'The flag is flying on the top of the bamboo pole.'

(17) *gatʃʰʈa pahaɽer matʰae   roetʃʰe.* [TRPS 65]
     tree.CLF hill.GEN head.LOC stay.PRS.PRF.3
     'The tree has been on the top of the hill.'

3.2 The postposition *opore*

The most frequent postposition used to represent these picture series is *opore* 'on, above' derived from a noun meaning 'high, up'. This occurs eight times in my translations and 12 times in the translation of the other speaker. It may be used with or without the locative marker. The form *opor/opore* is attested a total of eight times, in the pictures 1, 8, 13, 23, 29, 36, 40 and 59. With *die* it makes a complex postposition *opor die* 'over' in the picture 43. The other speaker replaced *matʰae* with *opore* three times (pictures 34, 56 and 65) and *gae* with *opore* (picture 3) once. The Trajector and the Landmark have direct contact in most of these pictures, except in picture 36 where there is no direct contact between the hill and the cloud, and in picture 13 where the bulb is above the table with no direct contact. This shows that the distinction between English 'on' (with contact) and 'above' (without contact) does not hold in Bangla.

In pictures 1 and 8, *opore* is used alternately with the locative marker to make the situation specific. The first picture has been explained in the discussion above. Similarly, for picture 8, if someone wants to provide some specific information about the location of the books to the addressee when the latter cannot find them, she has to use *opore* rather than the locative construction.

3.3 The postposition *modd^{h}e*

Modd^{h}e 'in', which is used to describe total containment, is the next most frequently occurring postposition, derived from a noun meaning 'middle'. This occurs six times in my data, for pictures 14, 19, 47, 60, 67 and 70. The other informant also uses *modd^{h}e* in all these situations along with two new cases where it may alternate with a locative construction. One is picture 11 where a boat is found floating on water. I translated the picture with the word *nodi* 'river' while she used the word *ʃomudro* 'sea'. It is quite interesting to note that the choice of lexical items guides the choice of the postposition. With *nodi* 'river', the postpositional use is completely out of the question. But with *ʃomudro* 'sea', there may be one general reading with the locative marker and one specific reading when it is necessary to mention that the boat is in the middle of the sea, not near the beach. This distinction comes with the physical dimension of the Landmark; a river is generally not so wide, but a sea is quite vast, with the other side not necessarily visible. To ensure that the boat is specified as quite far out in the sea, the postposition is used. The other additional use of *modd^{h}e* in the second informant's data is with picture 2. The distinction here is between a generic reading and a discourse-specific reading where a speaker wants to specify the location of the apple in case the addressee cannot find it.

We may conclude that the first type of locative construction is more general whereas the second type is more specific. This supports the finding of Feist (2009) from a set of cross-linguistic data where she concluded that there are two types of spatial terms across languages: one is generic and may occur in various contexts, and the other is more specific and occurs in specially defined contexts only.

3.4 The postpositions *nitʃe* and *tɔlae*

The two postpositions *nitʃe* and *tɔlae* are derived from spatial nouns, and the choice of the postposition also depends on the particular geometrical shape of the figure. Feist (2008) proposed that spatial language, like spatial cognition, is multi-dimensional and is influenced by three types of information: geometric, functional and qualitative physical information. For instance, the postpositions *tɔlae* and *nitʃe* may both roughly be translated as 'under' but the subtle choice of one over the other shows that *tɔlae* is used in the sense of 'underneath, beneath, below', where the shape of the Figure with some underlying layers guides the choice. The word *tɔlae* also comes from the noun *tɔla* meaning 'layer, floor'. The word *nitʃe* is derived from the word *nic* 'low'. *The ball is under the chair* (pic. 16) or *The fish is under the sea* would be translated with *tɔlae* where there is ground level below the chair, or where the sea water has many levels and fish can swim far below the surface level. However, *the spoon is under the napkin* (pic. 24) would be translated with *nitʃe* as there is no such level for the napkin and there is direct contact between the Trajector and the Landmark. However, the bed has levels such as the bedcover, bed sheet, mattress etc. and if a piece of paper is kept under the bed sheet, the use of *tɔlae* would be preferable in spite of direct contact between the Trajector and the Landmark. This observation is also confirmed in consultation with other speakers.

In the TRPS data, *nitʃe* 'under' is found in two pictures: 24 and 53. Both pictures show direct contact between the Trajector and the Landmark. *tɔlae* 'underneath' is used for two pictures: 16 and 31. In both these pictures, there is no contact between the Trajector and the Landmark.

3.5 Frame of reference postpositions *paʃe, ʃamne, petʃʰone*

Paʃe 'at the side' is derived from a Sanskrit noun *parʃwə* meaning 'side'. *paʃe* does not specify right or left. This postposition occurs only two times in the TRPS data. Bangla provides an intrinsic Frame of Reference in relation to the Landmark for this information. For example, the boy is sitting at the right of the fire (in relation to the fire) in picture 38. Avoiding this specific information, we may only use a vague *paʃe* for describing this picture.

(18) tʃʰeleṭa   aguner   paʃe   boʃe   atʃʰe.   [TRPS 38]
      boy.CLF   fire.GEN side.LOC sit.PFV   be.PRS.3
      'The boy is sitting next to the fire.' (vague as to which side of the fire)

In picture 49 also, the tree at the right side of the church may be mentioned when describing the location of the tree more specifically. Otherwise, only *paʃe* 'near' is used.

(19) gatʃʰṭa   girdʒar   paʃe   roetʃʰe.   [TRPS 49]
      tree.CLF   church.GEN side.LOC   stay.PRS.3
      'The tree is next to the church.' (vague as to which side of the church)

For *petʃʰone* 'behind', deriving from the noun *pechon* 'back', the intrinsic front and back concept is used when an object has one, as in picture 64 with the chair. When the object does not have an intrinsic Frame of Reference, a relative Frame of Reference may be used in relation to the speaker. The postposition occurs only once, for picture 64 in the TRPS data.

(20) tʃʰeleṭa tʃearer petʃʰone boʃe atʃʰe. [TRPS 64]
    boy.CLF chair.GEN back.LOC sit.PFV be.PRS.3
    'The boy is sitting at the back of the chair.'

The other speaker provides an alternate postposition ʃamne with picture 68. When the speaker is specific enough to provide information about whether the writing is on the front of the T-shirt or on the back, this postposition may be used. Here the intrinsic Frame of Reference of the T-shirt is also used.

3.6 Complex postpositions *opor die*, *moddʰe die* and *tʃaridike*

Opor die and moddʰe die are two of the complex postpositions consisting of two words, where the second word is *die*, a derivative of a verbal form *dea* 'to give'. *die* is a postposition which is used in different senses. One of its central senses is its use in a perceived motion situation. *opor die* is used when a motion is associated with a *where* question, as in picture 43 where a rope is kept over a tree trunk, crossing it from one side to the other. *madʒʰkʰan die* is used when an arrow has passed through the apple as an answer to 'where is the arrow?' in picture 30. Both *opor die* and *madʒʰkʰan die* are found to occur only once in the TRPS data.

(21) doriṭa gatʃʰer gūṛir opor die rakʰa atʃʰe. [TRPS 43]
    rope.CLF tree.GEN trunk.GEN above through keep.PASS be.PRS.3
    'The rope is kept over the tree trunk.'
(22) pʰɔlaṭa apeler madʒʰkʰan die gɛtʃʰe. [TRPS 30]
    arrow.CLF apple.GEN middle through go.PRS.PRF.3
    'The arrow has pierced through the apple.'

The other postposition found in the sense of encirclement in the TRPS is *tʃaridike*. This occurs only once with picture 15. This consists of two words *tʃar* 'four' and *dik* 'direction' and is used when a Trajector is situated within a boundary of the Landmark.

4 Result and discussion

Levinson and Wilkins (2006: 9) describes how the Topological Relation Picture Series contrast on a range of partially overlapping dimensions. The following table illustrates how Bangla encodes these semantic dimensions onto Basic

Locative Constructions through the use of some spatial postpositions and the Locative marker -e.

Tab. 1: Encoding of some semantic dimensions onto Basic Locative Constructions in Bangla

	Semantic dimension	How Bangla encodes it
1.	Horizontal support	Loc marker or *opore*
2.	Adhesion	*gae/opore*
3.	Liquid/mastic adhesion	Loc/*gae*
4.	Marks on surface	Loc
5.	Living creature on non-horizontal surface	Loc
6.	Attachment of projecting of Figure to Ground	Loc
7.	Attachment by cord	Loc
8.	Encirclement	*tʃaridike*
9.	Envelopment	*gae*
10.	Clothing/adornment	Loc
11.	Complete containment	Loc/ *modd^he*
12.	Partial containment	*modd^he*
13.	Containment in liquid or mass	Loc/*modd^he*
14.	Containment in encircling boundary	Loc/*modd^he*
15.	Attachment by piercing	Loc
16.	Negative space (holes, cracks)	Loc
17.	Vertical non-contact (above)	*opore*
18.	Behind	*petʃ^hone*
19.	In front of	*ʃamne*
20.	Under	*nitʃe, tɔlae*
21.	Next to	*paʃe*

For projecting the Trajector on the Landmark, a total of fourteen Spatial postpositions are used in the examples of Topological Relations Picture Series (TRPS) data. The distribution of these spatial postpositions on the basis of my discussion of data in the TRPS pictures is shown in the table below.

Tab. 2: Distribution of the postpositions in the TRPS

The postposition	Meaning	Number of occurrences in TRPS	Pictures in TRPS
gae	on the body	9	3,4,17, 25, 52, 55, 58, 66, 68
opor(e)	on, above	9	1, 8, 13, 23, 29, 36, 40, 43, 59
modd^{h}e	in the middle	6	14, 19, 47, 60, 67, 70
mat^{h}ae	On the top	3	34, 56, 65
nitʃe	under	2	24, 53
baire	outside	1	6
paʃe	At the side	2	38, 49
bhetore	inside	1	71
tɔlae	beneath, below	2	16, 31
tʃaridike	around	1	15
dɔgae	at the tip	2	20, 56
opor die	(Crossing) over	1	43
madʒ^{h}k^{h}an die	through	1	30
petʃ^{h}one	behind	1	64

4.1 Locative constructions in the TRPS data

The distinction between the concepts ON and IN is also not a universal one, as the locative marker can be used in Bangla for both of these concepts. In fact, in my own examples, a locative marker was used mostly to express the concept of ON (not IN). Out of a total of 32 uses of a locative case marker, 25 were in the sense of ON and four were in the sense of IN (pictures 2, 22, 32 and 54), one in the sense of WITH (picture 57) and two in the sense of FROM (pictures 9 and 27). The other speaker's data has even fewer occurrences of IN with the locative marker. She used a locative alternately with the postposition modd^{h}e for picture number 2. In all other cases, she used the postposition modd^{h}e. The use of a locative for expressing both typical ON and IN was also pointed out by Levinson et al. (2003) based on cross-linguistic evidence. Levinson and Wilkins (2006) also pointed out that languages differ as to how much spatial knowledge is encoded in semantics and how much is left to pragmatic inference. There are languages like English that distinguish between vertical support and containment using the lexical choice of the prepositions IN and ON, and there are languages like Bangla or

Tamil (Pederson 2006) which leave this distinction for the speakers to infer and use the locative case in both situations.

The locative is also used with the concept of ATTACHMENT WITH A CORD. The following sentence is the description of picture 57.

(23) ləketta ʧene lagano atʰe. [TRPS 57]
 locket.CLF chain.LOC attached be.PRS.3
 'The locket is attached to the chain.'

In short, a locative marker may be used in the TRPS data in most of the semantic dimensions except Adhesion, Liquid or Mastic Adhesion, Envelopment, Encirclement, Partial Containment, Vertical non-contact, Behind, In front of, Next to and Under. For Complete Containment, Containment in liquid or mass and Containment in encircling boundary, locative is used alternately with the postposition $modd^he$.

The study of the distribution of the locative marker in the TRPS data across many semantic dimensions qualifies it as the preferred and default marker. The language uses postpositions in many cases where the locative marker is not enough to understand the location of the Trajector. Therefore, we can say that it is a default marker for covering many semantic spatial dimensions. Bangla is a language where specific contextual information is provided only when the listener is not able to comprehend the vague locational information from the locative marker. Whenever a speaker has a choice between the locative marker and the postposition, the speaker confirms that the postposition would be used only in a conversation where the listener wants some more information about the Landmark. Even the geometric shape of the Landmark is crucial for using a postposition over the locative marker. For instance, in picture 59 a table is shown which has many drawers. In this case, the location of the pen on the table cannot be specified by a locative marker as it could be in a drawer or on the tabletop. Therefore, the postposition *opore* 'on' is used. Pederson (2006: 305) refers to this marking strategy as "pragmatically inferencing in that the more precise nature of a locative relationship need not be specified when adequately recoverable".

With respect to question 3, as stated in the introduction, we conclude that the constructions with postpositions are marked in the language in comparison to locative constructions. The postpositional constructions are default options only when a Frame of Reference is invoked. The fourteen postpositions which are used in the postpositional frames are all derived from some locative nouns and they themselves take a locative marker *-e*.

4.2 The role of verbs in spatial constructions

Ameka and Levinson (2007) classified the Basic Locative Constructions of the world's languages based on the type of verbs they use, as presented in Table 3.

Tab. 3: Basic types of Locative predications

Type 0	No verb in BLC
Type 1	Single Locative Verb 1a. Copula 1b. Locative (+existential) verb
Type 2	A small contrastive set of Locative verbs (3–7) 2a. postural verbs 2b. ground space indicating verb
Type 3	Multiverb positional verbs (9–100)

Cross-linguistically, certain verbs are very commonly found in Basic Locative Constructions. Many languages use specific postural verbs meaning *sit*, *stand*, *lie* and predicates like *hang* in Basic Locative Constructions (Levinson and Wilkins 2006: 15).

In Bangla, in the first type of locative constructions described in the previous section where only a locative marker is used with the Landmark, copula verbs meaning *have* or *remain* are used. But for describing some pictures, some other verbs are also used like *dʒʰola* 'to hang'. The verb meaning *rakʰa* 'to keep', *lagano* 'to be attached', *atkano* 'to be tied' and *pɔra* 'to wear, to tie' are also found in this type of construction followed by the copula 'have'. *pɔra* is used when the Landmark is a body part, as in pictures 21, 42 and 69 in my data. But the other speaker never used it; instead she directly used the copula 'have'.

In the second type of construction with a postposition attached to the Landmark, the number of verbs varies depending on the semantic dimension of the picture, generally followed by the copula meaning 'have'. Often, the verb also provides certain information about the location of the object. For example, for the semantic concept of *Adhesion* the verb *ʃāta* 'to stick' or *tʃepkano* 'to stick' is used as in (25), or for the concept of Attachment of an object to another by some means, the verb *lagano* 'to attach' is used as in (24).

(24) *ʈupiʈa   laʈhir   matʰae/dɔgae lagano atʰʰe.*
     cap.CLF   stick.GEN   top.LOC   stick   be.PRS.3
     'The cap is at the top of the stick.'

(25) stɛmpta   khamer   gae   ʃāta/tʃepkano   atʃʰe.
     stamp.CLF   envelop.GEN body.LOC   stick   be.PRS.3
     'The stamp is on the envelope.'

For the concept of Encirclement, as found in pictures 4 and 55, the verb *dʒɔɾano* 'to tie' is used.

(26) paipta   gūɾir   gae   dʒɔɾano   atʃʰe.   [TRPS 55]
     pipe.CLF   stump.GEN   body.LOC   tied   be.PRS.3
     'The pipe has been tied on the stump of the tree.'

Out of 71 constructions, ten (pics. 9, 13, 25, 27, 33, 37, 44, 45, 50, 63) have been described with the verb *dʒʰola* 'to hang' where the Trajector is supported against the Landmark by some means and it is hanging in the air. In pictures 9, 13, 27 and 63 where both the speakers' data use the verb *dʒʰola* 'to hang', a Trajector is attached to the Landmark by some means and is also hanging in the air. Sentences (27) and (29) use locative constructions whereas (28) uses the postposition *opore* and sentence (30) uses a postposition *theke* 'from' with the Landmark.

(27) kotta   henare   dʒʰultʃʰe /   dʒʰolano   atʃʰe.
     coat.CLF hanger.LOC   hang.PRS.PROG.3   hang.CAUS   be.PRS.3
     'The coat is hanging from the hanger.'/ 'The coat is hung from the hanger.'
(28) alota   tebiler   opore   dʒʰultʃʰe.
     light.CLF table.GEN   above   hang.PRS.PROG.3
     'The bulb is hanging above the table.'
(29) apelta   gatʃʰer   dale   dʒʰultʃʰe.
     apple.CLF tree.GEN   branch.LOC   hang.PRS.PROG.3
     'The apple is hanging in the branch of a tree.'
(30) alota   siliŋ   tʰeke   dʒʰultʃʰe.
     light.CLF ceiling   from   hang.PRS.PROG.3
     'The bulb is hanging from the ceiling.'

The verb *dʒʰola* occurs five times (with pics. 9, 13, 27, 63 and 66) in the data of the second speaker. There are other choices of verbs depending on dialectal variations. In two cases, viz., 44 and 37, an alternative verb *taŋano* 'hang up something in some height' has been used. *taŋano* 'hang up something in some height' is a causative form of the verb while *dʒʰola* is not. In pictures 45 and 50, a copula form *atʃʰe* 'has' is used. In picture 25, she used the verb *lagano* 'to attach'. Picture 33 is translated with the verb *atkano* 'to be attached'. Picture 66 is translated by me with a different verb *laga atʃʰe* 'to attach' and the other speaker used *dʒʰola* 'to hang'. In the remaining pictures, we find that *dʒʰola* 'to hang' and an alternative causative form of the verb *taɲano* 'to hang up something' are unambiguously used if the most part of the Trajector is in the air.

Other positional verbs like *sit* are also used five times in Frame of Reference constructions for the TRPS description.

(31) kukurṭa   orgʰɔrer   baire   boʃe   atʃʰe.   [TRPS 6]
     dog.CLF   its.kennel.GEN   outside   sit.PFV   be.PRS.3
     'The dog is sitting outside its kennel.'

Picture 70 may be described with a verb *dʰokano* 'to make something enter' or *aṭkano* 'to make something stick' or *gātʰa* 'to pierce something through something' followed by the copula *atʃʰ*.

From all these wide ranges of possibility for the use of verbs, we can conclude that the first type of locative construction of Bangla is either like type 1 or like type 2 but the second type of construction uses more than nine verbs and belongs to type 3.

4.3 A brief comparison with English

Languages like English, that encode spatial information entirely in the domain of lexical semantics, make distinctions through the use of spatial terms such as IN, ON, AT. However, as we have discussed above, Bangla does not make such distinctions and leaves a lot of information to pragmatics for inference, unless specifically asked for. Bangla, in this respect, is closer to Tamil, a Dravidian language (Pederson 2006). In Bangla as well as in Tamil, the default locative relation is expressed through the locative case marker. The unmarked locative marker is used in Bangla for all these concepts as well as for some others like WITH and FROM. Bangla also does not distinguish between the concepts of vertical support (ON) and vertical non-contact (OVER) as is the case with English. If vertical support is expressed explicitly by a postposition (it is not always required and can be expressed through the locative marker), it is the same as the postposition for vertical non-contact.

Though the Frames of References are not explored in this paper in detail, initial observations and analysis of the data of TRPS show that Bangla also uses a vague description in relation to the Frame of Reference unless specifically asked for. In pictures 38 and 49 the postposition *paʃe* 'near' is used, but a specific side (left or right) in relation to the Trajector is not mentioned. If required, as in

English, it describes the object by its intrinsic side if it has some intrinsic sides, as with a car or a chair. But if the object does not have any intrinsic side, such as for a table, egocentric relative frames, like in English, are evoked.

The development and use of some body-centric postpositions is also a distinct characteristic of Bangla and makes it different from English-like languages. Body-centric postpositions are also found in Persian (Moltaji 2016).

Some Locative copular verbs like *atʃʰ* 'to have' and *rɔa* 'stay, remain' are found in Basic Locative Constructions. However, apart from these, many more verbs can be used along with the copula in specific positional as well as default locative constructions. These verbs are often indicative of the type of semantic dimension of the situation. The number of verbs found with the locative semantics is also a point that makes the language distinct from English.

5 Conclusion

The study confirms that locative case markers and postpositions, as well as some verbs, play an important role in specifying the spatial semantics of a sentence. There are two major constructions associated with Basic Locative Constructions. One uses a Locative marker with the Landmark followed by a copula. A positional or locational verb may be used instead of a copula in some constructions. The second construction uses a postposition derived from a noun and is often marked with the Locative marker followed by a verb and a copula. The second type of construction is marked in the language and we find that a large number of verbs may be used in this type of construction for expressing the type of semantic dimensions. The locative case is the default spatial information provider in Bangla for most of the situations, except for those situations where either some specific information is needed, or some Frames of References are evoked. For Frames of Reference constructions, even Sanskrit and Prakrit (from which Bangla developed historically) used nouns rather than locative constructions.

The study is limited to the data covered by the 71 pictures of the TRPS data and it mainly focuses on topological semantic description. As a result, it does not elaborate on the Frames of References evoked in semantics of space except for some pictures of TRPS. The data for the TRPS has not been cross-checked in an experimental set-up with more native speakers. These are the limitations of the study. However, all important observations are discussed informally without an experimental setting with some other native speakers.

The Basic Locative Constructions may be more than what have been described in this paper because of the limitations of the data. We do not expect much variation in the use of the postpositions with Basic Locative Constructions. However, further extension of the study with more speakers may result in more variations in the use of verbs.

Abbreviations

CAUS=causative; CLF=classifier; LOC=locative; PRS=present; PROG=progressive; PFV=perfective; PRF=perfect; GEN=genitive; PASS=passive; 3= third person

Tansliteration

The IPA system of phonemic notation is used to transcribe the Bangla data and some Sanskrit words in this paper.

Acknowledgements

I am greatly indebted to the anonymous reviewers of the paper who helped to shape the paper in its present form by their positive comments. I also thank my former student Swagata Acharya and my family for helping me with the data.

Appendix: Topological Relation Picture Series

TRPS

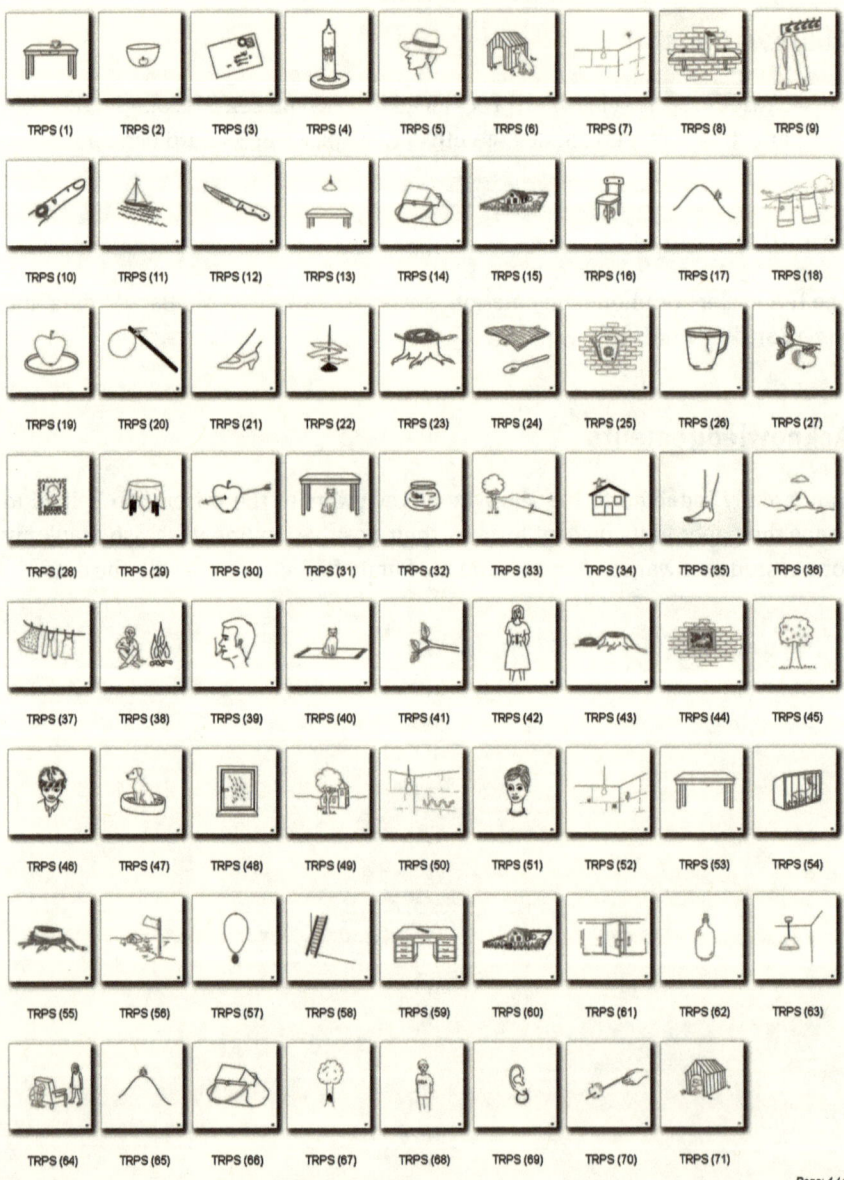

References

Ameka, Felix K. & Stephen C. Levinson. 2007. Introduction: The typology and semantics of locative predicates: Posturals, positionals and other beasts. *Linguistics* 45 (5). 847–872.

Bloom, Paul, Merrill F. Garrett, Lynn Nadel & Mary A. Peterson (eds.). 1996. *Language and Space*. Cambridge, MA: The MIT Press.

Bowerman, Melissa & Eric Pederson. 1992. Topological relations picture series. In Stephen C. Levinson (ed.), *Space stimuli kit* 1.2: November 1992, 51. Nijmegen: Max Planck Institute for Psycholinguistics.

Bowerman, Melissa & Eric Pederson. 2003. *Cross-linguistic perspectives on Topological spatial relationships*. Eugene: University of Oregon, and Nijmegen: Max Planck Institute for Psycholinguistics, MS.

Cuyckens, Hubert. 1991. *The semantics of Spatial Prepositions in Dutch: A cognitive-linguistic exercise*. Antwerp: University of Antwerp doctoral dissertation.

Ditte, Boeg Thomsen & Jan Heegård. 2018. Introduction: spatial language, cognition and environment. *Acta Linguistica Hafniensia* 50 (2). 123–128.

Feist, Michael I. 2000. *On in and on: an investigation into the linguistic encoding of spatial scenes*. Evanston: Northwestern University doctoral dissertation.

Feist, Michele I. 2008. Space between languages. *Cognitive Science* 32. 1177–1199.

Feist, Michele I. 2009. Spatial cognition through the lens of spatial language. *Cognitive Processing* 10 (Suppl 2). S212–S214. DOI 10.1007/s10339-009-0291-x.

Gentner, Dedre, Asli I. Özyürek, Özge Gürcanli & Susan Goldin-Meadow. 2013. Spatial language facilitates spatial cognition: Evidence from children who lack language input. *Cognition* 127 (3). 318–330.

Herskovits, Annette. 1986. Language and spatial cognition. An interdisciplinary study of the prepositions in English. Cambridge: Cambridge University Press.

Hickman, M. & Stephene Robert. 2006. *Space in Languages. Linguistic Systems and Cognitive Categories*. Amsterdam & Philadelphia: John Benjamins Publishing Company.

Khetarpal, Naveen, Asifa Majid, Barbara C. Malt, Steven A. Sloman & Terry Regier. 2010. Similarity judgments reflect both language cross-language tendencies: Evidence from two semantic domains. In S. Ohlsson & R. Catrambone (eds.), *Proceedings of the 32nd Annual Meeting of the Cognitive Science Society*, 358–363.

Khetrapal, Naveen, Grace Neveu, Asifa Majid, Lev Michael & Terry Regier. 2013. Spatial terms across languages support near-optimal communication: Evidence from Peruvian Amazonia, and computational analyses. In *Proceedings of the 35th Annual Meeting of the Cognitive Science Society*, 764–769.

Landau, Barbara & Ray Jackendoff. 1993. "What" and "Where" in spatial language and spatial cognition. *Behavioural and Brain Sciences* 16. 217–265.

Langacker, Ronald. 1987. *Foundations of cognitive grammar*. Vol. 1, *Theoretical prerequisites*. Stanford: Stanford University Press.

Levinson, Stephen C. 2004. *Space in Language and Cognition: Explorations in Cognitive Diversity*. Cambridge: Cambridge University Press.

Levinson, Stephen C. & David P. Wilkins. 2006. *Grammars of Space: Explorations in Cognitive Diversity*. Cambridge: Cambridge University Press.

Levinson, Stephen C., Sotaro Kita, Daniel B.M. Haun & Björn H. Rasch. 2002. Returning the tables: Language affects spatial reasoning. *Cognition* 84. 155–188.

Levinson, Stephen C. & Sergio Maira. 2003. Natural concepts in the spatial topological domain – adpositional meanings in crosslinguistic perspective. *Language* 79. 485–516.

Li, Peggy & Lila Gleitman. 2002. Turning the Table: Language and spatial reasoning. *Cognition* 83. 265–294.

Majid, Asifa, Melissa Bowerman, Sotaro Kita, Daniel B.M. Haun & Stephen C. Levinson. 2004. Can language restructure cognition? The case for space. *Trends in Cognitive Sciences* 8. 108–114.

Moltaji, Niloofar. 2016. *Spatial Relations in Persian: An investigation on the locative use of prepositions with comparison to English*. Stockholm: Stockholm University MA thesis.

Pederson, Eric. 2006. Spatial Language in Tamil. In Stephen C. Levinson & Wilkins P. David (eds.), *Grammar of Space: Explorations in Cognitive Diversity*, 400–436. Cambridge: Cambridge University Press.

Pinker, Steven. 1994. *The Language Instinct*. New York: Morrow.

Pütz, Martin & René Dirven (eds.). 1996. *The construal of space in language and thought*. Berlin: Mouton de Gruyter.

Saint-Dizier, Patrick. 2006. *Syntax and Semantics of Prepositions*. Dordrecht, The Netherlands: Springer.

Sinha, Chris & Lis Thorsheng. 1995. A coding system for spatial relational reference. *Cognitive Linguistics* 6. 261–309.

Schlesinger, Izchak M. 2006 [1995]. *Cognitive space and linguistic case: Semantic and syntactic categories in English*. 2nd edn. Cambridge: Cambridge University Press.

Svorou, Soteria. 1994. *The Grammar of Space*. Amsterdam: John Benjamins Publishing Company.

Talmy, Leonard. 1983. How language structures space. Conference paper in *Spatial Orientation: Theory, Research and Application*. DOI 10.1007/978-1-4615-9325-6_11.

Talmy, Leonard. 2000. *Towards a Cognitive Semantics*, Vol 2, Typology and process in concept structuring. Cambridge, MA: MIT Press.

Zlatev, Jordan. 2007. Spatial Semantics. In Dirk Geeraerts & Hubert Cuyckens (eds.), *Oxford Handbook of Cognitive Linguistics*, 318–350. Oxford: Oxford University Press.

John J. Lowe
Revisiting Pāṇini's generative power

Abstract: In this paper I revisit recent claims that Pāṇini's generative grammar has fully context-sensitive power. I show that in fact Pāṇini assumed acyclicity as a constraint on rule application, limiting the power of his superficially context-sensitive formalism in a way entirely parallel to much work in modern phonology.

Keywords: Generative power, Panini, acyclicity, constraint rules

1 Introduction

Pāṇini's *Aṣṭādhyāyī* has been hailed as the world's first generative grammar, composed more than 2,000 years before the advent of modern generative linguistics.[1] From the very beginnings of modern generative grammar, the questions of a grammar's generative power, and of the generative power required to model human language, have been central in the development of grammatical formalisms and in the evolution of the field.[2] A number of authors have analyzed Pāṇini's *Aṣṭādhyāyī* in these terms, including Staal (1965, 1966), Hyman (2007) and Penn and Kiparsky (2012). Pāṇini's *Aṣṭādhyāyī* is superficially a context-sensitive grammar, though this observation does not in itself answer the question of its generative power.[3] While Hyman (2007) claims that Pāṇini's system has only the power of a finite state transducer, Penn and Kiparsky (2012) seek to prove that

---

[1] Chomsky (1965: v): "it seems that even Pāṇini's grammar can be interpreted as a fragment of such a "generative grammar," in essentially the contemporary sense of this term".
[2] The term "modern generative grammar" encompasses a number of theories of grammar, from that of Chomsky's *Syntactic Structures* to the relative plethora of more modern theories such as Government & Binding Theory, the Minimalist Program, Lexical-Functional Grammar, Head-driven Phrase Structure Grammar, Sign-Based Construction Grammar etc.
[3] The focus here is on weak generative capacity. The driving principle behind Pāṇini's grammar is not the search for a theory of linguistic competence but the desire for the most concise and efficient description capable of generating all and only the grammatical utterances of Sanskrit; questions of strong generative capacity are therefore anachronistic to an analysis of the *Aṣṭādhyāyī*.

John Lowe, University of Oxford, The Oriental Institute, Pusey Lane, OX1 2LE, Oxford, UK. Email: john.lowe@orinst.ox.ac.uk

Pāṇini's formalism has the full power of a context-sensitive grammar (i.e. the power to generate all the context-sensitive languages). This paper revisits the claims of Penn and Kiparsky (2012), and reveals flaws in their argument. Pāṇini in fact assumed acyclicity as a constraint on rule application, significantly restricting the generative power of his formalism.

In section 1, I provide an overview of the issue of generative power of grammatical systems. In section 2, I discuss previous accounts of Pāṇini's generative power. In sections 3–4, I revisit the arguments of Penn and Kiparsky (2012) and show that Pāṇini assumed acyclicity.

2 Formal language theory and generative power

Chomsky (1957: 13) defined a *language* as: "a set (finite or infinite) of sentences, each finite in length and constructed out of a finite set of elements". Given this definition, the goal of linguistic analysis of a given language L is "to separate the *grammatical* sequences which are sentences of L from the *ungrammatical* sequences which are not sentences of L and to study the structure of the grammatical sequences. The grammar of L will thus be a device that generates all of the grammatical sequences of L and none of the ungrammatical ones" (Chomsky 1957: 13). Pāṇini's *Aṣṭādhyāyī* generates, or licenses the derivation of, all and only the possible grammatical sentences of Sanskrit, and in this crucial sense it can be understood as a generative grammar of the language.

Languages may have different levels of complexity, and may correspondingly require more or less complex grammars to generate them. In relation to the linguistic study of human languages, an important theoretical question is how complex human languages are, or can be. Related to this is a separate question: how complex must or should a grammar (or set of grammars licensed by a particular grammatical theory) be in order to both adequately and insightfully model human language?

The so-called "Chomsky Hierarchy" (Table 1) distinguishes four types of languages according to their computational complexity (based on Chomsky 1959): Type 0, the recursively enumerable or unrestricted languages; Type 1, the context-sensitive languages; Type 2, the context-free languages; Type 3, the regular languages. The type of grammars required to generate these languages differ in terms of the complexity of rules permitted in the grammars (or to look at it another way, in terms of the constraints placed on rule formulation in the grammars).[4]

Tab. 1: The Chomsky Hierarchy

Language class: grammar	Rule format	Conditions on rules
Type 0: Unrestricted grammars	A→B	A, B ∈ [$V_T \cup V_N$]*
Type 1: context-sensitive grammars	A→B / C __ D (or CAB→ CBD)	A ∈ V_N B ∈ [$V_T \cup V_N$]$^+$ C,D ∈ [$V_T \cup V_N$]*
Type 2: Context-free grammars	A→B	A ∈ V_N B ∈ [$V_T \cup V_N$]$^+$
Type 3: Regular grammars	A→a B	A ∈ V_N B ∈ [$V_N \cup \{\}$] a ∈ V_T

Each class of languages includes those classes below it on the hierarchy, such that Type 0 ⊃ Type 1 ⊃ Type 2 ⊃ Type 3. This means that regular languages also fall in the class of context-free languages, as well as in the classes of context-sensitive and unrestricted languages; context-free languages also fall in the class of context-sensitive and unrestricted languages, etc. But there are context-free languages which are not regular languages, context-sensitive languages which are not context-free languages, and context-sensitive languages which are not unrestricted languages. Likewise, a context-free, context-sensitive or unrestricted grammar could be written to generate any regular language, but a regular grammar can only generate regular languages. The grammars in the Chomsky Hierarchy correspond to machines of differing complexity: regular languages can be computed by finite state machines; context-free languages can be computed using push-down store automata; context-sensitive languages can be computed using linear bounded automata; and unrestricted languages can be computed using Turing machines.

Formal language theory investigates the properties of grammars by abstracting away from the messy reality of human languages and focusing on strings of abstract symbols which have a precise mathematical complexity. Consider a language to be a set of sentences, and consider a sentence to be a string of symbols (words, terminals). Then we can take sets of strings of abstract symbols, analyze

---

[4] In (1), V_T refers to the set of terminal elements in a grammar, and V_N to the set of non-terminals.

their mathematical complexity, and analyze the complexity required of grammars to model them. For example, the following regular (right linear) grammar models the language $\{a^n b^m \mid n, m \geq 1\}$:

(1) — Start symbol: A
    — Non-terminals: {A, B}
    — Terminals: {a, b}
    — Rules:
        — A → a A
        — A → a B
        — B → b B
        — B → b

The language $\{a^n b^m \mid n, m \geq 1\}$ consists of all the strings which contain one or more *a*s followed by one or more *b*s, so: *ab, aab, aaab, aaaab… abb, aabb, aaabb…, abbb…*etc. The number of grammatical strings in this language is infinite, and the regular grammar in (1) generates all and only these strings.

The language $\{a^n b^n \mid n \geq 1\}$ is too complex for a regular grammar. This language consists of all the strings which contain one or more *a*s followed by the same number of *b*s. This language also contains an infinite number of grammatical strings, though a subset of the strings in the language $\{a^n b^m \mid n, m \geq 1\}$. The additional complexity introduced by requiring that strings have the same number of *a*s and *b*s necessitates a context-free grammar:

(2) — Start symbol: A
    — Non-terminals: {A}
    — Terminals: {a, b}
    — Rules:
        — A → a A b
        — A → a b

To model the language $\{a^n b^n c^n \mid n \geq 1\}$, we require a context-sensitive grammar:

(3) — Start symbol: A
    — Non-terminals: {A, B}
    — Terminals: {a, b, c}
    — Rules:
        — A → abc / __
        — A → aAB / __

— cB→ Bc / __
— B → bc / b__c

The Chomsky Hierarchy and the question of what kind of grammar is required, or desired, to model human language, has had a significant impact on the development of modern grammatical theory. Following Chomsky (1957), it was long taken as evident that human languages are too complex to be modelled using a context-free grammar. Chomsky's initial attempt to formulate a richer model resulted in "transformational" grammar, with equivalent power to an unrestricted grammar. Pullum and Gazdar (1982) showed that most of the phenomena previously taken as evidence that human language is more than context-free could, in fact, be given a context-free treatment. This led to the development of Generalized Phrase Structure Grammar (Gazdar et al. 1985), a formal model of language explicitly restricted to context-free power. Subsequently, Huybregts (1984) and Shieber (1985) proved that Swiss German is not syntactically context-free but requires some context-sensitive power to account for cross-serial dependencies, and Culy (1985) showed that Bambara is morphologically more than context-free.

It appears, then, that human language is *mildly context-sensitive*: some power beyond context-free is required to model human language in general, but only a little, and not necessarily for all languages. Based on this observation, some authors sought to develop formalisms that are mildly context-sensitive, i.e. that can generate some but not all context-sensitive languages, and that are just a little more complex than context-free grammars, but not so complex as to be computationally intractable. Such formalisms include multiple component tree-adjoining grammars (Joshi et al. 1975) and multiple context-free grammars (Seki et al. 1991, Clark 2015).[5]

While one line of development therefore sought to restrict the power of grammatical formalism to the minimum required for modelling human language, the other approach taken was to use a more powerful formalism, but to state constraints within the formalism which limit the power of any individual grammar to a tractable level. This is the approach taken in frameworks such as Minimalism, Lexical-Functional Grammar and Head-driven Phrase Structure Grammar; Pollard (1996) points out that this is the standard approach in other sciences.[6]

---

[5] These are relevant in Penn and Kiparsky's (2012) account of Pāṇini's generative power, discussed below.
[6] See also Müller (2016: 529–533).

Generative power is therefore a considerably more complicated issue than the Chomsky Hierarchy itself suggests.[7] For example, if a context-sensitive grammar is permitted to include deletion rules (or if {} is included in the set of terminal symbols), then that grammar has the power of an unrestricted grammar (Coleman 1991: 128–130). From the other side, if deletion rules are removed from an unrestricted grammar, that grammar has at most the power of a context-sensitive grammar.

Constraints on rule application can also restrict the power of a grammar. As shown by Johnson (1972), if the rules of a context-sensitive grammar are prevented from applying cyclically to their own output ('acyclicity'), the grammar has only finite-state power, i.e. it can generate only the regular languages.[8] Notice that the grammar in (3) can only generate $\{a^n b^n c^n\}$ by allowing the rule A → aAB to apply cyclically to its own output; if we enforce cyclicity, the grammar can generate only the two strings *abc* and *aabbcc*. This will become important in what follows.

3 The *Aṣṭādhyāyī* as a formal system

3.1 The context-sensitive surface

Presentationally, at least, Pāṇini's grammar is context-sensitive: rules can be formulated with reference to a preceding and/or following context. Within the grammar, the Sanskrit case system is appropriated for technical purposes: cases are invested with technical functions (in addition to their ordinary uses, where required):

(4) — Nominative: an element added, or which substitutes for another element.
 — Genitive: an element which is replaced by the element given in the nominative.
 — Ablative: the preceding context for the operation.
 — Locative: the following context for the operation.

---

7 Coleman (1995: 333–340) has a very clear and useful summary of generative power; see also Kaplan and Kay (1994).
8 See also Kaplan and Kay (1994: 346), who state the restriction thus: "the part of the string that is actually rewritten by a rule is excluded from further rewriting by that same rule".

In schematic terms, we can reformulate Pāṇini's system into the familiar modern context-sensitive representation in the following way:[9]

(5) $A_{gen} \rightarrow B_{nom} / C_{abl} \_\_ D_{loc}$

By way of illustration, consider the following sandhi rule:

(6)   *ik-o   yaṇ   ac-i*   (72: *saṃhitāyām*)
       iK-GEN   yaN.NOM   aC-LOC   connection.LOC
       'In connected speech a sound of the group denoted by iK (i.e. *i, u, ṛ, ḷ*) is replaced by the corresponding sound of the group denoted by yaN (i.e. *y, v, r, l*) when one of the sounds denoted by aC (i.e. a vowel) follows.' (Aṣṭ. 6.1.77)

This is the rule that converts final vowels *i, u, ṛ, ḷ*[10] into corresponding semi-vowels in context before a vowel; e.g. *dadhi+atra* '(there is) yoghurt here' surfaces as *dadhy atra*. The following context is clearly indicated by the locative case marking on the pratyāhāra *a*C.[11]

But as we have seen in the preceding section, knowing that Pāṇini's *Aṣṭādhyāyī* is a context-sensitive grammar is insufficient, in itself, for determining its generative power. The *Aṣṭādhyāyī* does permit deletion, so it could, without further constraint, have unrestricted power. But Hyman (2007), focusing on the sandhi rules of the *Aṣṭādhyāyī*, claims that rules do not rewrite their own output, and thus the sandhi portion of the *Aṣṭādhyāyī*, at least, can be reduced to a regular grammar.[12]

---

9 For formal discussion of translating Pāṇinian replacement rules into standard CS representations as we are familiar with, see Staal (1965) and Cardona (1965).
10 *ḷ* vacuously, since this never occurs word finally.
11 Pratyāhāras are sequences of a grammatical element followed by a code letter (anubandha or 'it' – rendered in small caps), which serve to refer to sets of grammatical elements in the grammar, as iK in (6) refers to the segments *i, u, ṛ* and *ḷ*.
12 A slightly different association is sometimes made, between Pāṇini's formalism and context-free systems, in particular the 'Backus-Naur Form' which was centrally significant in the development of the historically important computer languages ALGOL58 (Backus 1959) and ALGOL60 (Backus et al. 1963). The Backus-Naur Form is a notation for context-free grammars, and the principles behind it were associated with the principles of Pāṇini's formalism by Ingerman (1967). However, the similarities relate specifically to the use of pratyāhāras to denote groups of symbols, and do not extend to the generative workings of the *Aṣṭādhyāyī* itself.

Joshi and Kiparsky (1979: 244–245) show that rules are permitted to apply cyclically in the sense that rules may apply multiple times in a given derivation. However, there are constraints on the reapplication of rules. Joshi and Kiparsky (1979: 244) refer to a paribhāṣā, an interpretative rule, attributed to Nīlakaṇṭhadīkṣita, which they understand to mean that "a rule cannot be conditioned twice in a derivation by the same context". Penn and Kiparsky (2012) refer to this as "Nīlakaṇṭhadīkṣitar's [sic] condition", and seek to show that it is a considerably weaker constraint than acyclicity, and does not itself reduce the power of the *Aṣṭādhyāyī* below full context-sensitivity.

3.2 Penn & Kiparsky's argument

As discussed in more detail below, Joshi and Kiparsky (1979) argue that Pāṇini presupposed a constraint on rule application to the effect that a rule may not reapply given the same (partial or complete) context as a preceding application, but that Pāṇini's system does not presuppose acyclicity, since Pāṇini states ad hoc constraints to ensure this when the constraint on reuse of contexts is not enough. Penn and Kiparsky (2012) accept this interpretation of Pāṇini's rules; below, I show that this interpretation is in fact problematic. For the time being, however, let us also adopt this interpretation, for the sake of argument, and investigate Penn and Kiparsky's claims.

Penn and Kiparsky (2012) begin by demonstrating that the constraint on reuse of contexts (their "Nīlakaṇṭhadīkṣitar's condition") is weaker than a full constraint on cyclicity. I here provide a slightly simpler demonstration than that provided by Penn and Kiparsky, using the following grammar:[13]

(7) 1. $aa \rightarrow bb$ / b__a
 2. $b \rightarrow a$ / b__a

Given the input *baaaa*, we have the following derivations. Rule 1 must apply first, giving *bbbaa*: the context for application of this rule in this case is the first and the fourth symbols, and the elements rewritten are the second and third symbols. Rule 2 must then apply, with the context being the second and fourth symbols, and the element rewritten being the third. This gives *bbaaa*. If we assume acyclicity, i.e. that a rule may not rewrite (all or part of) its own output, Rule 1 cannot

---

[13] This grammar is a reduced form of that provided by Penn and Kiparsky (2012), including only the first two rules.

be applied to the string *bbaaa*, since it would rewrite the third symbol, which was already rewritten by Rule 1 in its first application. Rule 2 can reapply, however, giving *baaaa*, and no further rule applications are possible, meaning that this grammar, assuming acyclicity, takes *baaaa* and returns only *baaaa*.

However, if we assume merely a constraint on reuse of contexts, there is another possibility at the stage *bbaaa*. Rule 1 may be reapplied instead of Rule 2, because the context is different from its first application: now the context of application of Rule 1 is the second and the fifth symbols. This gives *bbbba*. Rule 2 will then apply, with context of third and fifth symbols, to give *bbbaa*. This is the end of the derivation, because *bbbaa* does not provide a valid context for Rule 1, and Rule 2 has already applied to the string *bbbaa*, meaning that it cannot reapply without reusing the context used previously.

The constraint on reuse of contexts therefore outputs two strings given the input *baaaa*, and the grammar is therefore less constrained than if subject to acyclicity, which returns only one string. If neither constraint is applied, the grammar licenses infinite derivation chains.

Penn and Kiparsky (2012) try to demonstrate that Pāṇini's system, presupposing the constraint on reuse of contexts, has fully context-sensitive power. They provide a context-sensitive grammar which they say obeys the principles of Pāṇini's system, and which can model the language $\{a^n b^n\}$; given the formulation of this grammar, it can unproblematically be augmented to model any language defined by $C(j) = \{a_1{}^n a_2{}^n ... a_j{}^n | n \geq 0\}$, i.e. also $\{a^n b^n c^n\}$, $\{a^n b^n c^n d^n\}$, etc. The grammar they use is:

(8) – S → A / __
     – A → abA / __
     – A → ab / __
     – ba → X / __
     – X → ab / __

Essentially this is a way of generating $\{a^n b^n\}$ by producing arbitrarily long strings of the form *ab*, *abab*, *ababab*, *abababab* etc., and then flipping sequences of *ba* to give *ab*, until all *a*s precede all *b*s. The same thing can easily be done with the same basic structure for $\{a^n b^n c^n\}$, $\{a^n b^n c^n d^n\}$, etc.

Penn and Kiparsky (2012) relate this generative potential to the multiple context-free languages and the multicomponent tree adjoining grammars. These lie in generative power between context-free power and full context-sensitive power. For example, a multiple context-free grammar k-MCFG is generated by k context-free grammars in parallel, and can generate $C(j)$ for all $j \leq 2k$, such that 1-MCFG is equivalent to a context-free grammar, and can therefore generate $\{a^n b^n\}$, while 2-MCFG is a mildly context-sensitive grammar and can generate $\{a^n b^n\}$, $\{a^n b^n c^n\}$, $\{a^n b^n c^n d^n\}$. Since the grammar given in (8) can generate $C(j)$ for any j, it is as powerful as the most powerful MCFG, i.e. it has fully context-sensitive power. Penn and Kiparsky (2012) therefore claim that Pāṇini's system has very strong generative power, although the *Aṣṭādhyāyī* itself uses only a fraction of this power.

There are a number of problems with these claims of Penn and Kiparsky (2012). I will investigate these in the next section.

4 Revisiting Pāṇini's power

The first problematic aspect of Penn and Kiparsky's argument is as follows. They argue that the grammar in (8) does not violate the condition against reusing contexts, on the assumption that the null context is no context and therefore does not count. But the rule:

(9)   A → abA / _

is not really a null context rule, at least if we are taking the constraint on reuse of contexts seriously. It could be rewritten as:

(10) ϵ → ab / _A

and then it could only be reapplied by taking the same context repeatedly. To do it otherwise undermines the whole point of the constraint in question: as phrased in (9), Penn and Kiparsky (2012) nullify any restrictive power that the constraint on reuse of contexts might have, by putting the context into the input/output and assuming that a null context is no context. But if we phrase rules in such a way that a constraint on reuse of contexts can actually have an effect, then we will have to phrase as in (10), and such rules will not be able to apply multiple times in the same context.

Almost all the rules in (8) also depend on another assumption crucial to Penn and Kiparsky's argument: that Pāṇini's system permits input and output strings of length greater than 1. Three of the rules in (8) have output length greater than 1 (once 3, twice 2), and the fourth rule has input length of 2. To generate more complex languages would require more: for example, for $\{a^n b^n c^n d^n\}$ we would require a rule with output of length 5, in Penn and Kiparsky's formulation.[14] It is true that Pāṇini does technically allow input and output greater than length 1, but in practice this is highly restricted, and this practical restriction could reflect some restrictions in principle. The majority of cases of output greater than length 1 are cases of doubling: where one element in the input produces two instances of itself in the output. Other cases are much rarer, though they do occur: for example, affix insertion or replacement may be specified with concomitant insertion of a second element (an *āgama* 'augment'), as in the derivation of names like *indrāṇī* (Aṣṭ. 4.1.49). Going beyond two elements in the output is highly unusual and arguable; one such example, discussed in the ancient tradition for its complexity, is rule 6.4.47, which deletes the *r* and *s* segments from the root *bhrasj* and inserts *ra*M at the same time, i.e. three operations.[15] Now these are limitations on the actual rules formulated by Pāṇini, rather than necessary constraints on the kinds of rules that he could have formulated, but at least to some extent we can only determine the restrictions on rule formulations that Pāṇini assumed on the basis of the actual rules he formulated. Pāṇini may in fact have assumed an absolute constraint on output length of 3, for example.

Given these facts, it is clear that the grammar given in (8) is less constrained than Pāṇini's system, and its generative power will be significantly restricted if we take seriously the constraint on reuse of contexts and interpret the rule A → abA / _ as meaning ϵ → ab / _A. If we admit output of length 3, then it would be possible to generate the language $\{a^n b^n\}$ in Pāṇini's system, using something like the context-free grammar in (2) above. But note that this is only possible if we accept "Nīlakaṇṭhadīkṣitar's condition" as formulated by Penn and Kiparsky (2012). If it were the case that Pāṇini instead assumed acyclicity, even $\{a^n b^n\}$ would be ruled out. Penn and Kiparsky's understanding of Nīlakaṇṭha's constraint on rule application is based on Joshi and Kiparsky (1979: 244). In the next section, I revisit their claims regarding the inferences possible from Pāṇini's rules, as well as revisiting the formulation of the constraint itself.

---

14 I.e. A→ abcdA / _.
15 This is if we assume the input is the sequence of five segments bh-r-a-s-j. Alternatively, we might consider this a morphological rule affecting the single morphological element *bhrasj*, effectively replacing *bhrasj* with *bhaj* and inserting *ra*M, so only two operations.

5 Revisiting the constraint

As discussed, Joshi and Kiparsky (1979: 244) argue that Pāṇini assumed a constraint on rule application to the effect that "a rule cannot be conditioned twice in a derivation by the same context". They seek to demonstrate that this constraint was assumed by Pāṇini with two complementary arguments: in some cases the constraint must be assumed in order to get the right output, and in other cases Pāṇini states rules to explicitly prevent rules from re-writing their own output (i.e. to prevent cyclicity), when the assumed constraint on reuse of contexts is insufficient to guarantee this. In other words, Pāṇini uses soft constraints (rules within the grammar) to ensure acyclicity where necessary, but the presupposed constraint on rule reapplication (that "a rule cannot be conditioned twice in a derivation by the same context") is weaker.

To first illustrate multiple rule application, Joshi and Kiparsky (1979: 244) cite the form *bhūyāt*, 3sg. precative, which derives from *bhū+yās+st*, to which a rule applies which deletes -*s*- at the start of word final clusters or clusters before obstruents (8.2.29 *skoḥ saṃ yogādyor ante ca*). This rule, which has to apply twice, states that 'there is deletion of *s* or *k* which begin a cluster before a stop or fricative sound or at the end of a word'. So the first deletion affects the first *s*, because it is at the start of a cluster (*ss*) which precedes another obstruent. Then the second *s* is deleted because it is at the start of a cluster (*st*) which ends a word. So there are two applications of the same rule, but they do not have the same context.[16]

To illustrate the assumed constraint on reuse of contexts, Joshi and Kiparsky (1979: 245) cite rule 8.4.47, which I give along with the preceding rule, since this is also relevant:

(11) 8.4.46: *acaḥ rahābhyāṃ dve* 'All consonants except /h/ following an /r/ or /h/ following a vowel, are optionally (8.4.45) doubled.'
(12) 8.4.47: *anaci ca* 'All consonants except /h/ after a vowel and before a non-vowel are optionally doubled.'

In reference to 8.4.47, Joshi and Kiparsky (1979: 245) cite the word *atra* 'here', to which this rule may apply to give *attra*. They state that since the rule must not be allowed to reapply, to give *atttra, *attttra etc., this means that the left-hand context "after a vowel" cannot be reused. Note that this is only a partial context, since

---

[16] I show below that these two applications still respect cyclicity, but for now I present Joshi and Kiparsky's argument.

if the rule were to reapply, the right-hand context (the 'non-vowel') would be different in each iteration.

In fact this is not an optimal example, because there is another rule which can delete a stop or sibilant following a consonant and before a homophonous sound:

(13) 8.4.65: *jharaḥ jhari savarṇe* 'There is optional deletion of a stop or sibilant before a homophonous stop or sibilant and after a consonant (*halaḥ* inferred from 64).'

If 8.4.47 could apply multiple times in the same partial context, then 8.4.65 could also apply multiple times in the same partial context to effectively nullify all but one of the applications of 8.4.47.[17] Nevertheless, we still require the constraint on reuse of contexts, because 8.4.46–7 includes more consonants in its scope than 8.4.65. Semi-vowels and nasals do not fall under the scope of 8.4.65, but can be doubled by 8.4.46–7. So, the word *avyaya* 'unchanging, indeclinable' can be doubled by 8.4.47 to *avvyaya*, but the potentially infinite recursive reapplication of the same rule must be prevented. Similarly, 8.4.46 permits a word like *brahman* 'Veda, sacred text, knowledge' to be pronounced *brahmman*, but reapplication of the rule to produce *brahmmman, *brahmmmman, etc. is undesirable. Examples such as these therefore make a constraint on reuse of contexts both viable and necessary.[18] Notice that they would also, however, support a stronger constraint, i.e. acyclicity, which would have the same effect.

The second example that Joshi and Kiparsky (1979: 245) give is slightly different, and more problematic. The rule 7.4.59 *hrasvaḥ* specifies that a short vowel replaces the vowel of a reduplication syllable. The effect of this rule is therefore to shorten any long vowels found in reduplication syllables. In the formation of the perfect of *āp*, we have the following derivation sequence:

(14a) *āp+āp+a*
(14b) *ap+āp+a* (7.4.59)

---

[17] Assuming an intelligent user, this would license the correct output, but since 8.4.65 is optional (as are 8.4.46–7), from a purely mechanical perspective it would be possible to derive outputs such as *atttra, *attttra etc., or even infinitely long derivation chains. This possibility does therefore need to be ruled out.

[18] The need to prevent multiple applications of 8.4.46–7 was recognized and discussed by the later grammatical tradition, in the context of the *paribhāṣā* discussed in this section. See also fn. 23 below.

(14c) *a+āp+a* (7.4.60)
(14d) *āp+a* (6.1.101)

The first step shows the duplicated root followed by the 3sg. perfect ending *-a*. The first occurrence of *āp* here is the reduplication syllable, and the second is the original root syllable. In (15b) the shortening rule 7.4.59 applies to the reduplication syllable to give *ap-āp-a*. 7.4.60 then applies to delete the final consonant of the reduplication syllable (15c), and vowel coalescence then gives *āp-a* (15d). The resulting element *āp* technically counts as both the reduplication syllable and the stem (by 6.1.85). Crucially, 7.4.59 does not then reapply to the reduplication syllable to give *apa.

Joshi and Kiparsky (1979: 245) take this as another example of the constraint on reuse of contexts, but it is not clear what the context is here. Joshi and Kiparsky seem to assume that the context is 'in case of a reduplication syllable', but in fact this is not the context but the input to the rule. It is more appropriate to understand the non-reapplication of 7.4.59 as due to a constraint preventing cyclicity: 7.4.59 takes a reduplication syllable as input, and outputs the same syllable but with a short vowel. The same reduplication syllable cannot then be input to this rule again.

The other crucial part of Joshi and Kiparsky's argument is that Pāṇini explicitly prevents cyclicity where the constraint on reuse of contexts is insufficient. This provides crucial evidence, according to their argument, that Pāṇini must have presupposed a constraint on reuse of contexts but not a constraint on cyclicity. To argue this, Joshi and Kiparsky (1979: 245) discuss the derivation of another perfect form, *vivyādha*, perfect of *vyadh* 'pierce':

(15a) *vyadh+vyādh+a*
(15b) *viadh+vyādh+a* (6.1.17)
(15c) *vidh+vyādh+a* (6.1.108)
(15d) *vi+vyādh+a* (7.4.60)

This is partly parallel to the previous example, but here the form of the reduplication syllable is initially different, and has to undergo different alterations. Rule 6.1.17 causes vocalization of the semivowel in the reduplication syllable, giving *viadh-* (16b), which reduces to *vidh-* by 6.1.108 (16c), and to *vi-* by 7.4.60 (16d). Now we do not want the semivowel vocalization rule to reapply to *vi-*, to give something like *uivyādha. In this case, Pāṇini states a rule (6.1.37 *na samprasāraṇe samprasāraṇam*) which prevents vocalization applying to a semivowel which precedes a vocalized semivowel. Joshi and Kiparsky (1979: 245) claim that this provides evidence that Pāṇini did not assume acyclicity, but has to enforce it here because the constraint on reuse of contexts would not by itself prevent reapplication of 6.1.17.

We have seen already, however, that the other examples provided by Joshi and Kiparsky (1979: 244–245) in support of "Nīlakaṇṭhadīkṣitar's constraint" can also be understood if we take the constraint as a full constraint on cyclicity. In this case, the question is the relevance or redundancy of 6.1.37. If Pāṇini assumed acyclicity, then the need for 6.1.37 is not immediately obvious, because acyclicity is sufficient to prevent reapplication of 6.1.17 to the same reduplication syllable. Must we therefore assume that Pāṇini adopted a weaker constraint, such as a constraint on reuse of contexts? Not necessarily. The necessity of 6.1.37 had already been considered by the ancient grammatical tradition; the details of the issues involved go beyond the scope of this paper, but 6.1.37 is justified on the assumption that 6.1.17 would otherwise apply to all relevant semivowels in the input.[19] That is, 6.1.37 does not enforce acyclicity, but simply restricts the single application of 6.1.17 such that it affects only the second of two contiguous semivowels which come into its scope.

To return to the very first example given in this section, *bhūyāt*: Joshi and Kiparsky (1979: 244) gave this as an example of multiple application of a rule to the same form, but in fact the inputs to the two applications of the rule are the two separate s segments, so the two applications do not, in fact, violate acyclicity, as Joshi and Kiparsky imply. All subsequent examples discussed by them build on the assumption that cyclic rule application was possible, but in fact everything we have seen can be better interpreted if we assume that Pāṇini presupposed not a weak constraint on reuse of contexts, but a stronger constraint on the reapplication of a rule to its own output, i.e. acyclicity.

Joshi and Kiparsky (1979) interpret the supposed constraint on reuse of contexts from Pāṇini's rules, as we have discussed, but they and Penn and Kiparsky (2012) also understand this constraint to be directly stated in a paribhāṣā, an interpretative rule, which they attribute to the 18th century grammarian Nīlakaṇṭhadīkṣita.[20] If the constraint is in fact to be interpreted in the way Joshi and Kiparsky argue it should, this would support their claims regarding the above derivations. But in fact, it is not.

The paribhāṣā in question is in fact earlier than Nīlakaṇṭha, being first attested in Puruṣottamadeva's *Paribhāṣāpāṭha* (c. 12th century); Nīlakaṇṭha provides the first attested commentary on the rule, in his *Paribhāṣāvṛtti*. For both,

---

19 See Sharma (2001: 45–47) for a summary of the understanding of this rule.
20 This grammarian is discussed briefly by Coward and Kunjunni Raja (1990: 373).

see Abhyankar (1967: 160b, 313).[21] In Abhyankar (1967: 313) the text is given as follows, together with Nīlakaṇṭha's three lines of commentary. I also give the text and commentary of the preceding paribhāṣā, which is directly relevant:[22]

(16) 111: *parjanyaval lakṣaṇapravṛttiḥ.*
'kṛtakāri khalv idaṃ śāstraṃ meghavat' iti iko jhal (1.2.9) iti sūtrasthabhāṣyeṇa nyāyasiddheyam. tena ūkhatur ityādau hrasvasyāpy abhyāsahrasvatve tato dīrghe punar hrasvo na bhavati. lakṣye lakṣaṇasya sakṛd eva pravṛttir iti nyāyāt.
112: *lakṣye lakṣaṇasya sakṛd eva pravṛttiḥ.*
'yathoktaviṣayeṣu hrasvāpravṛttiḥ. 'irayo re' (6.4.76) iti dvivacananirdeśo 'syā jñāpaka iti spaṣṭam 'ekaḥ pūrvaparayoḥ' (6.1.84) iti sūtre bhāṣye.'

Translation:

(17) 111: The application of a rule is like the rain.
'Rules are like the rain in effecting something that is already done.' This paribhāṣā is established by principle in the *Mahābhāṣya* on the sutra *iko jhal* (Aṣṭ. 1.2.9). By this, in the shortening of the reduplication syllable even of one that is already short, (e.g.) at the start of the word *ūkhatuḥ*, the long vowel does not again become short. This is on the basis of the principle, the application of a rule to its target happens once.'
112: The application of a rule to its target happens once.
'As in the examples stated there is no occurrence of the short vowel. The indicator of this (paribhāṣā) is the specification of dual number in *irayo re* (Aṣṭ. 6.4.76). This is clear in the *Mahābhāṣya* (commenting) on *ekaḥ pūrvaparayoḥ* (Aṣṭ. 6.1.84).'

The first paribhāṣā given here is not directly relevant to the present discussion, but introduces the second paribhāṣā with reference to yet another example involving perfect tense reduplication. The form *ūkhatuḥ* is a 3rd person dual perfect

---

[21] The paribhāṣā in question does not however appear in Nāgeśa's *Paribhāṣenduśekhara*, although it is discussed under the *parjanyavat* paribhāṣā (see 16).
[22] The text of the crucial paribhāṣā is (trivially) slightly different as given by Joshi and Kiparsky (1979: 250) and Penn and Kiparsky (2012), who adopt the phrasing of Puruṣottamadeva's *Paribhāṣāpāṭha*: *lakṣye lakṣaṇaṃ sakṛd eva pravartate*.

form, which would correspond to a 3SG. *ūkha*. Crucial here is the first syllable, which in some respects is parallel to that of *āpa*, discussed above. The difference is that the root *ukh* has a short root vowel to start with. We therefore have the following derivation of the 3SG. *ūkha*:

(18a) *ukh+ukh+a*
(18b) *ukh+ukh+a* (7.4.59)
(18c) *u+ukh+a* (7.4.60)
(18d) *ūkh+a* (6.1.101)

The derivation chain is parallel to that of *āpa* above, except that the application of 7.4.59 in (19b) is vacuous, because the vowel of the reduplication syllable is already short. This is the point of paribhāṣā 111: just as the rain falls indiscriminately on land and on water (which is already wet), so rules apply even where their effects are vacuous. The fact that 7.4.59 has already applied, albeit vacuously, at stage (19b) is what prevents it from reapplying at stage (19d). The reason given for this is the second paribhāṣā, which is the one in question here: 'the application of a rule to its target happens once'.

In terms of the phrasing of the paribhāṣā, the crucial word is *lakṣya*. The application of a rule, *lakṣaṇa*, occurs (only) once *lakṣye* 'in *lakṣya*'. Joshi and Kiparsky (1979) and Penn and Kiparsky (2012) apparently take this to mean 'in a given context', but the primary meaning of *lakṣya* in grammatical literature is 'target of a rule', i.e. the element to which a rule applies, the element which is input to a rule.[23] Thus the most natural reading of the paribhāṣā is as a statement of acyclicity, not as a constraint on reuse of contexts. The translation given in (17) reflects this.

This reading is supported by the examples given. The case of *ūkha* or *ūkhatuḥ* is exactly parallel to *āpa* above: the non-reapplication of 7.4.59 is not to do with a reuse of context, because there is no context: the rule takes as input reduplication syllables, and it is only a constraint which prevents cyclic application of a rule to the same input which will give the desired outcome here.

The second example given in Nīlakaṇṭha's commentary on paribhāṣā 112 provides the exception that proves the rule: it shows a case where Pāṇini exceptionally permits cyclic application of a rule to its own output, something that would

---

[23] This is not the only possible sense of *lakṣya*, but the range of this word generally encompasses the element, form or word to which a rule is, could be or has been applied, and does not generally refer to material surrounding the element (/ form / word) to which a rule is (/ could be / has been) applied.

not have been necessary if he had not assumed acyclicity. The reference is to *Aṣṭādhyāyī* 6.4.76 *irayo re*: '*re* replaces *ire* (in various Vedic contexts)'. Although ambiguous due to sandhi, the tradition takes *irayo* to be genitive dual rather than genitive singular, which means the dual number has to be explained. The meaning must then be something like '*re* replaces *ire* twice'. The dual here is therefore understood to exceptionally allow this replacement to occur twice to the same element, i.e. the rule is allowed to rewrite its own output once. This is because the substitution *-ire* > *-re* sometimes occurs before roots where there will be secondary insertion of *-i* after the root, resulting in *-i-ire* > *-i-re*; the correct output in such cases, however, is simply *-re*, with secondarily inserted *i* also replaced, so we need to permit this rule to reapply to its own output. Since Pāṇini uses the dual here to license a single reapplication of a rule to its own output, we can infer that Pāṇini presupposes acyclicity.[24]

Altogether, then, it is clear from the phrasing of the paribhāṣā itself, and from the illustrations in the commentary, that this interpretative principle is what modern linguists call acyclicity; the supposed constraint on reuse of contexts is a phantom.

6 Conclusion

I have shown, contrary to Penn and Kiparsky (2012), that Pāṇini assumed acyclicity as a fundamental principle of his grammatical formalism; this can be inferred from the rules of his grammar themselves, and was also recognized and formulated as a principle by the ancient Indian grammatical tradition. As recognized by modern phonology, acyclicity is a fundamentally important constraint on rule systems, restricting the generative power of context-sensitive grammars to that of regular grammars and, correspondingly, making context-sensitive systems computationally tractable. It is a remarkable fact about the ancient grammarian Pāṇini that he anticipated this so precisely.

---

24 For technical reasons which go beyond the scope of this paper, later commentators such as Nāgeśa and Vaidyanātha do not take *irayo re* to be the authority for the principle of single rule application (which I interpret as acyclicity); instead, they derive the authority for this principle by a series of technical arguments related to the need to avoid multiple application of 8.4.47 (12); see e.g. Kielhorn (1874: 502).

Transliteration

The Sanskrit data is Romanized following the International Alphabet of Sanskrit Transliteration (IAST):
https://en.wikipedia.org/wiki/International_Alphabet_of_Sanskrit_Transliteration

Acknowledgements

I am very grateful to Jim Benson, Rishi Rajpopat, and John Coleman, for assistance and discussion of the issues addressed in this paper, and to Martin Everaert for his review of the paper. All errors are my own. The writing of this paper has benefitted from support from the European Research Council (ERC) under the European Union's Horizon 2020 research and innovation programme (grant agreement No. 851990 'LINGUINDIC').

References

Abhyankar, K. V. (ed.). 1967. *Paribhāṣāsaṃgraha: A collection of original works on vyākaraṇa paribhāṣās*. Poona: Bhandarkar Oriental Research Institute.
Backus, John W. 1959. The syntax and semantics of the proposed international algebraic language of the Zurich ACM-GAMM Conference. In *Proceedings of the International Conference on Information Processing*, 125–132. UNESCO.
Backus, John W., F. L. Bauer, J. Green, C. Katz, J. McCarthy, P. Naur, A. J. Perlis, H. Rutishauser, K. Samelson, B. Vauquois & J. H. Wegstein. 1963. Revised report on the algorithmic language Algol 60. *The Computer Journal* 5 (4). 349–367.
Cardona, George. 1965. On translating and formalizing Pāṇinan rules. *Journal of the Oriental Institute at Baroda* 14. 306–314.
Chomsky, Noam. 1957. *Syntactic structures*. The Hague: Mouton.
Chomsky, Noam. 1959. On certain formal properties of grammars. *Information and Control* 2. 137–167.
Chomsky, Noam. 1965. *Aspects of the Theory of Syntax*. Cambridge, MA: MIT Press.
Clark, Alexander. 2015. An introduction to multiple context free grammars for linguists. http://citeseerx.ist.psu.edu/viewdoc/summary?doi=10.1.1.714.8708.
Coleman, John S. 1991. *Phonological representations – their names, forms and powers*. York: University of York dissertation.
Coleman, John S. 1995. Declarative Lexical Phonology. In Jacques Durand & Francis Katamba (eds.), *Frontiers of Phonology: atoms, structures, derivations*, 333–383. London: Longman.
Coward, Harold G. & K. Kunjunni Raja. 1990. *The philosophy of the grammarians*, volume 5 of *Encyclopedia of Indian Philosophies*. Delhi: Motilal Banarsidass.

Culy, Christopher. 1985. The complexity of the vocabulary of Bambara. *Linguistics and Philosophy* 8. 345–351.
Gazdar, Gerald, Ewan H. Klein, Geoffrey K. Pullum & Ivan A. Sag. 1985. *Generalized Phrase Structure Grammar*. Oxford: Blackwell.
Huybregts, M. A. C. 1984. The weak adequacy of context-free phrase structure grammar. In Ger J. de Haan, Mieke Trommelen & Wim Zonneveld (eds.), *Van Periferie naar Kern*, 81–99. Dordrecht: Foris
Hyman, Malcolm. 2007. From Pāṇinian Sandhi to finite State Calculus. In Gérard Huet & Amba Kulkarni (eds.), *First International Sanskrit Computational Linguistics Symposium, Oct 2007*, 13-21. Rocquencourt, France: INRIA. http://hal.inria.fr/SANSKRIT/fr/.
Ingerman, Peter Zilahy. 1967. "Pāṇini-Backus Form" suggested. *Communications of the ACM* 10 (3). 137.
Johnson, C. Douglas. 1972. *Formal Aspects of Phonological Description*. The Hague: Mouton.
Joshi, Aravind K., Leon S. Levy & Masako Takahashi. 1975. Tree Adjunct Grammars. *Journal of Computer and System Science* 10 (2). 136–163.
Joshi, S. D. & Paul Kiparsky. 1979. Siddha and asiddha in Pāṇinian phonology. In Daniel A. Dinnsen (ed.), *Current Approaches to Phonological Theory*, 223–250. Bloomington: Indiana University Press.
Joshi, S. D. & Paul Kiparsky. 2006. The extended siddha-principle. *Annals of the Bhandarkar Oriental Research Institute* 2005. 1–26.
Kaplan, Ronald M. & Martin Kay. 1994. Regular Models of Phonological Rule Systems. *Computational Linguistics* 20 (3). 331–378.
Kielhorn, Franz. 1874. *The Paribhāṣenduśekhara of Nāgojībhaṭṭa, edited and explained*. Bombay: Government Central Book Depot.
Müller, Stefan. 2016. *Grammatical theory: From transformational grammar to constraint-based approaches*. Berlin: Language Science Press.
Penn, Gerald & Paul Kiparsky. 2012. On Pāṇini and the Generative Capacity of Contextualized Replacement Systems. *COLING* 2012. 943–950.
Pollard, Carl J. 1996. The nature of constraint-based grammar. Paper presented at the Pacific Asia Conference on Language, Information, and Computation, Kyung Hee University, Seoul, Korea. http://lingo.stanford.edu/sag/L221a/pollard-96.txt.
Pullum, Geoffrey K. & Gerald Gazdar. 1982. Natural languages and context free languages. *Linguistics and Philosophy* 4. 471–504.
Seki, Hiroyuki, Takashi Matsumura, Mamoru Fujii & Tadao Kasami. 1991. On multiple context-free grammars. *Theoretical Computer Science* 88 (2). 191–229.
Sharma, Rama Nath. 2001. *The Aṣṭādhyāyī of Pāṇini*, volume V. New Delhi: Munshiram Manoharlal.
Shieber, Stuart M. 1985. Evidence against the context-freeness of natural language. *Linguistics and Philosophy* 8. 333–343.
Staal, Johan Fritz. 1965. Context sensitive rules in Pāṇini. *Foundations of Language* 1. 63–72.
Staal, Johan Fritz. 1966. Pāṇini tested by Fowler's Automaton. *Journal of the American Oriental Society* 86 (2). 206–209.

Paroma Sanyal, Vyom Sharma, Ankita Prasad
Hindi root allomorphy: Insights from phonological and morphosyntactic theory

Abstract: For any systematic process of phonological reduction, the context where reduction applies is a priori designated as a marked position. In the case of Hindi verb roots, such a phonological neutralization process has been observed to systematically occur in a specific morphosyntactic context. Is this because this particular morphosyntactic context is a "marked" location in the derivation or is it simply possible that a language chose to mark a derivational cycle in a particular syntactic configuration with systematic phonological reduction? This paper shows that: (a) the phonological reduction process in Hindi is driven by the relatively higher weight of sonority-hierarchy-based stringency constraints in the derived roots √R2, and (b) the phonological reduction process that derives √R2 from √R1 root forms corresponds to the Spell-Out of the Voice head during lexicalization. This Voice head, being a cyclic head, is ordinarily outside the cyclic domain of the root, and therefore cannot access anything more than the spelled-out phonological form of the root for reduction. Thus, this process applies without root-specific allomorphy. In contrast, the *Voice head of anticausatives, being non-cyclic, can access the root. Thus, the phonological reduction associated with derived intransitives in Hindi is conditioned by root-specific allomorphic rules. Both the regular Spell-Out of Voice as well as of *Voice in anticausatives apply the same process of phonological reduction.

Keywords: Hindi, Root morphology, phonological theory, morphosyntactic theory

---

Paroma Sanyal, IIT, Department of Humanities and Social Sciences, Main Building, MS 611, New Delhi, India. Email: sanyalparoma@gmail.com
Vyom Sharma, IIT, Department of Humanities and Social Sciences, Main Building, MS 611, New Delhi, India. Email: vyom18@gmail.com
Ankita Prasad, IIT, Department of Humanities and Social Sciences, Main Building, MS 611, New Delhi, India. Email: ankita.9212@gmail.com

https://doi.org/10.1515/9783110753066-015

1 Introduction

The morphological module adds successive layers of inflections on the lexical base of the verb root. These layers correspond to the functional heads of tense, aspect and mood. In Hindi, many verbs also show what Bhatt and Embick (2017) call a "transitive alternation" in contexts such as the ones illustrated in (1a)–(1d).

(1) Transitive alternation pattern in Hindi verb roots:
    a. ɟaːɟdaːḍ **bə̃ʈ** rəhiː hɛ
        property divide PROG.F be.PRS
        'The property is dividing (i.e. being divided).'
    b. raːm-ne ɟaːɟdaːḍ **bãːʈ** diː
        Ram-ERG property divide GIVE.PFV
        'Ram divided the property.'
    c. məkaːn **ɟəl** rəhaː hɛ
        house.M burn PROG.M be.PRS
        'The house is burning.'
    d. ḍəkɛṱõ-ne məkaːn **ɟəl-aː** diː
        bandits.ERG house.M burn GIVE.PFV.M
        'Bandits burned the house.'
    (from Bhatt and Embick 2017: 94)

As is evident from the given examples, there is both a morphosyntactic as well as a phonological aspect to this "transitive alternation" pattern in Hindi. A holistic analysis of such a process not only gets us a better picture of the grammar of Hindi, but also furthers our theoretical understanding of how morphosyntax and phonology interface with each other through their respective correspondences with the lexicon. This paper aims to explore such an avenue by simultaneously analyzing the phonological as well as morphosyntactic aspects of this alternation pattern in a theoretically compatible frame.

The next section (section 2) of the paper describes the phonological contexts of Hindi root allomorphy. This includes a discussion on the nature of vowel reduction, followed by a formal analysis of the same. section 3 describes the syntactic contexts of the root alternation. Here, an introduction to the verb root classification given by Bhatt and Embick (2017) is followed by a discussion on the nature of *vocabulary insertion* in Hindi. We also provide a formal analysis of the verb root allomorphy in the syntactic context (section 3.3). section 4 presents and analyzes residual phonological issues with the verbs which are outliers to Hindi verb morphology. It also discusses some of the predictions of our syntactic analysis.

2 What is the phonological context for Hindi-Root allomorphy?

Hindi has eleven oral vowels in its repertoire (Ohala and Ohala 1992; Ohala 1994). The vowel /æ/ is only found in loanwords from English (Ohala 1994); hence it is not relevant to our analysis. All the vowels except schwa /ə/ and the loanword vowel /æ/ have nasal counterparts.[1]

Tab. 1: Hindi vowel repertoire

Vowels	Front	Central	Back
High	/iː/ /ĩː/		/uː/ /ũː/
	/i/ /ĩ/		/u/ /ũ/
Mid	/e/ /ẽ/	/ə/	/o/ /õ/
Low	/ɛ/ /ɛ̃/	/aː/ /ãː/	/ɔ/ /ɔ̃/
	/æ/		

(Ohala and Ohala 1992: 831)

The remaining ten vowels exhibit a three-way contrast along the front-back axis: there are four front and four back vowels, along with two central vowels—a mid-vowel /ə/ and a low vowel /aː/. The mid and low peripheral vowels show a height and tenseness contrast between the pairs /ɛ/ and /e/, and /ɔ/ and /o/. The high peripheral vowels also contrast tenseness, with a tense vowel which is also phonemically long (/iː//uː/) and a shorter lax vowel (/i//u/). It has been shown by Gordon et al. (2012) using acoustic measurements that the two pairs of high peripheral vowels in Hindi are mainly distinguished by duration and acoustic intensity.

---

[1] The intransitive (anti-causative) counterparts of transitive verbs with a nasal /a/ surface with nasalization on the /ə/ in phonologically reduced forms (for example, 1a and 1b), although nasalization in /ə/ is otherwise non-contrastive in Hindi.

One of the predominant ways to theoretically characterize phonological vowel length/duration is with respect to their differing moraic weight (Hyman 1984, 1985; McCarthy and Prince 1996). A short vowel is characterized as a single mora and a long vowel as two moras. This is a relevant distinction in Hindi since it is a weight-sensitive language (Pandey 1989). Thus, the moraic weight of Hindi vowels is likely to have implications in the domain of word minimality, which will be further discussed in section 2.1.

Following the view that there is a necessary correspondence between categories of morphology and phonology, as in Prince and Smolensky (1993) and the references therein, it is expected that the monosyllabic verb root in Hindi should meet the phonological requirements for a minimal prosodic word in the language. This requirement is formalized as the constraint in (2) below.

(2) Lx≈Pr *(MCat)*
A member of the morphological category *MCat* corresponds to a PrWd
(Prince and Smolensky 1993: 45)

The minimal prosodic word is a foot, which needs to be binary with either two syllables or two moras.

(3) Ft-Bin
Feet are binary under moraic or syllabic analysis
(Kager 1999: 156)

In Hindi, only five vowels (/aː/, /e/, /iː/, /ɔ/, /o/, /uː/) appear in monosyllabic verb roots with open syllables (cf. Table 2). Since these syllables have no coda consonant and the lexical word is monosyllabic, the entire moraic weight of the syllable, as well as the word, depends on the vowel. For the constraints Lx≈Pr and Ft-Bin to be satisfied, these vowels will have to be bimoraic. The absence of the short high peripheral vowels /i/ and /u/, and schwa /ə/ from this crucial context lends further support to the analysis that these five vowels form bimoraic feet in the verb roots and satisfy word minimality.

Tab. 2: Vowels in open verb roots (CV, V)

/aː/	/o/	/e/
aː-na: 'to come'	so-na: 'to sleep'	le-na: 'to take'
ɟaː-na: 'to go'	dʰo-na: 'to wash'	d̪e-na: 'to give'
gaː-na: 'to sing'	ro-na: 'to cry'	
laː-na: 'to bring'	kʰo-na: 'to lose something'	
kʰaː-na: 'to eat'		
paː-na: 'to get'		

/iː/	/uː/	
siː-na: 'to stitch'	cʰuː-na: 'to touch'	
piː-na: 'to drink'		

Unlike the open syllables in Table 2, monosyllabic verb roots in Table 3 with CVC closed syllables allow all the vowels in the repertoire. Here the presence of the moraic coda consonant in the rhyme of the syllable helps satisfy the minimality requirement of FT-BIN.[2] Note that although monosyllabic verb roots in Hindi with closed syllables allow all the vowels, the low peripheral vowels /ɛ/ and /ɔ/ have limited distribution in contrast to other vowels.

Tab. 3: Vowels in closed verb roots (CVC, VC)

/a/	/e/	/o/	/iː/
bʰaːg-na: 'to run'	let̪-na: 'to lie down'	kʰol-na: 'to open'	siːkʰ-na: 'to learn'
ɟaːg-na: 'to be awake'	pʰẽt̪-na: 'to mix'	bol-na: 'to speak'	piːt̪-na: 'to hit'
kaːʈ-na: 'to cut'	gʰer-na: 'to surround'	kʰod̪-na: 'to dig'	ciːkʰ-na: 'to scream'
d̪ãːʈ-na: 'to scold'	pʰẽk-na: 'to throw'	gʰol-na: 'to dissolve'	piːs-na: 'to grind'
haːr-na: 'to lose'	d̪ekʰ-na: 'to see'	ɟoɾ-na: 'to add'	biːʈ-na: 'to elapse'

/uː/	/i/	/u/	/ə/
gʰuːm-na: 'to roam'	kʰil-na: 'to bloom'	ʈʰuk-na: 'to bend'	bən-na: 'to be made'
pʰũːk-na: 'to blow'	gʰis-na: 'to rub'	ut̪ʰ-na: 'to get up'	kəɾ-na: 'to do'

---

[2] Hindi allows both bimoraic (VV, VC) as well as trimoraic syllables (VVC). So, FT-BIN is applied as a minimality restriction, and not a criterion for deciding the maximal syllable.

/uː/	/i/	/u/	/ə/
ʈʰuːl-na: 'to swing'	likʰ-na: 'to write'	sun-na: 'to hear'	bʰər-na: 'to fill'
luːʈ-na: 'to rob'	cʰip-na: 'to hide'	ruk-na: 'to stop'	dər-na: 'be scared'
ɖuːb-na: 'to sink'	gir-na: 'to fall'	bun-na: 'to weave'	ləɾ-na: 'to fight'

/ɔ/	/ɛ/
kʰɔl-na: 'to boil'	pʰɛl-na: 'to spread'
ɖɔɾ-na: 'to run'	
bʰɔ̃k-na: 'to bark'	
cɔ̃k-na: 'to startle'	

Many of the roots show alternate forms when they transitivize/ detransitivize and causativize. The base vowel in the root can predict which vowel will surface in the alternate form of the root (Bhatt and Embick 2017: 29). We refer to the full set of Hindi vowels in the base form as √ROOT₁ vowels. The predictable vowels that occur in the alternate forms are called √ROOT₂ vowels. The distribution of the two sets is illustrated in the data given in Table 4:

Tab. 4: Vowel alternation pattern in verb roots[3]

√ROOT₁ (VR₁) Vowels	√ROOT₂ (VR₂) vowels	
/iː/	siːkʰ-na: 'to learn'	sikʰ-aː-na: 'to cause to learn'	
	piːʈ-na: 'to hit'	piʈ-na: 'to be beaten'	
/i/	kʰil-na: 'to bloom'	kʰil-aː-na: 'to cause to bloom'	/i/
	gʰis-na: 'to rub'	gʰis-na: 'to be rubbed'	
/e/	leʈ-na: 'lie down'	liʈ-aː-na: 'to cause to lie down'	
	gʰer-na: 'suround'	gʰir-na: 'to be surrounded'	
/uː/	suːkʰ-na: 'to dry'	sukʰ-aː-na: 'to cause to dry'	
	luːʈ-na: 'to rob'	luʈ-na: 'to be robbed'	
/u/	jʰuk-na: 'to bend'	jʰuk-aː-na: 'to bend something'	/u/
	bun-na: 'to weave'	bun-na: 'to be woven'	
/o/	so-na: 'to sleep'	sul-aː-na: 'to cause someone to sleep'	
	kʰol-na: 'to open'	kʰul-na: 'to be opened'	

---

[3] The low peripheral vowels /ɔ/ and /ɛ/ do not participate in the verb root alternation. See section 4.1.2 for an analysis.

√ROOT₁ (VR₁) Vowels		√ROOT₂ (VR₂) vowels	
/ə/	pək-na: 'to cook' bədəl-na: 'to change'	pək-a:-na: 'to cause to be cooked' bədəl-na: 'to be changed'	/ə/
/a:/	ha:r-na: 'to lose' ma:r-na: 'to kill'	hər-a:-na: 'to cause someone to lose' mər-na: 'to die'	

(Data from Bhatt and Embick 2017: 112–115; Ramchand 2008: 156; Koul 2008: 93–98)

We discuss the phonological context of the root vowel alternation in the following subsections. section 3.1 discusses the syntactic context of this process.

2.1 The nature of phonological reduction

Although the environment and motivation for vowel change in Hindi verb roots is clearly morphosyntactic in nature, there is an aspect of phonological reduction to it as well. Referred to as a vowel simplification rule by Bhatt and Embick (2017: 113), it could be characterized as (4), since all three vowels (/ə/, /i/ and /u/) have been described as short (Shapiro 2003).

(4)   Correspondence between vowel length and weight
       [±LONG] → [-LONG]
       2μ   1μ

However, this rule fails to adequately capture the Hindi verb root allomorphy pattern described in Table 4 as the monomoraic vowels /e/ and /o/ also undergo a systematic qualitative shift. Further, the fact that the vR₂ vowels share no common values with respect to distinctive features such as [BACK], [ROUND], [HIGH], etc. that would help us distinguish them from the full set is a strong indication that we need a gradient perspective in order to formally understand the phonology of this process.

Co-existent with the feature-based binary approach to phonological processes, there has been a consistent tradition of conceptualizing phonological properties as gradient. One of the earliest and most common schematizations of this gradience was with respect to the property of sonority in speech sounds, for example the sonority-scale-based description of a syllable, which eventually developed into the Sonority Sequencing Principle (Seivers 1901; Steriade 1982; Selkirk 1984). If we analyze the vR₁ vowels in Hindi as per the sonority hierarchy

(Clements 1990; de Lacy 2004: 146), we find that they can be divided into four sets of increasing sonority.

Tab. 5: Sonority hierarchy of vowels in Hindi

low	⟩	mid peripheral	⟩	high peripheral	⟩	mid central
aː		e, o		iː, uː, i, u		ə

Note the split in the set of high peripheral vowels in Table 5. While the two bimoraic ones, /iː/ and /uː/, belong exclusively to the set of √R$_1$ vowels, the two monomoraic ones /i/ and /u/ occur in both √R$_1$ and √R$_2$ contexts (cf. Table 4). There are at least two ways to theoretically analyze this split. First, based on the evidence of this reduction process, we could propose that the vowels /i/ and /u/ are less sonorous than the vowels /iː/ and /uː/ and form another separate lower notch on the sonority scale that distinguishes them from the latter. The scale in Table 6 illustrates this hypothesis.

Tab. 6: Addition of a high non-peripheral segment to the Hindi sonority hierarchy

low	⟩	mid peripheral	⟩	high peripheral	⟩	high non-peripheral	⟩	mid central
aː		e, o		iː, uː		i, u		ə

Although there is cross-linguistic evidence, including from English, to substantiate the possibility of a difference in place of articulation between the long and short high peripheral vowels, whether this has a phonological consequence in Hindi is unclear. While Ohala (1994) has noted the tenseness difference in Hindi high vowels, the experimental analysis of Gordon et al. (2012) reports duration and intensity to be consistent markers of distinction in this set. Further, the syllable structure and word minimality restrictions in verbs discussed in section 1 also suggest that we need to factor in the moraic weight difference between the two sets of vowels as an important factor in the phonological grammar of Hindi.

Thus, in our proposed approach, the sonority scale indeed has four notches as in Table 5. These are further divided into two sets with the low and mid-peripheral vowels conflating to a higher sonority register, and the high peripheral and mid central vowels conflating to a low sonority register, as shown in Table 7.

Tab. 7: Two levels of sonority conflation in Hindi verb roots

a. high sonority			b. low sonority		
low	+	mid peripheral	⟩ high peripheral	+	mid central
aː		e, o	iː, uː, i, u		ə

Similarly, with respect to moraic weight, these vowels can also be divided into two sets.

Tab. 8: Two levels of weight conflation in Hindi verb roots

a. bimoraic (heavy/long)	b. monomoraic (light/short)
aː, iː, uː	⟩ e, o, i, u, ə

The intersection of both the low sonority set (Table 7 column b) and the monomoraic set (Table 8 column b) gives us the √R₂ vowels in Hindi. Further, in the correspondence between √R₁ and √R₂ vowels, the front to back axis of articulation is maintained as illustrated below.

Tab. 9: Vowel identity along the horizontal axis

√R₁		√R₂	Corresponding place position
ə, aː	→	ə	Central vowels
i, iː, e	→	i	Front vowels
u, uː, o	→	u	Back vowels

Therefore, although the mid-peripheral vowel /e/ is at the same point on the vertical axis as the central vowel /ə/, post-reduction it corresponds to the front vowel /i/ which is on the same horizontal axis. In the following sub-section (section 2.2) we present a constraint-based formal account of this generalization.

2.2 Formal analysis of the phonological context of reduction

In this section, we use the concept of stringency constraints (de Lacy 2004) to formalize the phonological generalizations regarding markedness reduction in

Hindi verb roots discussed in the preceding section. Stringency constraints form a universal set drawn from the universal sonority hierarchy. They ban non-sonorous elements in prominent positions (as in Table 10 column a) or sonorous elements in non-prominent positions (as in Table 10 column b).

Tab. 10: Stringency constraints for foot heads and non-heads:

a. Relative markedness of non-sonorous elements in the head of foot	b. Relative markedness of sonorous elements in non-head foot position
*H_{DFt}/ɨ	*$N_{ON-HDFt}$/ a,e.o,i.u,ə,ɨ
*H_{DFt}/ɨ,ə	*$N_{ON-HDFt}$/a,e.o,i.u,ə
*H_{DFt}/ ɨ,ə,i.u	*$N_{ON-HDFt}$/ a,e.o,i.u
*H_{DFt}/ ɨ,ə,i.u,e.o	*$N_{ON-HDFt}$/a,e.o
*H_{DFt}/ ɨ,ə,i.u,e.o,a	*$N_{ON-HDFt}$/a

Corresponding sonority scale: a) e.o) i.u) ə) ɨ   (de Lacy 2004: 147)

The core insight that this formulation presents is that prominent prosodic positions like the head of a foot have a negative bias for less sonorous vowels, while weaker positions have a negative bias for the more sonorous vowels. Given this set of stringency constraints, an output candidate which has the lowest sonority vowel /ɨ/ in the head foot position will incur violation of all five constraints, while vowels /ə/, /i.u/, /e.o/ or /a/ in the same position will incur 4, 3, 2 and 1 violations respectively. Thus, the relative well-formedness of the particular vowel in a particular position as per the sonority hierarchy gets formalized in the form of constraint violations. The √R₂ verb roots in Hindi correspond to the weak or non-head foot position above since they trigger similar sonority reduction. Furthermore, the dispreference for bimoraic vowels can also be encoded as a relative markedness constraint against more than one mora in the root vowel of √R₂.

Tab. 11: Stringency constraints for Hindi verb roots:

a. Relative markedness of sonorous elements in √R₂	b. Relative markedness of weight in √R₂
*√R₂ /a:, e.o, i:.u:.i.u, ə	*√R₂ / 2μ, 1μ
*√R₂ /a:, e.o, i:.u:.i.u	*√R₂ / 2μ
*√R₂ /a:, e.o	
*√R₂ /a:	

As discussed in section 2.1, the vowel correspondences between √R₁ and √R₂ maintain faithfulness along the front-back axis. In plotting the vowel chart acoustically, vowel height correlates with the values of the first formant (F1). The front-back axis does not correspond directly with the value of any one formant, rather, it is plotted using the difference between F1 and F2. Following that, we encode the input-output faithfulness for the horizontal axis in Hindi as the constraint IDENT (F1-F2).

(5) IDENT (F1-F2): assign one violation mark for every output segment whose (F1-F2) value does not match the (F1-F2) of the input segment

By deriving the √R₂ phonological forms from the √R₁ forms using the constraints in Table 11, we get the phonological grammar that corresponds to the verb root allophony in Hindi. In this paper, we use Harmonic Grammar (Legendre et al 1990; Boersma and Pater 2016; Pater 2009) to compute the violations and derive the phonological grammar. In the Harmonic Grammar evaluation table, each constraint violation is computed as [-1]. The violations are then multiplied by the weight of the constraint, for each candidate and each constraint. The harmonic value of a candidate is the sum of the violations, into weight, for each constraint. The candidate with the highest harmonic value emerges as the optimal candidate. The Tables 12–14 given below compute this relative well-formedness of the relevant output candidates with respect to the derivation of √R₂ phonological forms from the √R₁ forms.

Tab. 12: Reduction in the root vowel /aː/

√haːr₁	*√R₂/aː, eːo, iːuː,iːu, ə	*√R₂/aː, eːo, iːuː,iːu	*√R₂ /aː, eːo	*√R₂ /aː	*√R₂ / 2μ, 1μ	*√R₂ / 2μ	Ident F1-F2	Harmonic value
Weights	1	1	1	1	1	1	1.1	
a. √haːr₂	-1	-1	-1	-1	-1	-1		-6
b. √her₂	-1	-1	-1		-1		-1	-5.1
c. √hir₂	-1	-1			-1		-1	-4.1
☞ d. √hər₂	-1				-1			-2

In the Tables 12–14, we have taken the √R₁ forms of the words /haːr-naː/ 'to lose', /leṭ-naː/ 'to lie down', and /piːṭ-naː/ 'to beat up' as inputs respectively. In Table 12, even if we put equal weight on all the constraints, candidate (d) with /ə/ will still emerge as the optimal candidate. This is because the multiple factors of sonority, weight and IDENT (F1-F2) gang-up in a manner that ensures that the competing output candidates are much worse than (d).

Tab. 13: Reduction in the root vowel /e/

Vlet₁	*VR₂ /aː, e.o, iː.uː.i.u, ə	*VR₂ /aː, e.o, iː.uː.i.u	*VR₂ /aː, e.o	*VR₂ /aː	*VR₂ / 2μ, 1μ	*VR₂ / 2μ	Ident F1-F2	Harmonic value
Weights	1	1	1	1	1	1	1.1	
a. Vlet₂	-1	-1	-1		-1			-4
☞ b. Vlit₂	-1	-1			-1			-3
c. Vlət₂	-1				-1		-1	-3.1

Tab. 14: Reduction in the root vowel /iː/

Vpiːt₁	*VR₂ /aː, e.o, iː.uː.i.u, ə	*VR₂ /aː, e.o, iː.uː.i.u	*VR₂ /aː, e.o	*VR₂ /aː	*VR₂ / 2μ, 1μ	*VR₂ / 2μ	Ident F1-F2	Harmonic value
Weights	1	1	1	1	1	1	1.1	
a. Vpiːt₂	-1	-1			-1	-1		-4
☞ b. Vpit₂	-1	-1			-1			-3
c. Vpət₂	-1				-1		-1	-3.1

This is not the case in Table 13, where both the input and the optimal output are monomoraic. Therefore, weight plays no role in this evaluation table. Further, /ə/ being less sonorous than /i/, candidate (c) incurs one less violation of the stringency constraints than candidate (b). This is balanced by the additional violation of IDENT (F1-F2). Had the weights of these two constraints been at par, candidates (b) and (c) in Table 13 would have been equally well-formed. However, in Hindi we know that the mid-central vowel /e/ in VR₁ always corresponds to /i/ in VR₂. Therefore, we also know that the weight of the faithfulness constraint is at least marginally higher than the weight of the stringency constraint in Hindi. In Table 14, the crucial competition is between candidates (a) and (b), and the vital constraint that distinguishes between them is the stringency constraint that computes an additional violation for candidate (a) for being bimoraic. Without the mediation of this weight factor distinguishing them, these two candidate outputs would have been equally well-formed.

While presenting the phonological analysis of the vowel reduction process in Hindi, we have not discussed much about the syntactic context of this reduction process. In the following section, we use insights from generative syntax and Distributive Morphology to characterize the syntactic context of this process.

3 What is the syntactic context for Hindi root allomorphy?

Bhatt and Embick (2017: 105) have classified verb roots in Hindi based on transitivization/ causativization patterns into two classes:
- AA-class: This class of verbs roots has an overt affix -aː for the transitive form of the verb.
- NULL-class: This class of verb roots has no overt morpheme for the transitive form of the verb. The NULL-class verb roots can be causativized by suffixing -aː/-waː morpheme. They can also (but not always) be de-transitivized, as shown below.

The √R₁ form in all AA class verbs is the intransitive. These intransitives include both unaccusatives and unergatives.

Tab. 15: Transitive derivation unaccusative and unergative AA-class verbs

Unaccusative √R₁		Transitive √R₂
suːkʰ-na: 'to dry'	→	sukʰ-aː-na: 'to cause to dry'
gir-na: 'to fall'	→	gir-aː-na: 'to cause to fall'
biːṭ-na: 'to pass'	→	biṭ-aː-na: 'to cause to pass'

Unergative √R₁		Transitive √R₂
so-na: 'to sleep'	→	sul-aː-na: 'to cause someone to sleep'
leṭ-na: 'to lie down'	→	liṭ-aː-na: 'to cause to lie down'
gʰuːm-na: 'to travel'	→	gʰum-aː-na: 'to cause to travel'

Thus, with respect to the syntax, the √R₁ forms of AA class verbs correspond to two different derivational structures. While the unaccusative has an internal argument, and no external argument, the sole argument of an unergative is an external argument. In Figure 1, this contrast in syntactic structure is located as the difference in the functional head v. Following the analysis of Bhatt and Embick

(2017) we denote an agent-licencing head as v[AG] as well. The fact that both the unaccusatives and unergatives are phonologically realized as √R₁, irrespective of the difference in syntactic structure between them, suggests that the √R₁ form corresponds to the basic encyclopedic meaning of the verb root.

a. Syntactic structure of Unaccusatives   b. Syntactic structure of Unergatives

Bhatt and Embick (2017: 108 a, 123 b)

Fig. 1: Syntactic structure of Unaccusatives and Unergatives

What unifies them as a class is that the addition of a further external agent to each of these structures has the same consequences at PF; the v[AG] gets spelled out as an overt morphological marker -*a:*, and the verb root is reduced to its √R₂ form.

a. Spell-Out of transitivized unaccusatives   b. Spell-Out of transitivized unergatives

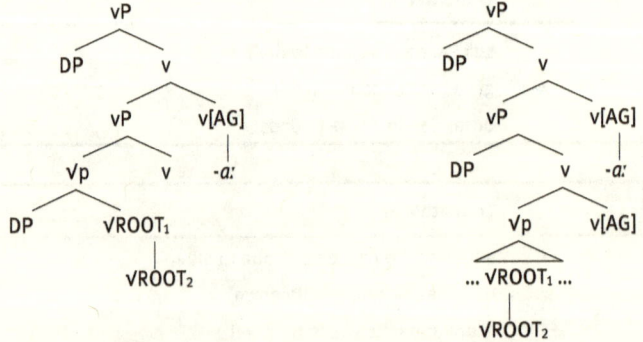

Fig. 2: Spell-Out of transitivized intransitive verbs

In the NULL class verbs, the encyclopedic meaning of the verb root corresponds to a transitive and therefore, the √R₁ form corresponds to the transitive. As observed by Bhatt and Embick (2017), this form lacks the morphological [-a:] marking despite containing the functional head of v[AG] in the syntactic structure.

Bhatt and Embick (2017) make a distinction between two kinds of transitive verbs in Hindi. The NULL class verbs belong to the first kind, and are characterized by the fact that each of them has a corresponding unaccusative form that appears to be derived from the transitive. These verbs can also form indirect causatives with [-a:/-wa:] markers. Both unaccusatives and indirect causatives surface with the √R₂ phonological form.

Tab. 16: Unaccusative and indirect causative derivation in NULL-class verbs

Intransitive √R₂⁴	Transitive √R₁	Indirect Causative √R₂
kəṭ-na: 'to be cut'	← ka:ṭ-na: 'to cut'	→ kəṭ-wa:-na: 'to cause one to cut'
ɟuɾ-na: 'to be joined'	← ɟoɾ-na: 'to join'	→ ɟuɾ-wa:-na: 'to cause to be joined'
luṭ-na: 'to be robbed'	← lu:ṭ-na: 'to rob'	→ luṭ-wa:-na: 'to cause to be robbed'

The second kind of transitive verbs are labelled "Ingesto-Reflexives/ Ingestives" since they refer to some sort of literal or metaphorical acts of ingestion. In Hindi, these verbs differ from NULL class transitive verbs in two respects. Unlike the NULL class transitive verbs, the transitive ingestive verbs do not have intransitive counterparts.

---

4 In English, some transitive verbs like *break* also have intransitive counterparts, e.g. "John broke the window" (transitive) versus "The window broke" (intransitive). Furthermore, some transitive verbs such as *cut* and *tear* can also form middle constructions without the external agent: "The paper tore easily" [middle]. In Hindi, all such verbs have intransitive forms corresponding to their transitive counterparts. These intransitives are not the passive forms, for they are ungrammatical with *dwa:ra:* 'by' phrases in Hindi.

Transitive	Intransitive
ɟɛ peɾ ka:ṭ rəha: hɛ	(*ɟɛ dwa:ra:) peɾ kəṭ rəhe hɛ̃
Jay tree cut PROG be.PRS	Jay by tree cut PROG.PL be.PRS.PL
'Jay is cutting a tree.'	'Trees are being cut.'
ɟɛ ka:gəz pha:ɾ rəha: hɛ	(*ɟɛ dwa:ra:) ka:gəz phəṭ rəha: hɛ
Jay paper tear PROG be.PRS	Jay by paper tear PROG.SG be.PRS.SG
'Jay is tearing up the papers.'	'The paper is being torn.'

Tab. 17: Direct and Indirect causative derivation from Ingestive verbs

Transitive √R₁	Direct causative[5] √R₂	Indirect Causative √R₂
kʰaː-naː 'to eat'	→ kʰi-l-aː-naː 'to cause one to eat'	→ kʰi-l-waː-naː 'to get one to eat'
siːkʰ-naː 'to learn'	→ sikʰ-aː-naː 'to cause one to learn'	→ sikʰ-waː-naː 'to get one to learn'
piː-naː 'to drink'	→ pi-l-aː-naː 'to cause one to drink'	→ pi-l-waː-naː 'to get one to drink'

Summarizing the core observations on the context of alternations between √R₁ and √R₂, we see that:

— √R₁ verb forms are associated with the encyclopedic meaning of the verb.
— These √R₁ forms can be transitive, for example *kaːʈ-naː* 'to cut'; unaccusative, for example *biːʈ-naː* 'to pass'; unergative, for example *naːc-naː* 'to dance'; and ingestive *kʰaː-naː* 'to eat'.
— All of them change to their corresponding √R₂ forms when the syntactic structure associated with them is causativized further by merging a v[AG]. This v[AG] introduces a further event, and is obligatorily marked with an [-aː] morpheme, e.g.:

    a. Transitive → Causative: kaːʈ-naː + v[AG] → kəʈ-aː-naː
    b. Unaccusative → Causative: biːʈ-naː + v[AG] → biʈ-aː-naː
    c. Unergative → Causative: naːc-naː + v[AG] → nəc-aː-naː
    d. Ingestive → Causative: kʰaː-naː + v[AG] → kʰil-aː-naː

---

5 Masica (1976: 319) has analysed [-aː] causativization in Hindi as the delinking of the reflexive nature of the base verb rather than the addition of a causative subevent:

    Intransitive/Reflexive: *utʰ-naː* 'to get up'
    Reflexive Delinking: *utʰ-aː-naː* 'to cause to get up/lift'
    Adding causative subevent: *utʰ-waː-naː* 'to cause to be lifted/raised'

Since ingestives imply identity between agent and patient theta roles, they are also semantically capable of encoding reflexivity. Alexiodou and Schäfer (2014) call them natural reflexive verbs. In Masica (1993: 476) a further distinction has been drawn between the [-aː] marked intransitives like *utʰ-aː-naː*, that can mean 'cause to get up' (indirect causative) or 'to lift' (transitive); and the [-aː] marked semi-transitive 'ingestive' verbs such as *ɖekʰ-naː/ ɖikʰ-aː-naː* 'to see', *sun-naː/ sun-aː-naː* 'to hear', *kʰaː-naː/ kʰil-aː-naː* 'to eat' which form double transitives like *show*, *tell* and *feed* rather than indirect causatives with the [-aː] marking.

Bhatt and Embick (2017) refer to the [-aː] and [-waː] causatives as transitive/direct causative and indirect causatives respectively. This is because unlike [-aː] which is associated with a v[AG], [-waː] is associated consistently with a v[AG] that has a v[Applicative]P as its complement.

In addition, the transitive verbs can also have unaccusative forms which surface with √R₂ forms. For example, transitive *ka:ʈ-na:* 'to cut' corresponds to unaccusative *kəʈ-na:* 'to be cut'.

In this paper, we focus on the specific morphosyntactic steps which correspond to the phonological reduction from √R₁ to √R₂. Therefore, in the following sub-section (section 3.2) we discuss our approach to how the correspondence is established between phonological material from the lexicon and the syntactic structure followed by our proposed analysis of the morphosyntax in section 3.3.

3.1 The nature of Vocabulary Insertion in Hindi

Within the domain of generative linguistics, there are two major theoretical perspectives on the interface between the phonological material in the lexicon, and the computational system of narrow syntax, which are commonly referred to as the lexicalist and non-lexicalist approaches. The core distinction between these two approaches is with respect to when, what and how the lexical material is accessed by the syntactic module.

In the lexicalist model (Chomsky 1970, 1995) all the lexical information, including syntactic, semantic and phonological features, enters the syntactic module before the syntactic derivation begins. All concatenation operations of word-formation take place within the lexical module before these items enter the syntactic derivation. The phonological rules in a language are also divided into two types; lexical and post-lexical. The lexical rules apply within the lexicon in alternating cycles of morphology and phonology. Therefore, these rules are sensitive to the morphological domains and word-formation mechanisms of the language and take place pre-syntactically. Unlike them, the post-lexical rules are pure phonological rules that are sensitive to phonological material only, and apply post-syntactically at the PF (Phonetic Form) stage of grammatical derivation. Were we to use this framework of correspondence between morphosyntax and phonology, the phonological process of reduction described in section 2 would have to be located within the lexicon since it is sensitive to morphological context.

In the non-lexicalist, realizational model of grammar, the lexical access for the generative process is distributed across multiple points in the derivation, and each of these lexical access points is parameterized to access a particular kind of information that is relevant to that particular stage of the derivation. Consequently, it is also called Distributive Morphology (Marantz 1997). There are a number of theoretical variants of this model, but the particular version we use in our analysis is the idea of morpheme, root and vocabulary items following Embick (2015).

a. Lexical Model of Phonology-Morphology

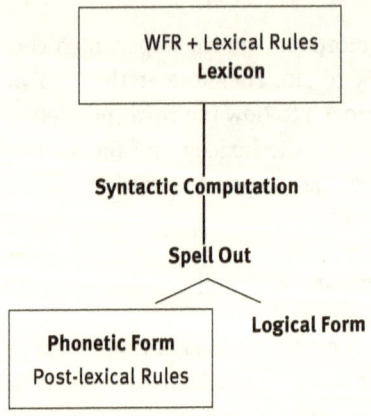

b. Distributive Morphology Model

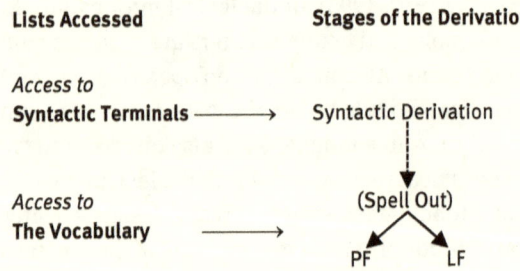

Fig. 3: (a) Lexical model of Phonology-Morphology; (b) Distributive Morphology Model (Embick 2015: 20)

In this model of grammar, there are two kinds of syntactic terminals: functional morphemes and roots. The roots are lexical material that enter the derivation at the beginning of the syntactic derivation. The roots contain no formal syntactic or semantic features, but include phonological features. For example, √k^{h}el 'play'. This is neither a noun or a verb but includes the string of speech sounds /k^h/, /e/ and /l/. Unlike roots, the functional morphemes contain only syntactic and semantic features (henceforth "synsem" features) like [+PAST] and no phonological features. Each root enters the syntactic derivation by merging with a functional morpheme and thus derives its syntactic category by virtue of the syntactic context into which it merges. Once the syntactic derivation is ready to be spelled out, there is a second retrieval of information from the lexicon.

At the point of Spell-Out, all the terminal nodes from the syntactic derivation which do not have any phonological material associated with them need to be valued with phonological content before entering the PF. Therefore, at this point lexical objects called Vocabulary Items are paired with synsem features on the syntactic terminals through an operation called Vocabulary Insertion. This post-syntactic addition of phonological material associated with inflectional morphology is called "late insertion", and is the reason this approach is referred to as a realizational approach to syntax.

With respect to a given syntactic structure with a number of synsem features, there will be a number of vocabulary insertion rules at Spell-Out. The Subset Principle, reproduced below, is one of the ways in which these vocabulary insertion rules are ordered with respect to each other.

(6) Subset Principle: The phonological exponent of a Vocabulary Item is inserted into a position if the item matches all or a subset of the features specified in the terminal morpheme. Insertion does not take place if the Vocabulary Item contains features not present in the morpheme. Where several Vocabulary Items meet the conditions for insertion, the item matching the greatest number of features specified in the terminal morpheme must be chosen. (Halle 1997: 128)[6]

---

[6] In Hindi, if we were to ignore phonological arguments that indicate that since the vR2 form is systematically predictable from vR₁, vR₂ should not be considered as a suppletive vocabulary item to be stored in the lexicon, we have a potential surface pattern of *ABA (Bobaljik 2012) in the NULL class.

Suppletive morphology in English   The context of allomorphy in Hindi
[went]↔√go + [past]   [kaːʈ]↔√kəʈ + v[AG] (intransitive to transitive)
[better]↔√good + [comp]

The now suppletive morpheme [kaːʈ] would form a better subset to the causative than the original root form [kəʈ]. So, by the subset principle, we would expect the causative form to surface as [kaːʈ-aː-naː], but it does not. It surfaces with an exponent which will be the equivalent of the universally non-attested *ABA principle that blocks exponence like good-better-goodest cross-linguistically (Bobaljik 2012). If we go by this analysis we get kəʈ-kaʈ-kəʈ-aː-na: for intransitive transitive-causative in Hindi. Clearly, this is not the case in Hindi because:
(a) Overwhelming phonological evidence that cannot be ignored points to the fact that no vR₁ form like [kaːʈ] should be considered as a suppletive morpheme;
(b) The pattern of alternation being the same in NULL class and AA-marked causatives/ transitives, there should not be unrelated, lexical exception based explanations for these;

In the following section, we present our proposal for the formal analysis of this morphology-phonology puzzle from Hindi.

3.2 Formal analysis of the syntactic context of reduction

Following Kratzer (1996) and Alexiadou (2014), we extend the basic event structure of the verb into three heads [Voice [Cause [v-Cat [Root]]]. A similar analysis of event structure where the cause argument is introduced by a Voice head has been used by Srishti (2011) in her analysis of Hindi causative constructions. Unlike her, since we are using the Distributed Morphology framework, the √ROOT morpheme enters the derivation by merging with a Categorizer. All Categorizers are cyclic heads.[7] A cyclic head is a head that triggers the Spell-Out of its complement domain. The Voice head is also such a cyclic head (Alexiadou 2014) because it acts as a boundary between the internal event structure and the external causation layer, which semantically constitutes another event. It has also been noted by Bhatt and Embick (2017), among others, that semantically the causatives constitute two events as opposed to transitives, which constitute a single event.

Based on the derivational mechanism, we divide the syntactic context for the phonological reduction of √R₁ to √R₂ into two types, namely, causatives and anti-causatives. By causative we mean constructions where irrespective of whether the verb is semantically a stative with an internal cause, or an eventive, the syntactic structure has a Cause head outside the syntactic structure of the basic event.

In the event structure of the causative verb, a category-less root merges with a v-categorizer to form a v, which projects to merge with the internal argument in transitives and unaccusatives. In case of a change of state predication, this v then forms the complement of a Cause head to form a CauseP, which is further selected

---

(c) The directionality of derivation from intransitive to transitive in the NULL class is clearly opposite of what cross-linguistically happens in the derivation of anti-causative and middle constructions from transitive ones.

We are grateful to an anonymous reviewer for pointing out that the phonological evidence is opposed to considering the verb root alternation pattern in NULL set as suppletive and therefore not a violation of *ABA.

7 Following Arad (2005) the specific meaning of a root is constituted through this merge of the root with the categorizer. For example, in Hindi when roots like √cʰaːp or √toɽ merge with a v-categorizer they are interpreted as transitive verbs with the meaning 'print' and 'break', and when the same roots merge with an n-categorizer, they become nouns with somewhat unpredictable meanings. In this case 'imprint' and 'solution'.

by a VoiceP. In case of an external causative construction, this VoiceP (which we will here onwards designate as Voice$_1$P) will be selected by a Cause$_2$ Head. This second Cause Head is further embedded within Voice$_2$P. As per our analysis of the relevant data from Hindi, this forms the maximal skeleton of the event structure of verbs.

Since the voice head is a cyclic head, the merge of Voice$_1$ head triggers the Spell-Out of its complement domain. This minimally includes the √ROOT and v-categorizer, but can also include other elements like the internal argument and Cause$_1$ head. The phonological form associated with this Spell-Out is always the √R$_1$ form, which is stored in the lexicon. Thus, the transitive, ingestive, unaccusative and unergative structure can all correspond to the √R^1 phonological form of roots.

The externalization of the complement of Voice$_2$ head forms the next cycle of Spell-Out operation. In this cycle, the Cause$_2$ head, which can be easily identified by the fact that it has a Voice P complement, is lexicalized by the following vocabulary insertion rule.

(7)   [a:] ↔ [$_{VoiceP}$[...]cause]]

The phonological form [a:] corresponds to a Cause head which has a VoiceP complement. There is also a phonological process of reduction associated with the Spell-Out of the Voice head.

(8)   [Phonological Reduction] ↔ [Voice]

This process reduces the spelled-out phonological form of the root spelled out in the preceding cycle to its corresponding R$_2$ form. We predict that, at this stage, since no encyclopedic semantics of the root is accessible, root-specific allomorphy is not possible. This prediction is borne out by the data from Hindi verbs that shows the phonological reduction associated with causatives to be exceptionless and operating with just the phonological information accessible after Spell-Out of the preceding cycle.

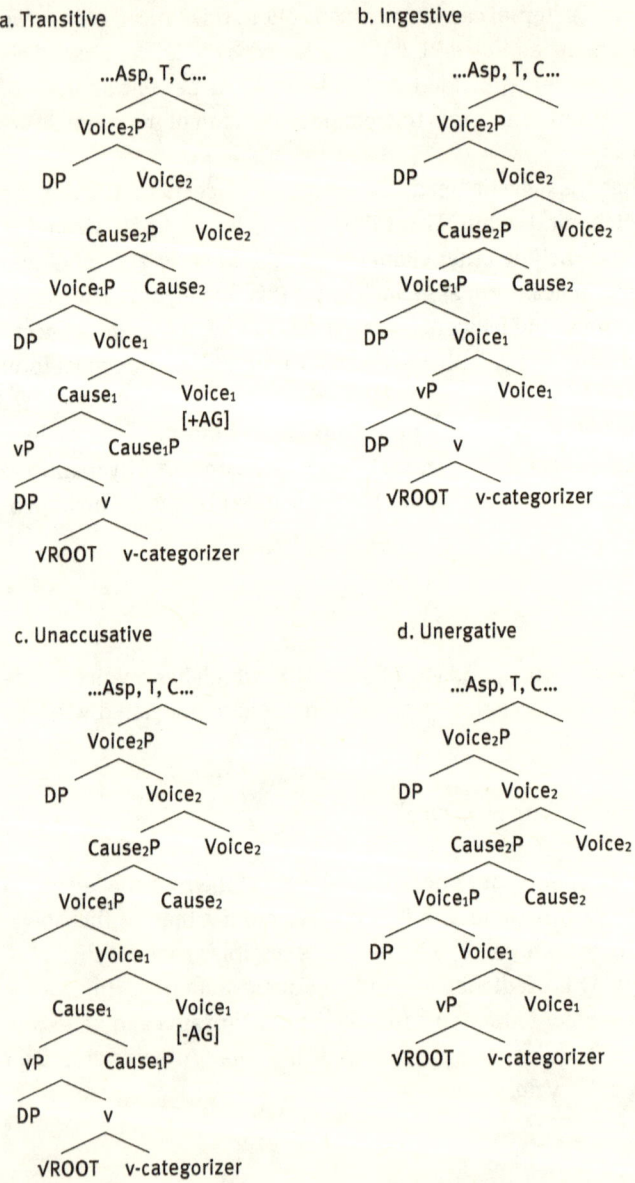

Fig. 4: Causative event structure of verbs

Anti-causatives (Alexiadou et al. 2006) are the intransitive counterparts of transitive verbs. These are similar to unaccusatives with respect to syntactic diagnostics. Bhatt and Embick (2017) designate these as unaccusative forms of transitive verbs and from our discussion in sections 3.1 and 3.2, we know that in Hindi these are homophonous with the √R₂ forms that appear in causatives. Our proposal is that similar to the case of Greek described in Alexiadou et al. (2006), in Hindi anti-causatives the [+AG] feature of the Voice head changes to [-AG] and as a result cannot license agentive arguments.[8]

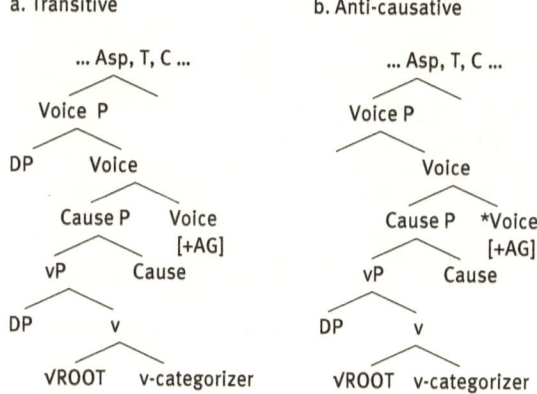

Fig. 5: Event structure of the transitives and anti-causatives

Notice that the structure of the anti-causative is identical to that of the unaccusative, except in one crucial aspect. The [-AG] feature on unaccusatives matches with the encyclopedic meaning of the verb, while in anti-causatives there is a mismatch. The encyclopedic meaning of these verbs corresponds to an internally or externally caused agent role, and the [-AG] feature on the Voice head makes this head syntactically defective. The consequence is that *Voice, unlike Voice,

---

[8] Also similar to the cases of Greek, German and English discussed in Alexiadou et al. (2006), we found that anti-causatives in Hindi can appear with a number of PPs though they cannot occur with the by phrase *dwa:ra:* used in passives. For example:
a. kʰiɾki: tu:ṭ gəji:
   window break.PFV
   'The window broke.'
b. həwa:=se/ tu:fa:n=mẽ kʰiɾki: tu:ṭ gəji:
   wind=instr/ storm=loc window break.PFV
   'The window broke in the storm/ due to wind.'
Since this is not directly relevant to the syntactic point we make in this paper, we are adding it as an additional observation about anti-causatives in Hindi.

is not able to function as a cyclic head, resulting in phase extension. Another morphosyntactic consequence of this syntactic structure is that *Voice, which is a non-cyclic head, can access the actual √ROOT morpheme which is in the same cyclic domain. This makes it syntactically possible for anti-causatives to have unpredictable root-specific suppletive morphology. This prediction is also borne out in Hindi where we find that some verb roots surface with irregular morphological exponents in the anti-causative.

Tab. 18: Irregular morphology in anti-causatives

Transitive	Irregular Anti-causative	Regular Causative
ṭoɽ-naː 'to break something'	ṭuːṭ-naː 'to break'	ṭuɽ-waː-naː 'to cause to break'
pʰaːɽ-naː 'to tear something'	pʰət-naː 'to tear'[9]	pʰaɽ-waː-naː 'to cause to tear'

For all the rest of the cases there is a vocabulary insertion rule (9b) that just allows phonological reduction whenever the complex [√ROOT-vCat-Cause-*Voice] is lexicalized together.

(9) Vocabulary insertion rules for anti-causatives in Hindi
 a. [ṭuːṭ] ⟷ [√ṭoɽ-vCat-Cause-*Voice]
  [pʰət] ⟷ [√pʰaɽ-vCat-Cause-*Voice]
  [cʰuːṭ] ⟷ [√cʰoɽ-vCat-Cause-*Voice]
  ...
 b. [Phonological Reduction] ⟷ [√ROOT-vCat-Cause-*Voice]

These rules are disjunctively ordered with respect to each other, with the more specific rules being ordered before the general ones.

4 Residual issues with Hindi root allomorphy

In this paper we have proposed a phonological analysis of vowel reduction in Hindi verbs in section 2, followed by a morphosyntactic analysis of the context

---

[9] Refer to footnote 4.

Hindi root allomorphy: Insights from phonological and morphosyntactic theory — 405

for the same in section 3. In this section, we will discuss and account for outliers to the phonological pattern of vowel reduction and theoretical predictions from the syntactic analysis of lexicalization of Voice head as the locus of phonological reduction.

4.1 Outliers to the pattern of Phonological reduction

While the pattern of phonological reduction analyzed by us in section 2 is consistent with most of the vocabulary, we also observed that there are two outliers to this phonological pattern. In the first case, the vowel hiatus context created by the addition of the inflectional [-aː] marker to CV verb roots is resolved by an epenthetic [l] which in turn has implications for vowel reduction. The second case pertains to high sonority peripheral long vowels that fail to undergo the expected reduction and have identical realizations for √R₁ and √R₂. In this section we briefly discuss these cases.

4.1.1 Hiatus resolution in CV roots

The phonological generalization of /aː/ in √R₁ reducing to /ə/ in √R₂ holds for all verbs in Hindi, except for CV roots containing /aː/. The vowel /aː/ in CV verb roots gets reduced to /i/, instead of the expected /ə/:

(10) kʰaː-naː: 'to eat' → *kʰə-waː-naː ~ **kʰil-aː-naː**: 'to cause to eat'

There is a systematic /-l/ insertion in the derivational context CV verb roots, when the following inflectional marker is a vowel. However while some words exhibit a glide insertion strategy to avoid potential vowel hiatus, others insert an epenthetic /-l/. In words with /-l/ insertion, the verb surfaces with /i/ in the √R₂ context in places where we expect a /ə/.

The choice of the epenthetic consonant that resolves vowel hiatus, and the effect that consonant has on the phonological reduction process in √R₂, are two processes related by separate factors. Since our focus is on the process that gets us the correct √R₂ form from the corresponding √R₁ form, we will ignore the case of [w] insertion since it is not an outlier to the vowel reduction process already analyzed. Then, we need to analyze why the sequence [il] is phonologically better than the sequence [əl]. Recall from our analysis in Table 12 that the central vowel /aː/ in √R₁ surfaced as /ə/ rather than /i/ in √R₂ because a) /ə/ being less sonorous than /i/ incurs one less violation of the stringency constraints, and b) /ə/ and /aː/

are on the same horizontal axis, while /i/ is not. Further, candidate (c) with /i/ was the second-best candidate in that table as well. So, for the second-best candidate to surface as the optimal one, the erstwhile optimal candidate (d) has to be blocked by the violation of at least one additional constraint.

Tab. 19: Transitive paradigm in Hindi CV verbs

√R₁ Vowels	√R₂ vowels
/a/ kʰaː-naː 'to eat'	kʰi-l-aː-naː 'to cause to eat'
/e/ ḍe-na: 'to give'	ḍi-l-aː-naː 'to cause to get'
/o/ so-naː 'to sleep'	su-l-aː-naː 'to cause to someone to sleep'
/iː/ piː-naː 'to drink'	pi-l-aː-naː 'to cause someone to drink'
/a/ gaː-naː 'to sing'	gə-waː-naː 'to cause someone to sing'

If we compare the surface phonological strings of [kəraːnaː] 'to make someone do', [cəlaːnaː] 'to make someone walk', and *[kʰəlaːnaː] / [kʰilaːnaː] 'to make someone eat', the ungrammaticality of *kʰəlaːnaː appears to be a puzzle. However, if we take into consideration the fact that all vowels except /ə/ can appear in word-final open syllables, the context becomes slightly clearer. The phonological reduction of √R₁ to √R₂ takes place independent of the phonological material associated with other synsem features.

Tab. 20: Blocking /aː/ to schwa reduction in CV roots

√kʰaː₁	*ə#	*√R₂ /aː, e,o, iː,uː,i,u, ə	*√R₂ /aː, e.o, iː,uː,i,u	*√R₂ /aː, e.o	*√R₂ /aː	*√R₂ / 2μ, 1μ	*√R₂ / 2μ	Ident F1-F2	Harmonic value
weights	3	1	1	1	1	1	1	1.1	
a. √kʰaː₂		-1	-1	-1	-1	-1	-1		-6
b. √kʰe₂		-1	-1	-1		-1		-1	-5.1
☞ c. √kʰi₂		-1	-1			-1		-1	-4.1
d. √kʰə₂	-1	-1				-1			-5

Another alternative explanation could be to analyze the low central vowel /aː/ in Hindi to be underspecified for the horizontal place of articulation. This would mean that whether /aː/ changes to /ə/ or /i/, in either case it will not incur any violation of IDENT F1-F2. The following revised evaluation tables present this analysis.

Tab. 21: Analysis as per Schwa Underspecification

√kʰaː₁	*ə#	*VR₂/aː, e.o, iː.uː.i.u, ə	*VR₂/aː, e.o, iː.uː.i.u	*VR₂/aː, e.o	*VR₂ /aː	*VR₂/ 2μ, 1μ	*VR₂ / Ident 2μ F1-F2	Harmonic value
Weights	1.1	1	1	1	1	1	1 1.1	
a. √kʰaː₂		-1	-1	-1	-1	-1	-1	-6
b. √kʰe₂		-1	-1	-1		-1	-1	-5.1
☞ c. √kʰi₂		-1	-1			-1		-3
d. √kʰə₂	-1	-1				-1		-3.1

Tab. 22: /aː/ to schwa reduction in CVC roots

√haːr₁	*ə#	*VR₂/aː, e.o, iː.uː.i.u, ə	*VR₂/aː, e.o, iː.uː.i.u	*VR₂/aː, e.o	*VR₂ /aː	*VR₂/ 2μ, 1μ	*VR₂ / Ident 2μ F1-F2	Harmonic value
weights	1.1	1	1	1	1	1	1 1.1	
a. √haːr₂		-1	-1	-1	-1	-1	-1	-6
b. √her₂		-1	-1	-1		-1	-1	-5.1
c. √hir₂		-1	-1			-1		-3
☞ d. √hər₂		-1				-1		-2

The contrast between the analysis in Table 21 and Table 22 is that there is marginal weight difference between the rest of the markedness constraints and *ə# in the latter. Further, Tables 21 and 22 clearly show why CVC verb roots with /aː/ reduce to /ə/ while CV verb roots with /aː/ reduce to /i/.

4.1.2 No reduction in Peripheral low vowels

The second phonological issue is with low peripheral vowels in Hindi, /ɔ/ and /ɛ/, which fail to reduce according to the usual process of "transitive alternation".

Tab. 23: Transitivization in mid-low vowels /ɔ/ and /ɛ/

ɖɔɽ-naː 'to run'	→	ɖɔɽ-aː-naː 'to make someone run'
pʰɛl-naː 'to spread'	→	pʰɛl-aː-naː 'to spread something'

Note that these vowels are always long and have an ambiguous status in the language with respect to a long monophthong or a diphthong. Phonetically, these vowels could either be pronounced as /ɔː/ and /ɛː/, or as the diphthongs /əu/ and /əe/. However, in this paper we are concerned primarily about their phonological representation in the minds of Hindi speakers and whether this blocking of reduction can tell us anything about that mental representation. If we start with the assumption that they are indeed /əu/ and /əe/ in the underlying representation, then both of them are diphthongs with rising sonority. Not having a homogenous character with respect to sonority can have the consequence of vacuously satisfying all the sonority-based stringency constraints that induce reduction. This will be true if the constraints incur a violation if and only if the segment occupied that same sonority position throughout the duration of the segment. The alternative would be to incur violations commensurate with both the sub-components of the diphthong. Table 24 and Table 25 compute the stringency constraint violations with respect to these conditions respectively.

Tab. 24: Blocking of vowel reduction in diphthongs

Vd̪əu[1	*ə#	*VR₂/aː, e.o, iː.uː.i.u, ə	*VR₂/aː, e.o, iː.uː.i.u	*VR₂/ aː, e.o	*VR₂/ aː	*VR₂/ 2μ, 1μ	*VR₂/ 2μ	Ident F1-F2	Harmonic value
Weights	1.1	1	1	1	1	1	1	1.1	
☞ a. Vd̪əu[2						-1	-1		-2
c. Vd̪u[2		-1	-1			-1		-1	-4.1
d. Vd̪ə[2		-1				-1		-1	-3.1

Tab. 25: Analysis with the sonority of diphthongs computed

Vd̪əu[1	*ə#	*VR₂/aː, e.o, iː.uː.i.u, ə	*VR₂/aː, e.o, iː.uː.i.u	*VR₂/ aː, e.o	*VR₂/ aː	*VR₂/ 2μ, 1μ	*VR₂/ 2μ	Ident F1-F2	Harmonic value
Weights	1.1	1	1	1	1	1	1	1.1	
a. Vd̪əu[2		-2	-1			-1	-1		-5
b. Vd̪u[2		-1	-1			-1		-1	-4.1
☞ c. Vd̪ə[2		-1				-1		-1	-3.1

The analysis in Table 24 reveals that since the diphthong vacuously satisfied the sonority-based stringency constraints, the optimal candidate for the phonological reduction in these cases is the same as the input candidate. In contrast, in

Table 25, the stringency constraints are assuming the two sub-parts of the diphthong as independent sonority units and computing their markedness separately. By doing so, Table 25 erroneously predicts candidate (c) with /ə/ as the optimal output candidate. Since the output candidate in Hindi matches candidate (a), it reveals that the sonority-based stringency constraints are vacuously satisfied in diphthongs as in the case of Table 24. This analysis also confirms that irrespective of phonetic and articulatory practices, native speakers of Hindi continue to phonologically process these vowels as complex segments of rising sonority.

4.2 Theoretical repercussions of the syntactic analysis

In section 3, we have proposed two vocabulary insertion rules in (9) that denote a correspondence between the phonological reduction process and the lexicalization of the Voice head at Spell-Out. Although there is a core syntactic difference between the two voice heads in our vocabulary insertion rules—namely, being a cyclic head or not being a cyclic head—it begs the further question of whether all Voice heads, in general, correspond to phonological reduction or whether it is context-specific. Based on the following two points of evidence, we suggest that the Voice↔Phonological Reduction correlation is a generalized PF rule in Hindi, and is blocked from applying in specific contexts.

4.2.1 Voice-T context in Hindi

Since the syntactic structure of all roots that merge into a syntactic derivation of event structure will contain a Voice head that will lexicalize in some cycle of the derivation, having a generalized rule of phonological reduction associated with Voice predicts that all roots that merge with a v-categorizer will only surface with √R_2 forms in PF. This is true for all cases except those where the Voice and T heads are in the same Spell-Out domain. Irrespective of whether it is a finite or non-finite T, if it is in the same cyclic domain as Voice, it blocks the process of phonological reduction associated with Voice. Therefore, we find √R_1 forms of the verb in finite clauses, non-finite relative clauses, and all such structures where no cyclic head intervenes between T and Voice.

(11a) Finite clauses with √R_1 form
  i. *ra:m səbzi   **ka:ʈ** rəha: hɛ*
     ram vegetable cut PROG be.PRS
     'Ram is cutting the vegetables.'

  ii.   ṭoṭa: əmru:ḍ **kha:** rəha: hɛ
     parrot   guava   eat   PROG   be.PRS
     'The parrot is eating a guava.'
  iii.   kəpɽe   **su:k^h** rəhe   hẽ
     cloth.PL   dry   PROG.PL   be.PRS
     'The clothes are drying.'

(11b) Non-finite clauses with √R$_1$ form
  i.   ra:m dwa:ra: **ka:ṭ-a:**   hua: a:m...
     ram by   cut-PTCP   be.PFV   mango
     'The mango cut by Ram...'
  ii.   ṭoṭe   dwa:ra: a:dha: **kha:-ja:** hua: əmru:d...
     parrot.OBL by   half   eat-PTCP   be.PFV   guava
     'The guava half-eaten by the parrot...'
  iii.   həma:re a:d^{h}e   **su:k^h-e** hue   kəpɽe...
     our   half   dry.OBL   be.PFV   cloth.PL
     'Our half-dried clothes...'

As has been noted earlier, the finite and non-finite constructions with anti-causatives are a special case where the vowel reduction rules are not blocked despite the *Voice and T being in the same cyclic domain.

(12a) Finite clauses with √R$_2$ form in anti-causatives:
   səbzia̰:   kəṭ rəhĩ: hẽ
   vegetable.PL   cut   PROG.PL   be.PRS
   'The vegetables are being cut.'

(12b) Non-finite clauses with √R$_2$ form in anti-causatives: B. Non-finite
   ra:m dwa:ra: kəṭ-i   hui   səbzia̰:...
   ram by   cut-PTCP   be.PFV   vegetable.PL
   'The vegetables cut by Ram...'

4.2.2 Deverbal nominals

Our morphosyntactic analysis of Voice as the locus for phonological reduction predicts that deverbal nominals, which are derived from roots that have already been categorized as verbs and contain the corresponding event structure, will always surface with √R$_2$ forms. This is because the n-categorizer is also a cyclic head that will trigger the Spell-Out of the Voice head. Further, it is also predicted that since the Voice and √ROOT are not in the same cyclic domain, there will be no irregular forms. These theoretical predictions are also borne out in Hindi.

Tab. 26: VR2 forms in the two kinds of deverbal nominals in Hindi

-a: Nominals		-ai Nominals	
cʰəp-a: 'printed'	gʰis-a: 'rubbed'	cʰəp-ai 'printing'	gʰis-ai 'rubbing'
kət-a: 'cut'	sil-a: 'sewn'	kət-ai 'cutting'	sil-ai 'sewing'
ləɾ-a: 'fought'	ḍikʰ-a: 'seen'	ləɾ-ai 'fight'	ḍikʰ-ai 'sight'
pis-a: 'crushed'	pəkɾ-a: 'caught'	pis-ai 'crushing'	pəkɾ-ai 'catching'
kʰĩc-a: 'pulled'	pəɾʰ-a: 'read'	kʰĩc-ai 'pulling'	pəɾʰ-ai 'reading'
piṭ-a: 'beaten'	sikʰ-a: 'learnt'	piṭ-ai 'beating'	sikʰ-ai 'learning'
bun-a: 'woven'	sun-a: 'heard'	bun-ai 'weaving'	sun-ai 'hearing'
bʰəɾ-a: 'filled'	likʰ-a: 'written'	bʰəɾ-ai 'filling'	likʰ-ai 'writing'

5 Conclusion

This paper has used the theoretical frameworks of Harmonic Grammar (Legendre, Sorace and Smolensky 2006; Pater 2009) and Distributed Morphology (Halle and Marantz 1993, Embick 2015) to analyze the process of verb root allomorphy in Hindi. Both these models allow for a comparison rubric where competing morphological or phonological objects from the language compete with each other to fit into the output representation. Each module of grammar can have different constraints, based on the nature of the entities whose well-formedness it is trying to compute. The object of the phonological grammar is to minimize markedness, and it will try to do that wherever it does not have the explicit requirement to maintain input-output correspondence in the encoding of lexical information. Our proposal shows that in the phonology-morphology interface of Hindi, this particular Faithfulness requirement is conditionally relaxed in the lexicalization of the Voice head. This results in an alternation between √R$_1$ and √R$_2$ forms of verb roots in Hindi.

Abbreviations and Transcription

The following abbreviations are used in glosses: PROG = progressive; F= feminine; PRS = present; ERG= ergative; PFV= perfective; PL= plural; SG=singular; PTCP= participle; OBL= oblique; M= masculine. Furthermore, the Hindi data is presented using IPA system of phonetic notation.

Acknowledgements

The syntactic analysis presented in this paper has undergone substantive revisions thanks to the comments and observations of anonymous reviewers. Paroma Sanyal is also grateful to Rajesh Bhatt for extensive discussions and insightful suggestions.

References

Alexiadou, Artemis, Elena Anagnostopoulou & Florian Schäfer. 2006. The properties of anticausatives crosslinguistically. In Mara Frascarelli (ed.), *Phases of interpretation*, 187–211. Berlin: Mouton de Gruyter.

Alexiadou, Artemis. 2014. Roots don't take complements. *Theoretical Linguistics* 40 (3-4). 287–297.

Alexiadou, Artemis & Florian Schäfer. 2014. Towards a Non-uniform Analysis of Naturally Reflexive Verbs. In Robert E. Santana-LaBarge (ed.), *Proceedings of the 31st West Coast Conference on Formal Linguistics*, 1–10. Somerville, MA: Cascadilla. [Proceedings Project. www.lingref.com, document #3001]

Arad, Maya. 2005. Word-level phases: evidence from Hebrew. *Perspectives On Phases, MIT Working Papers in Linguistics* 49. 29–47.

Bhatt, Rajesh & David Embick. 2017. Causative derivations in Hindi. *Indian Linguistics* 78 (1–2). 93–151.

Bobaljik, Jonathan David. 2012. *Universals in comparative morphology: Suppletion, superlatives, and the structure of words*. Cambridge, MA: MIT Press.

Boersma, Paul & Joe Pater. 2016. Convergence Properties of a Gradual Learning Algorithm for Harmonic Grammar. In John J. McCarthy & Joe Pater (eds.), *Harmonic Grammar and Harmonic Serialism*, 389–434. Sheffield, UK: Equinox.

Chomsky, Noam. 1970. Remarks on nominalization. In Roderick A. Jacobs & Peter S. Rosenbaum (eds.), *Readings in English Transformational Grammar*, 184–221. Waltham, MA: Ginn & Co.

Chomsky, Noam. 2014 [1995]. *The Minimalist Program*. [Current studies in linguistics series]. Cambridge, MA: MIT Press.

Clements, George N. 1990. The role of the sonority cycle in core syllabification. In John Beckman & Mary E. Beckman (eds.), *Papers in Laboratory Phonology I: Between the Grammar and Physics of Speech*, 283–325. Cambridge: Cambridge University Press.
Embick, David. 2015. *The morpheme: A theoretical introduction*. Boston & Berlin: de Gruyter Mouton.
Gordon, Matthew, Edita Ghushchyan, Bradley McDonnell, Daisy Rosenblum & Patricia A. Shaw. 2012. Sonority and central vowels: A cross-linguistic phonetic study. In Steve Parker (ed.), *The sonority controversy*, 219–256. Berlin: De Gruyter Mouton.
Halle, Morris. 1997. Impoverishment and fission. In Benjamin Bruening, Yoonjung Kang & Martha McGinnis (eds.), *Papers at the Interface. MIT Working Papers in Linguistics* (vol. 30), 425–449. MIT, Cambridge, MA.
Halle, Morris & Alec Marantz. 1993. Distributed morphology and the pieces of inflection. In Ken Hale & Samuel J. Keyser (eds.), *The View from Building 20*, 111–176. Cambridge, MA: MIT Press.
Hyman, Larry. 1984. *A theory of phonological weight*. Dordrecht: Foris Publications
Kager, René. 1999. *Optimality theory*. Cambridge: Cambridge University Press.
Koul, Omkar N. 2008. *Modern Hindi grammar*. Springfield, USA: Dunwoody Press.
Kratzer, Angelika. 1996. Severing the external argument from its verb. In Johan Rooryck & Laurie Zaring (eds.), *Phrase structure and the lexicon*, 109–137. Dordrecht: Springer.
De Lacy, Paul. 2004. Markedness Conflation in Optimality Theory. *Phonology* 21 (2). 145–199. www.jstor.org/stable/4615506. Accessed 30 June 2020.
Legendre, Géraldine, Yoshiro Miyata & Paul Smolensky. 1990. Harmonic Grammar – A formal multi-level connectionist theory of linguistic well-formedness: Theoretical foundations. In *Proceedings of the twelfth annual conference of the Cognitive Science Society*, 884–891. Cambridge, MA: Erlbaum.
Legendre, Géraldine, Antonella Sorace & Paul Smolensky. 2006. The optimality theory–harmonic grammar connection. In Géraldine Legendre, Antonella Sorace & Paul Smolensky (eds.), *The Harmonic Mind*, vol. 2, 339–402. Cambridge, MA: MIT Press.
Masica, Colin P. 1976. *Defining a linguistic area: South Asia*. Chicago: University of Chicago Press.
Masica, Colin P. 1991. *The Indo-Aryan Languages*. Cambridge: Cambridge University Press.
Marantz, Alec. 1997. No Escape from Syntax: Don't try Morphological Analysis in the Privacy of your own Lexicon. *University of Pennsylvania working papers in linguistics* 4 (2). 1–14.
McCarthy, John J. & Alan Prince. 1996. *Prosodic Morphology 1986*. Linguistics Department Faculty Publication Series. 13. Retrieved from https://scholarworks.umass.edu/linguist_faculty_pubs/13
Ohala, Manjari & John J. Ohala. 1992. Phonetic universals and Hindi segment duration. Paper presented at the *Second International Conference on Spoken Language Processing*, Banff, Alberta, Canada.
Ohala, Manjari. 1994. Hindi. Journal of the International Phonetic Association 24 (1). 35–38.
Pandey, Pramod. 1989. Word accentuation in Hindi. *Lingua* 77. 37–73.
Pater, Joe. 2009. Weighted Constraints in Generative Linguistics. *Cognitive science* 33 (6). 999–1035.
Prince, Alan & Paul Smolensky. 2002 [1993]. *Optimality theory: Constraint interaction in generative grammar*. Manuscript, Rutgers University and University of Colorado, Boulder. Retrieved from http://roa.rutgers.edu/files/537-0802/537-0802-PRINCE-0-0.PDF

Ramchand, Gillian. 2008. *Verb meaning and the lexicon: A first-phase syntax*. Vol. 116. Cambridge: Cambridge University Press.
Selkirk, Elisabeth O. 1984. On the Major Class Features and Syllable Theory. In Mark Aronoff & Richard T. Oerhle (eds.), *Language Sound Structure: Studies in Phonology Dedicated to Morris Halle by his Teacher and Students*, 107–113. Cambridge, MA: MIT Press.
Shapiro, Michael C. 2003. Hindi. In George Cardona & Dhanesh Jain (eds.), *The Indo-Aryan languages*, 276–315. New York: Routledge.
Sievers, Eduard. 1901. *Grundzüge der Phonetik: zur Einführung in das Studium der Lautlehre der indogermanischen Sprachen*. [Fundamentals of phonetics: An introduction to the study of phonetics in the Indo-European languages]. Vol. 1. Leipzig: Breitkopf & Härtel.
Srishti, Richa. 2011. *Hindi verb classes and their argument structure alternations*. Newcastle upon Tyne: Cambridge Scholars Publishing.
Steriade, Donca. 1982. *Greek prosodies and the nature of syllabification*. MIT doctoral dissertation.

Dinesh Ramoo, Cristina Romani, Andrew Olson
Lexeme and speech syllables in English and Hindi. A case for syllable structure

Abstract: Syllables are universal structures in articulation, but current speech production models disagree on whether syllables play a role only during the organization of phonemes during production or whether they play a more central role. Arguments against having syllables structure within the mental lexicon are resyllabification (phonemes moving from their lexical syllabic position to another syllable during connected speech, and the storage costs of having such information in the lexicon. This study used speech corpus analysis to quantify the resyllabification rates of English and Hindi as well as the storage costs of 3 prominent speech production models. The results show that English has a higher resyllabification rate than Italian or Hindi and that models that only use post-lexical syllabification actually have larger storage costs compared to models that store syllabic information. This indicates that having syllable structures within the mental lexicon might be a plausible scenario.

Keywords: Resyllabification, Information Theory, Speech Production

1 Introduction

Haugen (1956: 231) observed that: "the syllable has become something of a stepchild in linguistic description. While sooner or later everyone finds it convenient to use, no one does much about defining it". In the domain of the lexicon, the situation is even worse: the syllable is less of a stepchild than an exile. Linguists ban the syllable from lexical representation because it is a predictable unit, and lexical representations should include only those elements not predictable by more general grammatical principles (Chomsky and Halle 1968). Similar

---

Dinesh Ramoo, Thompson Rivers University, 805, TRU Way, Kamloops, BC V2C 0C8, Canada.
Email: dramoo@tru.ca
Cristina Romani, Aston University, Aston Street, Birmingham B4 7ET, UK.
Email: C.Romani@aston.ac.uk
Andrew Olson, University of Birmingham, School of Psychology, Edgbaston, B152TT, UK.
Email: a.c.olson@bham.ac.uk

https://doi.org/10.1515/9783110753066-016

reservations about the syllable can be seen in Gimson (1970), Steriade (1999), and Blevins (2003) as well.

Psycholinguists, too, have banished syllables from lexical representations. Phonemes are not linked to syllabic positions in the lexicon, it is argued, because the position a phoneme occupies can be reassigned within a phrase. The word-final coda, /k/, of *pick*, for example, becomes an onset in the phrase "pick over". Our intention here is to question this position and quantify the resyllabification costs which thus far have been a conjecture. We inquire as to whether storage of syllable structure linked to phonemes has advantages in terms of decreasing computational costs that offset the cost of storage as a whole.

We will not provide evidence that the syllable is part of lexical representations on empirical grounds, although highly detailed studies of errors made by Italian aphasic patients make this case strongly (Romani et al. 2011). Instead, we will evaluate the costs and benefits of including the syllable in lexical representations on computational grounds, and we will suggest a context in which it makes sense to think of the syllable as a critical grammatical unit that mediates between acoustically distinguishable sequences and a large content-addressable memory at input and between a content-addressable memory and rapidly evolving motor sequences at output.

Our argument will be that the syllable in lexical representations has clear advantages when considered in this context, and also that this context makes it clear that syllables are an abstract grammatical unit (that is, syllables provide the rules of combination for abstract phonemic sequences), not a unit that is an embodiment or restatement of more fundamental acoustic or articulatory dimensions (although, as an interface component, the syllable is formed, to some degree, in the crucible between the acoustic/articulatory demands of the periphery and addressing and storage demands of a mental dictionary).

2 The syllable

The syllable can be loosely defined as the smallest unit of articulation. While it is not contrastive, all speakers can distinguish it. The most basic evidence for the syllable in speech production is the fact that all speakers can easily distinguish and count the number of syllables in their own utterances (Ladefoged 1975). The need for the syllable as an indispensable unit in linguistics arises from the fact that many phonological generalizations are inconceivable without reference to it. Allophonic distribution in many languages is syllable-based and these phonological rules cannot be written economically as word-boundary conditions. The light /l/ and dark /ɫ/ in English are complementary, with the light /l/ occurring in onset and the dark /ɫ/ occurring in coda position. The aspiration of obstruents in a number of languages is also based on syllable boundaries. Syllable-initial obstruents are aspirated in English (Kahn 1976) and Kunjen (Sommer 1981) while syllable-final obstruents are aspirated in Yucatec Mayan (Straight 1976) and Sierra Popoluca (Elson 1947). Syllable-final obstruents are devoiced in German and Dutch. Here an underlying form such as /g/ or /d/ devoices to [k] and [t] when it is syllable-final (Vennemann 1968).

In addition to the linguistic evidence, there has been considerable evidence for syllables from psycholinguistic studies. These studies can be divided broadly between speech error analysis, chronometric data, frequency studies and language games. We will focus on speech errors and chronometric experiments as they are the major informants of the primary speech production models. Speech errors often – but not always – involve the movement or exchange of phonemes or phoneme sequences. Shattuck-Hufnagel (1983), Laubstein (1987), and Davis (1988) provide evidence from English speech errors to support the view of syllabic constituents. Davis (1988) in particular shows transpositions where syllable-initial segments, vowels and syllable-final segments exchange with their counterparts but it is extremely rare for syllable onsets and codas to exchange positions between each other (MacKay 1972; Motley 1973; Nootboom 1969; Shattuck-Hufnagel 1979). It is also interesting to note that segment sequences that cross syllable boundaries do not move together (Shattuck-Hufnagel 1983). Laubstein (1987) demonstrates, based on her investigations into naturally occurring speech errors, that while there was evidence for onset, peak and coda divisions, there was no evidence for the rhyme. Therefore, evidence for the internal structure of syllables is mostly derived from linguistic evidence. Meyer (1992) provides an extensive critique on the limitations of speech error analysis based on slips of the tongue (of normal speakers) stating that their movement errors should be contrasted with other errors arising from different levels of the speech mechanism. Aphasic patients, on the other hand, provide a better understanding of isolated errors as different brain lesions produce different errors.

To complement the evidence from speech error analysis, there has been an increase in chronometric experiments to find further evidence for the syllable in speech production. Compared to error analysis, which mostly deals with connected speech, these experiments focus on single word production. A number of studies have used priming in order to investigate whether syllables could be isolated as independent units. Priming studies have been conducted in a number of languages including Dutch (Baumann 1995), Mandarin Chinese (Chen et al. 2003), French (Brand, Rey and Peerman 2003; Ferrand, Segui and Grainger 1996) and English (Ferrand, Segui and Humphreys 1997). In these experiments, the orthographic form of the syllable is presented and masked before a picture or a word that may or may not share the first syllable. These studies did indeed find that congruent syllable primes lead to faster naming, with CV syllables being facilitated by CV syllables as opposed to CVC syllables. However, efforts to replicate these results in English (Schiller 2000), French (Brand et al. 2003), Spanish (Schiller, Costa, and Colomé 2002) and Dutch (Schiller 1998) have not been successful.

There has been more success with auditory priming in picture/word interference tasks (Costa and Sebastian-Galles 1998). In these experiments, the participants were required to name a picture while almost simultaneously (150 ms after the picture) hearing a word that did or did not share the first syllable with it. Costa and Sebastian-Galles (1998) found shorter reaction times when the word and picture shared the first syllable. In another study by Sevald, Dell and Cole (1995), participants were asked to repeat word pairs as often as possible within a four second period and it was found that the rate of speech was faster when the first syllables in the pair were structurally homologous. Interestingly, just having common segments did not especially facilitate the speech rate indicating that the syllable structure might be more abstract than just a phonotactic constraint on segments.

"Implicit priming" (introduced by Meyer 1990) also found positive results. Meyer (1990, 1991) had participants learn word pairs, requiring them to then reproduce the second word with the first being presented as a prompt. Words which were homogenous (i.e. shared a set of characteristics such as segments) were produced faster when they shared phonemes at the onset of the word. This suggests that the facilitation in naming stems from the ability to have part of the articulatory response prepared for the response. This paradigm was modified by Cholin, Schiller, and Levelt (2004) to study syllable structure. Their study used two sets of word pairs with one set sharing structure and content of the first syllable and the other sharing phonemes but not syllable structure in the first syllable. Their results show that both phonemes and syllable structure must be available for an efficient preparation of articulatory response. Many of these priming studies have not produced conclusive evidence for syllable priming effects but rather a segmental length effect. This may indicate that priming is not tapping into the required level of speech production to reveal syllable effects. It might also be the case that if only the structural information of syllables (as opposed to whole syllables) is stored, priming may not be able to produce significant effects.

The common assumption in many of the experimental designs has been to regard the syllable not as an abstract structure but as a phonotactic constraint which would affect the data selection. Studies that have tried to look at syllable structure have found more positive evidence suggesting that lexically represented syllable structure would be more consistent with the available data rather than articulatory representation. The overall economy that is claimed to be achieved by not storing syllables is efficient, but not at the expense of discarding the syllable altogether which actually requires more storage in the form of phonotactic constraints (which are themselves violated if not for syllabic information). While it is true that Occam's razor should be used in deciding on such matters, it must be borne in mind that it also stipulates that the application should be in the absence of contradictory evidence. As is clear from the literature, the evidence is far from conclusive in discarding the syllable.

Even though the importance of the syllable to various phonological rules is undeniable, it is notoriously difficult to get a phonetic definition of it. A common view was to define it in terms of prominence peaks (such as vowels). However, there are issues with syllable boundaries as can be seen in the violation of certain prominence peaks as in words like *extra* and *dogs*. However, most words in a language are open to unambiguous syllabification by native speakers. Theories of syllable structure often involve the assumption of a maximum syllable structure for each language. Generally speaking, these maximal consonants in a syllable are often only seen at word edges with word-medial syllables being rather simple as can be observed in English (Borowsky 1986), Greek (Steriade 1982), German (Giegerich 1989), Polish (Bethin 1992), and Georgian (Butskhrikidze 2002). Therefore, considerations of a maximal syllable structure often revolve around how to define word edges. Abercrombie (1967), Haugen (1956), Fudge (1969), Kahn (1976), Hammond (1999), and Blevins (2003) assume all consonants at word edges need to be part of the syllable so that *twelfths* would have a syllable structure of CCVCCCC. However, this does raise the issue of why word-medial syllables are simple. The argument that consonants cannot be pronounced without syllables is challenged by such utterances in English such as *shhh* [ʃ], and *psst* [pst]. However, if we consider these to be syllables, *twelfths* would be syllabified as [twɛ][lf][θs] which would not be accepted by speakers of English as syllables (consider also: *self*, *help*, and *serf*).

Selkirk (1982) gives an analysis whereby suffixes are not considered part of syllables yielding e.g. [twɛlfθ]s. Kiparsky (1981) provides an analysis that excludes coronals based on the observation that word-final consonants in English are often coronals. Other analyzes consider word-medial rhymes as maximal (Giegerich 1985; Borowsky 1986). All of these analyses face the issue of what to do with the extra consonants that are left over after syllabification. Duanmu (2009) proposes that these consonants can be accounted for by morphology.

However, this doesn't allow for words in English which have non-morphological complex clusters (e.g., *texts* [tɛksts]). These discussions show the difficulties faced by speech production models that attempt to formalize a method for accounting for psycholinguistics and linguistic evidence in trying to create formal rules for the organization of the syllable. This paper will take the assumption of the maximum onset principle as a foundation for syllabification as this is the avenue taken by the models discussed here. This principle states that a syllable's onset will take the maximum number of consonants allowed by a language's phonotactics leaving the rest to be part of the syllable coda. The [s] that appears in complex onsets in English would be assigned a special designation as a pre-marginal in this framework.

3 Segmental phonemes as the basis of phonological structure

Most models of language production assume that word-form representations are stored as segments rather than features or syllables (although the manner of storage and organization differs between models). Before we explore the various speech production models that will form the basis of this analysis, this assumption needs to be addressed. Are phonemic segments real components of phonological competence or historical by-products of alphabetic writing? Some researchers (Port 2007, 2010) have argued that segmental approaches to phonology correlate with cultures that have historically employed alphabetic writing. As this study is based on one language based on an alphabetic writing system (English) and another based on an alphasyllabic/abugida writing system (Hindi), this is an interesting issue to consider here.

The fundamental principle of analyzing speech as consisting of segments is based on the abstraction of the speech signal into minimally distinctive units. This principle also assumes that consonants and vowels are essentially the same type of unit. Firth (1936) challenged this view as erroneously integrating letters and sounds. He emphasized the vital role of syllables and other suprasegmental units (Firth 1948). He states that our seemingly intuitive sense of segments in speech is due to out familiarity with an alphabetic writing system. The fact that speech signals are continuous with limited means of identifying discrete segments has long been acknowledged (Liberman et al. 1967). The existence of allophones shows that the acoustic representations of segments identified as the same phoneme can vary depending on context. More recent challenges to segmental analysis of speech have been put forward by Günther (1986), Faber (1992), and Port (2006, 2007, 2010). Fowler, Shankweiler and Studdert-Kennedy's (2016) challenge that the widespread prevalence of alphabetic writing systems is evidence for the reality of segments is invalid as this is merely a historical accident. Indeed, the very fact that the independent emergence of writing systems often favor non-alphabetic systems of representation contests this view. Indeed, true alphabetic writing has only been invented once in history (Daniels 1992). Indian abugidas, graphemes that represent CV and V syllables, have often been used to argue that syllables are more natural than phonemes (Firth 1948).

The idea that Indian linguistics is essentially syllabic in its analysis has been challenged by Lowe (2020) with a linguistic analysis into Sanskrit. He provides extensive evidence from ancient Indian sources to show how a non-alphabetic and probably non-literate culture developed a segmental approach to phonology on linguistic grounds. He shows how the *varṇasamāmnāya* or inventory of sounds in Indian linguistics are vowel and consonant segments. The linguistic analysis of the sacred syllable *om* in the Aitareya Brāhmaṇa (5.32.2) defines it in terms of the segmental *varṇas* [a], [u] and [m] making these more fundamental than the syllable. This is also found in the Tamil grammar Tolkāppiyam which after defining vowels and consonants (1.1.4–9) explicitly mentions that consonants and vowels combine to form syllables (1.1.10). Unlike Sanskrit, which Lowe (2020) hypothesizes to have had a pre-literate linguistic tradition, the Tolkāppiyam is aware of the abugida writing system. However, it still employs a segmental analysis stating that consonantal graphemes without a vowel-nullifying dot (pulli) have an inherent [a] vowel attached to them (1.1.17). Lowe (2020) further states that the syllable has no significant role in the linguistic analysis of *Prātiśākhyas* (Vedic pronunciation manuals). He speculates that the necessity of analyzing initial and final segments in phonological processes such as sandhi rules helped Ancient Indian grammarians' awareness of segments.

The fact that 60–90% of all speech errors tend to be mono-segmental is given as psycholinguistic evidence for the existence of phonemes (Boomer and Laver 1968; Fromkin 1971; Nooteboom 1969; Shattuck-Hufnagel 1983). However, Stemberger (1983) and Shattuck-Hufnagel (1983) also note that 10–30% of all errors involve segment sequences, most of which are from the same syllable constituent. Berg (1989) also notes this characteristic in English and German where consonant clusters function as coherent units. Therefore, a speech production model must take into account the syllabic position of a segment in some form or another. Psycholinguistic evidence from Ziegler and Goswami (2005) shows that segment awareness appears to mostly derive from literacy of an alphabet. However, they also found that certain linguistic structures support awareness of phonemes even within the context of illiteracy.

Experimental evidence for segments comes from Roeloffs (1999) who used an implicit priming paradigm. Participants first learned a set of word pairs followed by a presentation of the first member of the pair as a prompt to produce the second member as quickly as possible. This basic test block was repeated as required. The blocks were either homogenous or heterogeneous with regard to phonological form. The homogeneous blocks either had shared onsets (e.g., all words beginning with /k/ or /g/), or segments differing only in voicing. In the heterogeneous blocks, initial segments contrasted voicing and place of articulation. The results indicated priming in homogeneous blocks when the targets shared an initial segment but not when all features but one were shared. This is evidence for the fact that whole phonological segments are being represented rather than distinctive features.

4 The syllable in speech production models

4.1 Dell model

Syllable position constraints from slip-of-the-tongue corpuses have been used by Dell (1986, 1988) and his collaborators (Foygel and Dell, 2000; Dell et al. 1997). Dell's model has a number of features which account for syllable position constraints following earlier models by Shattuck-Hufnagel (1979, 1983). Dell (1986) asserts that word-forms are represented in a lexical network. The network is composed of nodes that represent morphemes, segments and features. The nodes are connected by weighted bidirectional vertices. Figure 1 illustrates the representation of the word 'tiger' in the Dell model which can aid in understanding the following description.

During the process of phonological encoding, the morpheme node is activated. This activation spreads through the lexical network, with each individual node transmitting a proportion of its activation to its direct neighbor(s). A morpheme is mapped onto its relevant segments by selecting the segments or cluster nodes with the highest activation level. Therefore, speaking rate is an important factor in determining the time it takes to encode a syllable. The nodes that are selected are placed into slots of a syllable frame that is created independently.

The basic concept relies on syllable frameworks onto which phonemes are copied. However, the phonemes are distinguished according to syllable position so that those occurring in an onset are intrinsically different from those that can occur as coda. This accounts for allophonic distribution in many languages as well as syllable position constraints in speech errors. For example, in English, aspiration is found in onset-stops but not in coda-stops and there is a clear distinction between light and dark /l/ segments. Therefore, the system has to store two types of /l/ for onset /l/ and coda /ɫ/. Although a redundant solution to the problem of allophones, it has the advantage of distinguishing the order of phonemes within the syllable. The syllabic templates specific to word structure are linked to lexical nodes, which in turn are linked to phonological syllable nodes. The syllable nodes are linked to the corresponding phoneme.

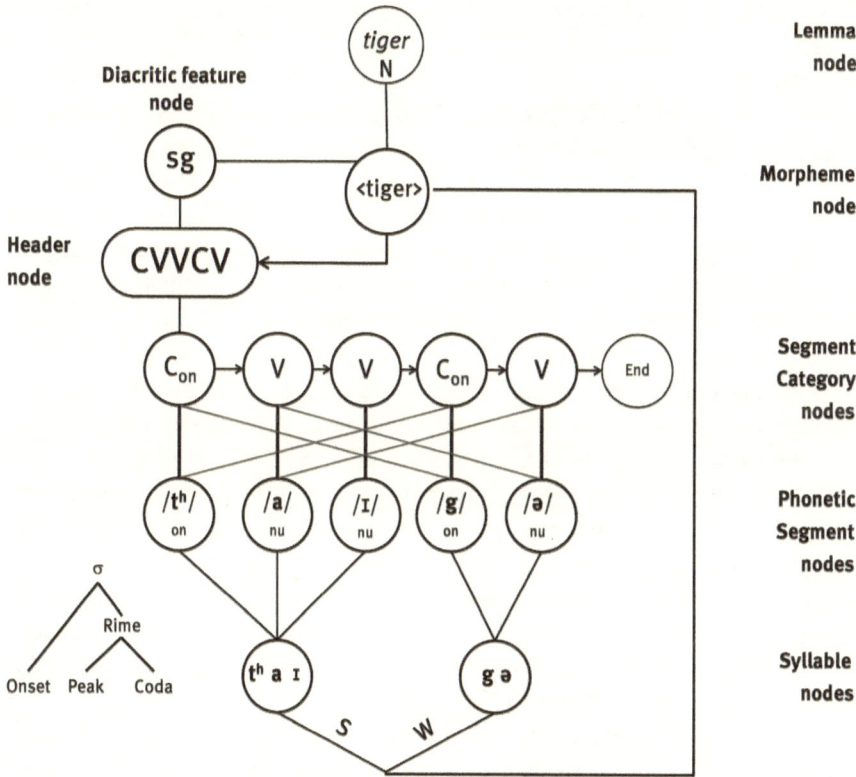

Fig. 1: Memory representation of the word form 'tiger' in the Dell model

The evidence from speech errors has been the most important data in informing this model as its most distinct feature is that phonemes are distinguished by syllable position (Dell 1986). The model ensures the preservation of the syllable

constraint as onset phonemes can only fit into their corresponding slot in the syllable template and the same is true for the peak and coda phonemes. It also implies that there is competition between phonemes of the same type to occupy their slots and explains tongue-twisters such as (a) and (b):
(a) "She sells sea shells by the seashore" ʃiː sɛlz siːʃɛlz baɪ ðiː siːʃɔː
(b) "Betty Botter bought a bit of butter" bɛtiː bɒtə bɔːt ə bɪt ɒv bʌtə

In the above examples, the errors made by speakers are assumed to be due to competition between phonologically similar segments that share the same syllable position. In the first example, this competition is between different onset phonemes while in the second example it is competition between segments competing for peak positions.

Dell (1988) proposes that each word is connected to a word-shape header node that contains the CV specification for the word-form. This node activates segment nodes such as onset consonant, vowel and coda consonant. This means that there is serial activation of segment category nodes instead of parallel activation. This accounts for the serial effects found through implicit priming studies (Meyer 1990, 1991). The model also accounts for a number of important empirical findings such as the influence of phonological similarity in semantic substitutions (Dell and Reich 1981), the tendency to produce real words rather than nonwords, the frequency distribution of anticipation-, perseveration- and transposition- errors (Nooteboom 1969) and the effects of speech-rate on errors (Dell 1986).

Semantic substitutions are seen as miscarriages in selecting lemma nodes. The word *mat* shares more segments with a target such as *hat* ($/æ/_{nu}$ and $/t/_{cd}$) than *cap* (only $/æ/_{nu}$). Therefore, the lemma node of *mat* will have a higher activation level than the lemma node of *cap* resulting in a likely opportunity for phonological word substitution error. The lemma node of *cap* shares semantic properties with *hat* and can also occur as a semantic word substitution error. The model accounts for lexical bias (i.e., the selection of words as opposed to nonwords) through feedback from phoneme to morpheme nodes (which exist for words but not for non-words).

According to Nooteboom (1969) anticipations are more likely than perseverations which are in turn more likely than transpositions. Anticipations involve the effect of a following segment before its original timed occurrence (e.g., *bed rock→red rock*) while perseverations involve the opposite (e.g., *bed rock→bed bock*). Transpositions on the other hand are pure exchange of segments (e.g., *bed rock→red bock*). The Dell model accounts for these differences in error type frequencies by having anticipation bias built into its architecture. Activation spreads through time so that upcoming words receive activation (albeit less than the current target). Transpositions occur the least because they involve both anticipation and perseveration. The effect of speech rate on errors is accounted for by the fact that activation is time-dependent. High speech rates mean that nodes may not have time to reach activation levels that are high enough making the system more vulnerable to speech errors.

Cutler (1981) brings into question the accuracy of the main evidence used in the Dell model: speech errors. Speech error data is influenced by biases in the perception of people listening for errors as well as the processes that produce errors made by speakers. It is suggested that the listener might misinterpret phonemes and that there is a bias towards locating errors at the beginning of words (accounting for a large percentage of onset errors). In addition, there is limited evidence for the existence of an abstract CV level in the mental lexicon. Speech errors do indicate a similarity of CV structure in the words involved. For instance, segment additions usually create clusters when the original word also had a cluster. However, the CV template similarities are not observed in all speech error corpora and CV similarities are found for onsets but not for nuclei.

The cost of storage and retrieval seems disproportionate to the economy of preserving syllabic information. Segments that can appear in numerous syllable positions (e.g., English light [l] in onset, dark [ɫ] in coda and syllabic [l̩] in nucleus) need to be stored more than once with each instance marked for different syllable positions. In addition, the different kinds of /l/ don't need to be stored because which type occurs is entirely predictable and these are not distinctive (i.e., used to distinguish words). It is also unclear why structural and segmental information is separated in the lexicon and combined each time a word is produced. The cost of storage seems disproportionate to the economy of preserving syllabic information. Instead of having a single phoneme /l/ and then predictable rules for how this is realized phonetically, the lexicon has to store three types of /l/ when the different types are never used to distinguish words. However, the apparent storage requirements of the Dell model need to be formally assessed and compared to those of other models.

The model also has difficulty with syllabification across morpheme and word boundaries (resyllabification). A segment in one morpheme or word may be syllabified with another morpheme or word during the production of polymorphic words or connected speech (e.g., Chomsky and Halle 1968; Selkirk 1984; Levelt 1989). Since the Dell model specifies segments according to their syllabic position, it has difficulty dealing with the need for flexible syllabification.

One of the major critics of the Dell model are Levelt (1989) and his collaborators (Meyer 1992; Roelofs 2000) who claim that reaction time is a more reliable indicator in gathering evidence for word production models.

4.2 Levelt, Roelofs, and Meyer (LRM) Model

One of the most complete models of speech production (from conceptualization through to articulation) is the one developed by Levelt, Roelofs and Meyer (1999) over a number of years. The model is based mostly on latency data from naming experiments. The LRM model is based on a top-down model in which information travels from more abstract levels to less abstract levels. While the model deals with all the levels involved in speech production, the main focus here will be on the lower levels where word-form encoding takes place. The Word-form Encoding by Activation and VERification (WEAVER) is the implementation of the LRM model developed by Roelof (1992, 1996, 1997a, 1997b, 1998, 1999) based on the theories of speech production put forth by Levelt (1989, 1992).

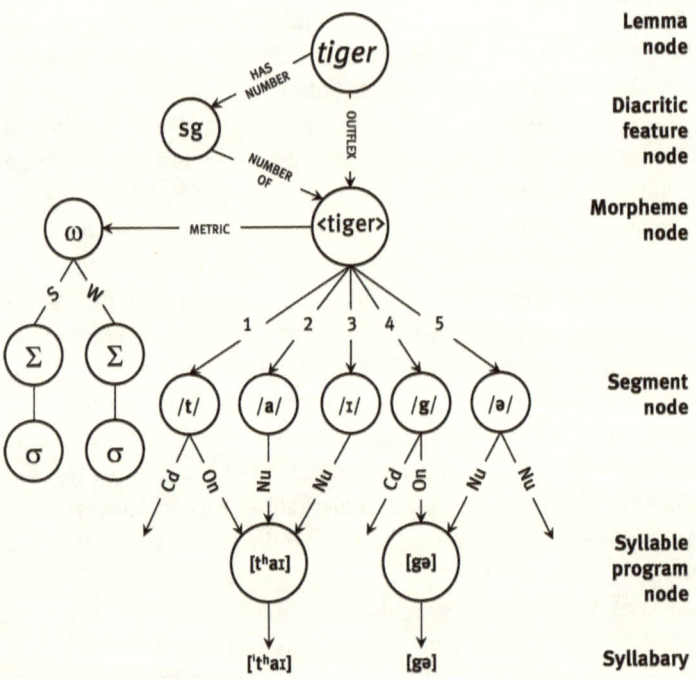

Fig. 2: Memory representation of the word form 'tiger' in the LRM Model

The model is inspired by Dell's (1986) hypothesis of word-form encoding via spreading activation and Levelt's (1992) articulatory syllabification with access to a mental syllabary (Levelt and Wheeldon 1994). It accounts for the evidence for syllable frequency effects and the ambiguous syllable priming data. So far, the model has had more success in reproducing syllable priming effects rather than frequency effects. Figure 2 shows the memory representation of the word *tiger* which can be used to understand the following descriptions. Syllabification in this model occurs when phonological information in the lexicon is associated with morpheme placeholders. The syllabification follows onset-maximization where the maximum number of consonants that can occur legally in an onset are syllabified with the following peak, provided they can occur word initially. If more than one word-form has been retrieved, word-final consonants may be resyllabified with word-initial vowels when permissible. From these processes, the output consists of a string of phonemes that are hierarchically structured into syllables and morphemes. The syllabic position of a segment is determined by the syllabification process; with every retrieved segment spreading activation to all the syllabic gestures in which it takes part. Then a "phonetic implementation" is required, where articulatory routines for each syllable are accessed from a mental syllabary. As storing all articulatory routines for all syllables would be not possible, the model needs another mechanism to compute less frequent syllables, storing only those that have high frequency. Separate mechanisms also exist to perform further modifications on loudness, pitch, and duration of the syllables.

Lexical information only includes phonemes and their order, with syllables necessary only to account for unusual stress patterns. For these stress patterns, lexical nodes are linked with prosodic nodes which provide the number of syllables and their stress. It is only at the time of output that full syllabification occurs where syllables are constructed from phonological segments. Articulatory syllables are made available based on their match with their phonological counterparts that are under construction. These are available based on frequency, with high frequency syllables being more readily available. However, this assumption seems to be essentially modular and its absence does not have a significant influence on the system's architecture.

The most prominent and radical feature in the LRM model is that, unlike Dell's model, syllable units or syllable templates have no place at the lexical level. Phonemes are defined only with regard to their serial position. However, like Dell's model syllables and phonemes merge at the articulatory level. The crucial difference is that during phonological encoding, segments are not assigned to syllable position, which is in contrast to Dell's model pre-syllabification of phonological codes. A prosodic template exists for words with unusual stress patterns. This template encodes the number of syllables in a phonological word and their relative stress assignment. But these prosodic nodes have no direct links to phonemes. One of the main arguments for not including syllable structure at an earlier stage in the LRM model is because of resyllabification. This refers to the phenomenon where phonemes in connected speech may be syllabified differently than in isolated words (e.g., *pick over* /pɪk/ /əʊ.və/ > [pʰɪ.kʰəʊ.və]).

Words need to be syllabified online for each production event as syllabification only occurs at the moment of output. These syllabified representations are then used to access a Mental Syllabary of articulatory motor programs. The thousands upon thousands of words in a language are made up of a smaller number of syllables. Less than 5% of the total number of syllables in languages such as English, Dutch and German are enough to produce almost 80% of all their speech (Schiller et al. 1996). The Mental Syllabary (which is essentially a store of syllabic motor programs) is a proposal made by Levelt and Wheeldon (1994) to account for the efficient and rapid production of these commonly occurring speech units. The correlation between syllable frequency and segment frequency in some of their experiments brings into question the evidence for syllable units and more controlled conditions in later experiments failed to show syllable or segment frequency effects (reported in Hendriks and McQueen 1996). In addition, the results can also be interpreted as of an influence of structural complexity as opposed to segmental information of syllable. The same output would be expected if syllable structures that are less complex were retrieved faster than more complex ones which correlate with syllable frequency. Alternatively, syllable structure links could be weighted according to frequency of use and may be strengthened or weakened accordingly.

4.3 Lexicon with syllable structure (LEWISS) Model

The LEWISS model is a new speech production model proposed by Romani et al. (2011) that attempts to explain linguistic and psycholinguistic data in terms of syllable structure. It organizes phonemes within a hierarchy of units based on syllable structure (see Figure 3). It bases this structure on the framework proposed by linguists such as Selkirk (1982), as well as Cairns and Feinstein (1982). Here the phonological segments are connected to syllable constituent nodes (i.e., onset, nucleus and coda), which are, in turn, connected to syllable nodes. The system computes the syllabification for words if a representation doesn't exist.

As the word is processed through the system in greater frequency, the weight between nodes for syllabic representation is strengthened until online syllabification becomes unnecessary. Phonological encoding in LEWISS involves retrieving the segments, as well as the word's structural information. This process is not a syllabification process because the syllable information is already stored. The LEWISS model does not store segments based on syllable position (like the Dell model), nor according to serial position (like the LRM model). The syllable structure provides the segments with their appropriate order within a word. In this sense, it has aspects from both the Dell and LRM models, but organizes the system in response to new empirical data.

The Standard Model for speech production acknowledges the need to include a metrical as well as segmental representation. The model also states that syllable-internal constituents are a part of this metrical representation (Meyer 2000). Starting with the most widely used psycholinguistic data: speech errors, it is evident that the elements that interact in errors are typically from the same syllable position: prevocalic onset, vocalic nucleus or postvocalic coda (Garrett 1975, 1980). This is also found in other languages such as Spanish (García-Albea, del Viso, and Igoa 1989) where 96% of all speech errors adhere to syllable position constraints.

It has been argued that while syllable-position constraints are evident in speech errors (Shattuck-Hufnagel 1983), it is also clear that more than 80% of all errors involve word onsets (Shattuck-Hufnagel 1987, 1992). This has been taken to argue that this phenomenon is simply a word onset effect rather than a syllable-position constraint (Wilshire 1998). However, the Spanish data (Garcia-Albea et al. 1989) contradicts this claim as there are more word-internal errors than word-initial ones.

Taking such evidence into account, Stemberger (1990) hypothesized structural frames for encoding the CV structure of words as proposed by autosegmental phonology (Clements and Keyser 1983; Goldsmith 1990). The analysis of German and Swedish speech errors was used to support the existence of a CV tier with length being specified by the number of C or V elements assigned to a segment (Stemberger 1984). However, English speech errors do not show evidence of an independent representation of length because English does not have geminates. Experimental evidence in Spanish comes from Costa and Sebastian-Gallés (1998) who used primed picture-naming. They found that picture-naming was facilitated by primes that shared their CV structure with the targets. Repeated pronunciation tasks in English also showed the effects of facilitation when CV structures were shared (Sevald, Dell and Cole 1995). While these studies support a CV structural representation, it is apparent that it alone cannot account for syllable-position constraints that divide CV representations with coda-onset boundaries. Therefore, models with CV representations such as Dell's model (Dell 1986, 1988) need to have segments marked for syllable position. LEWISS melds these concepts together to form a more efficient structural specification that can account for both syllable-position constraints and CV structural effects. While speech error studies involved accidental slips-of-the-tongue by normal speakers, a different source of obtaining large corpora of speech errors is by recording the speech errors made by aphasic patients. These speech errors are usually more consistent and could be used to infer the basic structure of the speech production system.

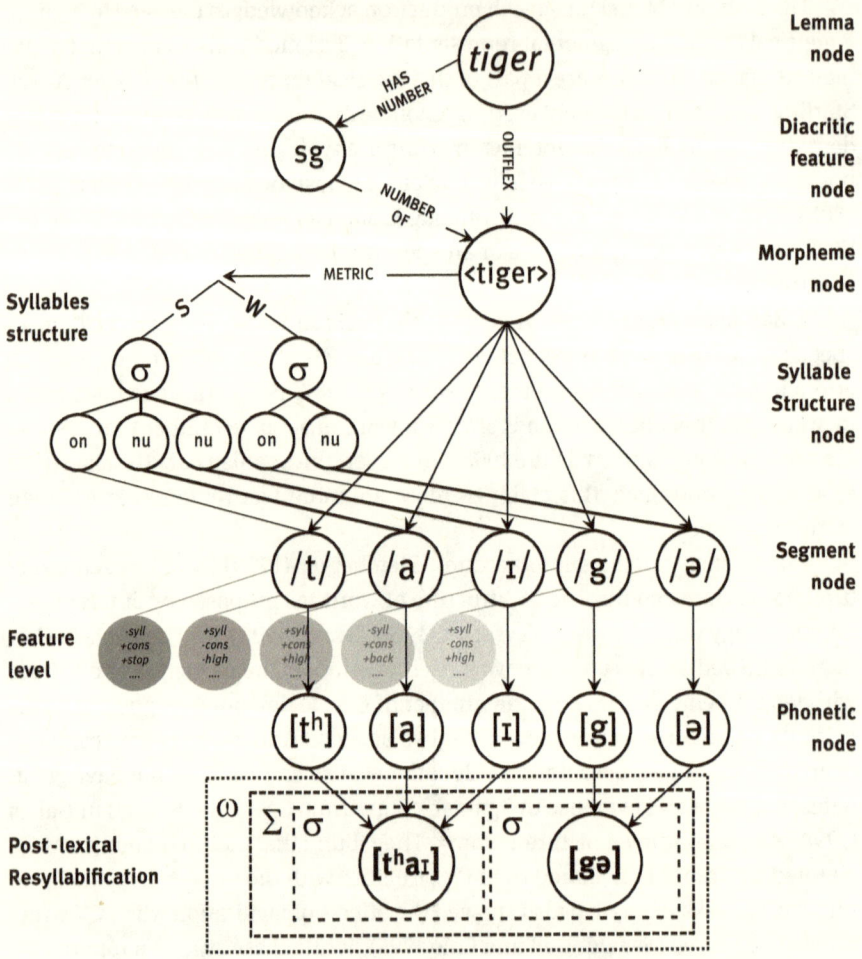

Fig. 3: Memory representation of the word-form 'tiger' in LEWISS

In a study done in Italian, Romani et al. (2011) showed that syllable structure has a strong influence in the speech errors of aphasic and apraxic patients. The patients performed repetition, reading and picture-naming tasks in Italian. Both sets of patients produced errors that targeted vulnerable syllable positions such as onset- or coda- satellites and pre-marginal position rather than onset- or coda-

cores and nuclei. This is consistent with a previous study by Den Ouden (2002). Den Ouden also found that among the speech errors, 95% of aphasic and 96% of apraxic errors preserved syllable structure, with most of the errors affecting the segments rather than the syllable structure of the target. This is also noted by other researchers (Wilshire, 2002). In a previous study of an apraxic patient, Romani and Calabrese (1996) found that geminates were more likely to be replaced by heterosyllabic rather than homosyllabic clusters (e.g., /dʒi.raf.fa/→/dʒi.rar.fa/ rather than /dʒi.ra.fra/). This data could also be explained by the Dell model as involving segments marked for syllable position. However, it was also found that segments could also move between syllable positions. This indicates that segments are abstract phonemes that don't include an intrinsic syllable position which would prevent these types of errors. All of this evidence has been used by Romani et al. (2011) to present a model that organizes words through abstract syllable structure. Given these three models and their varying representation of syllabic information, the question arises about which best accounts for observations of syllables and their behaviour in language production.

If language production is decomposed into its simplest parts, it can be roughly divided into storage, retrieval and computation. Human language production is efficient in that it is able to store, retrieve and compute phonemes, syllables, words and ultimately phrases at a rapid rate. This implies a high degree of efficiency. Two of the main arguments against lexical representation of syllabic information are that segments at word edges can be resyllabified during speech and the syllables are entirely predictable such that storing them would be redundant. The intention of this study is to question these two assumptions and provide a quantified value for the actual computational and storage costs of storing syllabic information. To that end, two languages: English and Hindi, were analyzed to see how resyllabification rates and information content varied cross-linguistically and how this impacts the assumptions of prominent psycholinguistic models of human speech production.

This study will not provide evidence that the syllable is part of lexical representations on empirical grounds, although recent, highly detailed studies of errors made by Italian aphasic patients make this case strongly (Romani et al. 2011). Instead, it will evaluate the costs and benefits of including the syllable in lexical representations on computational grounds, and will suggest a context in which it makes sense to think of the syllable as a critical grammatical unit that mediates between acoustically distinguishable sequences and a large content-addressable memory at input; and between a content-addressable memory and rapidly evolving motor sequences at output.

5 Resyllabification rates

Resyllabification is the reassignment of a syllable structure position that a phoneme undergoes during connected speech. The word final coda, /k/, of *pick*, for example, becomes an onset in the phrase "pick over" (/pɪk.əʊ.və/ → /pɪ.kəʊ.və/). This is a common phenomenon in English but the actual rate of resyllabification has been a conjecture. Here this assumption is put to the test to see if resyllabification is indeed as common as is assumed or whether it is a computationally bearable expense that is offset by other advantages in terms of storage and retrieval.

5.1 Method

5.1.1 Materials

As the analysis was conducted in two separate languages, two speech corpora had to be used as well as two syllabification algorithms. The materials for analysis for English were the Switchboard speech corpus (Godfrey et al. 1992) and the Moby dictionary. The switchboard corpus is a large multi-speaker database of telephone conversations collected at Texas Instruments. The corpus contains 2430 conversations with over 240 hours of recorded speech with over 3,000,000 words spoken by over 500 individual speakers in a variety of American dialects. As the processing consisted of characters rather than auditory segments, it was decided that the phonology and syllabification would be based on the Moby Dictionary with General American phonemes and syllabification rules. This analysis processed the first 1,000 conversations of the corpus.

For English, the dictionary was converted into an MS Access database file with two fields containing words and their phonological representation. As each word was read from the corpus, its phonological representation was retrieved from the dictionary for processing. If a word was not present in the dictionary, the program would prompt the user to enter the phonological representation which was then saved in the dictionary for future retrieval.

The process used for Hindi was slightly different due to the nature of the script and the lack of comprehensive lexicons in useable formats. The material used was from the EMILLE/CIIL corpus which contains transcriptions in a number of Indian languages. All transcriptions were in Unicode format, meaning that the Hindi text was in the Devanagari script. The Devanagari script is an abugida script with separate symbols for vowels but each consonant symbol has an inherent schwa. When vowels other than a schwa follow the consonants, they have diacritic marks added before, after, above or below it. Consonant clusters are created by melding together consonant symbols. While the script has a schwa-nullifier symbol (*virāma*) to delete the schwa (usually at the end of a word), this is not used in Modern Hindi as word-final and -medial schwa deletions are nor marked. A program was written in Java™ to convert the Unicode text into an ASCII based phonetic transcription with due regard to schwa deletion within and at the end of words. Then the words were processed in a similar manner to English.

5.1.2 Procedure

The resyllabification rate of each language (English and Hindi) was calculated from the above-mentioned material. Syllables can be reconstructed (computed) using language specific phonotactic information. The argument against storing syllabic information is that since resyllabification alters lexical syllabification, it is computationally more cost-effective to not store syllabified representations in the lexicon. Rather, it is considered less redundant to syllabify each output during production. If resyllabification is too high, then the cost of computing will indeed be too high and would invalidate the need to store syllabic information. If, on the other hand, resyllabification rates were low enough to be manageable, then the benefits of storing syllabic information offsets the relatively small computational cost of resyllabifying a relatively small number of word/morpheme boundaries.

Figures 4 and 5 illustrate a simplified representation of the steps involved in processing the speech corpora for English and Hindi. An algorithm was created in Java™ to read the speech corpus file and extract phrases that could be syllabified. Words in connected speech were considered to be those that were not broken by silences. As the speech corpus contained detailed timing information, it was possible to isolate each utterance. The syllabification algorithm that was created for this purpose was somewhat different from most of its predecessors. Each phoneme was assigned a particular object-oriented class that was a bundle of distinctive features. The distinctive features were represented as Boolean valued attributes (e.g., ±voice, ±front). The parent class of all the phonemes had methods to retrieve each attribute. The syllabification algorithm read the ASCII symbols into phoneme classes, inserted them into a matrix and then syllabified them according to phonotactic constraints and phonological rules. This allowed for the application of complex syllabification rules that were feature-based without overcomplicated and redundant coding. The main method of syllabification was onset-maximization. However, the algorithm also took into account the rules of stress attraction and syllables with primary stress did not allow their codas to be syllabified with the following syllable.

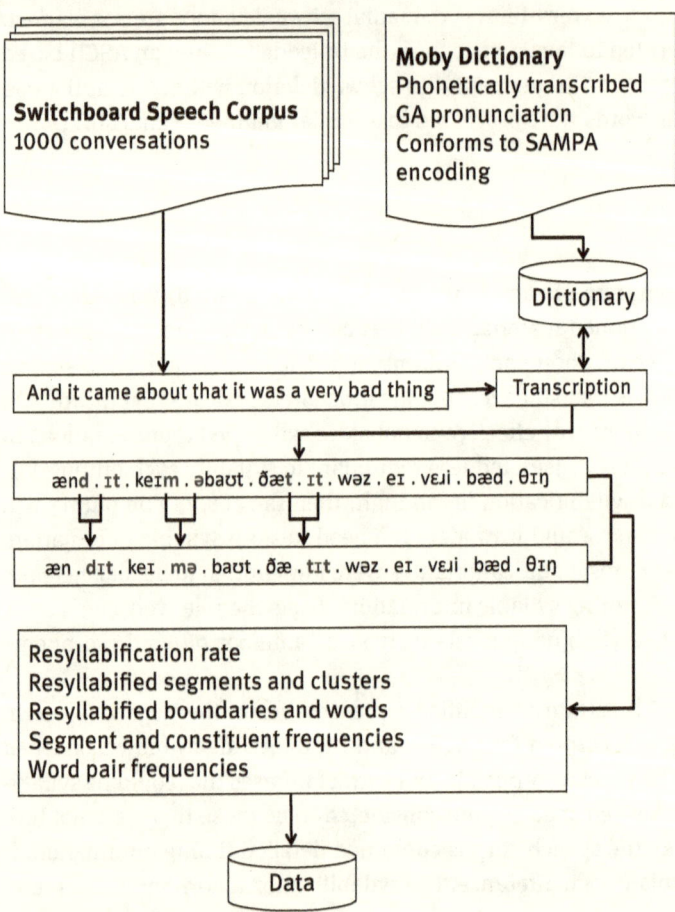

Fig. 4: Process for analyzing the English corpus

One of the major issues concerning the presence of syllable structure within the mental lexicon is the representation of morphemes. English has an abundance of morphemes and many of them are subject to resyllabification. However, it is unlikely that all words will be isolated from their morphemes in lexical representation.

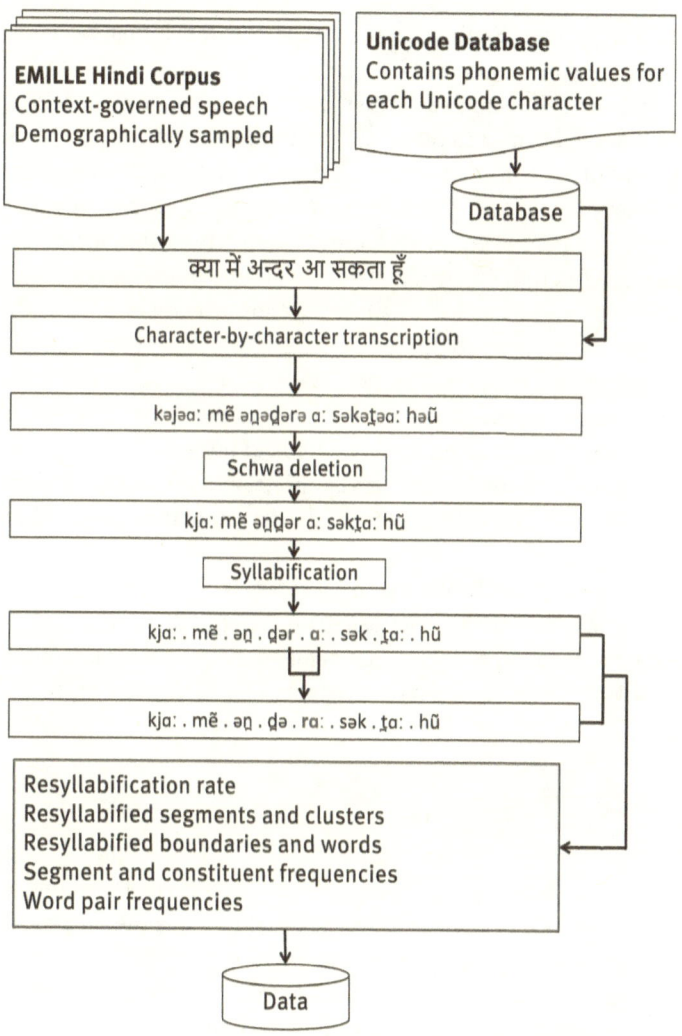

Fig. 5: Process for analyzing the Hindi corpus

It is to be expected that while the most frequent morphemes will be independent, the less frequent ones (while still being recognized as morphemes) will be part of the word's mental representation. For example, the word *governmental* could be linguistically parsed into three morphemes: *govern* (a free morpheme), *-ment* and *-al* (two bound morphemes). However, for all intents and purposes, one could safely assume that *government* would usually be stored as a single morpheme. The same is true for words such as *couth*, *shevelled*, *mayed*, and *plussed*, in that they are never used in modern English other than as negative forms: *uncouth*, *dishevelled*, *dismayed*, and *nonplussed* which can be safely assumed to be monomorphemic. To avoid erring too much on either side of the issue, it was decided to identify and resyllabify the most frequent morphemes, as listed in Ford, Davis and Marslen-Wilson (2010). The most frequent morphemes were: *-able*, *-ation*, *-er*, *-ful*, *-ish*, *-less*, *-ly*, *-ness*, *-ify*, *-ment*, *-ship* and *-ise*. After reading each phrase, the algorithm accessed the database to retrieve the phonetic transcriptions of the words or morphemes. After the phrase had been converted, the syllables at the word boundaries were combined and resyllabified according to onset-maximization. The resyllabified phrase was compared to the original phrase and if there was a difference, their characteristics (addition, deletion, etc.) and frequencies were recorded in another database. It will be evident from the above description that the resyllabification rate will be on the higher end of the scale. This was deliberate as erring on the side of the highest resyllabification rate possible in each language and will illustrate the maximum amount of computation required in each language.

While analyzing the resyllabification of utterances, the program also analyzed other linguistic variables within the lexical and speech utterances. These included the frequency of words, syllables, phonemes and syllable structures as well as any changes that existed between the original (lexical) utterances and resyllabified (speech) utterances.

5.2 Results

The analysis consisted of 1,000 conversations in English and 71 conversations in Hindi. The lower number in Hindi is due to the fact that this was the maximum number of spoken conversations in the corpus. The rest was from written sources. The resulting processing involved 811,458 words with 2,764,505 phonemes in English and 506,489 words and 1,899,093 phonemes in Hindi.

Figure 6 shows the distribution of place types in both languages as percentages of the total. We see that velar consonants are less frequent in both languages than labial and coronal consonants. Alveolar consonants are more frequent in English as this category includes the alveolar stops and nasals in this language. Hindi appears to show a more even distribution between labial, dental and alveolar consonants which are still more frequent than palatal and velar consonants.

Hindi has a retroflex place category which are consonants produced with the tongue rolled back. A surprising find is that while this place category is often seen as a typical feature of Indian languages such as Hindi, it is still less frequent than more frontal place categories. This indicates that there may be a markedness boundary between [-back], [+anterior] and [+back], [-anterior] phonemes in a language.

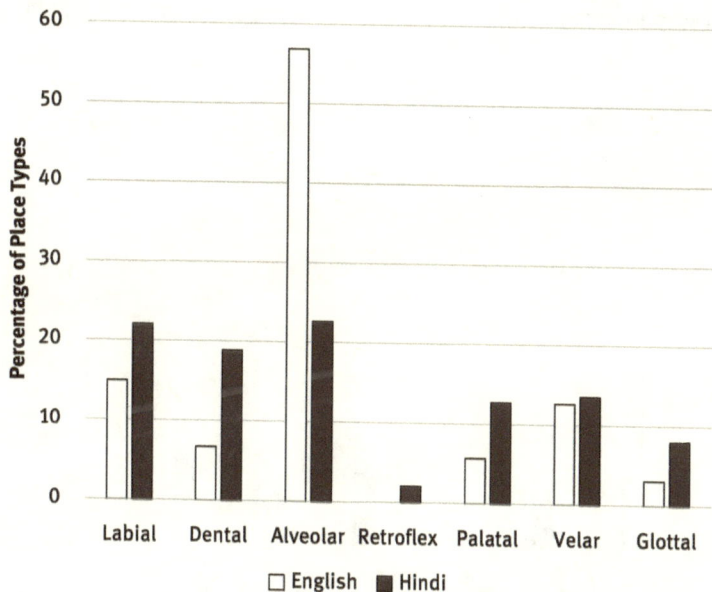

Fig. 6: Place type proportions in English and Hindi

Figure 7 shows the distribution of manner categories in both languages. Stops are most frequent in both languages, followed by fricatives and nasals. English has more fricatives than Hindi as it has labio-dental, dental, alveolar, post-alveolar and glottal fricatives whereas Hindi mostly has alveolar, post-alveolar, and glottal fricatives. Loan words from English and Persian have resulted in the labio-dental /f/ and alveolar /z/ as well as a minute number of velar fricatives /x/ and /ɣ/.

However, while these have modified Hindi graphemes that are evident in transcription, they are often assimilated into native phonemes by most speakers: /f/ → /pʰ/, /z/ → /dʒ/, and /x/ → /kʰ/. There is also a diglossia in terms of class as more educated speakers might use these phonemes more accurately in loan words. Such phonetic differences are not evident in transcribed speech. Differences were also observed in laryngeal features in both languages. The ratio between unvoiced and voiced consonants in was 35.3% and 64.7 % in English and 36.5% and 63.5% in Hindi. Voicing features in Hindi can also be divided based on the release of air. Unvoiced consonants are divided into aspirated and unaspirated phonemes. Aspirated phonemes accounted for 11% of unvoiced phonemes in Hindi compared to 89% of unaspirated consonants. This aspiration has a counterpart in voiced consonants as breathy voiced phonemes. These account for 1.7% of voiced phonemes in Hindi compared to 98.3% of normal voiced phonemes.

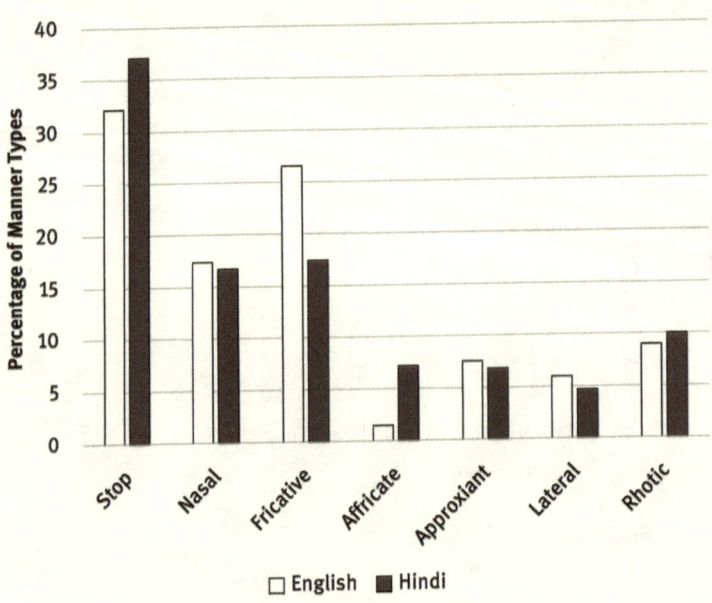

Fig. 7: Manner type proportions in English and Hindi

Table 1 shows a breakdown of the percentages of the frequencies across place and manner. This shows that while alveolar stops have a relatively high frequency in English, Hindi illustrated a more even distribution between labial, dental and velar stops. Similar patterns are discernable in nasals except that English and Hindi show similarities in velar nasals which are more often assimilated with the following velar stops in both languages.

Tab. 1: Percentage of phoneme types in English (ENG) and Hindi (HIN)

		Stops	Nasal	Fricative	Affricate	Appoximant	Lateral	Rhotic	Manner Total
Labial	ENG	5.43	4.37	5.15					14.96
	HIN	11.82	7.46	0.11		2.68			22.06
Dental	ENG			6.73					6.73
	HIN	11.22	7.64						18.86
Alveolar	ENG	20.23	11.00	10.74			5.96	8.92	56.86
	HIN			8.10			4.70	9.82	22.62
Retroflex	ENG								0.00
	HIN	1.67	0.22	0.02				0.18	2.09
Palatal	ENG			0.83	1.45	3.43			5.71
	HIN		0.35	1.09	7.17	4.15			12.76
Velar	ENG	6.53	2.02			4.10			12.66
	HIN	12.42	1.05	0.11					13.58
Glottal	ENG			3.08					3.08
	HIN			8.03					8.03
Place Total	ENG	32.20	17.40	26.54	1.45	7.53	5.96	8.92	
	HIN	37.12	37.12	17.47	7.17	6.82	4.70	10.00	

5.3 Resyllabification rate

The analysis of the resyllabification rate of these two languages provides us with some interesting insights into the costs and benefits of computing vs storing syllables for speech production. The CV structure of lexical and speech syllables varied due to resyllabification. As seen in Table 2 (Hindi) and Table 3 (English),[1] syllables in connected speech tend to be simpler than syllables in single words. The tables show the number and percentage of change from different syllable structures. Simplification of the lexical syllable structure in the corresponding speech syllable was 79.8% in English and 95.1% in Hindi. The majority of lexical syllables in Hindi were CV (32.6%), CVC (17.5%) and VC (10.3%) syllables. These percentages increased in speech syllables for CV (51.8%) and CVC (24.8%) syllables

---

[1] Structures with a lexical or speech frequency below 1,000 were removed from Table 3 (these resulted in the deletion of 4,954 items).

while remaining low for other structure types. The same is seen for English for CV (17.43%) and CVC (21.92%) lexical syllables. These increase in speech syllables in CV (24.94%), CVV (10.17%), and CVC (23.05%) structures. However, the relative distribution did not change, with CVC and CV syllables being the most frequent.

Of the total number of speech syllables 59.9% in Hindi and 50.41% in English were open syllables compared to open lexical syllables in Hindi (35.6%) and English (37.6%). The frequency of syllables can be highlighted with the Zipf-Mandelbrot law for linguistic systems. The essential statement of the law is that a small number of tokens would contribute to the majority of the distribution, while a large number of rare symbols create a long tail (Manning and Schütze 1999). This law is beautifully illustrated in the example of these two languages.

For English, the average percentage of the total number of syllables that were resyllabified was 33.8% (min 24.7%, max 39.4%). For Hindi it was 0.30% (min 0.27%, max 0.41%). Such a low rate of resyllabification indicates that storing syllable structure in the lexicon would not be computationally wasteful for Hindi since only a small amount of resyllabification is needed during production. Could these resyllabification rates also reflect other variables such as syllable frequency? To check this, we calculated the frequency of all the lexical and speech syllables and aligned them to see whether there was a change in the frequency of every syllable between the lexical representation and speech output.

There were 1,441 individual syllables from Hindi and 9,026 from English. As seen in Figure 8, English showed an almost equal percentage of syllables increased in frequency or remained the same frequency in speech as within the lexical representation. A higher percentage of syllables decreased in frequency in speech or were not found in lexical representation; only as speech syllables. The correlation between lexical and speech syllable frequencies in English was strong ($r=.862$, $p<.001$). Hindi had a large percentage (74.9%) which remained equally frequent in the lexicon as in speech with near equal increases and decreases. The correlation between lexical and speech syllable frequencies in Hindi was stronger than in English ($r=.978$, $p<.001$).

Tab. 2: Comparison between lexical and speech syllable frequency in Hindi

Outcome	Lexical Structure	Speech Structure	Change Frequency	
			Number	%
Simplification	CVC	CV	1074	35.9
	V	CV	176	5.9
	VC	CV	59	2.0
		CVC	460	15.4
		V	753	25.2
	VCC	CV	11	0.4
		CVC	1	0.0
		V	102	3.4
		VC	14	0.5
	CVCC	CV	27	0.9
		CVC	142	4.7
	CCVC	CCV	18	0.6
	CVCCC	CVCC	7	0.2
Complication	CV	CCV	46	1.5
	CVC	CCV	2	0.1
		CCVC	10	0.3
	V	CCV	12	0.4
	VC	CCV	7	0.2
		CCVC	42	1.4
	VCC	CVCC	23	0.8
	CVCC	CCVCC	3	0.1
	VCCC	CVCC	1	0.0
		CVCCC	1	0.0

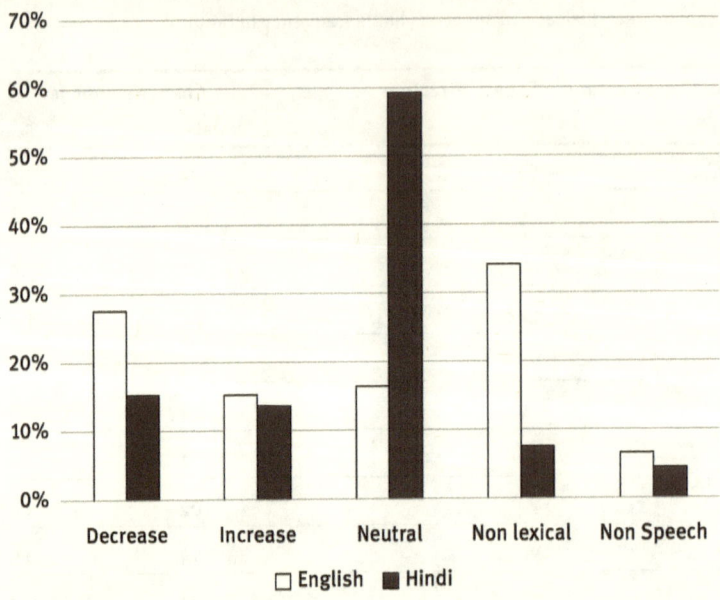

Fig. 8: Lexical and Speech Syllable Frequency Changes

In the distribution of resyllabified syllable pairs in English, 30% of all resyllabifications were produced by two pairs of syllables: *and uh* > 'an.duh' (21.3%) and *and it* > 'and.dit' (8.7%). The same is true for Hindi where the word for 'and' is /əuɾ/. The top two syllable pairs that together account for 28.75% of resyllabilifications were /əuɾ.əb/ and /əuɾ.ɪ/ in Hindi. The distribution was found to conform to Zipf's law: the frequency of these syllable pairs is a power-law distribution. This law holds for most natural languages and it has been proposed that it arises from the natural features of spoken language (Ferrer-i-Cancho and Solé, 2003). Neither participant in a conversation has a need to work harder than necessity dictates to reach understanding (a very high resyllabification rate might make it difficult for the listener to isolate word and morpheme boundaries). If resyllabification was not isolated to such a small set of syllable pairs, it would take much greater effort on the part of the listener in terms comprehension. Zipf's distribution is therefore the result of the distribution of effort.

Tab. 3: Comparison between lexical and speech syllable frequency in English

Outcome	Lexical Structure	Speech Structure	Change Frequency Number	%
Simplification	CVC	CV	63996	17.76
		V	909	0.25
	CVVC	CVV	11765	3.26
		VVC	343	0.10
		VV	143	0.04
	V	CV	13937	3.87
		VCCC	1	0.00
	VV	CVV	28881	8.01
	VC	CVC	58374	16.20
		V	18041	5.01
		CV	21199	5.88
	VVC	CVV	1677	0.47
		VV	2040	0.57
	VCC	VC	11122	3.09
		CVC	6698	1.86
		V	106	0.03
		CV	161	0.04
	VVCC	VVC	906	0.25
		CVVC	239	0.07
		VV	66	0.02
	CCV	V	202	0.06
	CCVC	CCV	8762	2.43
		VC	239	0.07
		V	151	0.04
	CCVCC	CCVC	1758	0.49
		VC	28	0.01
		CCV	48	0.01
		VCC	60	0.02

Outcome	Lexical Structure	Speech Structure	Change Frequency Number	%
Simplification	CCVV	CCCV	1	0.00
		VV	101	0.03
	CCVVC	CCVV	2257	0.63
		VV	31	0.01
		VVC	28	0.01
	CVCC	VC	191	0.05
		CVC	20891	5.80
		CV	2808	0.78
		VCC	357	0.10
		V	15	0.00
	CVCCC	CVC	150	0.04
		CVCC	2020	0.56
		VCCC	45	0.01
		CV	2	0.00
		VCC	7	0.00
		CCVC	3	0.00
	CVVCC	CVVC	4896	1.36
		CVV	492	0.14
		VVCC	74	0.02
		VVC	38	0.01
		VV	9	0.00
Neutral	V	CVC	8	0.00
Complication	CV	CCV	13415	3.72
		V	6770	1.88
		CVC	2483	0.69
		CVCC	36	0.01
		CCCV	42	0.01
		CCVCC	1	0.00
	CVV	VV	534	0.15
		CCVV	1492	0.41

Outcome	Lexical Structure	Speech Structure	Change Frequency	
			Number	%
Complication	CVC	CVVCC	47	0.01
		CVVC	253	0.07
		CCCVV	94	0.03
		CVCC	1985	0.55
		VC	2407	0.67
		CCVC	5174	1.44
		CVCCCC	4	0.00
		CCV	1846	0.51
		CCCVC	80	0.02
		CVCCC	190	0.05
		CCCV	22	0.01
		CVC	2	0.00
	CVVC	CVVCC	1813	0.50
		CCVC	1161	0.32
		CCVV	550	0.15
		CVVCCC	165	0.05
		CCCVC	21	0.01
		CCCVV	11	0.00
	V	CCV	346	0.10
		VC	104	0.03
		VCCCC	10	0.00
		CCCV	2	0.00
	VV	CCVV	532	0.15
		VVC	73	0.02
		CVVC	20	0.01
		VVCC	9	0.00
		CVVCC	4	0.00
	VC	CCVC	1838	0.51

Outcome	Lexical Structure	Speech Structure	Change Frequency	
			Number	%
Complication		CCV	544	0.15
		VCCC	142	0.04
		VCC	5322	1.48
		CVCCC	10	0.00
		VCCCC	44	0.01
		CVCC	57	0.02
		CVVC	4652	1.29
		VVCC	96	0.03
		CCVVC	61	0.02
	VVC	VVCCC	7	0.00
		CCVV	21	0.01
		VVCCCC	1	0.00
		CVVCC	3	0.00
		CVCC	12845	3.56
		CCVCC	199	0.06
		CCVC	70	0.02
	VCC	VCCC	100	0.03
		CCV	21	0.01
		VCCCC	15	0.00
		CVCCCC	6	0.00
		CVCCC	22	0.01
		CVVCC	316	0.09
	VVCC	CCVVCC	1	0.00
		CCVVC	1	0.00
	CCV	CCCV	444	0.12
		CCCVC	22	0.01
	CCVC	CCVCC	59	0.02
		CCVCCC	9	0.00

Outcome	Lexical Structure	Speech Structure	Change Frequency	
			Number	%
Complication	CCVCC	CCCV	9	0.00
		CCVCCC	236	0.07
		CCVCCCC	45	0.01
		CCCVCC	4	0.00
		CCCVC	1	0.00
	CCVV	CCCVV	16	0.00
	CCVVC	CCCVV	40	0.01
		CCCVVC	25	0.01
		CCVVCC	26	0.01
		CCVVCCC	2	0.00
	CVCC	CCVC	661	0.18
		CVCCC	904	0.25
		CCVCC	759	0.21
		CVCCCC	57	0.02
		CCV	20	0.01
		CCCVCC	7	0.00
		CCCVC	8	0.00
	CVCCC	CVCCCC	184	0.05
		CCVCC	68	0.02
		CCVCCC	73	0.02
		CVCCCCC	14	0.00
	CVVCC	CCVVC	333	0.09
		CCVV	12	0.00
		CCVVCC	91	0.03
		CVVCCC	88	0.02
		CVVCCCC	10	0.00
		CCCVVCC	5	0.00
		CCCVVC	5	0.00

5.4 Discussion

This part of the study analyzed the resyllabification rates of English and Hindi along with the distribution of phoneme and syllable types in these languages. The objective was to understand whether resyllabification was too high in these languages to sustain a model of language production that had syllabic information within the lexicon. The analysis showed that resyllabification in English is mostly a result of a high number of vowel-initial function words (e.g., *it*, *and*, *a*, *an*, *in*, *on*, *of*) whose equivalents in Hindi are usually not vowel-initial. Hindi appears to have a lower frequency of vowel-initial and high frequency function words. The above analysis makes it clear that it is not computationally uneconomical to have some syllabic information (such as syllable structure) within the lexicon as restructuring does not occur at a sufficiently high frequency to make it computationally wasteful.

6 Comparison of information content

The previous section showed how resyllabification concentrates on a small number of word edges and often in a limited set of lexical items. Resyllabifying these limited contexts would allow computational savings when compared to syllabifying all words each and every time they are produced. While storing syllable structure leads to computational savings, the trade-off is in storage costs. Storage of syllable structure necessitates another layer of information in addition to the phonemes of each word-form. How much more storage would be required? It is impossible to precisely estimate storage costs independent of a particular representational scheme, but one approach to this question is to quantify the minimal storage requirements under optimal conditions. One of the preferred methods of doing this is by calculating information entropy.

Since the inception of Information Theory by Shannon (1948), this branch of applied mathematics has broadened to a variety of fields including natural language processing and statistics. A key concept within Information Theory is "entropy". This is usually expressed as the average number of units (bits, nats, etc.) that are necessary for storage or transmission. The entropy of a discrete random variable is defined as the measure of the amount of uncertainty associated with it. If p is the probability mass function of a random variable X, then the entropy of X can be defined as:

$$H(X) = -\sum_{i=1}^{n} p(x_i) \log_b p(x_i)$$

where b is the base of the logarithm, the common values for which are 2 (for bits), e (for nats) and 10 (for dits). If applied to a simple example such as a coin toss, we can apply this equation for a fair coin to arrive at 1 bit as the information content. This means that in transmitting the outcomes of a coin toss, we need only 1 bit to store whether it is heads or tails and the uncertainty of the measure is equal to that.

While English is probably not a stationary ergodic process, it is still possible to arrive at an entropy rate. The earliest attempt to apply information theory in such a manner was by its founder. Shannon (1951) devised a guessing game in which he had human participants guess successive letters in a sample English text and arrived at the entropy of 1.3 bits per symbol (where the symbols consisted of 26 letters and a white space character). A later experiment (Cover and King 1978) using 12 subjects and a sample of 75 letters from the same source as Shannon (*Jefferson the Virginian* by Dumas Malone) arrived at an estimate of 1.34 bits per letter. All these experiments were conducted to study the entropy of written English.

The information content of written language has had much focus since the inception of Information Theory. However, the principles of Information Theory have rarely been applied in spoken outputs. Here we quantified the information content that is required for lexical storage in three different speech production models. The models we compared were Dell's spreading activation model (Dell 1986), the LRM model's serial phoneme representation (Levelt et al. 1999), and the LEWISS model with syllabic structure within the lexicon (Romani et al. 2011).

6.1 Method

The objective of this part of the project was to compare the storage costs of a model that stores syllable structure in the lexicon alongside established models that represent word forms using other methods. The English and Hindi corpora were analyzed to calculate the frequency distribution of various token types as they are defined within the lexicon. These frequency distributions were then used to calculate the entropy of each model.

The Dell model has phonemes differentiated according to their syllabic position. Therefore, the /p/ in *pit* would be an onset phoneme and is a different unit from the /p/ in *tap* which would be a coda phoneme. In exchange for storing the two phonemes separately, this representation allows a transparent account for syllable-initial aspiration and other syllable-based allophones. The tokens for this model were phonemes from onsets, peaks and codas.

The LRM model does not allow syllables to be located within the lexicon. This is justified as an economical way to deal with resyllabification. The word forms within the lexicon are connected to their phonological segments with their serial order encoded. Therefore, the tokens for this model were the frequency distributions of the individual segments in relation to their serial order in lexical words. This model also proposes the existence of a mental syllabary from which articulatory motor programs are retrieved. However, as lexical storage calculations involved the mental representation of word-forms as they are stored in the mental lexicon, the storage costs of a syllabary were not taken into account.

In the LEWISS model proposed by Romani et al. (2011), syllable structure is present within the mental lexicon. The tokens for this model were the structural and segmental information for each syllable. The structural information content was obtained by analyzing the frequency distribution of syllable-based onsets, peaks and codas, while the segmental information looked at the frequencies of individual phonemes (44 basic phonemes).

After the entropy rates of each of these scenarios were calculated, they were used to calculate the storage needs of all the monosyllabic words in a selected corpus. For English this was the CELEX dictionary (N=6,707). For Hindi (N=2,621), the list of monosyllabic words was derived from the EMILLE CIIL corpus analysis. A program written in Java™ isolated all the words consisting of a single syllable and applied the entropy rate to each segment and/or other lexical information (serial position, syllable structure, etc.). Monosyllabic words were used to gain a scaled comparison of the information requirements of the three models. A cursory glance of the information content required for a segmental or structural unit does not provide a good comparison. As the LEWISS model required storage of structural information (which varies from word to word), comparing only a few words is not sufficient. The overall information content of a fixed set of words defined according to some criteria (e.g., monosyllabic), provides a good comparison of information content across all three models.

6.2 Results

The CELEX dictionary consisted of 6,707 monosyllabic words. When compared together, the storage costs for the LRM model were considerably higher than the Dell or LEWISS models. Although the Dell model stores separate consonants for onset and coda positions, it saves storage costs by not having to specify where they connect to the word (since the consonants are marked for their position by nature). The LRM model needs to store the segments and their serial position, making for a higher storage cost. The LEWISS model comes between these two extremes. Phonemes do not need to be stored in separate copies that are specific to syllabic position, but another level of syllabic information (syllable structure) needs to be stored as well.

It must be noted that the bits that are mentioned here are not in any way meant to represent any unit of actual storage in the mental lexicon. Rather, it is a way in which to visualize and compare how storage needs contrast in terms of their information content and thereby deduce how they might apply in actual fact.

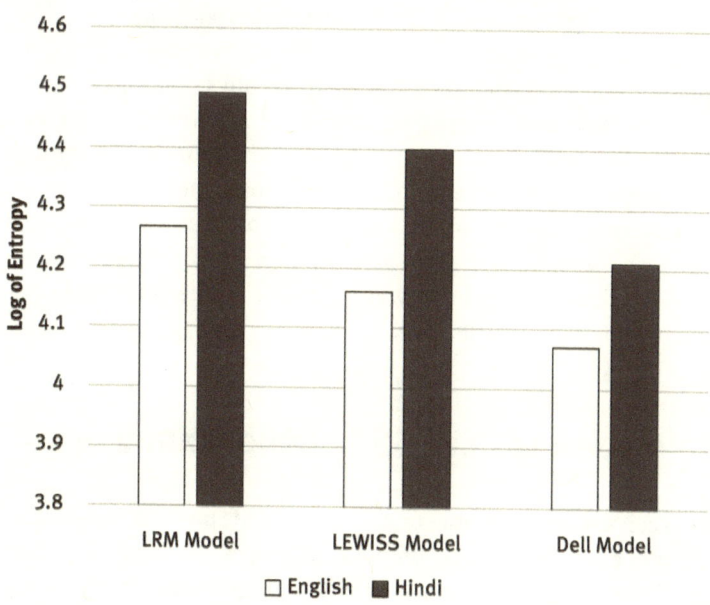

Fig. 9: Comparison between the Storage costs of different speech production models

6.3 Discussion

The results show that the entropy required for storing structural information within the lexicon comes between those for the LRM model and the Dell model. Intuitively, it might appear that the LRM model uses the least amount of storage as only phonemes are stored with no structural information or syllable frames. But the results show that overall, it requires more storage because the phonemes have no specification as to where they fit into a word other than serial position. The Dell model requires the least amount of storage because the units already have their syllabic positions intrinsically assigned to them. But they do not account for resyllabification and would require additional computational effort in order to change syllabic positions during resyllabification. Storing syllable structure requires less information than the LRM model as the structural information has been associated with the segments and does not require further computation. The only burden would be to resyllabify the word edges before output. However, as the segments do not have an intrinsic syllabic position (as in the Dell model), they can be resyllabified before phonetic transformation in a relatively less complex manner than in the Dell model. Roelofs (1997a) suggests a way Dell may be able to get away with some cross-morpheme syllabication for high frequency morphemes but the problem remains for low frequency morphemes.

The results are surprising in that while LRM purports to save storage by increasing computational costs, it appears to be costly in both storage *and* computational requirements. On the other hand, while it may appear that the Dell model is the most inefficient in terms of storage, the separation of phonemes according to syllable position saves overall storage costs as they do not need further information to link with a morpheme or word node. The compromise seems to be the LEWISS model, which comes between the two models by storing just enough information to specify syllable structure, while not requiring the storage of phonemes according to allophonic distribution.

7 The Application of LEWISS in Other Languages

While the LEWISS can explain a number of psycholinguistic phenomena, it must be noted that most of data comes from European languages. The languages that have been studied through this model (i.e., Italian, English and Hindi) are all Indo-European languages. A truly universal theory for speech production also has to be able to explain aspects of other languages. We have hitherto dealt with levels up to the phonological representations within the lexicon. But could stored syllable structure be an advantage for higher levels within the speech production system? What follows will be a speculation on how a completely different morphological system could be better explained though the LEWISS model.

An interesting feature that is rarely seen in European languages is nonconcatenative morphology. Most morphological modifications in languages such as English involve adding morphemes together. However, some morphological modifications involve modifying or adding segments in between the pre-existing root such as *foot→feet* in English and /mar-/ 'die' →/maːr-/ 'kill' in Hindi. While it is rare in English and Hindi, this kind of morphological modification is well developed in Semitic languages such as Hebrew and Arabic. The examples in Table 4 from Arabic illustrate this for the roots *s-l-m* and *k-t-b* (Wehr 1960).

Tab. 4: Morphological derivations of the roots s-l-m and k-t-b

Arabic	Meaning	Arabic	Meaning
(a) muslim	'person who submits'	(g) muktib	'literate person'
(b) salima	'he was safe'	(h) katiba	'he was reading'
(c) ʔislaːm(un)	'submission'	(i) ʔiktaːb(un)	'literature'
(d) salaːm(un)	'peace'	(j) kataːb(un)	'book'
(e) saːlim(un)	'safe'	(k) kaːtib(un)	'writing'
(f) salama	'he submitted'	(l) kataba	'he wrote'

This type of morphology represents an interesting challenge to how speech production models represent lexical items. The system has to be able to store the triconsonantal roots and be able to map them onto morphemes as required. LEWISS is able to accomplish this because the structural hierarchy can allow for segments to be mapped from the root.

In the example given in Figure 10 the word *islam(un)* is derived from the root *s-l-m*. As there is a syllable structural hierarchy, empty nodes can exist to be filled in by segments with the added advantage that each syllable constituent node only allows segments that are consistent with its position (consonants in onset and coda nodes, vowels in nucleus nodes).

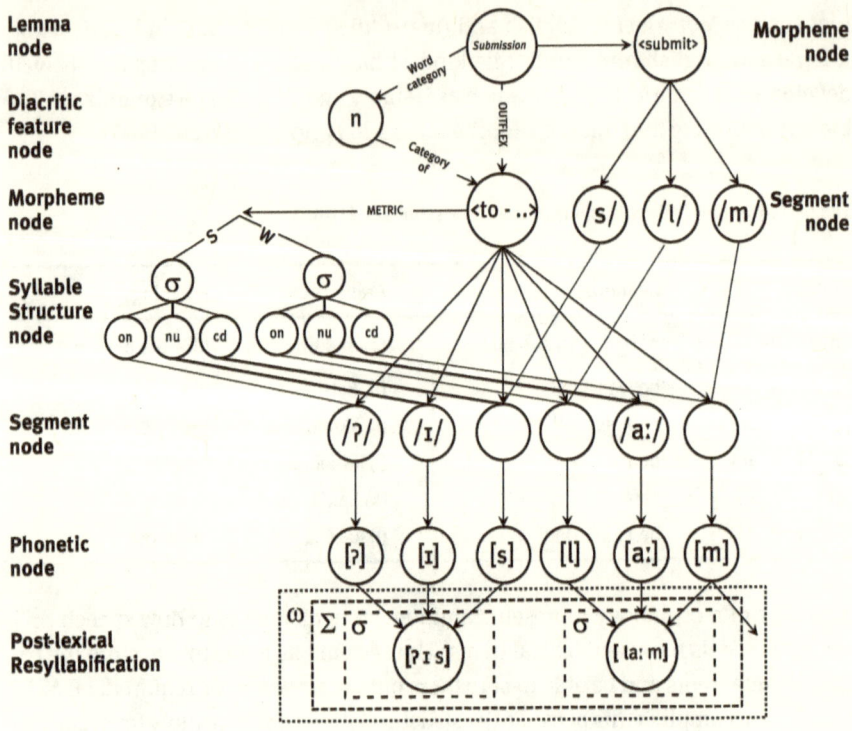

Fig. 10: Mental representation of the Arabic word for 'submission'

Models such as LRM which store phonemes according to serial position would find it difficult to impose such a system as any gaps in the serialized representation would muddle the order of the segments and the segments associated with the roots would have to have different serial positions for each morphological mapping (in effect violating the essence of nonconcatenative morphology). It could be argued that the LRM model could implement this kind of morphology by distinguishing between vowels and consonants as well as having blank serial positions (e.g., $m_1.u_2._3._4.i_5._6$ onto which k-t-b could be inserted). However, this model would have difficulty dealing with modifications that require gemination of a consonant. For example, /kut.ti.ba/, 'he was made to write' in Arabic (Wehr 1960) and /yik.kaː.teːb/, 'it is written' in Biblical Hebrew (Brown, Driver, and Briggs 1907). Here the same consonant which appears as a singleton in other morphological forms has to occupy two time slots. LEWISS can easily deal with such forms as the morpheme has to have a syllable structure with a single blank node connected to the coda position in the first syllable and the onset position in the second syllable. Storing syllable structure allows LEWISS to account for the gemination of certain consonants in morphological forms.

The Dell model can actually deal with nonconcatenative morphology with more success because it has the header node to indicate CV structures onto which the system can map segments. However, it would have issues in dealing with the triconsonantal roots interleaving into morphological structures leading to resyllabification. Segment would either be syllable onsets or codas depending on the segments within the morphemes. There is also phrase-final apocope which results in some word-final structures being dropped (*ʔislaːm(un)*> *ʔislaːm* at the end of a phrase) leading to resyllabification of /m/ from onset to coda. These changes would be difficult for the Dell model to handle with segments coded for syllable position.

The above account was just a single example of how the LEWISS model is able to take on the challenges posed by different language systems not just at the phonological and phonetic level (as discussed in this thesis) but also at other levels such as morphology. More evidence needs to be collected from such languages that may support this view.

8 Discussion

This article estimates the costs and benefits of a lexical representation of syllable structure in relationship to current models of speech production (Dell and LRM) and a more recent model where syllable structure is part of lexical representation. Costs were quantified in relationship to the actual rate of resyllabification in speech corpora and the lexical storage costs as estimated by information theory. The predictability of syllable boundaries using language-specific phonotactics has been used as a justification for not storing syllabic information within the mental lexicon. However, as empirical evidence from patients with acquired language disorders suggests, syllable structure is preserved by patients' segment errors even when this is not strictly necessary for phonotactic reasons (Romani et al. 2011). This makes a meaningful estimate of the true cost of lexical storage necessary and requires an estimate that takes into account properties of languages with different characteristics.

The first study looked at resyllabification and quantified the actual resyllabification rate of connected speech in English and Hindi. There is often at least some diglossia in many languages and the written variety (especially if taken from standard publications) is not reflective of its everyday use. Actual speech often contains speech disfluencies such as *uh* or *um* that are omitted in written forms and which might potentially resyllabify. Therefore, this analysis of speech transcriptions will perhaps encourage others to quantify spoken speech corpora in other languages.

The results show that, on average, 33.8% of syllables in a conversation are resyllabified in English while less than 1% were resyllabified in Hindi. While the resyllabification rate for English can be considered relatively high, this was mostly isolated to a small number of high-frequency syllables. Therefore, the potential storage savings from resyllabification are quite high. This picture could change in the context of other languages and their syllable typology. Many agglutinative languages would be intuitively expected to have a higher resyllabification rate. However, we must be careful in making such generalizations as some languages (e.g., Japanese) have a majority of CV syllables and may have a very low resyllabification rate (Itô and Mester 1995). As Japanese is mora-timed as opposed to stress-timed, syllabification will not be affected by stress assignment. Other languages (e.g., Telugu) almost always have word-final vowels and may therefore only resyllabify occasionally. The study of Dravidian languages might be interesting in this context as the spoken variety tends to encourage word-final vowels while simultaneously having an unusually large number of function words and morphemes that are vowel-initial (Zvelebil 1990). The implications of cross-linguistic differences in resyllabification might shed light on how syllable structure is represented cross-linguistically. The main point is that the major speech production models that are in current circulation are based primarily on European and particularly Germanic languages. While some of them provide a good understanding of speech production within their domain, there is a need for a larger sample from other languages. A good final estimate should take into account a range of languages with different properties, to avoid drawing a conclusion based on one language (English) that holds much less strongly for languages with different properties (assuming that this is a fixed property across languages and not subject to parametric variation).

The next study focused on the information content of various syllabic representations within the context of different speech production models. Storing syllable structure may lead to computational benefits, but the trade-off might be an inordinate increase in storage costs. The hierarchical structure that needs to be stored on top of the basic phonemic sequence adds to the capacity required by lexical representations, but by how much? Representations that are not syllabified require that the phonemic segments are stored along with their serial order. This is a minimal requirement. Since the phonemic content of words will be common to all accounts, this analysis (initially, at least) takes this to be a constant. The question is how much information is required to store the serial sequence in comparison to what is required by a hierarchical syllabic representation where the order of some positions is predictable based on grammatical principles. The analysis showed that this additional storage is relatively modest even when phonological content is attached to nodes at the bottom of a hierarchy. If phonological content is distributed over the hierarchy (as would be the case for feature-geometric accounts), all syllable-based representations were, in fact, less costly than representations without syllable structure.

The results showed that there was substantial savings for storing syllable structure as opposed to serialized phonemes (as in the LRM model). We also considered the advantages that stored syllable structure provides, over a serial representation of phonemes, for languages where consonant and vowel classes are associated with roots and inflections. Stored syllables structure naturally accommodates word-formation in these languages (e.g., Clements and Keyser 1983), but serial phonemes do not.

Our analysis showed the pitfalls of assuming costs of processes such as resyllabification and lexical storage without a formal analysis. More analysis may be required along the lines we have proposed here, but quantification is necessary, along with other evidence, to establish the proper place of syllable structure within speech production. The results show that when taken together, the resyllabification rate and the information content of storing syllable structure has substantial savings. While this is by no means a replacement for experimental data, it can be taken as a guide for future psycholinguistic experiments that can bring us closer to an accurate (and perhaps universal) speech production model. It is also hoped that this work will encourage psycholinguists (as well as provide them with some initial data) to conduct analyses of connected speech corpora. These are less often studied, but still a vitally important source of psycholinguistic evidence for models of speech production.

References

Abercrombie, David. 1967. *Elements of General Phonetics*. Chicago: Aldine publishing Company.
Baumann, Monika. 1995. *The production of syllables in connected speech*. Cambridge, MA: Massachusetts Institute of Technology doctoral dissertation.
Bethin, Christina Y. 1992. *Polish Syllables: The Role of Prosody in Phonology and Morphology*. Columbus, OH: Slavica.
Blevins, Juliette. 2003. *Evolutionary Phonology: The Emergence of Sound Patterns*. Cambridge: Cambridge University Press.

Borowsky, Toni J. 1986. *Topics in the lexical phonology of English*. Amherst, MA: University of Massachusetts Doctoral dissertation.

Brand, Muriele, Arnaud Rey & Ronald Peerman. 2003. Where is the syllable priming effect in visual word recognition? *Journal of Memory and Language* 48. 435–443.

Brown, Francis, Samuel R. Driver & Charles A. Briggs. 1907. *A Hebrew and English lexicon of the Old Testament*. Oxford: Clarendon Press.

Butskhrikidze, Marika. 2002. *The consonant phonotactics of Georgian*. Leiden, The Netherlands: University of Leiden doctoral dissertation.

Cairns, Charles E. & Mark H. Feinstein. 1982. Markedness and the theory of syllable structure. *Linguistic Inquiry* 13. 193–226.

Chen, Jenn-Yeu, Wei-Chun Lin & Ludovic Ferrand. 2003. Masked priming of the syllable in Mandarin Chinese speech production. *Chinese Journal of Psychology* 45. 107–120.

Cholin, Joana, Niels O. Shiller & Willem J. M. Levelt. 2004. The preparation of syllables in speech production. *Journal of Memory and Language* 50. 47–61.

Chomsky, Noam & Morris Halle. 1968. *The Sound Pattern of English*. New York: Harper and Row.

Clements, George N. & Samuel J. Keyser. 1983. *CV phonology*. [Linguistic Inquiries Monograph Series, No.9]. Cambridge, MA: MIT Press.

Costa, Albert & Nuria Sebastian-Gallés. 1998. Abstract phonological structure in language production: Evidence from Spanish. *Journal of Experimental Psychology: Learning, Memory and Cognition* 24. 886–903.

Cutler, Anne. 1981. Making up materials is a confounded nuisance, or: Will we be able to run any psycholinguistic experiments at all in 1990? *Cognition* 10. 65–70.

Daniels, Peter T. 1992. The syllabic origin of writing and the segmental origin of the alphabet. In Pamela A. Downing, Susan D. Lima & Michael Noonan (eds.), *The Linguistics of Literacy*, 83–110. Amsterdam & Philadelphia: John Benjamins Publishing Company.

Davis, Stuart. 1988. *Topics in syllable geometry*. New York: Garland.

Dell, Gary S. 1986. A spreading-activation theory of retrieval in speech production. *Psychological Review* 93. 283–321.

Dell, Gary S. 1988. The retrieval of phonological forms in production: Tests of predictions from a connectionist model. *Journal of Memory and Language* 27. 124–142.

Dell, Gary S. & Peter A. Reich. 1981. Stages in sentence production: An analysis of speech error data. *Journal of Verbal Learning and Verbal Behavior* 20 (6). 611–629.

Dell, Gary S., Myrna F. Schwartz, Nadine Martin, Eleanor M. Saffran & Deborah A. Gagnon. 1997. Lexical access in aphasic and nonaphasic speakers. *Psychological Review* 104 (4). 801–838.

Den Ouden, Dirk-Bart. 2002. *Phonology in aphasia: syllables and segments in level-specific deficits*. Groningen, The Netherlands: Groningen University doctoral dissertation.

Duanmu, San. 2009. *Syllable Structure: The Limits of Variation*. Oxford: Oxford University Press.

Elson, Ben. 1947. Sierra Popoluca syllable structure. *International Journal of American Linguistics* 13. 13–17.

Faber, Alice. 1992. Phonemic segmentation as epiphenomenon: Evidence from the history of alphabetic writing. In Pamela A. Downing, Susan D. Lima & Michael Noonan (eds.), *The Linguistics of Literacy*, 111–34. Amsterdam & Philadelphia: John Benjamins Publishing Company.

Ferrand, Ludovic, Juan Segui & Glyn W. Humphreys. 1997. The syllable's role in word naming. *Memory and Cognition* 25. 458–470.

Ferrand, Ludovic, Juan Segui & Jonathan Grainger. 1996. Masked priming of words and picture naming: The role of syllable units. *Journal of Memory and Language* 35. 708–723.

Ferrer-i-Cancho, Ramon & Richard V. Solé. 2003. Least effort and the origins of scaling in human language. *Proceedings of the National Academy of Sciences* USA, 100. 788–791.

Firth, John R. 1936. Alphabets and phonology in India and Burma. *Bulletin of the school of Oriental and African studies* 8 (2–3). 517–546.

Firth, John R. 1948. Sounds and prosodies. *Transactions of the Philological Society* 47 (1). 127–152.

Fowler, Carol A., Donald Shankweiler & Michael Studdert-Kennedy. 2016. Perception of the speech code' revisited: Speech is alphabetic after all. *Psychological Review* 123 (2). 125–150.

Foygel, Dan. & Gary S. Dell. 2000. Models of impaired lexical access in speech production. *Journal of Memory and Language* 43. 182–216.

Fudge, Erik C. 1969. Syllables. *Journal of Linguistics* 5. 253–286.

García-Albea, José E., Susana del Viso & José M. Igoa. 1989. Movement errors and levels of processing in sentence production. *Journal of Psycholinguistic Research* 18. 145–161.

Garrett, Merrill F. 1975. The analysis of sentence production. In Gordon H. Bower (ed.), *Psychology of Learning and Motivation* [Advances in Research and Theory Volume 9], 133–175. New York: Academy Press.

Garrett, Merrill F. 1980. Levels of processing in sentence production. In Brian Butterworth (ed.), *Language production: Vol. 1. Speech and talk*, 177–210. New York: Academic Press.

Geigerich, Heinz. 1985. *Metrical Phonology and Phonological Structure: German and English*. Cambridge: Cambridge University Press.

Geigerich, Heinz. 1989. *Syllable Structure and Lexical Derivation in German*. Bloomington: Indiana University Linguistics Club.

Gimson, Alfred C. 1970 [1962]. *An Introduction to the Pronunciation of English*, 2nd edn. London: Edward Arnold.

Godfrey, John J., Edward C. Holliman & Jane McDaniel. 1992. SWITCHBOARD: telephone speech corpus for research and development. *ICASSP-92: 1992 IEEE International Conference on Acoustics, Speech, and Signal Processing*, 517–520.

Goldsmith, John A. 1990. *Autosegmental and metrical phonology*. Cambridge, MA: Basil Blackwell.

Günther, Hartmut. 1986. Was the alphabet discovered or invented? On the alleged common processes in speech and writing. In Gerhard Augst (ed.), *New trends in graphemics and orthography*, 248–261. Berlin: de Gruyter.

Hammond, Michael. 1999. *The Phonology of English: A Prosodic Optimality Theoretic Approach*. Oxford: Oxford University Press.

Haugen, Einar. 1956. The syllable in linguistic description. In Morris Halle (ed.), *For Roman Jakobson*, 213–221. The Hague: Mouton.

Hendriks, Hanneke & James McQueen. 1996. *Annual Report 1995*. Max Planck Institute for Psycholinguistics, Nijmegen, The Netherlands.

Itô, Junko & Armin Meste. 1995. Japanese phonology. In John A. Goldsmith (ed.), *Handbook of Phonological Theory*, 817–838. Cambridge, MA: Blackwell.

Kahn, Daniel. 1976. *Syllable-based generalizations in English phonology*. Cambridge, MA: MIT doctoral dissertation.

Kiparsky, Paul. 1981. Remarks on the metrical structure of the syllable. In Wolfgang U. Dressler, Oskar E. Pfeiffer & John R. Rennison (eds.), *Phonologica*, 245–256. Innsbruck: Institut für Sprachwissenschaft der Universität Innsbruck.

Ladefoged, Peter, 1975. *A course in phonetics*. Orlando: Harcourt Brace.

Laubstein, Ann S. 1987. Syllable structure: the speech error evidence. *Canadian Journal of Linguistics* 32. 339–363.

Levelt, Willem J. M. 1989. *Speaking: From intention to articulation*. Cambridge, MA: MIT Press.

Levelt, Willem J. M. & Linda R. Wheeldon. 1994. Do speakers have access to a mental syllabary? *Cognition* 50. 239–269.

Levelt, Willem J. M. 1992. Accessing words in speech production: Stages, processes and representations. *Cognition* 42. 1–22.

Levelt, Willem J. M., Ardi Roelofs & Antje S. Meyer. 1999. A theory of lexical access in speech production. *Behavioural and Brain Sciences* 22. 1–75.

Liberman Alvin M., Franklin S. Cooper, Donald P. Shankweiler & Michael Studdert-Kennedy. 1967. Perception of the speech code. *Psychological Review* 74. 431–461.

Lowe, John J. 2020. Restricted access Segmental phonology in Ancient India? *Language* 96 (2). e97-e113.

MacKay, Donald G. 1972. The structure of words and syllables: Evidence from errors in speech. *Cognitive Psychology* 3. 210–227.

Meyer, Antje S. 1990. The time course of phonological encoding in language production: The encoding of successive syllables of a word. *Journal of Memory and Language* 29. 524–545.

Meyer, Antje S. 1991. The time course of phonological encoding in language production: Phonological encoding inside a syllable. *Journal of Memory and Language* 30. 69–89.

Meyer, Antje S. 1992. Investigation of phonological encoding through speech error analyzes: Achievements, limitations, and alternatives. *Cognition* 42. 181–211.

Meyer, Antje S. 2000. Form representations in word production. In Linda R. Wheeldon (ed.), *Aspects of language production*, 49–70. East Sussex: Psychology Press.

Motley, Michael T. 1973. An analysis of spoonerisms as psycholinguistic phenomena. *Speech Monographs* 40. 66–71.

Nooteboom, Sieb G. 1969. The tongue slips into patterns. In Abondio G. Sciarone, Arthur J. van Essen & A. A. van Raad (eds.), *Nomen: Leyden studies in linguistics and phonetics*, 114–132. The Hague, The Netherlands: Mouton.

Port, Robert F. 2006. The graphical basis of phones and phonemes. In Murray J. Munro & Ocke-Schwen Bohn (eds.), *Second Language Speech Learning: The Role of Language Experience in Speech Production and Perception*, 349–365. Amsterdam: John Benjamins.

Port, Robert F. 2007. How are words stored in memory? Beyond phones and phonemes. *New ideas in Psychology* 25. 143–170.

Port, Robert F. 2010. Language as a social institution: why phonemes and words do not live in the brain. *Ecological Psychology* 22 (4). 304–326.

Roelofs, Ardi. 1992. A spreading-activation theory of lemma retrieval in speaking. *Cognition* 42. 107–142.

Roelofs, Ardi. 1996. Computational models of lemma retrieval. In Ton Dijkstra & Koenrad De Smedt (eds.), *Computational psycholinguistics: AI and connectionist models of human language processing*, 308–327. London: Taylor and Francis.

Roelofs, Ardi. 1997a. Syllabification in speech production: Evaluation of WEAVER. *Language and Cognitive Processes* 12. 657–693.

Roelofs, Ardi. 1997b. The WEAVER model of word-form encoding in speech production. *Cognition* 64. 249–284.
Roelofs, Ardi. 1998. Rightward incrementality in encoding simple phrasal forms in speech production: Verb-particle combinations. Journal of Experimental Psychology: *Learning, Memory, and Cognition* 24. 904–921.
Roelofs, Ardi. 1999. Phonological segments and features as planning units in speech production. *Language and Cognitive Processes* 14. 173–200.
Roelofs, Ardi. 2000. WEAVER++ and other computational models of lemma retrieval and word-form encoding. In Linda R. Wheeldon (ed.), *Aspects of language production*, 71–114. East Sussex: Psychology Press.
Romani, Cristina & Andrea Calabrese. 1996. On the representation of geminate consonants: Evidence from aphasia. *Journal of Neurolinguistics* 9. 219–235.
Romani, Cristina, Claudia Galluzzi, Ivana Bureca & Andrew Olson. 2011. Effects of syllable structure in aphasic errors: Implications for a new model of speech production. *Cognitive Psychology* 62. 151–192.
Schiller, Niels O. 1998. The effect of visually masked syllable primes on the naming latencies of words and pictures. *Journal of Memory and Language* 39. 484–507.
Schiller, Niels O. 2000. Single word production in English: The role of subsyllabic units during phonological encoding. *Journal of Experimental Psychology: Learning, Memory and Cognition* 26. 512–528.
Schiller, Niels O., Albert Costa & Àngels Colomé. 2002. Phonological encoding of single words: In search of the lost syllable. In Carlos Gussenhoven & Natasha Warner (eds.), *Laboratory phonology: Vol. 7. Phonology and phonetics*, 35–59. Berlin: Mouton de Gruyter
Schiller, Niels O., Antje S. Meyer, Harald R. Baayen & Willem J. M. Levelt. 1996. A comparison of lexical and speech syllables in Dutch. *Journal of Quantitative Linguistics* 3. 8–28.
Selkirk, Elisabeth. 1982. The syllable. In Harry Van der Hulst & Norval Smith (eds.), *The Structure of Phonological Representations, Part II*, 337–384. Dordrecht: Foris Publications.
Selkirk, Elisabeth. 1984. On the major class features and syllable theory. In Mark Aronoff & Richard T. Oehrle (eds.), *Language Sound structure*, 107–136. Cambridge, MA: MIT Press.
Sevald, Christine A., Gary S. Dell & Jennifer S. Cole. 1995. Are syllables chunks or schemas? *Journal of Memory and Language* 34. 807–820.
Shattuck-Hufnagel, Stefanie. 1979. Speech errors as evidence for a serial ordering mechanism in sentence production. In William E. Cooper & Edward C. T. Walker (eds.), *Sentence processing*, 295–342. Hillsdale, NJ: Lawrence Erlbaum.
Shattuck-Hufnagel, Stefanie 1983. Sublexical units and suprasegmental structure in speech production planning. In Peter F. MacNeilage (ed.), *The production of speech*, 109–136. New York: Springer
Shattuck-Hufnagel, Stefanie. 1987. The role of word onset consonants in speech production planning: New evidence from speech error patterns. In Eric Keller & Myrna Gopnik (eds.), *Motor and sensory processing in language*, 17–51. Hillsdale, NJ: Erlbaum.
Shattuck-Hufnagel, Stefanie. 1992. The role of word structure in segmental serial ordering. *Cognition* 42. 213–259.
Sommer, Bruce A. 1981. The shape of Kunjen syllables. In Didier L. Goyvaerts (ed.), *Phonology in the 1980s*, 231–244. Ghent: Story-Scientia
Stemberger, Joseph P. 1983. Inflectional malapropisms: Form-based errors in English morphology. *Linguistics* 21. 573–602.
Stemberger, Joseph P. 1990. Word shape errors in language production. *Cognition* 35. 123–157.

Steriade, Donca. 1982. *Greek prosodies and the nature of syllabification*. Cambridge, MA: Massachusetts Institute of Technology Doctoral dissertation.

Steriade, Donca. 1999. Alternatives to syllable-based accounts of consonantal phonotactics. In Osamu Fujimura, Brian D. Joseph & Bohumil Palek (eds.), *Proceedings of LP '98: Item Order in Language and Speech Vol. 1*, 205–245. Prague: Karolinum Press.

Straight, Stephen H. 1976. *The Acquisition of Maya Phonology – Variation in Yucatec Child Language*. New York & London: Garland.

Vennemann, Theo. 1968. *German Phonology*. Los Angeles: University of California doctoral dissertation.

Wehr, Hans. 1976 [1960]. *Dictionary of Modern Written Arabic*. 3rd edn. [Translated and edited by J. Milton Cowan]. Ithaca, NY: Spoken Language Services, Inc.

Wilshire, Carolyn E. 1998. Serial order in phonological encoding: An exploration of the 'word onset effect' using laboratory-induced errors. *Cognition* 68. 143–166.

Wilshire, Carolyn E. 2002. Where do aphasic phonological errors come from? Evidence from phoneme movement errors in picture naming. *Aphasiology* 16. 169–197.

Ziegler, Johannes C. & Usha Goswami. 2005. Reading acquisition, developmental dyslexia, and skilled reading across languages: A psycholinguistic grain size theory. *Psychological Bulletin* 131 (1). 3–29.

Zvelebil, Kamil. 1990. *Dravidian Linguistics: An Introduction*. Pondicherry: Pondicherry Institute of Linguistics and Culture.

List of contributors

Tanmoy Bhattacharya is a Professor of Linguistics in the Department of Linguistics at the University of Delhi in India. Before joining the University of Delhi, he held different research and academic positions at various academic institutions such as SOAS, University of London, Universität Leipzig, University College London, M.S. University of Baroda and University of Hyderabad. In the domain of syntax, he has carried out extensive and original research on topics such as NP structures, WH-constructions, superiority, sluicing, clause-internal complementizers and polar questions in a number of Indo-Aryan and Tibeto-Burman languages. His most recent work has been on the topic of agreement in which he has brought to the fore the importance of many languages of Bihar (for example, Maithili, Magahi and Angika, among others), Jharkhand, Odisha (languages such as Santhali, Kurmali), Mizoram (especially Mara) and Nepal (Bantawa in particular) in forming a *sprachbund* of multiple agreement comprising a vast chunk of the Himalayan foothills, the East, and Northeast of India.

Dörte Borchers is a senior researcher in the Department of Linguistics at the University of Graz, Austria. She studied Social Anthropology, Burmese, and Classical and modern Indology in Göttingen and Heidelberg. After receiving her PhD in Linguistics from the University of Leiden, she conducted linguistic research in Nepal supported by an ELDP grant. Subsequently she held a position in Linguistics at the University of Münster for six years. She teaches courses on Empirical Linguistics, Tibeto-Burman linguistics, Typology, and language change, and has been invited to teach workshops on Language Documentation at the University of Jerusalem and at Jadavpur University. She has published about different aspects of Tibeto-Burman languages of Nepal and Burma. Her research interests cover language documentation, language politics, sociolinguistics, language typology, and Tibeto-Burman languages of South Asia, with a special focus on the languages Surel and Sunwar (Koints) in Nepal.

Jean-Luc Chevillard is a CNRS Researcher and a member of the research laboratory called UMR-7597 "Laboratoire d'Histoire des Théories Linguistiques" (HTL). After some initial training in mathematics, he began working in the field of "History of linguistics" in 1981 and has ever since devoted most of his time working on Tamil grammar and lexicographical texts which are commonly used as an essential tool to study classical Tamil literature. In addition, he has worked on the medieval Tamil devotional corpus (particularly Tēvāram), on the modern and pre-modern varieties of Tamil and reviewed Western scholars' approach to evaluate Tamil grammar and lexicography. From 2003 to 2014, he was the general editor of the journal Histoire Épistémologie Langage (HEL) and is currently preparing an electronic edition of an old Tamil-Portuguese dictionary "Vocabulario Tamulico com a Significaçam Portugueza" which was compiled by Antam de Proenca in 1679.

Martin Everaert is emeritus professor of Linguistics at Utrecht University. He works primarily on the syntax-semantics and the lexicon-syntax interface. His other areas of interest are typology and language evolution. He is, among others, co-editor of the Wiley-Blackwell Companion to Syntax and member of the editorial boards of Linguistic Inquiry and Journal of Linguistics.

Sanjukta Ghosh is an associate professor in the department of Humanistic Studies at Indian Institute of Technology (Banaras Hindu University) Varanasi, India. After receiving her PhD in Linguistics from the University of Hyderabad, she taught Linguistics at Banaras Hindu University from 2005 till 2018 before joining IIT (BHU) Varanasi. Her research interests include Cognitive Semantics, Pragmatics and Computational Lexical semantics. She has published on related topics in many Indo-Aryan languages including Bangla, Hindi, Bhojpuri and Maithili.

Mark Hale (PhD, Harvard) is professor in the department of Classics, Modern Languages and Linguistics at Concordia University in Montreal, Canada. His research focuses on three primary areas: Indo-European linguistics (especially syntax), Oceanic linguistics (especially Micronesian), and general diachronic phonology/syntax (and their interface). Within Indo-European linguistics, he is particularly interested in exploiting so-called "Wackernagel's Law" phenomena to determine basic clause structure in archaic Indo-Iranian languages. Within Oceanic linguistics, he is particularly interested in the historical phonology, morphology and syntax of Marshallese, Rotuman, and New Caledonian and Loyalty Island Languages. He has published widely on Sanskrit linguistics.

Madelyn Kissock (PhD, Harvard) is associate professor and chair in the department of Classics, Modern Languages and Linguistics at Concordia University in Montreal, Canada. Her current research focuses on several topics in the syntax of Telugu, a Dravidian language of South India. This work is part of a larger project on the syntax and phonology of Telugu. Her doctoral dissertation presented an analysis of Telugu reflexive-middle verbs. She has also worked on Rotuman phonology and the theoretical aspects of phonological acquisition. She has published widely on Telugu syntax and phonology.

Rajesh Kumar is a professor of linguistics in the Department of Humanities and Social Sciences at the Indian Institute of Technology Madras, Chennai. He obtained his Ph.D. in linguistics from the University of Illinois at Urbana-Champaign. Prior to joining IIT Madras, he taught at IIT Kanpur and IIT Patna in India and at the University of Texas at Austin in the USA. He has been a visiting faculty at the Tata Institute of Social Sciences in Mumbai in India. His book on Syntax of Negation and Licensing of Negative Polarity Items was published by Routledge in their prestigious series Outstanding Dissertations in Linguistics in 2006. He is associate editor of the journal Language and Language Teaching. He has been part of the language teaching program at all the institutions he has been affiliated with. The broad goal of his research is to uncover regularities underlying both the form (what language is) and sociolinguistic functions (what language does) of natural languages.

Bornini Lahiri is presently an Assistant Professor of Linguistics in the Department of Humanities and Social Sciences, Indian Institute of Technology, Kharagpur, India. In the past, she was involved with various language documentation projects such as "Scheme for Protection and Preservation of Endangered Languages" (SPPEL), hosted by Central Institute of Indian Languages and "Study and Research of Indigenous and Endangered Languages of India". She has worked extensively on typological and morpho-syntactic properties of several under-researched languages from different language families of India. Along with this, she has also collaborated on projects studying aggression and hate speech including an ongoing project on studying communal and misogynistic aggression, sponsored by Facebook Research. Her research papers have been published in various national and international journals and as book-chapters. Her recent books 'A typological study of Cases' and 'Dictionary of the Kurmali Language: Bangla-Kurmali-English-Hindi' (Co-authored) are in press with Routledge Publications and Jadavpur University Press, respectively.

John J. Lowe is Associate Professor of Sanskrit at the University of Oxford. His research covers Sanskrit and Indo-Aryan linguistics, with particular focus on syntax and semantics. He completed his D.Phil. at Oxford in 2012, working on syntax and semantics in Rigvedic Sanskrit, and has taught and researched at Oxford since then. Dr. Lowe's publications include *Participles in Rigvedic Sanskrit: The syntax and semantics of adjectival verb forms* (Oxford University Press, 2015), *Transitive nouns and adjectives: evidence from early Indo-Aryan* (Oxford University Press, 2017), and *The Oxford Reference Guide to Lexical-Functional Grammar* (Oxford University Press, 2019). He is currently the Primary Investigator on the five-year ERC-funded project "Linguistics from India: new ideas for modern linguistics from ancient India (LINGUINDIC)".

Adriana Molina-Muñoz is currently a researcher on the project "Uncovering Sanskrit Syntax" led by John Lowe, founded by the Leverhulme Trust, and hosted by the Faculty of Linguistics, Philology & Phonetics, University of Oxford. The project examines different syntactic phenomena in Sanskrit, including causatives, control and anaphora, using corpus data. She completed her PhD in Linguistics at the University of Illinois at Urbana-Champaign. Her research focuses on how syntactic phenomena are affected by other components of the language faculty, such as morphology and semantics/ pragmatics. She has investigated synchronically and diachronically different interface phenomena such as word order, compounding, relativization, ergativity, and aspect; focusing largely on Sanskrit and Hindi, but she has also worked on Bribri (Chibchan family, Costa Rica).

Miki Nishioka is an associate professor of Osaka University, Japan. She obtained her BA, MA and Ph.D. at Osaka University of Foreign Studies which was merged into Osaka University in 2007. After finishing her Ph.D. in 2001, she started teaching Hindi language and Hindi linguistics at universities in Japan. At the same time, she began teaching Japanese language to foreigners who study in various universities in Japan. She also taught Japanese language and linguistics at Jawaharlal Nehru University in 2014. Her research focuses on the comparison between Hindi and Japanese compound verbs, nominalization in Hindi and Bihari languages, and a comparative study of Hindi and Japanese discourse particles. She has extended her research area to corpus linguistics and has developed a web corpus called COSH to use in quantitative research on the topics.

Andrew Olson is a neuropsychologist who is interested in cognitive systems and how they be understood by studying the effects of brain damage. His particular focus is the organization of language in the brain. He works with patients with brain damage, children with developmental disorders and other special populations, including participants from the deaf community. He uses a wide variety of methods, including standard neuropsychological assessments, computerized experiments and eye-tracking. He is interested in computational and statistical models of cognition and in using explicit models for testing theories of language organization.

Ankita Prasad is a PhD research scholar at the Indian Institute of Technology, Delhi (IIT-D) in the Department of Humanities and Social Sciences (HuSS). Her current research focuses on sound change in Sylheti using an optimality theoretic framework. She has also worked on Hindi and Bengali phonology. Her broad areas of interest include Indo-Aryan phonology, optimality theory and harmonic grammar approaches to phonology, and morpho-phonological interactions modelled in the Distributed Morphology framework. She can be contacted via her institutional ID huz178133@hss.iitd.ac.in or personal email ankita.9212@gmail.com.

Dinesh Ramoo is a lecturer at Thompson Rivers University in Kamloops, Canada. After receiving his PhD in Psychology from the University of Birmingham in 2014, he has worked in the United Kingdom, Sri Lanka, and Turkey before moving to Canada in 2019. He has also served as a consultant linguist for Google Inc. and Oxford University Press. His research interests include word-form encoding in English as well as Indian languages such as Hindi and Tamil. He employs experimental data from neurological patients with acquired language disorders as well as computational models to study language production.

Cristina Romani is a Reader in Psychology at Aston University in Birmingham, UK. She is interested in cognitive and linguistic functions in different populations. Her goal is to reach a better understanding of normal cognition as well as better clinical management of individuals with cognitive impairments (due to stroke, developmental issues, or metabolic diseases). She is currently involved in research on acquired language impairments such as aphasia, reading, spelling and developmental dyslexia, as well as applied neuropsychological research (such as tracking the cognitive outcomes of metabolic diseases). She is dedicated to a theoretical, interdisciplinary approach between neuropsychology, linguistics, and cognitive science.

Gargi Roy is a Ph.D. candidate in Linguistics in the Department of Humanities and Social Sciences at the Indian Institute of Technology Madras, Chennai, India. Her research interest is primarily in syntax and syntactic convergence. Currently she is working on the clause structures in Kokborok (Tibeto-Burman) to capture the gradual syntactic change in the indigenous clausal patterns of Kokborok resulting due to the centuries' old contact with a genealogically unrelated language, Bangla (a New Indo-Aryan language) spoken in Tripura. She has presented research papers at University of Illinois, St. John's College (Cambridge University, U.K.), National Taiwan University of Science and Technology (Taipei, Taiwan), INALCO (Paris, France), University of Southern Denmark (Odense, Denmark) and other national gatherings. Some of her papers are published or accepted in several leading journals, including Studies in Language.

Paroma Sanyal is Associate Professor of Linguistics at the Department of Humanities and Social Sciences, Indian Institute of Technology Delhi. After completing her M.A in English, she earned her M.Phil and PhD in Linguistics at the English and Foreign Languages University, Hyderabad. Her research interests are in theoretical approaches to phonology and morpho-syntax. Specifically, she uses the theoretical frameworks of Optimality Theory and Harmonic Grammar for analyzing phonological data and Distributive Morphology and Minimalism for the analysis of morpho-syntactic aspects which are realized though phonological processes in particular natural languages. Earlier in the decade, she started her teaching career as a faculty in the Department of English at the University of Hyderabad and then Central University of Karnataka.

Ghanshyam Sharma is Professor of Hindi at INALCO, Paris. He received a PhD in Hindi form Agra University, India and a PhD in semiotics from the University of Bologna, Italy. Before coming to Italy for post-doctoral research with Umberto Eco in Bologna, he was a Research Assistant at the Central Institute of Hindi, Agra for five years. He had different academic positions at the University of Venice and the University of Bologna for about 20 years before joining INALCO in 2012. He is a semiotician with a keen interest in pragmatic aspects of Hindi grammar and Conditionals in Indo-Aryan languages. He has published numerous articles on topics in Hindi grammar and compiled the first-ever commissioned Italian-Hindi-Italian dictionary. He has also translated novels, from Italian into Hindi as well as from Hindi into Italian.

Vyom Sharma is pursuing a PhD in Linguistics from the Department of Humanities & Social Sciences, IIT-Delhi . He has more than 2 years of experience working as a Systems Engineer in the IT industry, but his passion for language and its structure persuaded him to begin a journey in the field of Linguistics. In his dissertation on negation in language, he tries to seek answers to questions which lie in the domain of Syntax-Semantics-Pragmatics. He has worked with language documentation team from JNU to write descriptive accounts of two languages of the Himalayan region namely Gaddi and Rongpo, and is part of the team of FLing@JNU (www.flingjnu.com), an online repository of field-work based research data from the Centre for Linguistics.

Karumuri V. Subbarao (or **Kārumūri V. Subbārāo**) – formerly a professor of Linguistics at the University of Delhi for many years and also Radhakrishnan Chair Professor in Humanities at the University of Hyderabad – is a renowned typologist. His research work is focused on the syntactic typology of South Asian languages in general and Tibeto-Burman and Austro-Asiatic languages in particular. One of his recent books *South Asian languages: A Syntactic Typology* (2012) is published by Cambridge University Press, Cambridge. He has been an elected member of the Linguistic Society of America since 2003, and the Linguistic Society of Nepal since 2005. He has taught at several universities in India and abroad. Currently, he is working on the grammars of three Tibeto-Burman languages, namely, Mizo, Rabha and Saihriem.

Anuradha Sudharsan was professor of linguistics at English and Foreign Languages University, Hyderabad, until 2014. Subsequently, she taught also at the Osmania University (Hyderabad) for two years. She received her MA in TESOL from Stony Brook University (USA) and an M.A. in linguistics from New York University (USA). After completing her PhD in linguistics at the Hyderabad Central University, she taught for many years at different institutions such as Tribhuvan University in Kathmandau (Nepal) and H.M. Patel Institute of English Training and Research in Gujarat (India). She was also a Guest faculty at South Gujarat University. Her main areas of interest are Dravidian linguistics, minimalist syntax, morphology, historical linguistics, and syntactic change. She has published several papers on Kannada syntax and now intends to embark on an ambitious research project: a book on Dravidian syntax.

The late Dr **Tabu Ram Taid** was professor of English at Cotton College, Guwahati University, Assam. Subsequently, he held the positions of Director of Higher Education and the Chairman of the Board of Secondary Education, Assam. Taid's publications include A Dictionary of the Mising Language, Mising Gompir Kumsung (2010) and An Introduction to Mising Phonology and Grammar (2016). He is a recipient of the prestigious Bhasha Samman award of the Sahitya Academy,

Delhi. He worked intensely for the preservation and the development of the Mising language, literature and culture.

Massimo Vai is an associate professor in linguistics at the University of Milan, Italy where he received a PhD in 1999. Subsequently, he was appointed as a postdoctoral research fellow at the University of Padua where he conducted research in the field of Indo-European syntax and participated in the group research activities of ASIt (i.e. Atlante Sintattico d'Italia). Between 1999 and 2000, he also held non-tenured professorship at the Free University of Languages and Communication Sciences (IULM) in Milan. At present, he teaches graduate courses in general linguistics and Historical and comparative linguistics at the University of Milan. His research interests lie in the field of comparative morphosyntax of ancient Indo-European languages, history of linguistics and the development of Italian dialects. He has published widely on various topics in these fields, particularly on Vedic syntax.

Index of authors

Abercrombie, David 419, 457
Abhyankar, K. V. 376, 379
Adams, James 25, 40
Adger, David 72, 101, 105, 115, 124, 153, 170
Åfarli, Tor A. 106, 115
Aghaei, Behrad 157, 170
Aissen, Judith 175, 187, 189
Akasegawa, Shiro 251, 259
Akiyama, Ken 241
Alexiadou, Artemis 44, 72, 73, 400, 402, 403, 412
Alizadeh-Sahraie, Mojtaba 74
Alrenga, Peter 124, 127, 160, 170
Ameka, Felix K. 353, 359
Amritavalli, Raghavachari 325, 326, 335
Anagnostopoulou, Elena 412
Andersen, Henning, 207, 240, 241
Annamalai, E. 273, 282, 283, 285, 287

Arad, Maya 400, 412
Aristar, Anthony R. 173, 188, 189
Arnaud, Rey 458
Arora, Harbir 315, 335, 337
Asher, Ronald 312, 318, 335
Aussant, Émilie 262, 287
Axel-Tober, Katrin 33, 35, 37, 40

Backus, John W. 367, 379, 380
Baerman, Matthew 197, 202, 203, 204
Baker, Mark 80, 86, 115, 140, 170
Baronian, Luc 197, 204
Bashir, Elena 313, 336
Baumann, Monika 417, 457
Béjar, Susana 101, 115
Belletti, Adriana 80, 82, 84, 115
Benincà, Paola 25, 40
Bergaigne, Abel 1, 20
Beschi, Constantius Joseph 270, 273, 277, 282, 286, 287, 288
Bethin, Christina Y. 419, 457
Bhanderi, Kalpesh 220, 241
Bhatia, Tej K. 258, 286, 287

Bhatt, Rajesh 43–45, 48, 62, 72, 81, 86–88, 99, 100, 106, 115, 126, 142, 169, 170, 311, 335, 382, 386, 387, 393–396, 400, 403, 412
Bhatta, V. P. 180, 189
Bhattacharya, Dipak 20
Bhattacharya, Tanmoy 77, 79, 80, 103, 115, 116, 174, 182, 189
Bickel, Balthasar 177, 189
Bieri, Dora 192, 199, 200, 201, 204
Blake, Barry 175, 189
Blevins, Juliette 416, 419, 457
Bloom, Paul 341, 359
Bobaljik, Jonathan David 399, 412
Boersma, Paul 391, 412
Borchers, Dörte 191, 193, 195, 196, 199–202, 204
Borowsky, Toni J. 419, 458
Bošković, Željko 101, 115, 116
Bossong, Georg 177, 187, 189
Bowerman, Melissa 339, 340, 359, 360
Brand, Muriele 417, 418, 458
Brants, Thorsten 75
Brereton, Joel P. 1, 5–8, 10, 11, 14, 15, 18, 20, 24, 41
Briggs, Charles A. 454, 458
Brown, Dunstan 203–205
Brown, Francis 454, 458
Bureca, Ivana 461
Burton-Page, John 241
Butskhrikidze, Marika 419, 458
Butt, Miriam 48, 72, 100, 116, 241

Cairns, Charles E. 428, 458
Calabrese, Andrea 431, 461
Campbell, Lyle 207, 241
Cardona, George 311, 335, 367, 379
Chandola, Anoop Chandra 44, 72
Chang, Franklin 53, 75
Chantraine, Pierre 33, 35, 40
Chatterji, Suniti K. 175, 189
Chen, Jenn-Yeu 417, 458

Chevillard, Jean-Luc 261, 262, 264, 284, 285, 287–289
Chhabra, Usha 241
Cholin, Joana 418, 458
Chomsky, Noam 80–82, 86, 101, 102, 106, 116, 121, 138, 145, 170, 323, 335, 361–363, 365, 366, 379, 397, 412, 415, 425, 458
Christophe, Vielle 289
Chumakina, Marina 205
Clark, Alexander 365, 379
Clements, George N. 388, 413, 429, 457, 458
Cole, Jennifer S. 418, 429, 461
Coleman, John 366, 379
Colomé, Àngels 418, 461
Corbett, Greville 197, 198, 202–205
Costa, Albert 418, 429, 458, 461
Creissels, Denis 178, 189, 298, 308
Culicover, Peter 58, 59, 74
Culy, Christopher 365, 380
Cutler, Anne 425, 458
Cuyckens, Hubert 342, 359

Dahl, Östen 175, 189
Daland, Robert 197, 202, 205
Danckaert, Lieven 26, 27, 40
Daniels, Peter T. 421, 458
Davies, William 121, 123, 125–127, 153, 170
Davis, Stuart 417, 436, 458
Davison, Alice 32, 38, 39, 40, 44, 45, 72
Dayal, Veneeta 44, 45, 48, 59, 69, 73
de Cat, Cécile 72
De Lacy, Paul 413
de Proença, Antam 261, 263, 273, 287, 288, 289
del Viso, Susana 429, 459
Delahunty, Gerald P. 123, 126, 127, 170
Delamarre, Xavier 31, 41
DeLancey, Scott 193, 205
Delbrück, Berthold 24, 33, 38, 39, 41
Dell, Gary S. 418, 422–429, 431, 449, 450, 451, 452, 455, 458, 459, 461
Den Ouden, Dirk-Bart 431, 458
Désoulières, Alain 286–288
Dirven, René 341, 360
Ditte, Boeg Thomsen 359
Dixon, Robert M. W. 188, 189

Donaldson, Susan 48, 73
Downing, B. T. 311, 335
Driver, Samuel R. 454, 458
Dryer, Mathew 124, 125, 151, 165, 170
Duanmu, San 419, 458
Dubinsky, Stanley 121, 123, 125–127, 153, 170
Duchier, Denys 75
Dunkel, George Eugene 31, 41
Dwivedi, Veena Dhar 45, 48, 60, 73

Elson, Ben 417, 458
Embick, David 382, 386, 387, 393–398, 400, 403, 411–413
Emeneau, Murray 292, 308, 318, 335
Ernst, Thomas 110, 116
Evans, Nicholas 194, 205
Everaert, Martin 291, 300, 308, 309, 312, 323, 337

Faber, Alice 421, 458
Farudi, Annahita 15–158, 170
Feinstein, Mark H. 428, 458
Feist, Michele 341, 347, 359
Ferrand, Ludovic 417, 418, 458, 459
Ferrer-i-Cancho, Ramon 442, 459
Féry, Caroline 74
Firth, John R. 420, 421, 459
Fischer, Silke 113, 116
Fortson IV, Benjamin W. 41
Fowler, Carol A. 421, 459
Foygel, Dan 422, 459
Francis, Elaine J. 45, 46, 51, 53, 58–60, 62, 68, 70, 73
Franco, Jon 84, 116
Fudge, Erik C. 419, 459
Fujii, Mamoru 380

Gaby, Alice 329, 330, 331, 335
Gair, James 308, 318, 319, 335, 336
Galluzzi, Claudia 461
Gambhir, Vijay 47, 48, 59, 71, 73
García-Albea, José E. 429, 459
Garrett, Merrill F. 359, 429, 459
Gast, Volker 291, 308, 318, 320, 336
Gazdar, Gerald 365, 380
Geigerich, Heinz 459
Geldner, Karl F. 8, 21

Genetti, Carol 192, 194–196, 202, 205
Geniušiene, Emma 308
Gentner, Dedre 341, 359
Ghoshal, Anindita 315, 336
Ghushchyan, Edita 413
Gibson, Edward 49, 51, 73
Gimson, Alfred C. 416, 459
Gleitman, Lila 360
Godfrey, John J. 432, 459
Göksel, Aslı 149, 170
Goldin-Meadow, Susan 359
Goldsmith, John A. 429, 459
Gollrad, Anja 74
Gordon, Matthew 383, 388, 413
Goswami, Usha 421, 462
Grainger, Jonathan 417, 459
Graßmann, Hermann 41
Grierson, George A. 175, 190
Griffiths, Arlo 2, 16, 17, 20
Grosu, Aslı 125, 170
Guéron, Jacqueline 59, 73
Günther, Hartmut 421, 459
Gupta, Sagarmal 53, 59, 73
Gürcanlı, Özge 359
Gwynn, John P. L. 312, 336

Hacker, Paul 241
Haddad, Youssef 317, 336
Haegeman, Liliane 101, 116
Haider, Hubert 110, 116
Hale, Austin 192, 199–201, 204
Hale, Kenneth 90, 116
Hale, Mark 1, 2, 20, 23–26, 41
Halle, Morris 197, 205, 399, 411, 413–415, 425, 458
Hammond, Michael 419, 459
Han, Hye Jin 123, 127, 152, 153, 170
Harris, Alice 207, 241
Haspelmath, Martin 164, 170, 322, 336
Haudry, Jean 36–38, 41
Haugen, Einar 415, 419, 459
Haun, Daniel B. M. 359, 360
Hawkins, John A. 51, 53, 69, 73
Heegård, Jan 359
Hein, Jeanne 270, 273, 276, 284, 288
Hendriks, Hanneke 428, 459
Henrique, Henriques 262, 269, 273, 288

Hermann, Eduard 23, 41
Herskovits, Annette 359
Hettrich, Heinrich 24, 29, 31, 41
Hickman, M. 341, 359
Hippisley, Andrew 198, 205
Hock, Hans Henrich 41, 44, 72, 313, 336
Holland, Gary B. 31, 41
Holliman, Edward C. 459
Hook, Peter E. 180, 190, 207, 218, 241, 258, 262, 288
Hopper, Paul J. 207, 242
Høyem, Inghild Flaate 113, 115
Hsu, Brian 27, 41
Huck, Geoffrey J. 58, 73
Humphreys, Glyn W. 418, 459
Huybregts, M. A. C. 365, 380
Hyman, Larry 384, 413
Hyman, Malcolm 361, 367, 380

Igoa, José M. 429, 459
Ingerman, Peter Zilahy 367, 380
Itô, Junko 456, 459
Iwasaki, Shoichi 146, 151, 170
Izadifar, Raheleh 74

Jackendoff, Ray 341, 359
Jacquesson, François 316, 336
Jagannathan, V. R. 243, 247, 255, 258
Jain, Dhanesh 311
James, Gregory 264, 273, 288
Jamison, Stephanie W. 1, 5, 10, 14, 18, 20, 24, 41
Jeyaraj, Daniel 273, 286, 288
Johnson, C. Douglas 366, 380
Johnson-Laird, Philip 177, 190
Joshi, Aravind K. 365, 368, 371, 380
Juge, Matthew 198, 201, 205

Kachru, Yamuna 44, 48, 50, 53, 69, 73, 77, 88, 90, 95, 110, 116, 180, 190
Kager, René 384, 413
Kahn, Daniel 417, 419, 459
Kakati, Banikanta 186, 190
Kaplan, Ronald 366, 380
Kasami, Tadao 380
Katre, Sumitra M. 175, 190
Kay, Martin 366, 380

Kayne, Richard 80, 87, 116, 164, 170, 317, 336
Kazenin, Konstantin 324, 336
Keenan, Edward 311, 336
Keine, Stefan 81, 86, 99, 115
Kellogg, Samuel Henry 243, 258
Kentner, Gerrit 74
Kerslake, Celia 149, 170
Keyser, Samuel J. 90, 116, 429, 457
Khetrapal, Naveen 359
Kidwai, Ayesha 48, 73
Kielhorn, Franz 378, 380
Kim, Jeong-Soo 13, 20
King, Tracy Holloway 48, 72
Kiparsky, Paul 23, 31, 41, 361, 365, 368, 380, 419, 460
Kita, Sotaro 359
Klein, Ewan H. 380
Konieczny, Lars 49, 73, 75
König, Ekkehard 291, 308, 318, 320, 336
Konow, Stan 195, 205
Kornfilt, Jaklin 146, 148, 170
Koster, Jan 124, 126, 160, 164, 170
Kothari, Anubha 48, 52, 60, 69, 73
Koul, Omkar N. 387, 413
Koul, Vijay K. 242
Krapova, Iliyana 27, 41
Kratzer, Angelika 400, 413
Krenn, Brigitte 75
Krisch, Thomas 25, 31, 41
Krishnamurti, Bhadriraju 312, 336
Kügler, Frank 74
Kulikov, Leonid 190
Kulinich, Elena 197, 204
Kulkarni, Aaditya 242
Kumar, Rajesh 311, 316, 323, 337
Kumari, T. C. 312, 318, 335
Kunjunni Raja K. 375, 379
Kuno, Susumo 71, 73

Ladefoged, Peter 416, 460
Lahiri, Bornini 173, 178, 190
Lakshmi Bai, Balachandran 312, 336
Lalitha Murthy, Balemarthy 320, 336
Lamers, Monique 177, 188
Landau, Barbara 341, 359
Langacker, Ronald 342, 359

Lasnik, Howard 121, 171
Laubstein, Ann 417, 460
Law, Paul 72
Lazard, Gilbert 187, 190
Lee, Seung-Ah 85, 116
Legendre, Géraldine 391, 411, 413
Lestrade, Sander 177, 188
Levelt, Willem J. M. 418, 425, 428, 449, 458, 460
Levinson, Stephen 341, 345, 349, 351, 353, 359
Levy, Leon S. 380
Lewis, Richard L. 49, 75
Li, Chao 173, 190
Li, Peggy 341, 360
Liang, Hsin-hsin 231, 242, 262, 288
Liperovskiĭ, Vladimir 247, 258
Lipták, Anikó 44, 73
Lohndal, Terje 101, 116, 126, 146, 160, 171
Longacre, Robert E. 184, 190
Longenbaugh, Nicholas 81, 117
Lopez, Carlos A. 8, 20
Lowe, John J. 29, 30, 42, 421, 460
Lubotsky, Alexander M. 16, 20, 33, 42
Lühr, Rosemarie 31, 33, 37, 42
Lust, Barbara 291, 299, 308, 318, 335

Maas, Utz 194, 205
MacDonald, Jonathan Eric 104, 117
Machida, Kazuhiko 286
MacKay, Donald G. 417, 460
Mahajan, Anoop 45, 73, 80, 88, 97, 100, 110, 115, 117
Mahapatra, Bijay. P. 180, 190
Maira, Sergio 341, 360
Majid, Asifa 341, 359
Malchukov, Andrej L. 173, 175, 188, 190
Manetta, Emily 45, 74
Manninen, Satu 46, 74
Marantz, Alec 397, 411, 413
Marlow, Patrick E. 44, 74
Masica, Colin P. 175, 180, 190, 243, 258, 292, 308, 396, 413
Matsumura, Takashi 380
Matsuoka, Tamaki 252, 258
May, Robert 59, 73
McCarthy, John J. 384, 413

McCawley, James 45, 48, 74
McCloskey, James 121, 171
McDaniel, Jane 459
McDonnell, Bradley 413
McGregor, Ronald S. 44, 74
McQueen, James 428, 459
Meinunger, André 72
Mel'čuk, Igor 198, 205
Meste, Armin 459
Meyer, Antje S. 417, 424, 429, 460
Michael, Lev 359
Miller, George A. 177, 190
Miner, Kenneth L. 140, 171
Miyata, Yoshiro 413
Mohanan, Tara 174, 177, 182, 190
Moltaji, Niloofar 356, 360
Motley, Michael T. 417, 460
Müller, Stefan 365, 380
Murofushi, Shinsuke 241
Muru, Cristina 262, 270, 288

Nadel, Lynn 359
Nadkarni, M. V. 129, 171
Nadkarni, Mangesh V. 312, 336
Narrog, Heiko 179, 190
Nedjalkov, Vladimir 322, 336
Neveu, Grace 359
Nevins, Andrew 101, 116
Nikolaeva, Irina 194, 205
Nilsen, Don L. F. 179, 190
Nishioka, Miki 243, 251, 258
Nooteboom, Sieb G. 421, 424, 460
Norris, Mark 106, 117
Nouguier-Voisin, Sylvie 298, 308

Oepen, Stephan 75
Œrtel, Hans, 28, 42
Ohala, John, 383, 413
Ohala, Manjari 383, 388, 413
Oldenberg, Hermann 8, 21
Olson, Andrew 415, 461
Ozarkar, Renuka 221, 242
Özyürek, Asli 359

Palancer, Enrique L. 190
Pandey, Pramod 384, 413
Paoli, Sandra 27, 42

Parasnis, Raobahadur D.B. 220, 242
Pardeshi, Prashant 207, 241
Parisi, Domenico 85, 117
Pater, Joe 391, 411
Patil, Umesh 48, 74
Patnaik, Manideep 320, 336
Pederson, Eric 339, 352, 355, 359
Peerman, Ronald 417, 458
Penn, Gerald 361, 365, 368, 375, 380
Pesetsky, David 101, 106, 117, 138, 171
Peterson, John 312, 319, 337
Peterson, Mary 359
Peust, Carsten 4, 21
Pierrehumbert, Janet 197, 202, 205
Pinault, Georges-Jean 1, 21
Pinker, Steven 341, 360
Pischel, Richard 8, 21
Polinsky, Maria 107, 117
Pollard, Carl J. 365, 380
Pollock, Jean-Yves 80, 115, 117
Pomino, Natascha 198, 205
Port, Robert F. 420, 460
Prasad, Rashmi 48, 74
Pray, Bruce 208, 242
Premchand, Munshi 242, 252, 258
Preminger, Omer 107, 117
Prince, Alan 384, 413
Pullum Geoffrey K. 365, 380
Purandare, Madhuri 242
Puri, Vandana 44, 74
Pütz, Martin 341, 360
Pytlowany, Anna 286, 289

Radhakrishnan, Sarvepalli 36, 42
Raina, Achla 218, 242
Ramachandrarao, B. 129, 171
Ramchand, Gillian 242, 387, 414
Rapacha, Lal Shankyarelu 192, 196, 199, 206
Rasch, Björn 359
Rasekh-Mahand, Mohammad 53, 58, 68, 74
Regier, Terry 359
Reich, Peter A. 424, 458
Reis, Marga 197, 206
Remberger, Eva Maria 198, 205
Řezáč, Milan 101, 115
Richards, Mark 87, 117
Rizzi, Luigi 23, 25, 39, 42

Robert, Stephene 341, 359
Rochemont, Michael 58, 74
Rocher, Ludo 286, 289
Roelofs, Ardi 425, 452, 460
Romani, Cristina 415, 428, 430, 449, 455, 461
Rosenbaum, Peter 123, 171
Rosenblum, Daisy 413
Roussou, Anna 158, 164, 171
Roy, Gargi 311, 316, 323, 337

Safir, Kenneth 121, 164, 171
Sag, Ivan A. 380
Saint-Dizier, Patrick 360
Sakata, Teiji 252, 259
Saksena, Anuradha 180, 190
Sarju Devi, T. 300, 309
Schäfer, Florian 396, 412
Schiffman, Harold 273, 282, 285, 289
Schiller, Niels O. 418, 428, 461
Schlesinger, Izchak 360
Schrapel, Dieter 21
Schulze, Marlene 192, 199, 204
Sebastian-Gallés, Nuria 429, 458
Segui, Juan, 417 459
Seki, Hiroyuki 365, 380
Selkirk, Elisabeth O. 387, 414, 419, 425, 428, 461
Sevald, Christine A. 418, 429, 461
Shankweiler, Donald 421, 459
Shapiro, Michael C. 387, 414
Sharma, Ghanshyam 207, 221, 242
Sharma, Jyoti 80, 103, 115
Sharma, Rama Nath 375, 380
Shattuck-Hufnagel, Stefanie 417, 421, 429, 461
Shaw, Patricia A. 413
Shieber, Stuart M. 365, 380
Shiller, Niels O. 458
Shree, Geetanjali 242
Sievers, Eduard 414
Siewierska, Anna 78, 117
Silverstein, Michael 175, 187, 190
Simpson, Andrew 151, 153, 171, 174, 182, 189
Sims, Andrea 197, 201, 205
Singh, Mona 59, 74
Sinha, Chris 342, 360

Skut, Wojciech 75
Smolensky, Paul 384, 411, 413
Snell, Rupert 44, 74, 243, 246, 259
Solé, Richard V. 442, 459
Sommer, Bruce A. 417, 461
Speyer, Jacob Samuel 36, 38, 42
Sridhar, S. N. 312, 337
Srishti, Richa 400, 414
Srivastav, Veneeta 44, 48, 59, 62, 69, 74
Staal, J. Fritz 361, 367, 380
Steever, Sanford 273, 282, 285, 289, 318, 337
Stemberger, Joseph P. 421, 429, 461
Steriade, Donca 387, 414, 416, 419, 462
Stolz, Thomas 300, 309
Stowell, Tim 124, 171
Straight, Stephen H. 417, 462
Strobel, Thomas 197, 206
Strube, Michael 48, 74
Strunk, Jan 45, 49, 51, 53, 59, 62, 68, 74
Studdert-Kennedy, Michael 421, 459
Stump, Gregory 197, 206
Subbārāo, K. V. 44, 48, 74, 291, 296, 298, 300, 303, 305, 308, 311, 312, 322, 335
Subramanya Ayyar V. M., 289
Sudharsan, Anuradha 119, 140, 146, 171
Svorou, Soteria 342, 360
Swart, Peter de 177, 188

Taid, Tabu 291, 300, 303, 306, 308
Takahashi, Masako 380
Talmy, Leonard 177, 190, 341, 360
Thani Nayagam, Xavier 289
Thompson, Sandra 125, 170
Thorsheng, Lis 342, 360
Thurneysen, Rudolf 30, 42
Torrego, Esther 101, 106, 117, 138, 171
Traugott, Elizabeth C. 165, 171, 207, 242
Tsimpli, Ianthi-Maria 159, 171
Tsoulas, George 72

Uszkoreit, Hans 51, 75

Van Hal, Toon 286, 289
Vasishth, Shravan 49, 59, 74
Velle, Ingvil Håberg 106, 117
Vennemann, Theo 417, 462

Verbeke, Saartje 177, 180, 190
Verma, Manindra 48, 59, 75
Vermeer, Hans 269, 273, 276, 284, 289
Veselinova, Ljuba 198, 201, 206
Vine, Brent 1, 21
Viti, Carlotta 29, 36, 42

Wackernagel, Jacob 25, 29, 40
Wali, Kashi 308
Walkow, Martin 81, 99, 115
Walther, Christoph Theodosius 273, 277, 286, 289
Wasow, Thomas 46, 53, 55, 75
Watanabe, Kuzuha 146, 151
Watkins, Calvert 30, 42
Wehr, Hans 453, 462
Weightman, Simon 259
Weiß, Helmut 197, 206

Wheeldon, Linda R. 426, 428, 460
Whitney, W. D. 5, 9, 12, 15, 21
Wilder, Chris 72
Willems, Klaas 190
Wilshire, Carolyn E. 429, 431, 462
Wurmbrand, Susi 107, 117

Yamashita, Hiroko 53, 75

Zehnder, Thomas 13, 21
Zeijlstra, Hedde 101, 107, 117
Ziegenbalg, Bartholomaeus 270, 273, 277, 288
Ziegler, Johannes C. 421, 462
Ziegler, Sabine 30, 42
Zlatev, Jordan 341, 360
Zvelebil, Kamil 456, 462

Index of languages

Angami 317
Angika 79, 178, 181, 184, 187, 188
Arabic 453, 454, 462
Asamiya 175, 176, 178, 179, 180–182, 185–187, 189

Bambara 365, 380
Bangla 173–180, 182–184, 187–189, 311, 312, 315–317, 320, 323, 331–334, 339–340, 343, 346, 348–353, 355–357
Beuil dialect 84
Bhojpuri 173, 175, 178, 180, 184, 187, 188
Bodo 312, 323, 324, 327–329, 331, 334, 335
Bolognese 84

Catalan 84
Corsican 84
Cremonese 84

Dakkhini 313–315, 335, 337
Dravidian languages 456
Dutch 417, 428, 461

Early modern Tamil 261
Eastern Indo-Aryan 173
English 44, 45, 48, 51, 53, 56, 59, 60, 62, 70–75, 119–121, 123, 125–129, 137, 146–149, 150, 153, 160, 162–165, 170, 171, 320, 321, 415, 417–421, 423, 425, 428, 429, 431–434, 436–440, 442, 443, 448–450, 452, 455, 456, 458, 459, 461

French 80–85, 87, 88, 116, 417

Georgian 419, 458
German 45, 51, 53, 59, 60, 62, 71, 74, 320, 321, 336, 417, 419, 421, 428, 429, 459, 462
Germanic languages 456
Greek 125, 146, 153, 158, 159, 162, 164, 171, 419, 462
Gujarati 207, 219, 220, 226, 229, 230–237, 239, 240, 242

Hindi 43, 48, 54, 56, 59, 68, 243, 246, 252, 381, 395, 399, 403, 411, 420, 431, 435, 448, 452, 455
Hindi-Urdu 77, 86, 90, 97, 100, 106, 113, 115, 207, 211, 218, 226, 232, 312, 314, 320, 337
Hmar 299, 303
Ho 79

Italian 84, 87, 117, 415, 430, 452

Japanese 146, 151, 158, 170, 243, 250, 252

Kannada 119, 127, 132, 140, 143, 145, 151, 158, 164, 171
Kashmiri 219, 242
Kharia 303, 312, 318, 331, 336
Khasi 298, 303
Kherwarian 79
Koints 191, 194, 201
Kokborok 311, 315, 322, 331
Konkani 313, 336
Korean 127, 146, 152, 171
Kunjen 417, 461
Kuuk Thaayore 329

Latin 26, 40

Māgadhi Prākrit 79
Magahi 79, 173, 175, 178, 184, 187
Maithili 79, 175, 177, 185, 187
Mandarin 320, 322
Marathi 146, 207, 219, 226, 242
Milanese 84
Mising 291, 297, 299, 303
Mizo 295, 299, 319, 336
Munda 312, 318, 331, 336
Munda languages 312, 318, 320, 331
Mundari 79

Nepali 173, 190
Norwegian 125, 146, 160, 171

Occitan 84
Odia 175, 178, 185, 187, 189
Old Egyptian 4
Old Irish 30, 41

Persian 125, 146, 154, 156, 162, 164, 170, 356, 360
Polish 419, 457
Prakrit 356

Rabha 312, 337

Sadani 312, 318, 320
Sanskrit 340, 348, 356, 421
Santali 79, 312, 320, 331
Sauraseni Prākrit 79
Sierra Popoluca 417, 458
Sinhala 318, 331, 335

Spanish 418, 429, 458
Sunwar 191, 204
Swahili 320, 322
Swiss German 365

Tamashek 203
Tamil 142, 144, 147, 165, 168, 352, 355, 360
Telugu 142, 144, 147, 165, 168, 171, 294, 299, 302, 309, 312, 314, 319, 335, 456
Thadou, 299, 303
Tibeto-Burman 191, 205, 311, 316, 320, 323, 331
Turkish 146, 158, 170

Vedic Sanskrit 1, 13, 23, 24, 27, 28, 29, 30, 31, 32, 33, 35, 37, 38, 39, 40, 41, 42

Yucatec Mayan 417

Index of subjects

ablative 179, 187, 189
accusative 174
acyclicity 361, 362, 366, 368, 369, 371–373, 375, 377, 378
adhesion 350, 352, 353
adjunction 83, 84
adnominal 43, 44, 47, 49, 50, 52, 54, 55, 58, 60–71, 74
adnominal modifier 193
adpositions 341
āgama 'augment' 371
agentivity 185
agent-licencing head 394
agreement 77, 78, 81, 82, 85, 88, 90, 91, 99, 115–117
Aitareya Brāhmaṇa 421
Aktionsart 209, 212
allomorphy 381–383, 387, 393, 399, 401, 404, 411
allophonic distribution 423, 452
anaphoric strategies 299
animacy 173, 177, 187, 189, 190
animate objects 173–189
animate verbs 183, 186, 188
anti-causatives 381, 400, 402–404, 410
anti-locality effects 49
Aṣṭādhyāyī 361, 362, 366–368, 370, 378, 380
Atharvaveda 1, 2, 5, 20, 21
automata
– linear bounded 363
– push-down store 363

Basic Locative Constructions (BLC) 340, 343, 350, 353, 356
behind 350, 352
benefactive marker 303
bimoraic feet 384
bimoraic vowels 390
Binding Theory 311, 323
body-centric postpositions 356

canonical subject position 119–127, 136, 138, 144, 147, 150, 151, 153, 154, 163, 168
case copying 296, 309
case feature 122, 137, 138, 142, 145, 157
case markers 173
case positions 119
case relations 340
caseless positions 119
case-marked 119, 121, 122, 124, 125, 127, 130, 133, 134, 137, 138, 140, 141, 144, 146, 147, 152–154, 156, 157, 159, 162, 164, 166
categorizers 400
causatives 381, 395, 396, 399–401, 404
causativization patterns 393
CELEX dictionary 450
Chomsky hierarchy 362, 363, 365, 366
chronometric data 417
clausal subordination 311
clauses of comparison 6, 7, 9, 10, 12, 17, 19
cognitive semantics 339
comitative 174
comparative clauses 1
complementizer 125, 128–130, 142, 147, 158, 162, 164, 167, 169
complementizer clauses 311
complete containment 352
complex predicates 243
compound strategy 322
compound verbs 243, 244, 246, 254, 256, 262, 274, 284
confusion matrix 67, 71
congruent syllable primes 418
constraint rules 361
containment
– in encircling boundary 350, 352
– in liquid or mass 350, 352
context-free grammar 364, 365, 369, 371
context-sensitive formalism 361
context-sensitive grammar 361, 364, 366, 367, 369, 370
context-sensitive power 361, 365, 369
contiguity 341

control
– backward 314
– forward 314
control constructions 311, 314
copula 339, 343, 344, 353–356
copy control 317
copying 106, 112
correlative strategy 311, 312, 316
correlatives 43, 72
CP clause 119, 122, 128, 130, 133, 135, 137, 138, 139, 143–145, 150, 152, 153, 157–159, 162–166, 168
cyclic head 381, 400, 401, 404, 409, 410
cyclicity 366, 368, 372, 374, 375

dative 174
declarative 248, 249
defectiveness 203, 204
definite marker 296, 297, 307
definiteness 59, 60
Dell model 422–425, 428, 431, 449, 450–452, 455
demonstrative 61
derived intransitives 381
derived roots 381
diglossia 437, 455
diglossic attitude 262
diphthongs 408, 409
Distributive Morphology 393, 397, 398

embedded clause 10–12, 14, 17, 311–314, 317, 323
emphatic marker 293, 303, 304
enclisis 39
encyclopedic meaning 394, 396, 403
end-weight 70
envelopment 350, 352
ergative 50, 64, 65, 69, 72, 138
ergative case 173
error matrix 67
eventive 400
exclamatory 248
Extended Projection Principle 120
externally headed relative clause 313

factored verb 207
factored verb complexes 211

final complementizer 315
finite state machines 363
Fisher exact test 50
frequency studies 417

gap strategy 312
Generalized Phrase Structure Grammar 365, 380
generative grammar 361, 362
generative power 361, 366
genitive marker 176, 178–181, 186
gerund 128, 130, 132, 133, 144, 147, 165, 166, 169, 240
givenness 58, 60
glide insertion strategy 405
grammatical compounds 279
grammatical weight 43, 53, 73
ground 340, 342, 350

Harmonic Grammar 391, 411, 412, 413
harmonic value 391
Head-driven Phrase Structure Grammar 365

idiomaticity 212, 214, 217
imperative 248
impingement verbs 184, 186, 188
implicit priming 418
implicit priming paradigm 422
in front of 350, 352
inanimate objects 173, 179, 183, 188
indicative 249
Indo-Aryan complementizers 23
Indo-European syntax 23, 42
information structure 43
information theory 415, 448, 449, 455
iva comparison clause 1

landmark 339, 342, 344, 352, 356
language contact 311, 315, 318, 332
language games 417
Left Edge Fronting 26
left periphery 23, 40
left-peripheral 45, 47, 58, 62
left-peripheral relatives 45, 48, 50, 53, 58, 64
lemma nodes 424
LEWISS model 428, 449, 455
lexeme 415

lexical nodes 423, 427
lexical representations 415, 431, 456
Lexical-Functional Grammar 361, 365
lexicalization 381, 405, 409, 411
linear distance 43, 51, 63, 69
locality 43, 48, 51, 68, 72, 74
locative 173, 177, 187, 339, 343, 346, 351, 359
locative marker-copula 339, 343
LRM model 426, 449, 454, 457

Madras Tamil Lexicon 268, 288
main clause 61
markedness constraints 407
markedness reduction 389
matrix clause 35, 38, 312, 323
matrix negation 1, 9, 13, 17
MC length 67, 71
mental syllabary 426, 428, 450, 460
mildly context-sensitive 365, 370
Minimalism 365
minimalist framework 130
minimality requirement 385
minimize domain 69
Moby dictionary 432
monoclausal 211, 215, 218
monoeventive 210, 215
moraic coda 385
moraic weight 384, 388
morpho-syntactic theory 381
multiple context-free grammars 365, 380
multiple-argument agreement 79

negative particle 243, 247, 251, 256
next 350, 352
nominal head 61
nominal modifier 193
nominal reciprocal 294, 304, 311, 319, 326, 331
nominalization 119, 158
nominalization of CP 119, 128, 147
nominalized clauses 119, 121, 127, 131, 133, 143, 146, 148, 153, 163, 165, 168, 171
nominative 47, 50, 63, 68, 132, 138, 143, 146, 151, 292, 296, 300, 307
non-nominalized clauses 119, 122, 125, 149, 158

objective case 173
oblique constructions 180
obstruents 417
Occam's razor 419
opaque instance 198
optionality 77
overt D head 119, 138
overt head 119, 138, 146, 169
overt nominal head 119, 122, 127, 133,

Pāṇini 361, 365, 374, 377, 380
parametric variation 456
paribhāṣā 368, 373, 375
partial containment 352
participles 77
Penn and Kiparsky's formulation 371
phonological reduction 381, 387, 397, 400, 404, 408
phonological theory 381
polar verb 208, 222
potential vowel hiatus 405
pronominal strategy 321
pronominals 79
proximity 341

quantificational strategy 321

RC length 53, 55, 61, 64, 67, 71
realizational approach to syntax 399
reciprocal marking 291
reciprocals 311, 322, 331, 335
reduplication 311, 322, 327, 333
reflexive 291
relative clause 43, 65, 67, 311
relative participle 261, 268, 274, 277
relative-correlative clause 312
relativized head 313
relay 105
resultative construction 247, 255
resyllabification 415, 425, 427, 431, 436, 439, 442, 448, 450, 452, 455
Ṛgveda 4, 13, 18, 21, 23, 26, 37, 42
root morphology 381

sandhi rule 367
Sanskrit case system 366
schwa-nullifier symbol 433

semantic roles 174
semantic void 191
sentential objects 119, 123, 149, 153, 159
sentential subjects 119, 123, 134, 153, 160, 165
serialised phonemes 457
serialized verb 215
sonority scale 388, 390
sonority sequencing principle 387
sonority-hierarchy-based stringency constraints 381
spatial constructions 339, 353
spatial postpositions 339, 350
spatial primitives 341
SpecCP 126, 153, 161
specifier-head-complement 130
SpecIP 120, 124, 127, 130, 133, 136, 138, 153, 157, 160
speech corpora 432, 455
speech error analysis 417
speech production 415, 422
speech production 460
speech syllables 415
Spell-Out 381, 394, 399, 409
storage and retrieval 425, 432
stringency constraints 389, 392, 405, 408
subjacency principle 49
subjecthood 120, 171
subjunctive 249
subset principle 399
substitution 83
suppletion 191, 194, 197, 201, 203, 205
suprasegmental units 420
swapping 299
Switchboard speech corpus 432
syllabification 427, 460
syllable structure 415, 428, 458
syllable templates 427
syllable typology 456
syllable units 427, 459
synsem features 399, 406
syntactic convergence 311, 336
syntactic locality 43, 49, 68
syntactic module 397
syntactic reanalysis 315
synthetic strategy 322
Tamil grammar 261

Tamil grammarians 276
Tamil script 264
Tolkāppiyam 421
topological relation picture series (TRPS) 339, 349, 358
trajector 339, 342, 348, 352, 354
trajector-landmark 339, 343
transitive alternation 382, 407
transitives 396, 399, 403
tree-adjoining grammars 365
Turing machines 363

unaccusative 138, 393, 400
under 350, 352
unergative 393, 396, 401
universal human experience 341
universal sonority hierarchy 390
unrestricted grammar 363, 365

V1-kar+V2 construction 222, 225
valuation 105
varṇas 421
varṇasamāmnāya 421
vector verbs 261, 274, 287
vectorality 228
vectored verb 207, 223
vectored verb complexes 208
Vedic clausal left periphery 23
Vedic syntax 23
verbal reciprocal 311, 318, 322, 331
verbal reflexive 291, 293, 295, 301, 303, 307
vertical non-contact 350, 352
vibhakti 340
virāma 433
vocabulary insertion 382, 397, 399, 401, 404, 409
vowel hiatus context 405

Wackernagel's Law, 25, 41
weight-sensitive language 384
word-final coda 416

yád 23, 26

Zipf's law 442
Zipf-Mandelbrot law 440

www.ingramcontent.com/pod-product-compliance
Lightning Source LLC
Chambersburg PA
CBHW030514230426
43665CB00010B/612